Cybercrime and Cloud Forensics:

Applications for Investigation Processes

Keyun Ruan
University College Dublin, Ireland

Information Science
REFERENCE

Managing Director:	Lindsay Johnston
Editorial Director:	Joel Gamon
Book Production Manager:	Jennifer Yoder
Publishing Systems Analyst:	Adrienne Freeland
Development Editor:	Austin DeMarco
Assistant Acquisitions Editor:	Kayla Wolfe
Typesetter:	Christy Fic
Cover Design:	Jason Mull

Published in the United States of America by
Information Science Reference (an imprint of IGI Global)
701 E. Chocolate Avenue
Hershey PA 17033
Tel: 717-533-8845
Fax: 717-533-8661
E-mail: cust@igi-global.com
Web site: http://www.igi-global.com

Copyright © 2013 by IGI Global. All rights reserved. No part of this publication may be reproduced, stored or distributed in any form or by any means, electronic or mechanical, including photocopying, without written permission from the publisher. Product or company names used in this set are for identification purposes only. Inclusion of the names of the products or companies does not indicate a claim of ownership by IGI Global of the trademark or registered trademark.

Library of Congress Cataloging-in-Publication Data

Cybercrime and cloud forensics: applications for investigation processes / Keyun Ruan, editor.
p. cm.
Includes bibliographical references and index.
Summary: "This book presents a collection of research and case studies of applications for investigation processes in cloud computing environments, offering perspectives of cloud customers, security architects as well as law enforcement agencies on the new area of cloud forensics"-- Provided by publisher.
ISBN 978-1-4666-2662-1 (hardcover) -- ISBN 978-1-4666-2693-5 (ebook) -- ISBN 978-1-4666-2724-6 (print & perpetual access) 1. Computer crimes--Investigation. 2. Forensic sciences--Data processing. 3. Cloud computing. 4. Computer crimes--Investigation--Case studies. 5. Cloud computing--Case studies. I. Ruan, Keyun, 1986-
HV8079.C65C95 2013
363.25'968--dc23

2012033552

British Cataloguing in Publication Data
A Cataloguing in Publication record for this book is available from the British Library.

All work contributed to this book is new, previously-unpublished material. The views expressed in this book are those of the authors, but not necessarily of the publisher.

Editorial Advisory Board

Joseph Carthy, *University College Dublin, Ireland*
Fred Cohen, *Fred Cohen and Associates, USA & California Sciences Institute, USA*
Jagdish Singh, *International Multilateral Partnership Against Cyber Threats (IMPACT), Malaysia*
Eugene H. Spafford, *Purdue University, USA*

List of Reviewers

Rafael Accorsi, *University of Freiburg, Germany*
Richard Adams, *Deloitte Australia, Australia*
John Crout, *NIST Cloud Computing Program, USA*
Dener Didoné, *Bank of Brazil, Brazil*
Monique M. Ferraro, *Technology Forensics, LLC, USA & Southern Connecticut State University, USA*
Tobias Hahn, *Fraunhofer Institute for Secure Information Technology, Germany*
Jacob Heilik, *www.heilik.com, Canada*
Joshua I. James, *University College Dublin, Ireland & An Garda Síochána eCrimes Unit, Ireland*
Andrew Jones, *Khalifa University, UAE, Edith Cowan University, Australia & University of South Australia, Australia*
Vasilis Katos, *Democritus University of Thrace, Greece*
Kenneth Kenapp, *University of Tampa, USA*
Dave Kleiman, *Computer Forensics LLC, USA*
Stephan Larson, *Slippery Rock University, USA*
Ricci Leong, *eWalker Consulting Limited, China*
Michael Losavio, *University of Louisville, USA*
Fabio Marturana, *University of Rome Tor Vergata, Italy*
Doug O'Halloran, *Meridian Credit Union, Canada*
Ernesto F. Rojas, *Forensic & Security Services Inc., USA*
Spyridopoulos Theodoros, *University of Bristol, UK*

Table of Contents

Detailed Table of Contents

Digital forensic evidence is subject to a variety of challenges, and these challenges apply in the Cloud. This chapter is an overview of these issues specifically oriented toward cloud computing environments.

Cloud computing is just one of many recent technologies that have highlighted shortcomings in the development of formal digital forensic processes, which up until now have been focused on a particular group of practitioners, such as law enforcement, have been too high-level to be of significant practical use, or have been too detailed and specific to accommodate new technology as it emerges. Because the tools and procedures employed by digital forensic practitioners are generally outside the knowledge and understanding of the courts, they need to be described in such a way that they can be understood by the layperson. This chapter looks at the issues surrounding digital evidence acquisition and introduces a new high-level process model that can assist digital forensic practitioners when it comes to presenting evidence in court that originated in the cloud.

This chapter focuses on a theoretical approach to proactive evidence collection and presents a conceptual approach for the Cloud. Forensic Readiness in the Cloud (FRC) calls upon technological and organizational strategies to address the risks that threaten organizational information. The two professions of Records Management (RM) and Digital Forensics (DF) can offer insights into how this might be achieved. In this chapter, the authors seek to explore the relationship between the two disciplines and the areas where collaboration and interdisciplinary work would be most beneficial. An initial overview of RM and its relationship to the wider field of Information Assurance (IA) precedes a more in depth comparison of the two related disciplines, using a model that integrates RM and DF. This is offered as a conceptual framework for making decisions about how to identify and manage the increasing quantities of evidence collected in networks.

Just about every technology magazine and article published today mentions virtualization or cloud computing. Technically, the two are different but very much intertwined. When environments use virtualization, there are artifacts an investigator can request that may provide valuable information. The content of this chapter explores the virtualization process, types of virtualized environments, and the part virtualization plays in cloud computing. A section is included that presents case scenarios to demonstrate the type of evidence gathered in each environment for forensic investigations. A final section includes recommendations for additional areas of research in the area of investigating environments containing virtualization integration with cloud environments.

Despite a growing adoption of cloud computing, law enforcement and the judicial system are unprepared to prosecute cloud-based crimes. This chapter illuminates legal problems in the United States for electronic discovery and digital forensics arising from cloud computing and argues that cloud computing challenges the process and product of electronic discovery. The researchers investigate how to obtain forensic evidence from cloud computing using the legal process by surveying the existing statutes and recent cases applicable to cloud forensics. A hypothetical case study of child pornography being hosted in the Cloud illustrates the difficulty in acquiring evidence for cloud-related crimes. For the first time, a sample search warrant is presented that could be used in this case study, and which provides sample language for agents and prosecutors who wish to obtain a warrant authorizing the search and seizure of data from cloud computing environments. The chapter concludes by taking a contrasting view and discusses how defense attorneys might be able to challenge cloud-derived evidence in court.

For the emerging field of cloud forensics, the development of validated and repeatable scientific processes for conducting cloud forensic investigations should include requirements that establish evidence collected is legally admissible. There is currently an uncertainty in the legal requirements for cloud forensics. Forensic investigations in the cloud introduce unique issues that must be addressed, and the legal environment of the cloud must be considered. The authors detail the process in criminal cloud forensic investigations for commanding production from cloud providers, including constitutional and statutory limitations and the civil and criminal admissibility processes. Decisions in court cases rely on the authenticity and reliability of the evidence presented. Ensuring cases involving cloud forensics follow the proper legal process and requirements will be beneficial for validating evidence when presented in court. Further, understanding legal requirements will aid in the research and development of cloud forensics tools to aid investigations.

Cloud Computing will be a disruptive technology that will ultimately change the face of computing. The unstoppable migration of data to the Cloud is undoubtedly due to numerous financial benefits, particularly for small- and medium-sized companies, which historically do not have the same capital budgets as larger enterprises. However, this boundless upside is not without risks from a legal and compliance perspective, making it all that more important for entities to look before they leap. Today, nearly every corporation is required to preserve and produce Electronically Stored Information (ESI), such as emails and other electronic documents, as part of their response to litigation, regulatory inquiries, and subpoenas. When the subject ESI happens to be stored in the Cloud, there are a handful of potential obstacles that serve to complicate the eDiscovery process. For some, this leads to sanctions and increased compliance risks. In order to navigate these potentially treacherous waters, organizations need to be proactive and follow a "measure twice, cut once" approach. This chapter discusses the basics of eDiscovery and explores ways to minimize potential compliance hurdles when migrating significant data stores to/from the Cloud.

Data acquisition and data recovery are essential to any e-discovery or digital forensic process. However, these two aspects seem to be considerably difficult in a cloud-computing environment. The very nature of the Cloud raises a number of technical and organizational challenges, which renders traditional approaches and tools inapplicable. Resource pooling, rapid elasticity, and geographical distribution of data are only a small part of the Cloud's features that hinder the forensic investigation. At the same time, there is significant absence of forensic readiness in the cloud computing policy framework. In this chapter, the authors discuss the challenges pertaining to data acquisition in a cloud environment and discuss possible directions for meeting these challenges by presenting representative cases and sketching the acquisition process and scenarios.

In today's dynamic information technology system, one area of tremendous focus and recent growth has been that of the cloud-computing model in its various offerings. With this growth, however, come new challenges within the realms of e-discovery and digital forensics, as we traditionally know it. The rapid growth of cloud computing services and the rate of acceptance and use by consumers are on the rise. Conversely, both legitimate and illegitimate activates can leverage the resources of the cloud to execute their operations. With the challenges growing to combat computer crime that utilizes the cloud ecosystem and the ease with which a criminal activity may be hidden using a cloud service, it is imperative that a cloud provider dedicate time, training, budget, and other resources to provide the facility for forensic investigators as well as law enforcement to combat this threat. The Cloud-Forensics-as-a-Service (FRaaS) model introduced later in this chapter can provide a comprehensive cloud forensics solution for creating a repeatable system. Such a system could be implemented as a standard forensics operational model for deployment within the cloud ecosystem regardless of environments and client service lines.

Cloud computing as a paradigm shift is transforming how services are being delivered. In this chapter, the authors present a Forensics as a Service (FaaS) model using cloud computing to deliver forensic services. This model leverages the flexibility, elasticity, and dynamics of cloud computing, and is affordable for business, government, or individuals in need due to its reduced cost. It also addresses the challenge of processing large volumes of forensic data by using MapReduce and distributed computing.

Foreword

Understanding technological change is really not that difficult. It is a repeated cycle of research, experience, adjustment, and examination. Research, combined with past experience and new infrastructures, leads to new technologies. When those new technologies offer lower cost or better features (or both), they become popular. Once deployed, those technologies are refined and eventually considered for evolution or replacement. It is not always obvious what a particular set of winning combinations and features may be, but therein lies the ongoing challenge for researchers, developers, and entrepreneurs.

Cloud computing is one example of such a technology advancement. Computing centers have been around for many decades, thus providing a long baseline of experience. Research in academia and experience with commercial systems—c.mmp/Hydra and Grapevine in the 1970s; Eden, ISIS, Clouds[1], and Apollo/Domain in the 1980s; RAID, NFS, Amoeba, Banyan, and Novell in the 1990s and beyond; and development of virtual environments and multicore systems in the 2000s—all laid the groundwork for current "cloud computing" to emerge. It required a special mix of hardware cost/performance, platform mix, and network bandwidth coupled with the experience from those earlier systems to make "cloud computing" economical and dependable enough for everyday use; it was not an "overnight" development.

There are opportunities with technology advancements applied to existing areas of endeavor. That is certainly the case with cloud computing and digital forensics. For example, one of the biggest problems for many researchers and investigative organizations is keeping copies of all of the images of systems that might be under investigation, and copies of all the various bits of malware, tools, and contraband that are used for comparison. Cloud computing offers the promise of vast storage, and better sharing of commonly used resources. Some research will need to be conducted to handle issues of integrity of evidence, and ensuring the authenticity of references, as well as how to ensure that there are usable backups of material, but approaches to these issues are not impossible to envision.

Another potential benefit of cloud computing is "Platform as a Service" or PaaS. This provides an opportunity to collect a "reference library" of possible system configurations, and load them as needed as remote, cloud-based images. Investigators can use these images for comparison, testing of software, tool benchmarking, hypothesis testing of malicious activity and code, and a number of other possibilities, all without the expenses and labor involved in having local machines. Furthermore, by having it "in the Cloud," other researchers can share the technology . . . and results.

There are potentially a host of other services that could be based "in the Cloud"—either public clouds or private clouds, or a hybrid combination—that could aid investigators and researchers. Having access to large amounts of storage, software, and virtual machines that would be too expensive or labor-intensive to maintain locally may open up many new possibilities for researchers and investigators alike.

However, some of the opportunities provided by new technologies are not what the designers of those technologies intended. Usually, the early development of any technology is oriented towards making the technology work—reliably—and then in reducing their cost. Issues of security, privacy, and compliance monitoring are often secondary thoughts . . . for the designers. There are those who see new technologies as new platforms for fraud, abuse, and the furtherance of illicit activities. The dual nature of new technologies is not limited to computing, either, but as a relatively new area of endeavor, we have less experience in coping with the associated complications. Cloud computing is certainly an example of note. Computers have brought us computer viruses, email has enabled spam, the WWW supports phishing, and networks enable all sorts of APT-style threats. We have yet to see what kinds of problems cloud computing might enable.

Digital forensics, as a field, is only slightly more than two decades old; consideration of what is available to us for local computing systems reveals gaps in our investigative methods for the Cloud. For example, crimes committed using virtual machines in PaaS-type environments are extremely unlikely to leave system residue (or images) that can be analyzed. As another example, shutting down a running cloud service to perform an investigation on petabytes (or larger) of storage is simply not feasible, both because of available methods and because of the potential for disruption of many innocent third parties.

There is often a small window of opportunity between the growing acceptance of a new technology and the emergence of associated threats. The key problem is getting a head start on the fixes (if possible) and countermeasures given that those who are concerned are usually not those who own the technologies and infrastructure where the threats will be manifest. This is where vision and creativity are critically important.

This volume is focused on the potential of "the Cloud"—both its promises and potential downsides. Herein you will find some foundational thinking about how to apply digital forensics in cloud computing environments. The coverage includes essays on everything from structure of an investigation, to data and tools, to legal requirements, to as-yet-unmet needs, to some methods of using the cloud paradigm itself to support digital investigations.

Cloud computing is here, and we cannot control its spread even if we wanted to. We can anticipate ways in which it may be used to support our activities, as well as how it may be used in furtherance of criminal activities, or abused within the confines of an organizational set of prohibitions. We can, and should, start thinking of how we might deploy those services to support our research and investigations. We also need to start thinking about how to investigate cloud-based incidents to gather the necessary digital evidence to identify with certainty the perpetrators and inform appropriate reactions to their deeds. Thus, if we are to try to stay ahead of the "bad guys" we need to start thinking about new methods of investigation, research, and forensics using cloud computing.

The editor and authors of these chapters have started that process. They have not yet solved all the challenges, but they have made significant steps toward defining the problems and setting forth how to address them. The problems that remain present a new set of challenges for practitioners, developers, and researchers. The cycle continues. Good luck with your portions of it!

Eugene H. Spafford
Purdue University, USA October 2012

Eugene H. Spafford *is a Professor of Computer Sciences at Purdue University, and is the founder and Executive Director of the Center for Education and Research in Information Assurance and Security (CERIAS). His research and education over three decades has contributed to many of the technologies used in modern computing system protection. Spaf's current research interests are in information security, cybercrime, software engineering, professional ethics, and security policy. Dr. Spafford is a Fellow of the ACM, AAAS, IEEE, ISC2, is a Distinguished Fellow of the ISSA, and has received many other awards for service, scholarship, and education.*

ENDNOTES

1 Yes, there was a distributed, boundary-less computing system named Clouds, developed at Georgia Tech in the 1980s. My Ph.D. dissertation was on building the prototype kernel for it. New ideas in the computing marketplace are not that new to researchers!

Preface

That life-changing moment looked like a pure coincidence. It was an ordinary evening in Dublin in 2009, and I was flipping through *Newsweek* and came across an article on cloud computing. After reading all the controversies and debates over the emergence of cloud adoption, I suddenly realized that I discovered a perfect research topic for my PhD. All of the sudden, I was so excited by that gigantic question mark over my head—how to investigate cyber crime and past incidents in the Cloud?—that I immediately started writing down all the interesting questions I could think of regarding digital investigation in the Cloud. Back in 2009, nobody seemed to have ever thought about these questions and their significant implications at all, and when I wrote down the term "Cloud Forensics" in the center of the question sheet, I was totally intrigued by a fascinating space of unknown. From that moment, I embarked on the bittersweet journey of trying to answer these questions.

This book is a collective brainchild from this process. With rapid global cloud adoption, cloud-computing environment is inevitably becoming a new battlefield for the evolving threat landscape as well as cyber crime. Cloud forensics, i.e., digital investigation in cloud computing environments, is a relatively green area that is rapidly emerging. This book is the world's first scholarly volume explicitly on the topic of cloud forensics. It is intended to collect different perspectives from both industry and academia on various challenges and possible solutions for carrying out cloud investigations, and I hope it will serve as a good reference book for digital forensic and cloud security researchers, practitioners, and professionals, who wish to carry out research and developments in the emerging area of cloud forensics.

This book opens with an introductory chapter on the background of cloud computing and digital investigation by my colleagues, Joshua James, Ahmed Shosha, and Dr. Pavel Gladyshev, at the Center for Cybersecurity and Cybercrime Investigation, University College Dublin. This chapter provides a comprehensive overview and literature review on the history and state-of-the-art of cloud computing and digital investigation in order to give readers adequate background knowledge on the subject matter.

In chapter 2, Mark Crosbie, security architect and head of the ethical hacking team at IBM Ireland and the CIO Office, introduces the evolving attack surface of cloud environments, where to look for potential evidence, and how digital investigators should think like a hacker.

The inventor of the first computer virus, Dr. Fred Cohen, gives an in-depth analysis of the challenges to digital forensic evidence throughout the evidence life cycle in the Cloud in chapter 3.

In chapter 4, Richard Adams, based on his vast experience from real-world investigations as the Principle in the Forensic Division of a Big4 professional services organization, argues why cloud-based storage demands a new digital forensic process model.

The next part of the book addresses various specific issues relevant to the investigation process in cloud computing environments, from forensic readiness in chapter 5 by Ferguson-Boucher and Endicott-

Popovsky, virtual forensics in chapter 6 by Prof. Diane Barrett, search and seizure in chapter 7 by Josiah Dykstra, to a foundational piece of comprehensive analysis on legal process and requirements for cloud investigations by Ivan Orton, Aaron Alva, and Endicott-Popovsky in chapter 8, followed by chapter 9 on eDisovery in the Cloud written by Dean Gonsowski, eDiscovery council at Symantec, and chapter 10 on data recovery strategies by Theodoros Spyridopoulos and Prof. Vasilios Katos.

Cloud computing poses significant challenges to digital investigation; however, it also brings a unique opportunity for groundbreaking novel approaches to address these challenges. The next part of the book is dedicated to Forensics as a Service. In chapters 11, 12, and 13, Jon Rav Gagan Shende, Dener, and Prof. Ruy J. G. B. de Queiroz from Brazil, Fabio, Dr. Simone Tacconi, and Prof. Giuseppe F. Italiano from Italy present three different models for delivering Forensics as a Service via cloud computing.

To leave the readers with a bit of optimism into the future, despite all the pressing cloud forensic challenges presented, this book concludes with my chapter on designing a forensic-enabling cloud ecosystem. Cloud computing is a major paradigm shift in the history of computing, and it is here to stay. The full impact of cloud computing is estimated to be about three years away (Forbes, 2012), and we are at a unique time to integrate forensic requirements, controls, and implementations into the cloud ecosystem in order to enable post-incident investigations and enhance the overall robustness of our cyber infrastructure.

Today, I am still on the journey of answering those questions I wrote down on that 2009 evening in Dublin, and I am happy that you are now joining this journey. I hope you will enjoy reading this book.

Keyun Ruan
University College Dublin, Ireland October 2012

REFERENCES

BBC. (2011, June 13). New Zealand quake: Christchurch hit by aftershocks. *BBC News*. Retrieved from http://www.bbc.co.uk/news/world-asia-pacific-13745359

Forbes. (2012, October 3). Cloud's full impact is still about three years away. *Forbes*. Retrieved from http://www.forbes.com/sites/joemckendrick/2012/10/03/clouds-full-impact-is-still-about-three-years-away-survey-predicts/

New York Times. (2012). Egypt news – Revolution and aftermath. *New York Times*. Retrieved from http://topics.nytimes.com/top/news/international/countriesandterritories/egypt/index.html

Slate. (2012, July 4). Power outages dampen July 4 parties. *Slate*. Retrieved from http://slatest.slate.com/posts/2012/06/30/washington_d_c_maryland_virginia_derecho_storm_leaves_2_mil_without_power_kills_4_.html

Acknowledgment

From signing the book contract in September 2010 to submitting the full manuscript in October 2012, the book took 2 years to complete, with 6 months of break in between due to my personal health issues. Some of the chapter authors dropped out due to natural disasters, such as the 2011 Christchurch Earthquake (BBC, 2011) in New Zealand, and political unrest, such as the Egyptian revolution (New York Times, 2012) in Cairo. Some of the chapter authors managed to complete the draft on time under unfavorable conditions, such as a serious power outage (Slate, 2012). This is my first book, and I completed it right after finishing my PhD dissertation, which felt like completing a marathon. The editing process was a tremendous learning experience. From sending out the call for chapters, coordinating peer reviews, to copy-editing, everything was new to me. I would like to thank the 21 contributing authors and 19 peer-reviewers from 14 countries and 6 continents, and the IGI Global editorial team for making this possible. I would like to thank my colleague Joshua James and my PhD supervisor Prof. Joe Carthy for supporting me in this project. I would like to thank Prof. Gene Spafford, Dr. Fred Cohen, Mr. Jagdish Singh, and Dr. Barbara Endicott-Popovsky for encouraging me throughout this process.

Finally, I want to thank Mom, Dad, Grandpa, and Auntie for understanding me for being always busy.

Keyun Ruan
University College Dublin, Ireland October 2012

Chapter 1
Digital Forensic Investigation and Cloud Computing

Joshua I. James
University College Dublin, Ireland

Ahmed F. Shosha
University College Dublin, Ireland

Pavel Gladyshev
University College Dublin, Ireland

ABSTRACT

This chapter aims to be a high-level introduction into the fundamental concepts of both digital forensic investigations and cloud computing for non-experts in one or both areas. Once fundamental concepts are established, this work begins to examine cloud computing security-related questions, specifically how past security challenges are inherited or solved by cloud computing models, as well as new security challenges that are unique to cloud environments. Next, an analysis is given of the challenges and opportunities cloud computing brings to digital forensic investigations. Finally, the Integrated Digital Investigation Process model is used as a guide to illustrate considerations and challenges during an investigation involving cloud environments.

INTRODUCTION

Cloud computing is a topic that has been gaining popularity with businesses and end users in recent years. A certain level of hype and inconsistent definition has lead to some confusion about what cloud computing is, and what services it can provide. Along with general confusion, some concerns have been raised about the security of cloud environments. As seen with traditional computing, a growing concern for security leads to consideration of incident response and eventually digital forensic investigation capabilities. This work endeavors to examine the implications of cloud computing on digital forensic investigations.

To accomplish this, a high-level introduction into fundamental concepts of both digital forensic investigations and cloud computing for non-experts will be given. A brief overview of

DOI: 10.4018/978-1-4666-2662-1.ch001

Copyright © 2013, IGI Global. Copying or distributing in print or electronic forms without written permission of IGI Global is prohibited.

the history and advancement of digital forensic science, legal considerations surrounding digital forensic investigations, the current state of digital crime, types of digital forensic examinations, and an introduction into current digital forensic investigation process models will be given to build the reader's understanding of digital forensic science. Next, fundamental concepts of cloud computing, such as service and deployment models, will be covered. Once fundamental knowledge of cloud computing is established, some cloud computing security issues will be examined, followed by an analysis of the challenges and opportunities cloud computing brings to digital forensic investigations. Finally, a digital forensic investigation model will be used as a guide to illustrate digital forensic investigation challenges when applied to cloud environments.

DIGITAL FORENSIC SCIENCE

This section is a brief overview of the history and advancement of digital forensic science. Legal considerations surrounding digital forensic investigations, primarily focused on law in the United States, are discussed as well as the current state of digital crime and how digital investigators are addressing this global problem. Key digital forensic definitions, types of digital forensic examinations, and an introduction into current digital forensic investigation process models are given to build the reader's understanding of the field.

History and Advancement of Digital Forensic Science

Digital forensics[1] is a branch of the forensic sciences that deals with the analysis of digital evidence from digital sources (Palmer, 2001). Unlike traditional forensic sciences, a digital forensic analysis attempts to analyze non-physical evidence, or evidence that cannot be directly observed by humans without interpretation. It is because digital evidence cannot be directly observed that the admissibility of such evidence in court is under constant scrutiny (Casey, 2004). To help establish digital forensics as a credible forensic science, digital forensic science was defined at the first Digital Forensics Research Workshop (DFRWS) in 2001 as:

The use of scientifically derived and proven methods toward the preservation, collection, validation, identification, analysis, interpretation, documentation and presentation of digital evidence derived from digital sources for the purpose of facilitating or furthering the reconstruction of events found to be criminal, or helping to anticipate unauthorized actions show to be disruptive to planned operations.

Digital investigation, however, predates this academic definition. Several notable but less developed definitions were previously proposed, such as those submitted by McKemmish (1999) and Civie and Civie (1998). Likewise, beyond academic definitions, research and digital investigations were already taking place prior to 2001. For example, Pollitt (1995) claimed that "[f]or a number of years now, law enforcement agencies have been seizing computers and other electronic devices." A growing interest in digital forensic investigation is confirmed by looking at other works of the early 1990s (Collier & Spaul, 1992a, 1992b; Clede, 1993; Spafford & Weeber, 1993). Hannan (2004) claims "forensic computing origins lay in the late 1980s…," which is when computer-based evidence was encountered more often by police (Jones, 2004), and is perhaps true for forensic computing as a field or separate science (Garfinkel, 2010), but from a legal perspective computers and computer evidence were topics of concern before then. For example, the U.S. Computer Fraud and Abuse Act was first enacted in 1984 (USDoJ, 2002), and also in the early 1980s *Computer in Court - A Guide to Computer Evidence for Lawyers and Computing Professionals* (Kelman & Sizer,

1982) was published that considers fundamental legal issues in relation to computer evidence. Even prior to this work, the admissibility of computer evidence from digital devices has been discussed as early as 1974 (Tapper, 1974), with references to computer technology in trials appearing as early as 1962. In the mid-1970s computer evidence became more of a focus (Roberts, 1974; DeHetre, 1975; Jenkins, 1975) rapidly evolving through the late 1970s when the computer was compared to an expert witness (Teubner, 1978), and the basic tenants for admissibility of computer evidence were explored (Connery & Levy, 1979); most of which is still relevant today. This increased interest in the mid-1970s correlates to the increasing reliance on computer systems in business, and an increasing availability and usage among the public (Polsson, 2011). Even with a considerable amount of evolution and previous work, Wilsdon and Slay (2005) claim that there are issues when it comes to implementation of past research and development in digital forensic investigations; a claim reiterated by Pollitt (2007) and Garfinkel (2010).

Despite a multitude of technological, and in some ways philosophical, changes to the field of digital investigation, the DFRWS definition is still widely accepted. Alternatives, or amendments, have been proposed (Hannan, 2004; Kent, et al., 2006), but the DFRWS definition has remained popular. Since the time of this definition, the areas of evidence preservation, collection, validation, identification, analysis, interpretation, documentation, and presentation have been continually developed, and various process models and standards for each phase of digital investigations have been proposed. However, no one standard has yet to see global acceptance (Wilsdon & Slay, 2005; Hunton, 2012; Lim, et al., 2012), and according to James and Gladyshev (2010) the majority of organizations are creating their own Standard Operating Procedures (SOP), which are not always directly based on a common standard. But regardless of the process used, when considering digital forensic investigations, the resulting evidence must be admissible in court (Carrier, 2006). As stated by Cohen (2010), "[o]n a global level, the most commonly applied standards are similar to the U.S. Federal Rules of Evidence and the Daubert decision." In the United States, the admissibility of scientific evidence was primarily examined using the Frye standard—from Frye v. United States, 293 F. 1013 (1923)—where accepted scientific evidence is based on the scientific community's general acceptance of the employed technique. The Frye standard was superseded in 1993 by the Daubert standard (Daubert v. Merrell Dow, 509 U.S. 579 [1993]; General Electric Co. v. Joiner, 522 U.S. 136 [1997]; Kumho Tire Co. v. Carmichael, 526 U.S. 137 [1999]), although not without criticism (Gutheil & Bursztajn, 2005; Giannelli, 2006). The Daubert standard allows a judge to determine the reliability of scientific evidence during what is called a "Daubert Hearing," usually before the trial. Four general categories are used as guidelines when assessing a scientific technique: testing, error rate, publication of the technique, and acceptance from the scientific community (Carrier, 2003). The Daubert standard was introduced to reduce the misuse of scientific evidence, but still not all states in the U.S. have adopted the Daubert standard; either keeping with the Frye standard or opting for their own testing methods (O'Connor, 2010). For additional information on global legal considerations concerning digital crime, digital forensic investigations, and admissibility of digital evidence, please see the Additional Reading.

The field of digital forensic investigation has had to cope with the rapid creation and adoption of digital devices. A growing number of interconnected devices can be exploited from almost anywhere in the world, but law enforcement still struggle with the concept of jurisdiction in an online world without borders, sometimes resulting in illegal, or at least questionable, cross-border actions by law enforcement (Lemos, 2001; Anderson, 2012). While research, legal and even practical foundations of digital forensics have been slowly forming, a continuing lack of communication between government, corporate and academic entities worldwide has been a limiting factor in the effectiveness of investigating global digital crimes (Broadhurst, 2006; Jang, 2012).

Continued Lack of Communication in an Increasingly Connected World

According to Internet World Stats (2011), from late 2000 to late 2011 there has been an estimated 528.1% worldwide growth in Internet users, numbering 361 million in 2000 to 2.267 billion at the end of 2011, a trend which is expected to continue (IBTimes, 2010; Meeker, 2012). Cisco (2012) estimates that there will be over 10 billion mobile-connected devices by 2016. Further, traditional and non-traditional digital devices - such as TVs and kitchen appliances - are expected to be increasingly connected to the Internet, contributing to a forecasted 50 billion devices connected by 2020 (Higginbotham, 2010). This growth in users, devices, and associated services has given rise new possibilities for business and communications, as well as digital crime. Statistics from the Internet Crime Complaint Center (IC3) (IC3, 2011), a US-based organization, show that there was a 3.4% increase in complaints filed from 2010 to 2011, with 303,809 and 314,246 complains per year, respectively. McAfee (2010) gives an overview of the growth of digital crime from 2000 to 2010, claiming that the cybercriminal community evolved from hackers simply looking for a challenge, to organized gangs looking to profit off the rapidly increasing use of connected devices and services. Some gangs are well established, and in 2011 a single highly-organized gang was suspected of being responsible for up to a third of all data thefts (Williams, 2011). Digital forensic investigators, however, not only need to deal with booming online criminal activity, but also the use of digital devices related to more traditional crimes. For example, Gogolin (2010) claims that most investigations today involve some sort of digital component. Cisco (2012) estimates that "[b]y the end of 2012, the number of mobile-connected devices will exceed the number of people on earth." In more saturated regions when a crime happens, both criminals and bystanders are likely to be producing digital information, which may be of use in the investigation of a non-digital crime. Amateur pictures and videos taken by cell phones have captured abuse, and even murder (Barnard, 2009; CNN, 2009), and have been used as evidence in court (Nguyen, 2012). Further, text messages, cell phone logs and geo-location services are also commonly analyzed by law enforcement in digital and non-digital crime investigation. This presents a difficult situation for digital forensic investigators. The field of digital forensic science is relatively new, technologies are rapidly advancing, and the scope of the digital investigator's job continually expands. Yet funding for digital investigators in law enforcement is slow to increase (Gogolin, 2010). This may change with the perceived[2] growing threat of a full-scale "cyber war[3]," and some countries may begin to focus budgets on digital investigation and security (Paul, 2012). Regardless, digital forensic investigators must attempt to keep up with rapidly advancing digital, as well as traditional, criminals while ensuring the integrity of the science of digital forensics. Rapid changes in digital forensic science, however, cannot come from digital forensic investigators alone. Improved collaboration and communication is needed between the currently siloed digital crime investigation players—military, law enforcement, corporate, and academia—and must be focused at a global, not national, level (Jones, 2012).

Digital Forensic Investigation

Carrier (2006) differentiates between 'digital investigations' and 'digital forensic investigations,' claiming that "[a] digital investigation is a process to answer questions about digital states and events," while "[a] digital forensic investigation is a special case... where procedures and techniques that are used will allow the results to be entered into the court of law." Under this definition, when an investigator is conducting a digital forensic investigation, the focus is on ensuring that the overall investigation process is able to produce evidence that is admissible in court. While this is a requirement for law enforcement, non-LE entities do not always consider the admissibility of evidence when beginning an internal investigation. This may lead to administrators or technicians unknowingly overwriting data of evidential value that may later be unusable by law enforcement once it was found that the case needed to be escalated to a criminal investigation. It is for this reason that all digital investigators should be competent, and able to consider how their actions could affect future legal recourse (ACPO, 2008). "[A]ny case involving computer forensics should always be treated as though it were going to court, and that any documentation and evidence will eventually be turned over to a prosecuting attorney" (Shinder and Cross 2008).

Digital forensic investigations are comprised of many different sub-fields. The general sub-fields include computer forensics, network forensics and cellular phone, or mobile device, forensics: each of which is comprised of more specific forensic studies, e.g. file system, memory, and software analysis. Further, specific sub-fields are forming with the advancement of technology, such as critical infrastructure investigations (Purdy, 2010) and Cloud forensics (Ruan, et al., 2011). While the technical aspects of an investigation may be specific to the suspect device, the examination and investigation process models can be generically applied.

Digital Forensic Investigation Phases

When considering digital forensic process models, there are essentially two layers of abstraction that are discussed: the depth of digital forensic examination, and the process phases of each type of examination. The depth of forensic examinations was not always considered, and each piece of suspect storage media normally received a fully in-depth analysis. Since the capacity of common data storage media has, and still is, growing rapidly—combined with a growing number of cases involving digital storage devices—some investigators are finding it impractical to conduct in-depth analysis on each piece of media. "[F]ew [Digital Forensic Laboratories] can still afford to create a forensic duplicate of every piece of media and perform an in-depth forensic examination of all data on those media... It makes little sense to wait for the review of each piece of media if only a handful of them will provide data of evidentiary significance" (Casey, et al., 2009). This philosophy has led to the growing acceptance of digital forensic triage (Rogers, et al., 2006; Koopmans, 2010; Mislan, et al., 2010), as well as the concept of a preliminary analysis; both of which will be discussed further.

Casey, Ferraro et al. (2009) described a three-tiered model of forensic examination to enable the "tailoring [of] forensic examination[s] of digital evidence to the type of crime or case under investigation." This model includes a survey/triage forensic inspection, a preliminary forensic examination, and finally an in-depth forensic examination. Many law enforcement agencies are currently considering, and even implementing this model (Goss, 2010). Though, corporate and contract-sector digital forensic analysts are currently more likely than law enforcement to use triage and preliminary analysis techniques (James & Gladyshev, 2010).

Triage Forensic Inspection

Koopmans (2010) proposed a definition of digital forensic triage that is derived from the definition of triage in the medical context:

A process for sorting injured people into groups based on their need for or likely benefit from immediate medical treatment. Triage is used in hospital emergency rooms, on battlefields, and at disaster sites when limited medical resources must be allocated.

Koopmans then applies the medical definition to computer forensics, resulting in computer triage being defined as: "A process of sorting computer systems into groups, based on the amount of relevant information or evidence found on these computer systems." Casey et al. (2009) defines triage as a "[t]argeted review of all available media to determine which items contain the most useful evidence and require additional processing." In Rogers et al. (2006), and later expanded by Mislan et al. (2010), triage is a process, normally performed on-scene, that is used to:

1. Assess the severity of a crime and prioritizing it accordingly;
2. Assess the offender's possible danger to society;
3. Obtain actionable intelligence in exigent circumstances (e. g., missing person, military operations, risk of evidence destruction);
4. Identify the richest sources of digital evidence pertaining to an investigation;
5. Identify victims that are or may be at acute risk;
6. Identify potential charges related to the current situation; and
7. Determine whether a certain item requires deeper inspection, such as recovery of deleted information or decoding of encrypted data.

Generally, the key point with digital forensic triage is that triage can be used to identify the 'richest sources' of digital evidence at the scene, allowing the detected media's in-depth examination to be focused and expedited. Triage is an extremely high-level examination, designed to be fast, not thorough. Under this philosophy, and Koopmans' definition, triage is not designed to normally remove media from needing further examination, and only allows for a shallow, focused view of found evidence—aka low hanging fruit—that helps in the prioritization of all the exhibits. However, some organizations, such as ADF Solutions (2011), claim that "triage can identify and eliminate negative computers with the same degree of confidence as can full forensic examinations." Differences in definition have caused some confusion within the digital forensic community. This claim, however, is very different technically and philosophically from triage as previously defined, and should instead be considered as a preliminary forensic examination.

Preliminary Forensic Examination

A more in-depth examination than triage, preliminary forensic examinations have "the goal of quickly providing investigators with information that will aide them in conducting interviews and developing leads" (Casey, et al., 2009). Depending on the results found during triage, the type of case, and the policy of the department, a preliminary analysis might be deep enough to justify discontinuing analysis on that particular media if nothing was found. Because preliminary analysis is more in-depth than triage, it usually takes longer, and as such may or may not be conducted on-scene. Several tools with various preliminary analysis workflows exist, such as SPEKTOR, ADF Triage-Examiner, and Cybercrime Technologies' Rapid Evidence Acquisition Project. Most are designed to be easy to use, and are highly automated. This allows first responders with minimal training to be able to conduct preliminary analysis. Again, depending on the organization's policy, if suspect traces are found during a preliminary analysis, the media will continue to receive an in-depth analysis with a focus on the already discovered traces. If no suspect traces were found, then further analysis may not be necessary.

In-Depth Forensic Examination

An in-depth forensic examination is usually analysis conducted with media that has been seized, and is much more thorough than the previous tiers of examination. Because of this, in-depth forensic examination also takes a considerable amount of time longer (Goss, 2010). This is also the most manual level of analysis; however, some tasks can be automated. Casey et al. (2009) defines an in-depth forensic examination as a "[c]omprehensive forensic examination of items that require more extensive investigation to gain a more complete understanding of the offense and address specific questions." This can be considered the standard depth of analysis. The type of case and the used digital forensic investigation process model dictates if the previous two tiers of examination will be used, but there will rarely, if ever, be a case where an in-depth analysis is not necessary to answer questions about suspect media.

Digital Forensic Investigation Process Models

"[T]he reality is that there is no single process for digital forensics" (Carrier, 2008). Various process models have been proposed, and commonly used models will be briefly discussed; however, as stated before, there is no one accepted standard, and the majority of organizations are creating their own SOP, which may or may not be based on an existing process model. For a comprehensive overview of other proposed models, see Additional Reading.

Digital Forensic Research Workshop 2001

In 2001 the Digital Forensic Research Workshop identified an investigative process for Digital Forensic Science (Palmer, 2001). This process included identification, preservation, collection, examination, analysis, presentation, and decision phases (see Figure 1). In Figure 1, the items in gray were the most agreed upon, and "were identified by the attendees as core processes [of digital forensic investigations]" (Pollitt, 2007).

National Institute of Justice

The U.S. Department of Justice (DoJ) National Institute of Justice (NIJ), created an electronic crime scene investigation guide for law enforcement in 2001. In this work, a four-phase process model was proposed. This model, however, was later expanded in the second edition of the guide (NIJ, 2008). The overall model consists of preparation, preservation, documentation, collection, examination, analysis, and reporting.

- **Preparation:** Knowledge about the types of devices commonly encountered, potential evidence sources, investigative tools, and equipment for collection, packaging and transportation of electronic evidence.
- **Preservation:** Securing and evaluating the crime scene; ensuring the safety of persons and protecting the integrity of all evidence.
- **Documentation:** Documentation of the scene, and electronic evidence.
- **Collection:** "The search for, recognition of, [and] collection of… electronic evidence."
- **Examination:** "Helps to make the evidence visible and explain its origin and significance."
- **Analysis:** "Looks at the product of the examination for its significance and probative value to the case."
- **Reporting:** "A written report that outlines the examination process and the pertinent data recovered completes an examination."

National Institute of Standards and Technology

The National Institute of Standards and Technology (NIST) proposed a four-phase model in the special publication 800-86 (Kent, et al., 2006). This model includes collection, examination, analysis and reporting phases (see Figure 2).

Figure 1. Digital forensic research workshop 2001 diagram of the digital investigation process where the gray area is the area of focus for the workgroup

Identification	Preservation	Collection	Examination	Analysis	Presentation	Decision
Event/Crime Detection	Case Management	Preservation	Preservation	Preservation	Documentation	
Resolve Signture	Imaging Technologies	Approved Methods	Traceability	Traceability	Expert Testimony	
Profile Detection	Chain of Custody	Approved Software	Validation Techniques	Statistical	Clarification	
Anomalous Detection	Time Synch.	Approved Hardware	Filtering Techniques	Protocols	Mission Impact Statement	
Complaints		Legal Authority	Pattern Matching	Data Mining	Recommended Countermeasure	
System Monitoring		Lossless Compression	Hidden Data Discovery	Timeline	Statistical Interpretation	
Audit Analysis		Sampling	Hidden Data Extraction	Link		
Etc.		Data Reduction		Spacial		
		Recovery Techniques				

Figure 2. National institute of standards and technology, four-phase digital investigation model proposed in SP 800-86 (Kent, et al., 2006)

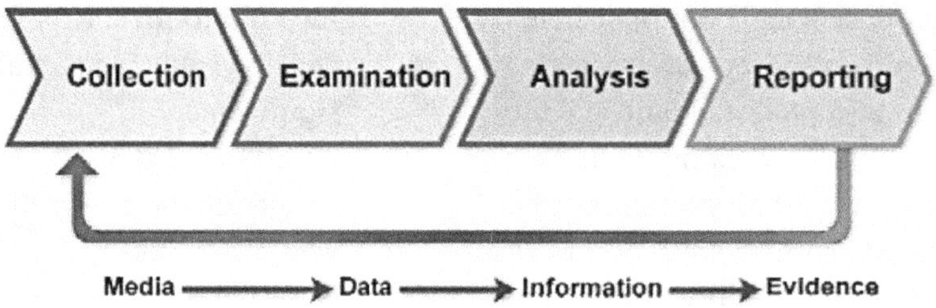

In this model each phase is defined as such:

- **Collection:** "Identify potential sources of data and acquire data from them"
- **Examination:** "Assessing and extracting the relevant pieces of information from the collected data"
- **Analysis:** "Study and analyze the data to draw conclusions from it"
- **Reporting:** "Preparing and presenting the information resulting from the analysis phase"

Integrated Digital Investigation Process

Carrier and Spafford (2003) proposed a investigation process model that considered the physical investigation along with the digital investigation

Figure 3. Integrated digital investigation process phases (Carrier & Spafford, 2003)

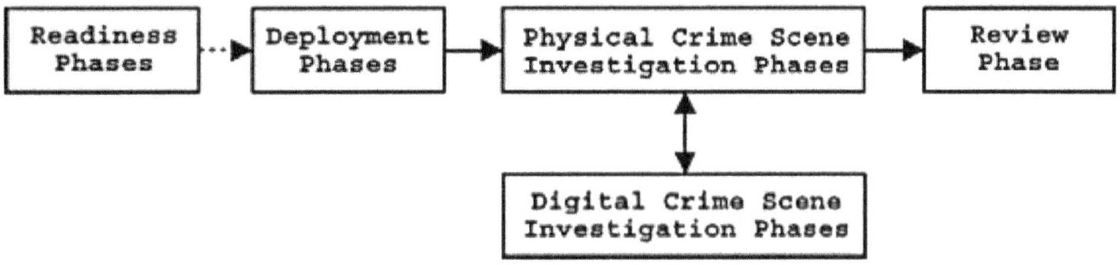

Figure 4. Integrated digital investigation process breakdown of physical crime scene investigation phase (Carrier & Spafford, 2003)

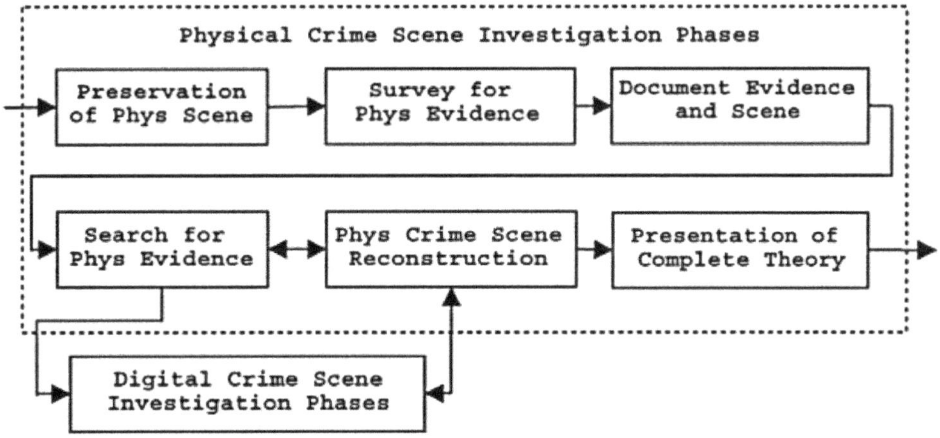

(see Figure 3). This model, named the Integrated Digital Investigation Process (IDIP), takes a holistic approach to crime scene investigation, where the physical crime scene reconstruction (see Figure 4) effects, and is affected by, the digital crime scene reconstruction (see Figure 5) to form a complete theory of happened events. Unlike the previous models, the IDIP feeds back between the physical and digital investigation phases. However, the overall model can be described as: Readiness, Deployment, Preservation, Survey, Documentation, Search, Reconstruction, Presentation, and Review.

All of the previously discussed process models have a common core. While each model has components that will continue to be debated, each model generally attempts to secure suspect data, analyze the secured data, and report on the findings in a way that is admissible in court. To accomplish this, preparation beforehand is necessary, as is meticulous documentation throughout the entire process. A particular model may be better suited to a certain organization, but generally each model will accomplish these main goals. One issue is in the standardization and verification of models used. Ensuring that the investigation and examination processes are valid is a topic of concern that can only begin to be alleviated when rigor is introduced into each phase of a digital forensic investigation.

Formal Methods

The concept of digital forensics as a science has been debated, and a call for formalizing digital forensic investigations has been proposed by academics and practitioners alike (Stephenson, 2003;

Figure 5. Integrated digital investigation process breakdown of digital crime scene investigation phase (Carrier & Spafford, 2003)

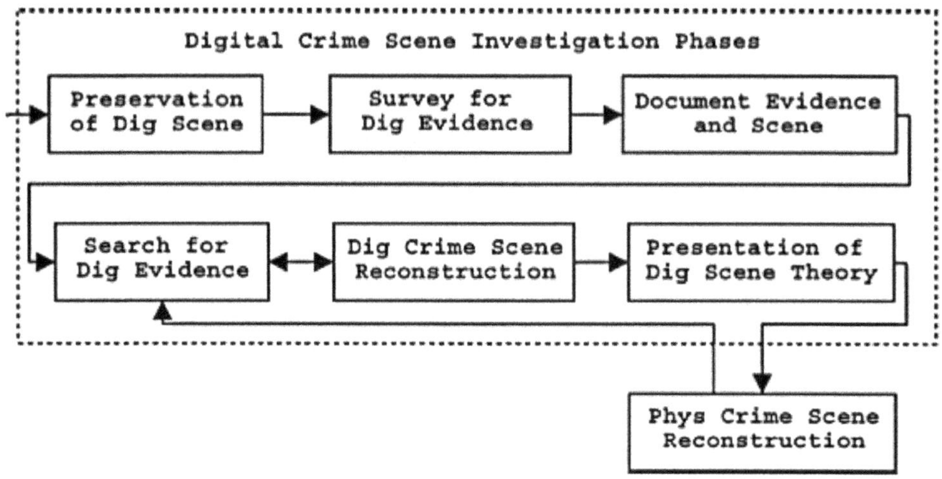

Gladyshev & Patel, 2004). "[T]he digital investigation process can be considered scientific if it formulates and tests hypotheses that are scientific" (Carrier, 2006). Various formal models have been proposed for digital investigation processes, such as the computer history model (Carrier & Spafford, 2006), finite state machine models (Gladyshev, 2004; James, et al., 2010), and others (Willassen, 2008; Rekhis & Boudriga, 2010). Research into the formalization of digital investigations is increasing, but these techniques are usually still too theoretical to be practically applied. Going forward, however, newly implemented digital investigation processes must be based on formal methods in order to ensure validation and integrity of the process, and to guarantee the field is backed by scientific, rather than improvised, methods.

Digital Evidence

The Scientific Working Group on Digital Evidence (SWGDE) define digital evidence as "[i]nformation of probative value that is stored or transmitted in binary form" (SWGDE, 2009). There are two states of data that digital forensic investigators must work with: live (non-persistent) data and post-mortem (persistent) data. Live data is data in a system that is powered on, and is more prone to change. Persistent data is data available when the system has been shut down. It must be said that all data has a degree of volatility, or susceptibility to change, and the speed in which data is likely to change, ordered from fastest to slowest, is known as the Order of Volatility (OoV). Farmer and Venema (2005) give an example of a "rough guide" for the order of volatility for different locations of data storage, assuming a live system (see Table 1).

Digital investigators must consider the implications of collecting each type of data, and be able to prioritize the data by the order of volatility. The order of volatility, and even availability of data, differs between a live system and an offline system.

Post-Mortem Data Forensic Acquisition and Verification

Many digital investigators have been taught to physically disconnect the power, or "pull the plug," on a suspect computer that is powered on at a crime scene (NIJ, 2008). Disconnecting the power would ensure that evidence would not be modified by processes running on the suspect system. Pulling

Table 1. Approximation of the lifespan of data by order of volatility

Registers, peripheral memory, caches, etc.	nanoseconds
[Random Access Memory]	nanoseconds
Network state	milliseconds
Running processes	seconds
Disk	minutes
Floppies, backup media, etc.	years
CD-ROMs, printouts, etc.	tens of years

the plug became standard practice until relatively recently when investigators, and the legal system in general, started considering volatile data, such as data in Random Access Memory, that was being lost. Once the power had been removed, a digital investigator was able to copy the persistent data, such as data written to the hard drive before powering down. Because persistent data is static, it is relatively easy to verify that the data has not changed over time. Verification of static data for digital forensic investigation purposes is normally done using a cryptographic hash.

"A hash function (H) is a transformation that takes an input m and returns a fixed-size string, which is called the hash value h (that is, $h = \mathrm{H}(m)$)" (Public-Key Cryptography Standards, 2009). Hash values are used in digital forensic investigations to verify the integrity of data. Hash value in the context of digital forensics are defined as "numerical values, generated by hashing functions, used to substantiate the integrity of digital evidence…" (SWGDE, 2009).

Once a suspect's device is shut down, an examiner can make a bit-by-bit copy of the storage media, known as a 'forensic image' (Shipley & Door, 2012). A common way to acquire the suspect's storage media is by removing the suspect hard drive, and attaching it to a workstation using a hardware or software write-blocker to ensure no data can be written. Once connected, many tools exist to make a bit-by-bit copy of either the whole physical disk, known as a physical disk image, or to make a copy of specific partitions on the disk, known as a logical disk image.

By hashing the suspect bit-level data on the media before acquisition, the resulting hash value becomes the standard with which to compare to ensure 1) the data on the suspect disk has not changed through actions of the examiner, 2) the created forensic image is an exact copy of the original suspect media, and 3) the suspect data can be verified by a third-party. Hashing static data at the time of acquisition allows investigators throughout the chain of custody to verify that any previous, or current, processes have not altered the data they are working with. Persistent data may be verified by utilizing the fact that the data should not change over time. Because of this, a hash of the data can be compared with the original, even years later. In the case of a post-mortem data analysis, the hard drive of a suspect computer can be removed and hashed, and a forensic disk image, or exact copy of the data, could be created. The disk image could then be hashed. If both hash values are exactly the same, then the data on the hard drive, and within the disk image, can be said to be the same. Hashing and imaging is normally done after powering down the suspect computer. The hashing process is not instantaneous, and shutting down ensures that no data changes while hashing process is taking place. In many situations, however, powering down a critical server may not be feasible, or data that is relevant to the case may not be persistent. In these cases, live data forensics may be the only alternative.

Live Data Forensic Acquisition and Verification

Live data forensics has been proposed to "provide additional information that is not available in a disk-only forensic analysis" (Adelstein, 2006). Live data forensics is conducted on a running suspect system, and is used to collect volatile data—such as the contents of RAM—that may contain encryption keys, chat fragments, active network connections, active processes, cache, etc.

Live forensic imaging of a suspect drive may also be done on critical systems that cannot be shut down. There are a number of benefits and drawbacks to live data forensics. Sometimes live data forensics is necessary because the system may be critical to business continuity, shutting down may create legal liability for examiners, or the system may have encrypted media that will be inaccessible when dismounted (Bilby, 2006). In these situations, live data forensics may be the best way to collect evidence, although not ideal. Several challenges with live data forensics must be considered.

First, the suspect system is still running, and data is likely to be changing as it is being collected. Because of this, it is impossible for a third party to verify that the data collected is correct. This is similar to previously discussed fingerprint extraction methods. Acquiring a copy of the fingerprint alters the original, making it impossible to be verified by a third party. In the case of digital forensics, to acquire RAM (from the suspect machine) a program must first be loaded into the suspect RAM. Meaning that to collect the data, some data must be altered. Further, acquiring RAM takes time, and during that time processes may be starting or stopping and users may be connecting and disconnecting from the suspect system. By the time the entire contents of RAM have been acquired, the state of the RAM has changed from when collection began. Hashing methods for verification of live data are only useful for the data that has been collected and is no longer changing. Data that has been collected cannot be verified after acquisition since the original data is constantly changing, and is no longer the same as at the time of acquisition. In addition, there is a possibility of crashing the suspect system when attempting live data forensics, which has potential to disrupt, or even corrupt, critical business data.

Second, when conducting live data forensics, the investigator will make changes to the system. However, in order to collect volatile evidence, the suspect's computer must remain on, and the suspect's operating system must be used to access the needed data[4]. When retrieving information from RAM, for example, a program must be loaded into the running memory, changing its contents. Even just inserting a USB key into a running suspect system will alter the system. However, Principle 2 of the ACPO guideline states:

In circumstances where a person finds it necessary to access original data held on a computer or on storage media, that person must be competent to do so and be able to give evidence explaining the relevance and the implications of their actions.

Principle 2 essentially allows the use of live data forensics in extraordinary situations, as previously mentioned, as long as the investigator is both competent, and knows the full impact of his or her actions.

Finally, live data forensics usually relies on the suspect system. Alternative methods of RAM acquisition, such as the so-called 'cold boot attack' (Halderman, et al., 2009) and FireWire acquisition methods (Martin, 2007; Gladyshev & Almansoori, 2010) have been proposed, but these methods also have associated risks. Carrier (2006) claims that the suspect system cannot be trusted. Rootkits or other malware in the suspect system can provide various anti-forensic functions, resulting in unreliable evidence (Bilby, 2006). To minimize the reliance on the suspect system, Carrier suggests that analysis applications should use their own file system code rather than relying on the kernel and system calls, and to use trusted binaries on write-protected media; a technique most live data forensic tools, such as Microsoft's Computer Online Forensic Evidence Extractor (COFEE) (Mansfield-Devine, 2010; Microsoft, 2010) are using. These techniques do not completely remove the risk of malicious code on the suspect system affecting a forensic investigation, but, assuming Principle 2 of the ACPO guideline has been met, they do reduce the risk to a level that tends to be accepted in court.

Regardless of the drawbacks, live data forensics is sometimes the only option for collecting evidence. Live forensic data has been accepted in court (Adelstein, 2006), and since computer systems are becoming increasingly more distributed, data center oriented, and services are becoming more 'Cloud' based, traditional post-mortem data forensics becomes less of an option.

CLOUD COMPUTING: SECURITY AND DIGITAL FORENSICS

This section introduces cloud computing, related terminology, and service and deployment models. Once fundamental knowledge of cloud computing is established, some key cloud computing security challenges will examined, followed challenges cloud computing brings to digital forensic investigations.

What is the Cloud?

The concept of cloud computing, and the services provided via the "Cloud," has received increasing interest from the public, private companies and even government organizations (Paquette, et al., 2010; Russell & Hammons, 2012), and as such are introducing more opportunities for cyber criminals and new challenges for law enforcement (Biggs & Vidalis, 2009). Many believe cloud computing is a computing paradigm shift, while others believe that cloud is a collection of old technologies with a new name for marketing purposes (Johnson, 2008; Armbrust, et al., 2009; Ellison, 2009). An obscure understanding of both the underlying technologies and new business model opportunities—and where each begin and end—has lead to some confusion in the definition of cloud computing. This confusion in definition appears to come from the fact that cloud computing is primarily comprised of three service layers[5]: infrastructure, platform, and application (Mell & Grance, 2011), each of which can be completely, or even partially, provided by any number of Cloud Service Providers (CSP).

Cloud computing encompasses each of these three service layers, which will be discussed further, but some layers are neglected when definitions focus on particular technologies rather than cloud computing as a whole concept (Vaquero, et al., 2008). Armbrust et al. (2009) submit that "cloud computing refers to both the applications delivered as services over the Internet and the hardware and systems software in the datacenters that provide those services." NIST (Mell & Grance, 2011) has proposed an arguably more comprehensive definition for Cloud Computing that is gaining in popularity:

Cloud computing is a model for enabling ubiquitous, convenient, on-demand network access to a shared pool of configurable computing researches (e.g., networks, servers, storage, applications, and services) that can be rapidly provisioned and released with minimal management effort or service provider interaction.

Further, NIST identifies five 'essential characteristics' of cloud computing, these being on-demand self-service, broad network access, resource pooling, rapid elasticity, and measured service. When each of these essential characteristics are met, it allows for "the illusion of infinite computing researches available on demand… [as well as] the ability to pay for the use of computing resources on a short-term basis as needed" (Armbrust, et al., 2009). In other words, computing resources can be sold to customers as a utility, much like water or electricity, where the customer is able to use as much as they want, when they want, and only pay for what they have used.

Armbrust, Fox et al. (2010) claim that when computing resources can be sold as a utility, there are at least three use cases that "favor utility computing over conventional hosting." The first is when a company must build their data center to be able to serve the peak load. At times when load is less than peak, infrastructure is being underutilized. They claim that "cloud computing lets an organization pay by the hour for computing resources, potentially leading to cost savings even if the hourly rate to rent a machine from a cloud provider is higher than the rate to own one."

The second case is when a customer does not yet know the demand for their services. Since computing resources in the Cloud can be provisioned as needed, as a user base rises or falls, so too can the amount of computing resources provisioned by the customer be added and removed. Rapid provisioning allows a customer to be more flexible in situations where load may be highly variable or rapidly increase as popularity grows.

The third case is for batch processing needs. Since the cost of processing using one machine for 1,000 hours, and 1,000 machines for one hour is the same, companies who require batch processing can potentially save time on their processing needs.

Choo (2010) expands on these points, considering the benefit of "avoid[ing] the expense and time-consuming task of installing and maintaining hardware infrastructure and software applications," claiming that hardware investments and administrative costs may be reduced when utilizing cloud infrastructure.

Although cloud computing may provide a number of benefits, it is not without potential drawbacks. Risks in terms of security and investigation will be discussed in later sections, but many potential risks, to both the CSP and the cloud customer, are dependent on the service and deployment models utilized.

Cloud Computing: Service Models

Cloud computing is primarily comprised of three service layers (Mell & Grance, 2011). These three layers are also essentially business models, or the level at which cloud services are normally sold by a Cloud Service Provider.

Infrastructure as a Service

The first of the three primary service layers is the infrastructure layer, which is comprised of computing hardware, and a software abstraction layer. Computing hardware in the Cloud is relatively unchanged from pre-cloud infrastructures; datacenters, for example, still largely use the same hardware. Some companies are attempting to market their hardware as specifically 'for cloud' (Duffy, 2009; Myslewski, 2009), which focus on faster delivery, convergence or multi-processing, but these technologies may also be useful for non-cloud infrastructures.

Still in the infrastructure layer, but on top of the hardware, is a software layer, termed hypervisor. "[The hypervisor] provides an abstraction layer that allows each physical server to run one or more 'virtual servers,' effectively decoupling the operating system and its applications from the underlying physical server" (Xen, 2011). For cloud services, at this layer is also a management stack that allows resource pooling. Many separate servers can then be added to the resource pool, creating the illusion of an infinite amount of resources. This concept is quite similar to distributed, or grid, computing[6]. The difference is in resource allocation for a task. With cloud computing the customer is allocated "a small fraction of the total cloud resource pool" (Eucalyptus, 2010), allowing multiple customers to use separate fractions of resources from the pool at the same time. In traditional distributed systems, a customer's task will attempt to utilize most, if not all, of the resource pool until their task is complete. This means other customers must wait in a queue until tasks before them are complete (McGuigan, 2011).

With cloud computing, a company effectively has a large pool of processing and storage of which a small portion of the whole can be rented to customers when needed, usually on a pay-per-usage scheme. This is referred to as Infrastructure as a Service (IaaS). To create the illusion of infinite resources IaaS requires a considerable investment in hardware, and has high associated running costs. Hobson (2010) claims that "Cloud Service Providers like Amazon, Google and Microsoft are driving the push, because they have excess capability to spare." As described previously, an attractive feature of IaaS to many companies is a possible operating cost reduction by letting an IaaS provider handle the hardware and maintenance, rather than buying and maintaining more hardware than they need, or running the risk of having too few resources during a spike in customer activity.

Platform as a Service

The second of the three primary service layers is the platform layer. The platform layer relies on the previously mentioned infrastructure layer, and has the goal of providing a Web-accessible platform for customers. The customer, however, normally has no control over the infrastructure layer that the platform is built upon. "This cloud computing model provides a platform for developers to code, test and experiment [with] new software without the complexity of setting up and maintaining test, development and production servers" (Brennels, 2010), and is known as Platform as a Service (PaaS).

The platform provided is usually either a base operating system or a full software stack[7] used to deliver a solution. Whatever the platform, the reason for it is generally storage, application development, and hosting, especially for providing services to many concurrent users. Some platform services, for example, are Google Apps, Microsoft's Azure, and Amazon's EC2. By utilizing the flexibility of the resource pool at the infrastructure level, the provided platform can quickly be allocated more or less resources, or multiple platforms—sometimes referred to as instances—can be created and configured, allowing the "increase or decrease [of] capacity within minutes, not hours or days" (Amazon, 2011).

Software as a Service

The third of the three primary layers is the software layer. At the software later, a provider's applications are provided to the customer. This is known as Software as a Service (SaaS). As the top tier, the software layer relies on both the platform and infrastructure layers for both hosting, and to allocate more or less resources for the application based on the application's needs. The customer, however, normally has no control over the platform and infrastructure layers that the application is running on. Google Docs and Apple's iCloud are examples of software as a service (Wang, et al., 2011). The applications are hosted by a provider, and are delivered to a client through a gateway. The client, in the case of Google Docs, for example, does not install any applications locally, and can save user data either locally or to available storage provided by the infrastructure and application layers.

Other Service Models

Other service models exist which are built on top of some, or all, of the three previously mentioned primary layers. One such example is Recovery as a Service (RaaS), which is essentially a backup of servers and data to a cloud that can be made live in case of failure or emergency. Gartner (Pettey, 2011) defines RaaS as "the managed replication of virtual machines and production data in a service-provider's cloud, together with the means to activate the VMs to support either recovery testing or actual recovery operations." Failing over to backed-up systems that can immediately be made live in the Cloud has a potential benefit of being faster than receiving and recovering from tape backups, with possibly less data loss in the process (Brennels, 2010).

Another proposed model is Security as a Service (SecaaS). The Cloud Security Alliance (2011) define Security as a Service as "the provision of security applications and services via the Cloud either to cloud-based infrastructure and software or from the Cloud to the customers' on-premise systems." In the same way cloud computing potentially reduces computing costs for companies, SecaaS may "... enable enterprises to make use of security services in new ways, or in ways that would not be cost effective if provisioned locally."

A final example is Forensics as a Service (FaaS). When conducting digital forensic investigations, large amounts of data must be processed. Efforts have begun to utilize the resources cloud computing provides, and apply them to digital forensic processing needs (Didone & de Queirozb, 2011; Carrier, 2012). The majority of work thus far has focused on utilizing processing capabilities, normally for law enforcement or consulting companies. But just like other described service models, cloud-based forensic services as software, or even a platform, could potentially be provided to users cloud-based infrastructure or on-premise systems. Potentially reducing the time from incident detection to forensic investigation.

These are only a few examples in a trend towards what Hewlett-Packard (2011) describes as "Everything as a Service" (XaaS).

Cloud Computing: Deployment Models

Organizations have a wide range of needs, and are looking to cloud computing to reduce operating costs. An organization, however, may not feel comfortable entrusting their entire infrastructure, hosting and storage needs to an off-site, uncontrollable CSP. Likewise, some organizations, such as government entities, may have higher security standards and requirements than average cloud customers. Three primary deployment models are commonly used to meet the almost endless combination of needs from organizations that still want to receive the benefits of cloud computing.

Private Cloud

NIST (Mell & Grance, 2011) defines a private cloud as "infrastructure [that] is provisioned for exclusive use by a single organization...." This allows the organization to utilize some of the benefits of cloud computing, such as resource pooling, hardware abstraction, robustness and fast instance deployment and configuration, while still keeping both physical and policy level control of all hardware, software and services. The resources in a private cloud are utilized only for the single organization, referred to as 'single tenant' environment. Operating a private cloud, however, still requires an investment in infrastructure and knowledge. Because of this, over or under provisioning of resources is still possible, and costs associated with infrastructure, running and maintenance may still be a burden on the organization. Since this model is single tenant the costs are not distributed, making it the most expensive model.

Public Cloud

Public clouds are cloud services offered to the public via a CSP. Unlike a private cloud, the organization running the cloud service does so to offer cloud resources to external customers. Multiple customers then lease resources from a shared resource pool, referred to as a 'multi-tenant' environment. The CSP then takes on the burden of installing, running, and maintaining the provided infrastructure. Since the infrastructure/platform/software security concerns are managed by the dedicated CSP, some organizations may benefit from better security practices than they would be able to create and implement in-house. Since this model is multi-tenant, the costs are distributed over a large number of customers, making it the least expensive model. With this model, cloud customers may trust the CSP for hosting, storage and general access to the customer's data—all of which could be revoked or removed by the CSP, e.g. if the customer stopped paying, or the CSP went out of business (Kravets, 2012). CSPs offer comprehensive Service Level Agreements (SLA) to define what they are and are not responsible for. While the customer may have some control over whether their data is stored nationally or internationally, they do not generally have physical access to their host, and can lose a great deal of policy-level control. Lower running costs and increased ease of deployment, however, are attractive for many organizations regardless of this loss of control.

Community Cloud

A community cloud is a deployment where multiple organizations pool their resources to achieve a common goal. By pooling the resources for the community, costs are distributed between the members, allowing for the benefits of a cloud while being less expensive than a private cloud. A community cloud works when each member has similar task, policy, and security needs, but liability, internal security, and distribution of investment and maintenance costs are all challenges with this deployment. For these reasons, this model may not be ideal for business critical hosting needs since a business may have less physical or policy control of their data without the assurance of an SLA.

Hybrid Cloud

For this work, the hybrid cloud deployment model will not be considered one of the primary models; however, it is a noteworthy, often used *extension* to the primary cloud deployment models. This model also has yet to see a widely accepted common definition. The debated definition from NIST (Mell & Grance, 2011) is:

The [hybrid] cloud infrastructure is a composition of two or more clouds (private, community, or public) that remain unique entities but are bound together by standardized or proprietary technology that enables data and application portability (e.g., cloud bursting for load-balancing between clouds).

This definition is also sometimes referred to as a combination cloud. Under this definition, two or more of the previously described deployment models are joined together, but still remain unique entities. The benefit of this model is one of flexibility, and also potential cost savings. Two common methods are normally used to achieve this goal, cloud bursting and cloud brokering.

"Cloud bursting combines existing cloud infrastructure with remote resources from one or more public clouds to provide extra capacity to satisfy peak demand periods" (Moreno-Vozmediano, et al., 2012). For example, an organization that has its own private cloud may temporarily exceed its internal capacity. Instead of increasing investment in infrastructure for a temporary overutilization, some services can be expanded to a public CSP. To take advantage of cloud bursting, an organization must first identify mission critical and non-critical data. The organization, then, could control what data is hosted on the public cloud, ensuring that mission critical data never leaves their area of physical or policy level control.

A cloud broker, according to Grivas et al. (2010), has knowledge of existing cloud service offerings from multiple CSPs, and the relation between business processes and the cloud services. A cloud customer is able to request a business process change, and the broker discovers and binds new services from one or more CSPs to provide the desired process changes for the customer. This allows customers to focus on their business processes instead of devoting time and resources towards discovering, testing and comparing the plethora of cloud service offerings. A cloud broker could potentially broker services for only one CSP or cloud deployment, but normally brokerage occurs across multiple CSPs (Bloomberg, 2011), potentially resulting in a hybrid cloud deployment for the customers.

Cloud Computing Security and Investigation Challenges

New concepts in cloud computing have created new challenges for security teams and researchers alike (Vouk, 2008). Cloud computing service and deployment models have a number of potential benefits for businesses and customers, but security and investigation challenges—some inherited from 'traditional' computing, and some unique to cloud computing—create uncertainty and potential for abuse as cloud technologies proliferate. This section looks at security challenges relating to cloud computing. Further, challenges cloud computing poses to digital forensic investigation will also be given.

Cloud Computing and Security Challenges

According to a survey from Ponemon Institute (2011), only 35% of IT respondents and 42% of compliance respondents believe their organizations have adequate technologies to secure their IaaS environments. The report shows that respondents believe IaaS is less secure than their on-premise systems, however, "[m]ore than half (56 percent) of IT practitioners say that security concerns will not keep their organizations from adopting cloud services." A drive towards cloud service offerings is reiterated by Gartner (2012), who forecasts that spending on cloud computing at each service model layer will more than double by 2016. At the same time Ernst and Young (2011) found that there is a perceived increase in risk by adopting cloud and mobile technologies, and many respondents believe that these risks are not currently being adequately dealt with. However, North Bridge (Skok, 2012) suggests that confidence in cloud computing is increasing, even though maturity of the technologies remains a concern[8].

An increased confidence in cloud computing and a drive to improve business processes while reducing costs are leading to security of such systems being a secondary concern. This attitude has been carried over from traditional computing, which could possibly result in the same, or similar, security challenges, such as those presented by the Computer Research Association (2003) in the *Four Grand Challenges in Trustworthy Computing*.

If both security and insecurity from traditional computing are inherited by cloud computing, both may be augmented with the increased complexity of the cloud model, the way that services are delivered, and on-demand extreme-scale computing. Each cloud deployment and service model has its own considerations as far as security and liability are concerned. For example, in a private, single-tenant cloud where all services may be hosted on-premise, the risks are similar to on-premise, non-cloud hosting. The organization has end-to-end control, can implement and target security systems, and can control critical data flow and storage policies. A challenge with this model is that the organization must have the expertise to be able to create, implement, and maintain a comprehensive security strategy for increasingly complex systems.

Several works have previously examined some cloud security concerns (Armbrust, et al., 2009; Jansen, 2011; Balduzzi, et al., 2012; Kui, et al., 2012; Zissis & Lekkas, 2012). The majority of these works can generally be classified as using a Confidentiality, Integrity, and Availability (CIA) model, extended by introducing the concept of 'trust.'

Confidentiality

In the CIA model, confidentiality is used to describe the limitation of access to data (or information) to only authorized users. Cloud computing introduces a number of confidentiality concerns. Some reasons for this include multiple—possibly competing—customers utilizing the same hardware, the remote and dispersed nature of the cloud service provider, possible layering of services from multiple CSPs, the legality of data disclosure to a third-party, and general access management, among others. Gellman (2009) states that "[c] loud computing has significant implications for the privacy of personal information as well as for the confidentiality of business and governmental information," claiming that a user's privacy and confidentiality risks vary significantly with the terms of service and privacy policy established by the cloud provider, and potentially along with the jurisdiction in which the data is physically stored.

Messmer (2011) claims that access control in cloud environments is somewhat difficult, and may not meet data protection regulations. Kui et al. (2012) identify access control in outsourced cloud environments as 'critical,' defining secure identity authentication as a challenge when data is outsourced to a CSP. "[The] data users and cloud servers aren't in the same trusted *domain;* the server might no longer be fully trusted as an omniscient reference monitor for defining and enforcing access control policies and managing user details." Kui et al. suggest that user authentication may be untrustworthy when outsourced due to server compromise beyond the customer's domain of control, or potential insider attacks from the CSP.

Balduzzi et al. (2012) demonstrated that potential confidentiality risks exist for users who create and distribute images for use in the Cloud, claiming that, for example, "an attacker can gather SSH private keys [from a virtual machine image] to break into other machines, or use forgotten Amazon Web Services (AWS) keys to start instances at the image provider's cost." In their research they were able to recover forgotten AWS and SSH keys that were immediately usable to start new instances at the key owner's expense; last login information that could be used to collect usernames, target machines, and potentially passwords; browser history, from which they found traces of a user's company and personal email login information; authentication credentials and potentially interesting commands to extract user and database login information, credit card information, VNC authentication, etc, by examining shell history; and in some cases they were also able to recover deleted files, such as the aforementioned keys and history logs.

Kui et al. (2012), Balduzzi et al. (2012), and Zissis and Lekkas (2012) all identify multi-tenancy as a confidentiality risk with could computing. Kui et al. claims, "side-channel attacks present new risks to cloud users' information in the multitenant environment." It has been shown that an attacker can force a machine under their control to co-locate on the same hardware as a victim, allowing for the possibility of side-channel attacks[9] (Ristenpart, et al., 2009). From this, stolen cryptographic keys and passwords, and general spying are possible. Likewise, Balduzzi et al. gave an example of scanning other VM instances on the network, and determining open ports and potentially vulnerable services. Zissis and Lekkas, on the other hand, submit, "Data [persistence] may lead to the unwilling disclosure of private data," claiming that "a user may claim a large amount of disk space and then scavenge for sensitive data."

While some confidentiality considerations can be reasonably remedied by choosing a reputable CSP that provides an SLA that suits the organization as well as "certifications of quality and operational control" (Ingthorsson, 2010), other implications, such as legal requirements of the CSP to produce details of customer activities to law enforcement may not be able to be avoided. For example, in some cases in the United States, the government may demand customer details from Internet Service Providers unbeknownst to the customer. "There have been thousands of such requests lodged since the [the Patriot Act] was passed, and the F.B.I.'s own audits have shown that there can be plenty of overreach... " (Zittrain, 2009). Legal, liability, and other jurisdiction issues are not necessarily new privacy considerations brought on by the use of cloud computing, but the level of outsourcing, and the possibly global dispersion of the CSP raises new concerns on the ease of information leakage.

Most of these privacy issues stem from the fact that an organization essentially loses control when their data is given to a *third party*. Cloud computing adds to this risk by introducing the multi-tenant and service-layering aspects, which could possibly be abused.

Integrity

Integrity in the CIA model normally refers to the trustworthiness of data or information. Jansen (2011) claims that using cloud services, especially in multi-tenant environments, may increase risk to the integrity of data, both in storage and processing. "Multi-tenancy in VM-based cloud infrastructures, together with the subtleties in the way physical resources are shared between guest VMs, can give rise to new sources of threats." For example, malicious code may circumvent VM isolation methods, and interfere with the hypervisor or other guest VMs. IBM (2010) claims that 35% of known vulnerabilities in server virtualization allow an attacker to escape from a guest virtual machine to either another guest or the hypervisor itself.

Even without circumventing isolation methods within the CSPs infrastructure, Balduzzi et al. (2012) showed that traditional software vulnerabilities, such as non-updated software, may still lead to malware infection that could result in questionable integrity of stored data and running services.

Another area that may have an impact on the integrity of data is computation outsourcing. Kui et al. (2012) submit that "the Cloud's operational details aren't transparent enough to users. Consequently, various motivations can cause the Cloud to behave unfaithfully and return incorrect results." Hardware problems, software bugs, or outsider or insider attacks could potentially compromise the integrity of processed data.

Zissis and Lekkas (2012) focus instead on the social aspect of integrity, claiming "the cloud model presents a number of threats including sophisticated insider attacks on [customer data]." They cite authentication as an issue in cloud environments "due to the increased number of entities and access points..." that could potentially lead to a manipulation of software that can affect the integrity of customer data.

Availability

Cloud computing resources are designed for high availability, however, Jansen (2011) submits that cloud service providers "can and do experience outages and performance slowdowns." Temporary outages have occurred with Amazon (Kosner, 2012), Google (2012), and Microsoft (Parnell, 2012) cloud services, caused by software, hardware or external issues. In these cases, service was eventually restored, but each left customers without access to services and data for a period of time.

Jansen also claims, "It is possible for a service provider to experience serious problems, like bankruptcy or facility loss, which affect service for extended periods or cause a complete shutdown." Cloud providers have gone out of business before, being bought by other companies that may allow current users a short period of time to retrieve their data (Scheier, 2009), while in other cases massive, irrevocable data loss has occurred (Bright, 2008). Missing a payment could be as drastic, and the only assurance of what will happen to a customer's is if the consequences are specified in an SLA with the CSP. However, an SLA may not always ensure data can be returned. For example, Megaupload, a once popular file-sharing portal, had company assets seized by New Zealand authorities, denying customers service since the seizure. Although the seizure and international sharing of seized data were deemed to be illegal by a New Zealand High Court (Chirgwin, 2012), service has not resumed, and customers are being denied access to legitimate data (Kravets, 2012).

Armbrust et al. (2009) believe that for high-availability, there should be no single point of failure. However, they claim, "the management of a Cloud Computing service by a single company is in fact a single point of failure," again citing hardware and software issues or CSPs going out of business. Further, Jansen and Armbrust, Fox et al. mention *Distributed Denial* of *Service* attacks (DDoS) that could potentially cripple cloud services, claiming that with enough computers, even cloud services could become saturated. Since multiple cloud service layers are used, each layer could be a potential point of attack to disrupt service to the client.

Jansen further claims that there is a 'value concentration' when data from multiple companies is hosted in the Cloud. This potentially means that cloud services may be more enticing to hackers since one CSP is likely to host data for multiple clients. If the hacker is able to penetrate the CSP, they may then gain data from multiple companies without targeting each of the companies individually.

The CSP is not the only potential point of failure. The client side that relies on cloud services may also be targeted. For example, anti-virus software is increasingly utilizing cloud computing for analysis of code. The response to cloud-based malicious code analysis was viruses that filter client-side network traffic to prevent the anti-virus agent from communicating certain information to the cloud service (Microsoft, 2011). Since client-server communication is a requirement the access cloud-based services, denial of service can be achieved by attacking any point of communication.

The distributed nature of cloud computing can allow for high availability if deployed correctly. A major challenge, however, is not only the traditional challenges of availability of data, but also the dependence on external third parties to be able to access critical data.

Trust

Some of the challenges mentioned previously are not unique to cloud computing, but a recurrent point in most work dealing with security in cloud computing is the concept of trust. In the traditional CIA model, critical data and services were normally under physical and policy control of the owner. In this case—except for insider threats—trust is implicit. The owner had a considerable amount of direct control over confidentiality, integrity, and accessibility. If any of these areas were lacking, the owner could make infrastructure or policy changes to improve, and for these reasons, the owner questioning their own level of trust was not explicitly stated. "In traditional architectures, trust was enforced by an efficient security policy, which addressed constraints on functions and flow among them, constraints on access by external systems and adversaries including programs and access to data by people" (Zissis & Lekkas, 2012). Trust in the Cloud, however, is not implicit. Many articles have been written questioning if data in the Cloud is more secure than on-premise systems (Kaufman, 2009). This is because many companies do not so easily trust external groups, even well known CSPs, to store and process critical data. For example, Ernst and Young (2011) found that "almost 90% of respondents believe that external certification would increase their trust in cloud computing."

Jansen (2011) claims that cloud customers are relinquishing direct control over many aspects of security. This "confers an unprecedented level of trust onto the service provider." This trust assumes that the CSP—and every CSP that is providing a service supporting the CSP the cloud customer is using—has proper controls and auditing in place to mitigate threats such as insider access, and vulnerabilities that each used cloud service introduces.

Zissis and Lekkas (2012) claim that in cloud computing the concept of perimeter security becomes "fuzzy." With traditional security, a perimeter of trust is created, and entities outside of this perimeter are considered suspicious. In the cloud model, critical data and business processes are outside of the perimeter of trust. For this reason, "the ability to clearly identify, authenticate, authorize, and monitor who or what is accessing the assets of an organization is essential to protecting an information system from threats and vulnerabilities." Zissis and Lekkas also propose that organizations should consider hybrid approaches, where critical systems, processes and data are isolated, and may be provided where the infrastructure is trusted, while non-critical systems, process and data maybe hosted by less-trusted CSPs.

Cloud computing is sold as a utility, or pay-per-use, service. Kui et al. (2012) identify that "because users might have little or no visibility into the cloud infrastructure, they're often unable to directly connect their actual cloud resource consumption and the usage charges." Without a guarantee on resource consumption measurement, and the ability to verify and audit charges, charges may be undisputable. For example, issues for which the customer should not be liable could cause excessive charges against which the customer may not be able to dispute. Further, charges could also potentially be falsified by the CSP. Without verifiable resource metering, a customer has no way to prove or disprove a claim.

When services are hosted in a public, multi-tenant, cloud, for example, the customer trusts the CSP for service. The customer is trusting that the CSP is able to competently create, implement and maintain a security strategy, not just for external attacks, but also from other tenants in the same cloud, and that their multi-tenant blanket approach to security will be adequate for all customers. Likewise, the customer must trust the CSP itself to not misuse the customer's data. Security comparisons of cloud deployments, and even between cloud and non-cloud infrastructures, is somewhat a moot point because "it is possible to deploy a private cloud in a way that is far less secure than the current batch of public clouds just as it is possible to deploy any infrastructure in an insecure way" (Wolski, 2010). Ultimately, it comes down to the organization's realistic evaluation of their capabilities and what amount of risk they are willing to take.

Other Cloud Security Concerns

Beyond the previously mentioned challenges, data and vendor lock-in is a concern with cloud services (Armbrust, et al., 2009; Kim, 2012). Data and vendor lock-in can become a challenge when Application-Programming Interfaces (API) are not standardized. If interfaces are not standardized, it may become difficult for cloud customers to move from one CSP to another, or even utilize multiple CSPs for data redundancy purposes.

Armbrust et al. also identify 'reputation fate sharing' as a risk. They state that "reputations do not virtualize well," claiming that one customer can impact the reputation of the CSP and all co-hosted users. For example, a spammer using the CSP's IP range, may get those IP addresses blacklisted (Kerbs, 2008). This could potentially disrupt service of legitimate cloud customers if they are later assigned an IP address that has been blacklisted.

Ernst and Young (2011) claim that "a company's physical boundaries are disappearing as more of its data is transmitted over the Internet." Because of the distributed nature of cloud computing, the physical location of data and the jurisdiction in which the data is located is a major concern that is seeing an increase in research (Ward & Sipior, 2010; Hu, et al., 2012; Vaciago, 2012).

The essence of the jurisdictional challenge is that a CSP may have data centers in multiple countries, each with unique laws about how and what data can be imported, exported, stored, and accessed. Depending on the CSP, and the underlying CSPs used to support the services, it may be difficult for a cloud customer to specify and audit the jurisdiction(s) in which they will allow their data to be stored. A customer having adequate knowledge of each of the legal systems where their data may be stored is a challenge that would require considerable resources for research on the side of the cloud customer. A mistake could allow critical data to be stored in countries with lax cybercrime and/or data privacy laws (Choo, 2010). Ruan et al. (2012) submit that service level agreements should define the level of control the cloud customer over the jurisdiction(s) in which customer data is allowed to reside, as well as allow the cloud customer or trusted third-party the ability to audit such restrictions. An SLA with the initial CSP must also include the ability to control and audit data stored on underlying CSP services.

Many of the previously discussed security considerations normally placed the cloud environment as the target of an attack, however, cloud services may also be used as the originator of attacks (Choo, 2010). For example, a proof of concept cloud-based DDoS infrastructure has been developed to conduct large-scale DDoS attacks using cloud resources for less than a similar criminal botnet would cost (Bryan & Anderson, 2010; Lemos, 2010).

Further, Roth (2011) demonstrated that the large amount of compute available in the cloud environment may be used as an extremely fast, and relatively inexpensive means of cracking passwords. Cloud computing allows the ability for a customer to design massively parallel and GPU assisted environments, applying the cost and time benefits of cloud computing to brute force[10] password cracking.

This work has described a number of security concerns for both CSPs and cloud customers. However, even though these are concerns, Kui et al. (2012) identify that "designing security into cloud benefits users and CSPs, [and] inevitably increased overhead for both." They submit that additional overhead (such as increased processing requirements) could increase the cost of the cloud services, which may conflict with the economic benefits that companies are hoping to realize by using these cloud services.

Finally, within organizations and between cloud customers and CSPs the ownership for security in the Cloud is not always precisely defined (Ponemon, 2011; Ruan, et al., 2012). If security tasks are not precisely assigned, a customer may be unwittingly vulnerable, and determination of liability when an incident occurs may be difficult.

For more security challenges in the Cloud see Additional Reading.

Cloud Computing and Investigation Challenges

Many of the technologies that make up cloud services, such as virtualization, have existed since before the utility computing business model was practical on a large scale. Because infrastructure, platform, and software hosting technologies have existed for business and personal use for some time, techniques for digital investigation of incidents relating to these technologies may be well known. For example, forensic acquisition and verification of hard drives is a common task in digital forensic investigations. Many times the same acquisition methods for a physical disk may also work for virtual disks associated with a virtual machine. Many of the digital forensic acquisition, verification, and analysis techniques may be able to be applied to cloud investigations, but cloud does pose some new challenges for digital forensic investigators. The following are a few of the many potential challenges cloud computing brings to digital investigation.

In traditional investigations, the suspect or victim's computers may normally be the main source of information about an incident. For example, in a child exploitation case, a suspect may have stored illicit images on their local hard drive. By finding and analyzing the images, the investigator may be able to determine that the images were, in fact, illegal. Other information, such as the recently opened files list, may be used to support that the suspect had knowledge of the images. However, if the suspect is using cloud-based storage, the images may not be stored locally. In this case, the investigator may be able to show that the suspect had knowledge of the images, but not whether the images were actually illegal. Saliba (2012) claims that cloud services may reduce the amount of direct evidence available on a suspect's disk, but sometimes provide more information about the user and cloud service that would help in acquiring a subpoena or warrant. As more data is stored in the Cloud, and services reduce the client-side impact, fewer evidential traces may be found. Instead, investigators will have to rely on more cooperation from CSPs that may not be in the same jurisdiction.

When suspect data is stored in the Cloud the data may be in one jurisdiction while the suspect machine connecting to the service may be in another jurisdiction. This scenario is becoming a challenge for law enforcement in many countries, especially with mobile cloud-attached devices. In many countries, investigators may access data stored remotely if given permission by the suspect (verbal conformation, entering the password, etc.). However, there has been very little definition of what to do if data is stored on a non-national cloud service that is currently connected while the investigator begins a live analysis of the suspect system. If the data is accessible, an investigator may save a considerable amount of time by acquiring the data from the connected service rather than waiting for international requests. However, authority on this matter is not always clear. In the author's experience, a lack of definition on the scope of acquisition of data on non-national remote connections sometimes depends on the country, and many times depends on the investigator's preliminary analysis of the remotely stored data as well as the likelihood of receiving the data if an international request was made.

Investigators physically accessing the CSP may also be more difficult, and may be impossible if the data is distributed over several geographic locations (Taylor, et al., 2011). In traditional investigations, a computer or server may possibly be taken down, and its physical disks imaged. Taking down production servers is increasingly rare for server environments since law enforcement may be liable for damages while the server is down. Taking servers down in a cloud environment may have an impact on many customers, creating more liability. Further, data may be stored on virtual storage spanning multiple servers, or even geographic locations, meaning that hard disk acquisition may not be practical, or even produce the desired data. Liability and reconstruction of virtual storage in cloud environments from physical disk images remains a challenge.

Storage in the Cloud is attractive to users because it is highly accessible and relatively cheap. As previously mentioned, the amount of data on personal hard drives is becoming too large for most law enforcement agencies to acquire and store all the data. Cloud services, however, are currently offering Gigabytes of space for free with the option to pay for more storage. The amount of stored data could quickly add up across multiple cloud service offerings, resulting again in too much data for law enforcement to process and store.

Since acquisition of a whole physical disk may not be practical or possible, and the quantity of data may be too large to effectively process and store, selective data acquisition may be required. Selective data acquisition implies a preliminary analysis, or some prior knowledge, to reduce the overall dataset an investigator is interested in. The challenge with this method is an intrinsic challenge in digital forensic investigations; how do we know what we do not know? In other words, even if all possible data could be acquired, how do we know that no evidence has been missed? If this question cannot be easily answered when all data is available, how can an investigator justify reducing the dataset, and potentially excluding inculpatory and/or exculpatory evidence? Some investigators are currently focusing on data sources that they believe are likely to provide the richest sources of information, but justifiable exclusion remains a challenge.

Because of the distributed, multi-layered nature of cloud computing, chain of custody for the data may be impossible to verify (Barbara, 2009).

Without strict controls it may be impossible to determine where exactly the data was stored, who had access, and was leakage or contamination of data possible. If data is stored in a cloud where multiple users and CSPs potentially have access, association of the data to the suspect is a challenge to establish beyond a reasonable doubt.

When an incident occurs on the side of the CSP, the CSP may be more concerned with restoring service than with preserving evidence. Further, the CSP may begin its own investigation into an incident without taking proper precautions to ensure the integrity of potential evidence. In more severe cases, CSPs may not report or cooperate in investigation of incidents for fear of reputational damage. The challenge in this case is with the competence and trustworthiness of the CSP. A CSP would be an effective, immediate first-responder, but questions about the integrity and chain of custody of the acquired evidence may make admissibility difficult. To meet this challenge law enforcement should work with CSPs, and ensure proper documentation is being created and forensically sound processes are being used.

Another challenge is with feature of rapid elasticity in cloud environments. Data associated with newly created virtual machine instances may only be available for a limited time. To this author's knowledge, no research has been conducted on determining available data associated with removed VM instances. If a new VM instance is created and either compromised or used to attack, evidential traces may be available in the VM. If the VM instance is then de-allocated, investigators currently do not know whether evidential traces or the entire VM instance cloud be recovered.

The final challenge in this non-comprehensive list is the issue of international communication. As mentioned previously, cloud computing blurs physical, policy, and jurisdictional boundaries globally. However, law enforcement at a global level has yet to find effective, timely, and efficient international communication and cooperation channels. Conferences such as the *International Symposium on Cybercrime Response* specifically discuss international law enforcement communication and collaboration efforts. Such conferences allow law enforcement to create informal communication channels, and sometimes help in the creation of bilateral agreements for cooperation, but these channels have their limits. Global law enforcement communication channels, such as INTERPOL's I-24/7 network or the G8 24/7 network, connect many countries, but are limited by their structure and bureaucracy. Many officers have found the global networks to be somewhat effective if the request was not overly urgent, however, these networks have failed to address real-time requests for help from countries under DDoS attack. Many times, law enforcement will prefer faster, informal channels to begin an international investigation, rather that traversing such networks. However, multi-country operations, such as "Operation Unmask" (Norton, 2012), show the potential of these networks to assist in large-scale coordination efforts. Overall, users, businesses and even criminals are utilizing technologies, such as cloud computing, to be able to rapidly find and share (and exploit) new ideas. These groups are no longer considering physical and political borders. Law enforcement, however, is currently restricted by a lack of effective global communication channels, political issues, and jurisdiction that make policing in a globally connected world even more of a challenge.

DIGITAL FORENSIC INVESTIGATION AND CLOUD COMPUTING

As more businesses and users adopt cloud computing, security challenges, such as those previously discussed, will be increasingly targeted and exploited. There are many technological and political challenges where investigation of potentially criminal incidents in the Cloud are concerned. Investigators, however, must still be able to acquire and analyze data in a methodical, rigorous, and forensically sound manner. This section explores the general application of a current digital forensic investigation process model—specifically the Integrated Digital Investigation Process—to cloud computing, and describes cloud investigation considerations at each phase of the model.

Readiness Phase

Carrier and Spafford (2003) state that "the goal of the readiness phases is to ensure that the operations and infrastructure are able to fully support an investigation." The operations readiness phase involves the on-going training of personnel, such as first responders and lab technicians, and the procurement and testing of equipment needed for the investigation.

Operation readiness should include education in cloud-related technologies, such as hypervisors, virtual machines, and cloud-based storage. Personnel should have general knowledge of how to interact with cloud technologies at the infrastructure, platform, and software layers, and understand the effect their actions have on the environment. They should understand the methods and tools available to collect investigation-relevant data in each layer of the Cloud. Different CSPs may have proprietary systems, so training on the use and investigation of these proprietary systems should be considered, if possible. Finally, personnel should have the hardware and software necessary to acquire relevant data from the Cloud.

Infrastructure readiness is an on-going process to ensure that investigation-relevant data is available when an incident occurs. Infrastructure readiness is a responsibility of the CSP, the level of which may be defined in the SLA between the CSP and the cloud customer. Because of the different in operations between CSPs, and the differing level of logging and data retention requested by cloud customers, law enforcement may have difficulty considering the type and amount of data that may be available.

The training of personnel, identification of potential risks, and identification of potential data sources before an incident occurs can greatly help in efficient incident response, and with the timely and sound acquisition of relevant data. For this reason, this work recommends that CSPs and law enforcement work together to model threats, their potential impact, and potential evidential trace data sources before an incident occurs. This will assist the CSP in preserving potential evidence during incident response, and will help law enforcement have a better idea of what data will be available, and how to handle such data, if a particular incident occurs.

To help in the identification of threats, their impact on a system, and their potential evidential traces, this work proposes an extension to the Spoofing, Tampering, Repudiation, Information Disclosure, Denial of Service, and Elevation of Privilege (STRIDE) model (Swiderski & Snyder, 2004). The STRIDE model is used to help understand the result of a specific threat being exploited in a system, and has previously been applied to probabilistic risk assessment in cloud environments (Saripalli & Walters, 2010). In this work, we propose to extend the STRIDE model beyond risk assessment and potential exploitation results, to add the identification of possible investigation-relevant traces produced by the exploitation. We term this the 'Investigation STRIDE model,' or I-STRIDE.

As shown in Figure 6, the I-STRIDE process is conducted by first deconstructing a service into its dependent components. A risk assessment is conducted per component, and risk mitigation techniques are derived. This work proposes that each risk identified by I-STRIDE, has associated investigation-relevant data sources. When a threat to a component has been identified, an investigator may determine what data is likely to be effected by the threat. From this subset of effected data, specific data sources that may be of evidential value can be identified. These potential evidential data sources may then be used for pre-investigation planning and data targeting purposes.

Application of I-STRIDE to a Deployed Cloud Architecture

To show the applicability of the I-STRIDE model to cloud environments, assessment of a small cloud computing infrastructure based on the Open Source distribution of Eucalyptus (2011) will be given as an example. The components of this platform will be explained, and an analysis using the I-STRIDE model will be conducted against this deployment.

The Eucalyptus architecture is composed of five high-level components that are essentially standalone Web services (Eucalyptus, 2010). These components include:

- **Cloud Controller (CLC):** The cloud controller is the main entry point for the cloud environment. CLC is responsible for "exposing and managing the underlying virtualized resources."
- **Cluster Component (CC):** CC is responsible for managing the execution of VM instances.
- **Storage Controller (SC):** Provides block-level network storage that can be dynamically attached by VMs instances.
- **Node Controller (NC):** Executed on every node that is designated for hosting and allows management of VM instances.
- **Walrus:** Allows the storage and management of persistent data.

Figure 7 shows the Eucalyptus components and their connection and communication channels.

The scope of this case will be limited to asset-centric[11] threat modeling. The assets in this case are will be defined as each of the Eucalyptus components, and will also include a cloud client. In this experiment, threats (see Table 2) were identified and exploited in the deployed Eucalyptus architecture. An analysis of which assets were affected and how, was conducted. After, an investigation was conducted to determine potential evidential data sources. Identified threats, their description, the affected asset, the impact on the asset, and the location of potential evidential data sources are listed in Table 2.

Using the I-STRIDE model could help CSPs and law enforcement identify an investigation starting point if a specific incident occurred. This level of readiness would potentially allow for improved pre-planning, first response and cooperation once an incident occurred.

Figure 6. The I-STRIDE process model for risk assessment, mitigation, and investigation

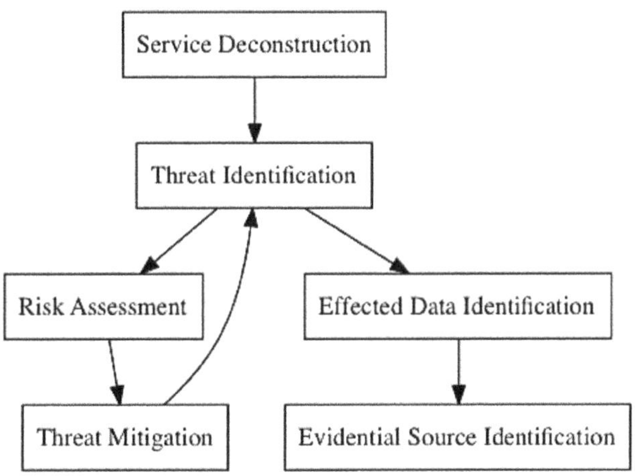

Figure 7. Deployed eucalyptus architecture

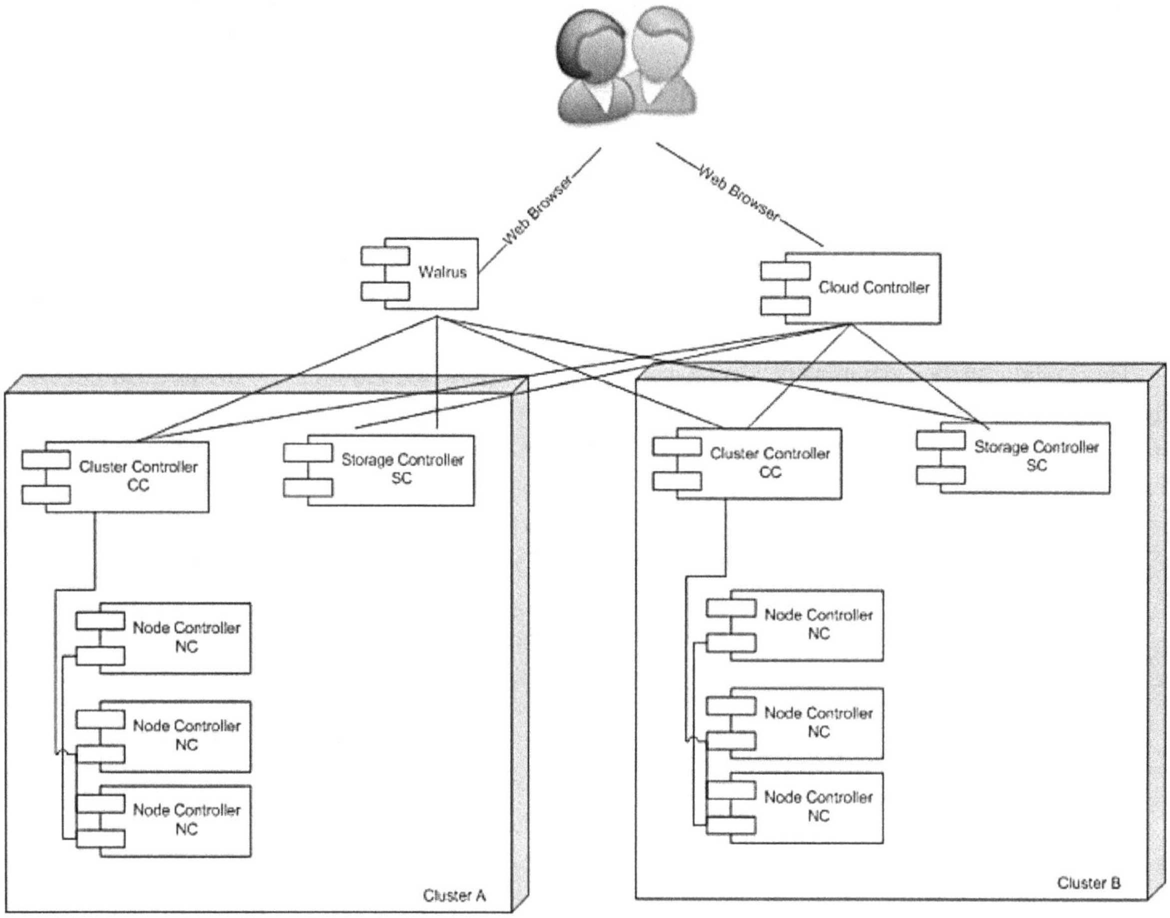

Deployment Phase

The deployment phase of the IDIP is split into detection and notification and confirmation and authorization phases. In the detection and notification phase, an incident is detected, and the appropriate people are notified. In the case of cloud, detection and notification may come from the CSP, cloud customer or a third party.

Once an investigator has been notified of an incident, they may then need to confirm the incident, and must get authorization to conduct an investigation. Authorization depends on the investigator's affiliation, and where the incident took place. For example, an investigator for the CSP may already have authorization from the CSP to investigate, where a law enforcement officer would need authorization to begin the case, and may need to procure warrants. Similarly, if the owner of the system in which the incident took place gives consent for the investigation, that may be all the authorization that is necessary, but if consent is not given, then other legal approval may be required.

Physical Crime Scene Investigation Phase

The IDIP includes a physical crime scene investigation phase. The purpose of the physical crime

Table 2. Threats, impact, and potential evidential data sources identified for a cloud environment using the I-STRIDE model

Threat	Description	Asset	Threat Impact	Potential Evidential Sources
XML Denial of Service	Attacker crafts XML message with a large payload, recursive content or with malicious DTD schema.	Cloud Controller Cloud Client	Denial of Service	XML parser logs at the cloud controller
Information Leakage	Web service fault messages contain information that attacker could use to compromise cloud privacy	Cloud Controller Cluster Controller Node Controller Cloud Client	Privacy Compromised (CSP/Customer)	Web Services Definition Language (WSDL) configuration file may contain traces of the leaked information
Replay Attack Flaws	Attacker could issue recurrence overloaded Simple Object Access Protocol (SOAP) messages over HTTP to overwhelm the CSP and stop the service	Cloud Controller Cloud Client	Denial of Service	SOAP message timestamp and message payload to identify the message flaws
WSDL Parameter Tampering	Attacker could embed command line code into WSDL documents or command shell to execute the command	Cloud Controller Cluster Controller Node Controller Cloud Client	Denial of Service	Detailed investigation of WSDL file could identify parameter tampering
WSDL Scanning	Attacker could use information in the WSDL file to guess the business rules and method, e.g. stock quoting and trading services	Cloud Controller Cluster Controller Node Controller	Privacy Compromised (Customer)	Detailed investigation of WSDL file could identify the compromised business rules and method
Schema Poisoning	Attacker could compromise the XML schema grammar and manipulate the data	Cloud Controller Cloud Client	Denial of Service	Detailed investigation of XML parser logs at the cloud controller may contain evidence of XML schema tampering
[12]Cross Site Scripting (XSS)	Attacker injects malicious client-side code into Web pages	Cloud Client	Privacy Compromised (Customer)	None

scene investigation is to extract physical evidence, and reconstruct the physical scene. Information from the physical crime scene investigation may later feed into, and provide context for, the digital crime scene.

When considering cloud computing, identification of *where* the relevant physical crime scene may be is a challenge. For example, if a hacker remotely accesses a cloud service to exploit another remote user, the physical crime scene may or may not be at the CSPs data center, depending on the exploit. The crime scene instead may be both at the suspect and victim's side, and possibly in different countries or jurisdictions.

The physical crime scene investigation phase is comprised of sub-phases including preservation, survey, documentation, search and collection, and reconstruction. These will be discussed further in the context of the digital crime scene investigation. However, "the search and collection phase of the physical crime scene is where the digital crime scene investigation begins" (Carrier & Spafford, 2003). The search and collection phase is used to collect evidence and provide more information that may be relevant.

Digital Crime Scene Investigation Phase

From the physical crime scene search and collection phase begins the digital crime scene investigation. Similar to the physical crime scene potentially being spread out among multiple physical locations, so too may the digital crime scene. For example, evidence may be on both the CSPs infrastructure as well as the victim's computer.

The first sub-phase on the digital scene investigation is preservation of the scene. If the crime scene can be identified, for example, where an incident occurred and evidential traces are likely to be found, then the scene must be preserved. If the crime scene is a victim's computer, preservation may be as simple as removing the computer from the network, or creating a forensic disk image. If, however, the crime scene is 'at' a cloud service, preservation becomes a challenge since many users may be accessing the service, potentially changing the scene. With a cloud service, and investigator should consider the best way to preserve the current state of the service, while having a minimal impact on the system.

Once preservation has taken place, as well as possible, a survey and acquisition of potential evidential sources takes place. Again, if the scene is a suspect or victim computer, traditional imaging and post-mortem triage and acquisition may be possible. Taking a cloud service offline, however, may not be possible. In the case where the scene must remain 'live,' live data forensics is necessary. The survey phase attempts to extract obvious pieces of digital evidence that will potentially give the investigator an idea about the suspect and crime. At this stage, the I-STRIDE model could be used to assist in conducting a targeted survey of the system. Once potential evidential sources have been identified, they are then forensically acquired. Depending on legal and technological restrictions, a computer's full physical disk may be acquired, or a targeted acquisition may be required.

The IDIP then proposes a documentation phase to document all digital evidence when it is found. Thorough documentation, however, should be conducted in parallel with all other phases in the IDIP. Thorough documentation can later be referred to if any part of the process is questioned. The documentation phase also includes data verification tasks, such as verifying the hash of acquired data. In the cases where live data forensics in necessary, some acquired data may not be able to later be verified. In these cases, precise documentation acts as verification for the investigator's actions.

Next is the search and collection phase. This phase is a thorough analysis of data and information acquired in the survey phase. If the data has been acquired in the survey phase, then data analysis should be similar irrespective of whether the data sources were acquired from a cloud environment or not. Some cloud-related challenges, however, might be in the analysis of unknown or proprietary data structures. This challenge is not unique to data acquired from cloud environments, but since cloud software that creates proprietary data structures would only be hosted in the Cloud, reverse engineering the data structure may be more difficult.

Once relevant data has been extracted, then the crime scene is reconstructed. "[The reconstruction phase] uses the scientific method to test and reject theories based on the digital evidence" (Carrier & Spafford, 2003). The reconstruction phase is where an investigator determines what the observed data means in relation to the investigation. This is also the phase where an investigator attempts to determine if there is sufficient evidence to support the theory, or whether more evidence would be necessary.

Based on the results from the reconstruction phase, survey and acquisition of the digital crime scene may again be required to collect data determined by the analysis to potentially be relevant. Otherwise, the digital crime scene theory is fed back into the physical crime scene investigation model, where more physical evidence may need to be acquired and analyzed, potentially starting another digital crime scene investigation.

Review Phase

The final phase of the IDIP involves reviewing the process and results, attempting to determine what worked, what did not, and what changes to the process need to take place. The review phase should be used to guide education, research and tool development efforts that feed back into the readiness phase. From the results of the review phase, new methods may be created to deal with before unknown situations that are specific to cloud environments.

CONCLUSION

Cloud computing has a number of benefits, such as high availability, potentially lower cost, and potentially improved security. However, cloud computing also has a number of associated risks. Some of these risks have been inherited from traditional computing models, while the cloud business model introduces others. As more businesses and end users move their data and processing to cloud environments, these environments will increasingly become the target, or even the originator, of malicious attacks. For this reason, digital forensic investigation methods must be tested against cloud computing environments with the help of CSPs to ensure digital evidence is available, and integrity can be maintained and verified.

This work has shown how current digital forensic investigation process models may be used to derive cloud-specific considerations when planning an investigation. In addition, in investigations of cloud environments the CSP will likely be involved. This work has proposed a risk and investigation assessment model (I-STRIDE) that can act as a base for CSPs and law enforcement to more effectively work together before and during the investigation of incidents in cloud environments.

Much more research is necessary concerning digital forensic investigations in cloud environments, but beyond technical challenges cloud computing is already testing the limits of communication and collaboration between international law enforcement. As cloud computing blurs geographical borders for businesses, end users and even criminals, law too must begin to look to a more open, global system; a system where everyone—law enforcement, private sector, academia, and even the public—can play a role to detect, research and reduce digital crime. Cybercrime affects every Internet connected country, and without effective international collaboration, laws, and efficient communication channels that support international collaboration, cybercrime will continue unchecked.

REFERENCES

Adelstein, F. (2006). Live forensics: Diagnosing your system without killing it first. *Communications of the ACM*, *49*(2), 63–66. doi:10.1145/1113034.1113070

ADF. (2011). *ADF solutions*. Retrieved 31 January, 2011, from http://www.adfsolutions.com/

Amazon. (2011). *Amazon elastic compute cloud (Amazon EC2)*. Retrieved 15 February, 2011, from http://aws.amazon.com/ec2/

Anderson, N. (2012). *Mega-victory: Kim dotcom search warrants invalid, mansion raid illegal*. Retrieved 11 July, 2012, from http://arstechnica.com/tech-policy/2012/06/mega-victory-kim-dotcom-search-warrants-invalid-mansion-raid-illegal/

Armbrust, M. (2009). *Above the clouds: A Berkeley view of cloud computing*. Berkeley, CA: University of California.

Armbrust, M. (2010). A view of cloud computing. *Communications of the ACM*, *53*(4), 50–58. doi:10.1145/1721654.1721672

Arms, W. (2000). *Digital libraries*. Retrieved 10 February, 2011, from http://www.cs.cornell.edu/wya/DigLib/MS1999/Glossary.html

Balduzzi, M., et al. (2012). A security analysis of amazon's elastic compute cloud service. In *Proceedings of the 27th Annual ACM Symposium on Applied Computing*, (pp. 1427-1434). Trento, Italy: ACM.

Barbara, J. J. (2009). Cloud computing: Another digital forensic challenge. *Forensic Magazine*. Retrieved from http://www.forensicmag.com/article/cloud-computing-another-digital-forensic-challenge

Barnard, A. (2009). Could your phone testify against you? *The New York Times Upfront*, 142.

Biggs, S., & Vidalis, S. (2009). *Cloud computing: The impact on digital forensic investigations*. Washington, DC: IEEE.

Bilby, D. (2006). *Low down and dirty: Anti-forensic rootkits*. Retrieved from http://www.blackhat.com/presentations/bh-jp-06/BH-JP-06-Bilby-up.pdf

Bloomberg, J. (2011). *Cloud brokering: Building a cloud of clouds*. Retrieved 23 July, 2012, from http://www.zapthink.com/2011/04/19/cloud-brokering-building-a-cloud-of-clouds/

Brennels. (2010). *Cloud 101 - Recovery as a service (RaaS) is here!* Retrieved 16 February, 2011, from http://cloudrecovery.info/2010/02/17/cloud-101-%E2%80%93-recovery-as-a-service-raas-is-here/

Brennels. (2010). *Cloud 101 - The four type of cloud services?* Retrieved 14 February, 2011, from http://cloudrecovery.info/2010/02/08/cloud-101-the-four-types-of-cloud-services/

Bright, P. (2008). Storms in the cloud leave users up creek without a paddle. *Ars Technica*. Retrieved from http://arstechnica.com/microsoft/news/2008/08/storms-in-the-clouds-leave-users-up-creek-without-a-paddle.ars

Broadhurst, R. (2006). Developments in the global law enforcement of cyber-crime. *Policing: An International Journal of Police Strategies & Management*, *29*(3), 408–433. doi:10.1108/13639510610684674

Bryan, D. M. N., & Anderson, M. (2010). Cloud computing: A weapon of mass destruction? In *DEFCON 18*. Las Vegas, NV: DEF CON Communications, Inc.

Carrier, B. D. (2003). Open source digital forensics tools: The legal argument. *@stake Research Report*.

Carrier, B. D. (2006). *Basic digital forensic investigation concepts*. Retrieved 28 January, 2011, from http://www.digital-evidence.org/di_basics.html

Carrier, B. D. (2006). *A hypothesis-based approach to digital forensic investigations*. (PhD Thesis). Purdue University. West Lafayette, IN.

Carrier, B. D. (2006). Risks of live digital forensic analysis. *Communications of the ACM*, *49*(2), 56–61. doi:10.1145/1113034.1113069

Carrier, B. D. (2008). *A brief introduction to the computer history model*. Retrieved 2 February, 2011, from http://www.digital-evidence.org/hist_model1.html

Carrier, B. D. (2012). *Sleuth kit hadoop*. Retrieved 22 July, 2012, from http://www.sleuthkit.org/tsk_hadoop/

Carrier, B. D., & Spafford, E. H. (2003). Getting physical with the digital investigation process. *International Journal of Digital Evidence*, *2*(2), 1–20.

Carrier, B. D., & Spafford, E. H. (2006). Categories of digital investigation analysis techniques based on the computer history model. *Digital Investigation, 3*, 121–130. doi:10.1016/j.diin.2006.06.011

Casey, E. (2004). *Digital evidence and computer crime: Forensic science, computers and the internet*. Amsterdam, The Netherlands: Elsevier Academic.

Casey, E. (2009). Investigation delayed is justice denied: proposals for expediting forensic examinations of digital evidence*. *Journal of Forensic Sciences, 54*(6), 1353–1364. doi:10.1111/j.1556-4029.2009.01150.x

Chirgwin, R. (2012). *Megaupload seizures illegal says NZ high court*. Retrieved 24 July, 2012, from http://www.theregister.co.uk/2012/06/28/dotcom_seizures_illegal/

Choo, K. K. R. (2010). Cloud computing: Challenges and future directions. *Trends & Issues in Crime and Criminal Justice, 400*, 381–400.

Cisco. (2012). *Cisco visual networking index: Global mobile data traffic forecast update, 2011–2016*. Retrieved 11 July, 2012, from http://www.cisco.com/en/US/solutions/collateral/ns341/ns525/ns537/ns705/ns827/white_paper_c11-520862.html

Civie, V., & Civie, R. (1998). Future technologies from trends in computer forensic science. In *Proceedings of Information Technology Conference, 1998*. IEEE Press.

Clede, B. (1993). Investigating computer crimes. *Law and Order, 41*(7), 99–102.

CNN. (2009). *CNN: Her name was Neda*. Retrieved from http://www.youtube.com/watch?v=b5KBrsz1oxs&feature=related

Cohen, F. B. (2010). Fundamentals of digital forensic evidence. *Handbook of Information and Communication Security*. Retrieved from http://all.net/ForensicsPapers/HandbookOfCIS.pdf

Collier, P. A., & Spaul, B. J. (1992a). A forensic methodology for countering computer crime. *Artificial Intelligence Review, 6*(2), 203–215. doi:10.1007/BF00150234

Collier, P. A., & Spaul, B. J. (1992b). Forensic science against computer crime in the United Kingdom. *Journal - Forensic Science Society, 32*(1), 27–34. doi:10.1016/S0015-7368(92)73043-6

Connery, E. M., & Levy, S. B. (1979). Computer evidence in federal courts. *Commercial Law Journal, 84*, 266–276.

CRA. (2003). *Four grand challenges in trustworthy computing*. Retrieved from http://www.cyber.st.dhs.gov/docs/CRA%20Grand%20Challenges%202003.pdf

DeHetre, J. D. (1975). Data processing evidence-Is it different? *Chicago-Kent Law Review, 52*, 567–599.

Didone, D., & de Queirozb, R. J. G. B. (2011). *Forensic as a service - FaaS*. Paper presented at the Sixth International Conference on Forensic Computer Science - ICoFCS 2011. Florianopolis, Brazil.

Duffy, J. (2009). *Cisco unveils cloud computing platform for service providers*. Retrieved 10 February, 2011, from http://www.infoworld.com/d/cloud-computing/cisco-unveils-cloud-computing-platform-service-providers-113

Ellison, L. (2009). *Why Larry Ellison hates cloud computing*. Retrieved from http://techpulse360.com

Eucalyptus. (2010). *Eucalyptus user guide*. New York, NY: Eucalyptus Systems, Inc.

Eucalyptus. (2010). *Resources*. Retrieved 9 February, 2011, from http://www.eucalyptus.com/resources/info/cloud-myths-dispelled - q2

Eucalyptus. (2011). *Eucalyptus: The open source cloud platform*. Retrieved 27 February, 2011, from http://open.eucalyptus.com/

EY. (2011). *Into the cloud, out of the fog: Ernst & Young's 2011 global information security survey: 34*. New York, NY: Ernst & Young.

Farmer, D., & Venema, W. (2005). *Forensic discovery*. Reading, MA: Addison-Wesley Professional.

Frye v. United States, 293 U.S. 1013 (1923). Daubert v. Merrell Dow Pharmaceuticals, 509 U.S. 579 (1993).

Garfinkel, S. L. (2010). Digital forensics research: The next 10 years. *Digital Investigation*, *7*(1), S64–S73. doi:10.1016/j.diin.2010.05.009

Gartner. (2012). *Forecast: Public cloud services, worldwide, 2010-2016, 2Q12 update*. New York, NY: Gartner.

Gellman, R. (2009). *Privacy in the clouds: Risks to privacy and confidentiality from cloud computing*. Paper presented at the World Privacy Forum. Washington, DC.

General Electric Co. v. Joiner, 522 U.S. 136 (1997).

Giannelli, P. (2006). *Judicature - Scientific evidence*. Retrieved from http://goextranet.net/Seminars/Ohio06/Tab%2002-Scientific%20Evidence-Gianelli/Judicature%20-%20Scientific%20Evidence.pdf

Gladyshev, P. (2004). *Formalising event reconstruction in digital investigations*. (PhD Thesis). University College Dublin. Dublin, Ireland.

Gladyshev, P., & Almansoori, A. (2010). Reliable acquisition of RAM dumps from intel-based apple mac computers over firewire. In *Proceedings of the Second International Conference on Digital Forensics and Cyber Crime (ICDF2C)*. Abu Dhabi, UAE: ICST.

Gladyshev, P., & Patel, A. (2004). Finite state machine approach to digital event reconstruction. *Digital Investigation*, *1*(2), 130–149. doi:10.1016/j.diin.2004.03.001

Gogolin, G. (2010). The digital crime tsunami. *Digital Investigation*, *7*(1-2), 3–8. doi:10.1016/j.diin.2010.07.001

Google. (2012). *Google mail - Service details*. Retrieved 24 July, 2012, from http://www.google.com/appsstatus-hl=en&v=issue&ts=1343170799000&iid=ccc3254047e72fb00c9cb8532281e28

Goss, J. (2010). *Forensic triage: Managing the risk*. (Master of Science Thesis). University College Dublin. Dublin, Ireland.

Grivas, S. G. (2010). *Cloud broker: Bringing intelligence into the cloud*. Washington, DC: IEEE. doi:10.1109/CLOUD.2010.48

Gutheil, T. G., & Bursztajn, H. J. (2005). Attorney abuses of Daubert hearings: Junk science, junk law, or just plain obstruction? *The Journal of the American Academy of Psychiatry and the Law*, *33*(2), 150–152.

Halderman, J. (2009). Lest we remember: Cold-boot attacks on encryption keys. *Communications of the ACM*, *52*(5), 91–98. doi:10.1145/1506409.1506429

Hannan, M. (2004). *To revisit: What is forensic computing?* Paper presented at the 2nd Australian Computer, Network & Information Forensics Conference. Perth, Australia.

Hewlett-Packard. (2011). *Everything as a service*. Retrieved 16 February, 2011, from http://www.hp.com/hpinfo/initiatives/eaas/index.html

Higginbotham, S. (2010). *Ericsson CEO predicts 50 billion internet connected devices by 2020*. Retrieved 27 January, 2011, from http://gigaom.com/2010/04/14/ericsson-sees-the-internet-of-things-by-2020/

Hobson, E. W. (2010). *What is cloud computing?* Retrieved 12 February, 2011, from https://sites.google.com/site/cloudinvestigations/whatis

Hu, Y. J. (2012). *Towards law-aware semantic cloud policies with exceptions for data integration and protection*. New York, NY: ACM. doi:10.1145/2254129.2254162

Hunton, P. (2012). Managing the technical resource capability of cybercrime investigation: A UK law enforcement perspective. *Public Money & Management*, *32*(3), 225–232. doi:10.1080/09540962.2012.676281

IBM. (2010). *IBM x-force 2010 mid-year trend and risk report*. New York, NY: IBM X-Force.

IBTimes. (2010). *Number of internet users in emerging markets to double by 2015: Report*. International Business Times.

IC3. (2011). 2011 internet crime report. *Internet Crime Complaint Center*. Retrieved from http://www.ic3.gov

Ingthorsson, O. (2010). Cloud computing - Data privacy and compliance. *Cloud Computing Topics*. Retrieved from http://cloudcomputingtopics.com/2010/03/cloud-computing-data-privacy-and-compliance/

Internet World Stats. (2011). *Internet usage statistics: The internet big picture*. Retrieved 11 July, 2012, from http://internetworldstats.com/stats.htm

James, J. (2010). Analysis of evidence using formal event reconstruction. *Digital Forensics and Cyber Crime*, *31*, 85–98. doi:10.1007/978-3-642-11534-9_9

James, J. I., & Gladyshev, P. (2010). *2010 report of digital forensic standards, processes and accuracy measurement*. Retrieved 22 December, 2010, from http://www.forensicfocus.com/2010-digital-forensics-standards-processes-accuracy

Jang, Y. (2012). Need of open network approach for cyber security organizational. In *Proceedings of the International Symposium on Cybercrime Response 2012*. Jung-gu, Republic of Korea: Cyber Terror Response Center.

Jansen, W. A. (2011). *Cloud hooks: Security and privacy issues in cloud computing*. Washington, DC: IEEE. doi:10.1109/HICSS.2011.103

Jenkins, M. M. (1975). Computer-generated evidence specially prepared for use at trial. *Chicago-Kent Law Review*, *52*, 600–609.

Johnson, B. (2008). *Cloud computing is a trap, warns GNU founder Richard Stallman*. Retrieved from http://guardian.co.uk

Jones, N. (2004). Training and accreditation - Who are the experts? *Digital Investigation*, *1*(3), 189–194. doi:10.1016/j.diin.2004.07.009

Jones, R. (2012). *Towards a global criminology?* Edinburgh, UK: Edinburgh School of Law Research.

Kaufman, L. M. (2009). Data security in the world of cloud computing. *IEEE Security & Privacy*, 7(4), 61–64. doi:10.1109/MSP.2009.87

Kelman, A., & Sizer, R. (1982). *Computer in court - A guide to computer evidence for lawyers and computing professionals*. London, UK: Gower.

Kent, K., et al. (2006). Guide to integrating forensic techniques into incident response. *National Institute of Standards and Technology*. Retrieved from http://cybersd.com/sec2/800-86Summary.pdf

Kerbs, B. (2008). *Amazon: Hey spammers, get off my cloud!* Retrieved 27 July, 2012, from http://voices.washingtonpost.com/securityfix/2008/07/amazon_hey_spammers_get_off_my.html

Kim, R. (2012). *Vendor lock-in and the challenge to platform as a service*. Retrieved 27 July, 2012, from http://gigaom.com/cloud/vendor-lock-in-and-the-challenge-to-Platform as a Service/

Koopmans, M. (2010). *The art of triage with (g) PXE. (Master of Science)*. Dublin, Ireland: University College Dublin.

Kosner, A. W. (2012). *Amazon cloud goes down friday night, taking Netflix, Instagram and Pinterest with it*. Retrieved 24 July, 2012, from http://www.forbes.com/sites/anthonykosner/2012/06/30/amazon-cloud-goes-down-friday-night-taking-netflix-instagram-and-pinterest-with-it/

Kravets, D. (2012). *Feds tell megaupload users to foreget about their data*. Retrieved 22 July, 2012, from http://www.wired.com/threatlevel/2012/06/feds-megaupload-data/

Kui, R. (2012). Security challenges for the public cloud. *IEEE Internet Computing*, *16*(1), 69–73. doi:10.1109/MIC.2012.14

Kumho Tire Co. v. Carmichael, 526 U.S. 137 (1999).

Lemos, R. (2001). *FBI hack raises global security concerns*. Retrieved 11 July, 2012, from http://news.cnet.com/2100-1001-256811.html

Lemos, R. (2010). *Cloud-based denial of serice attacks looming, researchers say*. Retrieved 27 July, 2012, from http://www.darkreading.com/security/news/226500300

Lim, K.-S. (2012). On-the-spot digital investigation by means of LDFS: Live data forensic system. *Mathematical and Computer Modelling*, *55*(1), 223–240. doi:10.1016/j.mcm.2011.05.019

Mansfield-Devine, S. (2010). Fighting forensics. *Computer Fraud & Security*, *1*, 17–20. doi:10.1016/S1361-3723(10)70112-3

Martin, A. (2007). *Firewire memory dump of a Windows XP computer: A forensic approach*. Retrieved from http://www.friendsglobal.com/papers/FireWire%20Memory%20Dump%20of%20Windows%20XP.pdf

McAfee. (2010). *A good decade for cybercrime*. Santa Clara, CA: McAfee, Inc.

McGuigan, B. (2011). *What is distributed computing?* Retrieved 10 February, 2011, from http://www.wisegeek.com/what-is-distributed-computing.htm

McKemmish, R. (1999). What is forensic computing. *Trends and Issues in Crime and Criminal Justice, 118*.

Meeker, M. (2012). Internet trends. *D10 Conference*. Retrieved 11 July, 2012, from http://allthingsd.com/20120612/mary-meeker-explains-internet-2012-in-17-minutes-the-full-d10-interview-video/?refcat=d10

Mell, P., & Grance, T. (2011). The NIST definition of cloud computing. *National Institute of Standards and Technology, 7*.

Messmer, E. (2011). *How one municipality is securing Google apps, docs*. Retrieved from http://csonline.com

Microsoft. (2010). *Computer online forensic evidence extractor (COFEE)*. Retrieved 4 February, 2011, from http://www.microsoft.com/industry/government/solutions/cofee/default.aspx

Microsoft. (2011). TrojanDropper:Win32/Bohu.A. *Malware Protection Center*. Retrieved 25 February, 2011, from http://www.microsoft.com/security/portal/Threat/Encyclopedia/Entry.aspx?Name=TrojanDropper%3AWin32%2FBohu.A

Mislan, R. P. (2010). The growing need for on-scene triage of mobile devices. *Digital Investigation*, *6*(3-4), 112–124. doi:10.1016/j.diin.2010.03.001

Moreno-Vozmediano, R. (2012). Key challenges in cloud computing to enable the future internet of services. *IEEE Internet Computing*, 99.

Myslewski, R. (2009). *Intel puts cloud on a single megachip*. Retrieved 10 February, 2011, from http://www.theregister.co.uk/2009/12/02/intel_scc/

Nguyen, L. (2012). *Tori Stafford trial: Cellphone record shows gap during abduction, murder*. Retrieved 13 July, 2012, from http://www.canada.com/life/Tori+Stafford+trial+Cellphone+record+shows+during+abduction+murder/6486178/story.html

NIJ. (2008). *Electronic crime scene investigation: A guide for first responders* (2nd ed). Retrieved 2 February, 2011, from http://www.ojp.usdoj.gov/nij/publications/ecrime-guide-219941/welcome.htm

Norton, Q. (2012). *25 alleged anons arrested in international crackdown*. Retrieved 27 July, 2012, from http://www.wired.com/threatlevel/2012/02/anonymous-arrested-interpol/

O'Connor, T. (2010). *Admissibility of scientific evidence under daubert*. Retrieved 26, January, 2011, from http://www.drtomoconnor.com/3210/3210lect01a.htm

Palmer, G. (2001). DFRWS technical report: A road map for digital forensic research. In *Digital Forensic Research Workshop*. Utica, NY: G. Palmer.

Paquette, S. (2010). Identifying the security risks associated with governmental use of cloud computing. *Government Information Quarterly*, *27*(3), 245–253. doi:10.1016/j.giq.2010.01.002

Parnell, B.-A. (2012). *Microsoft's Azure cloud down and out for 8 hours*. Retrieved 24 July, 2012, from http://www.theregister.co.uk/2012/02/29/windows_azure_outage/

Paul, W. (2012). Cyber war, formal verification and certified infrastructure. *Verified Software: Theories, Tools, Experiments, 1*(1).

Pettey, C. (2011). *Gartner says 30 percent of midsize companies will use recovery-as-a-service by 2014*. New York, NY: Gartner.

Pollitt, M. (1995). *Principles, practices, and procedures: An approach to standards in computer forensics*. Retrieved from http://www.digitalevidencepro.com/Resources/Principles.pdf

Pollitt, M. (2007). *An ad hoc review of digital forensic models*. Washington, DC: IEEE. doi:10.1109/SADFE.2007.3

Polsson, K. (2011). *Chronology of personal computers*. Retrieved 25 January, 2011, from http://www.islandnet.com/~kpolsson/comphist/

Ponemon. (2011). *The security of cloud infrastructure: Survey of U.S. IT and compliance practitioners*. New York, NY: Ponemon Institute.

Purdy, C. (2010). *Industry's first forensic-base critical infrastructure security solution*. Retrieved 29 January, 2011, from https://http://www.guidancesoftware.com/Media/NewsRoom/NewsRoomBlog.aspx?B=BlogContentDetails&Blog_S=NewsRoomMenu&newsroommenu_id=3503&image_id=1000000303&md_id=1000000296&id=1000000267&blogid=2523

Rekhis, S., & Boudriga, N. (2010). Formal digital investigation of anti-forensic attacks. In *Proceedings of the Fifth International Workshop on Systematic Approaches to Digital Forensic Engineering*. IEEE Press.

Ristenpart, T., et al. (2009). Hey, you, get off of my cloud: exploring information leakage in third-party compute clouds. In *Proceedings of the 16th ACM Conference on Computer and Communications Security*. ACM Press.

Roberts, J. J. (1974). A practitioner's primer on computer-generated evidence. *The University of Chicago Law Review. University of Chicago. Law School*, *41*(2), 254–280. doi:10.2307/1599148

Rogers, M. (2006). Computer forensics field triage process model. *Journal of Digital Forensics. Security and Law*, *1*(2), 27–40.

Roth, T. (2011). Breaking encryption in the cloud: GPU accelerated supercomputing for everyone. In *Proceedings of Black Hat DC 2011*. Black Hat.

RSA. (2009). *Public-key cryptography standards (PKCS)*. Retrieved 21 May, 2012, from http://www.rsa.com/rsalabs/node.asp?id=2176

Ruan, K., et al. (2011). Cloud forensics: An overview. I *Advances in Digital Forensics, 7*.

Ruan, K., et al. (2012). *Cloud forensics: Key terms for service level agreements*. Paper presented at the Eigth Annual IFIP WG 11.9 International Conference on Digital Forensics. Pretoria, South Africa.

Russell, K., & Hammons, S. (2012). *Citizen engagement platform*. Boulder, CO: Office of Information Technology.

Saliba, J. (2012). *Finding evidence in an online world - Trends and challenges in digital forensics*. Retrieved from http://www.cybercrimetech.com/2012/07/webinar-finding-evidence-in-online.html#!/2012/07/webinar-finding-evidence-in-online.html

Saripalli, P., & Walters, B. (2010). *QUIRC: A quantitative impact and risk assessment framework for cloud security*. IEEE. doi:10.1109/CLOUD.2010.22

Scheier, R. L. (2009). What to do if your cloud provider disappears. *Cloud Computing*. Retrieved from http://www.infoworld.com/d/cloud-computing/what-do-if-your-cloud-provider-disappears-508

Schneier, B. (2010). The threat of cyberwar has been grossly exaggerated. *Schneier on Security*. Retrieved from http://www.schneier.com/blog/archives/2010/07/the_threat_of_c.html

Security as a Service. (2011). *Security as a service defined categories of service 2011*. Washington, DC: Security as a Service Working Group. ACPO. (2008). *Good practice guide for computer based electronic evidence*. Washington, DC: ACPO.

Shinder, D., & Cross, M. (2008). *Scene of the cybercrime*. New York, NY: Syngress Media.

Shipley, T. G., & Door, B. (2012). *Forensic imaging of hard disk drives- What we thought we knew*. Retrieved 15 July, 2012, from http://articles.forensicfocus.com/2012/01/27/forensic-imaging-of-hard-disk-drives-what-we-thought-we-knew-2/

Skok, M. J. (2012). *Future of cloud computing 2012*. Waltham, MA: Northbridge Venture Partners.

Smith, S. E. (2011). *What is cyberwar?* Retrieved 28 January, 2011, from http://www.wisegeek.com/what-is-cyberwar.htm

Spafford, E. H., & Weeber, S. A. (1993). Software forensics: Can we track code to its authors? *Computers & Security*, *12*(6), 585–595. doi:10.1016/0167-4048(93)90055-A

Stephenson, P. (2003). Using a formalized approach to digital investigation. *Computer Fraud & Security*, *7*, 17–20. doi:10.1016/S1361-3723(03)08010-2

SWGDE. (2009). *SWGDE/SWGIT digital & multimedia evidence glossary version: 2.3*. Washington, DC: Scientific Working Group on Digital Evidence.

Swiderski, F., & Snyder, W. (2004). *Threat modeling*. Redmond, WA: Microsoft Press.

Tapper, C. (1974). Evidence from computers. *Rutgers Journal of Computers and the Law*, *4*, 324–406.

Taylor, M. (2011). Forensic investigation of cloud computing systems. *Network Security*, *3*, 4–10. doi:10.1016/S1353-4858(11)70024-1

Teubner, A. L. (1978). The computer as expert witness: Toward a unified theory of computer evidence. *Jurimetrics Journal*, *19*, 274–297.

USDoJ. (2002). *Prosecuting computer crimes*. Washington, DC: United States Department of Justice, Computer Crime & Intellectual Property Section.

Vaciago, G. (2012). *Cloud computing and data jurisdiction: A new challenge for digital forensics*. Retrieved from http://www.thinkmind.org/index.php?view=article&articleid=cyberlaws_2012_1_20_70033

Vaquero, L. M. (2008). A break in the clouds: Towards a cloud definition. *ACM SIGCOMM Computer Communication Review*, *39*(1), 50–55. doi:10.1145/1496091.1496100

Vouk, M. A. (2008). *Cloud computing-Issues, research and implementations*. IEEE.

Wang, W. Y. C. (2011). Toward the trend of cloud computing. *Journal of Electronic Commerce Research*, *12*(4).

Ward, B. T., & Sipior, J. C. (2010). The internet jurisdiction risk of cloud computing. *Information Systems Management*, *27*(4), 334–339. doi:10.1080/10580530.2010.514248

Willassen, S. (2008). Using simplified event calculus in digital investigation. In *Proceedings of the 2008 ACM Symposium on Applied Computing*. ACM Press.

Williams, C. (2011). *Cybercrime gang responsible for a third of all data thefts*. The Telegraph.

Wilsdon, T., & Slay, J. (2005). Digital forensics: Exploring validation, verification & certification. In *Proceedings of the First International Workshop on Systematic Approaches to Digital Forensic Engineering (SADFE 2005)*. IEEE.

Wolski, R. (2010). Top 5 questions posted on "cloud computing" [part 1/3]. *Eucalyptus*. Retrieved from http://www.eucalyptus.com/blog/2010/05/21/top-5-questions-posed-cloud-computing-part-13

Xen. (2011). *Xen hypevisor - Leading open source hypervisor for servers*. Retrieved 10 February, 2011, from http://www.xen.org/products/xenhyp.html

Zissis, D., & Lekkas, D. (2012). Addressing cloud computing security issues. *Future Generation Computer Systems*, *28*(3), 583–592. doi:10.1016/j.future.2010.12.006

Zittrain, J. (2009). Lost in the cloud. *The New York Times*.

ADDITIONAL READING

Amazon. (2011). *Amazon elastic compute cloud (Amazon EC2)*. Retrieved 27 February, 2011, from http://aws.amazon.com/ec2/

Armbrust, M. (2009). *Above the clouds: A Berkeley view of cloud computing*. Berkeley, CA: University of California.

Balduzzi, M., et al. (2012). A security analysis of amazon's elastic compute cloud service. In *Proceedings of the 27th Annual ACM Symposium on Applied Computing*, (pp. 1427-1434). Trento, Italy: ACM Press.

Baryamureeba, V., & Tushabe, F. (2004). The enhanced digital investigation process model. *Asian Journal of Information Technology*, *5*(7).

Carrier, B., & Spafford, E. (2003). Getting physical with the digital investigation process. *International Journal of Digital Evidence*, *2*(2), 1–20.

Carrier, B. D. (2006). *A hypothesis-based approach to digital forensic investigations*. (PhD Thesis). Purdue University. West Lafayette, IN.

Choo, K. K. R. (2010). Cloud computing: Challenges and future directions. *Trends & Issues in Crime and Criminal Justice*, *400*, 381–400.

CoE. (2001). *Concention on cybercrime*. Budapest, Romania: Council of Europe.

CSA. (2010). *Cloud security alliance top threats to cloud computing v1.0*. New York, NY: Cloud Security Alliance (CSA).

Dhanjani, N. (2009). *Hacking: The next generation*. Sebastopol, CA: O'Reilly Media, Inc.

Eucalyptus. (2010). *Eucalyptus community*. Retrieved 27 February, 2011, from http://open.eucalyptus.com/

Feliz, T. (2010). Cloud computing: 10 web operating systems. *AdmixWeb*. Retrieved from http://admixweb.com

Finley, K. (2010). *5 cloud-oriented operating systems available now*. ReadWrite Cloud.

Gellman, R. (2009). *Privacy in the clouds: Risks to privacy and confidentiality from cloud computing*. New York, NY: World Privacy Forum.

Google. (2011). *Top ten advantages of Google's cloud*. Retrieved 28 February, 2011, from http://www.google.com/apps/intl/en/business/cloud.html

Gustin, S. (2011). *GFail: Google very sorry after the cloud eats 150,000 gmail accounts*. Wired.

Higgins, K. J. (2011). *Proposed nonprofit would bridge law enforcement, enterprise security worlds*. Retrieved 27 February, 2011, from http://www.darkreading.com/smb-security/167901073/security/news/229100238/proposed-nonprofit-would-bridge-law-enforcement-enterprise-security-worlds.html

Hobson, E. W. (2010). *Digital investigations in the cloud*. White Paper. New York, NY: QinetiQ.

Home Office. (2010). *Codes of practice and conduct for forensic science providers and practitioners in the criminal justice system*. New York, NY: Crown Copyright.

NIST. (2010). *Cloud computing*. Retrieved 27 February, 2011, from http://csrc.nist.gov/groups/SNS/cloud-computing/

OpenNebula. (2011). *The open source toolkit for cloud computing*. Retrieved 27 February, 2011, from http://opennebula.org/

Pollitt, M. (2007). *An ad hoc review of digital forensic models*. Washington, DC: IEEE. doi:10.1109/SADFE.2007.3

Roth, T. (2011). Breaking encryption in the cloud: GPU accelerated supercomputing for everyone. In *Proceedings of Black Hat DC 2011*. Black Hat.

Thomas, K. (2010). Microsoft cloud data breach heralds things to come. PCWorld Business Center.

USDoS. (2011). *U.S. department of state freedom of information act (FOIA)*. Retrieved 27 February, 2011, from http://www.state.gov/m/a/ips/

Xen. (2011). *Xen cloud platform*. Retrieved 27 February, 2011, from http://www.xen.org/products/cloudxen.html

Zimmerman, S., & Glavach, D. (2011). Cyber forensics in the cloud. *IAnewsletter*, *14*(1), 4–7.

ENDNOTES

1 Also known as Computer Forensics or Cyber Forensics.

2 Some researchers believe various groups have exaggerated the threat of a cyber war (Schneier, 2010).

3 "Cyberwar is a form of war which takes places on computers and the Internet, through electronic means rather than physical ones" (Smith, 2011).

4 Some data, such as imaging Random Access Memory, can be acquired directly from an external FireWire connection (Gladyshev & Almansoori, 2010).

5 The layers of Cloud Computing can also be described in depth by using the Open Systems Interconnection (OSI) model.

6 Distributed computing – computing systems in which services to users are provided by teams of computers collaborating over a network (Arms, 2000).

7 A combination of programs that work together to produce a given result.

8 In this survey, 35% or respondents were customers and 65% were vendors. For these statistics, separation between customer and vender was not shown, and inclusion of venders could potentially bias results in favor of confidence in cloud services.

9 A side channel attack uses physical aspects of a system as sources of information about digital data or processes, such as power consumption, sound, and electromagnetic waves.

10 Brute-force password cracking is essentially attempting every possible key combination until the correct password is found.

11 Asset-centric threat modeling first identifies an organization's assets, and then focuses on identification of threats to the identified assets.

12 XSS is not specific to Eucalyptus, and is added to illustrate a threat to an asset—the cloud client—that will likely have no in-house traces associated, but is an in-house security issue.

Chapter 2
Hack the Cloud:
Ethical Hacking and Cloud Forensics

Mark Crosbie
IBM, Ireland

ABSTRACT

The goal of this chapter is to explain the challenges that the forensic investigator faces when investigating Cloud Crime and how they can learn from the techniques used by Ethical Hackers to improve their investigation technique. The security threat posed by hackers on the Internet is constantly evolving. Cloud computing provides new avenues for hackers to exploit organizations, giving rise to new classes of vulnerability, and new security challenges. The forensic investigator must learn to "think like a hacker" so that they can reconstruct the path the hacker takes through the cloud environment. This chapter will explain how an Ethical Hacker works, how the Ethical Hacker views the Cloud, and in doing so illustrate the new challenges facing a forensic investigator.

INTRODUCTION

The security threat posed by hackers on the Internet is constantly evolving. As security professionals improve the defensive posture of systems and networks, hackers have evolved their penetration techniques. Moreover, the nature of the attacks launched against the Cloud is changing. The rise of Web applications and Web services has provided a common foundation for hackers to exploit, independent of the underlying operating system or software stack. In the past hackers would have focused on system level exploits, requiring them to research, develop, and test a malware exploit that was fine-tuned for a particular operating system platform and version. Web application vulnerabilities are platform-neutral, and can be exploited using text-based scripting languages such as JavaScript.

As defined in Kent et al. (2006), digital forensics focuses on recovering electronic evidence for presentation in a court of law. The job of the forensic investigator is to reconstruct the activities of the hacker after-the-fact. Grobauer and Schreck (2010) identified the following forensic challenges within the cloud computing environment:

DOI: 10.4018/978-1-4666-2662-1.ch002

Copyright © 2013, IGI Global. Copying or distributing in print or electronic forms without written permission of IGI Global is prohibited.

- Separation of customer's data sources during evidence collection.
- Adapting forensic analysis methods to the Cloud.
- Improving live analysis techniques.
- Improving log generation and analysis techniques.

Hackers and criminals are aware that the forensic investigator will face these challenges, and will adapt their attack techniques to leverage the four challenges identified above. The remainder of this chapter explains how a hacker will target a Cloud with a view to committing a crime, and how they will use the very aspects of the Cloud that make it appealing to businesses against the forensic investigator.

The forensic investigator must have an awareness of the types of crimes possible in the Cloud. There are two scenarios to consider:

1. The Cloud is the target of the crime, and the likely victims of the crime are clients of a cloud provider.
2. The Cloud enables the crime to be committed, by providing services that would be otherwise unavailable to the criminals.

THE CLOUD AS THE TARGET

Enterprises who adopt cloud-computing models hope to see their costs reduced as applications and services, which were once provided in-house, are moved to a shared infrastructure. By outsourcing the provisioning and maintenance of hardware, software and applications they hope to see cost reduction while increasing their ability to rapidly deliver service. However, the cloud computing model also offers hackers a unique advantage; a concentration of valuable targets are one present on a single shared infrastructure model. Vulnerabilities in the underlying cloud provider infrastructure will likely compromise every customer resident in the Cloud.

Cloud computing is deployed in one of three service models. Mell and Grance (2011) have defined the three service models as Software as a Serivce (SaaS), Platform as a Serivce (PaaS) and Infrastructure as a Service (IaaS). By understanding how the hackers target the cloud service models the forensic investigator can prioritize how they gather data needed to prosecute the crime. For each service model, a hacker will target the underlying cloud infrastructure used to provision the applications. The cloud provider must provide functions to customers to manage the instances of the running applications they purchase. For example, a cloud provider may provide functions to add users into the services (termed on-boarding), delete dormant user accounts, and view user activity. If an attacker can compromise the cloud provider functions to manage the application they can gain access to the customer's data by adding themselves as a legitimate user (or administrator) of the application.

Software as a Service (SaaS)

In the Software as a Service model, the cloud provider is providing a hosted instance of an application. For example, a hosted email service offered by a SaaS cloud provider would provide a fully functional email application instance for customers to begin loading data into. Customers in the cloud provider do not have access to the underlying software stack, operating system, and hardware (nor do they wish to). The cloud provider is trusted by the customers to maintain the security and availability of the application to an agreed service level.

Typically, applications in a SaaS environment are Web applications. Web applications have a long history of known security flaws. The hacker can launch attacks against the application used by a customer and attempt to subvert the security of the application. This attack vector may also give the hacker access to data stored in the cloud provider belonging to other customers.

Platform as a Serivce (PaaS)

In the Platform as a Service model, the cloud provider delivers an integrated application stack to the customer. The application stack provides the building blocks upon which a customer can create their end-user application. The cloud provider provides basic components such as databases, Web servers, application servers, business logic engines, and an enterprise service bus, and it is the customer's responsibility to provision applications into the application stack provided by the cloud provider.

In an on-premise deployment, each of these building blocks would be contained within a controlled network perimeter. The expectation would be that the communication between the building blocks could be secured by partitioning it onto a separate physical network internally. This assumption is not valid in the Cloud; the cloud provider may not provide the controls necessary for the components to secure communication between each other. The security controls may be rudimentary, and not allow fine-grained protection of information flow up and down the application stack. The cloud provider may offer customers pre-built application modules to deploy onto the application stack to accelerate development of cloud applications.

A hacker will target the information flows between components in the PaaS stack. They will also attempt to exploit any weaknesses created by the multi-tenancy of the components in the PaaS stack, leading to information leakage. The application building blocks provided by the cloud provider to customers may themselves be vulnerable to many attacks.

Infrastructure as a Service (IaaS)

In the Infrastructure as a Service model, the cloud provider provides a virtualized set of components to the customer such as compute machines, raw storage, virtualized networks, and a control-layer to provision these. It is the responsibility of the customer to build the final OS (operating system) image and associated application stack in the IaaS environment.

The virtual machines that host computer servers typically do not have local storage in the IaaS model; remote storage must be purchased separately by the customer. Security on the connection between the virtual OS instance and the remote persistent storage is the responsibility of the customer, and not the cloud provider.

The hacker has a wider choice of targets in the IaaS environment. From a hacker's perspective the IaaS cloud model does not differ significantly from attacking a software stack deployed in an on-premise environment. The hacker will seek to exploit vulnerabilities in the OS choice by the customer; they will attempt to log into the underlying OS and install a rootkit or gather credential information, and will launch network attacks against the components in the IaaS environment mapped to the customer.

A hacker will usually begin by identifying their target or end goal. Hackers no longer want to break into a system out of curiosity. They operate in the same mode as criminals, profiling a target, selecting its weakest point and striking quickly and decisively to gain entry. The will spend a large portion of their time profiling the target they wish to attack in order to better understand it.

NEW FORMS OF CRIME IN THE CLOUD

The very aspects of cloud computing that make it attractive to legitimate businesses also makes it attractive to criminals. Criminals are drawn to the distributed nature of cloud computing; there is no single "failure point" for a criminal to be caught, no one computer in a group that holds all of the data necessary for the forensic investigator to reconstruct a sequence of events leading up to a crime. A criminal organisation can choose one cloud provider as a storage solution (e.g. Dropbox[1]), and obtain compute services from a second cloud provider (e.g. Amazon EC2[2]), and route all of their communications through a third (e.g. Gmail or Pastebin[3]).

Cloud computing offers computing power that would otherwise be unavailable to criminals with small budgets. For example, Google's AppEngine was used as a command-and-control network for a botnet in 2009[4]. It is to be expected that a cat-and-mouse game will evolve between Cloud providers offering compute services (such as Google or Amazon) and criminals who wish to use those services to commit crimes. Password cracking the Cloud is already offered as a service[5] by one security firm, and the Amazon EC2 compute service was used by a security researcher to crack wifi WPA-PSK passwords[6]. Criminals can use the power of on-demand Cloud computing to attack selected targets; Distributed Denial of Service (DDoS) attacks are a classic example where a large number of Internet-connected resources can overwhelm the availability of even a large commercial organisation. The Low-Orbit Ion Canon[7] is an example of a highly distributed DDoS tool.

The distributed nature of cloud computing enables a criminal organisation to maintain small "cells" of operation, with no one cell knowing the identity of any others. Data partitioning allows each cell in the criminal organisation to preserve their anonymity while still sharing information on likely victims, and the results of any criminal activities. The well known Anonymous[8] and Lulzsec[9] hacking groups adopt this method of operation, with individual members unaware of the identities of other members. A further refinement of this is for criminals to create entire fictitious identities online to link to their cloud accounts, creating excess "noise" for the forensic investigator to analyze. For example, most cloud providers will require a name, address, and credit card to register an account. Criminals can trivially obtain credit card numbers, and then create fake profiles on existing legitimate social media websites to make their cloud identity appear to have a corresponding equivalent in the "real world." A forensic investigator is then faced with the daunting challenge of obtaining data on the criminal identities from multiple online entities, many of whom are geographically spread around the world.

A forensic investigator needs to think like a hacker in order to catch a hacker. Breaking into an application is typically performed a sequence of small incremental steps where each step in the attack exploits what would appear to be a small vulnerability. This "stepping-stone" approach to exploitation also applies in the cloud space. Forensics investigators will not find a single "ah-ha" moment where an attack is launched and a system is compromised. Instead, they will likely find a series of tiny changes made in across dozens of systems and applications to enable an attacker to penetrate a Cloud.

In simple terms, hackers subvert the assumptions made by product designers about how they expect their application to behave in "normal" operating conditions. The "operational security" model of an application makes certain assumptions about the environment it is running in, the facilities available to it from the underlying operating system and platform and the type and behavior of the users in the application. Applications developed to be deployed in an on-premise data-center are often ill suited to a cloud deployment; the assumptions that they make about their operational environment are often invalid in a Cloud. For example, most applications deployed on-premise will assume that they can write a log-file to a local storage disk. However, in the Cloud, a compute instance may not have local persistent storage as all storage is through an object-store held remotely. Thus the operational security model of the application that assumes a secure local log file store is now broken when moved into a cloud environment.

Cloud computing has been enabled by the growth in Web applications and Web services. A Web application is an application accessed via a Web browser over the http/https protocol where there is minimal or no processing and storage of data on the client side. Web applications take advantage of the near ubiquity of the traditional Web browser client installed on almost all current client systems, from mobile phones through desktop computers to tablet devices. Web applications may have some processing elements run locally on the client browser, and these are typically coded in JavaScript. Unfortunately, JavaScript has been the target of many security vulnerabilities over time, and the most common attack vector against a Web application is to exploit poorly written JavaScript code.

A forensic investigator should assume that the attacker knows as much about the product as the development team. A dangerous assumption is that unusual or unique systems are more secure as knowledge about them is difficult to obtain. This is termed security through obscurity and can lead to poor security controls. Any hidden code, back doors, or hard-coded passwords can and will be found and exploited by attackers. A forensics investigator should always assume that an attacker can observe and record all network traffic to and from the cloud provider and will easily reverse-engineer any "proprietary" protocols used in the product. You should also assume that any proprietary encryption algorithms will be broken or bypassed by hackers. Particular attention should be paid to administrative accounts, functions or services present in the cloud provider, and obviously, these are the first targets a hacker will go after. Many cloud providers allow potential customers to sign up for trial accounts prior to purchasing a contract. Hackers will often use these disposable trial accounts to test the security controls in the cloud provider before launching an attack.

ETHICAL HACKING

In their famous paper "Improving the Security of your Site by Breaking into It," Farmer and Venema introduced the concept of the looking at the security of your site through an attacker's eyes as a way to assess it. Up until that point the traditional security posture was focused on building preventative controls against outside hackers; passwords, firewalls, encryption where needed. There was little public discussion around how to test these security controls. In their paper, Farmer and Venema stated that you could have little faith in the security of your site unless you took on the role of a hacker and attempted to subvert the security controls you had put in place.

The principles presented in their paper form the heart of the art and science of penetration testing, also known as *ethical hacking*. Despite being written over a decade ago the ideas and techniques they put forward are as valid today as they were before cloud computing.

The goal of the ethical hacker is to assess the security of products or infrastructure by subverting the operations of each product in order to determine how resilient they are to attack. A key goal is to undermine the security assumptions made during the development process and gauge the risk of exposure this will cause for customers. The outcome of the Ethical Hacking test process is a report identifying the weaknesses in the product, which require immediate attention and resolution.

For the purposes of this chapter, ethical hacker is defined as any person or team which conducts formal security testing against cloud providers, and the networks, network infrastructure elements, computing systems and servers, applications and Web applications that form part of a cloud environment. Ethical hackers are assumed to work for, or be contracted by, the owner of the application or system under test.

"Hackers" is defined to mean any malicious outsider or insider who is intent on subverting the security controls of a system. Hackers are operating without the authorization of the product or system owners.

Unlike hackers depicted in movies, an ethical hacking team adopts a formal structured process to ensure that products are tested in a systematic manner. Ethical hackers act as advocates for customers in security, questioning every aspect of a product's design, documentation, and deployment. Ideally, an ethical hacking team works in conjunction with the development team to ensure that lessons learned from each security testing cycle are incorporated into future product releases.

A forensics investigator can learn from an ethical hacker in terms of an approach and mindset to investigating crime in the Cloud. The goal of an ethical hacker is to duplicate the attack techniques used by a black-hat hacker, while retaining the formality of a rigorous software development process.

This chapter will present a series of techniques used by ethical hackers during their test execution that mirror the attacks launched by hackers, focusing on techniques that are used in cloud penetration testing. Understanding these techniques will help a forensics investigator called on to investigate cloud crime.

An ethical hacker will follow a well-defined series of steps when conducting a penetration test. These can be loosely grouped as:

1. Define the target of the attack, otherwise known as the attack surface.
2. Perform reconnaissance on the Cloud to gain an understanding of the potential vulnerabilities it may contain.
3. Penetrate the target using information gained in step 2 to demonstrate the existence of key vulnerabilities.

Step 1: Define the Cloud Attack Surface

A cloud environment is not a single system so a forensic investigator must establish exactly what the attack surface is so that they can determine the likely routes the attacker took to penetrate the Cloud systems. An attack surface is defined as "all of the reachable and exploitable vulnerabilities" in a Cloud[10].

The ethical hacker will consider five "perspectives" when calculating the attack surface of a Cloud:

- **System Perspective:** Examine the Cloud from the perspective of individual computing systems or servers. Enumerating the servers, and what services they offer, leads to a definition of the attack surface.
- **Network Perspective:** Examine the Cloud from the perspective of network elements such as firewalls, routers, switches, DNS servers, load-balancers, and proxies. Enumerating network services leads to a definition of the attack surface.
- **Service Perspective:** Examine the Cloud from the perspective of the Web services it offers to consumers. Web-services (and Web applications) are typically accessed over the http/https protocol and can use any number of standard application protocols. Enumerating the Web services leads to a definition of the attack surface.
- **Data Perspective:** Examine the Cloud from the perspective of the data it stores, transforms and transmits. Dataflow analysis between the cloud components is performed, and enumerating the dataflows leads to a definition of the attack surface.
- **Human Perspective:** Weaknesses in the human processes and training in the cloud provider, or in clients of the cloud provider.

Naturally, there is no perfect approach to defining the attack surface in the Cloud. An ethical hacker will take a combination of the above four approaches to iteratively refine a definition of a cloud attack surface; starting initially from a system perspective and ultimately being able to describe the attack surface in terms of dataflows and services. The forensic investigator should model the preservation and collection phases using a similar 5-perspective approach.

The System Perspective

In the system perspective, the ethical hacker views security in terms of controls in force on a system-by-system level. In this model, a database server, Web server, transaction server or an email server would each be treated as a separate entity and would be subject to penetration testing in isolation from other systems.

The system perspective has the advantage of simplicity, but does not scale effectively in a Cloud environment. Data is replicated across multiple systems in the Cloud, with no one database or server potentially holding all data. Processing is spread across multiple components; identification and authentication of a user may take place on one server and then their activity may be against a second. The system perspective also ignores the multi-tenant aspect of the Cloud; multiple customers executing on a shared resource. If a forensics investigator seized a single server, they may well end up analyzing data belonging to hundreds of potentially unrelated customers.

The Network Perspective

The network perspective of forensics, sees computing systems as interconnected networks. The elements in the network include network subnets, routers, switches, hubs and firewalls, and network services such as DNS, ARP, and VLANs. The network driven view takes the approach that hackers must cross network boundaries to reach systems, and will exploit vulnerabilities in the network infrastructure to compromise their end target.

The network perspective has the advantage that it can reconstruct hacker activity that may span multiple endpoints on the network. For example, if a hacker penetrates a firewall, followed by an email server, the network driven approach to forensics would follow the trace of network traffic from one system to the other. Naturally, a network-driven view of forensics relies on a reliable, complete, and available record of all network traffic.

A forensics investigator may take a network perspective when investigating a hacker in the Cloud. However a challenge in the Cloud is that networks are often virtualized and customers in the Cloud are partitioned using VLAN technology. A forensics investigator analyzing VLAN traffic will see only the traffic that is routed to the cloud customers' systems. This restriction may potentially lead the forensics investigator to miss important traffic that indicates an attack against a shared network element. For example, an attack against a firewall on customer A may compromise traffic on the network belonging to customer B, allowing the hacker to see traffic on both customers' networks. If a forensic investigator is only viewing logs for customer A, they will miss the attack against the shared network element, in this case a firewall.

The Service Perspective

This view sees the Cloud in terms of service endpoints that offer Web services to consumers. Customers of the cloud provider consume Web services in a loosely coupled fashion. The service view elements include XML, HTTP protocol, service endpoints, service definition languages, service discovery.

The service perspective is beneficial to a forensics investigator as most cloud offerings are built around either a Web services or a Web application model of use. Inbound requests to the cloud provider may be logged in a database allowing the forensics investigator to recreate a sequence of activity to and from the service endpoints defined by the cloud provider. The cloud provider may define a layer of management APIs that are called to allow customers to manage their compute and storage instances in the Cloud. These service endpoints are primary targets for hackers as they allow creation of user accounts, instantiation of additional servers, or may indeed allow the hacker to shutdown the customer's entire cloud instance.

The Data Perspective

The data perspective takes a "follow the data" approach. Analysis of data stored in files is a large part of a traditional forensics investigation. The forensics investigator would be trained in how to recover image files, text documents, video and audio files, and how to identify malware on a seized system.

Cloud computing models treat data as "objects" that can be stored and read by customers of the Cloud. Amazon, Dropbox, and *io.net* are among the cloud providers that offer file or object-based data storage in the Cloud. Customers of these services create, modify, load, read, and delete data content using an interface defined by the cloud provider.

A forensic investigator can adopt a data perspective on the Cloud by analyzing how and where data is accessed via the public interfaces defined by the cloud provider, and then reconstructing the activities of a hacker based on the use of these public APIs.

By analyzing the data flow through the Cloud, the actions that affect a data element are included in the scope of the investigation. The data perspective requires a forensic investigator can recreate all actions that changed, created or deleted data objects in the Cloud. If no detailed logs exist then the forensics investigator will have difficulty in investigating changes to the data elements in the Cloud.

The "Human" Perspective

One technique that is often overlooked by investigators is the art of social engineering that hackers use to exploit the weakest link in most security systems; the people who staff and run the data centers housing the cloud provider. A simple phone call to the main switchboard in most cloud providers will have a hacker connected to a network support engineer within seconds, and a skilled hacker will soon have fooled a support engineer armed with a few technical details gleaned from public sources such as those listed above.

Social engineering attacks are not unique to the Cloud, and have been used for many years to gain an initial entry point into computing systems (most famously perhaps by Kevin Mitnick[11]). The Cloud environment increases the number of potential avenues a hacker can explore for social engineering. A cloud provider may rely on other cloud suppliers to provide services that it in turn re-sells. A hacker has many more potential targets to attempt to hoodwink using basic social engineering. Once an entry point is gained into one company in the Cloud, a skilled hacker can use that as a stepping-stone to gain entry into subsequent targets.

Social engineering poses a challenge for a forensic investigator, as it typically does not manifest itself in system logs. A phone call to a support engineer may be logged, but the contents of the discussion may not be. Moreover, a cloud provider may claim to log and record all conversations to support engineers, but one of their cloud suppliers may not, creating a dead-end for the forensics investigator.

Step 2: Perform Reconnaissance on the Cloud

A hacker will begin by profiling the target system. Profiling enables them to get a sense of the size and scope of the system they wish to penetrate. The ultimate goal of profiling is to generate a list of potential attack vectors that the hacker can then exploit. Profiling is typically an "outside-in" view of the system, using only publicly available information and interfaces exposed by the cloud provider.

However, a skilled hacker may have already gained some insider knowledge about the cloud provider or its operations from social-networking sites, chatting with current or former employees, previous customers, forum postings or even dumpster diving.

Profiling a cloud provider is made easier by the fact that most cloud providers offer public interfaces to their clients. Often profiling is as simple as signing up for a free-trial account with a cloud provider to learn more about the services they offer, the versions of software installed and the endpoints of the cloud provider exposed on the Internet.

The ultimate goal of profiling is to define the attack surface for the cloud provider. The attack surface is the scope of entry points into a system that an attacker can exploit. For example, an administrative page that allows management of cloud compute instances is an entry point into a cloud provider and would form part of the overall attack surface. Likewise, a Web service API that can be consumed by external clients adds to the scope of the attack surface. The greater the number of interfaces, whether public or private, the larger the attack surface the system exposes. The goal of the reconnaissance phase is to determine the size of the attack surface.

Profiling is conducted using a two-phase approach, i.e., determine the footprint of the cloud provider, followed by the fingerprint of the cloud provider. Foot-printing takes a gross system level measurement of the attack surface, and fingerprinting refines it to enable targeting of attacks.

Establishing the Cloud "Footprint"

There are many public sources of data about a company that allow a hacker to determine its footprint. The most obvious initial starting point is to perform DNS queries on the domains of the cloud provider to find out where they are registered and which name servers are responsible for serving those domains. The Internet registrar (WHOIS) database[12] contains a mapping of all domains to owners, though in the case of cloud providers those owners are usually listed as corporate addresses. However, it is not unusual to find an individual's name, phone number, or email address listed in the WHOIS database for a domain. A hacker can use this information to launch a spear-phishing attack by attempting to impersonate that person in order to gain further information about the cloud provider systems from trusting insiders.

Hackers can retrieve the IP address range allocated to the cloud provider by querying any of the five global Regional Internet Registry (RIR) providers. The RIRs are responsible for allocating blocks of IP addresses. The RIRs are currently:

- African Network Information Centre (AfriNIC).
- American Registry for Internet Numbers (ARIN).
- Asia-Pacific Network Information Centre (APNIC).
- Latin America and Caribbean Network Information Centre (LACNIC).
- RIPE The Réseaux IP Européens Network Coordination Centre (RIPE NCC) for Europe, Middle East, and Central Asia.

Knowing the IP address ranges the hackers will next use commonly available Internet tools to understand the routes to and from the cloud provider, and the services offered by the cloud provider. Commonly used tools include traceroute[13] to see the route to the cloud provider, and nmap[14] to see the ports and services open on the servers the cloud provider has connected to the Internet. These tools have been used for many years to search for servers on the Internet.

However cloud computing brings an interesting twist; it is possible to create a map of the IP address range allocated by a cloud provider to compute instances given to customers to determine if a given virtual machine in the Cloud is located on the same physical server as another potential target VM, an attack termed "cloud cartography" (Ristenpart, et al., 2009).

Fingerprinting

Once the hacker has a list of networks and systems mapped for the cloud provider they will turn to fingerprinting techniques and tools to identify specific services on offer, protocols spoken by the services, any encryption techniques used, operating system versions, software versions etc. Fingerprinting is a more laborious process than footprinting, but the end results is a list of specific attack points in the cloud provider that the hacker can then exploit.

Profiling a cloud environment will not appear as a single entry in a log file. The attackers will spread their profiling activity over time so that their actions appear to be lost in the background network traffic. A forensic investigator will have to merge log files from multiple sources over a period of time to detect any indication of profiling the target in the Cloud. This will be a significant challenge given the diffuse nature of cloud environments, the lack of a standardized logging format (if any logs exist at all) and the reluctance of key suppliers to release log information.

A hacker will attempt to locate all of the resources inside the application in the Cloud, including data stores, user repositories, screens, UI elements, APIs, data flows, and application instances. This will typically be performed during the reconnaissance phase. Forensic investigators should look for traffic patterns to the Web application that indicate spidering attacks, following all of the links on all Web pages in the application in rapid succession. Such a traffic pattern would indicate that an automated tool is being used to probe the application for vulnerabilities.

Profiling a Cloud environment will include an assessment of the cloud infrastructure in addition to the applications deployed in the Cloud. The cloud provider will offer a public interface to a customer that allows them to manage instances of their applications in the Cloud. Hackers will focus their attention on the infrastructure interfaces during profiling to assess what routes into the Cloud exist that are outside of the control of any one cloud provider customer. The ideal target would be an interface that allows a hacker to create a seemingly legitimate customer instance in the Cloud. They can create dummy customer accounts, install applications, and test the security of the cloud provider from the inside. The forensics investigator should focus their attention on all traffic to and from the cloud provider infrastructure management interfaces.

Armed with knowledge about the attack surface for a Cloud the forensic investigator will be far positioned to recreate the series of actions taken by an attacker.

What can a forensics investigator learn from the techniques used by hackers to profile a cloud provider? Given the fact that a cloud environment is not a single system a forensic investigator must establish exactly what the attack surface is so that they can determine the likely routes the attacker took to penetrate the cloud systems. The forensics investigator should take the same foot-printing and fingerprinting tools available to hackers to determine the attack surface, i.e., hints from these tools can point the investigator to potential vulnerabilities the hackers used to break into the Cloud.

Step 3: Penetrating the Cloud

Attacks against the Cloud occur at the application level, and not the infrastructure level as has been common in the past. Application level attacks focus on exploiting vulnerabilities in code and applications deployed to provide a business service. Examples of applications deployed in the Cloud include corporate email systems, instant messaging systems, team collaboration space, Customer Relationship Management (CRM) and document storage and retrieval systems.

When infrastructure attacks were the most common entry point into systems a forensic investigator had to be an expert in network vulnerabilities and how they are exploited. A good forensic investigator would stay current on current network hacking tools, and also track the techniques used by hackers to exploit network services. As application level attacks become the major threat it should be immediately obvious that no forensic investigator can hope to be an expert in how all of these applications work. The attack surface in the Cloud has grown so dramatically with the explosion in applications and services that are now on offer. How should a forensic investigator proceed given the changing nature of the attacks on the Cloud?

A forensics investigator needs to understand how hackers are targeting the Cloud so that they can adapt their investigative methods to detect the attacks. Hackers are moving away from system level attacks to targeting Web applications and Web services. Hackers will attempt to penetrate the Web applications hosted in a Cloud to gain an entry point into the customer, and from there they will probe for system level vulnerabilities.

This section will describe a number of key attack vectors used by hackers in the Cloud, and how a forensics investigator can adapt their investigative methods to detect them. Rather than focus on specific attacks against the Cloud, this section will cover the general classes of vulnerabilities present in the Cloud and how the forensic investigator can reconstruct the attacks after-the-fact.

The The Open Web Application Security Project (OWASP)[15] has catagorised many of the vulnerabilities present in Web applications, which are common in cloud environments. These vulnerabilities are typically exploited using the standard HTTP protocols[16], and so will bypass firewalls that are focused on detecting network level attacks. Many of these vulnerabilities have been present in Web applications for over a decade. Cross-Site Scripting (XSS)[17] was first reported in the 1990s, and XSS vulnerabilities continue to be found in applications. Forensic investigators should be familiar with the body of work produced by OWASP, specifically the OWASP Testing Guide[18]. The OWASP testing guide explains how to conduct a security test against a Web application using commonly available tools to exploit the most common class of vulnerabilities

The OWASP Top Ten list for 2010[19] highlights ten critical vulnerabilities as occurring frequent in Web applications. Hackers will likely exploit these vulnerabilities in cloud applications, and a forensic investigator must be aware of how these exploits occur, and more importantly, what evidence they leave behind.

The OWASP Top Ten vulnerabilities are analysed from the perspective of the evidence left behind by an attacker, mapped onto four of five perspectives presented earlier, i.e., system, network, data, and service perspective. Table 1 summarises the likelihood that evidence exists if a forensic investigator uses that perspective to analyse the data available from the cloud provider.

The following terms are used in the table entries, and are defined as follows:

- **Possible:** There is a high probability that the investigator will find data that provides evidence of the attack occurring, and what the target of the attack was.
- **Likely:** There is a medium probability that the forensic investigator will find evidence of this attack by examining the Cloud from this perspective. The likelihood of finding evidence depends on how the application/system is designed, and operational considerations (e.g. whether or not verbose logging enabled).
- **Unlikely:** This is a low probability that the forensic investigator will find evidence for this attack by examining the Cloud from this perspective.

The forensic investigator should bear in mind that a hacker will build an attack out of a series of small steps. A successful attack is composed of many small exploits, any one of which is easy to miss. However taken together as a whole these exploits lead to a security compromise. Each of the vulnerabilities above is discussed in detail in the following sections.

Table 1. Likelihood of the existence of evidence from available cloud data mapped to the system, data, network, and service perspectives

Vulnerability	System	Data	Network	Service/Application
Injection Attacks	Unlikely	Possible	Unlikely	Likely
Cross-Site Scripting	Unlikely	Possible	Unlikely	Likely
Broken Session Management	Unlikely	Unlikely	Possible	Possible
Insecure Object References	Possible	Possible	Unlikely	Possible
CSRF	Unlikely	Unlikely	Unlikely	Possible
Security Misconfiguration	Likely	Unlikely	Likely	Likely
Insecure Cryptographic Storage	Possible	Likely	Likely	Likely
Restrict URL access	Unlikely	Unlikely	Likely	Likely
Insufficient transport protection	Possible	Unlikely	Likely	Likely
Invalidated redirects and forwards	Unlikely	Unlikely	Unlikely	Possible

Injection Attacks

In these attacks, malicious data is injected into the Web application in the Cloud in a manner that was not anticipated by the application designers. Examples include sending binary data into input fields that expect only text data, or crafting data to resemble executable content (see Cross-Site Scripting below).

Injection attacks are trivial for an attacker to execute; remote access to the cloud service over a network is sufficient, and often an authenticated session is not required. Injection flaws are common in legacy code, especially at the boundary layer between the application and the operating system where the cloud application is executing OS commands to perform key functions. A forensic investigator will likely find evidence for this class of attacks in logs for the cloud service, as injection attacks are often packaged in standard HTTP requests to a Web service. At a minimum, a corrupted log entry can be evidence that an attacker attempted to launch an injection attack; the side effect of the attack was to generate a corrupt log entry as the logging system was unable to handle the volume or encoding of the data sent in the attack.

Cross-Site Scripting (XSS)

In this attack the application takes an untrusted data input (typically entered in a form field on a Web page) and executes content derived from the input. Attackers can insert executable scripts into Web pages that are run whenever the page is displayed, or when a user clicks on a link.

Automated toolkits have made exploitation of XSS vulnerabilities a "point-and-click" exercise. It is trivial for an attacker to scan and exploit a cloud service for XSS vulnerabilities, and in doing so they will leave evidence behind in the form of service log file entries, and potentially network log entries.

Evidence for attacks exploiting this vulnerability will be contained in the log files for the cloud Web applications. A forensic investigator should look for Javascript embedded in *http* requests in the log files for the Web application. If the cloud provider has a Web Application Firewall (WAF) or Intrusion Prevention System (IPS) it is possible that the forensic investigator will find log file evidence for XSS attacks in those devices. Gaining access to the logs for an IPS or WAF maybe pose difficulties for the investigator, especially if the log files are rotated periodically to minimise storage space.

Cross-site scripting attacks can also leave evidence in data stores, especially if the attacker has launched a stored-XSS attack (see the OWASP guide referenced above for more details). A stored-XSS attack stores Javascript (or other content that is executed by a Web browser when rendering a Webpage) in the database backing a Web application. For example, if a Web application stores a "username" field in the database the attacker may modify it to append Javascript to the end of the username such that when displayed in victim's browser the Javascript executes and steals session tokens. The forensic investigator should look for evidence of script code in data stores associated with the Web application in the cloud provider. If the data store contains scripting code then it has likely been subjected to a stored-XSS attack.

Broken Session Management and Authentication

Session management is at the heart of Web application security. Session management ensures that user sessions remain isolated from each other; user A logged on to a Web application should not be allowed to interact with user B's session. Session management becomes especially important in the Cloud as separation of users must be enforced both within a customer (i.e. all users of customer A must be isolated from each other) but also across customers (i.e. all users of customer A must also be isolated from all users of customer B). Poor session management is one of the key attack vectors an ethical hacker will use to attempt an enumeration attack on the customers in a cloud provider; by manipulating the session token the ethical hacker will attempt to gain access to another user's authenticated session, in another customer instance in the Cloud.

Evidence for broken session management attacks is usually contained in the logs for the Web application under attack. Typical attack vectors to exploit these vulnerabilities involve manipulating session IDs that are embedded in URLs (URL re-writing) or stored in cookies. A pattern of repeated access to a specific Web resource will be obvious in the logs, with each request varying slightly as the attacker varies the session ID in an attempt to find a valid session to hijack. The forensic investigator should focus their attention on Web application logs as the primary source of evidence for this attack.

Insecure Direct Object References

A secure implementation of a Web application should not expose the details of how objects and data are stored in its database or file store. If an object reference vulnerability is present then an ethical hacker can manipulate object references in Web applications to gain access to resources outside of their authorized domain. A simple example is a corporate file-sharing application in the Cloud; users on project teams will share project documents with each other, but will not share these documents with users outside of a defined group. An ethical hacker will examine how the object references for these documents are stored and encoded in the Web application, and will attempt to gain access to a file that they otherwise would not have been able to view.

An attacker will exploit this class of vulnerability by attempting to access protected resources without having the correct authorization. A simple example is the case where the attacker modifies the parameters submitted in a URL to change their customer ID when accessing a resource in the Cloud. By modifying the customer ID the attacker is attempting to make a direct mapping to a resource that they should not see, but is not sufficiently protected by the cloud application.

The forensic investigator should look for evidence in the Web application logs to detect this attack. Typically, a Web application will record the modifications requests to stored objects performed by authenticated and authorized users. A forensic investigator should look for modifications to stored objects that do not correlate with requests in the access logs for the Web application.

Cross-Site Request Forgery (CSRF)

In this vulnerability, an attacker causes a request to be sent to a Web application that appears to originate from a legitimate user session. The Web application has no way of knowing if a user actually initiated the request by actively clicking on a link. A CSRF attack is an example of misplaced trust in the Web application; it assumes that all input received over an authenticated user session is valid, and was initiated by the user.

Evidence for this class of attack is most likely to be found in the logs for the Web application in the cloud provider. The forensic investigator should look for requests that attempt to change the state of the application but that do not contain a secret or unpredictable value to prevent the attacker from crafting malicious requests. CSRF exploits typically target administrative or privileged accounts as they can in turn change the state of the security of the application to the attacker's advantage.

Security Misconfiguration

Operational security demands that all computing resources conform to a known and measurable security policy at all times. In an on-premise deployment, security configuration is manageable, a cloud deployment significantly increases the challenge in managing security configurations. At a very basic level, customers in a cloud provider want to be assured that all of the services made available to them are configured to be secure. Yet cloud providers rarely can make that guarantee, especially if they themselves are re-selling services bought in from third-party cloud providers.

Security misconfigurations can occur at all layers of the cloud stack. For example, default accounts on servers may contain passwords that are well known. Likewise, an attacker may target the software stack in the cloud provider and attempt to exploit poorly configured administration accounts or functions to create backdoors. Error reporting is an often overlooked aspect of security misconfiguration; error reports often contain a stack-trace of the offending code module which allows an attacker to reverse engineer the design of the application or the cloud environment. This knowledge in turn allows them to improve the targeting of their attacks in the future.

A forensic investigator will be challenged to detect security misconfiguration. It is rare to find systems or applications that log when security configuration changes are made, and thus leaving a record for the investigator. The investigator will have to probe each layer of the cloud stack to pinpoint potential security misconfiguration.

Insecure Cryptographic Storage

A sign of poorly thought-out security model is an application that stores private or sensitive data in plaintext form, assuming that the database holding the information is a "secure server." Cryptographic libraries are available to perform all of the most common functions required to protect the confidentiality and integrity of data, yet developers are often ignorant as to how to use them properly. Most importantly, encryption keys are often generated in a weak manner, leading to keys that are easily guessed or broken.

Assumptions are often made by programmers about secure storage that are valid in an on-premise world are broken by the move to the Cloud. An ethical hacker will examine all data encryption performed by an application with a view to finding poor implementation of common cryptographic algorithms, weak or non-existent key generation (i.e. encryption keys hard-coded in the application) or storage of encryption keys in a publicly accessible location.The forensic investigator should take a data-driven approach to locating evidence to detect exploitation of insecure cryptographic storage. First, the investigator must identify the points in the Cloud where data is stored. Second, they must determine if the data is encrypted before being stored. Third, they must determine where the cryptographic keys are generated and stored for encrypting the data stored.

A review of the code for an application that has been the target of an attack will be required to determine if it correctly generates cryptographic tokens and encrypts all data stored or transmitted. If an attacker has targeted data that is not encrypted using strong cryptographic techniques, or which is stored in plaintext form, the forensic investigator should look for evidence of other attacks that access that data. For example; the investigator is tracking theft of identities and credit card information and discovers that a database containing credit card data is not encrypted when stored in a backup site. The investigator now knows that an attacker has a likely target in the cloud environment, and begins to look for evidence that the attacker exploit other weaknesses in the Cloud to target that database.

Failure to Restrict URL Access

Applications should perform a basic level of access control checks to determine if a user is permitted to access a certain page in a Web application. However, few applications will enforce these checks to a sufficient level. For example, in a Web application an administrator may have access to critical functions on a Web page that gives them the ability to create an delete user accounts. A standard user viewing the same page would have a limited set of operations to perform. Unfortunately, the application does not prevent a standard user entering the URL for one of the restricted actions and thus exceeding their authorization level. An ethical hacker will search for pages that perform state-changing actions such as adding or removing user accounts or access rights. The ethical hacker will test to see if these pages are accessible to non-administrative users. This class of vulnerability would have devastating consequences if it was present in the administration panel of a cloud provider that allows customers to create/delete/manage the instances of their applications in the cloud provider.

Evidence of exploitation of this class of vulnerability typically is found in the access logs for Web applications running in the Cloud. The investigator should look for patterns of access to URLs or Web resources in log files that indicate an attacker attempting to vary the URL being requested to bypass security checks. For example, an investigator should look for bursts of repeated requests that contain a fixed base URL followed by slight variations on a path to a page, because this indicates an attacker mapping the resources in a Web application in an attempt to locate a restricted resource.

Insufficient Transport Layer Protection

An assumption often made when applications are deployed on a corporate network is that the network is somehow "trusted" as it is behind a corporate firewall. Cleartext communication becomes the norm in accessing Web applications, as everyone on the inside of the firewall is assumed to be similarly trusted. Obviously, this model breaks completely when applications are moved into the Cloud. At a minimum, Web applications and services deployed in a Cloud should be accessed over SSL. SSL is an industry-standard encryption protocol that protects the confidentiality and integrity of the data exchanged over the network. Unfortunately, many Web applications only enforce SSL for an initial login page when a username and password are entered, and allow all subsequent communication to be in cleartext http. An ethical hacker will always assume that a hacker has complete access to the network, and can intercept all traffic to and from the customer's systems in the Cloud.

The forensic investigator may not find direct evidence that an attacker has exploited insufficient transport layer protections. Instead, the investigator should determine if the application enforces strong transport protection, as this would provide a likely attack vector for a hacker to exploit.

Invalidated Redirects and Forwards

In this class of vulnerability, an application allows redirection of a user towards another resource as part of providing a service. For example, an application that provides a help system may actually redirect the user to an external provider of content. Unfortunately, the vulnerability lies in how the application performs the redirection. All too often, no validation is performed on the redirection, so that the application can be tricked into redirecting a user to a site of the attacker's choosing. Users will assume that the links presented to them are to be trusted, as they are unaware that an attacker has modified the redirection to point to a malicious site. An attacker can use this technique to steal session cookies from a user's browser and hence perform a session-hijacking attack. Alternatively, an attacker can use this vulnerability as part of a cloud enumeration attack where they wish to find all users from all customers in the Cloud who are accessing a particular function in an application that is shared across the Cloud.

The forensic investigator should analyse the Web application to determine if it provides a redirect function as part of its normal functionality. For example, the investigator should look for URLs of the following form:

http://website.com/redirect.jsp?url=...

An attacker will use this redirect feature to forward victims to a malicious site as the base URL appears to be a trusted site and the victim will likely click on the link to follow it. Evidence for this will be found in the logs for the Web application.

The previous Top Ten list of vulnerabilities is not unique to cloud deployments of Web applications. On-premise deployments of Web applications are as likely to be vulnerable to these issues as a cloud deployment. However, vulnerabilities found in a Web application in the Cloud, especially one that is deployed in a shared SaaS environment, have a magnified business impact. With many customers sharing a common virtualized infrastructure a single vulnerability exploit can affect dozens if not hundreds of customers in a large cloud provider.

CONCLUSION

This chapter has explained what an ethical hacker is, and how they work. It has also explained the major classes of vulnerabilities that exist in the Cloud, especially given that most Clouds are built around Web applications. The challenge for the forensic investigator is to adapt their techniques for the Cloud. Data acquisition and integrity is a major challenge in the Cloud. There is no single central database that a forensic investigator can analyze to find all records pertaining to activity in the Cloud. There is no single server that houses "the Cloud," and as cloud providers layer services from other third parties a forensic investigator may find themselves chasing data across the globe.

The most important concept for a forensic investigator to take away from this chapter is that the nature of the attacks against the Cloud is accelerating, with Web application and Web service vulnerabilities providing the easy route for hackers to break into customers in the Cloud. A forensic investigator performing a disk-level analysis of a cloud server looking for malware and viruses is not working at the correct level to catch cloud crime; they should instead be analyzing the overall flow of data to and from all of the components in the Cloud. The forensic investigator has to move away from a model of performing analysis on a frozen system image, to a model of live cloud forensics where they may not have jurisdictional control over any of the systems involved. Learning from the ethical hacker will hopefully make the forensic investigators job easier.

REFERENCES

Farmer, D., & Venema, W. (2012). *Improving the security of your site by breaking into it.* http://www.porcupine.org/satan/demo/docs/admin_guide_to_cracking.html

Grobauer, B., & Schreck, T. (2010). Towards incident handling in the cloud: Challenges and approaches. In *Proceeding of the 2012 ACM Workshop on Cloud Computing Security Workshop*, (pp. 77-86). New York, NY: ACM Press.

Kent, K., Chevalier, S., Grance, T., & Dang, H. (2006). *Guide to integrating forensic techniques into incident response, special publication 800-86*. Gaithersburg, MD: National Institute of Standards and Technology.

Mell, J. P., & Grance, T. (2011). *The NIST definition of cloud computing*. Gaithersburg, MD: National Institute of Standards and Technology.

Ristenpart, T., Tromer, E., Shacham, H., & Savage, S. (2009). Hey, you, get off of my cloud: Exploring information leakage in third-party compute clouds. In *Proceedings of CCS 2009*. Retrieved from http://people.csail.mit.edu/tromer/papers/cloudsec.pdf

ENDNOTES

1 http://www.dropbox.com

2 http://aws.amazon.com/ec2/

3 http://pastebin.com

4 http://ddos.arbornetworks.com/2009/11/malicious-google-appengine-used-as-a-cnc/

5 https://www.wpacracker.com/

6 http://www.eweek.com/c/a/Security/Amazon-EC2-Used-to-Crack-Password-Encryption-on-Wireless-Networks-490541/

7 Low Orbit Ion Canon, distributed denial of service tool: http://sourceforge.net/projects/loic/

8 Anonymous hacking group news site: http://anonnews.org

9 Lulzsec, a splinter group from Anonymous: http://twitter.com/#!/LulzSec/

10 The Attack Surface Problem. SANS Institute Security Laboratory. http://www.sans.edu/research/security-laboratory/article/did-attack-surface

11 Social Engineering: The Basics. http://www.csoonline.com/article/514063/social-engineering-the-basics

12 WHOIS: http://www.whois.net/

13 Traceroute: http://en.wikipedia.org/wiki/Traceroute

14 Nmap: http://nmap.org

15 OWASP: http://www.owasp.org/

16 http://www.w3.org/Protocols/

17 Cross-Site Scripting: http://www.owasp.org/index.php/Top_10_2010-A2

18 OWASP Testing Guide: http://www.owasp.org/index.php/Category:OWASP_Testing_Project

19 OWASP Top Ten: http://www.owasp.org/index.php/Category:OWASP_Top_Ten_Project

Chapter 3
Challenges to Digital Forensic Evidence in the Cloud

Fred Cohen
All.Net, USA

ABSTRACT

Digital forensic evidence is subject to a variety of challenges, and these challenges apply in the Cloud as anywhere else. This chapter is an overview of these issues specifically oriented toward the Cloud Computing environments of today.

INTRODUCTION

Digital forensic evidence is identified, collected, transported, stored, analyzed, interpreted, attributed, reconstructed, presented, and destroyed through a set of processes. Challenges to this evidence may come through challenges to elements of this process. These processes, like all other processes and the people and systems that carry them out, are imperfect. That means that there are certain types of faults that can occur in these processes[1].

The emerging cloud-computing environment has three distinct features of note related to these issues: (1) distributed computing implies that evidence may exist in and reflect activities on many computers, (2) those computers may be at many locations, and (3) the computers may not be owned by the same entities as the content at issue. This chapter covers these differences in context of the previous work in the digital forensics area.

DOI: 10.4018/978-1-4666-2662-1.ch003

Faults and Failures

Faults consist of intentional or accidental making or missing of content, contextual information, the meaning of content, process elements, relationships, ordering, timing, location, corroborating content, consistencies, and inconsistencies. In the cloud context, the faults and failures may extend to multiple computers in multiple locations under control of multiple parties[2]. Thus, the opportunities for faults and failures are extended.

Not all faults produce failures, but some may. While it may be possible to challenge faults, this generally does not work and is unethical if failures

Copyright © 2013, IGI Global. Copying or distributing in print or electronic forms without written permission of IGI Global is prohibited.

are not demonstrable. Certain things turn faults into failures, and it is these failures that legitimately should be and can be challenged in legal matters.

Failures consist of false positives and false negatives. False negatives are items that should have been found and dealt with in the process but were not, while false positives are things that should have been discarded or discredited in the process but were not.

Legal Issues

In the United States, at the Federal level, evidence is admitted or rejected based on the relative weights of probative and prejudicial value. Other standards apply in different jurisdictions, but this standard is fairly common worldwide. Probative value is the extent to which potential evidence supports a legal claim. Prejudicial value is the extent to which that evidence potentially influences the trier of fact (usually a judge or jury). If more probative than prejudicial, evidence is admissible[3,4].

Part of the issue of probative value is the quality of the evidence. If the process that created the evidence as presented is flawed, this reduces the probative value. Impure evidence, evidence presented by an expert who is shown to lack expertise in the subject at hand, evidence that has not been retained in a proper chain of custody, evidence that fails to take into account the context, or evidence falling under any of the other fault categories shown in Figure 1, all lead to reduced probative value. If the effect of these faults is wrong results, the probative value may go to zero.

In the cloud context, these issues may be greatly complicated. For example, establishing a chain of custody is potentially problematic if evidence comes from or through many jurisdictions and providers, is gathered without direct physical access, was under the control of third parties, is stored in and moved between systems with a history of breaking, accessible from anywhere by anyone, or was protected only by a password that was one of millions of such passwords stolen in the last 6 months. Attesting to the reliability[5] of such evidence may be problematic[6].

Figure 1. Challenges overview

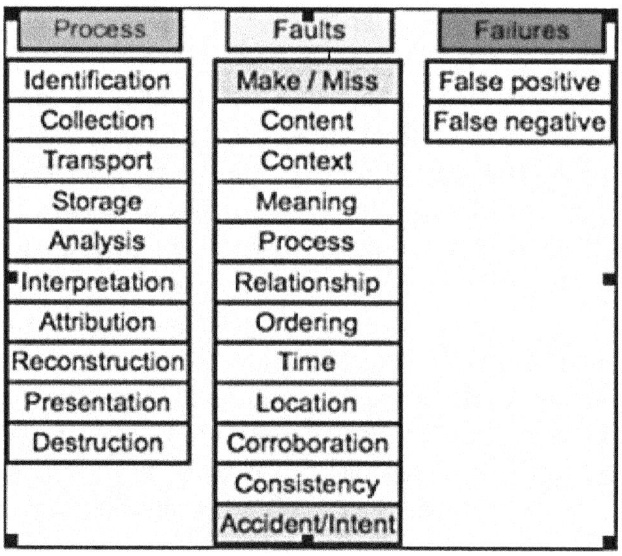

The Latent and Hearsay Nature of the Evidence

In order to deal with digital evidence, it must be presented in court. Since digital data is not directly observable by the finder of fact, it must be presented through expert witnesses using tools to reveal its existence, content, and meaning to the fact finders. This puts it into the category of latent evidence. Thus, it depends on the quality and unbiased opinion of the experts for each side.

In addition, digital evidence is hearsay evidence, in that it is presented by an expert who asserts facts or conclusions based on what the computer recorded, not what they themselves have directly observed. In order for hearsay evidence to be admitted, it normally has to come in under the normal business records exemption to the hearsay evidence prohibition or some other exception[7].

In the cloud-computing environment, tools in use typically depend on the execution of server software written for commercial use and not for forensic purposes, by unknown parties, used in unknown circumstances, and with at best limited visibility as to process[8].

Notions Underlying "Good Practice"

One of the results of diverse approaches to collection and analysis of digital forensic evidence is that it became increasingly difficult to show why the process used in any particular case is reliable, trustworthy, and accurate. As a result, sets of 'good practices' were developed by law enforcement in the UK, US, and elsewhere. The use of the term 'good practices' is specifically designed to avoid the use of terms like 'standards' or 'best practices.' This is because of a desire to prevent challenges to evidence based on not following these practices.

However, for cloud forensics, there are no such "good practices" defined or widely accepted yet. To the extent that existing practices are applied, they are applied without even this limited backing.

Overview of the Rest of This Chapter

The rest of this chapter will focus on identifying sources of faults that occur in and between elements of the forensic process and ways that those faults turn into failures. The failures are then used to challenge the process. Challenges can be couched in terms of the process, the fault, and the resulting failure and this makes for an effective presentation of the challenge. All of this will be viewed with examples and focus on cloud computing issues.

IDENTIFYING EVIDENCE

The first step in gathering evidence is identifying possible sources of evidence for collection. It is fairly common that identified evidence includes too little or too much information. If too much is identified, then court mandated search and seizure limitations may be exceeded. If too little is identified, exculpatory or inculpatory evidence may be missed. Commonly missed evidence comes in the form of network logs from related network components.

In most cloud computing environments, most of the evidence, and particularly most of the redundant traces, are not available or never generated or stored in the same way as they are in non-cloud environments. User-based login and controls are typically in the application rather than the operating system, so records tend to be limited to whatever the application designer decided to do.

The private and sometimes confidential details of the software used to produce records that may exist are typically unavailable to, and hard to characterize by, the examiner. For example, in a criminal case involving email through cloud service providers, the details of how drafts are turned into deliverable messages were unavailable, leading to the inability to prove whether or not a draft was ever sent (and more obviously, whether it was ever transmitted or received).

Unlike a commonly used computing environment to which the examiner might have access to perform experiments, in the Cloud, the details of what logs are produced, what other records are produced and/or kept, and where they might be found are opaque except through testimony of representatives of the provider. In many cases, these individuals are custodians of the records, but do not have detailed knowledge of technologies or actual records that might be found if sought. Indeed companies benefit from not keeping such records or having custodians with only limited knowledge.

Common Misses

There is a great deal of corroborating evidence that can be sought from connected systems that produce log files that can confirm or refute the use of a system by a party. If the evidence is not sought and the actions are in question, either in terms of taking place or in terms of their source, path, or content, the lack of intermediate audit trails may prevent a party from definitively showing what took place.

Other evidence that is commonly missed includes storage devices, networked computer contents, deleted file areas from disks, secondary storage, backups, and other similar information. Properly identifying information to be collected often fails because of missed relationships between computers and evidence in those computers. This evidence is often time sensitive and is lost if not identified and gathered within a short time frame.

These issues are exacerbated in outsourced cloud computing environments because of the lack of detailed knowledge and documentation for most customized environments. In effect, nobody knows what is actually generated or stored where in many of these systems, and they involve so many components. Things like individual disks are not even concepts presented to external users, and hardware is often changed out or reused over time in ways that make it infeasible in most cases to even look for many sorts of evidence that might be present.

Relevant information is often located in places not immediately evident from the original crime scene. In cases where evidence is stored for long periods and can be identified as missing in a timely fashion, the fault can usually be mitigated by additional collection. However, in cloud environments, such collection is often infeasible, since the specific locations of content are unknown, the volumes may be very high, and the protocols and mechanisms used to exchange information may be non-standard and poorly or not documented.

The time frame for much of this information is very limited, particularly in the case of server logs, connection logs, and similar network-related information. The chain of custody issues for such evidence can also be quite complex and involve a large number of participants from multiple jurisdictions. In distributed outsourced cloud computing, this commonly involves multiple countries on different continents. Indeed legal requirements for non-transit across jurisdictional boundaries are often bypassed by safe harbor agreements or simply ignored by companies and/or workers who are unaware and management who fails to identify and manage these issues properly.

Information Not Sought

In some cases, evidence is not sought. For example, when one side or another looks for evidence in a case, they may decide to follow-up or not follow-up on different facets of the case, pursue or not pursue various lines of inquiry, or limit the level of detail or sort of evidence they collect. These represent intentional non-identification of evidence. On the other hand, there are plenty of good investigators who miss all sorts of evidence for one reason or another. Evidence is often concealed and not found by investigators. Sometimes it is stored somewhere the investigators are unaware of or cannot gain access to. Sometimes the evidence is destroyed or no longer exists by the time it becomes apparent that it might be of value. These sorts of faults occur in every case, but they rarely rise to the level of a failure causing a substantial error in a case. People often do their best or focus their attention on what they think is important, and sometimes they miss things. Time and resources are limited, so certain lines are not always pursued. That is just how the world is.

False Evidence

On the other hand, there are also cases, rare as they may be, when evidence is made up "from whole cloth." This is increasingly difficult to do in many areas because of the improvements in record keeping practices and forensic examination over the years. It is very hard to make up digital evidence and have it survive expert challenges. However, in most cases, experts do not get involved in trying to challenge every piece of evidence, and the challenges of identifying false evidence in the cloud-computing environment are far greater than in non-cloud environments for the reasons already identified. The lack of redundancy and detailed records of how what traces are produced, the limited ability to perform experiments on the environment at issue to determine normal behavior, and related issues drive up the difficulty of separating false from real evidence.

Non-Stored Transient Information

Data that is not stored in storage media cannot be seized; it can only be collected in real time by placing sensors into the real-time environment. Such evidence must be identified in a different manner than evidence sitting on a desk or within a disk. This sort of evidence must be identified by an intelligence process, and special legal means must be applied in many cases to collect this evidence.

In most cloud environments, such intelligence is hard to come by, and most providers do not want to reveal the specifics of their operations. Such operations often change quickly with time, and many parties may be involved. For example, a cloud infrastructure may be composed of leased time on hundreds of systems around the globe, owned, and operated by scores of different providers. With records spread across such an infrastructure, even knowing where to look to place sensors is enormously problematic.

Today, for about $15/month each, computers can be leased in data centers almost anywhere. 100 such systems can be operated as a network for under $2,000/month using lessee encryption and keys. These sit inside a global infrastructure with millions of such computers, and the computers themselves are "virtualized" so that they may move from hardware and location to other hardware and location without the knowledge of the lessee. Attempts to capture traffic will involve potentially enormous resources, rapid movement of sensors from location to location, and an ability to deal with the encryption issues, all operating within high volume infrastructures. While governments are increasingly requiring providers to support government access for investigations of network-related activity, in civil matters, non-Federal government cases, and cases involving a lack of local government cooperation, dealing with such information is increasingly problematic.

Seizure Issues

The shared nature of much of today's cloud computing makes seizure of physical equipment problematic. Of course the problem starts with identifying what physical things are in fact to be seized. As discussed above, content and operational mechanisms may move rapidly from place to place, and often involve very large data centers and facilities that service from thousands to hundreds of millions of individuals. In some cases, shutting down a computer system may produce highly undesirable and unexpected side effects because of the interdependencies of systems. For example, shutting down a set of DNS[9] servers that are core to multiple processes can disrupt computers across the Internet and have ripple effects that can be global.

However, suppose you identify a particular set of hardware that may contain some sought after information. In order to seize it, you may have to shut down a lot of related systems and mechanisms. While cases have occurred where governments have shut down hundreds of businesses' computer capabilities in order to collect evidence associated with one party, these are problematic and likely to produce serious backlash. The situation is far worse for civil matters where hundreds of other companies may challenge attempts to gain an order to seize such hardware.

In most cases, seizure in the cloud-computing context has become a matter of collection of live data from live systems[10], rather than following the historical role of shutting down the computer(s) and doing detailed forensic analysis from the hardware up.

EVIDENCE COLLECTION

Most evidence is collected electronically. In other words, the process by which it is gathered is through the collection of electromagnetic signals. In order to trust evidence there needs to be some basis for the manner in which it was collected. For example, it would be important to establish that it comes from a particular system at which the human user sits. This implies some sort of evidence of presence in front of the computer at a given time.

Establishing Presence

Records of activity are often used to establish presence. For example, users may have passwords that are used to authenticate their identity. These may be stored locally or remotely and typically provide dates and times associated with the start of access, as well as with subsequent accesses. The verification process provides evidence of the presence of the individual at a time and place; however, such validations can be forged, stolen, and lent. In some environments, common passwords and user IDs are used, making these identifications less reliable.

In cloud computing, presence is nearly always remote. Thus, records local to the Cloud (e.g., virtual terminal identity used for access) are problematic, and records local to systems accessing cloud resources are likely required. While the use of authenticators, (e.g., user passwords or cookies stored on user computers) may be used to augment authentication, this does not prevent exploitation of those mechanisms (e.g., break-in to an end-user computer exploits the passwords and/or cookies on that computer to undertake acts falsely associated with an individual present at that computer) for false attribution. Contracts for usage may limit legitimate excuses for non-use, but this does not constitute a very substantial basis for presence.

Chain of Custody

Digital forensic evidence comes in a wide range of forms from a wide range of sources. Physical chain of custody within a given cloud service provider site is often feasible and records are often kept in such data centers at a higher level of detail and reliability than at local sites. However, as described earlier, data may reside across an infrastructure, possibly in separately stored and located parts, and over jurisdictional boundaries across multiple service providers.

Once procured, of course, the normal chain of custody applies. In some cases, it may be adequate to simply download the data with an identified method from a provider and maintain chain of custody from there. Establishment of origin and path is a somewhat different issue. In one civil matter, about a million postings were collected over the Internet using a script to download them from a server where they were stored for normal use. The authenticity[11] of these records was not challenged, even though it could have been. However, it is unlikely that such a challenge would have worked from a practical standpoint because such records are readily available to anyone over the Internet and are historical in nature. They were not being offered for the fact of their content, but rather as evidence of their existence and of the properties, they demonstrated. Parties who were not involved in the matter in any way had maintained multiple copies at multiple locations over periods of many years and these redundant copies were sufficiently similar that attempts to challenge authenticity on this basis would have likely failed. However, that does not apply to all cloud computing, and in most cases today, such properties do not exist for cloud-based records.

How the Evidence was Created

The information that becomes evidence may be generated for various purposes, most of which are not for the purpose of presentation in court. While the business records exception to the hearsay rule applies to normal business records, many other sorts of records may not be admitted, depending on how they are created, collected, maintained, and presented, and by whom. In most cases when information is gathered from systems as they operate, the systems under scrutiny are altered, however slightly or specifically, during the gathering process. While this does not necessarily taint the evidence, it provides an opportunity for tainting that should not be overlooked if there is a reason to believe that tainting may have taken place. Experimental demonstrations of what is tainted and what does not under what conditions may be necessary to clarify what is and is not reliable about such records.

Typical Audit Trails

Typical system audit trails include the date and time of creation, last use, and/or modification; identification information like program names, function performed, user names, owners, groups, and IP addresses, and other information, such as port numbers, protocol types, portions or all of the content, and protection settings. If this sort of information exists, it should be consistent to a reasonable extent across different elements of the system under scrutiny.

Cloud providers often have these sorts of audit trails for their systems, perhaps within virtual machines, and sometimes stored in central logging and analysis servers for various security and business purposes. However, most of these are unavailable from external locations, and many do not reflect the relevant material to the matter at hand. For example, a posting to a website may have no relevant logs as to who posted it, from where, under what identity, etc. Alternatively, that information may be entered at the sole discretion of the user. Dates and times may be generated from the cloud system or the user system, depending on the mechanisms in use. In essence, the sorts of audit trails of most interest are commonly purely discretionary and defined by the application. They are not typically externally available, and if sought, they may not be reliable, may change arbitrarily over time, and may not be retained.

Consistency of Evidence

For example, if a program is asserted to generate a file that was not otherwise altered, then the program must have been running at the time the file was created, must have had the necessary permissions to create the file, must have the capacity to create such a file in such a format, and must have been invoked by a user or the system using another program capable of invoking it. There is a lot of information that should all link together cleanly. If it does not, there are reasons to question it.

Cloud systems are problematic in many cases because far fewer redundant records are kept and the records are not kept as consistently either within or between systems. While this may well change over time, it varies dramatically from system to system. The integration of these systems further complicates the issues because a single display may contain records from many sources fused together for the user. Tracking down all of the relevant sources and putting them into relative perspective may be problematic. Indeed even the same Universal Resource Locator (URL) often provides different information on each visit. Thus, collection of output from activities must be collected at the time of inquiry and retained in order to get a snapshot in time, and that snapshot in time may not reflect other nearly contemporaneous snapshots.

Proper Handling during Collection

In most police-driven investigations, standard evidence handling processes and procedures are used for digital forensic evidence, with a few enhancements and exceptions. Photographs and labels are commonly used, and an inventory sheet is typically made of all seized evidence. Suspects and others at the location under investigation are interviewed, passwords and similar information is retrieved, and in some cases, this is used on site to gain access to computer systems. If proper procedures are not followed, then the evidence arising from this process may be invalidated. For example, if a suspect is arrested, not advised regarding their rights regarding making statements (in the US this is called the Miranda rights), and asked for a password to a computer system, then all of the evidence from that system may become unavailable for prosecution if the password is used to gain access to that information.

However, in the cloud environment, few law enforcement agencies have standard approaches, and approaches vary across organizations, stations, investigations, and individuals. While the American Association of Crime Laboratory Directors (ASCLAD)[12] has standards for preservation of evidence in general, in the digital realm, such standards do not exist to a level of specificity that allows uniform application, and in the cloud environment, such standards are not yet developed.

Selective Collection and Presentation

In some cases one side or the other may not do a thorough job of collecting or presenting evidence. They may prefer to seek out anything that makes the other side look bad and stop as soon as they reach a threshold required bringing the case to court. Many such parties may try to prevent the other party from getting the evidence, provide only paper copies of digital evidence, and so forth. In such cases, the other party should vigorously challenge the courts to require that the collection, preservation, and discovery of all of the evidence available, provided in the same digital forms, and for a similar amount of time.

In the cloud environment, it is essentially impossible in many cases to collect all of the potential evidence, to preserve evidence in its original form, or to examine it in full context. In most cases, access is only from external interfaces, and collection of evidence is done on active systems from limited remote access. This is problematic for many reasons, and the courts have failed to address this in the same way as it has addressed digital and other sorts of evidence historically. It seems that, for now at least, almost anything can be collected and presented, and the opponent increasingly bears more responsibility for refuting evidence than the propounding party does for authenticating it as to completeness.

Forensic Imaging

In order to address decay and corruption of original writing, common practice is to image[13] the contents of digital media and work with the image instead of the original. Reliable imaging must be done in such a way as to accurately reflect the original content. Studies done by the United States National Institute of Standards and Technology (NIST) to understand the limitations of imaging hardware and software and standards for forensic imaging are now widely available[14]. However, the same is not true of the cloud forensics space.

Except to the extent physical access to hardware can be attained, the methods of forensic imaging or hardware no longer apply.

In the cloud arena, remote imaging is done either by software that is pre-deployed into the systems under examination, by imaging software placed in those systems during operation, or by the available interfaces of those machines for external use[15]. Pre-deployed imaging software is rare. However, many cloud systems use underlying databases that retain transaction histories for rollback and replay. As such, these transaction histories may be used as a record that can be imaged by copying from the files they are stored in, assuming warrants can be secured and properly carried out. Modifying software in use in order to image is often problematic because the very system being imaged is being changed by the imaging process. However, the theoretical concern is rarely an issue in legal settings, where testimony by experts and custodians allows the evidence to be admitted. Admission, however, is not the same as authentication and reliability determination, and these are potentially areas for challenging the evidence.

The external interface access methods are in fact quite common today, and quite problematic in some cases. Two examples may help to clarify. In one case, emails stored on a cloud service provider system were imaged by an expert by using a user interface and downloading. The method used was adequate to show that an independent party got the same information, while the lack of an interface to allow alteration was adequate to assert that the content was as stored from first arrival in accordance with the normal business records processing of the provider. The headers contained in the messages were correlated to other information at other providers and the result was a chain of evidence that was adequate to meet the needs of admissibility and reliability to the extent necessary for the case at hand.

In a very different case, the archive.org "WayBack" machine[16] was used to produce an image of a website asserted to indicate, through the co-presence of text, images, and dates and times, that some events took place at some time frame. However, the depictions provided by this service reflect different components from different time frames co-joined so that they appear to have been present at the same time, even though they were not in fact ever present together on the same Web page at the same time. In this case, without the source used to produce the image, it would have been impossible to show that the time frames in the depiction were not simultaneous on the actual site. Thus, great care should be taken in accepting such productions, and challenges to productions without adequate backup material should be undertaken.

Non-Stored Transient Information

The collection of non-stored transient evidence typically involves a technical collection mechanism and often requires minimization in a law enforcement context (e.g., when recording telephone calls if the subject of the call is not related to the matter at hand, collection must be stopped). In most cloud computing environments, such information is not available, particularly between virtual machines within the same hardware substrate. High volume in shared infrastructure also presents many problems for minimization as well as for technical collections. Most packet sniffers have limitations in the form of collection rates, storage capacity, and ability to capture all packets. These limitations may be the basis for challenges involving missed information. Made data[17] is far more difficult to deal with in a packet sniffing technology. These technologies typically record what is sent through the media, but attribution to a source is more problematic.

Typical Ethernet interfaces use Media Access Control (MAC) addresses associated with packets[18] to identify the hardware device associated with a transmission. While these include manufacturer specified serial numbers that should be unique to a physical device, they can often be forged with software. If the environment was not examined for the presence of such software and if other hardware is present, it is a reasonable challenge to assert that the data may not have come from the identified computer. In the absence of corroborating evidence, tying traffic to a computer is not directly evident[19].

In order to assert that such data is legitimate as evidence there is a requirement that the manner in which it was gathered is demonstrated to be reliable. In cases involving communications media there may also be requirements to follow wiretap laws as opposed to other laws. In the cloud computing environment, there are far more opportunities for false and misleading signals to be present, and storage in cloud infrastructure is also potentially problematic because of additional access methods and paths.

Packaging for Transport

Packaging for transport of digital forensic evidence has requirements similar to those of other evidence, and it should be transported in a timely fashion to a facility where it can be logged into an evidence locker, chain of custody requirements must be met throughout the process, and it has to be kept in a suitable environment for preservation of the evidence.

If a claim of evidence tampering is to be made this will have to be shown to have taken place when it was in the custody of the person who is asserted to have taken this action. In one case, I was able to show that the amount of time available to an individual accused of tampering was inadequate to have planted the evidence asserted to have been planted. Tampering is not an easy thing to do without detection. Because of all of the inherent redundancy associated with digital forensic evidence as described earlier, tampering can often be detected by a detailed enough examination.

TRANSPORT AND STORAGE OF EVIDENCE

When digital evidence is taken into custody appropriate measures should be taken to assure that it is not damaged or destroyed, that it is properly labeled and kept together, and that it is not mixed up (e.g., co-mingled, lost in sequence, improperly labeled, or associated, etc.) or otherwise tainted. If these precautions are not taken, the results can be effectively challenged. This applies to cloud forensics as anywhere else.

Possession and Chain of Custody

It is common practice in some venues to videotape the evidence collection process, and this has been invaluable in meeting subsequent challenges in many cases. In any case, a sound chain of custody should be maintained, and things like emailing then deleting evidence not covered by message authentication, transmission of the original evidence in plaintext or without cryptographic checksums[20] through the Internet, or similar acts may break the chain of custody. All of these methods, however, can only demonstrate that once custody is initiated, it is maintained. It is wise to not place trust in cloud providers for custody, but increasingly, the volume of content is moving forensics toward cloud storage. In such cases, private or trusted cloud providers are vital, and the trust must be extensible to the point of providing adequate testimony about specific items of evidence across their lifecycle.

Storage

Evidence must be stored in a safe, secure environment to assure it is safe from alteration or destruction. Access must be controlled and logged in most cases. However, this is not enough for most digital evidence. Special precautions are needed to protect this evidence just as special precautions are needed for some sorts of biological and chemical evidence. Decay with time and evidence of integrity are issues in storage in general, and they are only exacerbated if storage is in the Cloud.

Some principles of what has been claimed to be "best practice" have been asserted, and one accepted set of principles may exist, but this has not been demonstrated in the community, and certainly not validated for cloud-based systems or storage[21].

Principle 1: No action should change data held.

Principle 2: In exceptional circumstances where examination of original evidence is required, the examiner must be competent to do it and explain relevance and implications.

Principle 3: Audit records or other records of all processes applied to digital evidence should be created and preserved. An independent third party should be able to reproduce those actions with similar results.

Principle 4: Some individual person should be responsible for adhering to these principles.

EVIDENCE ANALYSIS AND INTERPRETATION

Evidence analysis and interpretation are perhaps the most complex and error-prone aspects of dealing with digital forensic evidence. It is also the most subjectively applied in many cases. However, in almost all cases it should not and need not be subjective. It is subjective largely because of the failure of those undertaking analysis and interpretation to spend the time and effort to be careful in what they do. The effects of cloud computing on analysis are relatively small, but they should be accounted for to the extent analysis is undertaken in a cloud environment. Interpretation is a bit more of a stretch in most cases.

Content

Making content typically involves processing errors. For example, uncleaned media is used in the analysis process and the analysis finds evidence that was left over from a previous case. The challenge to this can come in many forms, and such challenges have a good chance of success if results cannot be independently verified. In cloud environments, where data may be subject to change from many sources and attribution and change control tend to be limited at best, this is even more problematic.

Missing content typically results from limited time or excessive focus of attention. Limited time is almost always an issue because there is usually an enormous amount of evidence present, most of which can only be peripherally examined with simple tools. Examining every bit pattern from every possible perspective is simply too time consuming to be feasible and is almost never necessary to get to the heart of the evidence. Excessive focus, on the other hand, is easier to avoid. By simply taking an open view of what could be meaningful evidence and being thorough in the evaluation process, such misses are avoidable. The challenge is simple. Did you look at everything? Is there any exculpatory evidence? Where did you look? Why did you not look in the other places? What technique did you use? Why did you not use a more definitive technique? Is there a more definitive technique? The questions can be nearly endless.

In some sense, cloud resources may be helpful in performing more analysis because of the higher volume of computation and storage available in most cloud systems compared to local systems. However, results, when found, need to be verifiable without the Cloud, and repeatability is potentially problematic when algorithms are not kept constant, as is often the case in cloud-based providers who do updates without warning or notice.

Contextual Information

Information only has meaning in context. Analysis can make context by making assumptions that are invalid or cannot be demonstrated. Context is missed when assumptions that are valid and can be demonstrated are not made. The challenge to made context starts with questioning the basis for assumptions. If assumptions cannot be adequately demonstrated, the context becomes dubious, the assumptions fall away, and the conclusions are not demonstrable. If an alternative context can be demonstrated with the same or better basis, that context can be substituted and the interpretation of the evidence altered. Missed context can be challenged with the introduction of alternative contexts. It then becomes the challenge of the other side to disprove these contexts.

An excellent example of this was a case where the defense challenged the validity of the evidence by introducing the potential that an attack on the computer system being examined caused the illicit effects rather than the user at the console. In the end, the prosecution could not convincingly demonstrate the validity of its assumption that the user that owned the computer carried out the behavior in question, and the case was dismissed. While many computer security experts assert that there was no evidence of the presence of such an attack, the absence of evidence of an attack by the defense is not the same as evidence of absence of such an attack by the prosecution.

Consider the implications of this in the cloud arena. Essentially every major cloud services provider in the public space has had break-ins, and most are reticent to discuss details. How can we trust the data they hold if they have been broken into and refuse to provide enough detail to assure that the content was actually provided by the claimed provider? Context in the Cloud changes almost continuously, and most providers do not provide reversion or the ability to test and analyze prior versions from times at issue in legal matters.

Meaning

The meaning of things that are found is obviously the basis for interpretation. Meaning that is missed may lead to a failure to interpret, and meaning that is made is an interpretation without adequate support. However, meaning in the cloud context is often problematic because of the lack of clear documentation and reconstruction capacity in examination.

For example, the presence of a file with a name associated with a particular program might not indicate that the program was present at any time in the past if the cloud provider simply chose that name for whatever reason. The filename could be a coincidence or it could have been placed there by other means such as part of a backup or restoration process. In most cases there are a variety of different meanings that can be applied to content, and determining the set of feasible meanings typically involves reviewing the different possible meanings relative to the rest of the environment.

The same applies to the content, presence, or absence of files, directories, packets, or any other things found in material under examination. Since the cloud provider is typically in complete control and access to the mechanisms in use is usually not available and may change without notice or explanation, this eliminates most available methods for determining what records actually mean in terms of their reflection of reality. Thus, the reliability of this evidence is hard to determine.

Realistically, meaning derived from traces in terms of causal chains leading to its existence requires an in-depth understanding of the potential paths through which traces may be produced. In even relatively simple computer systems, this is problematic if definitive causality is desired. In the present cloud environment it is far more complex. As analysis moves toward attribution, the ability to derive meaning from digital evidence across multiple systems gets far more complex and problematic[22]. Similarly, challenges become a more complex process to undertake if attribution has been undertaken with substantial results.

Process Elements

Content does not come to exist through magic. It comes to exist through a process. The notion that a sequence of bits appears on a system without the notion of how that sequence came to exist there makes for a very weak case. If the bits were created within the system, the means for their creation should be there unless it was somehow removed. If the bits were obtained from somewhere else, the process by which they got there should be identified. If there are alternative explanations for the arrival of the bit sequence, why is one interpretation better than the other?

In the outsourced cloud-computing environment, processes are not normally known to the examiner, may or may not generate audit records, and those records may or may not be made available or meaningfully interpreted. Files visible to the user may not have times associated with them or in fact be part of a file system as opposed to being merely entries in a database lacking metadata. Network-related activity may not be retained or monitored, and where fields within records or records themselves came from may be indiscernible to the examiner. Residual data is rarely available in a cloud situation, and if it is, where it came from is often problematic because of the level of sharing of resources involved. Without evidence of the process, alternative explanations may be offered with as much credibility as the explanation preferred by the other side. The plausibility of these explanations is key to the meaning of the content they refer to.

Relationships

Just as event sequences produce content, relationships between sequences and content produce content. The presence or absence of related content causes differences in the content generated by related processes. Similarly, the placement of content in the linked lists may indicate the differences in these relationships. There are many such relationships within systems and those relationships can normally be explored to challenge the assertions of those who make claims about them. However, in cloud systems, the information required to explore these issues is normally unavailable. Different components come from different and often distant systems and mechanisms and insufficient records are often retained for analysis.

Ordering or Timing

Sequences are a special case of orderings. More generally, orderings can involve things that cannot be differentiated from being simultaneous, while sequences are completely ordered. Timing often cannot be established with perfection, but partial orderings can be derived. The possible orders of events can make an enormous difference in some cases. One obvious reason for this is that ordering is a precondition for cause and effect. To assert that one thing caused another, it must be demonstrable that the cause preceded the effect. If this cannot be established by timing there is the potential to challenge based on the lack of causality.

While this may seem like a highly theoretical argument, many cases have been made or broken by the ability to show time sequences. If an accusation of theft and disclosure of trade secret information is made and it cannot be shown that the theft preceded the disclosure, then the basis for the claim is invalid. If an attacker was supposed to be present at a computer to commit a crime at a particular time and the accused can show that at that time they were not present at that computer, then the alibi will refute the claim. If the time is uncertain in a computer system, the entire process becomes suspect because computers usually keep time very well. If ordering or timing is missed, the lack of the ordering or timing information leads to challenges.

The most common challenge to computer-related times stems from the potential difference between a computer clock and the real-world time. Even accounting for time zone variations, which is often problematic, is an all too common problem that has to be addressed in the forensic process. If the time reference for the computer is not established at the time the evidence is collected, timing can sometimes be obtained by relating the timing of events within the computer to externally timed network events. Missed time can sometimes be made up for by correlation with outside events, while made time can often be demonstrated wrong by similar correlation. In cloud systems, time is usually coordinated via Network Time Protocol (NTP)[23] or similar mechanisms, making this challenge less likely to succeed, assuming the records are kept to the resolution of the available clocks. Additional complexities arise when time on cloud-based systems is used in conjunction with other time information, such as an eye witness identifying a time in Canada when the computer storing times is in Kenya reflecting a Web server in Australia, with metadata produced for different media and mechanisms from combinations of these sources.

Location

Everything that happens in computers has physicality despite any efforts to portray it as somehow ephemeral. Physicality tends to leave forensic evidence in one form or another. For example, when a person uses a keyboard, particles from hair and skin fall into the keyboard and tend to get stuck there. In a similar fashion, data in computers tends to be placed on the disk and to remain there. Computer systems have physical characteristics as well, and sometimes they are dead giveaways to location.

In one example of a missed and made location, an attack against a government computer system had an Internet Protocol (IP) address associated with a location in Russia. However, when observing the traffic patterns shown in log files, it was determined that the jitter associated with packet arrival times was very small[24]. Packet arrival time jitter tends to occur when packets are mixed in delivery queues across infrastructure. More infrastructures tend to lead to more jitter. The lack of jitter meant that the arriving packets were not being mixed much with other packets and that the computer responsible was therefore close, in terms of network hops, to the observation point. The attack was traced to a point only a few network links away from the surveillance point. Evidence such as this can make a compelling case, and it is easy to miss the real location and make a false location when such analysis is not thoroughly undertaken.

Unfortunately, there is usually little evidence of this sort available in cloud computing environments, and to the extent, it is available; it is rarely made available for examination.

Inadequate Expertise

We also face many low quality 'experts' and people with an axe to grind who are put up as experts. An excellent example of this was a case involving copyright infringement in which a court appointed special master made claims including: (1) the accuser may have altered data, (2) date and time information was unreliable, (3) the system never worked when returned to its owner after it was forensically investigated, (4) programs were destroyed, and (5) pre-existing data was no longer present. In this case, all of these claims were refuted by a better expert who used recorded statements, a videotape of the return process, some details of the physics of writing to disks that dismissed the possibility of forgery, and correlation with other records. It is important to note that under some circumstances all of the things asserted by this special master could have been true, so the claims were not outrageous in the general sense. It is only that they were not in fact true in this case. In the cloud computing space, real experts are particularly hard to find because the field is so new and so few cases have been through legal systems. As a result, people with limited expertise will end up as "experts" and the process of challenging their expertise with rigor is a worthy one to pursue.

Unreliable Sources

There are a lot of unreliable sources of digital content. For example, the Internet is full of the widest possible range of different content, only a portion of which is really accurate, and a significant portion of which consists of just plain lies. There is a tendency for people to believe some of these things, and once these things are believed, the belief transcends the original source. For example, when looking up information about the function of a hardware device or software program, at a detailed level, much of the information on the Internet is not accurate. It might reflect a different version, it may reflect a mistake by the author, it may reflect a simplification by the author for reader convenience, and it might be an intentional or malicious misstatement by a disgruntled ex-employee. While this information may be convenient or readily available and useful in many circumstances, it is not generally suited to the level of trust required for digital forensic evidence purposes.

As a good example, the question sometimes comes up of the list of all circumstances under which a file access date and time will be altered by a cloud-operating environment under normal use. It turns out that this is not an easy question to answer. The answer is different on different versions of operating environments, different applications may use different system calls for the same outcome with different side effects, and programs that deal with forensic processes typically do things differently than other operating system programs. Even such simple questions do not have easy answers and the Internet answers are not consistent or accurate in many cases, when there is information available at all.

Reconstruction

Digital crime scenes can sometimes be reconstructed, and this is a critical area for scientific evidence. While experts may assert any number of things about what might be within a computer, reconstruction provides the means to test hypotheses about causality in the forward direction, a necessity if effect is to be determined as to cause. While similar circumstances can be created, identical ones often cannot. As a rule of thumb, simple questions can often be answered by digital reconstructions, but complex sequences of events are far harder to confirm or refute.

In cloud-bases environments, reconstruction becomes very complex. While simple issues, like whether the entrance of a particular type of data produced a particular appearance may be produced for many such cases, reliability remains problematic unless the operating environment stability can be established. Furthermore, the lack of automation for most remote operations in such environments means that repetition of experiments for large numbers of situations may be very hard to accomplish. Variation of parameters is often problematic, and only a very limited set of causes can be explored from external interfaces.

If the goal is to prove that a cloud system could have generated an output based on hypothesized user actions, it may be far more complex, depending on the specifics. While some outputs are generated often or predictably, other outputs may be very situation-specific and involve complex interactions with the environment. In typical cloud environments, outputs are not strictly reproducible because of the aggregation of data from diverse sources, and this problem is further complicated by a lack of specifics on what is and is not relevant to the issues at hand. For example, pricing may be tied to history, which varies from use to use, and co-located data may vary based on identities associated with users from browser histories or similar mechanisms.

Reconstructing the entire environment may also be problematic if it involves things like network events that are usually out of the control of those doing reconstruction. There are forensic technologies that can largely accomplish these sorts of reconstructions, but they are rarely used and difficult to properly implement.

In almost all cases, a demonstration can be constructed to show some subset of the scenarios. If this is done, the challenge can be made on the basis that the space was inadequately covered, and additional data sought to counter it.

Good Practice in Analysis

It turns out that nobody has yet compiled a widely accepted collection of good practices for analysis of digital evidence. As a result, all of analysis is subject to expert interpretation and challenges of all sorts, and each case will be judged on its merits without appeal to some standard. However, there are some time-tested analysis techniques that should be covered despite the lack of any widely published good practices.

The Process of Elimination

It is generally considered good practice to use the process of elimination. In this process, a list of the possibilities is made and items on the list are eliminated one at a time or in groups for specific reasons that can be backed up by facts.

The challenges to the process of elimination start with the initial list. Is the list comprehensive? How do you know it is comprehensive? If I find one thing missing, does this invalidate the list as being less than comprehensive? What if I find two? Are there implicit assumptions in the list? What are they? Are they demonstrably true? What if they are wrong?

The next challenge comes in the application of the process. Was the test of each item on the list definitive? Was it properly done? What are the cases where this test would fail to be revealing? Does a positive or negative result in your test environment definitively show that the same result would be seen in the real environment? In other words, what are the possible differences between the real world and the test environment?

Finally, almost all such tests make assumptions about the independence of the items on the list or the elements within the computer systems involved. Suppose these things are not independent—would that invalidate this test? In many cases, these assumptions can be demonstrated to be incorrect under certain circumstances. In addition, in cloud environments, independence is one of the things rarely achieved or demonstrable.

The Scientific Method

The basis of the scientific method is that the truth can be only be confirmed by the failure of experiments that attempt to disprove an assertion. However, even one refutation implies that the hypothesis under test or that the testing method was incorrect in some respect.

The scientific method, and more generally, a scientific approach, is fundamental to success in digital forensics as elsewhere, and failure to take this approach seriously will likely result in errors in your analysis and successful challenges of it by competent legal or technical professionals.

In the cloud space, there has been too little scientific study to establish even the basic outlines of a theory, much less specific predictive models. As a result, the entirety of the scientific process has to be explored in each attempt at getting at the truth in this environment.

The Daubert Guidelines

Case law in the United States has led to the Daubert Guidelines for the admissibility and validity of scientific evidence[25]. These almost always apply to digital forensics in US Federal cases and most international cases. The tests of scientific evidence include four basic issues: (1) Has the procedure or technique been published? (2) Is the procedure generally accepted? (3) Can and has the procedure been tested? (4) What is the error rate of the procedure?

Most digital forensic analysis methods in use today have not been widely published, and this book represents one of the first attempts to move in this direction. Those that are published are rarely published in refereed scientific journals. In addition to these publications, there are manuals from products and books on special purpose topics. Finally, hardware and software design and source code information is rarely available for most elements of cloud computing today. These then form the literature in this area. The lack of published material leads to many challenges to the admissibility or validity of this evidence. Perhaps most importantly, most of the forensic examination and analysis tools made for sale do not address cloud issues and include trade secrets and unpublished content that forms the intellectual property basis, which creates competitive advantages and barriers to entry in the market. As a result, the most commonly used tools do not include the information required to determine precisely what they do and do not contain relevant material for cloud-based environments. Their use and their results can be strongly challenged on this basis.

In terms of being generally accepted, there are few generally accepted analysis techniques for digital forensics writ large[26], and none identified to date for cloud-based environments. In some sense, without publication, general acceptance is impossible, but almost any presentation of analysis of digital forensic evidence is challengeable on this basis. For example, if a forensic analyst asserts that a file contains some specific data and was created at some particular date and time, in addition to the technical limitations of this assertion, the methods used to derive this information can be questioned in great detail to try to shake confidence in the validity of the technique undertaken or the credibility of the witness. The problem with such a challenge is that it risks alienating the finder of fact and is likely to come down to things that users do every day but that are not documented as forensic processes. This approach is more applicable in cases where the technique is believed to have produced wrong results. In such cases, wrong results are usually easily demonstrated by following the specific steps taken by the examiner.

The error rate of forensic analysis tools is even harder to attest to because in almost all commercial products no error rate can be established without independent tests. As a result, while error rates for things like cryptographic checksums on forensic images can be estimated, error rates on cloud-based searches and depictions of images based on historical data are far harder to ascertain.

Digital Data is Only a Part of the Overall Picture

Almost every analysis of digital forensic evidence ultimately involves ties to the real world. In order for analysis to produce meaningful results, it must tie those results to the matter at hand. The analysis process, as a technical matter, can often be resolved and some set of resulting bit sequences with some time sequencing can be revealed to the finder of fact without significant disagreement. In fact, this is often done by stipulation, subject to an adequate presentation. However, the interpretation of those results is subject to far more variation than the setting of the bits.

The attribution of actions to actors is often hard to pin down. While there are cases where there are films of people using their computers and typing the material of interest to a legal matter, this is certainly the exception rather than the rule, and in cloud-based systems, it is rare indeed. Attribution has been and continues to be studied and while there are many indications that behavioral and biometric indicators can be used to attribute actions to actors, the amount of scientific study in this area to date is limited and the results are far from definitive.

Physical evidence can often be tied to digital evidence, but cloud-based systems are largely designed to separate physical access from the computation. For example, an online credit card theft may be challenged, but if the credit cards stolen resulted in purchases delivered to the defendant's address and the defendant did not question these items, try to return them, and is using them, the computer evidence of the theft may be hard to discredit. On the other hand, the lack of a nexus with real-world events should lead to a serious question about validity. Just because someone wrote about a credit card fraud scheme does not mean they perpetrated one. Even if their computer was involved in one that is similar to their writings, the lack of a physical nexus is a potentially fatal flaw.

Means, motive, and opportunity apply to the digital world, as well as the analog one. If the evidence shows a level of expertise in developing and hatching a scheme, and the individual on trial does not have the necessary expertise, the means does not exist. Digital systems are complex and a great deal about the knowledge of individuals is often revealed by records present, but far less such information is typically available in cloud-based systems than in end-user systems. Opportunity in cloud-based systems rarely requires presence.

Just Because a Computer Says So Does Not Make It So

This is perhaps my favorite basis for challenging the analysis of digital forensic evidence. The seeming infallibility of computers leads many to believe that if a computer says so it must be so. People are increasingly realizing that this is not so, but the point still must be made in many cases. The sources of errors in computers are wide ranging.

From computer viruses that leave pornographic content in computers to remote control via Trojan Horses that allow external users to take over a computer from over the Internet, to just plain lies typed in by human beings, computers are full of wrong information and malicious actors are constantly acting to subvert the integrity of computer systems and their content.

However, even without malice, some studies of data entry errors showed that error rates on the order of 10-20% are common. That is, one-in-five to one-in-ten data entries in a typical commercial database are not complete, accurate, and reflective of reality.

Care must be taken to properly understand and characterize digital evidence and properly place it in context.

CONCLUSION

Cloud-based computing is here in a big way and is likely to be here for a long time to come. From the perspective of forensic science, it adds several key challenges that have widespread effects. The basic issues of distributed computing over many locations, with disparate ownership and proprietary software and operations create more challenges than are typically present in end-user systems, but they also present some opportunities. For example, the lack of control by the user implies a limited capacity to subvert the mechanisms that are present, and independence of cloud service providers may imply less intentional subversion by those operators. In any case, the science has a long way to go, and challenges are likely to be present for a long time to come.

REFERENCES

Avizzienis, A., Laprie, J.-C., Randell, B., & Landwehr, C. (2004). Basic concepts and taxonomy of dependable and secure computing. *IEEE Transactions on Dependable and Secure Computing*, *1*(1). doi:10.1109/TDSC.2004.2

Cohen, F. (2007). *Challenges to digital forensic evidence*. New York, NY: ASP Press.

Cohen, F. (2012a). *Digital forensic evidence examination* (4th ed.). New York, NY: ASP Press.

Cohen, F. (2012b). *Update on the state of the science of digital evidence examination*. Paper presented at the Conference on Digital Forensics, Security, and Law. New York, NY.

Contini, S., Steinfeld, R., Pieprzyk, J., & Matusiewicz, K. (2007). *A critical look at cryptographic hash function literature*. Paper presented at ECRYPT Hash Workshop. Sydney, Australia: Macquarie University.

Duranti, L. (2010). Diplomatics. In *Encyclopedia of Library and Information Sciences* (3rd ed.). New York, NY: Taylor & Francis.

FBI. (2012). *A bibliography related to crime scene interpretation with emphases in forensic geotaphonomic and forensic archaeological field techniques*. Washington, DC: FBI Print Shop.

McKemmish, R. (2008). When is digital evidence forensically sound? In Ray, I., & Shenoi, S. (Eds.), *Advances in Digital Forensics 4*. Berlin, Germany: Springer. doi:10.1007/978-0-387-84927-0_1

ENDNOTES

1 The general approach taken here is from Cohen (2007).

2 For a more detailed discussion of the concepts of faults and failures see Avizzienis, Laprie, Randell, and Landwehr (2004).

3 For one opinion in a recent case, see "Lorraine v. Markel American Insurance Company" (241 F.R.D. 534) starting on page 5.

4 Another place to start your search is FBI (2012).

5 Reliability of a record relates to the extent to which it reflects the reality it purports. It is assessed on the basis of (1) completeness, which is to say, the record has all of the formal elements required by the administrative or legal system for achieving its purpose; and (2) the controls exercised in its creation, such as the competence of the author in terms of the authority and capacity to issue the record (Cohen, 2012a).

6 The term "reliability" like many other terms used here has different meanings in the technical literature than the legal literature. Where otherwise undifferentiated, we will use the legal definitions that stem from diplomatics and archival science (Duranti, 2010).

7 See for example, US Federal Rules of Evidence - Rule 801-802. An out of court statement offered in evidence to prove the truth of the matter asserted is hearsay, but there are many exceptions; most notably business records taken in the normal course of business and relied on for their accuracy and reliability as a matter of course in carrying out that business.

8 For a more detailed discussion of forensics tools and related issues see Cohen (2012a).

9 Domain Name System (DNS) provides the means by which Internet Protocol (IP) addresses are translated into host names and host names to IP addresses, as well as the identification of mail transfer (MX) records required for email. Most Internet operations require properly functioning DNS servers.

10 This process is not the same in most cases as current "live" forensics methodologies directed at a single operating system while in operation.

11 An authentic record is one that (1) preserves the same identity it had when first generated and (2) can be presumed or proven to have maintained its integrity over time (Duranti, 2010).

12 See: www.ascld.org

13 In digital forensics, the term "imaging" is often associated with an "exact" copy of the sequence(s) of bits present and the term "forensically sound" is often bandied about as meaning that the copy was exact in some sense. Imaging is also used in the media forensics community to deal with issues of graphical images. The usage here is intended to indicate any method by which digital content is made available for examination in any form other than the original physical means of storage, transit, and/or use.

14 The NIST Computer Forensics Tool Testing (CFTT) Project Web site is located at http://www.cftt.nist.gov

15 We assume that non-remote imaging is done in the same way as it is for traditional forensics work, including so-called "live" (while the media being imaged operates) and "dead" (the media is shut down) imaging.

16 See: www.archive.org

17 Made data in networks often results from protocol analysis errors and cognitive error mechanisms that produce things that look like valid, meaningful, authentic data when they are no such thing. In the presence of deception mechanisms, made data is commonly achievable by malicious actors because of the lack of integrity and attribution mechanisms in most protocol systems of today. Even more interesting is made data created by analysts who look at one kind of content and interpret it as another kind, thus making something that is not relevant data at all into something that ends up being treated as data for the purposes of analysis.

18 IEEE 802 standard – for details see http://en.wikipedia.org/wiki/IEEE_802

19 The so-called hardware address of Ethernet and similar interface cards is often forgeable by raw packet interface software. While some hardware devices prevent this, many do not, and forgery of MAC addresses and responses to protocols can lead to many sorts of failures of this sort. Having said this, it is also important to note that in the absence of such mechanisms, hardware addresses of interface cards and other similar information is often very reliable and identifies a computer interface to the individual machine as well as to the class of interface cards. This is often very strong evidence for individualization.

20 An excellent summary of related issues is in Contini, Steinfeld, Pieprzyk, and Matusiewicz (2007).

21 See McKemmish (2008).

22 See Cohen (2012a).

23 See http://www.ntp.org/

24 The notion of packet arrival time jitter was new to many of the experienced people who read this monograph, which is to say, it isn't a standard approach that is well documented. However, jitter is a well-known phenomena in electronics and timing issues abound in many areas of digital systems. Many papers on network performance discuss things like group delay and jitter because it is important to keeping high fidelity with low delay times in real-time processes such as audio and video signal processing. In many cases, new phenomena are identified that seem to show something of interest, and they fall into the category that is commonly called "Just Doesn't Look Right" (JDLR). When such things are identified, in order to be admitted for legal purposes, additional analysis and experimental work may have to be done to meet the standards for admissibility.

25 Daubert v. Merrell Dow Pharmaceuticals, 509 U.S. 579 (1993)

26 See Cohen (2012b).

Chapter 4
The Emergence of Cloud Storage and the Need for a New Digital Forensic Process Model

Richard Adams
Murdoch University, Australia

ABSTRACT

Cloud computing is just one of many recent technologies that have highlighted shortcomings in the development of formal digital forensic processes, which up until now have been focused on a particular group of practitioners, such as law enforcement, and have been too high-level to be of significant practical use, or have been too detailed and specific to accommodate new technology as it emerges. Because the tools and procedures employed by digital forensic practitioners are generally outside the knowledge and understanding of the courts, they need to be described in such a way that they can be understood by the layperson. In addition, they should also conform to some standards of practice and be recognised by other practitioners working in the field (Armstrong, 2003; Kessler, 2010). Unfortunately, as Cohen (2011) points out, the whole field of digital forensics lacks consensus in fundamental aspects of its activities in terms of methodology and procedures. There has been a lot of activity around different aspects of cloud computing, and in Australia this has centered on the protection of personal data (Solomon, 2010). On an international scale, there have been several articles written by lawyers (Gillespie, 2012; Hutz, 2012; Kunick, 2012) discussing other legal considerations of accessing data in the cloud; however, this chapter looks at the issues surrounding digital evidence acquisition and introduces a new high-level process model that can assist digital forensic practitioners when it comes to presenting evidence in court that originated in the cloud.

DOI: 10.4018/978-1-4666-2662-1.ch004

Copyright © 2013, IGI Global. Copying or distributing in print or electronic forms without written permission of IGI Global is prohibited.

BACKGROUND

Given the pervasive nature of information technology the nature of evidence presented in court is less likely to be paper-based and in most instances will be in electronic form (Stanfield, 2009). However, evidence relating to computer crime, regardless of definition, is significantly different from that associated with the more 'traditional' crimes for which there are well-established standards and procedures (Smith, Grabosky, & Gregor Urbas, 2004; Stanfield, 2009).

In Australian courts, the admissibility of evidence is governed by both statute and common law. Each state and territory have their own Evidence Act, with some combined to echo the Federal (Commonwealth) Evidence Act. The general principle adopted by these courts for copies of documents presented as evidence is that a copy of a document is recognised as equivalent to the original and that this applies to computer records. As with other types of evidence, the courts make no presumption that such evidence is reliable without some evidence of empirical testing in relation to the theories and techniques associated with the production of the copy (Mason, 2007). Edmond states that *"...reliability assessments should focus on the technique and its accuracy (as well as the proficiency of the operator/analyst)"* (Edmond, 2010, p. 94). This issue of reliability means that courts pay close attention to the manner in which electronic evidence has been obtained and in particular the process in which the data is captured and stored (Cohen, 2011; Grant v Marshall FCA 1161, 2003; Hargreaves, 2009; Kessler, 2010; Mason, 2007).

Because the tools and procedures employed by digital forensic practitioners are generally outside the knowledge and understanding of the courts and juries they need to be described in such a way that they can be understood by the layperson. In addition, they should also conform to some standards of practice and be recognised by other practitioners working in the field (Armstrong, 2003; Kessler, 2010). Courts may apply methods used for testing scientific evidence to digital evidence presented before them and this is commonly based on American practice (Abdullah, Mahmod, Ghani, Abdullah, & Sultan, 2008; Beebe & Clark, 2004; Palmer, 2001; Peisert, Bishop, & Marzullo, 2008; Stanfield, 2009; Moles, 2007; Stephenson, 2003). In this regard it is the practice of American Courts, when seeking to determine the reliability of scientific evidence, to apply the Daubert Test, named after the Daubert v Merrell Dow Pharmaceuticals case (Supreme Court of the United States, 1993). In this case the US Supreme Court determined that it was the duty of a trial judge to scrutinise evidence, particularly if it is of an 'innovative or unusual scientific' nature to ensure that it meets with the requirements of the Federal Rule of Evidence 702. This has been identified as the judge taking on the role of 'gatekeeper' (Kessler, 2010).

Based on the Federal Rule of Evidence 702 the process for determining the admissibility of evidence requires that any expert testimony must be derived from "scientific knowledge." However, "scientific knowledge" itself requires that "sound scientific methodology" has been applied based on the "scientific method" and this led to the court in the Daubert v Merrell Dow Pharmaceuticals case establishing what has become known as the Daubert Test. In practice the Daubert Test is often summarised as four components that provide clarity around determination of 'sufficient facts or data' and 'reliable principles and methods' (Gosh, 2004a; Stephenson, 2003):

1. Whether the theory or technique in question can be and has been tested.
2. Whether it has been subjected to peer review and publication.
3. Its known potential rate of error along with the existence and maintenance of standards controlling the technique's operation.
4. The degree of acceptance within the relevant scientific community

Another American case, that of Kumho Tyre Co. v Carmichael (1999), expanded the Daubert Test to allow for 'non-scientists' to give expert evidence, such as engineers and other technical witnesses, as noted by Gianelli (2007), Calhoun (2008), and Rogers (2006). Despite the fact that the Daubert case was heard in 1993 its influence is still strong in relation to digital evidence as demonstrated by the consultation paper issued by the Law Commission for England and Wales which effectively mimics the Daubert Test used in the United States (Edmond, 2010, p. 93). However, when applying the Daubert Test to cases involving digital forensic tools and techniques it appears that regarding digital forensics as a science causes some issues, in particular the lack of generally accepted standards and procedures (Carrier, 2002; Meyers & Rogers, 2004). Peisert et al. (2008) suggest a reason for this is that the discipline has been developed without the typical initial research that would have provided the sound scientific basis necessary for admitting digital forensic evidence. Contrary to the contention of Buskirk and Liu (2006) who suggest that digital evidence is 'automatically' presumed to be reliable we have a situation in which, in the absence of anything better, courts are often using methods that apply to 'classical' science to determine the reliability of objects from digital forensics (Calhoun, 2008; Cheng, 2007; Kenneally, 2005; Kessler, 2010; Limongelli, 2008; Meyers & Rogers, 2004).

ACQUIRING DATA FROM THE CLOUD

At first sight, it would seem that the issue of acquiring evidence from the cloud is really just an extension of current activities that are employed to acquire data from a network on the basis that the data is stored on a device other than the one being used to access the data. The similarities and fundamental differences between the two situations can be described under the headings of 'logical access,' 'physical access,' 'flexibility of methods,' 'segregation of data/evidence,' and (of particular relevance) 'legal implications.' These headings are now considered:

Logical Access

Network

In the case of a network acquisition, the Digital Forensic Practitioner (DFP) will be provided with access through a device that is attached to the client's network and also provided with authentication details. Although possible, it is less likely that external connections, i.e. using resources not owned by the client, will be used to access the device to be imaged and therefore the path that the data takes from the source storage device to the target storage device is fixed and known.

Cloud

Access to cloud resources will typically be provided through the normal process by which the cloud consumer connects to the hosted resources. The access from resources not owned by the cloud consumer is possible as the intermediate connection between source and target storage devices is provided by the Internet in most cases. However, it is not a simple matter to identify the path that the data takes from source storage device to the target storage device and this path may not remain fixed.

Physical Access

Network

In some situations, it may be necessary to acquire physical images of server storage devices rather than the logical data provided by the operating system. An organization's ability to make the physical device available for acquiring the data makes this a feasible activity, notwithstanding the practical implications such as ensuring that the impact on the organization's normal activities is minimized.

Cloud

As the cloud consumer that owns the data does not have physical control of the hardware on which the data resides the process of obtaining a physical image of the storage device is complex. From a practical perspective, the host server may be located in one or more locations around the world requiring the DFP to travel overseas with all the associated issues of time and cost—always assuming that they will be granted access to the host server in the first place.

From a technical perspective, the server running on the host resource is likely to be an instance of a virtual machine, which is also likely to be one of many on the same physical device. The options for acquiring the 'physical machine data,' i.e. all storage locations including file slack and unallocated space, require a copy of the virtual machine (and snapshots) which will, by necessity, have to be supplied by someone with access to the host server. However, this access is unlikely to be provided to the DFP working for the hosted client. A person with access to the host server may not be a DFP in their own right nor be aware of the actions to be taken in order to ensure that the evidence is admissible.

Flexibility of Methods

Network

The DFP will have a variety of methods available that will depend on the use to which the device to be imaged is being put (i.e. options will be more restricted if the device is the main company fileserver or email server). With a device on the company network that is to be acquired 'live' a common practice is to run a local 'agent' on the source device which then transmits the acquired data to another node on the network. Alternatively, the device may be powered down and the appropriate method selected from a variety of acquisition options such as removal of hard disk and attachment (via write blocker) to an acquisition device or booting the source device from a Linux or Windows-based forensic boot disk or USB.

Cloud

The options for acquiring the data remotely are more restricted in a cloud environment and will depend on the type of service being provided. For Platform as a Service (PaaS) the cloud consumer (and therefore the DFP) will not have any access to the hardware or operating system that is provided on the host. In this instance the DFP will have to rely on the Cloud Provider (CP) having the resources and the incentive to be able to acquire cloud consumer data in a forensically sound manner—complicated more if the data is physically stored on a device hosted by a subcontracted third-party.

For Software as a Service (SaaS) the DFP has even less visibility of the hardware on which the data to be acquired resides and to make matters more complicated not only may there be more than one cloud consumer being served by a particular host computer but the servicing of cloud consumer tasks may be distributed over multiple host computers. Again, the DFP will be reliant on the CP being willing and able to acquire the data in a forensically sound manner.

For Infrastructure as a Service (IaaS) the cloud consumer, and hence the DFP, will typically be provided with a virtual machine on which they can install their own operating system and applications. Despite the cloud consumer's virtual machine typically residing with numerous other virtual machines on the same hardware the DFP is able to take advantage of the fact that then operating system is accessible and can deploy the same tools as for a normal network acquisition.

Segregation of Data/Evidence

Network

Within a single organization there is usually no issue with having to identify and segregate different data for logical acquisitions as this will be accomplished during the normal course of identifying data of relevance as extraneous data will be wasteful of resources, especially the time to acquire, process, and review. The logical acquisition of data for a particular matter that is part of an investigation, such as for e-Discovery or compliance with a court order or notice (such as a notice served by the Australian Securities and Investment Commission under Section 30 ASIC Act) are situations whereby not all the data acquired will be involved in the proceedings due to issues of relevance, confidentiality, and privilege. This can often be the case when acquiring email server data, which will include all correspondence including that between an organization and their lawyers; however normally there is an agreed protocol to remove material that is not the subject of the warrant, notice etc. after it has been acquired.

Where there is more of a problem is when a physical acquisition is obtained from a device that has been used to store information from more than one legal entity. For an organization that may have several businesses sharing resources this issue can be relatively easily managed, as typically there are only a few parties involved and agreement can be reached on a protocol for segregating the data collected. There is more of a problem when the data that is to be acquired belongs to many other parties, such as data stored on the server of a law firm or firm of accountants. Although the number of entities involved may be quite large, it is ultimately possible to identify all of them and address the legal complications.

Cloud

None of the options provided by a CP enable physical access to the host computers and therefore this is unlikely to be an option available to the DFP. The fact that the data to be acquired may reside on one or more physical devices which themselves are being used by multiple cloud consumers and that the configuration of the devices may not be static makes it unlikely that the CP will be able to offer any form of physical acquisition.

The logical acquisition process for IaaS will follow similar line to that for a networked resource. But for cloud consumers that have purchased the PaaS and SaaS options the DFP will require the assistance of the CP.

Legal Implications

Network

When working on a network the legal aspects are relatively easy to identify and address. If the network is owned by the cloud consumer and their 'computer use' police clearly states that all data contained on their systems is, in effect, deemed to be their property then in many situations the work of the DFP is straight forward. The exceptions arise when, as mentioned earlier, the client or organization that owns the network may be storing information relating to third parties as in the case of lawyers, financial advisers and accountants. If the DFP is operating under a court order or warrant then they need to ensure that the details of the document are in order in that they authorize the intended activities of the DFP although it is often the case that the DFP may not be granted immediate access due to a legal challenge but these are, in many cases, resolved by the lawyers involved relatively quickly.

Cloud

There are several factors that have the potential to make the acquisition of data from the cloud far more complicated. Firstly, data may be distributed across hardware owned and operated by different entities. Secondly, these entities may be in more than one legal jurisdiction, and finally data may be co-mingled with data from other organizations who themselves may come under different legal jurisdictions. However, these issues should really only become a problem if physical acquisitions are required. For logical acquisitions, the location and nationality of the CP should not be an issue, as the DFP will be using the credentials of the cloud consumer to access the data as it is presented to them under their agreement.

For cases in which access to the physical storage devices are required the DFP will be reliant on their legal advisers to confirm that they have the authority to undertake the work on the basis of information supplied by the CP in relation to the physical location of the data—which may not be a simple or straightforward task. Furthermore, the DFP will also be reliant on one or more third parties to collect the data in a forensically sound manner, particularly if it resides overseas.

This section has highlighted some of the practical difficulties being faced by DFPs when they are considering acquiring data from the cloud. In essence, for logical acquisitions the process is only slightly more complicated than for a network acquisition and little different from that encountered when an organization has their datacenter hosted by a third party through a private network rather than across the Internet. The main issue arises when having to consider the physical locations of data when a 'live' or 'logical' acquisition is not an option.

A NEW DIGITAL ACQUISITION PROCESS MODEL

The amount of storage capacity being encountered by DFPs is making the process of undertaking a 'dead' acquisition impractical. Whilst storage capacity for the acquired data is relatively cheap, the speed with which the data can be collected is not keeping up with the increase in data volume with even entry-level laptops having 1TB of storage. If we look at what the DFP is trying to do, we can summarize this as collecting data in such a way that a court can make a determination of the reliability of any evidence that may be presented before it that formed part of that data. The technical aspects of the acquisition are not expected to be understood by the court but the process adopted by the DFP should be capable of being explained as well as all the aspects of the work that were taken into consideration.

In the early days of digital forensics, a lot of emphasis was placed on the ability to ensure that data had not been altered on the source device through the use of write-blocking devices and this was a relatively simple concept to explain in court. However, it soon became apparent that there were likely to be more and more situations in which it was not possible to shut down the computer storing the data and so the concept of 'least intrusion' evolved whereby the DFP identifies the likely changes that may occur to the data as a result of their activities together with their implications for any evidence contained within that data. We have rapidly seen an expansion in the volume of data being encountered and the impact of taking file servers or email servers offline recognized as being unacceptable in many instances.

We are therefore moving away from the utopia in which everything can be isolated as well as the concept that data can be located on a single physical device and this requires DFP to adopt alternative techniques. The courts want to see a clear process description for the activities undertaken by a DFP so that they can assess whether the DFP considered all the appropriate factors, such as authority to do the work, in undertaking their activities. With the advent of the cloud, the non-technical aspects of the DFP's work are assuming an ever-greater proportion of the data acquisition process. This is not to say that the courts will not want to query certain technical aspects of the DFP's work (usually by calling upon other experts) but they want to be able to place these in context with the other non-technical factors which could render the technical discussions irrelevant. In this regard, there is an urgent need for a process model that describes the activities undertaken by a DFP working in a commercial or a law-enforcement environment.

The multi-jurisdictional, multi-environmental nature of cases result in different applications of digital forensic principles being seen by courts in different ways, therefore the methodology employed by digital forensic practitioners will always come under scrutiny (Kessler, 2010; Rogers, 2006). This issue is not confined to the law enforcement environment as it applies equally to the activities of many commercial practitioners working in the field of digital forensics and incident response who may also be involved in legal proceedings (Kohn, Eloff, & Olivier, 2006; Meyers & Rogers, 2004; Peisert, et al., 2008; Turnbull, 2008).

Ciardhuáin has stated that "A comprehensive model of cybercrime investigations is important for standardising terminology, defining requirements, and supporting the development of new techniques and tools for investigators" (Ciardhuain, 2004, p. 1). Ciardhuáin goes on to suggest that a comprehensive model would have general benefits for IT managers, auditors and others not necessarily involved in the legal process due to the increasing incidence of 'crimes' involving computers. Going further still, Trcek et al. push the notion of an agreed "template legislation" that would harmonize the practice of digital forensics on an international basis (Trcek, Abie, Skomedal, & Starc, 2010). Yet, as Selamat et al. (2008) observe *"...there is no single framework can be used as a general guideline for investigating all incidents cases. Therefore, further research is needed to design a general framework to overcome this issue."* It is to address this issue that the model introduced in this chapter has been developed.

Given the rigorous standards that apply to material used in court there is an urgent need to establish a framework for digital forensics that assists courts in their determination of the admissibility of digital evidence (Ami-Narh & Williams, 2008; Brown, 2006; Rogers, 2004). The problem, according to many researchers (Carrier & Spafford, 2004; Meyers & Rogers, 2004; Peisert, et al., 2008; Sun, Yoon, & Yoo, 2008; Turnbull, 2008) is that there are several obstacles that must be overcome in order to develop such a framework, namely:

- There is no standard for the collection of digital evidence, although there are published guidelines in various countries.
- There is no standard of training/knowledge required of someone undertaking the collection of digital evidence.
- The environment in which digital evidence exists is not heterogeneous and is constantly changing requiring flexibility in the application of techniques and processes.
- The existing knowledge resides within a relatively small number of experienced practitioners and given the nature of the work there is little opportunity for passing this knowledge on in a timely manner to trainees.
- Often inexperienced investigators or IT personnel are required to collect electronic evidence.

There has been little progress in refining and defining a generic digital forensic process since an initial meeting of experts in 2001 concluded that this was necessary (Council of Europe, 2001; Nance, Armstrong, & Armstrong, 2010; Pollitt, 2009; US-CERT, 2008). Many researchers writing in this field have adopted their own terminology for describing process models which rather than being generic are aimed at particular environments, such as law enforcement (Rogers, 2006), and incident response (Cummins & Lowry, 2003; Mandia & Prosise, 2001; Stephenson, 2003b). Some researchers have tried to utilize existing formal languages and methods rather than invent their own terminology but they still have focused on a particular environment (Pollitt, 2007).

Standards and Guidelines

When considering 'standards' against which the DFP activities can be assessed by courts in Australia there is an aspect of definition that has to be addressed. The international body for 'standards,' the International Standards Organisation (ISO), defines a 'standard' as a "document, established by consensus and approved by a recognized body, that provides, for common and repeated use, rules, guidelines or characteristics for activities or their results, aimed at the achievement of the optimum degree of order in a given context." However, Australian Standards, the national body in Australia, considers that "Standards are published documents setting out specifications and procedures designed to ensure products, services and systems are safe, reliable and consistently perform the way they were intended to. They establish a common language which defines quality and safety criteria." Notwithstanding this issue, the relevant references are now considered individually.

ISO is the main international body that is relevant to standards within the field of digital forensics and is a non-government organisation that is composed of representatives from 157 national standards organisations, one of which is Standards Australia. ISO is based in Geneva, Switzerland and although it has no government-enforced powers ISO standards are often adopted by its member countries. In addition to the standards that it sets, ISO also publishes technical reports, guides and other technical literature, normally based on the output from special committees that are established for a particular purpose. One of these committees, JTC1 (the only joint committee of ISO), is the specialist standards-setting organisation for electrical, electronic and related technologies the IEC. At a meeting held in Kyoto in April 2008 a sub-committee of JTC1 (JTC1/SC 27 – IT Security Techniques) proposed a Study in the area of Evidence Acquisition Procedure for Digital Forensics. The ongoing contribution of the Australian Standards Working Group is currently being coordinated by Ajoy Gosh who has authored previous standards and guidelines in this area (Gosh, 2004a, 2004b) with input from practitioners working within law enforcement, education and commerce.

The BSI has produced a standard, BS 10008, whose title, 'Evidential Weight and Legal Admissibility of Electronic Information: Specification,' suggests that it may be related to the acquisition of electronic evidence. However, the standard relates to the production of electronic documents that may be required as evidence of business transactions and provides guidelines for practices and procedures involving information management systems.

The UK National Hi-Tech Crime Unit produces (on behalf of the Association of Chief Police Officers) the Good Practice Guide for Computer Based Electronic Evidence (Association of Chief Police Officers, 2003) which contains definitions of the four Principles of Computer Based Electronic Evidence (developed prior to the advent of cloud computing) which are as follows:

Principle 1: No action taken by law enforcement agencies or their agents should change data held on a computer or storage media, which may subsequently be relied upon in court.

Comment: This Principle will be difficult to follow in most, if not all, cloud environments without placing reliance on third parties (potentially other law enforcement personnel in the hosting country) and thus adding a further tier of complexity to task, notwithstanding the timing issues this raises.

Principle 2: In exceptional circumstances, where a person finds it necessary to access original data held on a computer or on storage media, that person must be competent to do so and be able to give evidence explaining the relevance and the implications of their actions.

Comment: For cloud computing this 'exception' is likely to become the rule.

Principle 3: An audit trail or other record of all processes applied to computer based electronic evidence should be created and preserved. An independent third party should be able to examine those processes and achieve the same result.

Comment: The audit trail and logging of activities from the cloud consumer access point should be straight forward; however the records from a third-party, such as a technician from the CP, may not potentially be of a suitable standard.

Principle 4: The person in charge of the investigation (the case officer) has overall responsibility for ensuring that the law and these principles are adhered to.

Comment: The inability to directly supervise the work undertaken by third-parties, such as the CP's technicians replicating a virtual machine, introduces considerable risks for the investigating officer.

Fundamental to the concept of work undertaken in a forensic environment is the ability to use material and information discovered in a court of law. As quoted above, Principles 1 and 2 require that, if possible, the original electronic data is not altered by any activities of the investigator or, if data has been altered, the person responsible is able to explain what was altered and the implications of this on the evidence being presented.

In general terms the ACPO rules are mirrored by the International Organization on Computer Evidence (IOCE) in its draft guidelines (IOCE, 2002) which themselves are based on the ISO 17025 Standard[1]. The IOCEs purpose is stated as being *"…to provide an international forum for law enforcement agencies to exchange information concerning computer investigation and computer forensic issues."*

The IOCE's guidelines can be summarised as:

- The general rules of evidence should be applied to all digital evidence.
- Upon seizing digital evidence, actions taken should not change that evidence.
- When it is necessary for a person to access original digital evidence that person should be suitably trained for the purpose.
- All activity relating to the seizure, access, storage or transfer of digital evidence must be fully documented, preserved, and available for review.
- An individual is responsible for all actions taken with respect to digital evidence whilst the digital evidence is in their possession.

The risks and issues identified in the ACPO rules are also present in the IOCE guidelines.

McKemmish (1999) introduces four Rules which he states must be followed by digital forensic practitioners during the course of their work. These Rules provide the framework under which the digital forensic practitioner should be working but they do not provide detailed guidance, although McKemmish does provide justification and examples of their application in context.

- **First Rule:** This involves the handling of evidence and requires that the original source of the data should be handled as little as possible and only to the extent needed in order to obtain an authenticated copy.

- **Second Rule:** Accommodating situations in which the practitioner has no choice but to undertake some activity that alters the data, such as entering a password to access a computer, the second rule requires the practitioner to account for changes they may make to any of the data, which comes under their control. Identifying and recording these changes will require the practitioner to have a deep technical knowledge of the environment such that they are aware of the implications of their actions.
- **Third Rule:** This states the need to comply with the rules of evidence such that the admissibility of the evidence cannot be brought into question. This involves adhering to the other Rules as well as maintaining a chain of custody and other documentation in order that any challenges relating to admissibility may be defended.
- **Fourth Rule:** This states that the digital forensic practitioner should not proceed with activities in a situation where they have exceeded their knowledge of the environment or situation. Given the ever-changing environment, this requires practitioners to keep their training program updated.

The McKemmish Rules follow the guidelines of ACPO and the IOCE but with particular emphasis on ensuring admissibility and working from a position of knowledge of the environment. This final point will be particularly challenging as, even if the CFP is knowledgeable with regard to the generic cloud environment, they are unlikely to be familiar with each particular cloud implementation that they may be called to deal with and thus require time to gather the necessary knowledge before they can proceed and this may not always be practical, particularly for law enforcement.

The document 'Guidelines for the Management of IT Records' (Gosh, 2004b) is intended to assist organisations manage the data stored on their systems in such a way that it may be readily accessed and provided in an admissible form in the event that it may be relevant in some form of litigation. Although digital forensic methods are referenced, the focus of this document is with Electronic Discovery rather than third party investigations and does not take into account the wider needs of digital forensic practitioners. In a similar vein the document 'Guidelines for Evidence Collection and Archiving' (Brezinski & Killalea, 2002) is a Network Working Group memo that is focused on incident response although it does provide advice on a range of digital forensic activities in the form of actions to be carried out under various headings, including 'chain of custody' considerations. However, despite this and the other references mentioned earlier, there has been little real progress since 2001 in refining the process for the acquisition of digital data to the point where there is a formal definition, generally accepted guidelines and reference to a standard that encompasses the activities of law enforcement, commercial, and incident response practitioners. Fundamentally, there even appears to be little agreement on the number of processes/stages involved. In January 2012, the US-CERT organisation included in its online 'reading room' a paper which suggests that we are also no further forward with regard to digital forensics becoming a 'mainstream' scientific discipline than we were at the time of the 2001 DFRWS and the paper includes the comment *"Because computer forensics is a new discipline, there is little standardization and consistency across the courts and industry. As a result, it is not yet recognized as a formal "scientific" discipline"* (US-CERT, 2008, p. 1).

The Daubert Test

The Daubert Test forms the basis on which many courts assess a particular 'scientific' process model (Gosh, 2004a; Stephenson, 2003) however, whilst the authors of many of the existing models can claim that they have been peer reviewed only a small number have undergone any form of testing and none of them are complying with any particular standard. This situation suggests that the Daubert Test is currently ineffective as a standard for determining the reliability of the process employed for acquiring digital evidence. Whilst there are several guidelines available for digital forensic practitioners these are focused on either law enforcement, electronic discovery or incident response and do not cover all the specific requirements of practitioners working in other areas. ISO is currently working on a standard for digital evidence collection with contributions from the Australian Committee IT-012-04, but this has not yet been published and this ISO document is also likely to be a 'Guideline' rather than a 'Standard' although it is intended to cater for the needs of digital forensic practitioners working in a number of different areas, including law enforcement and commercial practice. However, whilst the document itself contains 'baseline steps' for certain activities involving the collection and acquisition of electronic data there is no overall process model.

Previous Models

Agarwal et al. (2011) comment that there have been many initiatives to satisfy the need for a standard methodology that can be applied to the different environments in which digital forensics is practiced but that so far these models are mainly ad-hoc and further work is needed in this area. We are currently progressing towards having a separate process model for each new technology as it comes along. Therefore, rather than having a further ad hoc process model specifically for the cloud environment, we need a process model that can assist the DFP (and the courts) in relation to determining the reliability of electronic evidence by describing the acquisition process in a way that can be applied in different environments (such as law enforcement and commercial practice), is described formally, relates to recognized industry standards and accommodates new environments such as the cloud. Previous researchers have provided pointers to some of the key elements that could be included in a new generic model as detailed in the following paragraphs:

Rogers: The Digital Crime Scene Analysis Model (DCSA) (2004)

1. Supporting the adoption of a common approach by considering the similarities between physical and digital evidence.
2. Emphasizing chain of custody considerations.
3. Considering all areas of digital forensics rather than bias the model towards a particular group.
4. Acknowledging that in a fast-moving technological environment, the practitioners cannot be expert and experienced in all areas.
5. Promoting a pragmatic approach concentrating on the important areas on which other aspects of the work are dependant with an emphasis on data acquisition.
6. Emphasizing that a model should be tool and technology independent.
7. Recognizing that the high-level phases are dependent on the type of investigation.

Carrier and Spafford: The Integrated Digital Investigative Process (IDIP) (2003)

8. The concept of treating the computer as a digital crime scene
9. Identifying the important attributes for a model of the digital forensic process

Ciardhuain: An Extended Model of Cybercrime Investigations (EMCI) (2004)

10. Introducing the concept of 'information flow'
11. Covering all aspects of the investigation process

12. Identifying 'awareness,' 'authorization' and 'planning' stages
13. Incorporating the concept of iterations between stages (with Beebe and Clark)
14. Identifying that there may be both internal and external authorities involved

Reith et al.: The Abstract Digital Forensic Model (ADFM) (2002)

15. The concept of abstractly defined common steps from previous generic forensic protocols
16. Introducing the concept of 'digital forensics' as more encompassing than 'computer forensics'

THE ADVANCED DATA ACQUISITION MODEL (ADAM)

By combining the key contributions and considering previous models collectively the essential elements for a data acquisition activity can be summarized as comprising of three stages:

1. An initial preparation stage that incorporates activities that take place once the practitioner is notified or becomes aware of a potential requirement to undertake some work but prior to them gaining access to the 'incident scene[2]' (the detail of training, lab preparation and other activities prior to the notification/awareness point should not be the subject of a new model).
2. Actions that the practitioner undertakes to prepare for the acquisition of digital data once they have access to the 'incident scene' including, but not limited to, safety considerations, documentation, securing the scene and identifying potential locations for relevant digital data.
3. The actual process of acquiring digital data that may be of evidentiary value and its subsequent handling.

Carrier and Spafford (2003) state that digital forensic practitioners find the flexibility of objectives-based steps makes them more useful than a task-based 'tick-list' given that each 'crime scene' is unique and this is particularly relevant when we look at the possible permutations that can exist in a cloud environment. In addition, the principals under which the practitioner should be working are clearly stated (Association of Chief Police Officers, 2003) and these form the framework under which all the activities in the various stages are undertaken (Beebe & Clark, 2004). Shortcomings of previous models have been that:

1. Some tried to encompass all aspects of digital forensic activity in one model which became too wieldy and complicated.
2. Some confused the different activities of incident response and digital forensics leading to inappropriate activities (such as network-biased requirements) with a heavy emphasis towards an environment that does not represent a generic workspace for digital forensic practitioners.
3. Some are either very high-level descriptions providing no useful guidance or too low-level in which case they become too complicated to employ in practice.

The new model should therefore:

1. Have a narrow focus on the stages leading up to and including the acquisition of potential digital evidence.
2. Adopt terminology that is generic.
3. Be structured in such a way that digital forensic practitioners from different environments (law enforcement, commercial, etc.) will be able to easily adopt the model as a description of their processes whilst having the ability

to incorporate requirements specific to their own environment.

4. Introduce the concept of descriptors/prefixes for tasks, namely 'MUST' and 'SHOULD' to differentiate between activities that must always be carried out and those activities that may or may not apply in a given situation respectively. This will be done by using those keywords as defined in the document 'Keywords for use in RFCs to indicate Requirement Levels' [RFC2119] (Brezinski & Killalea, 2002).
5. Provide varying degrees of detail sufficient to assist the forensic practitioner at all levels whilst allowing for the simple, structured addition of new information to address the issues associated with advancing technology and tools.
6. Provide a well-defined process diagram (and associated narrative) for each stage such that it may be presented in court to help explain the work undertaken.
7. Be consistent with the ACPO Guidelines and draft ISO/IEC document CD27037 'Guidelines for identification, collection, acquisition, and preservation of digital evidence' as at July 2011, further adding to the credibility of the process described.

The new model, referred to as ADAM (Advanced Data Acquisition Model), addresses the 'Principles of Examination' stage of Noblett et al.'s (2000) Hierarchical Classification whilst allowing for the more detailed (lower level) organisational and situational aspects to be dealt with as necessary by the digital forensic practitioner.

In relation to the three-stage hierarchical model, ADAM:

1. Incorporates the principles of examination based on the guidelines from ACPO, ISO, and elsewhere.
2. Incorporates organizational policy and practice including guidelines, signing authorities, and other requirements.
3. Incorporates procedures and techniques that can be modified and expanded upon to accommodate new technological challenges (such as the cloud).

The ADAM itself consists of three stages associated specifically with the acquisition of electronic data. These stages were identified following the literature review (summarised in paragraph 3.4.3 Essential elements for the ADAM) and are described as:

Stage 1: The initial planning stage.

This is where high-level considerations are determined that relate to the documentation associated with the investigation, the investigation logistics, etc. This may involve a covert survey (sometimes carried out by private detectives) depending on the type and nature of the investigation being undertaken. In some instances, such as where law enforcement officers have already seized devices and present them for examination to the digital forensic practitioners, this stage may be very brief and simply consist of checking paperwork. In relation to cloud computing this may involve the CFP ensuring that they have the necessary knowledge within the team in relation to the particular environment and configuration that they are likely to encounter.

Stage 2: The onsite survey.

This is where all the gaps in knowledge relating to the location, size, and format of the devices holding the electronic data are filled in and the main acquisition plan is created. There may be instances in which this stage may be irrelevant as in the case for previously obtained devices mentioned above. However, in the case of cloud computing this information is likely to come from a third-party source, i.e. the CP who will be in a position to describe the particular environment configuration of relevance.

Stage 3: The acquisition of electronic data.

This will include both replication and storage of the acquired data.

The common factor associated with all the stages is documentation. Documentation is vital to ensure that a record is kept of all activity associated with the acquisition of the electronic data and subsequent transportation and storage as there is the potential for the whole process to come under close scrutiny in court (Brown, 2006; Casey, 2004; Jones, et al., 2006; Kruse & Heiser, 2002).

In order to avoid the complication of including a large amount of low-level detail the new model incorporates several key assumptions (in accordance with the current draft ISO/IEC document (ISO/IEC, 2011):

1. The digital forensic practitioner is authorised, trained and qualified with specialized knowledge, skills and abilities for performing digital evidence acquisition, handling, and collection tasks.
2. The digital forensic practitioner ensures that they and any members of their team comply with local jurisdictional laws and regulations—particularly relevant for the cloud environment where multiple jurisdictions may be involved.
3. The digital forensic practitioner observes the requirements that their actions should be auditable (through maintenance of appropriate documentation), repeatable where possible (in that using the same tools on the same item under the same conditions would produce the same results), reproducible where possible (in that using different tools on the same item would produce substantially similar results) and justified.

Having identified the three stages and the assumptions for the new model the next sections draw upon the contributions of previous researchers to develop the elements that go to make up each stage.

ADAM Stage 1: Initial Planning

McKemmish emphasises the importance of the initial planning stage in a document written for the Australian Institute of Criminology in which he says that the forensic process begins with the identification of digital evidence (McKemmish, 1999). McKemmish goes on to say that until the location and storage format of potential digital evidence are identified it is not possible to determine the most appropriate process for its acquisition (McKemmish, 1999). Casey (2004) identifies three topics related to the acquisition of electronic data, the first of which he describes as Authorisation and Preparation. Under this topic, Casey describes the processes that should be undertaken in preparing for a warrant and although he doesn't give a name to a plan he states that: "*Planning is especially important in cases that involve computers*" (Casey, 2004).

In the ideal world it would be possible to obtain perfect knowledge of the environment containing the electronic data to be acquired thus enabling a detailed plan to be created that would simply have to be followed on site, indeed Sammes and Jenkinson (2007) state in a book section titled 'Pre-Search Intelligence' that: "*It is vital that the number of computers, their types, operating systems and connections are all known before entry.*" However in practice the digital forensic examiner often has insufficient detail about the computer systems, quantity, and location of data, types of hard disk or the operating system involved to enable anything beyond a rough outline of a plan to be produced. Whilst agreeing with the earlier sentiments of Sammes and Jenkinson (2007), Brown (2006) adopts a more pragmatic approach than theirs and introduces the concept of 'boilerplates' which he describes as being guides that are: "*...general enough to be useful in a wide array of situations but detailed enough to be helpful.*"

Due to the fact that initial information relating to the specific onsite environment may be scarce, incomplete or simply inaccurate, the planning stage should concentrate on preparing for as many likely scenarios as possible, allowing for the fact that:

...each computer forensics collection operation can vary so greatly, investigators need to have a playbook from which to operate, similar to what a sports team coach would use to contain all the plays he intends to use (Brown, 2006)

Even if information can be obtained that provides some guidance on what to expect onsite., allowance always has to be made for errors or inaccuracies in this information. The planning stage is fundamental to the process of acquiring digital evidence and in one form or another is common across the different environments in which digital forensic personnel are employed. The ADAM provides more guidance than previous models in this regard, as it uniquely incorporates consideration of a number of constraints during the planning stage. These constraints are in relation to:

- Authorisation
- Physical
- Timing
- Data

The concepts behind each of these constraints will be covered in more detail in the following sub-sections, the results of which in practice would lead to the concluding activity for this first stage of the new model, i.e., the formulation of the Outline Plan.

Authorization Constraints

The primary consideration, before any of the process detail is considered, must be ensuring that you have the authority to undertake the work. This authority can be made up of several discrete aspects including authority from the organisation providing the services (internal authorisation), authority in law and authority from the owner of the resources containing the material to be acquired such as a CP (external authorisation).

The extent to which the authorization aspect of the Planning stage is covered in literature varies greatly. For instance, in their book 'Real Digital Forensics' (Jones, Bejtlich, & Rose, 2006) the authors do not mention the issue of planning and ignore preliminary background tasks by starting with instructions for acquiring data from a 'live' Microsoft Windows computer. This approach is also true for the authors of Forensic Discovery (Farmer & Venema, 2005) who again begin with the practical aspects of locating certain types of potentially relevant information on computer systems. Kruse and Heiser (2002) make a passing reference to authority under a paragraph entitled 'Legal Access' but only from the perspective of an in-house practitioner when they advise that the digital forensic practitioner must check that their company policies allow them access to the resources that are the focus of their investigation before commencing work. In contrast to the single paragraph, Casey (2004) devotes several pages to the issue.

Further support for the importance of this issue of authorization comes from Marcella and Menedez (2008) who provide a list of the basic steps for a 'cyber investigation' that begins with '1. Obtain proper authorization.' They then cover this issue in some detail beginning with:

Obtaining authorization to begin an investigation is critical, especially if the investigation involves an internal company employee and organizational management initiates the investigation. If the investigation is initiated by law enforcement, they too must follow established procedures for obtaining authorisation (Marcella & Menendez, 2008, p. 283).

For those working in a cloud environment the process of identifying what authorization is required and from whom may be a lengthy process.

Internal Authorisation

For a small specialist provider of digital forensic services the process of internal authorisation is relatively straight-forward and should consist of a signed agreement detailing the services to be delivered.

For a firm that provides digital forensic services as part of a larger service offering, for instance a global accounting firm, the procedure may be far more complicated in that various conflict checks and risk assessments will need to be undertaken (it would be a serious issue to turn up at an office to acquire a forensic image as part of some investigation only to find out that the premises belong to an audit client of the firm carrying out the investigation).

The conflict checks and risk assessments seek to mitigate potential conflicts of interest and form part of the due diligence procedures for many large organisations. The conflicts of interest may be focused on legislative rules and guidelines or commercial considerations, such as working on a matter for which an existing client is an opposing party.

The existing literature relating to corporate digital forensic investigations is primarily based on the digital forensic practitioner being employed within the organisation that owns the resources to be investigated and assumes that internal authorisation has been granted, although this process is not referenced in the text (Steel, 2006; Wiles, 2007). Digital forensic services being provided by a third party have not been covered in literature relating to process models.

Authority in Law

For commercial practitioners, in cases such as assisting with the serving of Anton Pillar orders or matters where government bodies have 'search and seize' powers, the investigator needs to ensure that they have the authority to provide the services in the manner in which they have been requested. This may involve being named on court orders or other documents.

Law enforcement practitioners will need to confirm the details of the appropriate warrant and any limitations imposed.

Court orders permitting access to a third party's property should be closely scrutinized, as the investigator may become the subject of litigation if they perform any actions not permitted by law. Where data is physically stored in one or more 'outside' jurisdictions, there may be a requirement to obtain multiple court orders.

Consideration should be given to the possibility of processing material that is covered by criminal law, for instance where there was a suspicion that child pornography may have been contained on one or more of the computer systems to be analysed.

Mere knowledgeable possession of child pornography, as well as certain other material, is a criminal offence in Australia and elsewhere and if there is a strong chance that this type of material could exist then the investigator needs to review the situation with the client in relation to discussing the matter and obtaining legal advice.

External Authority

When engaged to undertake work for an organisation that requires "their" systems to be accessed (such as in the case of a CP) the investigator needs to confirm that the entity giving the instructions has a right of access to the resources involved. For instance, there may be occasions in which data from more than one legal entity has been stored on a single computer system—this is often the case if the resources are held at a third-party IT provider, e.g. a provider of disaster recovery services holding a 'live' copy of several organisations' data or if the computers are used by an accountant or lawyer to store information from many clients. In addition, cloud solutions may involve resources from other sub-contracted entities who supply, for instance, storage resources.

Physical Constraints

Physical access to the systems containing electronic data is generally not considered in any great depth by other models and is often approached from the perspective of a commercial digital forensic practitioner simply needing to determine if data may be located at more than one site (Brown, 2006; Jones, et al., 2006; Marcella & Menendez, 2008; Steel, 2006; Wiles, 2007). The only other aspect of physical constraints that tend to be considered is in relation to dealing with external 'attacks' on systems involving the Internet which leads to a discussion of its technical characteristics. With regard to physical constraints, the new model involves two considerations that need to be addressed prior to undertaking the data acquisition.

Access

For non-cloud environments the first aspect of physical constraints to consider is that physical access to the resources containing the data to be acquired is needed in the majority of cases, obvious exceptions being data that can be accessed via the Internet or Internal/external networks, although in the later case there would need to be a good reason for obtaining the data remotely rather than using someone onsite. Commercial premises may be located on a site that is security controlled and require the appropriate authorisation to enter or there may be door access codes. Commercial premises may also be shared with other legal entities that may restrict access. Private premises may have limited access or restricted parking, such as private premises that have security gates thus requiring the lawyers to negotiate entry with the occupants in order to serve orders and begin the data acquisition process.

For cloud environments there is unlikely to be the option for the CFP to physically access the data storage devices and therefore reliance will be made on third parties; either resources from the CP or recognised CFPs that are local to the data.

Layout

The second aspect of physical constraints to consider is whether the data is held on resources at more than one location, either on separate sites or scattered between different offices or floors within the same building. This aspect may determine how many team members are required and how many sets of equipment are needed. Steel spends some time considering the physical aspects of accessing the data under a heading of 'Identifying the scene' (Steel, 2006). CPs may have a complex mixture of resources and on initial contact may not even know where particular data are stored.

Timing Constraints

An important aspect of the planning stage is determining constraints based on time. Several authors refer to choosing appropriate techniques or methods based on 'practical' considerations but do not include timing as part of their initial preparation (Casey, 2004; Wiles, 2007). Some authors, especially those basing their discussions on in-house digital forensic practitioners, don't consider the timing aspects at all (Marcella & Menendez, 2008; Steel, 2006). If data is known to be stored in the cloud then additional time should be allowed in order to understand the particular environment, obtain the necessary authorisations and make arrangements for third-parties. The ADAM requires consideration of three aspects of timing constraints, which are now considered individually.

Court Orders and Warrants

It is often the case with court orders that there are strict time limits placed on when the acquisition activities can take place and at what point they must be terminated regardless of whether the processing has been completed or not. Similar restrictions may also be contained within warrants. With the likely involvement of multiple jurisdictions for matters involving the cloud the identification of all relevant courts and completing the process of obtaining the necessary orders may have a significant bearing on how practical the proposed acquisition may be.

Private Premises

Engagements involving data located on private premises may require getting to the premises before the subject of the court order leaves for work (or some other activity) but preferably after partners and /or children have left the building. Of particular concern is the situation when data is stored in locations within different time zones in which case it may not be possible to synchronise activities to ensure that those under investigation have no opportunity to interfere with potential evidence after becoming aware of the activities of the DFP.

Commercial Premises

Engagements involving commercial premises often require a key holder to arrive and provide access to the offices following their review of the court order. Often there is a requirement to gain access to commercial premises after normal working hours and have the acquisition completed prior to employees turning up the following day. This may be to avoid business disruption or to ensure that employees suspected of some activity are not alerted to the investigation nor do they have the potential to destroy or remove data. The business disruption aspect is considered by Sammes and Jenkinson who also suggest a 'search briefing' that not only covers the allocation of tasks and the key objectives but identifies the provisions of the warrant or court order (Sammes & Jenkinson, 2007). If the data is held at multiple sites a suitable time frame needs to be allowed such that all forensic teams are able to co-ordinate their arrival to ensure that no one is alerted to the investigation before a team arrives. Although CPs will have support for their systems on a 24/7 basis the involvement of particular personnel to provide the required authority, access and/or technical assistance will restrict when certain activities in relation to acquiring the data can take place. In addition, for resources running multiple virtual servers such as used by CPs, there is unlikely to be a 'window of opportunity' when the resources can be taken offline without impacting on cloud consumers unrelated to the investigation.

Data Constraints

The data is the electronic information that is the target of the acquisition process and can take many forms. As for other aspects of the planning stage, it is not always clear at the outset whether there is in fact any data that is relevant to the investigation or where this data might be located.

It is common practice for authors of digital forensic books to list 'types' of electronic data and suggest possible locations for this data (Hutt, 1995; Brown, 2006; Casey, 2004; Farmer & Venema, 2005; Jones, et al., 2006; Marcella & Menendez, 2008). In addition, the ADAM also requires consideration of the potential quantity of data that may be acquired and therefore there are three aspects of data constraints that are covered in the following paragraphs.

Identification of Data

The type of data to be acquired can vary greatly. For example, it could be in simple text files, images, design drawings, accounting packages or even fragments of deleted material. If data needs to be previewed prior to acquisition then the means of identifying any relevant data needs to be addressed, for instance if relevant data is likely to be in the form of graphics images, i.e. pictures, then a keyword search will not be appropriate. There may be the need to have specialist software installed on a forensic workstation (such as a CAD application) if this is being used to preview the data in native format 'offline.' The processes undertaken in relation to identifying the relevant data may have a significant impact on the time required to carry out the work. A CP may be hosting an entire server or just application data that may exist on more than one physical machine. An entire virtual machine can be reproduced, through an appropriate technique and with the necessary audit trail, enabling examination of deleted material, registry information and other system files. However, if data is being stored within a hosted or shared application then a process of extraction will need to be undertaken which may only be possible through the CP.

Amount of Data

The amount of data to be acquired will have a direct impact on the amount of storage space required for the acquisition disks and also the amount of time that will be involved in the acquisition process itself. If a 'live' acquisition is being performed and there is likely to be an effect on network performance this needs to be communicated to the client/lawyers so that the impact on the business holding the data can be considered which may lead to negotiations on when and how the operation takes place. If data is being extracted remotely from a CP this may have a significant impact on their resources and interfere with other businesses and may therefore require some negotiations to be entered into in order to minimise this impact.

Location of Data

If the data to be reviewed and acquired is stored on backup tapes, e.g. the time period of interest is such that the data is not likely to be currently residing on any 'live' systems, access to a means of restoring the relevant backup tapes will need to be considered or a plan put in place to remove and duplicate the tapes offsite. It is becoming increasingly common for data to be held by a third party as part of a 'cloud' solution that is accessed via the Internet. This presents many potential difficulties, particularly in relation to authorization, but from a location perspective, it may not be possible to physically access the place in which the data is stored. There may not even be such a thing as a single location for the 'data' due to its nature and/or the fact that it is distributed across different physical devices that may be in different jurisdictions. This could make the drafting of the necessary court orders or authorisations very difficult.

The Outline Plan

Based on the outcome of the previous considerations the logistics of the acquisition exercise can be considered. Without a survey of the site(s), which is normally not practical due to the urgency of the work, only a reasonable estimate can be made at this stage with certain contingency measures put in place, e.g. somebody placed on 'standby' to collect and deliver additional storage media or other resources. A key part of the Outline Plan implementation is a briefing. Although Sammes and Jenkinson (2007) are writing from a law enforcement perspective when describing their 'Search Briefing,' this activity is no less relevant in the commercial field as it ensures that all those involved are aware of the information available at the time including any constraints imposed by court orders or other authorities. The following is based on the recommendations of Sammes and Jenkinson:

Answers to the following questions need to be addressed:

1. How many trained personnel are required?

2. How many teams are required, where do they need to be and at what date/time (this may be influenced by how many lawyers are available)?
3. How many sets of equipment are required and what should be in those kits?
4. Are any particular specialist skills required, if so how are they to be made available (e.g. someone with mainframe server knowledge may need to be at a specific location)?
5. How much storage media is required at each location and how can this be supplemented if necessary?
6. Will the services of another employee/contractor be required (e.g. a system IT administrator to assist with shutting down servers or locating backup tapes or a resource at a CP to acquire the data locally)?

The output of the Initial Planning stage should be the Outline Plan detailing:

1. Personnel required (with site allocations if applicable) and team composition.
2. Equipment required at each site (including software, dongles, write-blockers and image storage media).
3. Start time at each site.
4. Estimate of duration of acquisition stage.
5. Details of other personnel involved.
6. Contact numbers of team leaders/lawyers/client liaison distributed (if applicable).
7. Acquisition plan detailing target storage locations, protocol and key words (if applicable).
8. Applicable constraints—authorisation, physical, timing, and data.

Some authors delve into great detail in relation to the equipment that should be taken on site such as Sammes and Jenkinson (2007) whilst other authors such as Brown (2006) and Jones et al. (2006) include write-blockers of various types at the top of their recommendations for an 'onsite kit' (that are not included in Sammes and Jenkonson's list) as well as various software tools for acquiring digital data. The ACPO Guidelines make no recommendations at all for the equipment to be taken on site on the basis that the guidelines are for law enforcement personnel who would not normally deal with computers but whose role may cause them to come across computer equipment and their task is to seize that equipment. There is no consensus or standard set of guidelines for what equipment should be considered for inclusion in the onsite kit. The ADAM is not intended to provide this level of detail as the composition of the kit contents should be determined by the appropriate digital forensic professional.

ADAM Stage 2: The Onsite Plan

Having gained access to the site(s) in which relevant electronic data is thought to be stored, steps must be taken to ensure that the risk of potential evidentiary data being destroyed or removed is reduced as much as possible. Many writers of digital forensic guides, particularly those with a bias towards the work of law enforcement agencies, suggest that the whole 'crime scene' is immediately 'locked down' with the intention to obtain what Casey calls a "pristine environment" (Casey, 2004; Craiger, 2005; Sammes & Jenkinson, 2007). Whilst this may often be achievable for law enforcement investigations this is seldom practical in the commercial environment, a view supported by Kruse and Heiser (2002):

The ideal way to examine a system and maintain the most defensible evidence is to freeze it and examine a copy of the original data. However, this method is not always practical and may be politically unacceptable.

Brown (2006) suggests that one of the first actions upon arrival on site is to ensure the safety of the digital forensic practitioner(s) whilst some authors incorporate safety and security as one process (Sammes & Jenkinson, 2007). The ACPO

Guide (Association of Chief Police Officers, 2003) incorporates a section on safety and welfare but this is in relation to the potential for disturbing material being accessed during the course of the investigation. Guidelines for those involved in digital forensics within an organisation, normally involving incident response, tend to ignore the safety aspects. This may be because they have a more intimate knowledge of the environment, and tend to start with processing the electronic data. This approach has also been adopted in other circumstances such as the broader commercial environment (Casey, 2004; Farmer & Venema, 2005; Jones, et al., 2006). In order to provide a consistent and generic approach the ADAM contains basic procedures to be followed when attending the site as a pre-cursor to reviewing the Outline Plan. Rather than being too prescriptive and reducing the necessary flexibility required of a digital forensic practitioner the basic procedures are relatively 'high-level.'

Updating the Outline Plan

Once the digital forensic practitioner (or their proxy in the case of resources at a CP) is on site the Outline Plan needs to be reviewed and updated now that its various assumptions can be tested. There will often be areas of the plan that could not be completed at all prior to attending the site(s) containing the electronic data. If more than one site is involved there will be the need to have separate Onsite Plans to take account of the specific local circumstances. The overall goals will likely remain the same but the steps to be taken in order to achieve them may have to be altered. This is where the knowledge and experience of the digital forensic practitioner responsible for the particular site is critical. Few authors on forensic practice spare much time, if any, in describing a process for producing an onsite plan. Instead many simply state that the equipment likely to contain potential evidence should be identified (Baryamureeba & Tushabe, 2004; Casey, 2004; Pollitt, 2009). A more thorough approach is supported by Newman who suggests taking photographs of the scene, in line with most authors, but then goes on to list various activities that should be included in his 'Preliminary Survey':

1. Determine all the locations that might need to be searched.
2. Look for any specifics that must be addressed relating to hardware and software.
3. Identify possible personnel and equipment needs for the investigation.
4. Determine which devices can be physically removed from the site.
5. Identify all individuals who had access to the computer or electronic resources (Newman, 2007).

ADAM Stage 3: Data Acquisition

Some authors infer that the acquisition process is always undertaken in some 'ideal' environment where storage devices can be write-blocked (Jones, et al., 2006). McKemmish (1999) adopts a more practical view where he states that in certain circumstances "*changes to data are unavoidable*" (McKemmish, 1999, p. 1). His solution is to clearly identify and record the consequences of any actions undertaken. With a trend towards 'live' acquisition and given the technical nature of the devices (such as mobile phones and solid state drives), the environment (such as computer data stored in volatile memory) (Sutherland, Evans, Tryfonas, & Blyth, 2008), full disk encryption (Casey & Stellatos, 2008), and time/storage constraints (individual hard disk drives exceeding 2TB) (Gosh, 2004a) the concept of the 'ideal' environment is becoming even further removed from practice (Adelstein, 2006; Carrier, 2006; Leong & Leung, 2007). Given the many different potential scenarios, it would not be practical or appropriate to develop detailed guidelines that could be generally applied. Each organisation undertaking the acquisition of digital evidence should have developed their own procedures to supplement those of the ACPO and ISO Guidelines, but inevitably, it is down to the practitioner to decide how these guidelines are to be applied in a particular set of circumstances.

It is the role of the digital forensic practitioner to determine the most appropriate technique to be employed and maintain documentation of all activities associate with data acquisition. This will include starting the 'chain of evidence' and other documentation such that they will be able to describe their actions and reasons to a court. In situations in which a third-party resource is used and not directly supervised they must be issued with very clear instructions including the requirement to document all their activities.

MODEL VALIDATION

As part of the DSRP methodology, the ADAM was initially tested by undertaking a 'demonstration' activity in which the processes undertaken in three previous investigations were compared to those that form the ADAM. Differences were highlighted, considered and appropriate changes were made to the ADAM. Two experienced digital forensic practitioners were then approached (one from commerce and one from law enforcement) to provide feedback on the practical aspects of the ADAM from their respective environments prior to the ADAM being sent for review by a panel of experts that included notable researchers in the field of digital forensics. After the feedback from the panel of experts had been considered and implemented, a panel of practitioners was then asked to assess the model and provide feedback and this too was considered and implemented.

The final version of the ADAM consists of a set of Guidance Notes, a three-stage Operation Presentation in the form of a narrative, which includes ADAM Principles, and a set of UML Activity diagrams (one for each stage of the ADAM). Specific organization-based operating procedures can be integrated into the ADAM as well as 'best practice' guidelines to ensure relevance of the process model for its use in a particular environment as well as accommodating future advances in technology.

FUTURE WORK

Having created a model for the process of acquiring digital data that accommodates new and emerging technology whilst also allowing for the needs of groups of practitioners operating in different environments, the next stage for research is to consider following the same process used to develop the ADAM in order to model other aspects of the DFP work, i.e. analysis and presentation.

CONCLUSION

The issues surrounding the acquisition of digital evidence from the cloud may finally force the 'traditional' approaches that have been struggling to be relevant in networked environments to be superseded by a 'new generation' of process models, such as the ADAM, that both prescribe (as an aid to DFPs) and describe (as an aid to the courts) the activities of those whose task it is to acquire, analyze, and present digital evidence. Courts in Australia and New Zealand have already seen flowcharts introduced to assist the jury in understanding 'scientific' evidence in much the same way as the UML Activity Diagrams of the ADAM are intended with some of these flowcharts having been produced by judges themselves (Ogloff, Clough, & Goodman-Delahunty, 2006). This indicates that the proposed new model has a good chance of gaining acceptance as a useful tool in the legal environment and so what is now needed is the adoption by digital forensic practitioners of the ADAM or similar process model based on the same concepts to enable the field of digital forensics to justify its scientific credentials and accommodate new technologies as they arise.

REFERENCES

Adelstein, F. (2006). Live forensics: Diagnosing your system without killing it first. *Communications of the ACM*, *49*(2), 63–66. doi:10.1145/1113034.1113070

Agarwal, A., Gupta, M., Gupta, S., & Gupta, S. C. (2011). Systematic digital forensic investigation model. *International Journal of Computer Science and Security*, *5*(1), 118–130.

Armstrong, C. (2003). Mastering computer forensics. In Irvine, C., & Armstrong, H. (Eds.), *Security Education and Critical Infrastructures*. Dordrecht, The Netherlands: Kluwer Academic Publishers.

Association of Chief Police Officers. (2003). *Good practice guide for computer based evidence*. Retrieved from http://www.acpo.police.uk/asp/policies/Data/gpg_computer_based_evidence_v3.pdf

Baryamureeba, V., & Tushabe, F. (2004). *The enhanced digital investigation process model*. Paper presented at the Digital Forensic Research Workshop. New York, NY.

Beebe, N., & Clark, J. (2004). *A hierarchical, objectives-based framework for the digital investigations process*. Paper presented at the Digital Forensics Research Workshop 2004. New York, NY.

Brezinski, D., & Killalea, T. (2002). *Guidelines for evidence collection and archiving*. Retrieved from http://www.ietf/org/rfc/rfc3227.txt

Brown, C. (2006). *Computer evidence: Collection & preservation*. New York, NY: Charles River Media.

Buskirk, E. V., & Liu, V. T. (2006). Digital evidence: Challenging the presumption of reliability. *Journal of Digital Forensic Practice*, *1*(1), 19–26. doi:10.1080/15567280500541421

Calhoun, M. C. (2008). Scientific evidence in court: Daubert or Frye, 15 years later. *Legal Backgrounder, 23*(37).

Carrier, B. (2002). *Open source digital forensic tools: The legal argument*. Retrieved from http://www.digital-evidence.org/papers/opensrc_legal.pdf

Carrier, B. (2006). Risks of live digital forensics. *Communications of the ACM*, *49*(2), 56–61. doi:10.1145/1113034.1113069

Carrier, B., & Spafford, E. H. (2003). Getting physical with the digital investigation process. *International Journal of Digital Evidence*, *2*(2).

Casey, E. (2004). *Digital evidence and computer crime*. London, UK: Elsevier Academic Press.

Casey, E., & Stellatos, G. J. (2008). The impact of full disk encryption on digital forensics. *SIGOPS Operating Systems Review*, *42*(3), 93–98. doi:10.1145/1368506.1368519

Cheng, E. (2007). Independent judicial research in the Daubert age. *Duke Law Journal*, *56*, 1263–1318.

Ciardhuain, S. O. (2004). An extended model of cybercrime investigations. *International Journal of Digital Evidence*, *3*(1).

Cohen, F. (2011). Putting the science in digital forensics. *Journal of Digital Forensics. Security and Law*, *6*(1), 7–14.

Craiger, J. P. (2005). *Computer forensic procedures and methods*. Retrieved from http://ncfs.org/craiger.forensics.methods.procedures.final.pdf

Daubert v Merrell Dow Pharmaceuticals Inc 509 US at 579, 113 S.Ct. 2786, 125 L.Ed.2d 469 (1993).

Edmond, G. (2010). Impartiality, efficiency or reliability? A critical response to expert evidence law and procedure in Australia. *The Australian Journal of Forensic Sciences, 42*, 83–99. doi:10.1080/00450610903258128

Farmer, D., & Venema, W. (2005). *Forensic discovery*. Reading, MA: Addison-Wesley.

Giannelli, P. C. (2007). *Scientific evidence* (4th ed.). Newark, NJ: Lexis Law.

Gillespie, A. A. (2012). Jurisdictional issues concerning online child pornography. *International Journal of Law and Information Technology, 20*(3). doi:10.1093/ijlit/eas007

Gosh, A. (2004a). *Guidelines for the management of IT evidence*. Paper presented at the APEC Telecommunications and Information Working Group. New York, NY.

Gosh, A. (2004b). *HB 231:2004 information security risk management guidelines*. Sydney, Australia: Standards Australia.

Grant v Marshall FCA 1161 (2003).

Hargreaves, C. J. (2009). *Assessing the reliability of digital evidence from live investigations*. Cranfield, UK: Cranfield University.

Hutz, R. E. (2012, May 22). E-discovery: The relationship between cloud computing, e-discovery and privilege. *InsideCounsel*.

IOCE. (2002). *Guidelines for best practice in the forensic examination of digital technology*. Retrieved from http://www.ioce.org/fileadmin/user_upload/2002/Guidelines%20for%20Best%20Practices%20in%20Examination%20of%20Digital%20Evid.pdf

ISO/IEC. (2011). *Draft - Guidelines for identification, collection, acquisition, and preservation of digital evidence, CD 27037: ISO/IEC*. Retrieved from http://www.iso.org

Jones, K. J., Bejtlich, R., & Rose, C. W. (2006). *Real digital forensics*. Reading, MA: Addison-Wesley.

Kenneally, E. E. (2005). Confluence of digital evidence and the law: On the forensic soundness of live-remote digital evidence collection. *UCLA Journal of Law and Technology, 5*.

Kessler, G. C. (2010). *Judges' awareness, understanding, and application of digital evidence*. Davie, FL: Nova Southeastern University.

Kruse, W. G., & Heiser, J. G. (2002). *Computer forensics: Incident response essentials*. Reading, MA: Addison Wesley.

Kumho Tire Company v. Carmichael 526 U.S. 137; 1999 (1999).

Kunick, J. (2012, June 15). Technology: The promises and perils of the cloud. *InsideCounsel*.

Leong, R., & Leung, H. (2007). Deriving cse-specific live forensics investigation procedures from FORZA. In *Proceedings of the 2007 ACM Symposium on Applied Computing*. ACM Press.

Limongelli, V. (2008). Digital evidence: Findings of reliability, not presumptions. *Journal of Digital Forensic Practice, 2*(1), 13–16. doi:10.1080/15567280701721913

Marcella, A. J., & Menendez, D. (2008). *Cyber forensics: A field manual for collecting, examining and preserving evidence of computer crimes* (2nd ed.). New York, NY: Auerbach Publications.

Mason, S. (2007). *Electronic evidence: Disclosure, discovery & admissibility*. London, UK: Butterworths.

McKemmish, R. (1999). *What is forensic computing?* Retrieved from http://www.aic.gov.au/publications/tandi/ti118.pdf

Meyers, M., & Rogers, M. (2004). Computer forensics: The need for standardization and certification. *International Journal of Digital Evidence, 3*(2).

Moles, R. N. (2007). *The role and function of the expert witness*. Retrieved from http://netk.net.au/Reports/ExpertWitness.asp

Newman, R. C. (2007). *Computer forensics: Evidence collection and management*. London, UK: Auerbach Publications.

Ogloff, J., Clough, J., & Goodman-Delahunty, J. (2006). *The jury project: Stage 1 - A survey of Australian and New Zealand judges*. Melbourne, Australia: Australian Institute of Judicial Administration.

Peisert, S., Bishop, M., & Marzullo, K. (2008). *Computer forensics in forensis*. Paper presented at the Third International Workshop on Systematic Approaches to Digital Forensic Engineering. Oakland, CA.

Pollitt, M. (2009). The good, the bad and the unaddressed. *Journal of Digital Forensic Practice*, *2*, 172–174. doi:10.1080/15567280902882852

Reith, M., Carr, C., & Gunsch, G. (2002). An examination of digital forensic models. *International Journal of Digital Evidence*, *1*(3).

Rogers, M. K. (Ed.). (2004). *DCSA: A practical approach to digital crime scene analysis* (5th ed., *Vol. 3*). New York, NY: Taylor and Francis.

Rogers, M. K. (2006). DCSA: Applied digital crime scene analysis. In Tipton & Krause (Eds.), *Information Security Management Handbook* (5th ed.). New York, NY: Auerbach.

Sammes, T., & Jenkinson, B. (2007). *Forensic computing: A practitioner's guide* (2nd ed.). Berlin, Germany: Springer.

Smith, R. G., Grabosky, P. N., & Urbas, G. (2004). *Cyber criminals on trial*. Cambridge, UK: Cambridge University Press. doi:10.1017/CBO9780511481604

Solomon, A. (2010). *Privacy and the cloud*. Paper presented at the Cloud Computing Conference and Expo. New York, NY.

Stanfield, A. (2009). *Computer forensics, electronic discovery & electronic evidence*. London, UK: Reed International Books.

Steel, C. (2006). *Windows forensics: The field guide for conducting corporate computer investigations*. New York, NY: Wiley Publishing.

Stephenson, P. (2003). A comprehensive approach to digital incident investigation. *Information Security Technical Report*, *8*(2), 42–54. doi:10.1016/S1363-4127(03)00206-1

Sutherland, I., Evans, J., Tryfonas, T., & Blyth, A. (2008). Acquiring volatile operating system data tools and techniques. *SIGOPS Operating Systems Review*, *42*(3), 65–73. doi:10.1145/1368506.1368516

US-CERT. (2008). *Computer forensics*. Retrieved December 2008 from http://www.us-cert.gov/reading_room/forensics.pdf

Wiles, J. (Ed.). (2007). *The best damn cybercrime and digital investigations book period*. New York, NY: Syngress Publishing.

ADDITIONAL READING

Carrier, B., & Spafford, E. H. (2003). Getting physical with the digital investigation process. *International Journal of Digital Evidence*, *2*(2).

Carrier, B. D. (2006). Risks of live digital forensics. *Communications of the ACM*, *49*(2), 56–61. doi:10.1145/1113034.1113069

Cohen, F. (2011). Putting the science in digital forensics. *Journal of Digital Forensics. Security and Law*, *6*(1), 7–14.

Daubert v Merrell Dow Pharmaceuticals Inc 509 US at 579, 113 S.Ct. 2786, 125 L.Ed.2d 469 (1993).

Edmond, G. (2010). Impartiality, efficiency or reliability? A critical response to expert evidence law and procedure in Australia. *The Australian Journal of Forensic Sciences*, *42*, 83–99. doi:10.1080/00450610903258128

Kumho Tire Company v. Carmichael 526 U.S. 137 (1999).

Mason, S. (2007). *Electronic evidence: Disclosure, discovery & admissibility*. London, UK: Butterworths.

ENDNOTES

1 This is the main standard used by testing and calibration laboratories and was first published in 2001. This is a general purpose document concerned with management and quality procedures that do not specifically relate to computer forensic labs.

2 The environment in which the evidence is thought to reside.

Chapter 5
Forensic Readiness in the Cloud (FRC):
Integrating Records Management and Digital Forensics

Kirsten Ferguson-Boucher
Aberystwyth University, UK

Barbara Endicott-Popovsky
University of Washington, USA

ABSTRACT

This chapter focuses on a theoretical approach to proactive evidence collection and presents a conceptual approach for the Cloud. Forensic Readiness in the Cloud (FRC) calls upon technological and organizational strategies to address the risks that threaten organizational information. The two professions of Records Management (RM) and Digital Forensics (DF) can offer insights into how this might be achieved. In this chapter, the authors seek to explore the relationship between the two disciplines and the areas where collaboration and interdisciplinary work would be most beneficial. An initial overview of RM and its relationship to the wider field of Information Assurance (IA) precedes a more in depth comparison of the two related disciplines, using a model that integrates RM and DF. This is offered as a conceptual framework for making decisions about how to identify and manage the increasing quantities of evidence collected on networks. Organizational Network Forensic Readiness (NFR) has emerged as a method for supporting collection of digital evidence from networks using suggested checklists, procedures, and tools. This chapter elaborates upon a previously documented life cycle methodology for 'operationalizing' organizational NFR and integrates this with best practice from RM in FRC. FRC provides a conceptual approach to proactive evidence collection and identifies the phases at which RM approaches and processes might be most effectively employed in the Cloud.

DOI: 10.4018/978-1-4666-2662-1.ch005

Copyright © 2013, IGI Global. Copying or distributing in print or electronic forms without written permission of IGI Global is prohibited.

INTRODUCTION

Whilst many of the tools, strategies and processes have, and are being, developed in *reaction* to significantly increased malicious activity, they also prove invaluable means for addressing wider evidentiary requirements of organizations. Many internal investigations and civil or contractual disputes require forensic attention. Information required to preserve the historical memory of the organization or for the capture of social capital when much of the workforce is now mobile, short term and technology dependent, rests on the ability to verify the information held. In an environment where commercial organizations are often merging, governments retiring departments and the buzzwords are 'transparency,' 'accountability' and 'compliance,' network forensic readiness is an area that provides a means for meeting organizational recordkeeping requirements. It has drawn research interest in recent years and many of the established principles can be applied to the cloud environment.

The emergence of cloud computing as a new model for delivering computing resources has proven to be one of the most significant changes in how technology is accessed and provisioned. Commercial and public entities are increasingly taking advantage of the flexibility and scalability it offers as well the obvious financial benefits. Research by KPMG (2012) into the global governmental uptake, found that many governments are now focusing on cloud strategies, similar to those already implemented in the US, and more recently the UK (Censer, 2011, HM Government, 2011). Whilst reduced spending, higher flexibility and scalability, ease of use, improved reliability and security of scale can clearly be anticipated (Ferguson-Boucher, 2011), there are also some potentially less positive outcomes: the opportunity to modernize business processes and explore options for business continuity and disaster recovery are balanced against integration, interoperability, compliance, e-discovery, and life cycle challenges. It is an interdisciplinary, global challenge, one which is further complicated by the increasing sophistication of cybercrime and the complexity of the information ecology we have created with the Cloud.

"The rise of cloud computing not only has exacerbated the problem of scale for digital forensic activities, but also created a brand new front for cybercrime investigation with various challenges...cloud computing is a new battlefield of cybercrime, as well as a new ground for novel investigative approaches" (Ruan, et al., 2011). With regard to cybercrime perspective, recent research undertaken at Aberystwyth University, Wales (Convery & Ferguson-Boucher, 2011) found that for information professionals, storage in the Cloud, for example, merely adds to the complexity that they face when managing information across the organization's systems and infrastructure. Information lifecycle management, retention, and providing evidence that records are authentic, reliable and possess integrity are the main challenges. "Retrieval and destruction of information encompasses a range of issues relating to how information can be identified, searched, and destroyed once it has been stored in the Cloud. The ability to attach and maintain metadata as well as to apply retention decisions to information stored in the Cloud depends on the cloud service's systems functionality" (Convery, 2010). Deletion in the Cloud is often in fact based on the deletion of nodes pointing to information in virtual instances. Whether the deletion of the information (which is actually held on physical hard drives) has been fully achieved needs to be assessed and proven. Likewise, pathways for retrieval are dependent on cloud providers offering sufficiently sophisticated mechanisms for access.

BACKGROUND

This chapter will explore the relationships between RM and DF and analyze NFR as a tool for identifying and retaining records relevant for legal purposes in a cloud environment. The wider context for this study is that of Information Assurance (IA). IA evolved from the Information Security discipline and provides the technical and managerial measures designed to ensure the confidentiality, integrity, and availability of information—sometimes called the "CIA" of information management. The term "information assurance" gained acceptance within the US government in the mid-1990's and has since achieved common parlance across industry. An early model of IA known as the McCumber Cube highlights the relationship between confidentiality, integrity, and availability, the information states: transmission, storage and processing, and the measures: human, policies and practices and the technology (McCumber, 1991).

Records Management

RM is one of the disciplines within the broader context of communities with a fundamental stake in IA. For the limited purpose of this study, a history of modern Record Keeping (RK) commences with 1930's America rather than 5000BC Sumeria (Benfell, 2007), at which time the US archives introduced the concept of the "life cycle" of records. This is generally considered the foundation of all modern records management principles, methods and techniques (Webster, 1999). Other significant RK periods include the Second World War years, when the practice of offsite records storage and retention scheduling were introduced, as well as the publication of the first article on the life cycle concept. In the late twentieth century, less centralised communication patterns, virtual shared workspaces and integrated systems altered working practices significantly. Transaction Processing Systems, "computerized systems that perform and record the daily routine transactions necessary to the conduct of business" (Laudon & Laudon, 1999) perfected the creation of "current, accurate, and consistent" data, in vast quantities. The Internet, email, social media, and mobile technologies now provide constant challenges. Evidence of business activities like workflow programs, database, and Web applications require "a fundamental shift in perception to focus on the intellectual control of records" (Shepherd, 1994).

In 2001, ISO 15489 (Information and Documentation—Records Management) was broadly accepted throughout the RM profession. It defines RM as "the field of management responsible for the efficient and systematic control of the creation, receipt, maintenance, use, and disposition of records, including the processes for capturing and maintaining evidence of, and information about, business activities and transactions in the form of records." Records themselves are defined as "information created, received, and maintained as evidence and information by an organization or person, in pursuance of legal obligations or in the transaction of business" (ISO 15489-1:2001). The characteristics of records, also articulated in ISO 15489, further illuminate the status of a "record." It is this evidential status, which is of particular relevance for this research (Bailey, 2008). A key element of RM is its ability to provide evidence of an activity. Historically, if evidence could be provided of an event, it was deemed to have happened in that way. Records can be powerful tools in the hands of those in positions of authority who seek recognition and verification of, the *status quo*, in situations where power structures are shaping and reshaping (Clanchy, 1993; Harris, 2000; Jonker, 2011). Control of records, and therefore evidence, enables the construction of "truth," affecting standing within the international community and ultimately global power structures (Hurley, 2011). In the late 1990s, Frank Upward created the Record Continuum Model, which sought to contextualize records in the paper and digital environment. He highlighted 'evidentiality' as one of the four axes and posed questions regarding the use of the term "evidence" in RK as it related to legal evidence (Upward, 2005). ISO 15489 identifies the RM role as ensuring that records will be accepted as evidence in a court of law, should this be required ISO 15489-1:2001:

The principles of good practice in Record Keeping (RK) are of value, even if the need to produce electronic records in court never arises. The effort and resources required to comply quickly bring business benefits, whether the original is in court or not.

The tools available to the records manager include:

- **iGAFT (Information Governance and Assurance Functional Taxonomies):** To gain intellectual control and categorize records in a systematic and consistent way (a more comprehensive approach than the security classification familiar to security specialists). These focus on the functions of the organization and how business critical information, both now and for the longer term can be arranged according to function and rules applied to their management and use.
- **Appraisal Strategies:** To determine which records are deemed to have ongoing value, aligning with the current business objectives and longer-term drivers.
- **Retention Schedules:** To determine how long they should be kept, and
- **Disposition Plans:** To ensure these decisions as to value and management are implemented.

The Principles of IA and RM

ISO 15489 states that records must possess content, context, and structure. Content reflects the facts about the activity that they should be accurate and complete. Context, i.e. the circumstances of creation and use, include the activity, function, and administrative context of the record. Structure reflects the relationships within the record, and external to it, and organizes the content in such a way as to denote context (Shepherd & Yeo, 2003). Context has always been pivotal to the RM profession, specifically the content in which records are created, i.e. if this is not known, the "record" ceases to be relevant and evidential. ISO 15489 further isolates four qualities that records should possess: *authenticity*, *reliability*, *integrity*, and *usability*. *Authenticity* is linked to the accuracy of the records; *reliability* pertains to the records being a full and accurate representation of the activity/transaction. *Integrity* relates to the fact that records are complete and unaltered. Finally, *usability* refers to records being retrievable, presentable, and interpretable. Although the language relates to the "record," increasingly it is accepted that in order to maintain the above characteristics in records, it is the systems and the information architecture that must be proven to meet these requirements. "Modern evidential law has shifted focus away from the record as a material object to a record as the outcome of reliable business processes" (Lacovino, 2006).

IA, as defined by the National Security Telecommunication and Information Systems Security Instruction (NSTISSI), concerns information operations that protect and defend information and information systems by ensuring confidentiality, integrity, availability, authentication and non- repudiation. This includes providing for the restoration of information systems by incorporating protection, detection, and reaction capabilities (National Security Agency, 1999). The IA requirements of *confidentiality*, *integrity*, and *availability*, Machonagy et al. expanded to include *authentication*, and *non-repudiation* (Maconachy, Schou, Ragsdale, & Welch, 2001). These are known as the 5 pillars. "Authentication and non-repudiation are not attributes of information or systems, but are attributes used to describe the procedures or methods used to assure the integrity and authenticity of information, and to protect the confidentiality of those same. Authenticity is the attribute of being authentic or of established authority for truth and correctness (Verification)—genuine—not fabricated. Non-repudiation is the attribute of assuring that the conclusions of an analysis are the complete and only relevant truth and cannot be repudiated" (Dardick, 2010). Dardick also mentioned the Parkerian Hexad, introduced by Donn B. Parker in 1998, which added authenticity, utility, and possession to the CIA, utility being defined as usability or usefulness.

Although the exact meaning and underlying assumptions are different, there is a synergy between IA and RM principles. Both RM and IA seek to address issues relating to the integrity, authenticity, and security of the content of systems, which impact directly on private, organizational and societal personas. IA wishes to maintain the integrity of the system and the data held in it; RM is focused on establishing integrity of a record. Authentication and authenticity have some relation to one another. Authentication in IA refers to the ability of a system to identify and allow access to appropriate users. Authenticity in RM refers to the "trustworthiness of a record, consisting of its accuracy, reliability, and authenticity" (Duranti, 2009). One might assume that if authentication and non-repudiation were in play, the authenticity of a digital record could be established. Indeed the definition of Information Security given in ISO 27001 (Information technology—Security techniques—Information security management systems—Requirements), as highlighted by Lomas, when commenting on the synergy between the two standards (27001 and 15489) includes the word *authenticity*: "preservation of confidentiality, integrity and availability of information; in addition, other properties such as authenticity, accountability, non-repudiation, and reliability can also be involved" (Lomas, 2010).

Confidentiality and non-repudiation are exclusively within the realm of IA, linked to issues of security and the privacy of information. Whilst RM does not explicitly refer to either, it could be argued that non-repudiation is an aspect of reliability of a record. Further, RM constantly works within the confines of specific legislation, particularly freedom of information and data protection laws. These form a natural tension between what society considers appropriate in terms of accountability of organizations and confidentiality demanded by citizens and customers. Access rights and data security are key elements in the management of digital records, as is evidenced by their prominence in MoReq2010 specification (Modular Requirements for Records Systems) published by the DLM Forum Foundation (MoReq2010). In some respects, ISO 15489 itself was devised in order to address issues of non-repudiation. By following the principles and recommendations enshrined in the standard, it would prove more difficult to repudiate records provided as evidence of activities.

According to the international standard, *usability* refers to the retrievability, presentability, and interpretability of records. Availability, however, is applied to systems and the ability for these to be accessed at any time. The issue is one of emphasis and approach. Availability is very much in the operational sphere, i.e. if systems are unavailable to customers and there is a period of "downtime," whereas usability addresses how records are rendered, how accessible they are both to current and future users of systems. The accessibility of records and systems would appear to be a concern for both disciplines. The synergies and convergences of language and meaning are balanced by dissimilarities and homographs.

Digital Forensics (DF)

DF can perhaps further advance an approach, which seeks to facilitate the collection of cloud information. DF is defined as the use of scientifically derived and proven methods for the purpose of acquiring evidence derived from digital sources (Digi 01.2001). The process of acquiring evidence is largely agreed upon: identification, preservation, examination/analysis, and documentation/presentation (Stippich & Stippich, 2005; Ward, et al., 2007). It is a two-stage process of the technological—i.e., discovery, recovery, preservation, and control of electronic data or documentation—and the legal—i.e., the analysis, verification and presentation of e-evidence in court or in investigation. Reith, Carr, and Gunsch have extended this process to include Preparation, Approach Strategy, Collection, and Returning evidence (Reith, Carr, & Gunsch, 2002), in an effort to provide a non-technology specific methodology.

Forensics is an extremely complex procedure, fraught with potential dangers; booting up or shutting down a computer risks losing or overwriting data (contamination); the copy made must be an exact one and only the mirror image is used for analysis (Ward, Sipior, Volonino, & Peterson, 2007). The metadata, as well as the original data must be copied and all other sources of information established; removable media, backup tapes, logs, and deleted files are all potential evidence containers. File slack1, swap files and unallocated disk space all provide suitable locations for relevant information. This relates to not only the physical evidence but also the derived evidence. "Continuity means that the defence team has to be in a position to trace back from the helpful derived evidence to the raw material from which it has been drawn. This is not only to ensure that the evidence has not been altered during processing, but also to establish that no mistakes have been made by the analyst or the tools deployed—and also for the defence to be able to argue that other selections and analyses may produce very different results" (Sommer, 2012).

The principles of DF are akin to forensic science: freeze the scene, maintain continuity of evidence (chain of custody), and keep extensive contemporaneous notes of all actions undertaken. "At the most basic level, forensic practices are geared towards establishing the authenticity of files, conducting analysis to discern their characteristics and generating documentation about what has been done and when" (Kirschenbaum, Ovenden, & Redwine, 2010). The Association of Chief Police Officers (ACPO) UK Good Practice Guide (2003) has 4 principles on which it bases law enforcement CF: giving precedence to the inviolate nature of the evidence and the skill base and methodologies which must be employed to ensure its usefulness in court. The characteristics of evidence as viewed from the CF perspective focus on admissibility, authenticity, accuracy, completeness, and its ability to convince juries (Sommer, 2002). Admissibility refers to "the legal rules which determine whether potential evidence can be considered by a court" (Sommer, 2002). The Banker's Books Act 1891 introduced the concept of applying this to documents and section 24 of the Criminal Justice Act 1988 to "business documents," specifically. "...an admissible business record is a document created or received by a person in the course of a trade, business, profession or other occupation…; and the information contained in the document was supplied by a person…who had…personal knowledge of the matters dealt with" (Smith, 2007).

It may still be deemed inadmissible for a series of other reasons unrelated to its nature as digital evidence; however, if deemed admissible, it must then be "persuasive and probative" i.e. authentic, accurate, and complete. Authenticity is associated with the ability to link files and data to individuals and events through access controls, logging and crypto-based authentication. Accuracy refers to the computer processes, not data content, and completeness implies that the data "tells within its own terms a complete story of particular circumstances" (Sommer, 2009). Potential sources of evidence include cloud providers as third party record holders and the integrity and completeness of the tendered documents may require different forms of verification if they rest with an outsourcing agency (Sommer, 2012).

In the United States, in the case of Zubulake v.UDS Warburg (2003) five categories of stored data were identified: active online data, near-line data and offline storage/archive data, all of which were deemed reasonably accessible, and backup tapes and erased, fragmented or damaged data, which require more time and effort on the part of DF experts to access (Volonino, 2003). Recent changes to Federal Rules of Evidence (FRE) have sought to compensate for the unique issues specific to Electronically Stored Information (ESI), its prevalence and scope, and its impact on the discovery process. "The challenges confronting organizations in meeting e-discovery requirements underscores the necessity for proper ERM [Electronic Records Management] to reduce the complexity, time-consuming nature, and expense of the e-discovery process" (Ward, Sipior, Volonino, & Purwin, 2010). This includes the metadata associated with records and a duty to preserve "what I knows or reasonable should know is relevant in the action" (William T. Thompson Co. v. General Nutrition Corp., Inc., 1984; in Ward, et al., 2010). "The evidential nature of records derives from their creation in context of an action and their retention as evidence of that action and related processes" (Lacovino, 2006).

RECORDS MANAGEMENT AND DIGITAL FORENSICS

In this context, activities which may benefit recordkeeping and forensics intervention are not exclusively those in the law enforcement sphere. They include fraud, civil claims, contractual disputes, and internal investigations (Van Horenbeeck, 2005). A preventative approach to activities benefits a wider range of activities: due diligence, audit, regulative compliance, as well as more technical activities like redeployment, retirement or sanitisation of data, event reconstruction and monitoring, business continuity, troubleshooting anomalies, correcting vulnerabilities, verifying corporate procedures like disk wiping and encryption implementation (Stippich & Stippich, 2005). This proposed shift in focus has been illustrated by the use of forensic tools for arguably non-forensic purposes. Previous usage had been limited to police investigations after a computer crime was suspected. Now, if applied in a preventative manner, DF is being used for correcting vulnerabilities. One example is the process of reverse engineering…the ability to reverse engineer that specific transaction at any point in time to its original source, and being able to document that process for purposes of error correction or process examination (Gallegos, 2005). It is also being used to verifying corporate procedures like disk wiping and disk/network encryption implementation (Nickkel, 2006). There is a growing community of commentators who envisage a pre-planning stage, which would encourage organizations to collect evidence in advance (Volonino, 2003, Gallegos, 2005). This is a concept which will be explored in more detail later in relation to cloud computing.

There are different challenges that networked computing pose to the collection, storage, and retrieval of valid evidence on a network. A typical incident response presents time-pressured technicians with networks that provide little support for forensic data collection (Endicott-Popovsky & Frincke, 2006; Adding the fourth 'R': a systems approach to solving the hacker's arms race). The requirement to restore productivity often drives technicians to network restoration, even when the result is alteration of key files, limiting their value as courtroom evidence. Since there continues to be relatively limited interest in pursuing legal action, the rational choice for those administering networks often is the expedient one—restore productivity by restoring network functionality as rapidly as possible, and apply minimal effort to collecting and preserving forensically sound information for later courtroom use (Endicott-Popovsk & Frincke, 2006; Embedding forensic capabilities into networks: addressing inefficiencies in digital forensics investigations).

The following enumerates the challenges of collecting evidence across the life cycle of forensic data:

1. **Gather:** Identify where to find it and where to look in the system. The tools are designed for other purposes, but here they will be used as evidence of some activity.
2. **Store:** How to store and how long for. How to maintain consistency across systems. Each device maybe managed differently because they are designed for other purposes and short term use. In this case, it may be needed in the long term.
3. **Retrieve:** This can be difficult. It requires going back through the system and to find the data. It will not necessarily be in the same place each time because paths through the system are based on a most efficient algorithm and so a forensic specialist will need to piece together the path each time.
4. **Available:** It needs to be available when you need it and implies a consistent standard for storage, etc.
5. **Tamper-Proof:** It should be secure from tampering if it is to be admissible in court.
6. **Repeatable Process:** According to the US Rules of Evidence. The courts need to be able to rely on the process and it cannot therefore, be not *ad hoc*, but carefully designed and thought through.

The authors envisage the use of DF and RM in meeting the requirements for preserving evidence in networked environment. "The Records Continuum" and the theories of Frank Upward (Irons, 2006) have been employed to explore the relationships between these two disciplines. Upward's "continuum modeling is meant to work at this persisting conceptual level, modeling complexity not complication" (Upward, 2000). This tool relies on the structuration theory of Giddens and his "memory traces." Upward places axes or grain upon the backdrop of Giddens "time-space distanciation." He refers to an information-processing continuum, "space-time stretching processes related to the role of recorded information in embedding narratives into our existence. Giddens time-space distanciation continuum is represented in the model in the same order in which the points were presented in his work—interaction, routinisation, space-time distancing, and societal totalities" (Upward & Stillman, 2007).

By using the dimensions (represented by concentric circles in Figure 1) of create (interaction), capture (routinisation), organize (space-time distancing), and pluralize (societal totalities), as a backdrop for all record keeping activities, axes can be created that focus on any aspect of societal Record Keeping (RK). The record keeping dimensions remain as depicted. This constant rhythm of information processing applies to all activities—we create, capture into a RK system; we organize and ultimately pluralize in some way. Technology has, if anything, offered new and instant means by which our creations can be transformed and reused.

Figure 1 is the product of the integration of Upwards dimensions with digital forensics by one of the authors (Ferguson-Boucher, 2007). "It is precisely their topological constancy when dealing with such a complex and changing field as information and communication technologies that makes them useful as exploration and discovery tools within projects and research" (Upward & Stillman, 2007). The axes, or "grain," reflect the specific focus. The superimposition of a particular *grain* (Upward, 2005) on the process continuum requires the identification of the four major themes in the discipline of Digital Forensics.

The four major requirements proposed are:

1. Weight of Evidence
2. Curation of Evidence
3. Patterns of Evidence
4. Manifestation of Evidence

These requirements are mapped to the upward continuum to produce the model in Figure 1. It is proposed that this model could be used to ensure forensic readiness in the event of having to provide digital evidence to a court of law.

Figure 1. The digital forensics continuum

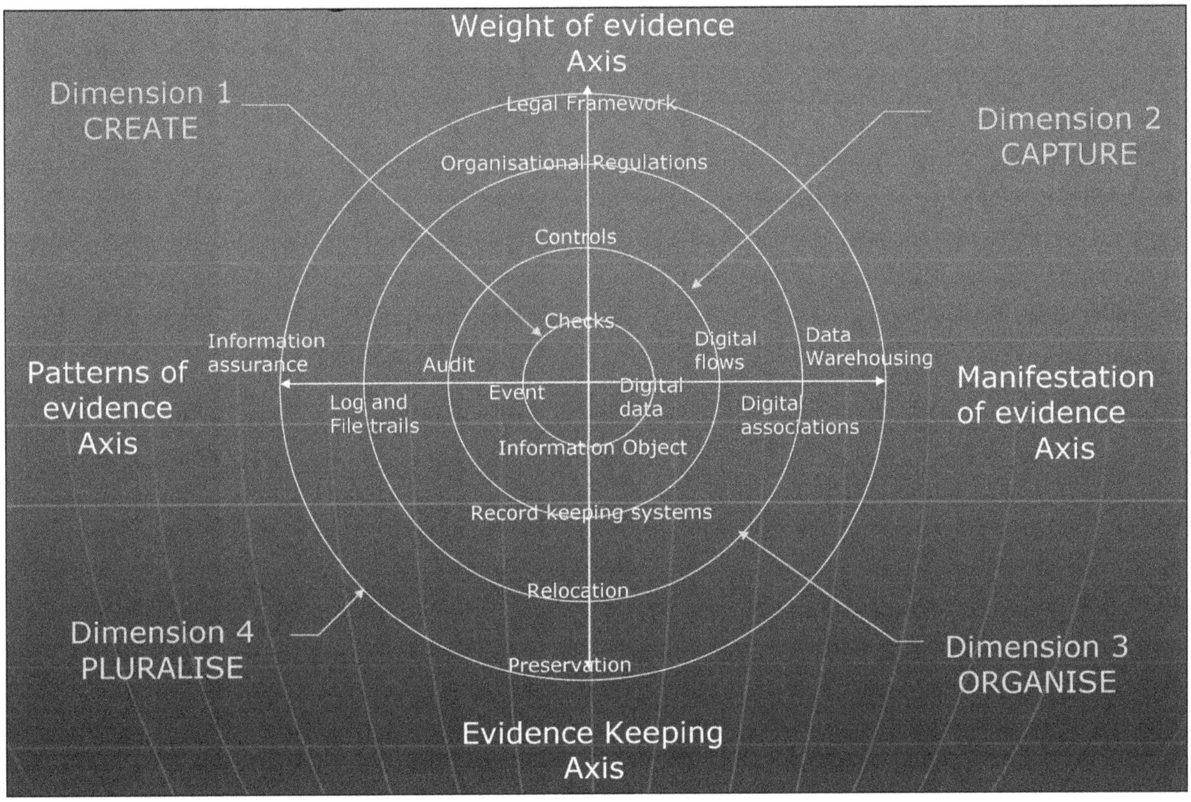

Perspectives: The Dimensions and Axes

The key to the DFC is the rhythm of the dimensions and their constancy in contrast to the axes, which can be realigned, in this case to align with digital forensics. In each dimension, the four points of intersection provide the focus for the consideration and application of RM and DF principles and tools. The creation dimension encompasses the information object itself, the data it contains, the checks that need to be applied to it and the specific events it relates to. The capture dimension encompasses the RK systems into which the information object has been registered and maintaining the flows of data which provide the context for the record. The controls are systematically applied, through policies and procedures and technical audit. In the organize dimension, the concern shifts to that of the continual relocation of records to ensure sustainability and integrity. The challenge is to ensure that the digital associations are not broken and that the organizational regulations are still applied and can be proven to have been applied. This is possible using the log and file trails, which are discernible for all activities relating to the contents of the record keeping system, serving to further support their ability to act as evidence. The leap into the pluralize dimension, which may occur at any time in the process, must ensure that the preservation of digital evidence has been achieved and that the demands of the legal framework have been met. Information assurance is used here to represent the existence of information in this wider public arena, in whatever space-time, and its ability to be held as trustworthy. The manifestation of this evidence in the digital environment is data warehousing (Ferguson-Boucher, 2007).

A second perspective is via the Axes rather than the dimensions. By focusing on these co-ordinates, each of the key aspects of DF is considered: the legislative, archival, assurance, and storage requirements of information that requires evidential status. Weight of Evidence refers to the assessing of ESI for evidential weight. This is given credence by the mechanisms of checks, controls, regulation, and legislation. The co-ordinates on the model are: Checks->controls->organizational regulations->legal framework. Curation of Evidence refers to the movement of the records through time in whatever form enables access and therefore recovery, i.e. RK systems and digital preservation/curation. The co-ordinates are Information Objects->Record keeping systems->relocation->preservation. Patterns of Evidence refer to the observable physical traces and imprints on the technological systems left by the happenings and events. The co-ordinates: Event->audit->log and file trails->information assurance. Finally, Manifestation of Evidence refers to that which emanates from the flows, associations, and digital evidence discoverable within entities. The co-ordinate are Digital data->digital flows->digital associations->data warehousing.

Perspectives: Lifecycles and Continuum

Having explored the relationship between DF and RM through the DFC, the Network Forensics Development Life Cycle was used to map the DFC to the forensic process. In previous papers, we have discussed the idea of embedding forensics in systems as a means to make this process more efficient (Endicott-Popovsky & Frincke, 2006; Embedding Forensic Capabilities into Networks: Addressing Inefficiencies in Digital Forensics Investigations). It has been suggested that embedding forensics would be accomplished through the Network Forensics Development Life Cycle (NFDLC) described below as a modification of NIST's ISDL, Information Systems Development Lifecycle. For systems to become forensically ready, therefore, a change in network protection strategies is required and selective implementation of NFR would benefit both legal action and documentation of due care in supporting the security and defensibility of network systems (Endicott-Popovsky & Frincke, 2007).

In the Initiation Phase, a preliminary risk assessment would include determination of what assets on the network would warrant digital forensic protection. The Acquisition/Development Phase ensures that the system requirements would include assurance that any device or procedure collecting forensic data on the system will do so in a manner acceptable in a courtroom. Implementation Phase would include base lining the network (or network segment) in order to understand how it functions; and network segments/devices involved in collecting evidence would be verified/calibrated in order to understand how they perform across a range of characteristics. In operation or maintenance terms, audits would be performed at regular intervals, and as the network grows and changes, confirming the results of previous baseline and verification/calibration tests. Finally, the Disposition Phase would concentrate of the chain of custody procedures, which would be incorporated to ensure preservation of potential evidence residing in a retired system.

To the extent that forensic capabilities are embedded in networks, forensic investigations most likely will require less investigator time and effort. It is expected that organizations will recognize that key data assets on the network warrant the protection that embedded forensic capabilities can provide. Establishing how to determine the rules for storing and maintaining digital forensic evidence collected on the network will be a key element of the process. Therefore, the mapping of the Digital Forensics Continuum (DFC: see Figure 1) against the NFDLC (see Figure 2) demonstrates the suitability of Forensic Readiness strategies as a mechanism for meeting some of the authenticity and evidential requirements for digital information. In Table 1, the phases of the ISDLC, with the NFDLC additions are mapped against the Axes of the DFC.

Sremack refers to the need for research into "using case specific knowledge of a system to determine what information is critical, thereby minimizing the amount of extraneous information that is collected and analyzed and guarantee that no critical data is missed" (Sremack, 2004). Sommer (2012) proposes the use of risk scenarios to elucidate the kinds of digital evidence that are likely to be required because "regular risk analysis often fails to identify the types of evidence that could and should be captured. In addition, various lower level situations—for example, disputes about transactions or employment—fall below the horizon of conventional security analysis." ISO 15489 catalogues an eight-stage procedure for RM programs, the first five of which relate to establishing the current position and identifying the *requirements* for records. This common objective of defining what records/information/data are *required* (records being defined as information, which is likely to be needed for evidential and legal purposes) can be achieved through a risk/warrant analysis.

By pre-identifying certain categories of evidence, on the basis of a risk assessment, it would be possible to provide special treatment for those requiring full DFR protection, at whatever stage of the process i.e. can be applied to the data itself, the flows between systems, the associations between related data without which it will be meaningless and storage/warehousing. Risks would be identified through the tools of the RM; namely the creation of an intellectual map of the organization and what it does, in order to gain intellectual control of content; an assessment of the legal, operational, and cultural requirements and the application of a program of destruction,

Figure 2. The NFDLC: a modification of NIST's ISDLC

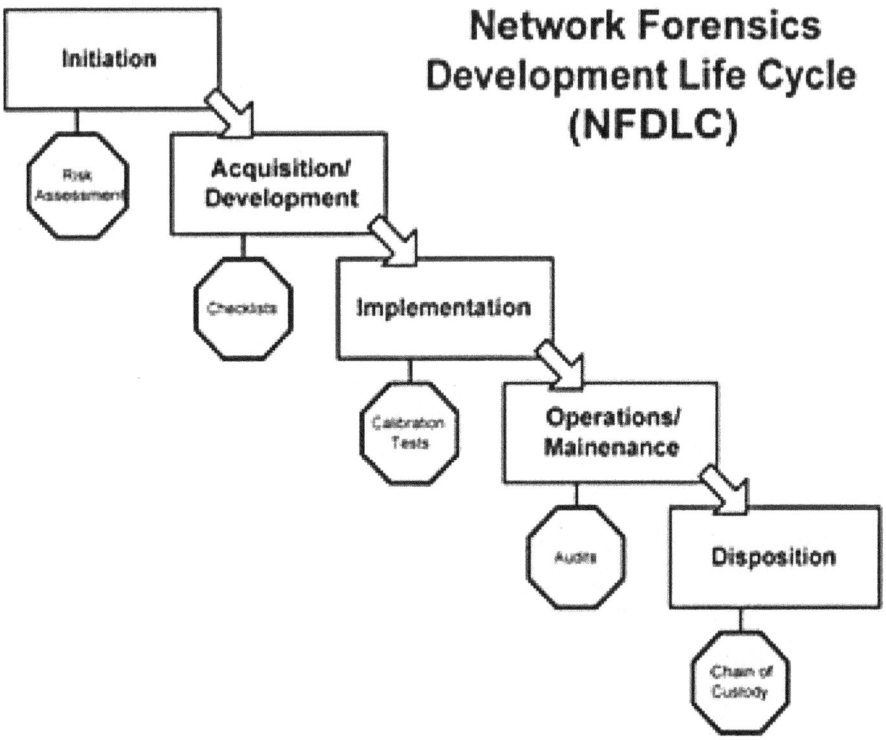

Table 1. Mapping of DFC with NFDLC and applicability of the DFC to phases of the NFDLC

PHASE	ISDLC Phases	NFDLC Additions	DFC and NFDLC
PHASE 1	Initiation Phase: preliminary risk assessment	Determine what warrants digital forensic protection	*Phase one: Risk and warrant – Manifestation* (digital data, data flows, data association and data storage/ warehousing)
PHASE 2	Acquisition/ Development Phase	Adhere to Rules of Evidence in system requirements	*Phase two: Rules of Evidence – Weight* (checks, controls, regulation and legislation)
PHASE 3	Implementation Phase	Perform baseline testing, network/ mechanism verification/ calibration tests	*Phase three and four: Validation and audit – Patterns* (events, audits, log and file trails and information assurance)
PHASE 4	Operation/ Maintenance Phase	Conduct verification/calibration audits	
PHASE 5	Disposition Phase	Incorporate chain of custody/ evidence preservation procedures	*Phase five: Preservation – Continuity* (Objects, systems, relocation and preservation)

archival and preservation strategies applied on that basis to each intellectual unit. The application and ongoing monitoring of regulation and legislation changes specific to information, lie with not only the RM profession, with its knowledge of compliance and retention for legal, operational and heritage purposes, but also the legal and computing profession, specifically those in DF since they have specialist and increasingly successful experience in the prosecution of crimes based on digital evidence (Van Horenbeeck, 2005). By making decisions as to the value and potential need for information to meet compliance and governance demands, the volume of records to be managed is lessened and the rationale for actions taken to manage them is made more transparent. The checks, controls, organization wide regulations should ultimately align with the legislative framework in which the organization operates. In a global environment, this can be particularly challenging and cross-disciplinary teams are essential in ensuring full cognisance of the related information, legal and operational implications.

One of the authors has in previous papers contended that a change from reactive to proactive practice not only requires a redefining IA to include forensics, but also a more focused approach to digital evidence and the requirements of a courtroom. Calibration testing may help to address issues of compliance with evidence standards for courtroom admissibility by ensuring expert testimony relating to the various network devices used to collect network traffic data cannot be compromised. Intrusion detection systems (IDS), for example, were not designed to act as evidence-gathering devices, rather as tools to assist decision-making. Modification would include uniform archiving and retention periods (rather than random) and sensor location near assets determined by risk analysis to warrant a strategic approach (Endicott-Popovsky & Frincke, 2007).

Disposition can also be readily addressed using existing skills and understanding in the RM and archival spheres. Digital preservation and curation is an area which has attracted considerable research interest as governments, academic institutions, and commercial organizations strive to ensure that the digital data and information they hold that will be required for the longer term can be guaranteed to be available. A key concept in the IA field, availability, could prove to be considerably more difficult in the longer term, without specific consideration of the sustainability and curation of digital evidence.

FORENSIC READINESS IN THE CLOUD

The following model resulted from the mapping of the DFC against the NFDLC in Table 1. It represents a single view of the issues and challenges of forensic evidence collection, with four areas of synthesis and four dimensions. The model provides a lens through which proactive evidence collection could be viewed and analyzed in relation to the Cloud (see Figure 3).

Having examined key concepts within the fields of RM, IA, and DF, and modelled DF against RM using the continuum to identify shared meaning, and further mapped the DFC against the concept of NFR, the resulting model provides a conceptual framework for exploiting RM and DF approaches in exploring how to collect evidence in the Cloud most efficiently and effectively. FRC offers a holistic approach to the issues and challenges that need to be taken into account when approaching forensics readiness in the Cloud. DF is not limited to investigation and detection, to purely reactive and retrospective activities. "Digital forensic practitioners must extend digital forensics knowledge and tools into cloud computing environments, and help cloud organizations, to establish a forensic capability in order to reduce cloud security risk" (Ruan, et al., 2011). FRC is achievable through consideration in a continual and cyclical fashion of all the facets presented in the model. The manifestation, weight, patterns, and continuity of digital evidence viewed across each of the dimensions of information processing presents an opportunity to fully address the issues of acquiring and managing digital evidence in the Cloud (see Figure 4).

The following sections make reference to the analysis of cloud benefits and challenges recently researched and published by Ruan et al. (2011). By applying the model to the specific issues raised in this research, its validity as a combined RM/DF conceptual tool can be explored. Initial consideration is given to Manifestation:

Figure 3. The model

Figure 4. High-level concerns

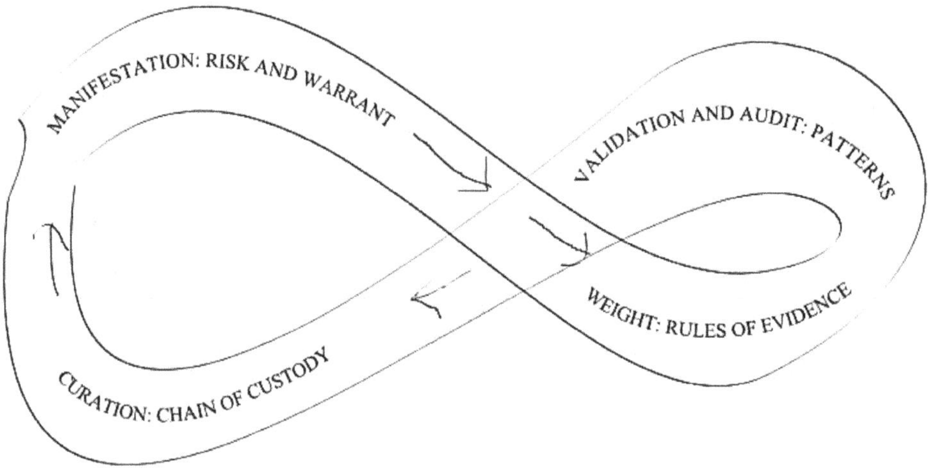

risk and warrant: what assets warrant digital forensics protection and Patterns: verification and audit: how this can be applied in the Cloud?

Ruan et al. have identified various uses to which cloud forensics can be put, including due diligence and regulatory compliance. The need to assist organizations in exercising due diligence and compliance using DF techniques to protect sensitive information and maintain records for audit purposes, using iGAFT to identify for example information held on customer transactions, contractual arrangements and details. These could be identifiable prior to the incident or request, earmarking them in advance and making decisions as to their suitability for the Cloud either in processing or storage and ultimately the level of forensic readiness required. Ruan et al. also refer to investigative uses, which would enable the provision of admissible evidence in court: Weight: rules of evidence. Whilst those listed are reactive, application and embedding prior to incidents occurring would ensure admissibility and incur less cost, for example, by companies building their own dedicated forensic servers in the Cloud, ready for use only when required. Ruan et al. mention log monitoring: "collecting, analyzing, and correlating log entries across multiple systems in the Cloud, assisting in auditing, due diligence, regulatory compliance, and other efforts." Again, a proactive approach to collecting this evidence in the Cloud would reap wider benefits, for example: "pay per use storage of logs allows more comprehensive logging without compromising performance" (Ruan, et al., 2011).

Perhaps the most significant challenge in the Cloud is Continuity: chain of custody: how to achieve preservation and continuity in the Cloud? Considerable work is being done across the disciplines and sector in this area. In the broadest sense, continuity can be defined as "the unbroken and consistent existence or operation of something over a period of time" or "a state of stability and the absence of disruption" (Oxford Dictionary Online). Digital Continuity specifically is defined as the ability to use digital information in the way that you need, for as long as you need (The National Archive, 2011). Cloud continuity is therefore a part of this wider challenge for the short and longer-term survival of our digital assets. A related concept and one which has particular relevance in the cloud ecology is that of sustainability, which is defined as "pertaining to a system that maintains its own viability by using techniques that allow for continual reuse" or "able to be maintained or kept going, as an action or process" (Dictionary.com). Data Resilience is also becoming a wider acknowledged term which reflects the cross disciplinary approaches to continuity in any digital environment including the Cloud. "Resilience is an increasingly important topic in the provision of digital services. Digital technology offers the prospect of '24/7' services, a model which can only be sustained through constant monitoring and planning to ensure continuity of service. Increasing demands on the networks, increasing concerns about security, and increasing economic and social consequences from their failure, makes resilience a pressing concern" (Digital Preservation Coalition). There are curation tasks, which could be carried out very effectively in the Cloud and would benefit from rapid provisioning, elasticity and widespread access. Equally the transfer of responsibility, i.e. stewardship of information and potential legal complexities can make decision relating to mission critical information difficult without a "preservation guarantee," namely proof of retrievability and possession (Aitken, McCann, McHugh, & Miller, 2012). This notion of trust and proof are being addressed by projects like DuraCloud, Timbus, and Ensure to name a few examples. DuraCloud offers a software platform and a brokering service and aims to mitigate risk by building a preservation solution on clouds with which researchers can engage relatively easily. The stated goal of predictability in the Cloud is built on the premise that the community has similar needs and this service, through a Web-based dashboard, "health checks," validation tools, file format ID, online backup, and open source/interoperability focus enables discovery/retrieval and a trustworthy solution (Cohen, Marberg, & Nagin, 2012).

Enabling Knowledge Sustainability Usability and Recovery for Economic Value (Ensure) considers the cost and value of differing solutions in managing the quality of digital objects over time and providing "content-aware long term data protection" (Edelstein, Factor, King, Risse, Salant, & Taylor, 2011). Timbus (Digital Preservation for Timeless Business Processes and services) on the other hand, focuses more on scenarios where the "important digital information to be preserved is the execution context with which data are processed, analyzed, transformed and rendered." Their 3 E's: Expediency of effort, Execution of process and Exhumation of assets resonates with many of the proactive evidence collection goals of the FRC, providing accessibility to business processes and aligning (in this case) preservation actions more fully with enterprise risk management and business continuity management (Edelstein, et al., 2011).

Business continuity planning continually refines and extends these protections to ensure that the right services are supplied to the right people at the right time. This aspect of managing cloud assets is one which brings together the Records and Information Governance players with a much wider team of specialists: archival and curation specialists, risk and business continuity colleagues and security and forensic teams. By looking at what is happening in the various fields with this as a concern, both in the heritage and commercial sectors, much can be gained from sharing knowledge, approaches and the technologies which are currently being explored and tested. The preservation, continuity, sustainability and resilience, of information held in the Cloud adds value and by managing each aspect of the model, information (not IT) governance issues are addressed, not in the narrow sense of control but in terms of value and alignment for business benefit.

ESI, for example, is discoverable and eliminating or obfuscating retrieval in an arbitrary manner, e.g. purging after a certain date or not having a coherent and transparent strategy is not acceptable in e-discovery cases. The legal and compliance requirements are stringent and the risk of failing to preserve is becoming a visible at board level. The solutions provided by the market for the Cloud are limited and from sectors with a collaborative and ECM rather than resilience focus. Once again using the Cloud as one of the most current and challenging aspects of the digital landscape, application to, and consideration of, each dimension can also facilitate comprehensive planning of evidence collection procedures for e-discovery and retrieval purposes.

Finally, if the model is mapped to challenges highlighted by Ruan et al., it is noted that they cluster predominantly around the organization and pluralise dimensions. Some correlate to the capture dimension, or routinization, for example, *weak registration,* a "control." This enables cyber-criminals to conceal their identity and therefore become harder to trace. The inability to exactly locate data in the Cloud means decreased access to forensic data, when it is on the move ("digital data" and "digital flows"). Audit logs and issues with time synchronisation across multiple physical machines, regions, between infrastructures and Web clients can hinder the collection of meaningful and defensible evidence ("audit"). Most, however, operate in the organize and pluralize or space-time distancing and societal totalities dimensions (see Figure 5).

Forensics is rarely considered when records are created and, indeed, captured into cloud systems. It is very much a 3rd and 4th dimension activity, i.e., its impact is felt at organizational and wider societal levels when information is being used subsequently for purposes for which it was not originally intended (both criminal and forensic).

In the Cloud, issues for the organise dimension include:

- **Relocation:** The process of relocating critical assets to ensure that they are managed more rigorously than none essential data is currently limited by the technological ability to audit cloud systems. What it is and where it resides remains key to the employment of FRC.
- **Digital Associations:** Unless proactively managed, there may be a decrease in access to metadata, which maintains the associations in the Cloud.
- **Organizational Regulations:** In the Cloud, the chains of dependency and levels of complexity are increasing and make regulations difficult to apply and monitor.
- **Log/File Trails:** There tends to be decreased access in the Cloud to log/file trails and also the unification of log formats is problematic.

In the pluralise dimension, which Upward refers to in terms of "space-time distanciation," where information processing and records exist as societal totalities:

- **Preservation:** Continuity of data can be compromised if access to deleted data is limited by the removal of mapping.
- **Digital Warehousing:** Storage and warehousing in the Cloud can prove problematic in an environment where data can be overwritten very quickly and conversely data are hard to erase completely in line with destruction schedules.
- **Legal Framework:** One of the more significant legal issues for storage and processing is confidentiality. Segregation is logical rather than physical. On the physical level, system audit logs, etc., are shared with multiple tenants.
- **Information Assurance:** Information assurance is hard to achieve. The hypervisor alone monitors and provisions the instance of servers run as virtual machines and this makes it a target for malicious activity. If targeted successfully, it is then difficult to ensure that evidence will be admissible.

Across both of these dimensions, investigations operate cross jurisdictionally. The distributed nature of the environment means legislation, assurance, preservation, and storage (all axes) can be compromised relatively easily. In addition,

Figure 5. Full model

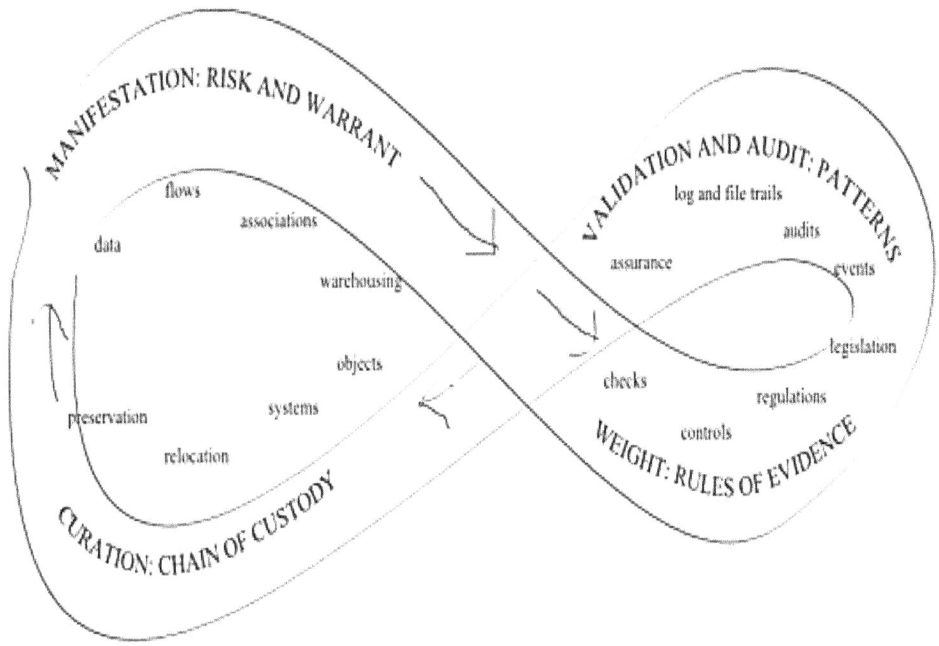

research into assurance, storage, and preservation technologies and legal frameworks are slow in comparison with the pace of technology and DF itself is in its infancy (Ruan, et al., 2011).

CONCLUSION

Records managers analyze the processes in an organization before they identify the record creating processes. Only then are they able to identify those that require "special treatment" (i.e. critical business assets in current business terms) (Cook, 2005). The level of accountability and the operational requirements of the organization and their perception of legal risk, compliance, and business decision-making will define which transactions require full evidential protection. Critically, the relationships between the essential business entities need to be apparent and maintained for current and future usage (Ferguson-Boucher & Endicott-Popovosky, 2008), not just the data themselves. RM offers tools which narrow down the number of information objects which should be considered critical—those more likely to be called upon in court or for evidential purposes, and therefore have a requirement to be trustworthy. Therefore, from a DF point of view, knowing where (i.e. in what processes) to apply the techniques more rigorously would be a benefit. FRC can then be applied to a more limited set of processes.

The fact that *create* and *capture* dimensions are underrepresented is significant. FRC would help to ensure that these dimensions were considered throughout the lifecycle by seeking to embed forensic capabilities. This is only achievable through planning prior to incidents and proactive evidence collection for high-risk data, information, and records. The "digital data" itself, the "digital object," the "event" to which it relates, and the "checks" that need to be applied to ensure its evidential value for all unintended uses forms the nucleus of the planning and implementation process. The "digital flows" between locations (cloud data is most vulnerable when in transit) the capture into a "RK system," i.e. one which can demonstrate sufficient control to provide digital evidence (this is not necessarily electronic document and records management systems), and the "audits" and "controls," which support both the legal and system requirements, are equally represented in the model. From an RM perspective, the ability to prove that techniques have been employed to assist in verifying a system—and that therefore the records that creates possess integrity and authenticity—is a significant benefit (Duranti, 2008).

We cannot know how, or which, single document/data set/ record will be challenged in the future, but we can seek to manage those most likely to be required. RM procedures are set up to determine which of these are most likely to be and to capture them into a system, which meets the necessary RK requirements (MoReQ2010). Making early decisions regarding risk to the organization and to the wider society of keeping, or not keeping, records and by using RM and DF practices and procedures to ensure their reliability and accessibility may reduce discovery, spoliation and preservation costs in the Cloud. This chapter has looked in detail at the concept of Records and RM in the Cloud. It has considered the need for the Retrieval of digital evidence from risk and readiness perspectives. Ultimately, it has provided a potential Response via the FRC model, as a conceptual framework for making decisions about how to identify and manage increasing quantities of evidence collected in the Cloud, by identifying which RM and DF approaches and processes might be most useful in contributing to a structure for information governance and assurance in the Cloud.

In a court of law each item of evidence is examined in its own right and then in conjunction with other items of evidence before making a judgment. This approach to providing more dependable digital evidence on the basis of employing FRC, may add to the collection of evidence and the reliability of cloud information provided. RM can assist in narrowing the volume and focusing the lens on critical data assets that have network access.

Having developed a conceptual framework, areas for further research have been identified. These will form the basis for our future research.

- More detailed consideration of how tools like iGAFT, Retention Schedules and Appraisal and Disposition Strategies can be applied in a cloud environment.
- Examination of current digital preservation methods and theory to enable application of evidence collected as part of FRC to ensure authenticity, availability, and resilience of information required for the longer term.

REFERENCES

Aitken, B., McCann, P., McHugh, A., & Miller, K. (2012). *Digital curation and the cloud. Technical Report*. New York, NY: Digital Curation Centre.

Association of Chief Police Officers. (2003). *Good practice guide for computer based electronic evidence* (Version 3). London, UK: NHTCU. Retrieved 15 August, 2012 from http://www.met.police.uk/pceu/documents/ACPOguidelinescomputerevidence.pdf

Bailey, S. (2008). *Managing the crowd: rethinking records management for the web 2.0 world*. London, UK: Facet Publishing.

Benfell, P. (2007). Great expectations: Heliocentrism, semantics and records management. *Records Management Journal*, 7(2), 74–81. doi:10.1108/09565690710757878

Censer, M. (2011). Major players zero in on cloud computing market. *The Washington Post*. Retrieved 15 August, 2012 from http://www.washingtonpost.com/business/capitalbusiness/major-players-zero-in-on-cloud-computing-market/2011/04/27/AFN1slTF_story.html

Clanchy, M. T. (1993). *From memory to written record: England 1066-1307*. Oxford, UK: Blackwell Publishing.

Continuity. (2012). *Oxford dictionary online*. Retrieved August 15, 2012 from http://oxforddictionaries.com/words/about

Convery, N. (2010). Cloud computing report. *Archives and Records Association*. Retrieved 15 August, 2012 from Retrieved 15 August, 2012 from http://www.archives.org.uk/images/documents/Cloud_computing_report_final-1.pdf

Convery, N., & Ferguson-Boucher, K. (2011). Storing information in the cloud – A research project. *Journal of the Society of Archivists*, *32*(2), 221–239. doi:10.1080/00379816.2011.619693

Cook, T. (2005). Macro-appraisal in theory and practice: origins, characteristics and implementation in Canada, 1950-2000. *Archival Science*, *5*(2-4), 101–161. doi:10.1007/s10502-005-9010-2

Dardick, G. S. (2010). Cyber forensics assurance. In *Proceedings of the 8th Australian Digital Forensics Conference*. Perth, Australia: Edith Cowan University.

Digi 01. (2001). *A road map for digital forensics research*. Paper presented at the First Digital Forensic Research Workshop. Utica, NY. Retrieved 15 August, 2012 from http://www.dfrws.org/2001/dfrws-rm-final.pdf

Digital Preservation Coalition. (2012). *Website newsroom*. Retrieved 15 August, 2012 from http://www.dpconline.org/newsroom/not-so-new/852-digital-resilience-and-digital-preservation-registration-opens-for-members

DLM Forum Foundation. (2011). *MoReq2010®: Modular requirements for records systems — Volume 1: Core services & plug-in modules*. Retrieved 15 August, 2012 from http://moreq2010.eu/

Duranti, L. (2008). *It's all about trust: The reliability, accuracy and authenticity of digital records*. Retrieved 15 August, 2012 from http://www.liv.ac.uk/lucas/Archived_News_and _Events.htm

Duranti, L. (2009). From digital diplomatics to digital records forensics. *Archivaria*, *68*, 39–66.

Edelstein, O., Factor, M., King, R., Risse, T., Salant, E., & Taylor, P. (2011). Evolving domains, problems and solutions for long term digital preservation. In *Proceedings of the 8th International Conference on Preservation of Digital Objects (iPRES 2011)*. Singapore, Singapore: iPRES.

Endicott-Popovsky, B., & Frincke, D. (2006). Adding the fourth 'R': A systems approach to solving the hacker's arms race. In *Proceedings of the Thirty-Ninth Annual Hawaii International Conference on System Sciences: Symposium: Skilled Human-intelligent Agent Performance: Measurement, Application and Symbiosis*. Kauai, HI: IEEE.

Endicott-Popovsky, B. E., & Frincke, D. A. (2006). Embedding forensic capabilities into networks: Addressing inefficiencies in digital forensics investigations. In *Proceedings of the 7th IEEE Workshop on Information Assurance*. West Point, NY: U.S. Military Academy.

Endicott-Popovsky, B. E., & Frincke, D. A. (2007). Embedding Hercule Poirot in networks: Addressing inefficiencies in digital forensic investigations In *Proceedings of the Human Computer Interact (HCI) Conference*. Beijing, China: HCI.

Ferguson-Boucher, K. (2007). *ESI: Without a trace: A comparative study of records management and digital forensics*. (Dissertation). Aberystwyth University. Aberystwyth, UK.

Ferguson-Boucher, K. (2011). Cloud computing: A records and information management perspective. *IEEE Security and Privacy*, *9*(6), 63–66. doi:10.1109/MSP.2011.159

Ferguson-Boucher, K., & Endicott-Popovosky, B. (2008). *Digital forensics and records management: What we can learn from the discipline of archiving*. Paper presented at the Security, Compliance and Risk Management Institute Conference: Where Information Technology, Law and Risk Management Converge. Seattle, WA.

Gallegos, F. (2005). Computer forensics: An overview. *Information Systems Control Journal*, *6*, 13–16.

Government, H. M. (2011). *Government cloud strategy*. Retrieved 15 August, 2012 from http://www.cabinetoffice.gov.uk/sites/default/files/resources/government-cloud-strategy_0.pdf

Harris, V. (2000). Law, evidence and electronic records: A strategic perspective from the global periphery. *Comma: International Journal on Archives*, *41*, 29–43.

Hurley, C. (2011). *Strength below and grace above: the structuration of records*. Retrieved 15 August, 2012 from http://www.infotech.monash.edu.au/research/groups/rcrg/publications/strength-below.pdf

Irons, A. (2006). Computer forensics and records management—Compatible disciplines. *Records Management Journal*, *16*(2), 111. doi:10.1108/09565690610677463

ISO 15489-1:2001. (2001). *Information and documentation: Records management – Part 1: General*. Retrieved from http://www.iso.org

Jonker, A. (2011). *The past that wasn't*. Paper presented at the International Symposium on the Law of Unintended Consequences: The Right to be Forgotten, the Duty to Remember. Vancouver, Canada. Retrieved 15 August, 2012 from http://www.slais.ubc.ca/people/students/student-groups/aca/symposium2011/index.html

Kirschenbaum, M., Ovenden, R., & Redwine, G. (2010). *Digital forensics and born-digital content in cultural heritage collections*. Washington, DC: Council on library and information resources. Retrieved 15 August, 2012 from http://www.clir.org/pubs/reports/pub149/pub149.pdf

KMPG. (2012). *Government: Exploring the cloud: A global study of government's adoption of the cloud*. Retrieved 15 August, 2012 from http://www.kpmg.com/Global/en/IssuesAndInsights/ArticlesPublications/Documents/exploring-cloud.pdf

Lacovino, L. (2006). *Recordkeeping, ethics and law: Regulatory models, participant relationships and rights and responsibilities in the online world*. Dordrecht, The Netherlands: Springer.

Laudon, K. C., & Laudon, J. P. (1999). *Essentials of management information systems*. Englewood Cliffs, NJ: Prentice Hall.

Lomas, E. (2010). Information governance: information security and access within a UK context. *Records Management Journal*, *20*(2), 182–198. doi:10.1108/09565691011064322

Maconachy, W. V., Schou, C. D., Ragsdale, D., & Welch, D. (2001). A model for information assurance: An integrated approach. In *Proceedings of the 2001 IEEE Workshop on Information Assurance and Security,* (pp. 306-310). West Point, NY: United States Military Academy.

McCumber, J. (1991). Information systems security: A comprehensive model. In *Proceedings of the 14th National Computer Security Conference*. Baltimore, MD: National Institute of Standards and Technology.

National Archives. (2011). *Identifying information assets and business requirements*. Retrieved 15 August, 2012 from http://www.nationalarchives.gov.uk/documents/information-management/identify-information-assets.pdf

National Security Agency. (1999). *National security telecommunication and information systems security instruction no 4009. National Information Systems Security (INFOSEC) Glossary*. Washington, DC: NSA.

Nickkel, B. J. (2006). *The role of digital forensics within a corporate organization*. Paper presented at the Gartner IT Security Summit. London, UK.

Reith, M., Carr, C., & Gunsch, G. (2002). An examination of digital forensic models. *International Journal of Digital Evidence*, *1*(3).

Ruan, K., Carthy, J., Kechadi, T., & Crosbie, M. (2011). *Cloud forensics: An overview*. Retrieved 15 August, 2012 from http://cloudforensicsresearch.org/publication/Cloud_Forensics_An_Overview_7th_IFIP.pdf

Shepherd, E. (1994). Records management in Britain – A review of some developments in professional principles and practice. *Business Archives*, *67*, 13–25.

Shepherd, E., & Yeo, G. (2003). *Managing records: A handbook of principles and practice*. London, UK: Facet Publishing. doi:10.1108/00220410310506349

Smith, G. J. H. (2007). *Internet law and regulation*. London, UK: Sweet and Maxwell.

Sommer, P. (1998). *Digital footprints: Assessing computer evidence* (*Special Edition*, pp. 61–78). Criminal Law Review.

Sommer, P. (2002). Digital evidence: Emerging problems in forensic computing. *University of Cambridge*. Retrieved 15 August, 2012 from http://www.cl.cam.ac.uk/research/security/seminars/2002/2002-05-21.pdf

Sommer, P. (2009). *Directors and corporate advisors' guide to digital investigations and evidence*. London, UK: Information Assurance Advisory Council.

Sommer, P. (2012). *Digital evidence, digital investigations and e disclosure: A guide to forensic readiness for organizations, security advisors and lawyers*. London, UK: Information Assurance Advisory Council.

Sremack, J. (2004). *Formalizing of analysis: A proof-based methodology*. (Master of Science Thesis). North Carolina State University. Raleigh, NC.

Stippich, M. J., & Stippich, C. J. (2005). A holistic perspective on the science of computer forensics. *Journal of Information Privacy and Security*, *1*(1), 27–39.

Sustainable. (2000). *Dictionary.com*. Retrieved 15 August, 2012 from http://dictionary.reference.com/browse/sustainable

Upward, F. (2000). Modeling the continuum as paradigm shift in recordkeeping and archiving processes and beyond – A personal reflection. *Records Management Journal*, *10*(3), 121. doi:10.1108/EUM0000000007259

Upward, F. (2005). The records continuum. In McKemmish, S. (Eds.), *Archives: Recordkeeping in Society*. New South Wales, Australia: Charles Stuart University.

Upward, F., & Stillman, L. (2007). Community informatics and the information processing continuum. In Stillman, L., & Johanson, G. (Eds.), *Constructing and Sharing Memory: Community Informatics, Identity and Empowerment* (pp. 318–332). Cambridge, UK: Cambridge Scholars Publishing.

Van Horenbeeck, M. (2005). *Forensic investigation and its relationship with information assurance and corporate governance*. (Certificate of Multidisciplinary Forensic Investigation Thesis). Katholieke Universiteit Leuven. Flanders, Belgium.

Volonino, L. (2003). Electronic evidence and computer forensics. *Communications of the Association for Information Systems*, *12*(27), 457–468.

Ward, B. T., Sipior, J. C., Volonino, L., & Peterson, G. (2007). Computer forensics, e-discovery, and spoliation: Impact of the new federal rules. In *Proceedings of the Americas Conference on Information Systems*. Keystone, CO: IEEE.

Ward, B. T., Sipior, J. C., Volonino, L., & Purwin, C. (2010). *Electronic discovery rules and electronic evidence: A United States perspective*. Paper presented at the European and Mediterranean Conference on Information Systems. Abu Dhabi, UAE.

ADDITIONAL READING

Adam, S. (2010). Preserving authenticity in the digital age. *Library Hi Tech*, *28*(4), 595–604. doi:10.1108/07378831011096259

Alberts, I., Schellinck, J., Eby, C., & Marleau, Y. (2010). Bridging functions and processes for records management. *Canadian Journal of Information and Library Science*, *34*(4), 365–390. doi:10.1353/ils.2010.0010

Askhoj, J., Sugimoto, S., & Nagamori, M. (2011). Preserving records in the cloud. *Records Management Journal*, *21*(3), 175–187. doi:10.1108/09565691111186858

Bell, A. (2010). Understanding data and information systems for recordkeeping. *Journal of the Society of Archivists*, *31*(2), 232–235. doi:10.1080/00379816.2010.507924

Castillo-Soto, A., & Baker, G. (2011). A new approach to records management with the information workplace platform. *Records Management Journal*, *21*(3), 205–213. doi:10.1108/09565691111186876

Chen, H., Nunes, M. B., Zhou, L., & Peng, G. C. (2011). Expanding the concept of requirements traceability: The role of electronic records management in gathering evidence of crucial communications and negotiations. *Aslib Proceedings: New Information Perspectives*, *63*(2/3), 168–187.

Cook, T. (2005). Macroappraisal in theory and practice: Origins, characteristics, and implementation in Canada, 1950-2000. *Archival Science*, *5*, 101–161. doi:10.1007/s10502-005-9010-2

Cumming, K., & Findlay, C. (2010). Digital recordkeeping: Are we at tipping point? *Records Management Journal*, *20*(3), 265–278. doi:10.1108/09565691011095292

Davenport, T. H., & Prusak, L. (1997). *Information ecology: Mastering the information and knowledge environment*. Oxford, UK: Oxford University Press.

DIRKS. (2003). *Strategies for documenting government business: The DIRKS manual*. New South Wales, Australia: State Records Authority of New South Wales. Retrieved 19/08/2012 www.records.nsw.au/recordkeeping/dirks-manual/introducing-the-dirks-methodology/dirks-methodology-and-manual

Finnell, J. (2011). Records management theory's dilemma: What is a record? *Library Philosophy and Practice*. Retrieved from http://www.webpages.uidaho.edu/~mbolin/finnell.htm

Gilliland, A. J. (2011). Reflections on the value of metadata archaeology for recordkeeping in a global, digital world. *Journal of the Society of Archivists*, *32*(1), 103–118.

Ismail, A., & Jamaludin, A. (2009). Towards establishing a framework for managing trusted records in the electronic environment. *Records Management Journal*, *19*(2), 135–146. doi:10.1108/09565690910972084

Jafari, M., Safavi-Naini, R., & Sheppard, N. P. (2011). A rights management approach to protection of privacy in a cloud of electronic health records. In *Proceedings of the 11th Annual ACM Workshop on Digital Rights Management*, (pp. 23-30). New York, NY: ACM Press.

James, R. (2010). Records management in the cloud? Records management IS the cloud! *Business Information Review*, *27*(3), 179–189. doi:10.1177/0266382110377060

Lappin, J. (2010). What will be the next records management orthodoxy? *Records Management Journal*, *20*(3), 252–264. doi:10.1108/09565691011095283

Man, E. (2010). A functional approach to appraisal and retention scheduling. *Records Management Journal*, *20*(1), 104–116. doi:10.1108/09565691011039870

Mas, S., Maurel, D., & Alberts, I. (2011). Applying faceted classification to the personal organization of electronic records: Insights into the user experience. *Archivaria*, *72*, 29–59.

Milne, C. (2010). Developing information architecture through records management classification techniques. *Aslib Proceedings: New Information Perspectives*, *62*(4-5), 366–386.

Montana, J. (2010). *How to develop a retention schedule*. Overland Park, KS: ARMA International.

Moss, M. (2010). Without the data, the tools are useless: Without the software, the data is unmanageable. *Journal of the Society of Archivists*, *31*(1), 1–14. doi:10.1080/00379811003658443

National Archives. (2012). *Managing digital records without an electronic records management system*. Retrieved 19/08/2012 from www.nationalarchives.gov.uk/documents/information-management/managing-electronic-records-without-an-erms-publication-edition.pdf

Roitblat, H., Kershaw, A., & Oot, P. (2010). Document categorization in legal electronic discovery: Computer classification vs manual review. *Journal of the American Society for Information Science and Technology*, *61*(1), 70–80. doi:10.1002/asi.21233

Saffady, W. (2009). *Managing electronic records* (4th ed.). London, UK: Facet Publishing.

Serewicz, L. (2010). Do we need bigger buckets or better search engines? The challenge of unlimited storage and semantic web search for records management. *Records Management Journal*, *20*(2), 172–181. doi:10.1108/09565691011064313

Sommer, P. (2007). *Identity management systems: The forensic dimension*. Paper presented at the 19th Annual First Conference. Seville, Spain. Retrieved 15 August, 2012 from http://www.first.org/conference/2007/papers/sommer-peter-slides.pdf

Stuart, K., & Bromage, D. (2010). Current state of play: Records management and the cloud. *Records Management Journal*, *20*(2), 217–225. doi:10.1108/09565691011064340

Tough, A. (2011). Accountability, open government and record keeping: Time to think again? *Records Management Journal*, *21*(3), 225–236. doi:10.1108/09565691111186894

Trace, C. B. (2011). Beyond the magic to the mechanism: Computers, materiality and what it means for records to be born digital. *Archivaria*, *72*, 5–27.

Upward, F., McKemmish, S., & Reed, B. (2011). Archivists and changing social and information spaces: A continuum approach to recordkeeping and archiving in online cultures. *Archivaria*, *72*, 197–237.

Ward, B. T., Purwin, C., Sipior, J. C., & Volonino, L. (2009). Recognizing the impact of e-discovery amendments on electronic management. *Information Systems Management*, *26*(4), 350–356. doi:10.1080/10580530903245721

Wettenhall, R. (2010). Organisational amnesia: A serious public sector reform issue. *International Journal of Public Sector Management*, *24*(1), 80–96. doi:10.1108/09513551111099235

Xie, S. L. (2011). Building foundations for digital records forensics: A comparative study of the concept of reproduction in digital records management and digital forensics. *The American Archivist*, *74*(2), 576–599.

Yeo, G. (2008). Concepts of record (2): Prototypes and boundary objects. *The American Archivist*, *71*(1), 118–143.

KEY TERMS AND DEFINITIONS

Cloud Computing (CC): A model for enabling ubiquitous, convenient, on-demand network access to a shared pool of configurable computing resources (e.g., networks, servers, storage, applications, and services) that can be rapidly provisioned and released with minimal management effort or service provider interaction.

Digital Forensics (DF): The application of science to the identification, collection, examination, and analysis of data while preserving the integrity of the information and maintaining a strict chain of custody for the data.

Forensic Readiness in the Cloud (FRC): Maximizing the ability of the Cloud to collect credible digital evidence while minimizing the cost of an incident response.

Information Assurance (IA): Measures that protect and defend information and information systems by ensuring their availability, integrity, authentication, confidentiality, and non-repudiation. These measures include providing for restoration of information systems by incorporating protection, detection, and reaction capabilities.

Network Forensic Readiness (NFR): Maximizing the ability of an environment to collect credible digital evidence while minimizing the cost of an incident response.

Record Keeping (RK): Making and maintaining complete, accurate, and reliable evidence of business transactions in the form of recorded information.

Records Management (RM): The field of management responsible for the efficient and systematic control of the creation, receipt, maintenance, use, and disposition of records, including the processes for capturing and maintaining evidence of, and information about, business activities and transactions in the form of records.

ENDNOTES

1. File slack is "the unused space at the end of the file or the hard drive" and swap files are created when "Windows moves a portion to the hard drive, creating virtual RAM (Ward, et al., 2007).

Chapter 6
Security Architecture and Forensic Awareness in Virtualized Environments

Diane Barrett
American Military University, USA

ABSTRACT

Just about every technology magazine and article published today mentions virtualization or cloud computing. Technically, the two are different but very much intertwined. When environments use virtualization, there are artifacts an investigator can request that may provide valuable information. The content of this chapter explores the virtualization process, types of virtualized environments, and the part virtualization plays in cloud computing. A section will be included that presents case scenarios to demonstrate the type of evidence gathered in each environment for forensic investigations. A final section will include recommendations for additional areas of research in the area of investigating environments containing virtualization integration with cloud environments.

INTRODUCTION

With more emphasis placed on going green and power becoming more expensive, virtualization offers cost benefits by decreasing the number of physical machines required within an environment. A virtualized environment offers reduced support by making testing and maintenance easier. On the client side, the ability to run multiple operating environments allows a machine to support applications and services for an operating environment other than the primary environment (Barrett, 2010). Since most organization look to maximize machine utilization while reducing administrative costs, virtualization decreases upgrade costs and allows more uniformity in desktop environments.

In the third quarter of 2011, roughly 40% of all servers were virtualized with 80% of surveyed organizations planning to increase virtualization in the next year (Veeam, 2011). According to Gartner, the global desktop virtualization market will reach 65.7 billion unit sales, equivalent to about 40% of the worldwide business desktop market, in 2013 (Gartner, 2011). At the 2011 Gartner

DOI: 10.4018/978-1-4666-2662-1.ch006

Copyright © 2013, IGI Global. Copying or distributing in print or electronic forms without written permission of IGI Global is prohibited.

Symposium IT/Expo, managing vice president and infrastructure teams, chief of research, David Cappuccio, said that virtualization would ultimately drive more companies to treat IT like a business. Virtualization is a critical component in increasing density and vertically scaling data centers. When utilized properly, average server performance can reach 40% to 50%, yielding huge benefits in floor space and energy savings (Cooney, 2012). 4- and 8-core processors are common in regular systems, with 16 and 32 core processors common in higher end systems. This provides a very conducive environment for virtualization.

According to Gartner, in 2011 more than 20 percent of organizations began storing customer-sensitive data in hybrid architecture and by 2016, more than 50 percent of Global 1000 companies will have stored customer-sensitive data in the public cloud (Gartner, 2011). The venture into virtualization has encouraged the use of this technology to extend as far as mobile devices. Estimates are that in 2012, more than half of all new smartphones shipped will include virtualization support. One such example is VMware's Horizon Mobile. An installed guest operating system in a virtual machine keeps the users work and personal environments, applications, and data isolated. LG and Samsung have both agreed to build phones containing VMware's mobile hypervisor. In late 2011, Verizon entered into an agreement with VMware to sell the virtualized Android smartphones. The phones, expected to hit the market shortly, include a virtualized SIM (Higgenbotham, 2011).

These predictions along with the fast pace as which technology is moving, means encountering a virtualized environment during a forensic investigation will become the norm as opposed to the exception. The relationship between virtualization and cloud computing is a complex one. Not all virtualized environments are cloud environments but generally cloud computing includes virtualized components. Virtualized components include everything from servers to routers.

Technological advances in virtualization, cloud computing and portable desktop environments leave very little trace on the host system. Locating pertinent evidence is no longer as simple as examining the local hard drive. Often the investigator finds only small traces of evidence on the host machine, provided the investigator knows how to recognize virtualization products. Virtualization, in-memory computing, and cloud computing will all affect the current forensics investigative processes, forcing the community to produce new methods and procedures for investigations in this type of environment.

There is not a lot of literature published on examining virtual environments. The first published text to address the examination of virtualized environments is Barrett and Kipper's (2010) Virtualization and Forensics. While the book does not go into detail about the examination of more complex environments, it does provide a forensic investigator with basic information needed to recognize various environments and the associated files.

Fiterman and Durick (2010) delved into the examination of ESXi environments by co-authoring an article published in Digital Forensics Magazine titled 'Ghost in the Machine.' In addition to the article, Durick maintains a blog where he posts additional virtual machine examination research. Bares (2009) presented a paper at the IEEE International Conference on Security and Intelligence Informatics that explored how the physical memory of a machine is actually allocated in the use of virtual machines.

To emphasize the issue with lack of research in this area, Haletky (2009) observed that despite the increasing number of critical applications and secure data on virtual infrastructures, few forensics tools exist to be sure a VM is locked down, or find out why it wasn't once it's been compromised. Although there is some published research on the examination of virtual environments, a need exists for conducting more research especially in more complex environments. Peppered throughout the chapter are correlations to the techniques and concerns expressed in the writings and observations of the above-mentioned authors. The information contained herein is an attempt to offer a better understanding of how virtualization happens, where different products store information, and how to investigate virtualized environments using case examples.

BACKGROUND

Virtualization has been in use since the 1960s, but recently has garnered attention as a way to take advantage of the more robust processing power provided by today's computers. Virtualization allows a component to run in an environment other than the native environment. The component can be items such as an application, operating system or a piece of hardware.

In order for virtualization to happen, an intermediary called a hypervisor is used (Ali & Meghanathan, 2011). The hypervisor controls the virtual environment's access to the physical computer's processors and memory. Further explanation of these concepts is provided in the next section.

Due to the nature of the way virtualization works, the forensic examination of the environment may happen differently than the forensic processes normally used. In a live examination, the processes more closely resemble the examination of a non-virtualized environment. In a dead drive analysis and an actual virtual machine acquisition, the processes differ between virtualized and non-virtualized environment.

The Virtualization Process

In order to have a discussion on virtualization, there must be a distinction made between a physical machine and a virtual machine. A physical machine is a hardware-based device such as a personal computer, server, or router running at the electronic level as opposed to the logical level. Physical machines operate with much more direct access to the hardware, whereas users of virtual environments relate to the data accessed based on the name of the virtual machine file.

The fundamental concept of a Virtual Machine (VM) revolves around a software application that behaves as if it were its own device. This concept originates in the job sharing mechanism prominent in mainframes. It was around this time that, Popek and Goldberg (1974) described a virtual machine as an efficient, isolated duplicate of a real machine.

In the case of operating system virtualization, the VM application or guest runs its own self-contained operating system within the actual host machine. Virtual machine software products allow an entire stack of software to be encapsulated in a VM. The encapsulation starts at the operating system and runs all the way up to the application level (Barrett, 2010). This type of technology has the ability to run more than one virtual machines on a single physical computer if the computer has sufficient processing power, memory, and storage. Figure 1 shows the premise behind virtualization.

Individual virtual machines are isolated from each other to provide a compartmentalized environment (Barrett & Kipper, 2010). Each virtual machine contains its own environment just like a physical server and includes an operating system, applications, and networking capabilities. The virtual machine management happens individually, similar to a physical environment. Unlike a physically partitioned machine, virtual machine products allow multiple operating systems to exit on one partition. The virtual operating system can be any operating system as so can the host operating system (Barrett, 2010).

In order for virtualization to happen, a hypervisor is used. A hypervisor or Virtual Machine Monitor (VMM) is a virtualization platform that provides more than one operating systems to run on a host computer at the same time (Barrett, 2008). There are a few different types of hypervisors including bare metal, hardware assist, and hosted.

Figure 1. Concept of virtualization

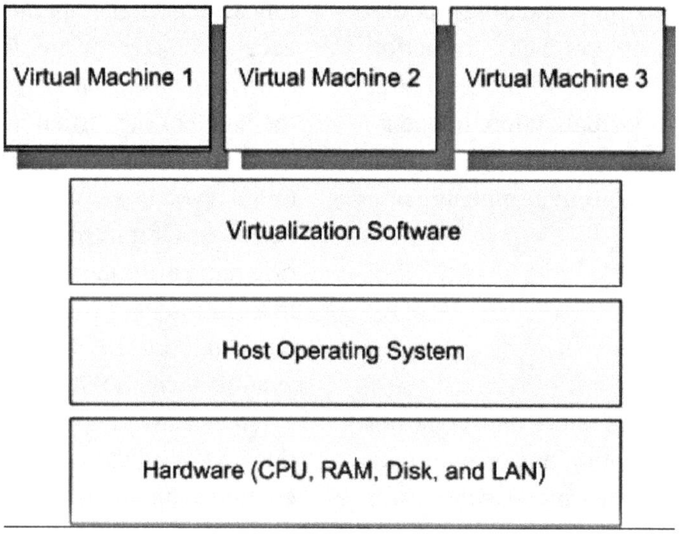

Virtualization Models

There are several virtualization models including full virtualization, paravirtualization, and operating system-level virtualization. Full virtualization is a virtualization technique that completely simulates the underlying hardware using a hypervisor to provide each VM with all the services of the physical system. Users can run multiple different guest Operating Systems (OSs) simultaneously and the OSs are separated from each other so that one does not know about the other (Fowler, 2009).

Paravirtualization allows the systems to know about one another level. The OS kernel acts as a bridge between the applications and the processing done at the hardware. Each operating system manages its own resource needs. Paravirtualization requires porting of the guest operating system. Paravirtualization involves modifying the OS kernel to replace nonvirtualizable instructions with hypercalls that communicate directly with the virtualization layer hypervisor. The hypervisor also provides hypercall Application Binary Interfaces (ABI) for other critical kernel operations such as memory management and interrupt handling (VMware, 2007). Figure 2 shows the concept of paravirtualization.

In OS-level virtualization, the base OS runs the virtualization. In OS-level virtualization, the kernel allows for multiple isolated instances of an OS instead of just one. This technology is very similar to the chroot mechanism on a UNIX or Linux OS. All OSs both physical and virtual must run the same type of OS such as a Windows base with only Windows.

Hardware assist virtualization allows the same binary kernel image to run under a variety of hypervisors, or, with the right ROM, in native mode on the bare hardware. This type of virtualization provides additional execution modes known as root mode and non-root mode.

Part of hardware assist virtualization is Second Level Address Translation (SLAT). SLAT is a technology introduced in both Intel and AMD processors used to reduce the overhead incurred during virtual to physical address mapping performed for virtual machines (Carbone, 2009). A further discussion of memory mapping occurs in the section on live analysis Figure 3 shows the concept of hardware assist virtualization.

Figure 2. Concept of paravirtualization

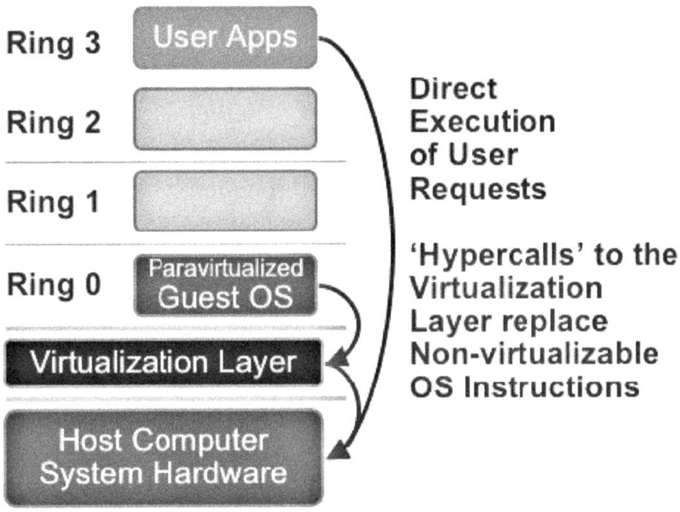

Figure 3. Concept hardware assist virtualization

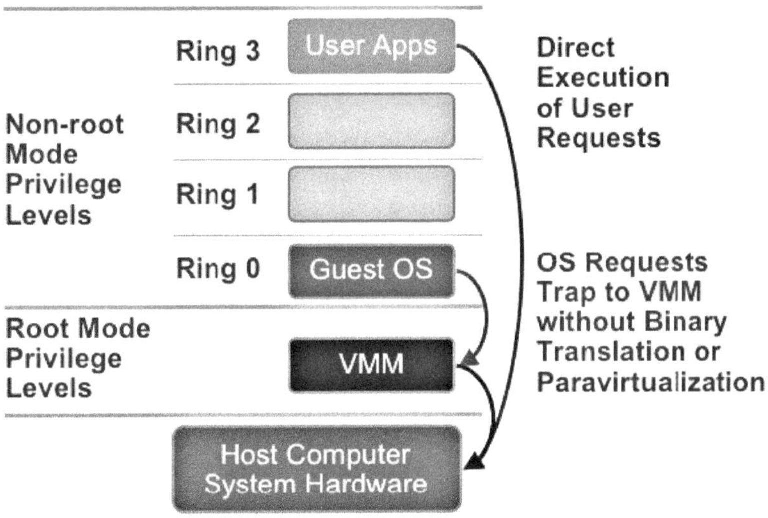

Hypervisor Types

The hypervisor manages the system's processor, memory, and other resources to allocate what each operating system requires. A Type 1 native hypervisor, also known as a bare-metal hypervisor, is software that runs directly on a hardware platform (Barrett, 2008). The guest operating system runs at the second level directly above the hardware. These are hardware-bound virtual machine emulators, which rely on the actual, underlying CPU to execute non-sensitive instructions at native speed (Ferrie, 2007). In hardware virtualization, the hypervisor translates all operating system instructions on the fly and caches the results for future use, while user level instructions run unmodified at native speed. VMware and Citrix Systems have releases of a client-side Type 1 hypervisor that can are embedded. Examples of embedded hypervisor technology include use in systems to control automated machinery on a manufacturing floor or large medical devices.

A Type 2 or hosted hypervisor is software that runs within an operating system environment and the guest operating system runs at the third level above the hardware. The hypervisor runs as an application or shell on another already running operating system. These operating systems running on the hypervisor become guest or virtual operating systems. This type of virtual machine is composed entirely of software and contains no hardware components whatsoever (Barrett & Kipper, 2010). Thus, the host can boot to completion, and launch any number of applications as usual, with one them being the virtual machine emulator.

The wide variety of hypervisor options allows for the occurrence of virtualization on any number of environments. Virtualization can occur at the operating system level, application level, device level, and on embedded devices. Virtualized environments can become complicated quickly, especially when virtualized components include desktops, servers, storage, and routers.

Types of Virtualization

In addition to virtualization models and hypervisor types, there are different types of virtualization, which include: hardware, server, application, network, storage, and service. Hardware virtualization, sometimes called platform virtualization, executes on a particular hardware platform by host software. Essentially, it hides the physical hardware. The hypervisor creates a simulated computer environment for the guest software that could be anything from user applications to complete operating systems. The guest software performs as if it were running directly on the physical hardware. However, access management to physical resources such as network access and physical ports occurs at a more restrictive level than the processor and memory (Adams & Agesen, 2012). Guests are often restricted from accessing specific peripheral devices. Managing network connections and external ports such as USB from inside the guest can be challenging.

Server virtualization is actually a subset of hardware virtualization. This concept is most prominently found in datacenters to implement energy cost-effective measures and utilize the increased hardware resource capability of servers. In server virtualization, many virtual servers can be contained on one physical server. This configuration is hidden server users. To the user, the virtual servers appear exactly like physical servers (Barrett, 2008). This type of virtualization allows load balancing for even distribution of workloads across multiple servers.

Application virtualization is a concept different from virtualizing hardware such as Type 1 and Type 2 virtualizations. Application virtualization is different from platform virtualization in that with platform virtualization the virtualization encompasses the whole OS as opposed to only specific applications (Barrett, 2010). In application virtualization, the virtualization involves a local device and an actual installed application in a remote location. Another name for application virtualization is thin client technology. Virtualizing applications allows applications to run in environments that do not suit the native application by providing stability through isolating the application from the OS. Application virtualization is not possible in some instances, especially when the application requires heavy OS integration.

The concept of network or local area network virtualization involves virtualizing Internet Protocol (IP) routing, forwarding, and addressing schemes. Network virtualization provides a way to run multiple networks, each customized to a specific purpose, at the same time over a shared network using virtual IP management and segmentation (Creeger, 2010). Network virtualization also provides for either merging multiple physical networks into one virtual network or logically segmenting a single physical network into multiple logical networks.

Storage virtualization is a common component of Storage Area Networks (SANs). A SAN system, design is such that all the separate storage disks on the network become part of individual groups and those groups become part of an array. Servers can then access the array as though it were a local storage device (Barrett & Kipper, 2010). SANs components include disk arrays and switches. Figure 4 shows the concept of storage virtualization.

Service virtualization is associated with Service-Oriented Architecture (SOA). A SOA is fundamentally a collection of services that communicate with one another with some means of connecting services. This means of connecting the services to one another is usually a service intermediary sitting between the service client and the service implementation.

Benefits and Drawbacks of Using Virtualization

There are many benefits to virtualization with the primary one being a cost benefit by decreasing the number of physical machines required within an environment. Other benefits that virtualization offers are more effective disaster recovery and business continuity, better resource management including server consolidation, and testing (Orakwue, 2009). Virtual machines consist entirely of software, so transportation to an offsite location can be done just like transmitting a data file. This ability alone can reduce downtime in the event of system failure. The use of virtual environments for isolating and testing malware actions is a common activity. Another important role of virtualization is its use in forensic investigations by allowing the investigator to view the environment as the suspect used it (Shavers, 2008). Virtualization has many benefits but it may not be appropriate for every situation or environment and there are costs associated with virtualization. Although virtualization purports to be green, a physical

Figure 4. Storage virtualization

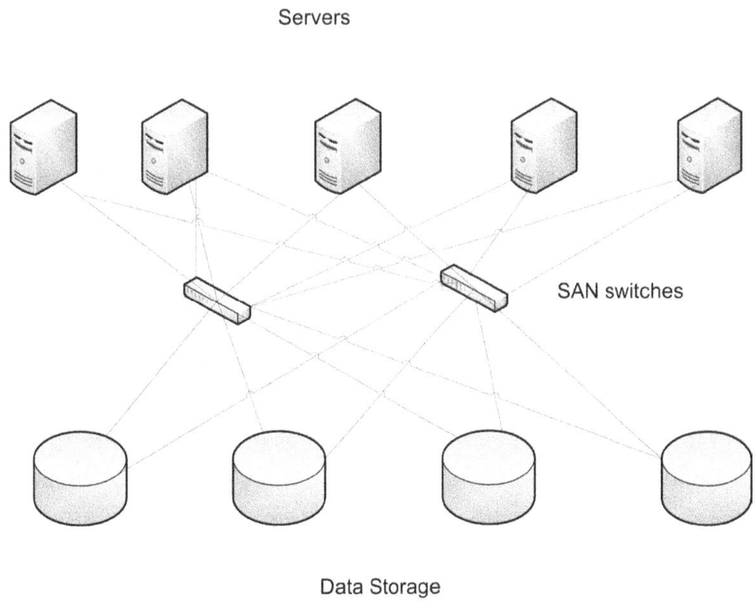

server running many virtual machines may run at a constant or higher utilization rate than if there was single use. The ability to quickly mass produce virtual machines can present not only a licensing compliance issue but also storage issues. A virtualized infrastructure is often more complex to manage than the conventional physical server environments. If there is a compromise of a virtual machine, an intruder could possibly gain control of all the guest operating systems. In addition, because virtualization allows for hardware sharing, most virtual machines run with very high privileges. This can allow an intruder who compromises a virtual machine to compromise the host machine.

If VMs that contain sensitive information are hosted on the physical machines that contain VMs for testing, the risk to the sensitive information is greatly increased. When financial applications are hosted in a virtual environment in which there is shared hosting or a Storage-Area Network (SAN) environment, special considerations for the data must be made. Some of the VM software is freely available and downloadable. Employees can independently install these applications onto their laptops, workstations, or removable media creating security and licensing issues.

Now that one has a basic understanding of virtual environments, it is time to move on to extracting forensic evidence from each of the various environments. There are a variety of environments, techniques, and methods to be covered. These include not only operating systems but memory as well.

VM ENVIRONMENTS AND FORENSIC EVIDENCE

Using virtual machines in forensics investigations to create contained environments for malware isolation or to examine suspect machines has been a practice for a long time. For example, VMware can mount a dd image and applications such as LiveView and Virtual Forensic Computing (VFC) can create a VMware virtual machine out of a raw disk image or physical disk. Virtual Forensic Computing (VFC) uses a combination of VMware's VMPlayer and the forensic disk mount tool Mount Image Pro to create and mount the disk. This allows the forensic examiner to boot the image or disk in a virtual environment and view the system in a user-level perspective of the system. This method is a controlled setting that does not modify the host operating system and after the investigator examines the subject system, the changes can be discarded (Shavers, 2008). The original machine is preserved and used without any adverse effects.

However, the tide has shifted recently. Instead of using virtual environments to examine the suspect's machine, the virtual environments themselves have become cause for examination. As noted earlier, virtualization technology transcends all facets of corporate environments from datacenters to virtual desktops. Additionally, portable applications allow mobile employees to leave hardware behind and take only software with them. Entire environments exist on micro devices such as a USB drive or an iPod. Operating systems on removable media and external devices can function on its own (Barrett & Kipper, 2010). It is possible with removable media that the only place that evidence is located is in the RAM, which empties when the computer powers off. The exploration of this concept expands in the case scenarios later in the chapter. Portable environments, combined with the concept of downloading a virtual machine through a browser on any machine, and accessing data anywhere via cloud computing have changed the evidence landscape. All these technological changes present new challenges to the traditional methods of performing forensic analysis (Barrett, 2010).

Many forensic examinations still use the traditional method of creating a forensic copy of the suspect's drive, using a write-blocker, and then using that image for further analysis. Although this method allows the investigator to locate files associated with virtual environments, it may not allow the investigator to see inside the virtual machine as we can with other file types. Virtual machines are merely files on a hard drive, and these files are easily copied, deleted, or stored in remote locations, but are not easily viewable. For example, clicking on a Microsoft Word file in most forensics software will automatically open the document. When a virtual environment is used, the examiner may need to mount the environment in order to examine the files inside. There may even be case where the only way to examine the virtual environment is by using the tool that created the environment itself (Barrett & Kipper, 2010).

Each virtualization technology installs and creates different files or virtual devices that are exclusive to the particular vendor's virtual machine. The file extensions are unique as is how the application stores information. Some forensic software lists the file extensions as unknown file types. An investigator should be familiar with the files because if one of these files is present, it may be an indication that a virtual machine existed on the media and warrants further investigation. The following sections describe some of the more popular environments. This is by no means an exhaustive list; the focus is on the ones an investigator will most likely encounter.

VMware

Arguably, the best-known virtualization vendor is VMware. VMware invented its virtualization tool for the x86 platform in the 1990s to address underutilization in computer hardware. The VMware platform installs and runs as an application and a type II hypervisor on top of a Windows or Linux host operating system (Barrett & Kipper, 2010). The VMware Server or Workstation application is responsible for isolating each VM from both the host operating system and all the other VMs that may be running at the time. VMware creates virtual adapters as well as files with extensions: .vmx, .vmdk, .vmsn., and .vmss. Posted on VMware's website (2012) is an explanation of all the files extensions that are associated with VMware Workstation along with the purpose of the file. A brief explanation of the file names and extensions is summarized in Table 1.

In addition to the above listed files, there is .log file created for each virtual machine. This file is stored in the directory that holds the configuration (.vmx) file.

Microsoft

Microsoft's virtual products, just like VMware's products have proprietary files associated with the virtual machine. Microsoft virtualization products use a .vhd extension. The files and their descriptions are as follows:

- **.vmc:** Virtual machine configuration file.
- **.vhd:** The virtual hard disk file.
- **.vsv:** Virtual machine saved-state files associated with the virtual machine.
- **.vud:** Virtual machine undo disk files associated with the virtual machine.

Table 1. VMWare file extensions

Extension	Usage
.vmdk	virtual hard drive for the guest operation system
.vmem	backup of the virtual machine's paging file
.vmsn	snapshot file
.vmsd	snapshot metadata
.nvram	virtual machine bios information
.vmx	virtual machine configuration file
.vmss	virtual machine suspended state file
.vmtm	team data configuration
.vmxf	supplemental team configuration file

The saved-state and undo disk files are stored in the same folder as the virtual machine configuration (.vmc) file. If the user saves the state of a virtual machine, instead of shutting it down, all data from the virtual machine's memory is stored in a saved-state file (.vsv file) as opposed to a .vhd file. Microsoft recommends that the user either restores the virtual machine or discard the changes, and then shut down the virtual machine before moving or copying a .vhd file (Microsoft, 2012).

Some file systems, such as the FAT32 file system, have a 4-GB limit on file size. To accommodate for this, versions of Microsoft Virtual Server and PC prior to 2005 supported splitting of disk images when the disk image grew larger than the maximum supported file size on the host file system. For example, if the hard disk image expands more than 4 GB, Microsoft Virtual PC 2004 will split the hard disk image into another file. The split files are stored in the same directory as the main hard disk image. The split file only has raw data, no headers or footers except for the last one, which has a footer stored at the end of the file. The first file in the split disk image has an extension of .vhd. The subsequent split files use a number convention similar to an Encase image, so they would show as .v01, .v02, and so on. The maximum number of split files that can be present is 64 and the size of the split file is not alterable.

Citrix Xen

Citrix Xen offers wide variety of products from servers to virtual desktop infrastructure (VDI) in a box, which includes several different formats, i.e., an Open Virtualization Format (OVF), Virtual Hard Disk (VHD) file format, and an Open Virtual Appliance (OVA) package. OVF is an XML file format defined by the DMTF that contains the guest virtual machine metadata (Xen, 2012). A single OVF can contain information on several guest VMs. A Virtual Hard Disk (VHD) file is the disk image of the virtual machine as described in the previous section. This is the same format that Microsoft has adopted, but works a little differently in Xen. Each VHD represents a virtual disk than when joined with an OVF can characterize multiple virtual machines. The last type of format supported by Xen is called an OVA Package, which contains the OVF and VHD in an individual uncompressed tape archive (TAR) file (Xen, 2012). An OVA Package is created after exporting an OVF and is the format used for Xen's virtual appliances. In some Citrix Xen products, the logging is not enabled by default. If an investigator has to examiner one of these environments, the process is more difficult. Citrix XenApp and XenDesktop clients record information about the last logon in a log file under the users Application Data folder. Figure 5 demonstrates the Xen paravirtualization environment architecture.

Cisco and Virtual Routers

Cisco provides a variety of network virtual solutions for datacenters, unified communications, switching, storage, and networking. Cisco's Data Center 3.0 targets virtualization and automation using an appliance called VFrame Data Center. This appliance moves provisioning of virtual resources from what was a storage function to the networking side by linking computing, network, and storage infrastructures. Cisco's intention with this approach is to increase networking virtualization options by combining the Nexus 1000V virtual network switch and Virtual Machine Fabric Extender (VM-FEX) with Microsoft's Hyper-V hypervisor. For example, the Nexus 1000V virtual switch runs in VMware's virtualization environment. Integrating and running it in conjunction with Microsoft's Hyper-V allows an entire virtual network to operate as an extension of the physical network. Using the Nexus 1000V with the Virtual Machine Fabric Extender (VM-FEX) enables traffic from network end points to be sent to a master physical switch where the network poli-

Figure 5. Xen paravirtualization (http://www.virtualizationsoftwares.com/what-is-paravirtualization/)

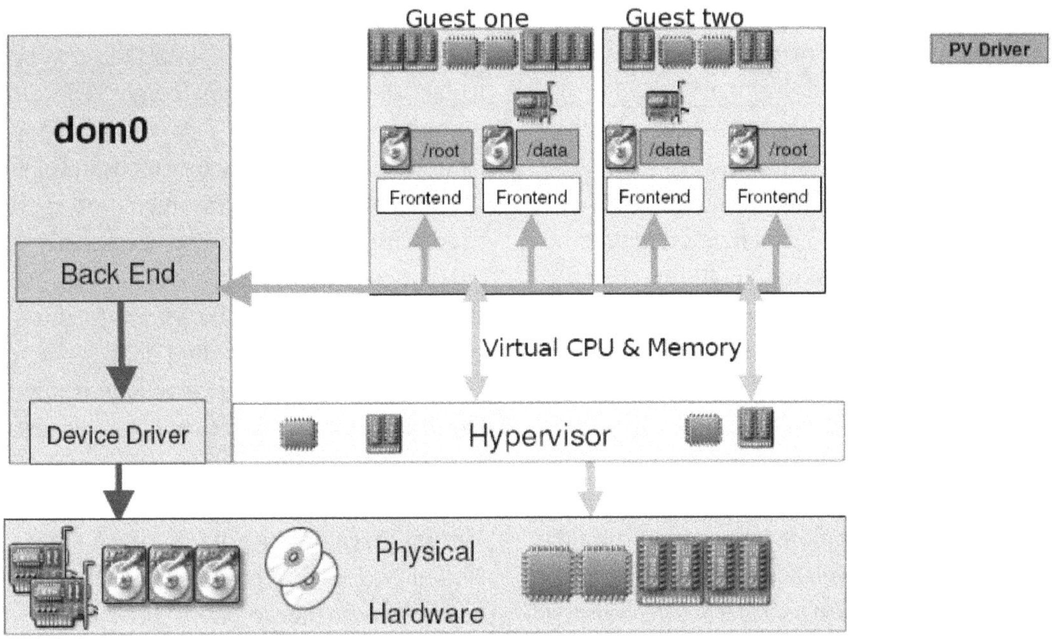

cies and controls are applied. Using the Nexus 1000V in conjunction with Cisco virtual services allows for central management of tasks like intrusion prevention, intrusion detection, and firewall security functions. According to Cisco (Mullins, 2011) there is widespread deployment of the 1000V in VMware environments, particularly when integrated with Cisco's Unified Computing System infrastructure.

Not quite as prominent as Cisco, but another virtual networking environment that an investigator should be familiar with is Vyatta. Vyatta provides Network OS virtual machines. Vyatta is a commercially supported, open-source networking, security, and service solution (Vyatta, 2011). Vyatta is a virtually secure router with flexible deployment options and the ability to ingrate other applications into the virtual machines. Vyatta can be implemented into VMware, Citrix XenServer, Xen and Redhat KVM hypervisor environments. Vyatta also provides OVF and XVA virtual appliances for adding routing and security to VMware ESX and XenServer environments.

Virtual Desktops, Appliances, and Portable Environments

Desktop virtualization is similar in form to server virtualization but with some differences, specifically in usage and the performance demands. Desktop virtualization is often the most dynamic of all the virtualized environments having far more changes made inside the environment both locally and over the network than a virtualized server. A virtual desktop is based on a computing architectural model in which a VM detects and responds to changing business requirements on demand. This allows for all types of configurations which can be created, deleted, copied, archived, and downloaded over a network or remotely hosted with administration times dropping from hours to minutes (Barrett & Kipper, 2010).

One example of this type of environment is a Virtual Desktop Infrastructure (VDI). Desktop operating systems and applications run inside virtual machines that reside on servers in data center. An organization can migrate to a newer OS without upgrading the physical PCs. The virtual machines are easily ported to the newer OS by allocating more CPU and memory resources and are not affected by the end user hardware.

There is a newer cloud-based VMware solution for desktop virtualization called VMware View. This solution provides virtual desktops as a managed service from a virtualization platform that delivers the entire desktop, including the operating system, applications, and data. VMware View desktops reside in the Cloud and are not tied to a physical computer. End-users can access a VMware View desktop anytime, anywhere and whenever needed.

Virtual appliances are VM images, usually with a specific configuration, designed to run on a virtual platform such as VMware, Parallels, and VirtualBox. The purpose of a virtual appliance is to reduce or eliminate the installation, configuration, and maintenance costs associated with running large or complicated suites of software. Preconfigured virtual appliances are available from a variety of vendors including VMware, Microsoft, and Parallels. Virtual appliances come ready to start up. They have a preinstalled, preconfigured OS inside a virtual machine environment. The user merely downloads the appliance and loads it. Virtual appliances are fundamentally changing how software is developed, distributed, deployed, and managed (Microsoft, 2012). In addition to commercial virtual appliance marketplaces, open-source vendors are also supporting the virtual appliance model. Some examples of preconfigured open source appliances are Ubuntu Server Edition JeOS, Lime JeOS, and Red Hat's Appliance Operating System (Barrett & Kipper, 2010). There are also virtual appliances available for download from vendor Web sites specifically built for conducting forensic investigations. An example of this environment is the SIFT workstation from SANS.

Virtual emulators are a bit different from virtual machines. Virtual emulators allow OS to be run that have different processor requirements. In other words, emulators simulate an entire environment, not just the OS. An example of this is running Windows Vista on a Mac-based PowerPC. Due to fact that the entire environment is simulated, emulators tend to be slower than VMs. Some examples of emulators are Bochs and DOSBox.

Portable virtual environments are applications used with PCs that do not necessarily alter the current environment, but instead can use a Universal Serial Bus (USB) device to run a virtual environment. This method leaves the original system intact while the virtual environment runs from a portable device such as thumbs drives, iPods, and cell phones. Examples of this type of environment are MojoPac, MokaFive and Portable Virtual Privacy Machine. Figure 6 shows what a MokaFive Live PC looks like. The application will be explore further in one of the case scenarios.

RELATIONSHIP BETWEEN VIRTUALIZATION AND THE CLOUD

Although cloud computing and virtualization appear to be synonymous, they are two different concepts. They both provide for provisioning of resources and access to environments other than what installs on the physical machine. The biggest difference between the two concepts is that virtualization is technology based and cloud computing is model based. To further contrast, virtualization is one physical computer pretending to be many computing environments whereas cloud computing is many different computers pretending to be one computing environment. The initial purpose of virtualization is to maximize machine resources, while cloud computing provides a way for businesses to have access to resources without having to maintain the physical environment.

Cloud computing is an approach for the delivery of services with virtualization being one service available for delivery. Many providers use virtualization as the basis for building a cloud based environment but it is not required. Because

Figure 6. MokaFive live PC

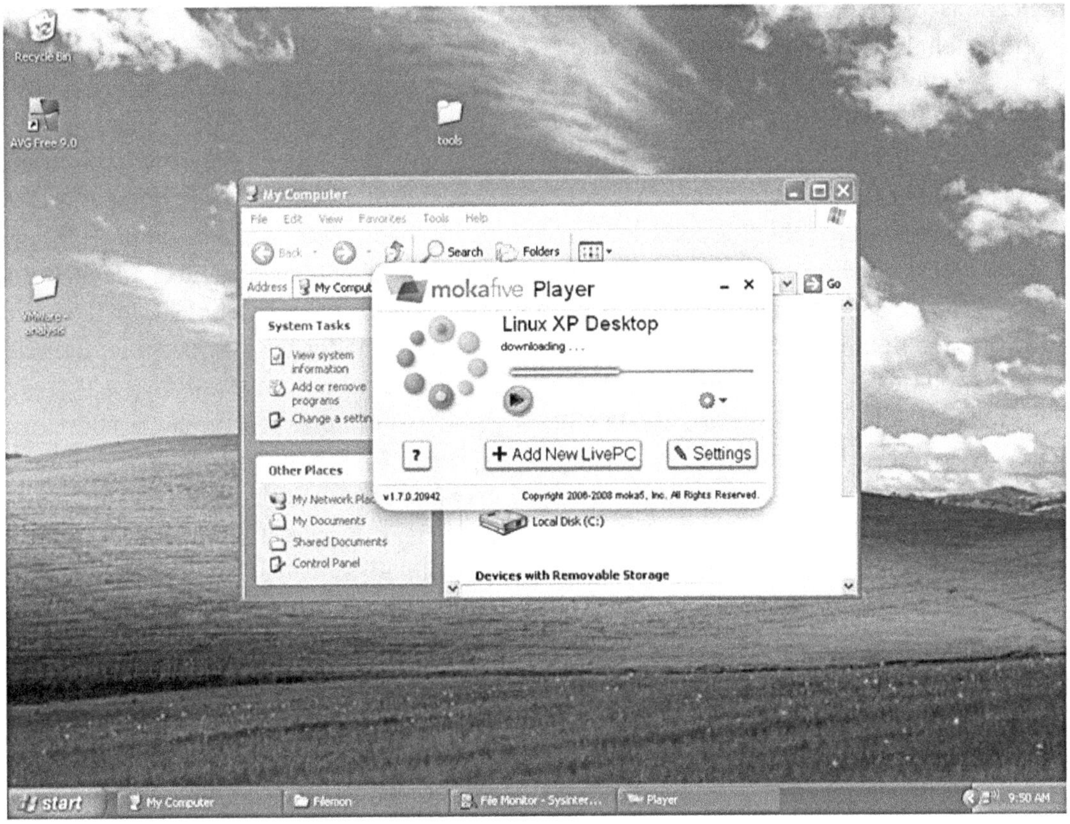

virtualization provides flexibility and ease of VM movement, it is often a counterpart for cloud computing. For example, if an organization wants to implement a virtual environment, it will weigh technology factors such as server bandwidth, the number of hosted VMs per server, and the type or hypervisor used. If an organization wants to implement a cloud environment, it will weigh business model factors such as the type of service needed, public or private cloud implementation, and pricing model. Although virtualization may be part of the cloud solution, it is a subset of the service requirement for meeting organizational needs (Phillippi, 2010).

VM Architecture and the Cloud

VM architecture is a bit different from cloud architecture. Fundamentally the way each one works is unique starting with the basic underlying structure of a hypervisor through security. Since cloud computing is a service model, when you run an application in a cloud environment, there is not a cloud layer comparable to a hypervisor that communication must pass through in order to leverage the physical infrastructure. One facet of cloud computing is multitenancy. Multitenancy is a design approach to enable scalability, availability, management, segmentation/isolation, and operational efficiency by leveraging the shared infrastructure across many different users (Barrett & Kipper, 2010). The hypervisor used in virtualization helps enable the scalability of cloud computing. Hypervisors allow operating systems and applications to install to a consistent hardware profile, even though they run on a variety of actual physical system implementations. In many cloud instances, there is virtualization involved, but the existence of virtualization and hypervisors does not necessarily indicate that the resources are a cloud environment. Cloud technology is based on physical resources operating to deliver abstracted IT resources on-demand, at scale, and usually in a multi-tenant environment. Hypervisors allow servers to be multitenant without rewriting applications to be multitenant (Urquhart, 2009).

Security is area where the architectures between virtualization and cloud environments differ. In a strictly virtual environment, best practice dictates that financial data and a testing environment do not reside on the same physical box in the event of a compromise. The network topology will include a mapping of which virtual servers will reside on which physical servers and the established level of trust that is required for each system. The planning of the environment takes trust crossover into consideration for Demilitarized Zones (DMZs), PCI cardholder data environments, site-specific zones such as segmentation according to departments or functions, and application-defined zones such as the three tiers of a Web application (Hau, Araujo, Chudgar, Hustad, & Chaubal, 2009).

In cloud environments, typically the lowest common level of security is the standard in a multitenant environment, which can quickly lead to insufficient security for VMs that require more locked down environments. When using VM technology in cloud services, it is very important to ensure that appropriate compartmentalization, network security, and separation of virtual environments occurs and that proper protection of the VM systems happens. When a cloud environment uses virtualization, other considerations include the type of virtualization used, the security controls of and beyond the VMs, the VM image integrity, and how VM isolation occurs (Barrett & Kipper, 2010).

Using the Cloud to Run VMs

Cloud services at the infrastructure, platform, or software level often go hand-in-hand with virtualization in order to create economies of scale. The use of technologies that intertwine with virtualization such as cloud computing, Desktops as a Service (DaaS), and streaming OSs are very promising, but there are still challenges. Some of these challenges are technical; for example, performance challenges may occur for users located across the country or the globe. Although some desktop virtualization products take advantage of networking protocols designed for wide area networks, they still have bandwidth and latency challenges. Bandwidth limits the amount of data transmitted, as well as limiting the number of users who can access the virtualized environment. Latency prevents applications from performing as though they were local to a traditional desktop (Barrett & Kipper, 2010).

Cloud computing is very flexible. It is an on-demand self-service, sold based on the needs of the user usually in minute-by-minute or hour-by-hour increments. As with all successful services, it is designed to fit the needs of the users and adjust with them. Virtualization is maturing rapidly, and similar to other technologies used today, there is a convergence of functionality (Birk, 2011). Cloud computing is often the blending of virtualization, distributed computing, and prevalent high-speed bandwidth. Public cloud computing providers offer virtual servers with assigned Internet Protocol (IP) addresses and chunks of storage space based on the user's needs.

Virtualization by its very design assumes the hardware management duties of the OS; added to this is the growing number of applications that are moving to the Web which now assume the application management duties from the OS. This produces a very interesting set of conditions that could lead to the creation of a truly disposable OS created from a combination of hypervisor functions and Web applications that operates for a single session and is then dismantled completely when shut down. Since the very nature of cloud computing is abstraction, many technological implementation functions that are common in traditional client/server environments will change in part or disappear because of virtualization.

INVESTIGATIVE CASE SCENARIOS FOR VIRTUALIZATION AND THE CLOUD

Perhaps the best way to see how a virtual environment in the Cloud present challenges to a forensic investigator is to look at some scenarios. This section presents several different types of virtualized environments that an investigator may encounter in a cloud environment. It will also include some recommendations on where to look for evidence and in some cases suggest procedures for proper acquisition of the environment. The use of private cloud scenarios allow the focus to be on the examination of the virtual environment as opposed to the additional complications associated with the acquisition of files in a public cloud environment.

Microsoft Virtual Environment Scenario

A case requires an investigator to examine a virtual desktop environment. The organization uses a private cloud to host VMware based Windows 7 desktop operating systems. The organization provides the VMware container to the investigator in the form of a vmdk file. During the course of the examination, the investigator finds several files with .vhd extensions.

The investigator must address several issues here: the processes behind the basic use of the environment, sharing of the environment, and the storage of individual data. Another concern is the evidence of files with the .vhd extension. This is an indication of the possible use of a virtual environment inside of the virtual desktop. At this point, the investigation focus shifts to the vhd files.

To investigate this environment, a starting point could be searching for the associated Microsoft Virtual PC files: the virtual machine configuration (.vmc) file, the virtual hard disk (.vhd) file, any virtual machine saved-state (.vsv) files, and virtual machine undo disk (.vud) files. The absence or presence of one of these files could help indicate if the virtual environment was created and copied from another location or actually locally in the VMWare image. Just about every application that runs on Microsoft operating systems touched the registry in some way. The registry would be another area to explore for evidence of a local Virtual PC installation along with file extensions listed under HKEY_CLASSES_ROOT, file associations. Another registry area to check is the MRU cache. Other files that will help in the investigation are:

- Link files
- Prefetch files
- Page file
- Any unique identifiers associated with the program
- Artifacts in unallocated space

The Prefetch (XP) or Superfetch (Vista and 7) folder and the "layout.ini" file will defragment itself every 72 hrs. In addition to self-clean older Prefetch files from your system. The Microsoft operating system can only hold 128 Prefetch files in the Prefetch folder; after that, no new Prefetch files can be added or created (Buckley, 2010). An example of the Prefetch folder is shown in Figure 7. The investigator should also look to see if any snapshots exist. In Microsoft Virtual PC, these are called differencing disks and have the same extension as the virtual hard disk, which could explain why there is more than one .vhd file. Snapshots allow the virtual machine to revert back to the state when the snapshot was taken. The concept behind snapshots is similar to Windows restore points. It is possible that if snapshots exist, there will be evidence in these files as well. Additionally, forensically mounting the vhd files should help determine exactly what is inside the VMs.

VMware Virtual Environment Scenario

A case requires an investigator to examine a virtual machine running on VMware ESXi 4 server that has experiencing some suspicious activity. The client believes there is a compromise of the VM. The organization uses a private cloud to host VMware based servers running on ESXi. The organization provides server access to the investigator since the server hosts many VMs and it is not feasible to shut the server down for a complete image.

Properly investigating this environment requires generating an image without invoking any code within the guest VM, establishing the integrity and the authenticity of the acquired evidence files, and supporting a proper chain of custody. The first step is collecting a snapshot of the VM and the .vmsn file. A live system acquisition will not capture the .vswp file. It is possible that the partition on which the file resides will require acquisition as well. Next, connect to the ESXi service console over SSH, and then determine where the VM files are saved using the CLI (Fiterman & Durick, 2010). The esxcfg-info command is helpful for this purpose. Then capture and hash the pertinent files such as .vmx, .vmsn, and .vmdk files. This can be done through the console since ESXi 4 Update 1 comes with an implementation of OpenSSL. The last step is to verify the acquisi-

Figure 7. Prefetch folder contents

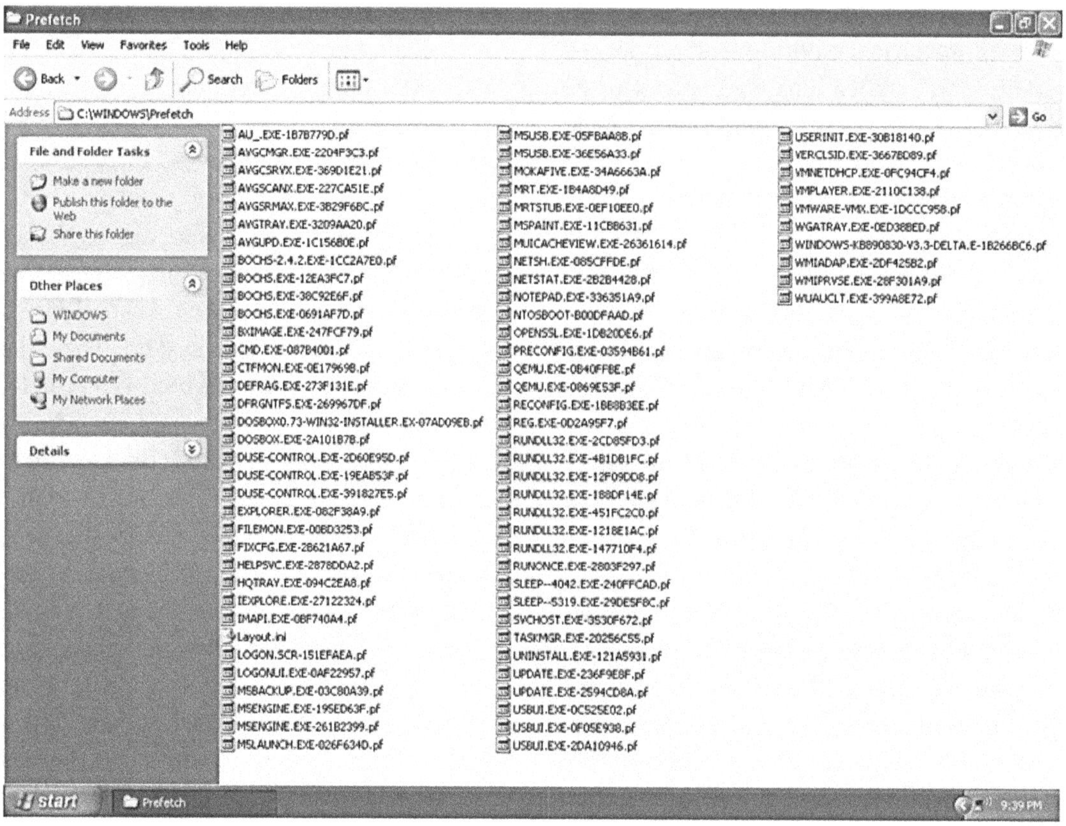

tion. Once these steps are complete, the virtual environment can then be mounted and examined for the suspicious activity. Figure 8 shows a VMware VM and associated files.

VirtualBox Virtual Environment Scenario

A case requires an investigator to examine a VirtualBox virtual environment found installed on a Windows Server 2008 machine. The organization uses a private cloud to host VMware-based Windows 7 desktop operating systems. An employee recently left the organization to join a major competitor. During examination of her external hard drive, there were remnants of Oracle VirtualBox files located in the unallocated space. Upon VM audit and inventory, the administrator discovers that there are several .vdi files on one of the Windows 2008 servers. The client believes the two are connected. The focus of the investigation is the server.

To investigate this environment, it is possible to take a two-fold approach. Conducting a live analysis could determine if there was an installation of any applications on the server and conducting a dead analysis will determine what is actually in the .vdi files. Although it is unlikely that the suspect was this sophisticated, the investigator should be aware that VirtualBox can display virtual machines remotely. This concept works in such a way that a virtual machine can execute on one machine even though the machine displays on a second computer, and the machine will be controlled from there as well, as if the virtual machine was running on that second computer (VirtualBox, 2012). This happens through the VirtualBox Remote Display Protocol (VRDP). A user can use any standard RDP viewer to connect to a remote virtual machine just as they would when using any other virtual desktop infrastructure model. VirtualBox also supports remote USB devices. When a user plugs a USB device into the client, the remote VirtualBox can access it. How this

Figure 8. VMware VM and associated files

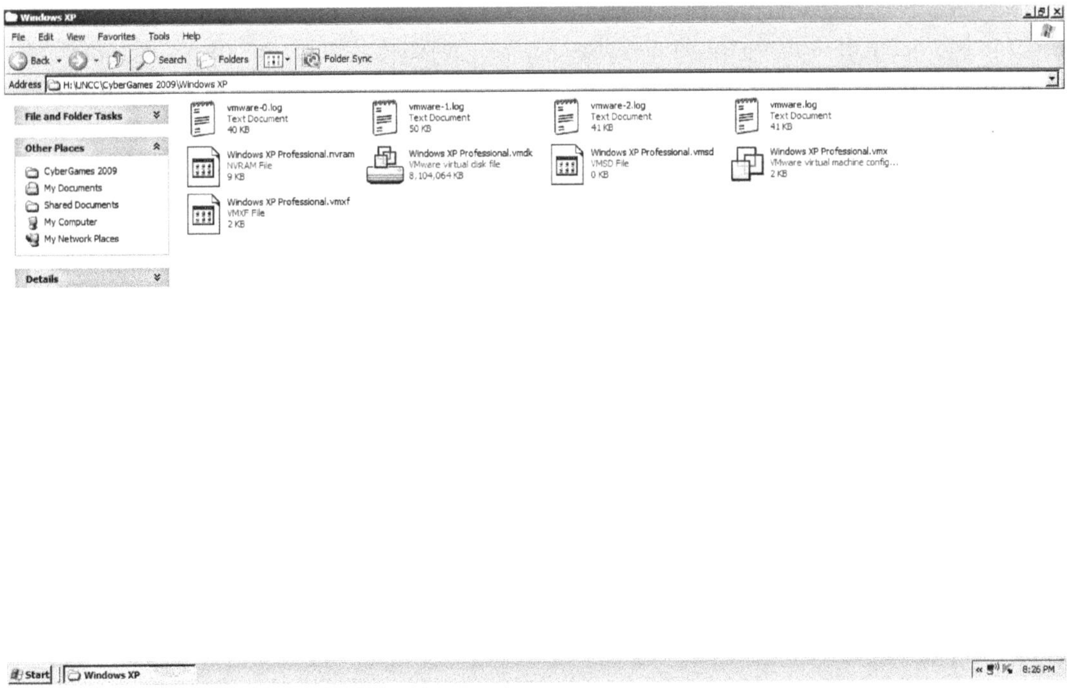

affects an investigation is that if the employee had an USB drive plugged into a home computer or vice versa, it could be accessed from inside a VirtualBox VM using RDP. What an easy way to steal corporate data with very little trace evidence.

VirtualBox contains built in tools for converting vmdk files to vdi fomat, so depending on the level of access the suspect had it is possible that the conversion of some VMware VMs to VirtulaBox VMs took place. A search for files associated with the QEMU emulator and XML VM configuration settings file may hold clues. This scenario shows how quickly the examination of virtual environments becomes complicated.

Portable Virtual Environment Scenario

A case requires an investigator to examine odd files found installed on a hosted VM. The organization uses a private cloud to host VMware based Windows 7 desktop operating systems. For compliance and internal auditing purposes, it is standard practice to randomly select, store, and run individually used VMs against the baseline image. The audit revealed several .lpc files and references to Moka5 in the startup folder and registry. The organization provides the investigator with the .vmdk file for examination. The focus is on the odd files found.

To investigate this environment, conducting research on the files extension and Moka5 reference would be a good place to start. The environment is associated with a portable environment that runs from a USB drive. The ability to run complete environments from USB drives is not new and as security concerns with mobile workers rise, it will be commonplace to find this type of environment to carry everything from data to servers. For example, it is possible to install VMware ESXi3.5 and ESXi4.0 on a USB key. Encrypted USB solutions targeting military and government workers are the IronKey and MXI Stealth Key.

The MokaFive uses the same technology as VMware for its Live PC except that instead of using a .vmdk extension, it stores the data in a flat.0 file in the cache folder with the .lpc used as a pointer file. This concept is shown in Figure 9.

The .0 extension is a compressed hard disk data format. The MokaFive engine streams and pre-fetches Live PCs. The application captures any changes made during a session in a separate file system on a RAM disk. Browsing and multimedia history stays inside the virtual machine. From actual examination of the MokaFive Live PC software behavior originally published by Barrett and Kipper (2010), areas of interest to an investigator are:

- Folders created in the *My Documents* folder for Live PCs and Live PC documents, which remain intact when the drive ejects. These folders are shown in Figure 10 at the end of the section.
- The application asks whether the user wants to leave it installed for easier load next time. There will be evidence in both the Temp folder and the Application Data folder with VMware references
- An entry in the user's Startup folder for MokaFive USB Clean 2238 points to an executable file in the host machine's C: drive: C:\Documents and Settings\Local Settings\Temp\m5usb-2238\ m5usb.exe.
- A Folder labeled m5usb-2238 located inside the Temp folder contains MokaFive-related files.
- Evidence exists of registry keys created or modified.
- A Log file containing information on MokaFive automatically updates the client on the host machine and the path of the MokaFive engine on the thumb drive.
- The application phones home for updates upon launch.

Figure 9. MokaFive folder contents

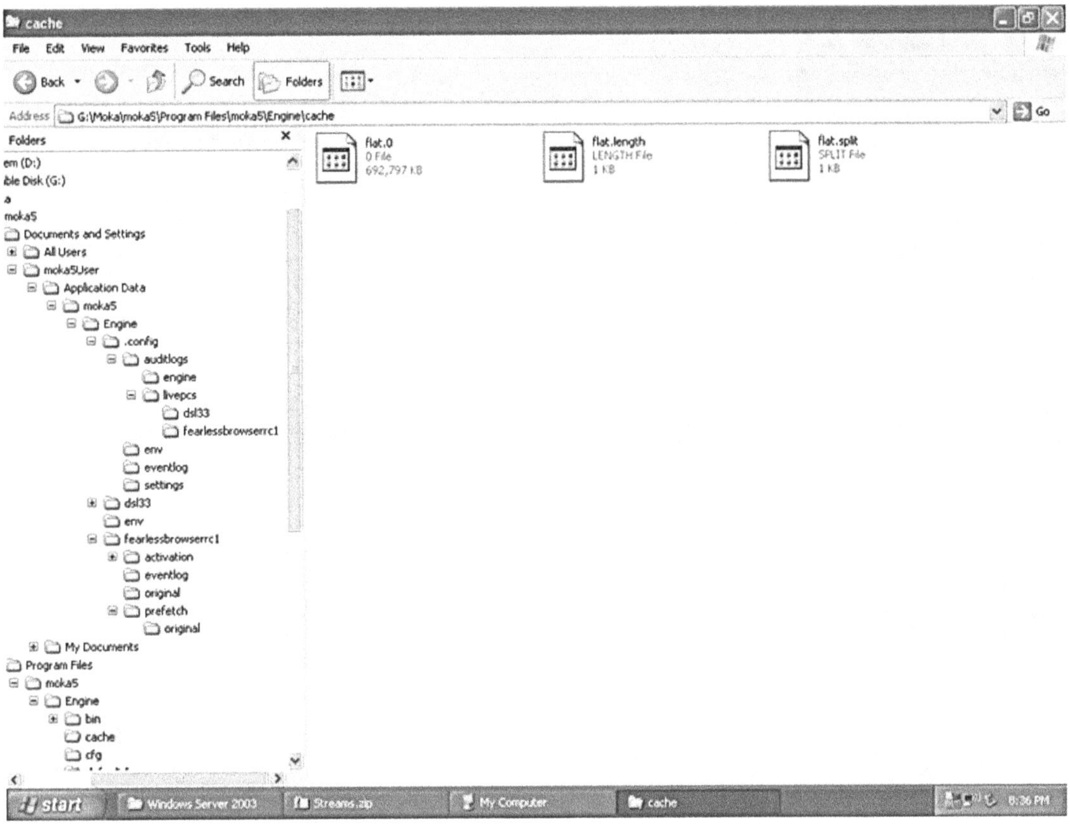

- The only way to examine this environment is to load it into the MokaFive application because of the proprietary file format.

It is worth noting that although in this instance the examination example takes place on an older version of MokaFive on a thumb drive, the current enterprise solution can run Live PCs using either a Type 1 or Type 2 hypervisor on all operating systems, removable media, and even a BlackBerry. Users can download a LivePC from a Web interface into a variety of VM environments such as VMware Player, VMware Fusion, or VirtualBox. A distinguishing part of the MokaFive Suite is that it allows a roll back of the operating system, IT-installed applications, or user-installed applications, without touching the user data and settings in the virtual machine. VMware ended availability for its client virtualization solution, Assured Computing Environment (ACE) and is steering ACE customers toward MokaFive, which means encountering this type of environment is greatly increasing.

Virtual Routing Environment Scenario

A case requires the investigation of network traffic to discern odd connection events found in the event logs of a Windows 2008 server hosting VMs. The organization uses a hybrid cloud solution. Internally it host the VMs on a XenServer environment and uses Vyatta deployed on the Riverbed Services Platform (RSP) as a consolidated edge protection solution.

Figure 10. MokaFive live PC folders

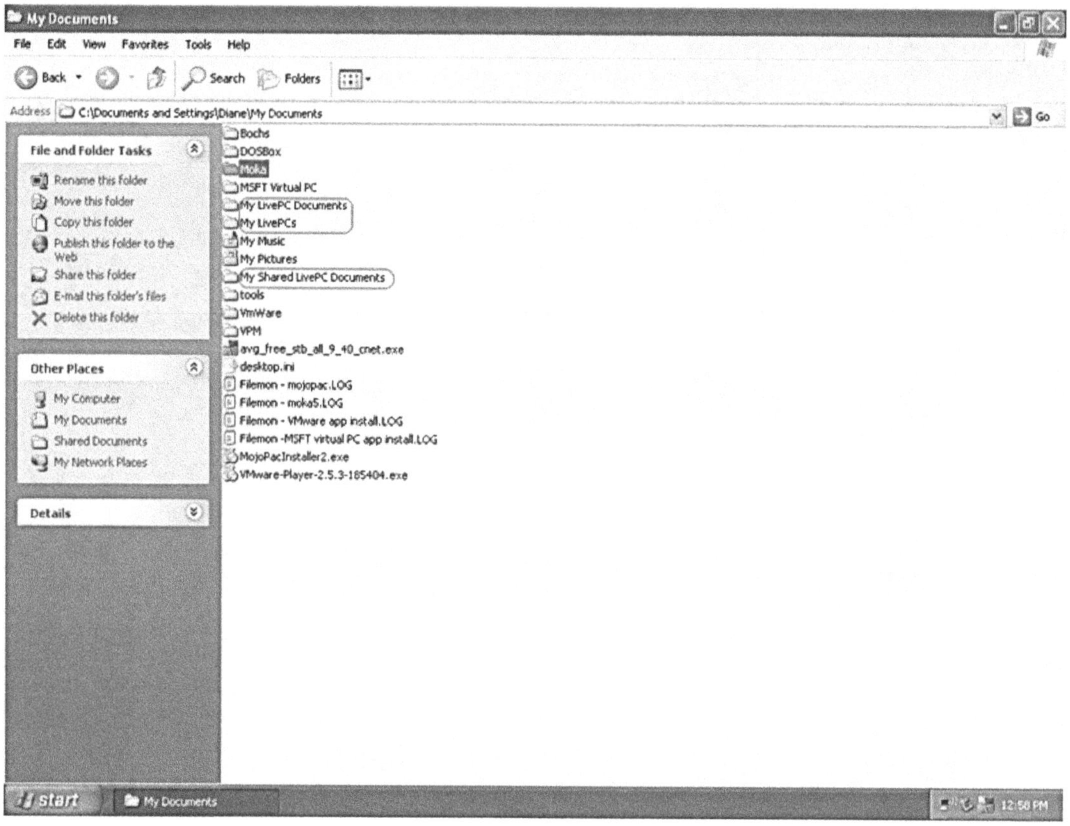

To investigate this environment, determining the network layout and what functionality Vyatta provides would be a good place to start. Since Vyatta is a Network OS VM and includes a stateful firewall, network intrusion prevention, IPSec and SSL-based OpenVPN, it is important to determine what logs the VM can provide (Meadows, 2009). In addition, since Vyatta is used with RSP, there may be logs on the Riverbed appliance that would be helpful. This situation presents an interesting situation in that the investigator must decide whether to take only the necessary logs or the entire VM (Kroeker, 2009). Granted the fact that the logs would be easier to acquire, but the entire VM may provide additional clues. In the event the entire VM is to be taken, the process would be similar to the one presented in the VMware ESXi server scenario. The acquisition requires generating an image without shutting down the appliance or invoking any code within the guest VM during the acquisition.

SOLUTIONS AND RECOMMENDATIONS

Absent from the case scenario discussions is the topic of memory acquisition. In a live response, along with the running processes and services, an investigator normally performs a memory acquisition. In a virtual environment, there is a certain amount of memory allocated to the VM when it is set up. Limits can be set for each virtual machine and the amount of the host computer's memory that the virtual machines use. Additionally, the extent to which the host OSes allows the memory manager to swap virtual machines out of physical Random Access Memory (RAM) can be set, but the memory modules do not reserve any specific area of memory for the VM. For example, in case of a compromised VM hosted on a server, the investigator cannot do a memory acquisition and know what part of that acquisition belongs to the individual VM, which part belongs to other VMs, and which part belongs to the host OS. A VM can reserve the amount of host RAM it uses, but the memory is not allocated in advance and any unused RAM is available for use by other applications if the VMs are not using it. However, if the entire amount of allocated RAM is in use by the VMs, the host OS itself or any other application cannot use it.

Bares (2009) used a NTFS partition as the testing environment to determine the recoverability of files based upon how much memory was allocated to three VMware server VMs. The test VMs were respectively allocated 256, 512, and 1024 MG of RAM. The recovery attempt consisted of e-mail communications, instant messenger traffic, creation of a Word document, and Web traffic. One of the interesting findings of the research is that the amount of RAM allocated to the individual VMs has a minimal effect on the number of recoverable files and hits. Most of tests conducted on the VM with the largest amount of allocated RAM resulted in fewer recoverable files and hits than the tests conducted on the VMs with less RAM. This result is mostly likely due to the way that VMware server reserves RAM for virtual machines and how the hypervisor interacts with physical memory. The tests in the VM with the smallest amount of RAM consistently proved that there was no decline in the total data recoverable from the swap file as the amount of RAM increased. What this means to an investigator is that data recover capability from RAM when using a VM has little bearing on the amount of RAM allocated to the VM. Using both the VM swap file and the memory analysis helps to correlate evidence.

The next issue that the scenarios did not cover is the imaging of the partition or drive. Whether there is value in acquiring an image of an entire drive is dependent the situation. In the case of a compromised host it may be necessary to determine if the entire server is compromised or just one VM. If the VM itself is the only item of interest, there may not be a need to acquire the entire drive. In certain situations, it may not even be possible to image the entire drive, such as in the case of a SAN, or an ESXi server that may be hosting multiple VMs. The case for imaging the entire drive would be that the VM might have shared folders on the host machine. For example, MokaFive installs folders on the host machine where live PCs can be stored. Additionally, the .lpc extension that it used is merely a pointer file. It is likely the investigator will miss evidence by not capturing the entire environment.

If imaging the entire drive any running VM must be properly shutdown before the physical machine is shutdown. The biggest factor in determining how successful the investigator will be in file recovery is whether the VM is properly shutdown. When VMs are improperly shutdown, less information is recoverable (Bares, 2009). The investigator must determine exactly what information is necessary to conduct the investigation when deciding if an image is required.

The VMware scenario provided a procedure for connecting to the ESXi server and acquiring the VM. With many forensic vendors offering enterprise solutions, the use of small programs called servlets, applets, or agents allows remote acquisition of running processes, services, memory, and entire environments. This is an option organizations may have in place when an investigator inquires about the environment. If the machine in question does not already have software program installed, if the environment is virtual, it may not install. Virtual environments have a configuration option to use the host adapter instead of having a separate IP address. Most live network forensic programs push out the software based on IP address. In an environment where the organization is hosting virtual desktops, pushing out an applet work mostly likely would work, provided the applet could install in a VM. In a situation where a VM is running inside a VM or where the VM uses the host IP address, pushing out an applet would be successful but only for the host machine environment. The investigator may be able to see the user running the VM but not be able to capture any information from inside the VM. In this instance, it is necessary to acquire the VM and then examine it (Barrett, 2010).

As our tools advance to account for virtual environments, the likelihood of capturing the required evidence from these environments will increase significantly. With all the options for managing, provisioning, and monitoring VMs investigators have more options for finding evidence. In the meantime, any organization that combines forensic monitoring with virtualized environments should be sure to check with software vendors about the capability of the tool to monitor the environment. If building VMs for desktop distribution, installing the applet inside the environment will probably prove to be successful so that the machine can be monitored the same as a physical machine. Another area of concern is tracking the applet inside the VM from machine to machine. For example, how or if the organization monitors the VM when employees drop the VM to a thumb drive or take it home is a determining factor in whether evidence is recoverable. Determining the processes in place with the use of live forensic tools is pertinent for a successful investigation.

The last issue not addressed in the scenarios is file systems. The VMware scenario used an implementation of ESXi. When using VMware ESX Server, the administrator can create a partition and format it with the VM file system (VMFS). VMFS is a distributed, clustered file system. Analysis of a cluster file system can be a bit tricky. Our forensic tools by nature analyze data from individual computers not huge data stores. It is possible to acquire a VM residing on a cluster file system and although efforts to capture the file system data may be successful, analysis of the underlying blocks may not be possible using current tools.

Forensic analysis of the VMFS is still developing. Hankeln (2010) formulated a potential process to extract data such as isos, vmdks, and vmem files from a server with a raid of scsi-disks formatted with VMFS. Durick (2010) formulated a process uses the Open Source VMFS Driver. This process enables read-only access to files and folders on partitions formatted with the Virtual Machine File System (VMFS). The investigator must determine if it is truly necessary to acquire the underlying file system. Before acquiring the entire VMFS, a defined examination process must be in place such as the one suggest by Hankeln. The Open Source VMFS Driver enables read-only access to files and folders on partitions formatted with the Virtual Machine File System (VMFS).

FUTURE RESEARCH DIRECTIONS

Hypervisors are moving from the software level down into the hardware level and out to storage. How to conduct investigations in an environment that includes complex virtualized solution is an area for further investigation. Haletky (2010) proposed an interesting scenario based on the setup at VMWorld. In 2010, the provisioning of over 100,000 VMs happened during that one week. 512 servers hosted 14,000 VMs. In the Cloud, there are perhaps a few hundred thousand constantly moving machines. An organizations data may never be at rest in the Cloud. There is very little forensic research in the proper way to handle the large data stores used by virtual infrastructures. For example, how an investigator acquires a VM when it spans multiple data stores and includes Raw Disk Maps, uses iSCSI initiators, USB over IP, or N_Port ID Virtualization SAN attachments (Haletky, 2009) is relatively unknown. Collecting a VM from a SAN environment such as the one in Figure 11 presents challenges to an investigator.

Another unknown area for further investigation is the analysis of VMFS. If the investigator acquires a drive formatted with VMFS and has the tools to analyze the file system, the defined process for locating the required VM when the format is not known has yet to be explored.

Virtualization is quickly moving into the mobile arena. Cell phone companies are investigating the applicability in providing multiple phone environments on the same hardware. It is entirely possible that in the near future a user can choose a handset and then specify how many OSs to install. For example, the user could install Blackberry OS alongside Windows Mobile. Shortly the Verizon market offering will include virtualized Android smartphones. The phones include a virtualized SIM. In an exploding mobile market, virtualization adds a layer of complication never before experienced on mobile devices. It is imperative further investigation occurs in this area.

Finally, procedure for live forensics and the use of servlets, applets, or agents could warrant further investigation. When a VM is running inside a VM or where the VM uses the host IP address, what actually happens in these situations deserves research and documentation. Conducting research into the capability of live forensic software to capture the state of a running VM could help determine processes for encountering this type of environment.

CONCLUSION

Cloud computing has definite hold on the market and many companies are developing products for this type of environment. In many instances, these cloud offerings include virtualization. New technologies always present challenges for forensics investigators. These challenges range from the added layer of complexity for litigation holds and e-discovery of virtual environments to the acquisition and analysis of complex virtualized cluster file systems. When an investigator receives an order to locate information in a cloud environment, being aware of information stored in VMs is a necessity. Although we have made great strides in methodologies and products, we may miss vital information associated with virtual environments or end up with other unintended data. We are

Figure 11. SAN environment

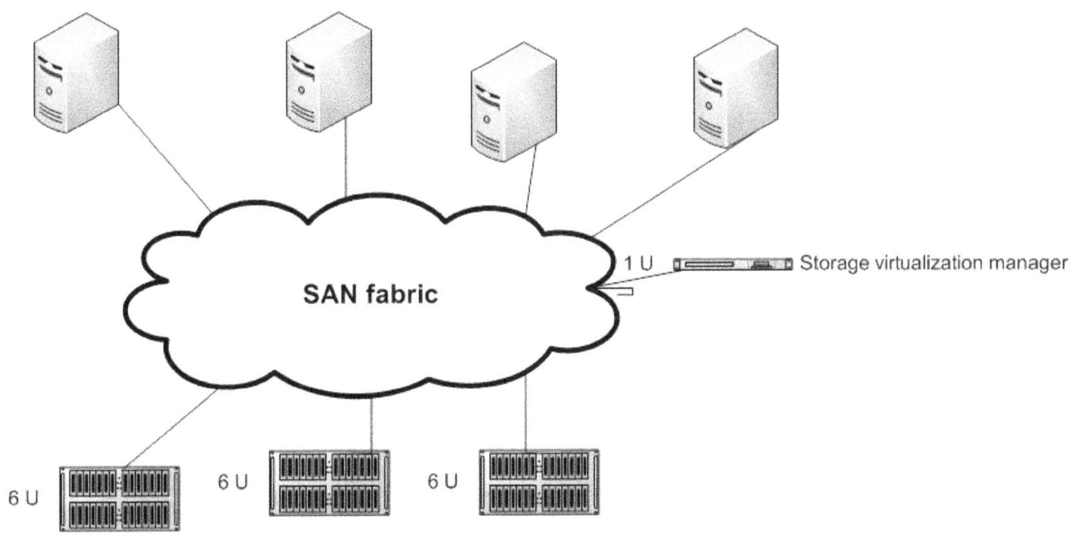

moving to more of a dynamic environment where organizations are pushing out virtual operating systems to desktops from a server and streaming applications on an as-needed basis. At the end of day, everything goes away and the user environment starts fresh the next day. Tracing crime thorough fluid environments goes against all the basics principles of sound forensic investigations. Having kiosks where a user downloads a virtual environment through a browser, commits a crime, and then deletes the virtual machine forces the industry to explore new methods of investigation. Currently there is a lack of documented processes, procedures, and case precedence with regard to the examination of many virtualized environment scenarios such as the ones just mentioned.

The possibility of court challenges based on virtual environment acquisition and analysis is real. As investigators find new ways to examine virtual machines, opposing experts will question the validity of the original evidence file and forensic procedures followed. Continued diligence, research, and sharing of findings are essential if the industry is to keep up with technology.

REFERENCES

Adams, K., & Agesen, O. (2012). *A comparison of software and hardware techniques for x86 virtualization.* Retrieved July 30, 2012 from http://www.vmware.com/pdf/asplos235_adams.pdf

Ali, I., & Meghanathan, N. (2011). Virtual machines and networks - Installation, performance, study, advantages and virtualization options. *International Journal of Network Security & Its Applications*, *3*(1), 1–15. doi:10.5121/ijnsa.2011.3101

Bares, R. A. (2009). Hiding in a virtual world: Using unconventionally installed operating systems. In *Proceedings of the 2009 IEEE International Conference on Intelligence and Security Informatics*, (pp. 276-284). IEEE Press.

Barrett, D. (2008). How virtualized environments affect computer forensics. In *Proceedings of the Conference on Digital Forensics, Security & Law*, (pp. 39-50). IEEE.

Barrett, D. (2010). Forensic challenges in virtualized environments. *Journal of Advancing Technology*, *10*(2), 15–25.

Barrett, D., & Kipper, G. (2010). *Virtualization and forensics: A digital forensic investigator's guide to virtual environments*. Burlington, MA: Elsevier.

Birk, D. (2011). *Technical challenges of forensic investigations in cloud computing environments.* Retrieved July 30, 2012 from http://www.zurich.ibm.com/~cca/csc2011/submissions/birk.pdf

Buckley, D. (2010). *Windows timeline prefetch analysis*. Retrieved July 30, 2012 from http://www.fishnetsecurity.com/Resource_/PageResource/White_Papers/FishNet_Security_WindowsTimelinePrefetchAnalysis.pdf

Carbone, J. (2009). *The new second level address translation (SLAT) feature in windows server 2008 R2 hyper-V.* Retrieved July 30, 2012 from http://www.virtualizationadmin.com/articles-tutorials/microsoft-hyper-v-articles/general/second-level-address-translation-benefits-hyper-v-r2.html

Cooney, M. (2012). *Gartner: 10 key IT trends for 2012 virtualization, social media, energy are top issues IT will have to contend with.* Retrieved July 30, 2012 from http://www.networkworld.com/community/blog/gartner-10-key-it-trends-2012

Creeger, M. (2010). Moving to the edge: A CTO roundtable on network virtualization. *Communications of the ACM*, *53*(8), 55–62. doi:10.1145/1787234.1787251

Decker, M., Kruse, W., Long, B., & Kelley, G. (2011). *Dispelling common myths of "live digital forensics"*. Retrieved July 30, 2012 from http://www.dfcb.org/docs/LiveDigitalForensics-MythVersusReality.pdf

Ferrie, P. (2012). Attacks on more virtual machine emulators. *Symantec Advanced Threat Research*. Retrieved from www.symantec.com/avcenter/reference/Virtual_Machine_Threats.pdf

Fiterman, E. M., & Durick, J. D. (2010). Ghost in the machine, forensic evidence collection in the virtual environment. *Digital Forensics Magazine*, *2*, 73–77.

Fowler, B. (2009). *Securing a virtual environment*. Retrieved from http://www.infosecwriters.com/text_resources/pdf/BFowler_VIrtual_Environment.pdf

Gartner. (2011). *Gartner reveals top predictions for IT organizations and users for 2012 and beyond: Predictions show IT budgets are moving out of the control of IT departments*. Retrieved July 30, 2012 from http://www.gartner.com/it/page.jsp?id=1862714

Haletky, E. (2009). *VMware vSphere and virtual infrastructure security: Securing the virtual environment*. Boston, MA: Pearson.

Hankeln. (2008). *How to read VMFS or any other file system with MOA*. Retrieved July 30, 2012 from http://sanbarrow.com/latest-videoesxi-exe.html

Hau, W., Araujo, R., Chudgar, V., Hustad, R., & Chaubal, C. (2009). *How virtualization affects PCI DSS: A review of the top five issues*. Retrieved July 30, 2012 from http://whitepapers.techrepublic.com.com/abstract.aspx?docid=1086319

Higginbotham, S. (2011). *VMware and Verizon team up for mobile virtualization*. Retrieved July 30, 2012 from http://gigaom.com/2011/10/18/vmware-and-verizon-team-up-for-mobile-virtualization/

Meadows, R. (2009). *Cisco router and switch forensics: Investigating and analyzing malicious network activity*. Burlington, MA: Elsevier.

Microsoft. (2012). *Microsoft virtualization from the datacenter to the desktop*. Retrieved July 30, 2012 from http://technet.microsoft.com/en-us/virtualserver/bb676673.aspx

Mullins, R. (2011). *Cisco's virtualization play with windows server 8*. Retrieved July 30, 2012 from http://www.informationweek.com/news/tech-center/storage-virtualization/231602145

Orakwue, E. (2009). Rise of the virtual machine. *ISSA Journal*. Retrieved from http://www.issa.org/Library/Journals/2009/February/Orakwue-Rise%20of%20the%20Virtual%20Machine.pdf

Phillippi, N. (2010). *The difference between virtualization and cloud computing*. Retrieved July 30, 2012 from http://www.erpsoftwareblog.com/2010/08/the-difference-between-virtualization-and-cloud-computing/

Popek, G. J., & Goldberg, R. P. (1974). Formal requirements for virtualizable third generation architectures. *Communications of the ACM*, *17*(7), 412–421. doi:10.1145/361011.361073

Shavers, B. (2008). *Virtual machine forensics, a discussion of virtual machines related to forensics analysis*. Retrieved July 30, 2012 from http://www.forensicfocus.com

Urquhart, J. (2009). *Cloud is an operations model, not technology*. Retrieved July 30, 2012 from http://news.cnet.com/8301-19413_3-10249486-240.html

Veeam Software. (2011). *V-index.com virtualization penetration rate in the enterprise*. Retrieved July 30, 2012 from http://www.v-index.com/pdf/v-index_full_report_q3_2011.pdf?button_btm

VirtualBox. (2012). *Remote virtual machines*. Retrieved July 30, 2012 from http://www.virtualbox.org/manual/ch07.html

VMware. (2011). *What files make up a virtual machine?* Retrieved July 30, 2012 from http://www.vmware.com/support/ws55/doc/ws_learning_files_in_a_vm.html

VMware, Inc. (2007). *Understanding full virtualization paravirtualization and hardware assist*. Retrieved July 30, 2012 from http://www.vmware.com/files/pdf/VMware_paravirtualization.pdf

Vyatta. (2011). *On demand networking for virtual environments*. Retrieved July 30, 2012 from http://www.vyatta.com/solutions/virtual

Xen. (2012). *Xen hypervisor project*. Retrieved July 30, 2012 from http://www.xen.org/support/documentation.html

ADDITIONAL READING

Amoah, S. (2010). Cloud computing and network forensics in the eyes of computer forensic examiner. *Decision Group*. Retrieved from http://www.edecision4u.com/lawful%20interception%20article_02.html

Barrett, A. (2012). *VMware makes the case for PCI DSS compliance*. Retrieved from http://searchservervirtualization.techtarget.com/news/1338681/VMware-makes-the-case-for-PCI-DSS-compliance

Beckman, M. (2009). Cloud computing deep dive. *InforWorld*. Retrieved from http://www.slideshare.net/dyang10/infoworld-cloud-computing-deep-dive

Bem, D., & Huebner, E. (2007). Computer forensic analysis in a virtual environment. *International Journal of Digital Evidence*, *6*(2).

Cargile, A. (2009). Hypervisor security concerns. *The Coffee Desk*. Retrieved from http://charette.no-ip.com:81/programming/2009-12-30_Virtualization/

Coates, J., & Jarrat, J. (1989). *What futurists believe*. New York, NY: JF Coates, Inc.

Distributed Management Task Force, Inc. (2012). *DMTF creates open standard for system virtualization management*. Retrieved from http://www.dmtf.org/newsroom/pr/view?item_key=70d5d3ba78d39488626f838397a3d1e9812e5d40

Frost & Sullivan. (2009, November 30). *Although in its nascent stage, the future of virtualization market in India looks promising*. Retrieved from http://www.frost.com/prod/servlet/press-release.pag?docid=185829213

Garfinkel, T., & Rosenblum, M. (2012). *When virtual is harder than real: security challenges in virtual machine based computing environments*. Palo Alto, CA: Stanford University.

InfoWorld. (2009). *InfoClipz: Cloud computing*. Retrieved from http://www.infoworld.com

King, S. T., Chen, P. M., Wang, Y.-M., Verbowski, C., Wang, H. J., & Lorch, J. R. (2006). SubVirt: Implementing malware with virtual machines. In *Proceedings of the 2006 IEEE Symposium on Security and Privacy*, (pp. 314-327). IEEE Press.

Knowledge Exchange, I. T. (2012). *Defragmenting virtual machine files*. Retrieved from http://itknowledgeexchange.techtarget.com/virtualization-pro/defragmenting-virtual-machine-disk-files/

Kotsovinos, E. (2011). Virtualization: Blessing or curse? *Communications of the ACM*, *54*(1), 61–65. doi:10.1145/1866739.1866754

Law.com. (2012). *How virtualization affects EDD collection*. Retrieved from http://www.law.com

McAfee. (2012). *How virtualization affects PCI DSS part 1: Mapping PCI requirements and virtualization*. Retrieved from http://www.mcafee.com/hk/resources/white-papers/foundstone/wp-how-virt-affect-pci-dss-part-1.pdf

Microsoft. (2012). *Virtual hard dive specifications*. Retrieved from download.microsoft.com/.../Virtual%20Hard%20Disk%20Format%20Spec_10_18_06.doc

MojoPac. (2012). *RingCube*. Retrieved from http://www.mojopac.com/enterprise/products/index.html

Moka5. (2012). *LivePCs*. Retrieved from http://www.moka5.com/products/index.html

Mortman, D. (2012). *How to find virtual machines for greater virtualization compliance*. Retrieved from http://searchsecurity.techtarget.com/tip/How-to-find-virtual-machines-for-greater-virtualization-compliance

Murphy, A. (2012). *Virtualization defined – Eight different ways F5*. Retrieved from http://www.f5.com/pdf/white-papers/virtualization-defi ned-wp.pdf

Ohlhorst, F. J. (2012). Virtualization management brings the ultimate in efficiency. *Eweek, 29*(1), 10–11.

Security, C. I. (2012). *CIS level 1 benchmark for virtual machines*. Retrieved from http://www.cisecurity.org/tools2/vm/CIS_VM_Benchmark_v1.0.pdf

Siebert, E. (2012). *How to steal a virtual machine and its data in 3 easy steps*. Retrieved from http://searchvmware.techtarget.com/news/1378347/How-to-steal-a-virtual-machine-and-its-data-in-3-easy-steps

Stagner, H. (2005). *How to examine the compromised microsoft virtual server 2005 host server after a security breach*. Retrieved from http://searchservervirtualization.techtarget.com/tip/How-to-examine-the-compromised-Microsoft-Virtual-Server-2005-host-server-after-a-security-breach

Stagner, H. (2012). *How to detect rogue virtual machines on a network*. Retrieved from http://searchservervirtualization.techtarget.com/tip/How-to-detect-rogue-virtual-machines-on-a-network

Tech Target. (2012). *Data center virtualization: Four steps to compliance*. Retrieved from http://searchcompliance.techtarget.com/tip/Data-center-virtualization-Four-steps-to-compliance

Vanover, R. (2010). *The inner workings of the vStorage virtual machine file system*. Retrieved from http://searchvmware.techtarget.com/tip/The-inner-workings-of-the-vStorage-Virtual-Machine-File-System

Virtualization Information. (2012). *Install and configure ESX server*. Retrieved from http://virtualizationinformation.com/docs/Notes%20on%20VI%203.pdf

VMWare. (2012a). *Network segmentation in virtualized environments*. Retrieved from http://www.vmware.com/files/pdf/network_segmentation.pdf

VMWare. (2012b). *Understanding full virtualization paravirtualization and hardware assist*. Retrieved from http://www.vmware.com/fi les/pdf/VMware_paravirtualization.pdf

VMWare. (2012c). *Understanding virtual machine snapshots in VMware ESX*. Retrieved from http://kb.vmware.com/selfservice/microsites/search.do?language=en_US&cmd=displayKC&externalId=1015180

VMWare. (2012d). *Virtualization: Architectural considerations and other evaluation criteria*. Retrieved from http://www.vmware.com/pdf/virtualization_considerations.pdf

VMWare. (2012e). *GSX server documentation*. Retrieved from http://www.vmware.com/support/gsx25/doc/performance_memory_reserved_gsx.html

VMWare. (2012f). *Knowledge base, some space missing from a new VMFS data store due to hidden files*. Retrieved from http://kb.vmware.com/selfservice/microsites/search.do?language=en_US&cmd=displayKC&externalId=1001618

Chapter 7
Seizing Electronic Evidence from Cloud Computing Environments

Josiah Dykstra
University of Maryland, Baltimore County, USA

ABSTRACT

Despite a growing adoption of cloud computing, law enforcement and the judicial system are unprepared to prosecute cloud-based crimes. This chapter illuminates legal problems in the United States for electronic discovery and digital forensics arising from cloud computing and argues that cloud computing challenges the process and product of electronic discovery. The researchers investigate how to obtain forensic evidence from cloud computing using the legal process by surveying the existing statues and recent cases applicable to cloud forensics. A hypothetical case study of child pornography being hosted in the Cloud illustrates the difficulty in acquiring evidence for cloud-related crimes. For the first time, a sample search warrant is presented that could be used in this case study, and which provides sample language for agents and prosecutors who wish to obtain a warrant authorizing the search and seizure of data from cloud computing environments. The chapter concludes by taking a contrasting view and discusses how defense attorneys might be able to challenge cloud-derived evidence in court.

INTRODUCTION

Crime committed using cloud computing resources and against cloud infrastructures is inevitable. In early 2011, Sony was the victim of an online data breach that took down the PlayStation Network. In a widely cited report, Bloomberg News reported that the intruder used Amazon's public cloud to commit the crime (Galante, Kharif, & Alpeyev, 2011). The report also stated that the FBI was investigating the crime, but that neither Amazon nor the FBI would comment on whether the former had been served a search warrant or subpoena. No further information about the case has been made public. This is the first public case of a cloud-related crime, though many more are bound to emerge soon.

Companies are embracing cloud technology to offload some of the cost, upkeep, and growth

DOI: 10.4018/978-1-4666-2662-1.ch007

Copyright © 2013, IGI Global. Copying or distributing in print or electronic forms without written permission of IGI Global is prohibited.

of equipment that they would otherwise have purchased themselves. Cloud infrastructure offers an attractive prize for hackers, with exceptional bandwidth, storage, and computing power, and a consolidated repository of data. While many people have lamented how users of the cloud and their data are protected, few of these discussions have considered the difficulty of responding to and prosecuting security breaches, including forensics and criminal prosecution.

Cloud computing introduces new and significant challenges in prosecuting cloud-based crimes that differ from traditional electronic evidence and electronic crime. The very attributes that make cloud computing attractive can be at odds with forensic and legal goals. For example, the cloud offers location independence so that data are available from anywhere, even though location may determine jurisdiction. Another example is the rapid self-creation and destruction of cloud resources, a powerful feature for customers, but a severe challenge for evidence preservation.

This chapter discusses the legal seizure of data from cloud computing related to the prosecution of cloud-based crimes. We explore the legal problems in the United States for electronic discovery and digital forensics arising from cloud computing as an infrastructure service and explain how cloud computing challenges the process and product of electronic discovery. We investigate how one might obtain forensic evidence from cloud computing using legal process by surveying the existing statues and recent cases applicable to cloud forensics. While this is not legal advice, we approach the problem from a computer science perspective and with a background in digital forensics. This technical perspective is intended to inform forensic practitioners about legal problems, and aid legal practitioners with prosecuting cloud crimes.

We use a hypothetical case study of child pornography being hosted in the Cloud to illustrate the difficulty in acquiring evidence for cloud-related crimes. While fictional, it describes a common computer crime where the cloud is an accessory to a crime. For the first time we present a sample search warrant affidavit that could be used in this case study. This provides an example and sample language for agents and prosecutors who will soon need to obtain a warrant authorizing the search and seizure of data from cloud computing environments.

We conclude by discussing how defense attorneys might be able to challenge cloud-derived evidence in court. It is important for both prosecution and defense to understand how cloud evidence may be challenged in court today. Some of these issues include complexity of the environment and lack of jury comprehension, the failure of cloud forensic evidence against the *Daubert* test, and changing attitudes of the US Supreme Court regarding privacy.

BACKGROUND

Before looking at the laws affecting the process of seizing evidence of cloud evidence, we provide some context and background about cloud computing, digital forensics, and the law.

Cloud Computing

Let us being by defining the scope of our discussion. It would be easy to let a discussion on cloud computing grow to encompass all Internet-enabled services as "cloud computing." There are good reasons for discussing forensic investigations of Facebook and Twitter specifically because those services are involved in many cases, but we will take a more formal definition. One often-cited definition of cloud computing comes from the National Institute of Standards and Technology (NIST) (Mell & Grance, 2011), which reads in part:

Cloud computing is a model for enabling ubiquitous, convenient, on-demand network access to a shared pool of configurable computing resources (e.g., networks, servers, storage, applications, and services) that can be rapidly provisioned and released with minimal management effort or service provider interaction.

"Cloud" is a generic term that refers to a network where the physical location and inner workings are abstracted away and unimportant to the usage. Telephone networks and the Internet are examples of Clouds. Cloud computing, however, is concerned with providing customers with raw remote computing resources such as computation or data storage, and the ability to provision those resources themselves.

There are many providers of cloud services, and even those that provide similar services have proprietary implementations. Amazon Web Services (AWS) is one example of a cloud service provider. AWS provides a variety of Infrastructure as a Service (IaaS) cloud services. The Elastic Compute Cloud (EC2) is a platform where customers can purchase computing power in the form of a computer connected to the Internet that the customer can control. The Simple Storage Service (S3) is a cloud storage offering, essentially acting like a large disk drive accessible from the Internet. Other examples of cloud service providers are Microsoft Azure, Salesforce, and Google App Engine.

For the purposes of our discussion about seizing evidence, we focus on gathering evidence from IaaS cloud providers. Online services, including social networking sites and Web-based email, inherently have different data of interest in e-discovery. Technical and legal experts have already analyzed many issues related to e-discovery of these services, including the publication of real subpoenas and search warrants. Concentrating on IaaS cloud services, we will take as broad a view as possible. However, remember that each provider may implement their cloud services in a proprietary manner that may influence the forensic data available, how those data are collected, and who has access to the data.

Digital Forensics and the Law

Digital forensics holds a unique place in the wider world of forensics distinguished by its meaning. In forensic odontology or forensic anthropology, for example, forensic investigators are concerned with applying their discipline to evidence of crimes and answering questions of interest to the legal system. In particular, these questions relate to how a crime was committed or how an individual died. "Digital forensics," on the other hand, has come to encompass a wide variety of activities. The term is so encompassing that it often refers to non-legal questions. Some people would say that any file recovery, such as an accidentally deleted term paper, is an example of digital forensics. Others would say that enforcing corporate policy is digital forensics, such as investigating an employee's computer to see if he or she were violating corporate policy against checking sports scores during work hours. This ambiguity in meaning threatens the credibility of the discipline.

In a recent online survey of forensic experts, primarily forensic investigators, 61% agreed or strongly agreed with the way the phrase "digital forensics" is used today (Dykstra, 2012). The respondents overwhelming felt that digital forensics did not need to involve a civil or criminal offense. However, of five published definitions of "digital forensics," they most agreed with those including the phrases "reconstruction of events found to be criminal" (43.8%) or "in a manner that is legally accepted" (39.3%).

The difficulty lies in the fact that there is no other accepted term to describe forensic-like digital investigations. Both legal and non-legal investigations may use the same software, procedures, and techniques. When the investigation must be legally sound, additional requirements are levied on the process, including chain-of-custody and authenticity. Our survey showed that given five alternative phrases, respondents preferred "digital investigation" and "digital examination" (see Figure 1).

Figure 1. Which of the following terms would best describe forensic-like activities that are not intended for legal process and are not bound by legal soundness?

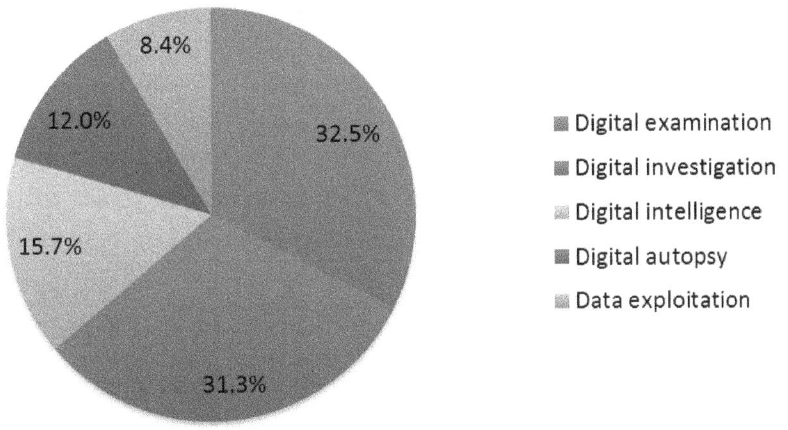

For the purposes of these discussions, we assume that digital forensics is concerned with the acquisition and analysis of digital evidence to inform legal proceedings. Digital forensics is an umbrella term for any digital data that encompass sub-disciplines such as computer forensics, network forensics, database forensics, mobile device forensics, and video forensics. Even modest crimes involving digital devices require blending these disciplines, since nearly every computer is interconnected to another. Cloud computing, by its nature, draws upon computer forensics and network forensics since a networked computer is always involved. Other digital forensic disciplines may also be involved depending on the crime.

Related Work

We are unaware of any published template for writing a search warrant for cloud data. In 2006, a California attorney published an article titled "Search Warrant Language for Cellular Phones," describing how to obtain data from cell providers (Morgester, 2006). Several law enforcement manuals, which describe what data are available to law enforcement and how to request them, for Webmail and social networking Websites have leaked online. These may hint at similar data available for cloud services. Several search warrants have appeared in the press for services like Facebook (Willamette Week, 2011) and Gmail (Van Horn, 2009). The Department of Justice Search and Seizure Manual (2009) includes sample subpoenas, orders, and warrants which we used for guidance, but none of these were for cloud data.

Stephen Wolthusen (2009) highlighted a number of research challenges for forensic discovery in distributed environments. While he enumerated some of the legal challenges, he did not analyze the applicability of existing laws. Another study (Taylor, Haggerty, Gresty, & Lamb, 2011) looked more closely at UK-specific issues.

Other authors have taken a careful look at privacy related to cloud computing, the most common topic of law review articles related to cloud computing. Stylianou (2010) studied changes in the privacy terms of cloud services, and found that more private information was being surrendered to third parties but that companies were treating that data with more respect. Barnhill (2010) explained that court decisions extend no reasonable expectation of privacy in emails stored with third. Couillard (2009) wrote, "users expect their information to be treated the same on this virtual cloud as it would be if it were stored on their computer, phone, or iPod."

OBTAINING FORENSIC EVIDENCE FROM THE CLOUD

In criminal cases, discovery is the pre-trial phase where the prosecutor obtains information or evidence that may be used against a defendant during the trial. Electronic discovery refers to the exchange of Electronically Stored Information (ESI). Therefore, search and seizure of cloud-based evidence falls in the discovery phase of criminal prosecution.

In the United States, numerous constitutional and statutory provisions govern search and seizure, including that of forensic evidence from cloud providers. Since we focus on criminal cases, we will explore the Federal Rules of Criminal Procedure (FRCrP) and the Fourth Amendment. In this section, we show how these statues might apply to acquisition of cloud-based ESI. We intend only to introduce the array of issues rather than to dive deeply into each one.

One statute plays an important part in cloud forensics: the Electronic Communications Privacy Act of 1986 (ECPA), codified at 18 U.S.C. §§2510-22. ECPA includes two definitions that are important when discussing cloud computing and the law. The first is an "Electronic Communication Service" (ECS) that is "any service which provides to users thereof the ability to send or receive wire or electronic communications" (18 U.S.C. §2510). Title II of ECPA is referred to as the Stored Communications Act (SCA), 18 U.S.C. §2701-12, which adds the second definition. A "Remote Computing Service" (RCS) that is "the provision to the public of computer storage or processing services by means of an electronic communications system" (18 U.S.C. §2711). Different rules apply to the two services, and a cloud provider might be an ECS or RCS or both, depending on the services it provides.

Federal Rules of Criminal Procedure

The Federal Rules of Criminal Procedure (FRCrP) are a collection of 61 rules that govern the process of how criminal prosecutions are conducted in United States district courts. They were last amended in December 2011. In this section, we will consider six topics that describe how the Rules relate to seizing cloud-based data.

Available Data

The first question in considering cloud-based data is what data are available. FRCrP (2010) Rule 16 permits the ability to request data "in the defendant's possession, custody, or control." The respondent for discovery of cloud evidence will either be the cloud provider or a customer of the cloud service. The repackaging and reselling of cloud services introduces potential for legal complexity, since end-users may interface with a provider, which in turn uses cloud computing. Dropbox is an online storage service that uses AWS for data storage (Dropbox, 2012). Dropbox states that "All files stored online by Dropbox are encrypted and kept securely on Amazon's S3 in multiple data centers located around the United States." Customers negotiate services directly with Dropbox, not Amazon. If a Dropbox customer were under investigation, data could be requested from either Dropbox or Amazon or both. As we will see below, the petitioner's choice depends on what data are sought.

Unfortunately, the complete set of forensic data available to a requestor is publically unknown. The public cloud providers have thus far withheld their capabilities, possibly because they are protecting the proprietary cloud implementation that gives them competitive advantage. We speculate about data that are likely available, but cannot speculate about the provider's practical ability to collect these data. To discuss what data are in the cloud provider's control, it is important to understand what data might be available. Infrastructure as a

Service can be thought of as many layers of a cake, each independently providing part of the cloud service. The top layer of the cake contains the consumer's data and applications, which may be exposed to the Internet in the form of a Webpage or database. These data are the first that may be available, and by definition of IaaS are owned and controlled by the consumer. The next layer is the guest virtual machine, which in IaaS is also owned and controlled by the consumer. The third layer of the cake is the hypervisor, special software that runs on a provider's computer (called the host) and allows many virtual machines to run independently on a single physical machine. Below the physical machine is the distributed array of storage disks. The base of the cake is the computer networking that interconnects the components, and provides high bandwidth to the Internet.

Law enforcement policy manuals have not been made public by any of the major cloud providers that describe the records and data available under a search warrant. The providers control data related to subscriber information and billing records. As customers are billed based on their usage, records relating to service usage should also be available. Beyond these obvious requests, consider other data that the providers likely keep for some period of time. Connection information, sometimes called NetFlow records, that record the two endpoints of Internet communications are non-content data that can be useful as a historical record. Cloud services are provisioned by an out-of-band channel, usually on a special management website or through an Application Programming Interface (API). The provider may be able to produce logs showing successful and unsuccessful logins, from where those logins came, and when they occurred. If services can be provisioned programmatically, similar logs may be available. While it is not important to the functioning of the system for humans to know where data are located (*e.g.*, server or data center), the underlying infrastructure must know where they are. The provider may be recording system logs that describe where the data are, who created them, and when they were created, modified or deleted. In sum, law enforcement today has no template search warrants for cloud data and does not know what they can or should ask for.

Access to Data

Having considered what data are available, the next issue is the access to that data. With IaaS, data inside a consumer's virtual machine, such as a Webpage, are hidden even from the provider unless the consumer makes it available on the Internet. The cloud provider, whose ownership and responsibility extend to the hypervisor and below, could access the computer files that make up the virtual machine, and could provide a copy of the virtual machine during discovery. The provider also has other ample opportunities to collect content and non-content forensic evidence, all of which are in the provider's custody, possession, and control: they could collect network packet captures of all ingress and egress network traffic from their cloud; they have billing data about the provisioning and usage of cloud resources; they could collect logs showing the physical storage locations of data. The language of the contract between the provider and the customer will determine how much access the customer has to these data. In *Flagg v. City of Detroit* (2008), for example, the court ruled that text messages held by a provider were subject to the city's control, given that the city had some contractual right of access to the data. To complicate matters, there are data in the provider's possession over which the customer may not have legal custody (*e.g.*, infrastructure logs), and there are data in the provider's possession over which they may not have legal custody (*e.g.*, customer's data).

With most cloud providers, IaaS customers can usually collect network captures from inside their virtual machine, but they see only their own traffic. The Communications Assistance for Law Enforcement Act (CALEA, 1994) requires telecommunications carriers to assist law enforcement in performing electronic surveillance pursuant to court orders. However, the term "telecommunications carrier" does not include "persons or entities insofar as they are engaged in providing information services" (47 U.S.C. §1001(8)(C)(i), 1994). The law does not require cloud providers to provide real-time interception capabilities. In a statement before the House Judiciary Committee's hearing on *Going Dark: Lawful Electronic Surveillance in the Face of New Technologies* (2011), the FBI and others identified this as a shortcoming (p. 23).

Preserving Evidence

Once law enforcement knows what data are available, and who has access to the data, the data must be preserved until it can be lawfully acquired. Preservation is an essential tool in electronic discovery, particularly with highly volatile and elastic data. The bar is very low to compel a provider to preserve a snapshot of potential evidence. In Section 2703 of the Stored Communications Act (2000), ECS and RCS providers "upon the request of a governmental entity, shall take all necessary steps to preserve records and other evidence in its possession pending the issuance of a court order or other process" for 90 days, which can be renewed for an additional 90 days. Section 2704 describes how a governmental entity, in a subpoena or court order, may order the provider to create a backup copy of the contents of the communications. Cloud providers need some mechanism for preservation, if they do not have one already. On one hand, the providers have an advantage in preserving even large volumes of data since they advertise broad storage resources. This alleviates traditional concerns about cost, such as in *Viacom Int'l Inc. v. YouTube Inc.* (2008), where the court ruled that the need for 12 terabytes of data overweighed the expensive and burdensome of production. Additionally, IaaS resources such as virtual machines inherently enable snapshots to be taken of the running machine at any time. On the other hand, the providers may have no way to prevent the de-provisioning of resources or deletion of data.

Consider the following example where cloud practices inhibit preservation. Cloud resources, such as virtual machines, are launched using a user's private key. A hacker steals the key from the legitimate owner, and uses it to launch hundreds of machines that flood a popular website and take it offline. The prosecution, wishing to subpoena data from the legitimate user, might ask for logs of activity showing who launched the machines, and copies of the machines themselves. However, the legitimate user may have no logs to produce, and the attacker may have deleted the hundreds of malicious machines. In traditional digital forensics, investigators create a bit-for-bit image of a hard drive that the examiner can search for deleted files. Tragically, while providers know when files are deleted in their storage array, and may have logs to prove it, they probably lack the ability to recover deleted files or to produce complete hard disk images. The Service Level Agreement for Microsoft Azure reads "You're responsible for backing up the data that you store on the service…Data that is deleted may be irretrievable" (Microsoft Corporation, 2010).

With the elasticity of cloud computing, ephemeral data will be problematic. In *Columbia Pictures v. Bunnell* (2007), the court concluded that Random Access Memory (RAM) data was discoverable. *Bunnell* also concluded that IP addresses were discoverable. In the Cloud, both data and infrastructure are potentially fleeting. Cloud providers ultimately must at least know when resources are provisioned and de-provisioned, since those activities directly determine billing of the customer. Elasticity also demands a method to preserve evidence either due to standard business practices or negligent destruction, known as spoliation. The courts have mandated preservation when litigation is reasonably anticipated (Zubulake v. UBS Warburg, 2003; AAB Joint Ventures v. United States, 2007). In civil cases, the Federal Rules of Civil Procedures in section 37(E) also protect the provider if data are "lost as a result of the routine, good-faith operation of an electronic information system." There is no exact analog in the FRCrP, where willful, intentional destruction falls under obstruction of justice. Even so, "only persons conscious of wrongdoing" can be held liable, as Chief Justice William Rehnquist wrote when the Supreme Court overturned Arthur Anderson's conviction of willfully destroying documents related to Enron (Arthur Andersen LLP v. United States, 2005).

Legal Right to Data

Ownership issues should be detailed in the contract between the cloud provider and consumer. Amazon Web Services has such a customer agreement (2012). In this contract, "content" is defined as "software (including machine images), data, text, audio, video, images or other content" (Amazon Web Services, 2012). In Section 8.1, Amazon clams "no rights under this Agreement from you or your licensors to Your Content, including any related intellectual property rights" (Amazon Web Services, 2012). The document defines "Service Offerings" as "the Services (including associated APIs), the AWS Content, the AWS Marks, the AWS Site, and any other product or service provided by us under this Agreement" (Amazon Web Services, 2012). In Section 8.4, Amazon clams that "we or our affiliates or licensors and reserve all right, title, and interest in and to the Service Offerings" (Amazon Web Services, 2012). In other words, the consumer explicitly owns their virtual machines, and does not own the IP address, hardware, or cloud-hosted infrastructure. Microsoft contracts contain similar language. "Except for material that we license to you, we don't claim ownership of the content you provide on the service. Your content remains your content" (Microsoft Corporation, 2010). "Content" is not defined in this service agreement.

In cases where content is not defined, we must look to case law. In *Flagg* (2008), the court found that the city had a contractual right to text messages held by a third party provider. *Flagg* did not address the ownership of other data, such as the provider's logs. In the issuance of a subpoena or search warrant, it will be vital to differentiate what data are in the custody, possession, or control of the provider verses the client.

Jurisdiction and Venue

Jurisdiction for cloud computing is somewhat different from other jurisdiction jurisprudence to date. Even in cases regarding online data, the cases almost exclusively revolve around websites. Online services such as Facebook and Gmail, though they comply with legal process for information, have neither been challenged about the backend geographic location nor locations of the resultant data. In the Cloud, the issue compounds since data will certainly be stored in several jurisdictions, and may be stored across international boundaries whose laws may be in conflict. In *United States v. Drew* (2009), the defendant was tried in California because she was accused of violating a social networking site's terms of service, and the site's owner was located in California. Courts have recently been applying the "effects test" for personal jurisdiction, based on "(1) intentional actions, (2) expressly aimed at the forum state, (3) causing harm, the brunt of which is suffered—and which the defendant knows is likely to be suffered—in the forum state" (Core-Vent Corp. v. Nobel Industries AB, 1993). Under that framework, one would expect most cloud-based litigation to occur in the cloud customer's forum state. Many people assume that the laws protecting data are those where the data physically exists. However, there is no precedent or case law supporting this assumption. The effects test would lead us to believe that in most cases, crimes are committed against the data owners in their forum state, and not with the intent to cause harm in the forum state of the data.

FRCrP Rule 18 (2010), which says, "…the government must prosecute an offense in the district where the offense was committed," is no longer a straightforward issue. When a suit is brought where the cloud is the object of the crime, four options exist for venue of the trial: the perpetrator's forum, the cloud provider's forum, the cloud customer's forum, or the online data location forum. Cloud service providers may dictate the venue in their contract. Barring contractual establishment of venue, allows for offenses committed in one district to "be inquired of and prosecuted in any district in which such offense was begun, continued, or completed." The Supreme Court held in *United States v. Beddow* (1992) that determining the proper venue "is best described as a substantial contacts rule that takes into account a number of factors—the site of the defendant's acts, the elements and nature of the crime, the locus of the effect of the criminal conduct, and the suitability of each district for accurate fact finding…" None of these factors are obvious in determining venue for cloud-based crimes. Any of the four venues we identified could make a compelling case to host the trial.

Cloud computing and most other Web services exist without deference to geographical location. We contend, however, that consumers have a "reasonable expectation of location" for their data. In general, users sensibly believe that if they are using a service provided by a US company that their data reside in the United States. They may also look at top-level domain names and assume that data stored by www.state.md.us, for example, is in the United States while that for *mail.ru* is in Russia. Most Service Level Agreements (SLA) for online services do not specify the location where data will be stored. Unless they have reason to believe otherwise (*e.g.*, Amazon Web Services allows customers to specify the geographic region where data is stored), consumers and end-users will make assumptions about the location of their data, and subsequently the laws governing it.

How to get Data

Finally, we consider the vehicles available to compel data from a provider. Traditional search warrants are authorized under FRCrP Rule 41. This type of warrant can be used to seize physical evidence, but only (with few exceptions) for objects in the court's jurisdiction. ECPA offers five mechanisms for the government to obtain electronic information from a provider, including its own kind of warrant. These five mechanisms are:

1. Subpoena;
2. Subpoena with prior notice to the subscriber or customer;
3. § 2703(d) court order;
4. § 2703(d) court order with prior notice to the subscriber or customer; and
5. Search warrant.

According to the DOJ Search and Seizure Manual (2009), "Department of Justice policy favors the use of a subpoena or other less intrusive means to obtain evidence from disinterested third parties, unless use of those less intrusive means would substantially jeopardize the availability or usefulness of the materials sought" (p. 111). Loss of availability is of paramount concern given the elasticity of the cloud. Regardless of the vehicle used, we have already seen a difference in what data are in the provider's possession, custody, or control, and what data are in the cloud customer's possession, custody, or control. To complicate the matter, 18 U.S.C. §2701 et. seq. prohibits a provider from disclosing user content in response to a civil subpoena. This was affirmed in *Flagg* (2008), saying "[The Stored Communications Act] lacks any language that explicitly authorizes a service provider to divulge the contents of a communication pursuant to subpoena or court order." This decision on communication and the SCA provide drastically different protection for data storage in an ECS versus a provider of RCS, where 18 U.S.C. §2703(b) allows a cloud provider acting as a provider of RCS to disclose the contents of an account used for remote storage without a warrant, and without notifying the customer or subscriber. Kerr (2010) suggested that this is unconstitutional.

The final issue to consider is time. Typically, the issuing party will allow between 10 and 30 days to comply, except where the issuing court's local rules dictate a minimum time period for compliance. Given the ease with which cloud data could be destroyed by a criminal, and the lack of mechanisms likely available for providers to preserve evidence, the threat of spoliation is dramatically increased. One solution is to require faster compliance with court orders. The primary detractor to this approach is that it requires human intervention at the cloud provider and doesn't scale well. Another solution is to empower data owners and investigators to gather forensic evidence themselves. We are actively exploring this area.

Costs of Data Production

Upon execution of a warrant, the cost of cloud-based ESI production could be extensive. The situation is not entirely analogous to Zubulake v. UBS Warburg (2003). In Zubulake, the majority of the $273,649 production costs arose from the restoration of five offline magnetic tapes and attorney fees. Data stored in the Cloud are online and available for access. The physical act of locating and copying the data may still take considerable time. For example, Amazon (2012) offers an export service that enables customers to have their data copied to a storage device and mailed to them. This service costs $80.00 per storage device handled plus $2.49 per data-loading hour. These costs are unlikely to approach the costs of magnetic tape restoration; however, the analysis costs of large data volumes will dwarf the data production costs. If a cloud customer arbitrarily had two terabytes of data in the Cloud, it would take nearly 10 hours to copy to a USB hard drive, totaling $104.90. Degnan (2011) estimates forensic analysis at $1000 per gigabyte, bringing two terabytes to $2 million. Importantly, an IaaS cloud provider may be unable to search the corpus of data and produce specific evidence (*e.g.*, a particular file), but rather would have to hand over the whole data set.

Fourth Amendment

Search and seizure for evidence of crimes committed in or against the Cloud must be valid under the Fourth Amendment. This amendment reads:

The right of the people to be secure in their persons, houses, papers, and effects, against unreasonable searches and seizures, shall not be violated; and no Warrants shall issue but upon probable cause supported by Oath or affirmation, and particularly describing the place to be searched, and the persons or things to be seized (U.S. Const., amend IV).

In this section, we will examine how the Fourth Amendment applies to cloud computing in three areas: expectation of privacy, requirements for a warrant, the execution of search warrants, and exceptions to the warrant requirement.

Expectation of Privacy

For simplicity, and given the previous work in this area, we assume that cloud computing customers have a reasonable expectation of privacy for their data, even though they have entrusted it to a third party. We also proceed under the current doctrine that applies the Fourth Amendment to online data. Therefore, under Katz v. United States (1967) and its progeny, we grant that a search is performed in obtaining cloud data, and that the Fourth Amendment is implicated by the violation of the reasonable expectation of privacy. Instead, we explore the issues surrounding the execution of a warrant for cloud data.

Requirements for a Warrant

Before a lawful warrant can be issued, a number of basic requirements must be met. First, the warrant must be approved by a court of law. Second, the Fourth Amendment requires probable cause, in a sworn statement, that the law enforcement officer requesting the warrant believes that the search will reveal criminal activity. Third, the Amendment requires that a warrant "particularly" describe the person, place, or thing to be searched. This third requirement presents an issue for cloud-based crimes.

In previous sections we examined the location-independent nature of cloud computing. This is clearly counter to the requirements of the Fourth Amendment. In addition to physical location, pin-pointing the data to be searched is also problematic. In recent years, warrants for Web-based email could specify a particular sender, receiver, and timeframe, preventing the unnecessary production of the entire corpus of email. In IaaS, the warrant may equally narrow the search for data by filename, creation time, or author. Lawyers like to use an analogy between hard drives and filing cabinets. Given the nature of digital evidence, electronic searches do not overcome the need to scan the container for the evidence. Just as one would leaf through a filing cabinet looking for a particular document, so too must the investigator interrogate the computer looking for the particular file (Kerr, 2005). Unfortunately, distributed cloud data may require the leafing through many filing cabinets in many warehouses in many locations, where data is co-mingled with other user's data. Despite the potential for an unprecedented and overwhelming volume of ESI from cloud crimes, search warrants in these cases have a unique opportunity to address the particularity issue often associated with digital searches. Unfortunately, since cloud providers are opaque about their infrastructure, it would be impossible for the warrant to specify the search strategy or approach of execution ahead of time. With a basic understanding of cloud computing technology, magistrates should decline to impose conditions of issuing cloud-targeted warrants.

Execution of Search Warrants

The Fourth Amendment makes no explicit statement about who should execute the warrant, in other words, who should carry out the intentions of the warrant. Today, most search warrants for online data are served to the provider, and subsequently executed by the provider. The legal authority for the provider to execute a warrant comes from statute and case law. In particular, 18 U.S.C. § 2703(g) says "Notwithstanding section 3105 of this title, the presence of an officer shall not be required for service or execution of a search warrant issued in accordance with this chapter requiring disclosure by a provider of electronic communications service or remote computing service of the contents of communications or records or other information pertaining to a subscriber to or customer of such service." In United States v. Bach (2002), the court held that "The Fourth Amendment does not explicitly require official presence during a warrant's execution; therefore, it is not an automatic violation if no officer is present during a search." The practical reason is also germane: law enforcement does not have the resources or expertise to execute the warrant themselves. When the provider executes the warrant at the bequest of law enforcement, they may become agents of the government, a potentially undesirable state. In US v. Richardson (2010), the court held that America Online was not acting as an agent for the government when it uncovered and report child pornography in a user's email. However, this activity was not done at the government's request. Steven Morrison (2011) recently suggested that ISPs be treated as state actors for any search of user's email. Cloud providers may also look for ways to empower customers and law enforcement to acquire forensic data. This capability is admirable and would free the provider from the burden of doing all the work, and be an attractive feature to potential security-minded clients. Whether the provider or law enforcement does the search, it leads to two new questions: where can the search be done, and whose law applies?

Consider an example that illustrates this problem. Imagine a cloud provider incorporated in California has a data center in Virginia. A judge in Washington, DC, issues a warrant for data that resides in the Virginia data center. A resident of New York is the owner of the data. If executed by the provider, the search is done from a computer terminal in California. The provider also makes it possible for the FBI to execute the search remotely from their offices in DC. We propose that it does not matter where the search is done (inside of the United States), and that the search must comply with California law. The interconnected, networked nature of a national or global company makes it irrelevant where the search is done. Even if the provider executes the search in California, they will remotely access the data, across many interstate networks, in the Virginia data center. It follows, however, that the provider, being incorporated and governed by California law, ought to have jurisdiction over the search no matter where it happens.

Exceptions to the Warrant Requirement

The Fourth Amendment does not apply, and warrants are not required, in a number of circumstances. Two of these situations—consent and plain view—are considered here. In cloud crimes where a crime has been committed against an innocent data owner, that party can give consent to a search, and a warrant is not required. Someone whose website, hosted in the Cloud, has been hacked or whose data has been stolen, for example, is likely to cooperate with law enforcement in the criminal investigation. Another type of cloud-based crime is that where the party controlling the cloud resources is committing the crime. For example, if some party is distributing child pornography on a cloud-hosted website, it would be immediately apparent to an officer that incriminating evidence is hosted on the site. This situation is known as plain view, and no warrant is required to seize that contraband. Bear in mind, however, that after an officer identifies the contraband in plain view, a warrant based on the plain view evidence discovered is required for subsequent searches.

SEARCH WARRANTS FOR CLOUD DATA

Having considered some of the applications and implications of the law for seizing cloud-based ESI, we now turn to the act of acquiring the evidence. In preparation for a full search warrant example, let us walk through some of the cloud-specific parts of the warrant.

The first part of a search warrant must describe what is to be seized. The law requires "reasonable particularity" in the description of the evidence, contraband, fruits, or instrumentality of crime that the agents hope to obtain by conducting the search.

In cloud computing environments, the "property to be seized" should contain a description of information (such as computer files) rather than physical hardware, regardless of the role of the computer in the offense. By definition, the physical hardware of a cloud provider is not owned by the suspect (unless the provider is the subject). Seizure of physical hardware yields no benefit that data alone cannot provide, and in fact may be disruptive to other cloud clients sharing that hardware. The "property to be seized" described in the warrant should fall into one or more of the categories listed in FRCrP Rule 41(b):

1. "Property that constitutes evidence of the commission of a criminal offense."

This is a very broad authorization, covering any item that an investigator reasonably believes would reveal information that would aid in the investigation. "Property" has come to include tangible and intangible property. Case law has established that electronic data are also "property" that may be searched and seized.

2. "Contraband, the fruits of crime, or things otherwise criminally possessed."

In cloud environments, contraband could take one of the following forms. Contraband, including child pornography, pirated software, and other copyrighted materials, may be kept in cloud storage or inside of cloud virtual machines. When a hacker breaks into a machine hosted in the Cloud, that machine could be the fruits of the crime—that property acquired as the result of the crime of unauthorized access.

3. "Property designed or intended for use or which is or had been used as a means of committing a criminal offense."

Cloud environments could be used as the instrument of a crime in several ways. Cloud storage could be used to transmit child pornography, and cloud-based virtual machines could be used to produce it. A virtual machine could be used for hacking, or used to host websites with illegal content. In each case, the cloud contains property used to commit an offense.

The second step in drafting a warrant is to describe the property's location. The law, rooted in the physical world, is interested in where the property is. The location, which must be noted with reasonable particularity, has historically been a safeguard to citizens that limit the scope of the warrant. Search warrants for online Webmail have traditionally specified only the email address as the "place to be searched." "Location" requires special consideration when dealing with online data, especially with cloud computing. Only rarely will data be stored on a single server at the address of the data custodian. In many cases, the servers will be dispersed across state or international boundaries. Further, cloud data are often replicated to multiple datacenters. This seemingly presents a problem when describing the "location to be searched," since the agent or prosecutor may not know where the data containers are.

The search warrant for cloud-based data should not specify a physical address to be searched, lest the search exclude data stored at other physical locations. Instead, the warrant should specify the desired data and the warrant served to the data custodian.

Here is an example of how to describe the location of cloud-based data in some datacenter owned and controlled by Amazon:

Data, metadata, and account information created, stored, or controlled by Amazon Web Services LLC, 410 Terry Avenue North, Seattle, WA 98109-5210, related to IP address 1.2.3.4 for the time period beginning 12:01 a.m. CST (January 1, 2012) through 12:01 a.m. CST (July 1, 2012).

The terms "data" and "metadata" include all of the foregoing items of evidence in whatever form (such as virtual machines, user-created content, log data, packet captures, intrusion detection alerts, billing records) and by whatever means they may have been created or stored, including any electrical, electronic, or magnetic form (such as volatile and non-volatile information on an electronic or magnetic storage device, including hard disks, backup storage, live memory, as well as printouts and readouts from any storage device), in any physical location controlled by the provider where the data may reside.

The third step in drafting a warrant is to set the parameters for executing the warrant. Federal warrants allow the specification for the time of day during which to execute the warrant, and the date by which to execute the warrant. These are further safeguards to ensure a limited lifetime of the warrant and minimal disruption (*e.g.* "in the daytime between 6:00 a.m. to 10 p.m.") to the subject of the warrant.

The elasticity and near instant provisioning and de-provision of data poses a legal challenge in cloud computing. Unless physical machines are seized or virtual machines are turned off, execution of the warrant is unlikely to impact or disrupt the data owner, but in fact risks spoliation if announced. The search warrant can be executed at any time in the day or night, but should be executed as soon as possible to preserve evidence. The traditional response time of 10 days should be shortened as much as possible, within reason of the logistical constraints of the cloud provider.

An affidavit to justify the search and seizure of cloud-based computer data should include, at a minimum, the following sections: (1) definitions of any technical terms used in the affidavit or warrant; (2) a summary of the offense, and, if known, the role that a targeted computer plays in the offense; and (3) an explanation of the agents' search strategy.

While agents and prosecutors should resist the urge to pad affidavits with long, boilerplate descriptions of well-known technical phrases, cloud computing is a new discipline and currently requires special attention to defining new terms. As a rule, affidavits should only include the definitions of terms that are likely to be unknown by a generalist judge and are used in the remainder of the affidavit. Figure 2 shows a sample definition for "cloud computing" which could be used in the affidavit. This, and several others, is included in the sample search warrant later in the chapter.

These concepts are embodied in the sample search warrant that follows. The key thing to remember is that the seizure should focus on data rather than hardware, and that the data may be distributed across physical locations.

Case Study

To illustrate the application of the concepts presented so far, we will now look at a hypothetical case study of a cloud-based crime. This case study was previously used to explain technical issues in cloud forensics (Dykstra & Sherman, 2011). After analyzing the scenario, we can then construct a sample search warrant that could be used in this case.

Here is the hypothetical crime:

Polly is a criminal who traffics in child pornography. He has set up a service in the Cloud to store a large collection of contraband images and video. The website allows users to upload and download this content anonymously. He pays for his cloud services with a pre-paid credit card purchased with cash. Polly encrypts his data in cloud storage, and he reverts his virtual Web server to a clean state daily. Law enforcement is tipped off to the website and wishes both to terminate the service and prosecute the criminal.

This is a case where the computer is incidental to the offense. Let us assume that this scenario took place in Amazon EC2. Let us assume that law enforcement first contacts the cloud provider with a preservation order to retain evidence pend-

Figure 2. Definition of "virtual machine" for use in a search warrant

Virtual Machine ("VM")
Virtualization is a technique whereby special software, called the hypervisor, can run many virtual (rather than physical) machines. The hardware on the single machine is emulated so that each virtual instance of a computer, called a virtual machine ("VM"), does not require dedicated physical hardware, but each VM believes it has its own hardware. The hypervisor has special access to control all of the virtual guests, but it should also be able to isolate the guests from each other.

ing a warrant. Preservation is authorized under 18 U.S.C. §2703(f)(1) which says "A provider of wire or electronic communication services or a remote computing service, upon the request of a governmental entity, shall take all necessary steps to preserve records and other evidence in its possession pending the issuance of a court order or other process." Tracking down the user is the more difficult task.

The examiner has no technical ability to image the virtual machine remotely since the cloud provider does not expose that functionality, and in doing so would alter the state of the machine. Deploying a remote forensic agent, such as EnCase Enterprise, would require the suspect's credentials, and functionality of this remote technique within the Cloud is unknown. Simply viewing the target website is enough to confirm that the content is illegal, but it tells us nothing about who put it there. Additionally, no guarantee can yet be made that the target Web server has not been compromised by an attacker, or that the examiner's request to the Web server was not the victim of DNS poisoning, man-in-the-middle, or some other alteration in transit.

Consider other possible sources of digital evidence in this case: credit card payment information, cloud subscriber information, cloud provider access logs, cloud provider NetFlow logs, the Web server virtual machine, and cloud storage data. Assistance from the cloud provider is paramount here. Law enforcement can issue a search warrant to the cloud provider, which is adequate to compel the provider to provide any of this information that they possess. Law enforcement need not execute or witness the search. The warrant specifies that the data returned be an "exact duplicate," the forensic term that has historically meant a bit-for-bit duplication of a drive. Since child pornography is a federal offense, the provider must comply with the order. A technician at the provider executes the search order from his or her workstation, copying data from the provider's infrastructure and verifying data integrity with hashes of the files. Files may have been distributed across many physical machines, but they are reassembled automatically as the technician accesses them. Though the prosecution may call the technician to testify, we have no implicit guarantees of trust in the technician to collect the complete data, in the cloud infrastructure to produce the true data, nor in the technician's computer or tools used to collect the information correctly. Nonetheless, the provider completes the request, and delivers the data to law enforcement.

To reconstruct the crime, the forensic investigators need evidence to help them piece together the following:

- A copy of the virtual machine in order to understand how the Web service works, especially how it encrypts/decrypts data from storage;
- Keys to decrypt storage data, and use them to decrypt the data;
- Copies of all files in order to confirm the presence of child pornography; and
- Cloud access logs or NetFlow to identify possible IP addresses of the criminal.

By viewing the website it is clear that it contains illegal content, but not who the data owner is. Timestamps and other file metadata may prove useful, provided they are available and accurate. For this reason, complete bit-for-bit copies of the original evidence are important.

Case Study Search Warrant

The appendix presents one example of an application for a search warrant in the hypothetical case study. Note how the request focuses on data rather than on hardware. For this reason, it is written as an ECPA §2703(d) warrant. An FRCrP Rule 41 warrant would have been used to seize hardware or imaging disk drives on-site. A template warrant can be found at http://cisa.umbc.edu/warrant/. The document is an academic example and is not legal advice. The warrant should not be used in practice without seeking legal counsel.

Paragraph 1 establishes the request for cloud data in investigation of the crime. Paragraph 4 details the cloud crime and presents probable cause that the provider has relevant evidence. The technical background in paragraphs 5-12 is specific to cloud computing, using Amazon as the example. They describe how the service works and what data may be available. Paragraphs 13-23 are similar to language found in any request for electronic evidence.

CHALLENGING CLOUD EVIDENCE

Earlier in the chapter, we discussed the details of seizing cloud data. This section describes defenses that may be asserted to discredit that evidence. Some issues parallel the scrutiny of any evidence, while others arise explicitly from the use of cloud technology. We consider four topics here: issues with jury comprehension, problems with the execution of the search, the *Daubert* test for scientific validity and relevance, and whether now is the right time for judicial decisions.

Jury Comprehension

By nature, the cloud-computing environment is more complex than a single computer or a server. The environment has many layers of implementation that must be trusted to produce authentic data (Dykstra & Sherman, 2012). In 2009, for example, Kostya Kortchinsky (2009) at Immunity demonstrated a working exploit to break out of a virtual machine and attack the host. In a real world situation this may have eroded confidence in the forensic evidence. The courts have repeatedly said that the *possibility* of an action is insufficient to say it is so (Noblesville Casting Div. of TRW v. Prince, 1982). That opinion also said that "Of course, an expert's opinion that something is "possible" or "could have been" may be sufficient to sustain a verdict or award when it has been rendered in conjunction with other evidence concerning the material factual question to be proved." There are numerous "what if" scenarios for data tampering in the Cloud. A non-comprehensive list includes: data could be tampered with in transit over the network inside the cloud network; redundant copies of the data could have gotten out of sync; the credentials of the data owner could have been compromised resulting in false data creation or data tampering; there could have been opportunities for insider threats at the provider; the hypervisor may be insecure allowing a malicious user to manipulate other virtual machines; the host operating system could be compromised; there could be weak or no encryption on the provider's internal infrastructure for data in transit or data at rest allowing malicious actors to change the data. Nevertheless, computer malfunction and malfeasance must be investigated and can raise doubt in the confidence of the evidence. The hypervisor is especially vulnerable to scrutiny given its powerful position to see and manipulate all of the virtual machines that it controls, including the data therein. Many cloud service providers use custom, proprietary hypervisors that have not been seen or audited independently by the global security community.

Complexity of evidence also stands to challenge judges and juries who lack knowledge about cloud computing. This kind of complex litigation might leave the lay juror "spinning with information too strange to digest and often too intimidating to ponder" (Broyles, 1996). Much has been written, particularly over the last 20 years, about jury comprehension of complex evidence, including highly scientific evidence such as DNA. In *Citizen Comprehension of Difficult Issues: Lessons from Civil Jury Trials* (Cecil, Hans, & Wiggins, 1991), the authors recommended comprehensive examination of how courts handle scientific and technological complexity in litigation. While 78% of American adults—and potential jurors—use the Internet as of August 2011, according to The Pew

Internet and American Life Project (2011), this says nothing about their comprehension about how it or their computer works. Cloud computing is one of the most complex computing environments today, likely to challenge even the most technically inclined juror. Evidence and expert witness testimony must be artfully presented.

Execution of the Search

In the status quo, cloud providers execute search warrants and subpoenas on behalf of law enforcement. In this regard, cloud providers act no differently than any other Internet-based entity. Doing so raises a conflict of interest. The cloud providers have an interest in protecting their reputations, and may not be disinterested parties in an investigation. Furthermore, the provider may not have authority or discernment about what other evidence is in plain view. The courts, in fact, have been split about the issue of plain view for digital evidence (United States v. Williams, 2010; United States v. Mann, 2010). Rigorous guidelines, such as how to challenge the scope and procedure of the search, are lacking today. Barring these changes, it would be preferable for an independent third party to execute the warrant or subpoena at a cloud provider. Until the process of how a search is executed by the provider is well understood, the prosecution should call the technicians to testify about how records are created and the methodology used to retrieve them. As has been noted before, "the Government need not call each of the technicians who did the search so long as it" presents a witness who can "`explain and be cross-examined concerning the manner in which the records are made and kept'" (United States v. Cameron, 2009).

In Covad Communications Co. v. Revonet, Inc. (2009), Judge Facciola wrote, "it is the rare case that a litigant does not allege some deficiency in the production of electronically stored information…" Production of cloud-based evidence will be no different, particularly since that kind of evidence is entirely new to the courts. Some of the issues that could be raised about the deficiency of production of cloud-based ESI include: Who at the provider executed the search warrant, what were their credentials, and how was the search done? Can the technician who executed the search attest to the reliability and authenticity of the data, including, but not limited to, the security of the workstation used to execute the search, the security of the network to prevent data tampering over the network, and a record of who had access to the data? Does the provider maintain aggressively enforced records management policies that can provide authenticity and authentication of the data, perhaps in the form of data provenance? Can the provider attest to the reputation and integrity of the cloud infrastructure, including the hypervisor and host operating system? Were the data located on drive, or distributed over many? If multiple, are the timestamps of those systems internally consistent? Is it possible that important evidentiary data once existed and has been deleted, and if so, is there any record of it? As these questions illustrate, the most vulnerable aspects of cloud discovery are expert witness testimony and the forensic methodology used.

The Daubert Test

The Daubert standard, from the landmark Supreme Court case Daubert v. Merrell Dow Pharmaceuticals, Inc. (1993), can be used to measure the scientific validity and relevance of forensic evidence. Daubert includes factors such as whether a theory or technique has been tested, whether it has been subject to peer review and publication, where there is a known error rate, and whether the theory or technique is generally accepted within the relevant scientific community. Because cloud forensics is a new discipline, the answer to each of these factors is "no." Popular forensic tools such as EnCase have passed the Daubert test, given in part to their commercial availability, testing by the government, long-term use by the community, and extensive acceptance in court. On the contrary, techniques for remote forensics, let alone cloud forensics, do not enjoy any consensus in the forensic community.

Tools designed specifically for cloud investigations have not yet appeared, and forcing existing tools into this role may be ill advised. Forensic practitioners, unfamiliar with cloud environments, will be tempted to use their existing tools like EnCase when first investigating cloud crimes. According to Guidance Software (2011), "There are more than 40,000 licenses of EnCase technology worldwide, the EnCase Enterprise platform is used by more than sixty percent of the Fortune 100, and thousands attend renowned Guidance Software training programs annually." Even so, the advertised features of commercial tools, including EnCase, which can be used for remote forensics, have not been tested for correctness or error rate, and have not yet been presented in court. In the United States, the National Institute of Standards and Technology's (NIST) Computer Forensic Tool Testing (CFTT) group is charged with testing digital forensic tools, measuring their effectiveness, and certifying them. NIST (2012) evaluated EnCase 6.5 in September 2009, but has never evaluated EnCase Enterprise which includes the remote forensic features. This software is not without fault. In 2007, a vulnerability was found in the authentication between the remote EnCase client and the server which could allow an attacker to corrupt or falsify data (Giobbi & McCormick, 2007).

When to Rule

Finally, cases emerging today involving cloud-based evidence are unlikely to produce judicial guidance, particularly from the Supreme Court, on ripeness grounds. Ripeness refers to the fact that because the technology is new, legal decisions are contingent upon future changes that cannot be anticipated. Cloud computing technology has evolved over time and continues to change on a regular basis. Amazon Web Services announced new features or service changes at least one time per month during 2011. Other providers have a similar pace of change. Adjudicating too narrowly on cloud-specific issues would be premature, even though broad application of established principles (*e.g.,* Fourth Amendment search and seizure) are apropos. In fact, recent comments by US Supreme Court Justice Sotomayor reveal potentially changing attitudes about the expectation of privacy in data given to third parties, a decision whose consequences would affect cloud computing. In United States v. Jones (2012), she wrote "More fundamentally, it may be necessary to reconsider the premise that an individual has no reasonable expectation of privacy in information voluntarily disclosed to third parties."

FUTURE RESEARCH DIRECTIONS

Because cloud crimes are not yet widespread and public, it is difficult to predict how the legal system will handle them. Public cases could reasonably be predicted in the next one or two years. These proceedings will test the viability of search and seizure of ESI in cloud environments. Successful legal prosecution will rely on continued education of the players involved, legal interpretation by the courts, and technical capabilities of forensic investigators.

The global, distributed nature of cloud computing will require scholars in other countries to consider how laws in their countries may apply to cloud crimes. Further, ample work remains for establishing how law enforcement will cooperate in cross-boundary cloud investigations.

CONCLUSION

Cloud computing is an advancement in the history of computation due in large part to the convergence of technologies. The economics of the paradigm will drive growth and adoption rates from companies and individuals. Where the people, the data, and the money go, so does crime. While investigators struggle with the new problems of acquiring and analyzing cloud data, the law must prepare for the legal challenges associated with acquiring and presenting cloud data in court. The first public cases involving cloud-based ESI are likely to appear soon, and the people involved in those cases have a unique opportunity to set a new legal precedent.

When these cases emerge, each player's actions will be shaped by an interpretation of how traditional discovery rules govern the cloud crime. As we saw, applying these rules can be murky and unclear. Preservation, ownership, jurisdiction, and search warrant execution are just some areas where we saw non-trivial challenges.

Examining a concrete case study helped highlight the practical implication of the complex considerations for acquiring evidence. However, the case study introduced a context against which to build a search warrant. As a first public example, this language arms law enforcement agents with topics to consider when they draft their first warrant for cloud data. Arming the prosecution also led us to outline some of the areas that defense teams could incorporate into their own strategies.

Now is an exciting time for cloud computing as innovative new product offerings emerge. The legal community is also at the threshold of a wave of cloud-based crimes. Our exploration of seizing electronic evidence from cloud computing provides a foundation to forensic investigators and legal professionals as they investigate and prosecute of cloud-based crimes.

REFERENCES

AAB Joint Ventures v. United States, 75 Fed. Cl. 432 (2007).

Amazon Web Services. (2012a). *AWS customer agreement*. Retrieved from http://aws.amazon.com/agreement/

Amazon Web Services. (2012b). *AWS import/export*. Retrieved from http://aws.amazon.com/importexport/

Arthur Andersen LLP v. United States, 544 U.S. 696 (2005).

Barnhill, D. S. (2010). Cloud computing and stored communications: Another look at Quon v. Arch Wireless. *25. Berkeley Technology Law Journal*, *27*, 621–671.

Broyles, K. E. (1996). Taking the courtroom into the classroom: A proposal for educating the lay juror in complex litigation cases. *64. The George Washington Law Review*, *714*, 721–722.

Cecil, J. S., Hans, V., & Wiggins, E. (1991). Citizen comprehension of difficult issues: Lessons from civil jury trials. *40. The American University Law Review*, 727–774. Retrieved from http://www.wcl.american.edu/journal/lawrev/40/cecil.pdf

Columbia Pictures Inc. v. Bunnell, 245 F.R.D. 443 (C.D. Cal 2007) (2007).

Communications Assistance for Law Enforcement Act of 1994, 47 U.S.C. §§ 1001-1010 (1994).

Core-Vent Corp. v. Nobel Industries *AB*, 11 F.3d 1482, 1486 (9th Cir. 1993) (1993).

Couillard, D. A. (2009). Defogging the cloud: Applying fourth amendment principles to evolving privacy expectations in cloud computing. *Minnesota Law Review*, *93*, 2205–2239.

Covad Communs. Co. v. Revonet, Inc., 2009 U.S. Dist. LEXIS 47841 (D.D.C. May 27, 2009) (2009).

Daubert v. Merrell Dow Pharmaceuticals, Inc., 509 U.S. 579 (1993).

Degnan, D. (2011). Accounting for the costs of electronic discovery. *Minnesota Journal of Law. Science& Technology*, *12*, 151–190.

Dropbox. (2012). *Where does Dropbox store everyone's data?* Retrieved from https://www.dropbox.com/help/7

Dykstra, J. (2012). *Survey of digital forensics and the law*. Unpublished Raw Data.

Dykstra, J., & Sherman, A. T. (2011). Understanding issues in cloud forensics: Two hypothetical case studies. In *Proceedings of the 2011 ADSFL Conference on Digital Forensics, Security, and Law*, (pp. 191-206). ADSFL.

Dykstra, J., & Sherman, A. T. (2012). Acquiring forensic evidence from infrastructure as a service cloud computing: Exploring and evaluating tools, trust, and techniques. *Digital Investigation*. Retrieved from http://www.csee.umbc.edu/~dykstra/DFRWS_Dykstra.pdf

Flagg v. City of Detroit, 252 F.R.D. 346, 353 (E.D. Mich. 2008) (2008).

Galante, J., Kharif, O., & Alpeyev, P. (2011). Sony network breach shows Amazon cloud's appeal for hackers. *Bloomberg*. Retrieved November 2, 2011, from http://www.bloomberg.com/news/2011-05-15/sony-attack-shows-amazon-s-cloud-service-lures-hackers-at-pennies-an-hour.html

Giobbi, R., & McCormick, J. (2007). *US-CERT vulnerability note VU912593 - Guidance EnCase enterprise uses weak authentication to identify target machines*. Retrieved from http://www.kb.cert.org/vuls/id/912593

Guidance Software. (2011). *Leading eDiscovery, forensics, and cybersecurity solutions – Encase*. Retrieved from http://www.guidancesoftware.com

Katz v. United States, 389 U.S. 347 (1967).

Kerr, O. S. (2005). Searches and seizures in a digital world. *Harvard Law Review*, *119*, 531–585.

Kerr, O. S. (2010). Applying the fourth amendment to the internet: A general approach. *Stanford Law Review*, *62*, 1005–1029.

Kortchinsky, K. (2009). *CLOUDBURST: A VMware guest to host escape story*. Retrieved from http://www.blackhat.com/presentations/bh-usa-09/KORTCHINSKY/BHUSA09-Kortchinsky-Cloudburst-SLIDES.pdf

Mell, P., & Grance, T. (2011). *The NIST definition of cloud computing*. Retrieved from http://csrc.nist.gov/publications/nistpubs/800-145/SP800-145.pdf

Microsoft Corporation. (2010). *Microsoft services agreement*. Retrieved from http://explore.live.com/microsoft-service-agreement

Morgester, R. (2006). Search warrant language for cellular phones. *Cyber Crime Newsletter*. Retrieved from http://www.olemiss.edu/depts/ncjrl/pdf/May-June%202006%20Final%20Copy.pdf

Morrison, S. R. (2011). What the cops can't do, internet service providers can: Preserving privacy in email contents. *Virginia Journal of Law & Technology*, *16*, 253–300.

National Institute of Standards and Technology. (2012). *Disk imaging*. Retrieved from http://www.cftt.nist.gov/disk_imaging.htm

Pew Internet and American Life Project. (2011). *Internet adoption*. Retrieved from http://www.pewinternet.org/Trend-Data/Internet-Adoption.aspx

Stored Communications Act of 1986, 18 U.S.C. §§ 2701-2712 (2000).

Stylianou, K. K. (2010). An evolutionary study of cloud computing services privacy terms. *The John Marshall Journal of Computer & Information Law*, *27*, 593–612.

Taylor, M., Haggerty, J., Gresty, D., & Lamb, D. (2011). Forensic investigations of cloud computing systems. *Network Security, 3*, 4–10. doi:10.1016/S1353-4858(11)70024-1

United States v. Bach, 310 F.3d 1063 (8th Cir. 2002) (2002).

United States v. Beddow, 957 F.2d 1330, 1335 (6th Cir.1992) (1992).

United States v. Cameron, 573 F.3d 179, 183 (4th Cir. 2009) (2009).

United States v. Drew, 259 F.R.D. 449 (C.D. Cal. 2009) (2009).

United States v. Jones, 132 S. Ct. 945 (2012).

United States v. Mann, 592. F.3d 779, 782 (7th Cir. 2010) (2010).

United States v. Williams, 2010 U.S. App. LEXIS 1327 (4th Cir. Jan. 21, 2010) (2010).

US Department of Justice. (2009). *Searching and seizing computers and obtaining electronic evidence in criminal investigations*. Retrieved from http://www.justice.gov/criminal/cybercrime/docs/ssmanual2009.pdf

US Government. (2010a). *Federal rules of civil procedure*. Retrieved from http://www.uscourts.gov/uscourts/RulesAndPolicies/rules/2010%20Rules/Civil%20Procedure.pdf

US Government. (2010b). *Federal rules of criminal procedure*. Retrieved from http://www.uscourts.gov/uscourts/RulesAndPolicies/rules/2010%20Rules/Criminal%20Procedure.pdf

US House of Representatives Committee on the Judiciary. (2011). *Going dark: Lawful electronic surveillance in the face of new technologies*. H.R. REP. NO. 112-159. Washington, DC: US House of Representatives Committee on the Judiciary.

Van Horn, C. (2009). *Chris Coleman documents and search warrants*. Retrieved from http://www.examiner.com/article/chris-coleman-documents-and-search-warrants

Viacom Int'l Inc. v. YouTube Inc., 2008 WL 2627388 (S.D.N.Y. 2008) (2008).

Willamette Week. (2011, April 8). You look like Obama: FBI seeks Facebook records for person of interest in mosque arson. *Willamette Week*. Retrieved from http://www.wweek.com/portland/blog-26890-you_look_like_obama_fbi_seeks_facebook_records_for.html

Wolthusen, S. (2009). Overcast: Forensic discovery in cloud environments. In *Proceedings of the Fifth International Conference on IT Security, Incident Management, and IT Forensics*, (pp. 3-9). IEEE.

Zubulake v. UBS Warburg, 220 F.R.D. 212 (S.D.N.Y. 2003) (2003).

Zubulake v. UBS Warburg LLC, 216 F.R.D. 280, 291 (S.D.N.Y. 2003) (2003).

KEY TERMS AND DEFINITIONS

Daubert Test: The *Daubert* Test is based upon the US Supreme Court decision in *Daubert v. Merrell Dow Pharmaceuticals*, which establishes a set of standards for dealing with the reliability of scientific techniques used in forensics. The four factors are: testability, peer review, error rates, and acceptability.

Electronic Communication Service: Electronic Communication Service is defined in 18 U.S.C §2510 as "any service which provides to users thereof the ability to send or receive wire or electronic communications."

Electronic Discovery: Electronic discovery, or e-discovery, is the process of seeking, locating, collecting, and producing electronic data as evidence in a civil or criminal legal matter.

Evidence Preservation: Preservation broadly refers to the process involved in ensuring continued access to evidence, including protection against destruction or deterioration of evidence.

Remote Computing Service: Remote Computing Service is defined in 18 U.S.C §2711 as "the provision to the public of computer storage or processing services by means of an electronic communications system."

Search Warrant: A search warrant is a legal document which authorizes law enforcement to search and seize a person or location for items named in the warrant as evidence of a crime. In the United States, searches must be reasonable and specific under the Fourth Amendment of the US Constitution.

Seizure: Legal seizure is the confiscation of property, against the will of the possessor or owner, by legal process.

APPENDIX: Sample Warrant

UNITED STATES DISTRICT COURT

FOR THE ____WESTERN DISTRICT OF WASHINGTON____

IN THE MATTER OF THE SEARCH OF INFORMATION ASSOCIATED WITH THE WEBSITE POLLYONLINE.NET THAT IS STORED AT PREMESIS CONTROLLED BY AMAZON WEB SERVICES, LLC	Case No.

APPLICATION OF THE UNITED STATES

FOR AN ORDER PURSUANT TO 18 U.S.C. § 2703(D)

I, JOHN DOE, being first duly sworn, hearby depose and state as follows:

INTRODUCTION AND AGENT BACKROUND

1. I make this affidavit in support of an application for a search warrant for information associated with certain Amazon Web Services (AWS) accounts and Internet Protocol ("IP") address that are stored at premises owned, maintained, controlled, or operated by Amazon Web Services (the "Company"), LLC, a Web services company headquartered at 410 Terry Avenue North, Seattle, Washington, 98109 (the "Premises"), which functions as an electronic communications service provider and remote computing service. The information to be searched is described in the following paragraphs and in Attachment A. This affidavit is made in support of an application for a search warrant under 18 U.S.C. §§ 2703(a), 2703(b)(1)(A) and 2703(c)(1)(A) to require AWS to disclose to the government records and other information in its possession, pertaining to the subscriber or customer operating the Web site.
2. I am a Special Agent (SA) with the Federal Bureau of Investigation (FBI), and have been since January 2003. I am currently assigned to the Baltimore Field Office, Cyber Squad. Since joining the FBI, I have been involved in investigations of computer intrusions, intellectual property right violations and Internet fraud. I have also been assigned to investigate Sexual Exploitation of Children (SEOC) violations of federal law. I have gained experience conducting such investigations through training and everyday work related to these investigations.

3. The facts in this affidavit come from my personal observations, my training and experience, and information obtained from other agents and witnesses. This affidavit is intended to show only that there is sufficient probable cause for the requested warrant and does not set forth all of my knowledge about this matter

PROBABLE CAUSE

4. On April 1, 2012, an anonymous tip was submitted to the FBI's Baltimore Field Office that the website www.pollyonline.net contained and was distributing child pornography, in violation of 18 U.S.C. §§ 2252 and 2252(a). I determined that the IP addresses for the website hosting the material resolved to one assigned to Amazon Web Services. On April 3, 2012, a preservation request was sent to AWS related to this website and its IP address. Accordingly, this application sets forth specific and articulable facts showing that there are reasonable grounds to believe that the materials sought are relevant and material to an ongoing criminal investigation.

TECHNICAL BACKGROUND

5. Based on my training and experience, I use the following technical terms in this Affidavit and Attachments A and B to this Affidavit:
    a. "Cloud" is a generic term that refers to a network where the physical location and inner workings are abstracted away and unimportant to the usage. "The cloud" was first used to describe telecommunication networks, where the consumer was blissfully unaware of the inner workings of how their telephone conversation was transmitted to the remote end. The term was later used to describe computer networks, and ultimately to describe the Internet specifically. Knowing the physical location of a website is unimportant to using that service. Cloud computing also takes advantage of this definition of cloud, as it is also a service connected to a network, often the Internet. However, cloud computing offers specific services whereby customers rent remote computing resources such as processing power or data storage, and provision those resources themselves.
    b. "Cloud computing" is a model for enabling ubiquitous, convenient, on-demand network access to a shared pool of configurable computing resources (e.g., networks, servers, storage, applications, and services) that can be rapidly provisioned and released with minimal management effort or service provider interaction. This cloud model is composed of five essential characteristics, three service models, and four deployment models.
        i. "Infrastructure as a Service" (IaaS) allows a consumer to provision processing, storage, networks, and other fundamental computing resources where the consumer is able to deploy and run arbitrary software, which can include operating systems and applications. The consumer does not manage or control the underlying cloud infrastructure but has control over operating systems, storage, and deployed applications; and possibly limited control of select networking components (e.g., host firewalls).

ii. "Platform as a Service" (PaaS) allows a consumer to deploy onto the cloud infrastructure consumer-created or acquired applications created using programming languages, libraries, services, and tools supported by the provider. The consumer does not manage or control the underlying cloud infrastructure including network, servers, operating systems, or storage, but has control over the deployed applications and possibly configuration settings for the application-hosting environment.

iii. "Software as a Service" (SaaS) allows a consumer to use the provider's applications running on a cloud infrastructure. The applications are accessible from various client devices through either a thin client interface, such as a Web browser (e.g., Web-based email), or a program interface. The consumer does not manage or control the underlying cloud infrastructure including network, servers, operating systems, storage, or even individual application capabilities, with the possible exception of limited user-specific application configuration settings.

c. "Cloud Service Provider" (CSP) is the entity that offers cloud computing services. CSPs offer their customers the ability to use infrastructure, platform, or software as a service. These services may include offerings such as remote storage, virtual machines, or Web hosting. Service is billed as a utility based on usage.

CSPs maintain records pertaining to the individuals or companies that have subscriber accounts with it. Those records could include identifying and billing information, account access information in the form of log files, account application information, and other information both in computer data format and in written record format. CSPs reserve and/or maintain computer disk storage space on their computer system for the use of the cloud service subscriber for both temporary and long- term storage of electronic data with other parties and other types of electronic data and files. Such temporary, incidental storage is defined by statute as "electronic storage," and the provider of such a service is an "electronic communications service" provider. A cloud service provider that is available to the public and provides long-term storage services to the public for electronic data and files, is providing a "remote computing service." CSPs may be able to provide some of the following, depending on the type of services they provide:

NetFlow
Full Packet Captures
Firewall and Router Logs
Intrusion Detection Logs
Virtual Machines
Customer Account Registration
Customer Billing Information

d. "Virtual Machine" (VM) is a system where the hardware is virtual rather than physical. Virtualization is a technique whereby special software, called the hypervisor, can run many virtual (rather than physical) machines. The hardware on the single machine is emulated so that each virtual instance of a computer, called a VM, does not require dedicated physical hardware, but each VM believes it has its own hardware. The hypervisor has special access to control all of the virtual guests, but it should also be able to isolate the guests from each other.

e. "NetFlow Records" are collections of network statistics collected by a service provider about traffic flows. A traffic flow is a sequence of data packets from a source to a destination. NetFlow is collected when it is impractical to collect all of the data packets for a flow. Providers may use these logs for quality control, security, or billing. For any particular network flow, NetFlow can include the source and destination IP addresses, network ports, timestamps, and amount of traffic transferred. A provider may only collect a sample of all possible sessions, and may only store the NetFlow for a short time.

6. Amazon Web Services (AWS) is an IaaS Cloud Service Provider, a subsidiary of Amazon.com, Inc., that does business online at http://aws.amazon.com. AWS allows its users to establish accounts with the company, and users can use their accounts to purchase the use of a variety of cloud computing resources offered by AWS.
7. AWS requires users to provide basic contact information during the registration process. This information includes the user's full name, contact e-mail address, physical address (including city, state, and zip code), telephone number, credit card information, and billing address. Users must read and agree to the AWS Customer Agreement. The final step in the registration process is identity verification where an automated system at AWS calls the phone number provided with a verification code that must be entered online.
8. AWS users have the ability to store and retrieve data in the Amazon Simple Storage Service (S3). S3 can store an unlimited number of data objects, which may be documents, photos, videos, or other data. Each object is retrieved using a unique, user-specific key. AWS users are billed based on the amount of data stored, and the transfer into and out of the cloud.
9. AWS provides its users the ability to purchase computing resources on the Amazon Elastic Compute Cloud (EC2). EC2 is a virtual computing environment that allows users to create, use, and manage an unlimited number of virtual machines. Each virtual machine is associated with the user that created it. The user has complete freedom to configure and use the VM as they wish, including installing software and services such as a Webserver. AWS users are billed based on the type of VM they choose, and the number of hours that the VM is running.
10. AWS stores user-generated data in more than one physical location. They state "Objects are redundantly stored on multiple devices across multiple facilities in an Amazon S3 Region." (http://d36cz9buwru1tt.cloudfront.net/AWSRiskandComplianceWhitepaperJanuary2012.pdf). User-generated data are unlikely to be stored at the Premises. However, system administrators, using the software that controls the cloud infrastructure, have the ability to identify the physical and geographic storage location of the disk drives containing the data.
11. Cloud Service Providers like AWS typically retain information about their users' accounts, such as the types of service utilized, the date and time of when the services were started and stopped, and connection information (such as the Internet Protocol ("IP") address from where the request initiated).
12. Therefore, the computers of AWS are likely to contain all the material just described, including user-created content, stored electronic communications, and information concerning subscribers and their use of AWS, such as account access information, transaction information, and account application.

INFORMATION TO BE SEARCHED AND THINGS TO BE SEIZED

13. I anticipate executing this warrant under the Electronic Communications Privacy Act, in particular 18 U.S.C. §§ 2703(a), 2703(b)(1)(A) and 2703(c)(1)(A), by using the warrant to require Amazon Web Services to disclose to the government copies of the records and other information (including the content of communications) particularly described in Section I of Attachment B. Upon receipt of the information described in Section I of Attachment B, government-authorized persons will review that information to locate the items described in Section II of Attachment B.
14. As described above and in Attachment A, this application seeks permission to search and seize records that might be found on the Premises or data centers controlled by AWS, in whatever form they are found. I submit that for some computers or electronic medium found on the Premises or in data centers controlled by AWS, there is probable cause to believe those records will be stored in that computer or electronic medium, for at least the following reasons:
    f. Based on my knowledge and experience, I know that Cloud Service Providers bill customers based on the usage of services, and that current and historical billing records are likely to be kept for resources currently being used.
    g. I know that Cloud Service Providers have a tremendous amount of storage capacity, and that this storage is distributed across physical storage media (i.e., hard drives) in multiple data-centers in multiple geographic locations. I also know that software keeps track of how data is stored in this environment, and that it has the ability to identify the physical location of any piece of data and reconstruct the pieces into their original format.
    h. I know from training and experience that child pornographers generally prefer to store images of child pornography in electronic form as computer files. The computer's ability to store images in digital form makes a computer an ideal repository for pornography. Even a small portable disk or computer hard drive can contain many child pornography images. The images can be easily sent to or received from other computer users over the Internet. Further, both individual files of child pornography and the disks that contain the files can be mislabeled or hidden to evade detection. In my training and experience, individuals who view child pornography typically maintain their collections for many years and keep and collect items containing child pornography over long periods of time; in fact, they rarely, if ever, dispose of their sexually explicit materials.
15. In this case, the warrant application requests permission to search and seize images of child pornography, including those that may be stored on a virtual machine. These things constitute both evidence of crime and contraband.
16. I know that when an individual uses a website to distribute child pornography over the Internet, the Web server will generally serve both as an instrumentality for committing the crime, and also as a storage device for evidence of the crime. The computer is an instrumentality of the crime because it is used as a means of committing the criminal offense. The computer is also likely to be a storage device for evidence of crime. From my training and experience, I believe that a computer used to commit a crime of this type may contain: data that is evidence of how the computer was used; data that was sent or received; notes as to how the criminal conduct was achieved; records of Internet discussions about the crime; and other records that indicate the nature of the offense.

17. Because several people share the Premises as customers of the cloud service, it is possible that the Premises will contain data that are predominantly used, and perhaps owned, by persons who are not suspected of a crime. If agents conducting the search nonetheless determine that it is possible that the things described in this warrant could be found with those intermingled data, this application seeks permission to seize that data as well.
18. Based upon my knowledge, training and experience, I know that searching for information stored in cloud providers may result in a large amount of electronic storage to be searched later by a qualified computer expert in a laboratory or other controlled environment. This is often necessary to ensure the accuracy and completeness of such data, and to prevent the loss of the data either from accidental or intentional destruction. This is true because of the following:
    i. The volume of evidence. Computer storage devices (like hard disks) can store the equivalent of millions of pages of information. Cloud computing offers a vast amount of storage for very little cost. Additionally, a suspect may try to conceal criminal evidence; he or she might encrypt the data or store it in random order with deceptive file names. This may require searching authorities to peruse all the stored data to determine which particular files are evidence or instrumentalities of crime. This sorting process can take weeks or months, depending on the volume of data stored.
    j. Technical requirements. Searching computer systems for criminal evidence sometimes requires highly technical processes requiring expert skill and properly controlled environment. The vast array of computer hardware and software, and non-traditional data formats used to support a cloud environment requires even computer experts to specialize in some systems and applications, so it is difficult to know before a search which expert is qualified to analyze the system and its data. In any event, however, data search processes are exacting scientific procedures designed to protect the integrity of the evidence and to recover even "hidden," erased, compressed, password-protected, or encrypted files. Because computer evidence is vulnerable to inadvertent or intentional modification or destruction (both from external sources, destructive code imbedded in the system, or malicious insiders, a controlled environment may be necessary to complete an accurate analysis.
19. The information requested should be readily accessible to Amazon Web Services by computer search, and its production should not prove to be burdensome.
20. I anticipate executing this warrant under the Electronic Communications Privacy Act, in particular 18 U.S.C. §§ 2703(a), 2703(b)(1)(A) and 2703(c)(1)(A), by using the warrant to require AWS to disclose to the government copies of the records and other information (including the content of communications) particularly described in Section I of Attachment B. Upon receipt of the information described in Section I of Attachment B, government-authorized persons will review that information to locate the items described in Section II of Attachment B.

CONCLUSION

21. Based on my training and experience, and the facts as set forth in this affidavit there is probable cause to believe that on the computer systems in the control of Amazon Web Services there exists evidence of a crime, contraband, and fruits of a crime. Accordingly, a search warrant is requested.

22. This Court has jurisdiction to issue the requested warrant because it is "a court of competent jurisdiction" as defined by 18 U.S.C. § 2711, 18 U.S.C. §§ 2703(a), (b)(1)(A) and (c)(1)(A). Specifically, the Court is "a district court of the United States… that – has jurisdiction over the offense being investigated." 18 U.S.C. §2711(3)(A)(i).
23. Pursuant to 18 U.S.C. § 2703(g), the presence of a law enforcement officer is not required for the service or execution of this warrant.

REQUEST FOR SEALING

It is respectfully requested that this Court issue an order sealing, until further order of the Court, all papers submitted in support of this application, including the application and search warrant. I believe that sealing this document is necessary because the items and information to be seized are relevant to an ongoing investigation into the criminal organizations, as not all of the targets of this investigation will be searched at this time. Based upon my training and experience, I have learned that online criminals actively search for criminal affidavits and search warrants via the Internet and disseminate them to other online criminals as they deem appropriate, i.e., post them publicly online through the carding forums. Premature disclosure of the contents of this affidavit and related documents may have a significant and negative impact on the continuing investigation and may severely jeopardize its effectiveness.

Respectfully submitted,
JOHN DOE
Special Agent
Federal Bureau of Investigation
Subscribed and sworn to before me on ___________:

____

UNITED STATES MAGISTRATE JUDGE

ATTACHMENT A

Property to Be Searched

This warrant applies to information associated with the website www.pollyonline.net resolving to IP address 23.20.70.250 that is hosted at premises owned, maintained, controlled, or operated by Amazon Web Services, a company headquartered at 410 Terry Avenue North, Seattle, Washington, 98109.

ATTACHMENT B

Property to Be Searched

I. Information to be disclosed by Amazon Web Services
To the extent that the information described in Attachment A is within the possession, custody, or control of AWS, AWS is required to disclose the following information to the government for the IP address listed in Attachment A:

(a) All contact information, including full name, user identification number, birth date, contact e-mail addresses, physical address (including city, state, and zip code), telephone numbers, screen names, websites, and other personal identifiers of the user or users of services associated with the IP address;
(b) IP logs, including all records of the IP addresses that logged into the accounts associated with the IP address;
(c) Firewall, router, and intrusion detection logs associated with the IP address;
(d) The length of service (including start date), the types of service utilized by the user or users associated with the IP address, and the means and source of any payments associated with the service (including any credit card or bank account number).

II. Information to be seized by the government
All information described above in Section I that constitutes fruits, evidence and instrumentalities of violations of 18 U.S.C. §§ 2252 and 2252(a) involving www.pollyonline.net from April 1, 2012 to April 30, 2012, including information pertaining to the following matters:

(a) The virtual machine assigned to the IP address in question on April 1, 2012;
(b) A list of other IP addresses assigned to the virtual machine in question, and the dates and times they were assigned;
(c) Packet captures of traffic to and from the virtual machine in question;
(d) Data stored in any other cloud service, including S3 and DynamoDB, associated with the account running the virtual machine;
(e) Records relating to who created, used, or communicated with the website.

Chapter 8
Legal Process and Requirements for Cloud Forensic Investigations

Ivan Orton
King County Prosecuting Attorney's Office, USA

Aaron Alva
University of Washington, USA

Barbara Endicott-Popovsky
University of Washington, USA

ABSTRACT

For the emerging field of cloud forensics, the development of validated and repeatable scientific processes for conducting cloud forensic investigations should include requirements that establish evidence collected as legally admissible. There is currently an uncertainty in the legal requirements for cloud forensics. Forensic investigations in the cloud introduce unique issues that must be addressed, and the legal environment of the cloud must be considered. The authors will detail the process in criminal cloud forensic investigations for commanding production from cloud providers including constitutional and statutory limitations, and the civil and criminal admissibility processes. Decisions in court cases rely on the authenticity and reliability of the evidence presented. Ensuring cases involving cloud forensics follow the proper legal process and requirements will be beneficial for validating evidence when presented in court. Further, understanding of legal requirements will aid in the research and development of cloud forensics tools to aid investigations.

DOI: 10.4018/978-1-4666-2662-1.ch008

Copyright © 2013, IGI Global. Copying or distributing in print or electronic forms without written permission of IGI Global is prohibited.

1.0. INTRODUCTION

Cloud forensics introduces unique legal issues beyond those encountered during traditional digital forensics cases and presents a challenge to the legal system, which is not well equipped to handle such cases. This chapter will examine issues regarding commanding and producing in court digital evidence resident in the cloud. The "commanding production" section will focus on the criminal law. The "producing in court" or admissibility section will apply to both civil and criminal practice.[1]

To date, there is limited guidance available from case law that can govern decisions involving admissibility of cloud-based evidence. Our analysis is founded on an extensive review of the constitutional and statutory limitations that apply to cloud forensic investigations, as well as a walkthrough of admissibility standards for digital evidence including issues unique to cloud-based evidence.

Cloud computing is in its infancy. This chapter identifies the ways in which digital evidence in the cloud differs in substance from digital evidence gathered from computer hard drives and networks under the control of parties engaged in legal actions. The material presented begins to identify the issues surrounding cloud forensics uncertainty, comparing these issues to those raised in more traditional digital forensics cases.

The authors recognize that addressing barriers to conducting effective cloud forensic investigations will require a concerted effort by stakeholders involved in the process, including the cloud provider.

Development of new tools and procedures for cloud forensics may not currently address the complex legal requirements that must be met in order for cloud-gathered evidence to be admissible in court. Incorporating the need to collect admissible evidence in system design can improve the ability of system operators to identify, collect, store and retrieve valid evidence. It is particularly important for potential cloud customers to analyze this before moving to the cloud since cloud customers lose the ability to control this process once information is moved to the cloud (Convery, 2010). Understanding the legal requirements for admissible cloud evidence allows for incorporation of those concepts into information systems, creating a forensically ready design that will improve the efficiency of valid evidence collection.

1.1. Cloud Forensics Definitions

The emerging field of cloud forensics combines the disciplines of digital forensics and cloud computing (Ruan, Carthy, Kechadi, & Crosbie, 2011b). Cloud computing is defined by the U.S. National Institute of Standards and Technology (NIST) as "a model for enabling convenient, on-demand network access to a shared pool of configurable computing resources (e.g., networks, servers, storage, applications, and services) that can be rapidly provisioned and released with minimal management effort or service provider interaction" (Mell & Grance, 2011).

Digital forensics is the study of evidence from attacks on computer systems in order to learn what has occurred, how to prevent it from recurring, and the extent of the damage. This field initially was divided into digital disk forensics—retrieving admissible evidence from a computer disk—and network forensics—retrieving evidence throughout a network system wherever it may reside or flow. Based on network access and architecture, cloud forensics is a subset of network forensics (Ruan, Carthy, Kechadi, & Crosbie, 2011b).

With traditional disk forensics, the model by which investigations are conducted rely on the acquisition of physical disks, and require a clear chain of custody be maintained on the physical items (Pollitt, Caloyannides, Novotny, & Shenoi, 2004). By contrast, cloud forensics requires a different approach due to characteristics of the cloud environment where physical assets are not under the control of the user and may not be identified and located easily due to the dynamic nature of cloud provisioning.

1.2. Legal Background

Cloud forensics, like traditional digital forensics, requires that technical and legal practitioners have a strong integrated understanding of computer science and the law. U.S. courts operate through a combination of procedural rules and case law precedent as guidance when ruling on evidentiary issues (Kuntze, Rudolph, Alva, Endicott-Popvsky, Christiansen, & Kemmerich, 2012). Other countries where cloud data may reside may have a different basis for legal decision-making, complicating the collection of cloud-based digital evidence.

Case law precedent is based on the concept of *stare decisis*, which establishes that the court rules by using precedence to guide decisions on cases that are similar in nature (Re, 1975). In other words, courts will make decisions on the basis of rulings that have already been decided and what will be ruled on has the potential to shape how the court rules on cases of similar nature in the future. Since the field of cloud forensics has not established best practices to the level of similar fields such as digital forensics (Christiansen, 2010), early rulings could be based on faulty science, complicating the development of adequate case law and setting faulty first precedent.

Our research emphasizes the procedural rules and decisions that guide the admissibility of data as valid evidence in the U.S. legal system. In that system, admissibility decisions are the purview of the judge who is permitted significant discretion. While the decision lies with the judge, the burden is on opposing counsel to objecting to admissibility (Lorraine v Markel American Insurance Company, 2007). It is our expectation that raising and examining the issues of admissibility of cloud forensics evidence in advance of significant case law being established, will avoid some of the pitfalls of rulings based on poor science.

1.3. Literature Review

With the field of cloud forensics in its infancy, little in the relevant literature details the legal aspects of admissibility of cloud forensic data; however, publications that have discussed cloud forensics have mentioned, in passing, that legal requirements are important to consider. Examples include: Biggs and Vidalis (2009), Birk and Wegener (2011), Broadhurst (2006), Ruan, Carthy, Kechadi, and Crosbie (2011b), Spyridopoulos and Katos (2011), Taylor, Haggerty, Gresty, and Hegarty (2010), Taylor, Haggerty, Gresty, and Lamb (2011), Wolthusen (2009), and Yan (2011).

2.0. COMMANDING PRODUCTION

As noted at the outset, our focus in this section will be on the criminal investigation process.

2.1. Introduction

This section discusses the laws and rules governing the issuance of legally binding directives and the circumstances under which they must be used. Within each topic, these are discussed; first, in general, and then second, as these laws and rules relate to storage in the cloud. In doing so the authors will attempt to identify issues unique to, or causing special problems for, the forensic examination of cloud stored data.

For the purposes of our discussion, a "legally binding directive" is a court order that mandates compliance by the recipient and meets all necessary constitutional and statutory requirement. Two observations:

First, where the constitution or relevant statute mandates a particular form of order (such as a warrant supported by probable cause, for example), failure to utilize the proper order can lead to adverse results, such as suppression of any evidence obtained and/or civil or criminal liability for providing/obtaining such information.

Second, the absence of constitutional or statutory protection does not mean the cloud provider *must* provide a third party access to cloud data. Even where the constitution or statutes do not prevent the cloud service provider from allowing third party access, because of Service Level Agreements, Privacy Policies and other factors, it is highly unlikely that an investigator will be able to access records stored in the cloud without producing a legally binding directive to the cloud provider.

It is important for the reader to understand this; even if there is no legal barrier preventing a provider of cloud services from providing access to cloud-stored-data to third parties, absent some contractual obligation to the contrary the service provider can still refuse to provide access. A legally binding directive thus serves two purposes. It meets any constitutional or other barriers to disclosure and it mandates disclosure, whether there is a barrier or no.

It is also important to understand that a directive can be legally binding in that it requires the recipient to comply or face contempt or other court action, and still not be legally sufficient in terms of complying with the constitution or statute. For example, in most jurisdictions, attorneys in civil and criminal cases routinely issue "trial subpoenas duces tecum" compelling the attendance of witnesses in court with specified documents. If properly served, a witness receiving such a subpoena must appear or contest the subpoena or face possible contempt of court citation. But if this subpoena was issued for constitutionally protected documents, requiring a warrant supported by probable cause, or for documents covered by specific statutes limiting government access, the subpoena will not be sufficient to save the documents from suppression or the provider and government from civil sanction, or both.

2.2. Legal Limits on Access by Law Enforcement

Legal limits on access to cloud data by or on behalf of law enforcement flow from two sources: constitutional limits (Federal and state), and statutory limits.[2] These restrictions on searches have different impacts. Searches that violate constitutional protection are likely to be suppressed. Searches that violate statutory restrictions may be subject to suppression, but more typically, while providing a civil remedy to the aggrieved party, do not provide suppression as a remedy. Either way, it is wise to insure one is using a legal production mechanism. Section 2.3 will consider the Constitutional limitations in detail and Section 2.4 will discuss the Statutory Limitations.

2.3. Constitutional Limitations

The below discussion relates to the requirements of the U.S. Constitution. These requirements set a floor below which protection must not fall. The courts of several states, however, have interpreted their state constitutions to be more protective of privacy than the Fourth Amendment. Investigators in those states must be aware of the standards in the state or states in which they operate.

Constitutional limitations flow from the Fourth Amendment's prohibition against unreasonable searches and seizures.

The right of the people to be secure in their persons, houses, papers, and effects, against unreasonable searches and seizures, shall not be violated, and no Warrants shall issue, but upon probable cause, supported by Oath or affirmation, and particularly describing the place to be searched, and the persons or things to be seized." U.S. Const. amend. IV.

There are three questions to be asked in the Fourth Amendment context: Does the Fourth Amendment apply to the situation; Is there a legal warrant or warrant equivalent; and, if there is not a legal warrant, Does the search fall within the exceptions to the warrant requirement?

2.3.1. Does the Fourth Amendment Apply to the Situation?

This determination requires two separate considerations:

1. Is there a reasonable expectation of privacy?
2. Is government action involved?

2.3.1.1. Is There a Reasonable Expectation of Privacy?

2.3.1.1.1. Reasonable Expectation of Privacy in General

One unique aspect of cloud computing is the data is stored, not at the user's home or office, but away from that location, in the hands of third parties. Another unique aspect is that the user may be viewed as having given explicit or implicit consent for others to access the data. These two factors have the potential to preclude a user from having any reasonable expectation of privacy in cloud data.

This is a new and developing area of the law. When this developing law is coupled with evolving societal and legal concepts of when one is entitled to privacy, little can be said with certainty about how courts will ultimately determine the issue of whether, and under what circumstances, there can be a reasonable expectation of privacy in cloud data.

Because this can be a confusing area of the law, we devote significant time to explanation and exploration of this topic.

In determining whether there is a reasonable expectation of privacy, courts look at two factors: the subjective expectation of the person asserting a privacy interest and whether society accepts that as objectively reasonable (California v Greenwood, 1988). The highest privacy interest is attached to private dwellings (Welsh v Wisconsin, 1984). A computer inside a private dwelling will certainly be accorded a similar privacy status.

Expectation of privacy in the contents of a computer is less clear when the computer is not in the home or when the contents of the computer are routinely shared with others or members of the public. Cloud computing often involves situations where a computer in the home (or workplace) connects to or accesses data stored outside the home (or workplace). Furthermore, while data in the cloud may be considered to be "shared" with the cloud provider, it is highly unlikely that cloud users intend this to mean their data is shared with the public unless the user explicitly takes such action. This hybrid of within-the-home/outside-the-home, private/shared-with-the-provider computing can create challenges to courts attempting to discern the boundaries within which one has a reasonable expectation of privacy.

To understand the law in this area, some background is needed. In Katz v. United States (1984), the Supreme Court expressly held that "what a person knowingly exposes to the public, even in his home or office, is not a subject of Fourth Amendment protection."[3] The Supreme Court "consistently has held that a person has no legitimate expectation of privacy in information he voluntarily turns over to third parties" (Smith v Maryland, 1979; see US v Miller, 1976; Couch v US, 1973).

This general principle, that one has no reasonable expectation of privacy in information he shares with third parties, can be justified in two ways.

The first, often referred to as "disclosed to the public," deals with the manner and nature of the sharing. If an individual shares information with the public in general, whether through standing on a street corner and yelling, publishing it in publications intended for the public at large, or posting it in a public forum, there can be little disagreement that the individual has no privacy interest in the information. This meets neither test—there is no subjective expectation of privacy and society is not willing to recognize a claim of privacy under those facts (California v Greenwood). Data disseminated in this manner, cloud stored or otherwise, is not protected under the Fourth Amendment. For example, many blogs are stored on third party servers. If those blogs are "published," i.e., made available to the public at large, then there is no reasonable expectation of privacy.

The second justification, usually referred to as the "third-party doctrine" focuses on the risk the individual assumes, in disclosing information to a third party, that the third party will disclose the information to others, including law enforcement. This is the form of shared information that is important in the cloud context.

Prof. Orin Kerr at George Washington University Law School has argued that the "third-party doctrine" should more properly be viewed under the consent exception to the warrant requirement, rather than as a determinant of whether the defendant had a reasonable expectation of privacy (Kerr, 2009). Though Prof. Kerr's analysis is convincing, courts have continued to view third-party involvement under the reasonable-expectation-of-privacy analysis and so shall we. We will return, however, to the consent exception to the warrant requirement later in this chapter.

2.3.1.1.2. Reasonable Expectation of Privacy in the Cloud

With that background information, the question becomes does an individual or entity have a reasonable expectation of privacy in data she has stored in the cloud? Does storing data on third party computers constitute "exposing it to the public" or "voluntarily turning it over to third parties" so as to vitiate any privacy expectation?

Although, as noted earlier, this is a two-part test (does the individual have a subjective expectation of privacy and does society recognize that expectation as reasonable), most decisions in this area are decided under the second part of the test—whether the expectation of privacy is reasonable.[4]

The problem in answering that question is that, as the Supreme Court has noted, "We have no talisman that determines in all cases those privacy expectations that society is prepared to accept as reasonable" (O'Connor v Ortega, 1987).

Still, scholars have attempted to discern, from court decisions, the logical framework behind these decisions (LaFave, 2008; Kerr, 2007), but have largely concluded that the perceived logical framework is more useful in characterizing decisions than in providing guidance for future decisions (Kerr, 2007).

Nonetheless we will attempt to characterize, from case law, some factual and policy elements that make a finding of a reasonable expectation of privacy more, or less, likely.

2.3.1.1.2.1. Reasonable Steps Taken to Conceal the Contents

This category includes the steps taken by the individual to minimize the likelihood that the data can be viewed by anyone other than those the individual voluntarily exposes it to. In the non-cloud world this includes using opaque containers and keeping those containers in close proximity (Bond v United States, 2000), locking luggage or a briefcase (United States v Presler, 1979), or password protecting or encrypting files, directories, or a computer (United States v Ziegler, 2007).

These steps go directly toward demonstrating a subjective expectation of privacy by decreasing the likelihood or probability of disclosure to others. Likewise, the use of such concealment mechanisms, such as unlisted URL, password protected access and data encryption in cloud storage are strong indications of a subjective privacy expectation.

2.3.1.1.2.2. Nature of the Contents

Courts sometime correlate a reasonable expectation of privacy to the nature of the container and its contents. For example, U.S. v. Friere (1983) held the defendant had a reasonable expectation of privacy in a briefcase he had entrusted to a third party, noting that "fewer places outside one's home justify a greater expectation of privacy than a briefcase."[5]

Courts have viewed the contents of a computer as similar to the contents of a briefcase, and equally entitled to a heightened expectation of privacy (United States v Andrus, 2008). There is reason to believe that courts will find the same heightened expectation of privacy in the same kind of data stored in the cloud.

2.3.1.1.2.3. Absence of Evidence of Abandonment of Expectation of Privacy

No person can have a reasonable expectation of privacy in property he has abandoned (Hester v United States, 1924). To demonstrate abandonment the Government must establish that the defendant's voluntary words or conduct would lead a reasonable person to believe that the defendant relinquished his property interests in the item searched/seized (United States v Stephens, 2000).

Absent some specific statement by the defendant the only thing that would allow a court to consider the defendant to have abandoned her expectation of privacy in cloud data would be a sustained period of inactivity in the account.[6]

2.3.1.1.2.4. Were the Documents in Question Created by the User or Were They Created by the Third-Party

The Supreme Court case in which they found no constitutional expectation of privacy in bank records, United States v. Miller, dealt with the bank's records, specifically the business records created or by the bank that detailed transactions with the defendant. That is, the defendant took certain actions regarding his bank account—a withdrawal or deposit for example—and the bank created records of these transactions. Sometimes the record is one totally created by the bank, such as monthly account statements. Other records maintained by the bank are copies of items created by the user, such as checks. In all instances, however, the records actually disclosed were copies made from the microfiche copies the bank maintained. United States v. Graham (2012) applied the same logic, that the records disclosed were the third party's records, not the individual's records, to cell site location records.

This "who-created-the-records" standard is not always followed. For example, the Supreme Court found no reasonable expectation of privacy in records the taxpayer provided to an accountant, even though these were original records of the taxpayer (Couch v US).

To the extent who created the records determines whether there is a reasonable expectation of privacy, in the cloud context the actual files were created by the user, not the cloud provider. If the records sought consist, instead, of transactional records, such as log files of cloud access, created by the cloud provider, it is less likely that courts will find the user to have a constitutional privacy interest in those records.

2.3.1.1.2.5. Whether the Nature of the Relationship between the Individual and the Third-Party Requires the Third-Party to have Access to the Contents Provided

An easy example of a relationship that requires access to the contents of the information provided is the banking relationship. When you write a check that is ultimately presented to your bank, the bank does more than note that a check has been written against your account. Numerous substantive content items are examined by the bank including the account and check number imprinted on the check, the amount, the signature, and in many instances, the payee and endorsement.

A contrary example is the telephone company who, for legitimate business reasons, needs to know what numbers you've called, and when, but ordinarily has no legitimate reason to monitor the content of your calls.

This approach in the cloud context—providing protection to transmission to/through third parties where the relationship only requires the third party to examine "routing information" (the electronic equivalent of the address on the outside of an envelope) but not finding a reasonable expectation of privacy in relationships where the third party is expected to or entitled to examine the content of the relationship—has been advocated by Professor Kerr (2010), but has not always been given a warm reception by courts.[7]

One case discussed the related issue of privacy expectation in stored email where the service provider had a contractual right of limited access. In Warshak v. United States (2010), the government obtained the defendant Warshak's stored emails by subpoena (after first requesting NuVox, the ISP holding the emails, to preserve emails in storage and prospectively, after receiving the subpoena). Warshak sought to suppress these emails as having been obtained in violation of the Fourth Amendment. The court analyzed the issue as we have, first determining that Warshak had a subjective expectation of privacy in his email, and then examining whether society was willing to recognize this expectation as legitimate. In analyzing this latter issue the court examined the protection afforded other forms of communication that pass through intermediaries (telephone conversations and letters) and concluded that it would defy common sense to give emails less protection than letters and phone calls.

The court then addressed the government's contention that is relevant to our discussion. The government argued that the terms of service between Warshak and NuVox allowed NuVox to access Warshak's emails for some purposes.[8] The court dispensed with the government's argument as follows:

First, the court noted that the mere *ability* of a third party to access contents of a communication was not sufficient to extinguish a privacy right.

Second, and more important, the court noted that a *right* of access also did not extinguish an otherwise existing privacy right. The right of access referenced was the same as was available to many telephone companies, the right to access and use information in the operation of the service and as necessary to protect the service. The degree of this access did not operate to extinguish the privacy right in the stored email. The court likened this agreed access to that granted by hotel guests to cleaning maids, and apartment tenants to repairpersons, noting that neither of those types of access vitiated any existing privacy interest.

Finally, the court commented that their holding did *not* mean that a subscriber agreement could *never* be broad enough to snuff out a privacy right, giving as an example a reserved right by the provider to "audit, inspect, and monitor" a subscriber's emails being sufficient access to eliminate any privacy right.

The court found the government's access to Warshak's emails without a warrant to be a Fourth Amendment violation, but allowed the evidence to be used under the "good faith" exception (Illinois v Krull, 1987).

This decision makes it clear that the exact nature of the relationship between the provider and user, and any agreed access the user provides in the service agreement, can have a major impact on whether a reasonable expectation of privacy will be recognized.

2.3.1.1.2.6. The Contractual Relationship between the Individual and the Third-Party

A closely related question is whether the contract or service agreement provides that the third party may "mine" the content stored by the third party? If so, the user is tacitly providing the third party not only custody of the data but also access permission. While such permission may not be conclusive on the issue of whether a reasonable expectation of privacy exists, the absence of any such content permission argues in favor of a finding of a protected privacy interest.

2.3.1.1.3. Conclusion as to Reasonable Expectation of Privacy in Cloud Data

As noted, cloud storage creates some fairly unique issues regarding reasonable expectation of privacy because of the shared or quasi-shared nature of the storage. Resolution of this issue—whether there is a reasonable expectation of privacy in data stored in the cloud—will ultimately be made by the courts, and the trend appears to be in the direction of finding a protected privacy interest.[9] Two respected commentators have urged the courts to hold that such protection exists.[10] In the interim, the prudent investigator will proceed on the assumption that privacy rights exist, and will only proceed with a warrant or warrant equivalent or under one of the exceptions to the warrant requirement. When this reasonable-expectation-of-privacy question is viewed as a consent issue, however, the answer may show this privacy interest to be useless if the cloud provider can consent to a search (as discussed in 2.7.1).

2.3.1.2. Is There Government Action?

The Fourth Amendment only applies to the actions of the government and third parties acting as agents of the government. The exclusionary rule was not intended and does not apply to the actions of private citizens or foreign law enforcement agents (including law enforcement of another state). The government may use information gathered by private citizens and foreign law enforcement under the "silver platter" doctrine.

2.3.1.2.1. The Silver Platter Doctrine

The silver platter doctrine arose in the early 1900s when federal search and seizure law was more restrictive than state search and seizure law, and suppression was a remedy for violation of the federal law. When state law enforcement officers conducted a search legal under state law but illegal under federal law, could the fruits of the search be used in federal courts? The answer was yes, if the federal authorities received the fruits on a silver platter, i.e., they were not so involved in the illegal search as to require suppression.

The "silver platter" doctrine withered on the vine after the protections of the Bill of Rights were extended to the states in Wolf v. Colorado (1949) and state and Federal protections were equal; however, starting in the 1980s, some state courts began holding their own constitutions to be more protective than the Federal constitution and the flow of evidence started moving the other way. Now Federal law enforcement (or law enforcement of other states), facing less stringent legal requirements, started providing evidence to state police on this same silver platter (NJ v Mollica, 1989). At best, of course, this only means that the higher state standard may be avoided. Compliance with the Federal standard as a floor is always required.

Courts view a transfer from a Federal official to a state official as analogous to a transfer from a private citizen to a state official. Searches by private citizens, not acting as the agent of law enforcement, are not entitled to constitutional protection.

2.3.1.2.2. Conclusion as to Government Action and the Cloud

The standard will almost certainly be the same for cloud data as for local data. The primary difference is that the nature of the relationship and the service agreement between the user and the cloud provider may create more situations where the provider will monitor, and even examine, cloud data for contraband. For example, under a Federal statute, since repealed,[11] AOL monitored communications for child pornography and reported any such material to a tip line which then reported the tip to law enforcement. This was found not to violate any Fourth Amendment right of the defendant because the scanning was done by a private entity to recognize files possibly detrimental to their system (United States v Richardson, 2010). Similar logic would likely apply to other monitoring done by cloud providers, such as monitoring for material violating copyright or to data mining done under the service agreement.

2.3.1.3 Conclusion re Applicability of the Fourth Amendment to Cloud Data

If either of these elements is missing—reasonable expectation of privacy or government action—the Fourth Amendment does not apply. If the statutory protections described below do not apply then there is no legal requirement to obtain a warrant, court order or subpoena.[12]

If both of these elements are present then the investigator must have either a warrant (or warrant equivalent) or fall within one of the consent exceptions described below.

2.4 Statutory Limitations: Electronic Communications Privacy Act

In response to decisions like Miller,[13] finding no expectation of privacy in bank records, Congress has passed a number of laws to provide statutory privacy protection for bank records (Right to Financial Privacy Act, 2000), cable television viewing and video rentals (Cable Privacy Act, 2000; Video Privacy Protection Act, 2000). Congress also extended the wiretap statute to provide some privacy protection to records related to electronic communications in the Electronic Communications Privacy Act.[14] Thus, at the Federal level, in many situations involving third party record holders, any privacy protection in third parties records stems from statutes, not the constitution.

The most relevant of these to our discussion is the Electronic Communications Privacy Act.

The Electronic Communications Privacy Act ("ECPA") updated the wiretap statute[15] and added the Stored Electronic Communications Act ("SCA").[16] Although it is common to reference ECPA in discussing limitations on computer searches, most often it is the specific provisions of SCA that are in play.[17]

2.4.1. Provisions of the SCA

2.4.1.1. What Does the SCA Cover?

The act covers the contents of electronic communications while in electronic storage by an "electronic communications service."[18] An electronic communications service is "any service which provides to the users thereof the ability to send or receive wire or electronic communications."[19] The act also covers the contents of electronic communications in a "remote computing service."[20] A remote computing service is one that provides "to the public … computer storage or processing service by means of an electronic communications system."[21]

2.4.1.2. What Does the SCA Prohibit?

The act prohibits providers of electronic communication service or remote computing service from disclosing contents of electronic communications or customer records and transactional data to the government, except as provided.

2.4.1.3. When Is a Disclosure to the Government Allowed?

This complex topic is discussed in great depth in many readily available sources (Office of Legal Education Executive Office for United States Attorneys, 2009). A discussion of this topic in similar depth is beyond the scope of this chapter. As a general rule of thumb, however, all records, except the content and record of real-time communications, can be obtained by a warrant supported by probable cause. Many, but not all records can be obtained by subpoena or court order.

2.4.1.3.1. Subscriber or Customer Records

2.4.1.3.1.1. Records Obtainable by Subpoena

Subscriber or customer records (name, address, telephone toll billing records, telephone number or other subscriber number or identity, and length and type of service for a subscriber or customer) may be obtained by subpoena (or higher process like a warrant or court order.)

The USA PATRIOT Act (2001) made other subscriber/customer records, such as transaction history, IP logs, etc. available by subpoena. Previously they had been available only by warrant or court order.

Under the PATRIOT Act, a subpoena can be used to obtain basic subscriber information including customer's name; address; length of service; means and source of payment (including any credit card or bank account number); local and long-distance telephone toll billing records; and records of session times and durations, as well as any temporarily assigned network address.[22]

Other sections of the SCA, not discussed here, allow access to opened email under a subpoena with notice to the customer. Provision is made for delayed notice in some circumstances.[23]

2.4.1.3.1.2. Records Obtainable by Court Order

Under the SCA, a court order, sometimes referred to as an "articulable facts order" or "§ 2703(d) court order," may be sought to obtain all other subscriber information except the content of an unopened e-mail that has been stored for 180 days or less.[24] To obtain a "§ 2703(d) court order," there must be specific and articulable facts showing that there are reasonable grounds to believe that the specified records are relevant and material to an ongoing criminal investigation. These records would include complete audit trails/logs, Web sites visited, identities of e-mail correspondents, cell site data from cellular/PCS carriers, and opened e-mail. As a practical matter, a "§ 2703(d) court order" can also be used to obtain basic subscriber information. Notice to the subscriber is only required when opened e-mail is requested from the provider.[25]

2.4.1.3.2. Contents of Electronic Communications

In general, the contents of an electronic communication may be disclosed with the consent of any party to the communication. The consent of all of the parties to the communication is not needed—only one party need consent.[26]

A government entity can compel the production of the contents of stored electronic communications by warrant. As previously noted, however, communications in storage for more than 180 days can be obtained by subpoena.

2.4.1.4. What Is the Remedy for Violation of this Act?

2.4.1.4.1. Criminal Liability

The SCA provides for criminal liability for one who "(1) intentionally accesses without authorization a facility through which an electronic communication service is provided; or (2) intentionally exceeds an authorization to access that facility; and thereby obtains, alters, or prevents authorized access to a wire or electronic communication while it is in electronic storage in such system."[27] Punishment can be up to two years imprisonment.

2.4.1.4.2. Civil Liability

The act creates a civil cause of action for violations, including damages and attorney's fees with punitive damages if the violation was willful. Although one early decision held that only the cloud provider, not the government, was civilly liable for violations (Tucker v Waddell, 1996); a later decision found liability in the government official who obtained the information (McVeigh v Cohen, 1998). Changes in the SCA made in 2001 reconciled the provisions that led to these discrepant results, and courts have more routinely found exposure to civil liability for the government (Freedman v America Online, Inc., 2004).

2.4.1.4.3. Suppression

Suppression is not a remedy for non-constitutional violations of SCA.[28] This protection, as noted, does not preclude suppression for constitutional violations under state constitutions. As noted earlier, in the Federal arena, the Sixth Circuit, in a since-vacated opinion, held that contrary to *U.S. v. Miller*,[29] an individual had a reasonable expectation of privacy in the content of his emails notwithstanding the fact that a third-party provider of Internet communication services had access to those messages (United States v Warshak, 2010). If this decision is embraced by the other circuits or the Supreme Court, some provisions of the SCA may themselves be unconstitutional.

2.4.1.4.4. Good Faith

Section 2707(e) of the SCA states that "reliance on … a court warrant or order, a grand jury subpoena, a legislative authorization, or a statutory authorization … is a complete defense to any civil or criminal action brought under this chapter."[30] The Tenth Circuit used this provision in *Davis v. Gracey*[31] to reject the defendants' civil claim under SCA. The court noted that because the officers relied on a warrant supported by probable cause they were entitled to a "good faith" defense.[32] A number of states do not incorporate the good-faith defense into their own constitution (State v Afana, 2010). It is not known what impact that doctrine will have on the good-faith provisions of the SCA in the context of civil or criminal liability.

2.4.2. Does the SCA Apply to Cloud Stored Data?

Other than the evolving interpretations of the constitutional reasonable expectation of privacy issue described earlier, the real question for this chapter is whether the SCA applies at all to cloud computing.

There are two issues that determine the answer to that question:

- Does the SCA's limitations on access to records of electronic communications imply limitations on access to information stored in the cloud; and
- Are cloud providers included within the definitions of "electronic communication service" or "remote computing service"?

2.4.2.1. Does the SCA's Limitations on Access to Records of Electronic Communications Imply Limitations on Access to Information Stored in the Cloud?

The SCA defines "electronic communication" as any transfer of signs, signals, writing, images, sounds, data, or intelligence of any nature transmitted in whole or in part by a wire, radio, electromagnetic, photoelectronic or photooptical system that affects interstate or foreign commerce.[33]

Since data is transferred to the cloud electronically, does this definition cover all data transferred to the cloud or does it only cover electronic communications (primarily email) stored in the cloud. There are no known court decisions on this issue.

2.4.2.2. Are Cloud Providers Included within the Definitions of "Electronic Communication Service" or "Remote Computing Service"?

"Electronic Communication Service" means any service, which provides to users thereof the ability to send or receive wire or electronic communications.[34] Online email cloud providers like Gmail and Hotmail appear to fall within that definition. Other cloud providers, providing only storage, would appear not to be within the definition.

"Remote Computing Service" means the provision to the public of computer storage or processing services by means of an electronic communications system.[35]

Using just this language it would appear that cloud providers are providing remote computing services. The SCA is, however, extraordinarily complex. The section of the statute that limits disclosure to the government, only applies that limit to data that is maintained by the provider "solely for the purpose of providing storage or computer processing services to such subscriber or customer, if the provider is not authorized to access the contents of any such communications for purposes of providing any services other than storage or computer processing."[36]

One commentator has concluded that:

The applicability of the RCS provisions in the Stored Communications Act will, therefore, always require examining the cloud provider's terms of service agreement and privacy policy. If a customer authorizes access to her data for the provision of contextual or targeted advertising services, the Act will not apply and the data will be at risk of disclosure to the government or another third party (Robinson, 2010).

2.4.3. Conclusion as to Applicability of the SCA to Cloud Data

Except for cloud providers of email services, and cloud providers who have no contractual right to access the contents of cloud data, the provisions of the SCA appear not to apply to cloud data. Making such a determination, however, requires familiarity with the details of the service agreement for any service whose data one wishes to access.

If one concludes that Fourth Amendment protections apply to cloud data then a warrant is required anyway, so the question of applicability of the SCA may be moot, but Fourth Amendment law includes exceptions to the warrant requirement, described below. If an investigator is acting without a warrant under one of these exceptions, he is walking on firm constitutional ground but may still be violating the SCA.

2.5. What Qualifies as a Legal Mandatory Directive?

2.5.1. When May a Subpoena be used to Obtain Constitutionally Protected Information

Where the Constitution or statutes require a warrant, the warrant must meet constitutional standards described below. However, there may be circumstances where, because the data that is sought is in the possession of third parties, a subpoena may be used. Grand jury subpoenas and administrative subpoenas are permitted to reach areas protected by the Fourth Amendment under a variety of theories related to the historic role grand juries have played in criminal investigations.[37] The Supreme Court standard for such subpoenas is "reasonableness."[38] Some state courts have permitted a grand jury subpoena to reach things protected by the Fourth Amendment so long as the subpoena is supported by probable cause (People v Watson, 2005). Other courts have implied that so long as a subpoena gives prior notice and an opportunity to object a subpoena can reach otherwise protected area of privacy (State v Miles, 2007).

Courts have often excused a subpoena from some of the more stringent requirements of a warrant because of the different ways evidence is obtained under the two. Under a warrant the evidence is *seized.* Under a subpoena the evidence is *demanded.* Courts have stated that use of a subpoena supported by probable cause often provides procedural safeguards that even a warrant does not provide (People v Mason, 1999).

The importance of this distinction flows from the fundamental difference between cloud forensics and non-cloud forensics. While in non-cloud forensic situations the investigator will be working with the actual hard drive(s) at issue which have been seized under a warrant, mandatory disclosure processes to obtain cloud data, whether warrant or subpoena in form, will, except perhaps in the most severe national security context, always be executed as if they were a subpoena, i.e., a document will be served on the record holder and that record holder will examine her files and produce the responsive data. Several courts have noted that warrants, supported by probable cause, but executed as subpoenas, where the civilian record holder actually conducts the search, provide more privacy protections (United States v Bach, 2002).

It remains to be seen whether this concept will actually result in warrants-executed-like-subpoenas being held to a lower standard.

2.6. What Constitutes a Valid Warrant?

As with other portions of this paper, this section will first describe, in general terms, the requirements for a valid warrant and then highlight any special issues involved in a warrant for cloud data.

2.6.1. The Application for the Warrant Must Demonstrate Probable Cause to Believe That Evidence of a Crime Will Be Found in the Place to Be Searched

If there is probable cause to believe *both* that a crime has occurred *and* that evidence of the crime will be found at a particular location, then a search warrant may be obtained.

2.6.1.1. Evidence of a Crime

Establishing probable cause that evidence of a crime will be found is usually a non-issue. The nature of the investigation, the nature of the crime and the nature of the evidence sought usually provide a sufficient basis for making this showing. Even though usually easy to establish, courts have made it clear that failing to establish a nexus between the crime and the items to be searched will result in suppression.[39]

There will likely be no unique problems associated with cloud storage with regard to establishing this nexus.

2.6.1.2. Will Be Found in the Place to Be Searched

This is the most commonly overlooked element in search warrants: 'What is the probable cause for believing that evidence of the crime you are investigating will be found in the location you wish to search?' This requires much more specificity than some generic "where else would it be" explanation. Articulable facts pointing to the location are required.

This is often problematic in any application seeking to search a computer for, at the very least, you must establish probable cause to believe that the evidence you are seeking will be found in a particular residence.

It could prove to be especially problematic in the cloud context. The application for the warrant must point to specific facts demonstrating the likelihood that the data being sought will be found not on the defendant's computer(s) in general, but specifically at the cloud location the application seeks to search. This topic is discussed in more detail in section 2.4.3.

2.6.2. Signed by a Neutral and Detached Magistrate

The warrant must be signed by a magistrate who has authority to issue the warrant. Obviously, the judge must occupy a position that has been properly created and has authority to issue warrants.[40]

Special problems can arise in the context of searches of locations outside the issuing court's jurisdiction. This will almost always be the case in searches for data stored in the cloud. The judge must have authority to authorize a search of the location covered by the warrant. Statutes and court rules in some states expressly limit a judge's search warrant authority to within that state. A warrant issued by a judge from one of those states, to search a cloud provider in another state is beyond that judge's authority. If the defendant had a recognizable privacy interest in the evidence provided under the warrant, the evidence is subject to suppression.

In other states, it is less clear that there are such jurisdictional limits on warrants. For example, where a warrant issued under probable cause is being executed like a subpoena (i.e., no "search" takes place—the warrant is served on the third party who then provides the evidence requested by the warrant), it is not clear that jurisdictional limits make such a warrant invalid.[41]

Several states, including California, Florida, Minnesota, and Washington, have laws requiring entities doing business in their state to accept that state's process for their business records, no matter where stored. These laws also generally provide that entities incorporated in that state must accept process from other states.[42]

This process has at least two limitations. First, as noted, only a small handful of states have such laws. Second, while the law purports to give judges in those states jurisdiction to *issue* such warrants or other compulsory process, it is not clear that they establish a valid mechanism for *enforcement* of the warrants and other process. What can the issuing court do if the party served with an order of production (whether in the form of a warrant supported by probable cause or other procedure) refuses to comply, or more specifically, simply ignores the order. The law of the extra territorial impact of warrants and other orders has only rarely been litigated (Kerr, 2010), and it is simply unknown whether such an out of state order, even if properly issued, can be enforced.

There are other options as well. One possibility is for law enforcement in the jurisdiction desiring the data to provide an affidavit to law enforcement in the jurisdiction in which the data is located. The data location law enforcement will obtain a local warrant for the data, incorporating the referring state's affidavit. This is commonly referred to as "domesticating" a warrant.

A second option is use of the Uniform Act to Secure the Attendance of Witnesses from Without a State in Criminal Proceedings.[43] This law, a version of which exists in every state, creates procedures under which a party to a criminal case in one State can obtain the presence of a witness located in another State. This can include compelling a witness to produce evidence located in another State. The Supreme Court has found this process to be constitutional (New York v O'Neill, 1959).

Each of these last two options can be enforced. However, none of the options give state courts authority over data located outside the United States. Obtaining such data requires reference to treaties, if any, between the United States and the foreign jurisdiction and requires the involvement of the Department of Justice.[44]

Of course, federal law enforcement has access to judicial districts covering the entire United States. While cumbersome, it is possible for federal law enforcement to obtain warrants in each of the districts in which the sought-for data might be found.[45] Federal law enforcement has the same limitations and options regarding out-of-country data.

2.6.3. Reasonably Precise in Describing the Place to be Searched and the Items to be Seized

There appear to be no particularity problems regarding the "items to be searched" that are unique to cloud searches. The problem relates to limits on describing the "place to be searched." While in general this should not be more burdensome for cloud searches than for other searches provided the warrant limits itself to searching for data within the target's area of the cloud, the varying and usually proprietary nature of storage and retrieval systems may present problems. Since such an area is likely demarked logically rather than physically, proof of the precision of the search may require presenting some information to the magistrate about the nature of file allocation utilized by the target cloud provider. Cloud providers may be hesitant to provide such information except under a protective order.

The precise location of cloud stored information may not be known at crucial early stages of an investigation. This could be a major stumbling block.

Even more onerous, defining "the place to be searched" in a cloud context raises many questions. Does "the place" mean the location of the business or registered agent's office for the cloud provider? Does it mean the location of "central server," if there be such a beast, for the cloud provider? Does "the place" mean the physical location of every storage device containing responsive data?

In the above section, we discussed how the requirement that a warrant be signed by a neutral and detached magistrate raised the issue of jurisdiction. What is at issue here is a related, but different, location issue.

If the investigator cannot tell the warrant judge where he wants to search because he does not know where the data actually is stored, can he obtain a valid warrant?

This is a crucial, but rarely analyzed problem. Even the 2009 version of the comprehensive and highly regarded Department of Justice's Computer Search Manual[46] does not discuss the constitutional problems associated with specifying the search location in warrants for cloud based data.[47]

The Fourth Amendment requires that warrants "particularly describ(e) the place to be searched."[48] The precision required is determined by whether the warrant describes the place to be searched with "sufficient particularity to enable law enforcement officers to locate and identify the premises with reasonable effort" and "whether any reasonable probability exists that the officers may mistakenly search another premise" (United States v Turner, 1985).

The kinds of cases where an absence of absolute precision has been excused include where the house is specifically and uniquely described but the wrong address is given, or other situations where sufficient specific information was provided to the searching officer so as to minimize the possible of a mistaken search of another premise.

On the other hand, finding a lack of particularity in describing the place to be searched, courts have declined validity to, and suppressed the results of, a warrant that did not specify a location other than within the issuing judge's jurisdiction - the Western District of Wisconsin (United States v Nafzger, 1992). Courts have made it clear that a warrant for a specific item at a specific location is limited to a search of that location. Officers may not use this warrant to seize the item after it was moved to a different location without a new warrant (Maryland v Garrison, 1987).

This legal requirement may prove to be a fatal stumbling block in seeking a warrant where the location of the data in the cloud is unknown or cannot be determined.

One possible solution flows from the language of the state statutes, discussed above, authorizing state judges to compel the production of evidence, regardless of where that evidence is located. The premise of these statutes is that any entity doing business in a state is generally required to have designated a "registered agent" in the state to accept process. The process, served as a subpoena even if it is a warrant supported by probable cause, puts a legally enforceable burden on the entity possessing the records to produce the evidence regardless of where stored. The focus of the inquiry is on the legal location of the entity possessing the evidence, not the location of the evidence itself.

What this "solution" does not solve is situations where the jurisdiction where the evidence is physically located imposes limitations on access to the evidence that is inconsistent with the terms of the warrant from the investigating state. These situations arise in situations where data is stored in a foreign country, where presumably the MLAT between the countries resolves the dispute. It may also arise, however, in situations where the required data is located in another state. [49]

2.6.4. Conclusions as to Requirements for a Valid Warrant for Cloud-Based Data

Obtaining a valid search warrant for cloud-based data involves overcoming two obstacles largely unique to such data. The first is that the application for the warrant demonstrates probable cause to believe that the data sought is actually at the cloud location for which search is requested. The second is that, given the opaque and often proprietary processes that cloud providers use to allocate a user's data to the cloud servers, it may be difficult to meet the requirement that the warrant be reasonably precise in describing the location to be searched. Many of the issues in this obstacle are correlated to meeting the authenticity requirement for admission of cloud data, discussed in section 3.1.2.

2.7. Exceptions to the Warrant Requirement

There are exceptions to the rule that evidence obtained without a warrant is inadmissible. These are, of course, the "few, specific, established, and well-delineated exceptions" developed under the Fourth Amendment (Schneckloth v Bustamonte, 1973).

Only two of these exceptions—consent and exigent circumstances—may justify the search of a cloud server without a warrant. These are discussed below.

It is important to remember that these exceptions simply allow the evidence to be used if it can be obtained. These two exceptions do not themselves provide authority for mandating a cloud provider to provide access.

2.7.1. Consent[50]

If the suspect or other person with authority over the property consents to a search, then a warrant is not required. In the context of cloud based data storage, the key questions for constitutionality analysis are: (1) who has the authority to consent, (2) is the consent given voluntarily and intelligently, and (3) is the consent limited?

As just noted, valid consent makes the acquisition of the data valid constitutionally. The cloud provider is not obligated to honor any consent other than that of the account holder. Nor is the cloud provider itself obligated to consent to a search, even if the provider is constitutionally capable of giving consent.

2.7.1.1. Who May Consent?

Obviously, the suspect may consent to a search of his own premises and effects, subject to such consent being given voluntarily and intelligently. As for third party consent, the general rule is that one "who possesses common authority over or other sufficient relationship to the premises or effects sought to be inspected" has the authority to consent to a search (US v Matlock, 1974).

The crucial analytical test is whether the defendant has a reasonable expectation of privacy in the premises or effects to which another has consented to be searched. In most instances of shared premises and effects, the courts have ruled there is a reduced expectation of privacy in the premises or things shared with another (US v Ladell, 1997). As the Ninth Circuit stated: "Although there is always the fond hope that a co-occupant will follow one's known wishes, the risks remain. A defendant cannot expect sole exclusionary authority unless he lives alone, or at least has a special and private space within the joint residence" (US v Morning, 1996). The consent given by a third party may not be valid if the area involved has been set aside, or rented, for the exclusive use of the defendant (State v Mathe, 1984).

While consent issues in cloud-stored data are not unique, consent issues will almost always arise because of the sharing of data with the cloud provider inherent in the cloud relationship. There are a wide variety of consent related issues involved in computer searches including when an employer can consent, when a parent or spouse can consent, etc. There is a rich body of law in these arenas that are applicable to cloud and non-cloud searches alike. Since our focus is on legally issues unique to or pervasive in cloud searches, the below discussion is limited to special instances of consent relevant to cloud based data, including the ultimate question of whether the cloud provider can consent to a search of a customer's data.

2.7.1.1.1. Parent

Courts generally find third-party consents easier to sustain "if the relationship between the parties—parent to child here, spouse to spouse in other cases—is especially close" (US v Ladell, 1997).

In the computer context, the more the computer is a shared item, both in terms of use and location, the more likely it is that a parent can give a valid consent. Even when the computer belongs to the child or is used by them exclusively and is located in their room or private space, parents can generally consent to a search of such a computer so long as the child is "essentially dependent" on the parent. If the child pays rent or in other ways is independent of the parent, the parent may lack the authority to give valid consent to a search of the child's effects or private space (US v Rith, 1999).

Parental consent is somewhat different in the cloud situation, because the physical storage location is not within the house. The crucial issue is likely going to involve shared access or ownership of the cloud *account,* not the local computer accessing the cloud-stored data.

2.7.1.1.2. Spouse

Spouses are generally considered to have joint control and equal right to occupancy of the premises and access to computers on the premises, and so may give a valid consent. If, however, the computer is used exclusively by the non-consenting spouse and is kept in a separate room (especially if locked), the other spouse may not be able to give valid consent. (See below section for discussion of encrypted or password protected files.)

The same analysis just made in the parental consent context applies here. The determinative issue is not shared occupancy and access to a local computer. It is instead shared ownership or access to the cloud account.

2.7.1.1.3. Co-User

Generally, allowing co-use results in a greatly reduced expectation of privacy. Whether password restricted or encrypted areas are the equivalent of locked bedrooms and thus not subject to a consent search by a co-user is a fact specific issue.[51] Under a 2007 4th Circuit decision, the use of password protected or encrypted files by the suspect prevents a co-user (including a spouse) from having actual authority to consent, but if the officer has no indication of the presence of password protected or encrypted files, the co-user may have apparent authority to consent (US v Buckner, 2007). Until you learn otherwise, however, assume that a co-user *cannot* give consent to search such objectively private areas of a computer.

For cloud computing the question is again, what authority over, and access to, the cloud account, as opposed to the computer, does the third party have?

2.7.1.1.4. Co-Tenants

Although the cloud providers system for storing user data may not physically segregate data by user, relying instead on logical segregation to track each user's data location, such intermingling should not create a consent issue regarding co-tenants as, unless specifically permitted by a user, users do not have access to each other's data.

2.7.1.1.5. Third Parties

When an item has been left in the custody of a third party the courts may find limits on the third party's authority to consent to a search of the item. In *United States v. James,*[52] the Eighth Circuit held the third party did not have authority to consent to the search of a packet of computer CDs left in his possession by the defendant. The court focused on its perception of the defendant's intent and held that the defendant did not intend to give the third party any authority to consent to the search of the disks. He gave them solely for the purpose of storing the disks.

This view of a suspect's ability to limit the scope of authority given to a third party holding the defendant's item conflicts with decisions like *United States v. Falcon.*[53] The defendant left a cassette at his brother's apartment labeled "confidential" and "do not play." Notwithstanding these instructions, the *Falcon* court held the brother's consent to search the cassettes to be effective because the brother "could have played (the tape) at any time, whether by design or by accident."[54]

One way of reconciling these two lines of thought is that in the James case the CDs were contained in a sealed envelope and the envelope was further encased in tape. Thus, they could not have been viewed by accident. More importantly, the police came to third party in the *James* case because they intercepted a letter from James to the third party instructing the third party to destroy the envelope and its contents.

Whether the specific facts of *James* will form the basis of future limits on consent searches is unknown, but the case does provide support for the more widely held view that where the defendant has taken extra steps to insure the privacy of computer files, such as by encrypting or password protecting them, the authority of the third party possessing, or having access, to the computer containing those files to consent to the search of those files is greatly limited.

2.7.1.1.6. The Cloud Provider

The cloud provider is not acting as a parent or spouse. To the extent they have authority to consent to a search it would be because they are deemed a co-user, co-tenant, or third party with possession, with access authority sufficient to meet the law's requirements. It seems clear that the only thing that provides the necessary access authority is the terms of use contract, or some other authority given to the provider by the user outside the contract.

Clearly if the terms of use allow the provider to fully access or consent to another's access, that provides sufficient authority. The more important question is whether the terms of use authorize more limited access that a reviewing court would consider sufficient to allow the provider to consent to a search. The previous discussion at 2.3.1.1.2.6, regarding whether terms of use allowing the provider to mine the user's data for advertising purposes defeat a reasonable expectation of privacy is merely a different view of the same topic. In both situations the unique nature of the individual contracts and the lack of any case law in this arena make it impossible to predict the circumstances under which qualified access under the terms of agreement will be held to authorize the provider to consent to access by others including law enforcement. What can be said clearly is that the terms of use are highly relevant in this regard. It is doubtful that most users understand the exposure to third party access those terms can provide.

2.7.1.2. Consent May Be Limited and May Be Withdrawn

Consent may be limited and withdrawn. A search of areas for which consent was not given, or after consent is withdrawn, is invalid.[55]

Some courts have held searches invalid when the officers, acting under general consent, broke open locked or sealed containers (Florida v Wells, 1990). Is a search of hidden, password protected or encrypted files under a general consent to search a computer open to the same attack? To the extent that analogy to the physical world is applicable, the answer is probably no. The line of cases represented by *Wells,* focus on the destruction of property necessary to open the sealed or locked container. Since there is no comparable destruction in accessing hidden, password protected or encrypted files, the search may be upheld.

An interesting question, equally but perhaps not uniquely involved in cloud forensics, is what happens when someone with consent authority consents to a search of cloud data, the data is downloaded to a local police drive, and then, before the drive is actually examined, consent is withdrawn. May the police nonetheless search their drive containing an image or copy of the cloud data?

The authors have found no cases directly on point. In analogous situations, courts have held that where the IRS obtained tax documents by consent and then consent was subsequently withdrawn, the IRS must return, without further examination, any documents they have not examined, but may retain any incriminating documents they had already examined before the consent was withdrawn (United States v Ward, 1978).

2.7.2. Exigent Circumstances

The exigent circumstances exception allows a warrantless search of premises where the officer has probable cause and exigent circumstances exist. The determination of whether exigent circumstances exist includes an examination of many factors.[56]

We have long recognized that the imminent destruction of evidence may constitute an exigency excusing the failure to procure a warrant. This risk is particularly weighty where narcotics are involved, for it is commonly known that narcotics can be easily and quickly destroyed. ... We held that a police officer can show an objectively reasonable belief that contraband is being, or will be, destroyed within a home if he can show 1) a reasonable belief that third persons are inside a private dwelling, and 2) a reasonable belief that these third persons are aware of an investigatory stop or arrest of a confederate outside the premises, so that they might see a need to destroy evidence (US v Dawkins, 1994).

In the cloud context, the most likely scenarios of exigent circumstances are where law enforcement is concerned that the defendant, or someone on her behalf, may delete cloud data before the data can be obtained under a warrant. This situation could arise where law enforcement does not have time to request/direct the cloud provider to "freeze" the data, or where the cloud provider is unwilling or unable to do so.

Assume the police are executing a lawful warrant and see, on an active computer screen, evidence that the computer is connected to a cloud server. Assuming they fear that an accomplice to the defendant may delete this cloud data before they can preserve it, may they download the cloud data to a portable police hard drive under a claim of exigent circumstances and then seek a warrant to search it?

A fascinating case that is the subject of a book by the AUSA prosecuting the case (Schroeder, 2011) was described by the court as follows:

Following an extensive national investigation of a series of computer hacker intrusions into the computer systems of businesses in the United States emanating from Russia, Alexey Ivanov was identified as one of the intruders Around June 2000, the FBI set up Invita, a "sting" computer security company in Seattle. On/about November 10, 2000 Mr. Ivanov, along with his "business partner," Defendant Vasiliy Gorshkov, flew from Russia to SeaTac.

In Seattle, the two men met with undercover FBI agents at the Invita office located in Seattle During the meeting and at the behest of the FBI, Defendant Gorshkov used an FBI IBM Thinkpad computer ("IBM") ostensibly to demonstrate his computer hacking and computer security skills and to access his computer system, "tech.net.ru," in Russia. After the meeting and demonstration, both Gorshkov and Ivanov were arrested.

Following the Defendants' arrest, without Defendant Gorshkov's knowledge or consent, the FBI searched and seized the IBM and all key strokes made by the Defendant while he used it, by means of a "sniffer" program which allowed the FBI to track and store the information. The FBI thereby obtained the Defendant's computer user name and password that he had used to access the Russian computer.

Armed with this information the FBI logged onto the subject computer(s) located in Russia. Faced with the possibility that a confederate of the defendant could destroy the files in the Russian computer, the FBI decided to download the file contents of the subject computer(s). This was done without reading same until after a search warrant was obtained (United States v Gorshkov, 2001).

The court denied the defendant's motion to suppress this evidence under two theories. One, not relevant to this discussion, was the court's conclusion that the Fourth Amendment has no extraterritorial reach. The other justification was exigent circumstances—the agents had a legitimate fear that the data would be deleted before a warrant could be obtained. So long as the agents had probable cause for seizing (downloading) the data, and a valid warrant was obtained before the downloaded data was examined, there was no Fourth Amendment violation.[57]

2.7.3. Conclusion as to Applicability of Exceptions to Warrant Requirement to Cloud-Stored Data

The consent exception is equally applicable to cloud data and may arise in most if not all instances because of the user's sharing of their data with the cloud providers and the possible or probable finding of consent implicit in such an arrangement. While this vitiates the warrant requirement, law enforcement is nonetheless dependent on voluntary cooperation from the cloud provider in gaining access to the data.

The exigent circumstances doctrine may be available for cloud-stored data in situations where (1) law enforcement has probable cause to believe that evidence of a crime is stored in that data, and (2) they have some mechanism for downloading the data. The last requirement is true because without a warrant the cloud provider is not obligated to allow access even under exigent circumstances. Exigent circumstances excuses the absence of a warrant, but it does not provide for mandatory compliance.

2.8. Conclusion Regarding Commanding Production

There are six issues relating to commanding production that are unique to, or provide special problems for, forensic examination of cloud-stored data:

2.8.1. Does the Sharing of Data with a Third Party, Inherent in Cloud-Stored Data, Eliminate a Reasonable Expectation of Privacy for the User (and the Directly Related Consent Issue Stated in 2.8.5 Below)?

We believe that it is unlikely that simply the act of storing data with a third party is not sufficient to defeat a claim of privacy. We also note that certain actions, such as encrypting the data can increase the likelihood that the courts will accept an argument that the user has a subjective expectation of privacy.

The two most important considerations are those expressed in the *Warshak* opinion discussed earlier, that email is akin to other forms of communication through third party intermediaries like phone conversations and mail and as such, is entitled to similar protection, but that the terms of the service agreement regarding access by the provider can be such that any privacy right is extinguished.

2.8.2. Does the SCA Regulate Disclosure by Cloud Providers?

We conclude that in some circumstance, where the cloud provider also provides electronic communication service, like Gmail, or where the cloud provider has no contractual right of access to the data, the SCA will apply. Outside those areas, the SCA does not apply (but the reader is cautioned that the 4th Amendment may apply.)

2.8.3. Does Cloud-Stored Data Create Difficulties Associated with Meeting the Requirement that There must be Probable Cause to Believe the Sought Evidence will be at the Location You Seek to Search and that a Warrant be Reasonably Precise in Describing the Location to be Searched?

These two questions revolve around the same stumbling block—the likely inability of the investigator to know precisely where (in a geographical or physical sense) in the cloud the sought for data is located. Without such information the affidavit can neither describe the location to be searched with any adequate degree of particularity nor state probable cause to believe the data will be at that location.

There are two possible solutions. The first is to use a subpoena mechanism to serve warrants, i.e., serving the document on the cloud provider's physical offices and requiring them to produce the requested documents wherever they are. This "solution" is limited to those states, which allow a warrant to reach data located outside the state. It is further limited by complications associated with enforcing the warrant, and conflicting limitations on access to the data imposed by the state/nation where the data is located.

The second possible solution is not discussed in this paper for there is no data upon which to base an expectation of the solution. That solution is for the law to recognize, either in the form of changed rules and statutes, or in the form of case evolution, that brick and mortar concepts of location are not appropriate in these contexts and the real test should be on the adequacy of the logical separation of data between users and law enforcement's ability to articulate with specificity the logical location of data and the probability that evidence of a crime will be found at that logical location.

2.8.4. May the Cloud Provider Consent to a Search of Cloud-Stored Data?

As noted, this is in many ways, simply a different construct for the questions asked in the "reasonable expectation of privacy" inquiry and the answer is the same; the terms of the SLA and the degree of access, if any, given by the user to the service provider is largely determinative.

2.8.5. Are the Consent and Exigent Circumstances Exceptions to Warrant Requirements Helpful if They Permit but do not Require Disclosure by the Cloud Provider?

This question focuses not on large, constitutional issues, but on practical ones. If there are no constitutional prohibitions on disclosure, how does the investigator gain access to stored data? We conclude that SLAs, Privacy Policies, and the related expectations of the users will mean that providers will insist on being served with binding legal directives before they will disclose cloud data, even if there is no prohibition on the disclosure.

3.0. ACTUAL PRODUCTION IN COURT

Once obtained, evidence will be of little use if it is not actually accepted as evidence in a case—or accepted as evidence into a case. The Federal Rules of Evidence, or similar rules specific to the jurisdictional state, guide the process of admissibility. While there have been some modifications to these rules over the past few years to address the increasing role digital evidence is playing in the legal system (K&L Gates, 2006), most decisions regarding the admissibility of digital evidence rely on rules originally designed for paper documents. Even more alarming is the fact that the legal education system has woefully failed to keep pace with these changes in the forms of evidence and lawyers and judges alike are often woefully unprepared to argue for, challenge, and rule on the admissibility of digital evidence (Alva & Endicott-Popovsky, 2012).

The seminal court opinion in the 2007 case *Lorraine v. Markel American Insurance Company*[58] provides both a devastating critique at current practices in the digital evidence arena as well as a useful and comprehensive overview of the procedural requirements for admissibility of "Electronically Stored Information" (ESI) as guided by the Federal Rules of Evidence.

Because the general digital evidence legal arena is undeveloped, it is necessary to discuss the ways that digital evidence can be admitted or challenged before delving in to the unique problems presented by evidence obtained from cloud providers.

Judge Paul Grimm's opinion in *Lorraine*, with his exhaustive treatise of the rules governing admissibility of digital evidence, provides both a helpful road map to guide us through this area of the law and insight into what parts of the admissibility process are particularly problematic for evidence obtained from forensic examination of cloud based data.

Unlike the previous section, which presented problems largely unique to the criminal investigatory process, this discussion of admissibility is largely applicable to both the civil and criminal process.[59]

Before addressing the specific rules, it is important to note three things about the admissibility process. First, it is not stringently linear. As *Lorraine* states, there is a burden on opposing counsel to object to admissibility. Objections by counsel can be made based upon any one of the Rules of Evidence without regard to order.[60]

Second, a judge's role in the admissibility process is to act as a gatekeeper. The bar for admissibility is generally low. Admitting evidence does not mean the evidence is persuasive or convincing. Admission simply acknowledges that the evidence can be presented to the jury and the jury will determine what weight to give the evidence. Judges will frequently acknowledge this by responding to an objection by saying "that goes to weight, not admissibility."[61] A common example of this in the ESI arena is an objection to the admissibility of a digital photograph on the grounds that it could have been altered. Absent any proof of alteration, such an objection goes to the weight the jury gives the evidence not its admissibility.

The importance of this two-step evaluation of evidence to a non-lawyer cannot be overemphasized. The first step is admissibility, the second step is persuasiveness. One way this could be viewed is to think of admissibility being the "weigh-in" of boxers before a match, where they must pass certain minimal but crucial eligibility and health requirements. Being allowed to enter the ring in no way guarantees success. However, while the crucial, qualitative determination is made once the boxers are in the ring, where the goal is to win the boxing match, failure to meet the eligibility requirements to enter the ring is fatal.

The same is true in the courtroom. Getting evidence admitted does not guarantee a verdict in your favor, but failing to have the evidence qualify for admission can be fatal. In fact, significant effort is frequently exerted in both civil and criminal cases in pretrial stages to qualify or disqualify evidence's admissibility. Often a victory or loss at the pretrial stage can set the ground for a settlement or guilty plea.

The third thing to note about the admissibility process is that trial judges have very wide discretion over admissibility and appellate courts generally defer to trial courts' determinations of admissibility. This puts an even greater emphasis on the determination of admissibility stage of the proceedings for trial court decisions regarding admissibility are only infrequently reversed on appellate review.

3.1. General Rules Applicable to all Electronic Evidence and Application to Cloud Context

Judge Grimm's discussion of the admissibility requirements of the evidence rules were in the context of email, but the rules discussed are generally applicable to all evidence, including other forms of digital evidence. He argues that five substantive areas for admissibility must be considered whenever Electronically Stored Information is offered as evidence. These are: relevance, authenticity, hearsay, original evidence, and probative v. prejudicial.[62] These categories are discussed in general below, and then in reference to unique problems associated with each category in cloud-based evidence.

3.1.1. Relevance

When ruling on admissibility, one of the first questions is whether the evidence presented has relevance: "(a) does it have the tendency to make a fact more or less probable than it would be without the evidence; and (b) is the fact of consequence in determining the action"[63]. The bar for determining relevance is low, at "more probable than it would be without the evidence"[64]. Sufficiency is immaterial to admissibility based on relevance, as the evidence only needs to be shown to logically alter the probability of a fact of consequence.

Judge Grimm notes that establishing ESI as relevant is generally not difficult, although it is clear that "evidence that is not relevant is never admissible"[65]. Thus, relevance is generally not an issue.[66]

3.1.1.2. Unique Cloud Issues: Relevance

The authors contend that there is nothing inherently unique to relevance with respect to the cloud.

3.1.2. Authenticity

To meet the authenticity requirement, the proponent must show that "the ESI is what it purports to be."[67] The Federal Rules of Evidence provide non-comprehensive examples for how evidence can be authenticated:

1. Testimony of a Witness with Knowledge.
2. Nonexpert Opinion About Handwriting.
3. Comparison by an Expert Witness or the Trier of Fact.
4. Distinctive Characteristics and the Like.
5. Opinion About a Voice.
6. Evidence About a Telephone Conversation.
7. Evidence About Public Records.
8. Evidence About Ancient Documents or Data Compilations.
9. Evidence About a Process or System.
10. Methods Provided by a Statute or Rule.[68]

The two most relevant ways in which cloud-based evidence can be authenticated are through the testimony of a witness with knowledge (Fed. R. Evid. 901(b)(1)) and through evidence about a process or system (Fed. R. Evid. 901(b)(9)); both ways are discussed below.

3.1.2.1. Testimony of a Witness with Knowledge

In order to establish that evidence is authentic, the proponent will likely call a witness who can testify that the evidence is what it purports to be. "A witness may be appropriately knowledgeable through having participated in or observed the event reflected by the exhibit."[69]

In the case of digital evidence, it is generally sufficient to produce a person, such as a custodian or other qualified witness, with personal knowledge of the procedure that generated the records (States v Kassimu, 2006). Depending on the complexity of the system, the person may need more than a superficial knowledge of the system, however. As noted by Judge Grimm the witness must have a working knowledge of the process of producing the information:

(I)t is not required that the authenticating witness have personal knowledge of the making of a particular exhibit if he or she has personal knowledge of how that type of exhibit is routinely made. It is necessary, however, that the authenticating witness provide factual specificity about the process by which the electronically stored information is created, acquired, maintained, and preserved without alteration or change, or the process by which it is produced if the result of a system or process that does so, as opposed to boilerplate, conclusory statements that simply parrot the elements of the business record exception to the hearsay rule or public record exception. (Internal citations omitted.)[70]

3.1.2.2. Evidence about a Process or System

If the proponent seeks to authenticate evidence by offering evidence about a process or system, the process/system itself may be subject to an additional test—the *Daubert* test. This test or standard, required to be conducted for cases in all U.S. Federal Courts, is used to determine admissibility of scientific, technical, or specialized evidence.[71] The *Daubert* test, complements Federal Rules of Evidence 702, which states:

A witness who is qualified as an expert by knowledge, skill, experience, training, or education may testify in the form of an opinion or otherwise if: (a) the expert's scientific, technical, or other specialized knowledge will help the trier of fact to understand the evidence or to determine a fact in issue; (b) the testimony is based on sufficient facts or data; (c) the testimony is the product of reliable principles and methods; and (d) the expert has reliably applied the principles and methods to the facts of the case.

Under Daubert the judge acts as a "gatekeeper," limiting such evidence to that which is reliable and scientifically valid. This determination is made by asking four questions:

1. Whether the proferred knowledge can or has been tested.
2. Whether the theory or technique has been subjected to peer review and publication.
3. The known or potential rate of error, and
4. Whether the theory or technique has gained general acceptance in the relevant scientific discipline.

These four questions are often summarized as testing, peer review, error rates and acceptability in the relevant scientific community. Later court decisions have made it clear, however, that this should be a flexible test, tied to the particular facts of the case. These factors are neither an exhaustive list nor a required checklist.[72]

3.1.2.3. Unique Cloud Issues: Authenticity

The main barrier for cloud forensics is one of authenticity. In particular, the challenge is to show that the data, both technically within the cloud environment and throughout the investigative process, is what it purports to be.

If the only authenticity challenge to cloud based evidence is whether the item produced in court is the item produced by the cloud provider the matter is akin to a chain of custody discussion, wherein all you must show is that what was provided by the cloud provider is what is being produced. Any number of witnesses can provide probative testimony, from a representative of the cloud provider who can compare the item presented in court to their record of what was produced, to a witness from the evidence proponent's staff who can testify from personal knowledge that what is produced in court was what he or she was given by the cloud provider. In fact this form of authenticity challenge is so easily met that it would rarely be raised.

The more meaningful authenticity challenge is to whether the item produced in court is in fact from the cloud storage records associated with a particular user. When evidence is seized from an individual's computer, there can be little doubt that it came from that person's computer. To be sure, in a shared use environment the issue of what user actually used, possessed, created (or whatever other connection with the data is relevant) the data can be challenged, usually as a matter of weight, but there can be no sustainable challenge regarding what computer or hard drive was associated with the data.

In the cloud context, however, the data of multiple users is kept logically separate but is, by virtue of the nature of hard drives, physically comingled. If the authenticity challenge is to the proof that the data produced is the data associated with a particular user, some evidence or testimony must be produced to provide assurance that the thing is what it purports to be - data associated with a specific user.

Where the authenticity of a cloud-based document is challenged (i.e., is this document associated with the user's account), the person testifying to this will likely be a representative of the cloud provider who can testify about the process of associating data with specific users.

At one level this authenticity can be established by a witness from the cloud provider who can testify to the challenged fact, that the data offered was associated with a specific user when they produced it. This would be akin to a bank records custodian authenticating that a particular check was associated with a specific individual's account. A cloud provider witness would testify regarding their method of retrieving and producing the requested information ("I queried the system for all records associated with this user's account, copied that information onto a CD (or more realistically a hard drive) and delivered that CD/hard drive to the requestor.")

The more difficult question, and the more difficult authenticity proof requirement, arises when what is challenged is the core method of allocating, tracking, and retrieving data associated with an individual account in the cloud. This is particularly true where mere possession of the item, like child pornography, with no other connection to the user is sufficient for conviction.

Meeting such a challenge requires proof of the reliability of the process or system controlling the data storage. The focus is on the reliability of the system rather than the reliability of the person describing the system.

Because of the newness, complexity, and likely proprietary nature of the cloud provider's file allocation procedures, it is highly likely an expert witness will be called upon to testify. The authenticity of the evidence gathered is at least partially dependent upon the qualifications and experience of the investigator—a cloud provider employee in the case of cloud forensic investigations.

An even more onerous potential authentication problem arises related to how forensics is done in the cloud environment. Specifically, the rapid provisioning of resources within a single cloud environment creates a challenge to provide sufficient proof that the file(s) in question were actually those used, modified, or otherwise by the person in question. Cloud forensic investigations involve production of forensic evidence from the cloud provider, delivered to law enforcement. With traditional digital forensics, a potential authenticity issue within the chain of custody could be overcome because the evidence in question—the contents of the original hard drive can be physically presented to the court if necessary. Reexamination could be conducted with the physical evidence to provide additional proof of authenticity. With cloud forensic data, there is no fallback to physical evidence. Evidence presented for forensic investigations is reliant upon a proof that the process used by the cloud provider to attribute the questioned data to a particular user is reliable, for the original cloud servers would rarely, if ever, be available for in court examination.

The inability to ever produce the data in its original, as-stored-in-the-cloud-condition, makes the role of the process or system and the testimony about the process/system uniquely critical. Whether cloud providers will be willing to reveal this potentially highly proprietary information is an unknown.

3.1.3. Hearsay

Hearsay has been described as:

an out-of-court statement offered in court to prove the truth of the matter asserted by the out-of-court declarant. It is offered into evidence through the testimony of a witness to that statement or through a written account by the declarant. The hearsay rule excludes such evidence because it possesses the testimonial dangers of perception, memory, sincerity, and ambiguity that cannot be tested through oath and cross-examination (Rice, 2005).

The rule favors live testimony where such would help the fact finder assess the veracity and perception of the person making a statement being offered for its truth.

In general, where a statement is offered for its truth, the person making the statement must testify. A classic example of a hearsay statement is a witness in an automobile accident case testifying that the police officer investigating the accident told him (the witness) the defendant was speeding. If the officer is not present, then she cannot be cross-examined about the basis for her statement. Since the statement of the officer, given by the witness, is likely only relevant for the truth of what the statement asserts (the defendant was in fact speeding) the witness' testimony about what the officer said is clearly inadmissible hearsay.

Hearsay is an extremely complex area of evidence law and is the subject itself of many learned treatises and books. We cannot even begin to explore the intricacies of this subject in this chapter. A reader, uninitiated in this subject, would be well served by referring to the often-cited Judge Grimm and his decision in Lorraine v. Markel American for an excellent summary of hearsay law in the context of ESI.[73]

Judge Grimm summarized the hearsay rule as requiring the application of five separate questions:

(1) Does the evidence constitute a statement, as defined by Rule 801(a); (2) was the statement made by a "declarant," as defined by Rule 801(b); (3) is the statement being offered to prove the truth of its contents, as provided by Rule 801(c); (4) is the statement excluded from the definition of hearsay by rule 801(1); and (5) if the statement is hearsay, is it covered by one of the exceptions identified at Rules 803, 804 or 807.[74]

Some of Judge Grimm's assessments of the application of the hearsay rule to ESI are worth repeating.

Electronic evidence generated by a computer process (log files for example) is not hearsay because they are not 'statements'[75], with a statement being "a person's oral assertion, written assertion, or nonverbal conduct, if the person intended it to be an assertion"[76].

Such electronic evidence would also not be considered a statement made by a declarant (under the given definitions for "person" and "declarant" from Fed. R. Evid 801) because "when an electronically generated record is entirely the product of the functioning of a computerized system or process... there is no 'person' involved in the creation of the record, and no 'assertion' being made. For that reason, the record is not a statement and cannot be hearsay"[77]. It is important to note that this is only for electronic records produced by a system or process, and does not directly apply to electronic writings where a person makes an assertion in his or her statement.

Several important hearsay exceptions—including business and public records—reinforce the importance of authentication. The business records exception and others can allow admission provided that it meets the proper qualification and that "neither the source of information nor the method or circumstances of preparation indicate a lack of trustworthiness."[78]

3.1.3.1. Unique Cloud Issues: Hearsay

Most of the hearsay analysis applicable to ESI in general will be applicable to ESI stored in the cloud. The five-step analysis prescribed by Judge Grimm must be followed whether the data being offered comes from the defendant's local hard drive or from cloud-based storage. The one area where hearsay rules are more frequently applicable in the cloud context is in establishing the authenticity of the cloud-based data (with authenticity meaning producing evidence that the data in question is data associated with the relevant user account).

We have previously described, at 3.1.2.2, how such authenticity could be established by showing the process or system involved in attributing data to a particular account. A proponent of an exhibit obtained from cloud storage might seek to authenticate an exhibit without calling a witness from the cloud provider, arguing that a written certification that the exhibit was a record of regularly conducted activity was sufficient under Fed. R. Evid 902(11). That is, the cloud provider would provide a certification stating that the exhibit was stored in a location attributable to the user in question at or near the time it was transmitted to the cloud provider by the user, that it was maintained in that location in the course of the regularly conducted activity of the provider, and that it is the regular practice of the provider to conduct this activity.

It seems to stretch the business records exception beyond any logical meaning to allow it to be used in this manner, to avoid providing the proprietary details of the storage and allocation system, but it is not a stretch to believe that some enterprising attorney, faced with a recalcitrant cloud provider unwilling to provide proprietary details, might attempt such use.

A more likely use of the business records exception would be to use that exception, together with the argument that log files of customer access are statements of a computer, not a person, as a way of admitting such log files without calling a witness to authenticate the log files.

This again emphasizes the importance of authentication and methods of meeting authentication objections in the cloud environment.

3.1.4. Original Evidence

The Original Writing Rule is the next hurdle Judge Grimm sets out for electronic evidence admissibility. Fed R. Evid. 1002 requires the proponent offer the "original" of a writing, recording, or photograph unless the Rules provide otherwise. Fed. R. Evid. 1003 states that "A duplicate is admissible to the same extent as the original unless a genuine question is raised about the original's authenticity or the circumstances make it unfair to admit the duplicate."

Offering a duplicate or copy of an original, thus, is generally only a problem when there is a genuine question original's authenticity.

3.1.4.1. Unique Cloud Issues: Original Evidence

Any unique cloud issues relating to the original writing rule turn on the authenticity questions discussed earlier. So long as the proponent can show that the offered item is what it purports to be (which in the cloud context means that the document offered is a copy of information that can be shown to have come from an area of the cloud assigned to the defendant) there should be few original evidence issues with regard to cloud based data.

As with all the other admissibility questions, there could easily be obstacles to the admission of documents stored in the cloud related to the documents themselves and not to the fact they were stored in the cloud.

The challenges of admissibility with respect to the unique nature of the cloud stem primarily from the fact that the "original" evidence—the multitude of hard drives containing the data attributable to the defendant—will almost never be available. The inability to 'go back' and obtain the original again is a unique issue that presents challenges for cloud forensic investigations from an authenticity standpoint.

The unique requirement placed upon actual production is that cloud providers conduct the investigation. This requires that cloud providers comply with actual production requests. Would inability to access original evidence halt an investigation? Federal Rules of Evidence 1004 states (a) that an original is not required if, among other conditions, (b) an original cannot be obtained by any available judicial process; or (c) the party against whom the original would be offered had control of the original; was at that time put on notice, by pleadings or otherwise, that the original would be a subject of proof at the trial or hearing; and fails to produce it at the trial or hearing." Thus there may be a potential to gather evidence on the surface, though no accompanying metadata, logs, or other data indicating proper authenticity would be available. Depending on the case and evidence sought, production may not be possible. If cloud providers did not comply with production, the authors note that the burden in determining authenticity of any evidence collected through other means would be higher, and potentially unattainable.

3.1.5. Probative vs. Prejudicial

The final admissibility question noted by Judge Grimm is probative value against the potential for unfair prejudice. This admissibility test is governed by the Federal Rules of Evidence 403, which protects against unfair prejudice. When counsel "analyzes the admissibility of electronic evidence, he or she should consider whether it would unfairly prejudice the party against whom it is offered, confuse or mislead the jury, unduly delay the trial of the case, or interject collateral matters into the case."[79] With ESI evidence, Judge Grimm states that the courts are likely to consider whether the evidence would be unduly prejudicial for several reasons including when there is a concern as to the "reliability or accuracy of the information that is contained within the electronic evidence" (St. Clair v Johnny's Oyster & Shrimp, Inc., 1999).

3.1.5.1. Unique Cloud Issues: Probative vs. Prejudicial

This admissibility question will apply equally to cloud and non cloud-based evidence. It might be possible for a party to seek to restrict reference to the fact that data was stored in the cloud if that fact might be prejudicial, but the authors are unaware of a case where this argument has been made.

3.2. Conclusions Regarding Admissibility of Cloud-Based Data

3.2.1. Authenticity

As emphasized, authenticity is likely the most critical admission criteria unique to the cloud. Because individual user data is almost always comingled physically it will be necessary to establish the validity of the process of attributing specific data to specific users. The unique aspects of cloud-based evidence present challenges in authenticity that must be considered throughout a cloud forensic investigation. Judge Grimm's opinion strongly advocated diligence in evidence authentication: "the inability to get evidence admitted because of a failure to authenticate it almost always is a self-inflicted injury which can be avoided by thoughtful advance preparation"[80]. A technical effort to certify systems are forensically ready; a well-documented investigative process; and a clear legal argument for admissibility would be indicative of 'thoughtful advanced preparation' required to overcome the unique barriers for the authentication and admissibility of cloud forensic evidence.

Even with such a system in place, those seeking to admit cloud data are dependent upon the provider to produce the witness(es) necessary to describe the system.

The ultimate answer to questions involving authenticity of cloud data will turn, thus, on the validity of the system used to logically allocate data to individual users, and the ability of the proponent of such evidence to find a persuasive way to describe such a system. This will involve the following questions as a summary of authenticity issues for potential cloud based evidence:

3.2.1.1. Was the Process Used to Attribute Data to User Reliable?

The actual production of evidence will be carried out through a warrant or subpoena provided to a cloud provider. An employee of the cloud provider would then produce the evidence and present findings. While forensic investigations are allowed to occur without the presence of law enforcement,[81] the validity of the investigation and the processes used to gather the evidence are subject to proper authentication. How do we know the evidence gathered by a cloud provider is what it purports to be? What proof is there than the process used by the cloud provider to attribute evidence to a particular user is reliable?

The two most meaningful ways to show authenticity under the Federal Rules of Evidence are 1) Evidence About a Process or System, and 2) Testimony of a Witness with Knowledge.[82]

In both options, a representative from the cloud provider would likely be necessary to connect the evidence in question to the cloud customer.

3.2.1.2. Was the Process Used to Obtain Forensic Data from the Cloud Reliable?

At its most basic level, proof of authenticity for cloud-based data is proving that the data is what it purports to be—data from the cloud storage area associated with a specific person. The most convincing way to do this is to show that process used to extract cloud data (and by necessity, the process used to allocate and track the location of data associated with a specific person) is reliable. This can be done by describing the results of testing the process, by describing the logic behind the process, and by having expert testimony about the reliability of the process. The newness, complexity, and likely propriety nature of the cloud provider's data allocation procedures require the cooperation of the cloud provider and establishing reliability may, at least until the process is widely accepted as reliable, be a formidable task.

3.2.1.3. Can the Cloud Forensics Process Pass a Daubert Test?

The *Daubert*[83] test sets a higher bar for authenticity, and is an additional measure to validate the process used to obtain forensic data and other authenticity questions. This test is required in U.S. Federal Cases for scientific, technical, or other evidence requiring specialized knowledge, including digital evidence. There are four lines of inquiry that an expert witness is questioned on for the evidence in question: 1) whether the proffered knowledge can or has been tested; 2) whether the theory or technique has been subjected to peer review and publication; 3) the known or potential rate of error; and 4) whether the theory or technique has gained general acceptance in the relevant scientific discipline.

The requirements described by the *Daubert* test provide a charge to the academic and industry community of cloud forensics researchers and practitioners. Beyond all other legal requirements that must be considered, one crucial gate by which cloud forensic evidence would be admitted in a court case rests on reviewed and published techniques; knowledge of the rate of shortcomings; and acceptance by the cloud forensics community of the processes used to attribute data in the cloud to an individual user. For an emerging area, this monumental, but necessary, challenge calls for a cohesive 'best practices' approach motivating the field of cloud forensics such that evidence from cloud forensic investigations can be used in court.

3.2.1.4. Is the use of Duplicates Sufficient? Is the Inability to Access the Underlying Original Data Fatal to establishing Authenticity?

Where a local drive is the subject of forensic analysis, one unspoken fact usually undercuts and deters most challenges to the accuracy of the forensics process—regardless of how the data was found, the original drive is usually available to demonstrate that the data is in fact on that drive. While examination of the original drive in this manner would be a rare act, the potential to do so is always present. The existence of the possibility can deter many theoretical challenges.

The absence of such underlying original data will likely not be fatal to a legal challenge where the issue is being decided by a judge, but where the jury is the ultimate determiner of relevance, which is in itself dependent on a piece of evidence being what it purports to be, the inability to produce the original evidence may be faced with lay skepticism. The jury is being asked on faith to accept the validity of the process used to obtain the evidence.

The problem with the absence of the original underlying data is difficult enough where the evidence copy has been obtained through the forensic practices of the provider. When the copy is acquired without the use of acceptable forensic practices, in this case due to access issues, the difficulty of establishing authenticity may be insurmountable.

4.0 ADDITIONAL LEGAL REQUIREMENTS

This section will detail commonly cited legal issues for cloud forensics, and will discuss whether or not each issue presents a unique legal challenge with respect to the cloud. These legal requirements should be considered throughout cloud forensic investigations.

4.1. Multi-Jurisdiction

Multi-jurisdictional issues are consistently noted as the primary issue in cloud forensic investigations, and digital forensic investigations as a whole (Ruan, Carthy, & Kechadi, 2011a). The location of data affects the ability to compel production of such data and may, although unlikely under most states' long arm jurisdiction rules, affect the determination of where a case involving cloud data must be filed/prosecuted.

4.1.1. Criminal Cases

Criminal cases involve criminal charges brought by the government under criminal sections of the U.S. Code or state counterparts. The jurisdictional issue for where such a case may be filed usually turns on questions of where the victim is located, where the defendant is located, and where the criminal acts occurred or where their impact was felt. Often jurisdiction is not exclusive, i.e., several states or the federal government and one or more states may each legitimately assert jurisdiction. Subject to double jeopardy limitations, prosecution in multiple jurisdictions is possible.

In general, jurisdiction for a case will be in the jurisdiction investigating and filing the case, although this is largely a tautological decision for usually the selection of what jurisdiction will investigate a case is decided by the determination of which jurisdiction may prosecute the case. In cases with multiple possible jurisdictions, so long as the valid statutory jurisdictional requirements are met, the ultimate decision as to which will prosecute is usually a policy question.

For criminal cases, the controlling substantive, procedural, and constitutional rules (including the Rules of Evidence) are those of the government asserting jurisdiction and bringing the case.

4.1.2. Civil Cases

Cases where one person or entity brings a claim against another person or entity for a failure of a legal duty are considered civil cases. The government can be a party, either as plaintiff or defendant; the key requirement is that the cause of action is civil. For civil cases, an understanding of jurisdiction is more complicated. When the data and entities involved in the case are in different geographic areas, the primary jurisdictional requirement is that the "forum" state (the state where an action is brought) has "enough connection with a problem to satisfy constitutional and statutory requirements" (Richman & Reynolds, 2002). Some courts contend that location of a server is not sufficient enough to qualify as a connection for jurisdiction decisions.

Issues other than determining jurisdiction can be involved in multi-jurisdictional cases. One significant issue is whose substantive law applies when the parties and evidence are located in different jurisdictions? A large and complex area of law called "Conflict of Law" has been developed to resolve these issues. This body of law is beyond the scope of this chapter and will not be addressed here.

The most important point to be made for this chapter is that the issues associated with the multi-jurisdictional nature of cloud based data storage are not unique. These issues arise frequently in disputes completely outside the realm of cloud storage.

4.2. Multi-Tenancy

Multi-Tenancy issues are endemic to cloud forensic investigations due to the shared storage nature of cloud computing. There are two issues, each already discussed in the previous two sections. The first is the validity-of-the-warrant issues relating to establishing probable cause to believe that evidence of a specified crime will be found at the location for which search permission is sought, and the related issue of the need for particularity in the warrant regarding the identification of the place to be searched.

The second issue is authenticity. If data from multiple tenants is stored at the location to be searched, there must be a sufficient basis for claiming that the offered data is that of the defendant and only the defendant.

Where the investigator cannot specify with precision the location of the sought after data there may be temptation to seek "cloud-wide" warrants or other compulsory production orders. Such over broad orders may look to a reviewing court like a fishing expedition. Such overbroad, general warrants are unlawful searches, and the results of such searches will almost certainly be suppressed.

Such a broad warrant, one that does not limit itself to a specific user's data, can be overbroad in two ways. First, such a warrant almost by definition is reaching or has the potential to reach the data from tenants with no involvement in the matter before the court. This could conceivably rise to a trespass or invasion of privacy action against the party seeking the evidence. Second, it could involve reaching data of the target outside the scope of the warrant or subpoena. Either of these flaws can lead to suppression.

4.3. Service Level Agreements (SLA)

Service Level Agreements (SLAs) govern the relationship between the customer and the cloud service provider. As such, the terms agreed to within the SLA may provide information on how forensic investigations will be handled. A large majority of cloud forensics survey participants noted that tools, techniques and other information for forensics investigations should be included in SLAs (Ruan, Carthy, & Kechadi, 2011a). While a review of current SLAs is outside the scope of this chapter, it is important to provide a brief overview on the legal implications of SLAs and how SLAs effect investigations.

Legally, SLAs are almost always binding fall under U.S. contract law. SLAs can be of importance particularly when setting terms for collection of forensic data. The most common burden SLAs place on the cloud provider are with respect to uptime for the customer, though several have advocated that these agreements include how incidents will be handled (Grobauer & Schreck, 2010), including the processes for conducting investigations that respect the laws of multiple jurisdictions (Ruan, Carthy, Kechadi, & Crosbie, 2011b).

From an investigative standpoint, the SLA dictates the availability of forensic data for the customer that could be collected in the event of an investigation. While much of the focus of this chapter has related to obtaining cloud data in an adverse relationship (i.e., the government seeking the defendant's cloud data), in many instances the cloud data at issue belongs to the victim, and the issue is not how to command such production but rather the rights the user has to her own forensically accurate data. If the SLA does not include notice of what type of process or forensic data will be provided for the customer, then the cloud provider has no contractual duty to provide such information. This does a couple of things legally: 1) it binds access to forensic data that may otherwise be available; 2) lowers quality of best evidence available. The SLA may govern what type of forensic data is collected and the process in which it is stored.

It is important to note that an SLA is only binding between the parties and does not restrict the information that may be sought under a warrant or subpoena. An SLA that denies any provider responsibility to give a user log files is not a shield against a warrant asking for log files. If they exist they must be produced.

4.4. Chain of Custody

A crucial component of admissibility of evidence in court is whether a well-documented and validated chain of custody is maintained for such evidence (Kuntze, et al., 2012). When evidence is "susceptible to alteration by tampering or contamination," then a "substantially more elaborate foundation" may be required (Losavio, 2005). There are many factors that present chain of custody concerns for cloud forensic investigation that would introduce susceptibility, and thus a more rigorous requirement for a proper chain of evidence.

The first potential failure of the chain is with the cloud provider. At this point, as we asserted earlier, forensic evidence will be obtained by the cloud provider and presented to law enforcement as evidence. With this reality, there is no control on the forensic investigation with respect to procedure, process, or person; the collection of evidence is conducted 'behind doors.' While it is allowed under the Fourth Amendment for search and seizure without the presence of law enforcement,[84] diligence must still be conducted for a proper chain of evidence. The burden of documenting the chain of custody rests on the cloud provider, and such documentation is critical to ensuring the chain is maintained. Detailed documentation should include the person conducting the investigation, the steps taken to ensure the evidence has not been modified, and verification through hashes.

With regards to the person—particularly when there are multiple persons—conducting the investigation, a proper chain of evidence must be maintained through logs and comprehensive notes to detail who conducted what elements of the investigation as well as how the evidence was handed off and stored securely. Additionally, establishing the person(s) on the cloud provider side had familiarity with the investigation process used by the company may be a useful step in admissibility for authentication (United States v Cameron, 2011). This would be in line with authentication through expert witness testimony as previously discussed.

Ensuring the evidence has not been modified also must be established. A proper process and inclusion of verification through hashes should be conducted and documented to confirm evidence had not been modified, which will stand as verification in court (Jarrett, Bailie, Hagen, & Judish, 2009). However this may be a technical problem in cloud forensic investigations where cloud images may not be able to be validated using cryptographic hashes (Dykstra & Sherman, 2011).

Another issue with ensuring a proper chain of evidence is that many cloud providers use proprietary file systems for provided services. This introduces questions of validity, and presents a gap in familiar digital forensics practices handling hard drives.

5.0. FUTURE RESEARCH DIRECTIONS

To our knowledge, this is the first comprehensive work on the legal process and requirements for cloud forensics and cloud-based investigations. Our work in this chapter has established a foundation for further research in the legal aspects of cloud forensics. We plan to build on this work through several research directions.

From the legal perspective, there is an alarming gap in the understanding of digital evidence—including emerging areas such as cloud-based evidence. This lack of education for members of the legal community can result in serious miscarriages of justice and disruption of the legal system (Alva & Endicott-Popovsky, 2012). We actively plan to extend this research by identifying necessary elements that must be taught in schools of law, and to current members of the judiciary. This includes the development of curriculum to include interdisciplinary courses that will improve digital evidence literacy among law students and educate on evidentiary rules relevant in cloud forensics cases. As the cloud becomes more prevalent, we will begin to see case law develop around how cloud-based evidence is handled. We will expand our research to include a through analysis of new cases from the courts in this area. Such research would inform the legal and technical communities of potentially new legal requirements set by the courts, and also provide any new guidance for how to approach cloud forensics.

The area of cloud forensics must include collaboration between the technical, organizational, and legal perspectives (Ruan, Carthy, Kechadi, & Crosbie, 2011b). This work sets a firm legal foundation that must be combined with other areas to build multidisciplinary solutions. We plan to conduct research to combine legal requirements with technical solutions to ensure cloud-computing environments are forensically ready. There is a need for best practices and guides for cloud providers, cloud customers, and other stakeholders to understand the process and requirements we detail in this work, which we will seek to provide through collaborations. We also plan to research the legal barriers for eDiscovery of data stored in the cloud, including the economic costs that may be incurred by businesses for cloud forensic investigations.

Additionally, there are areas related to cloud forensics not detailed in this work. Such areas include specifics on how network data is handled in court cases; the differences between the acquisitions of physical disks and cloud data; and the legal considerations on the storage of forensic data in the cloud with regard to providence and a valid chain of custody. These are all potential avenues for further research that should be sought to extend the field.

And of course, there is the expansion of the analysis contained in this chapter to the civil arena, particularly in regard to the processes of obtaining cloud data.

Overall, there are many avenues for research that must be explored in order for the emerging field to develop reputable findings generally accepted by the field, in turn, be used to aid in the admissibility of cloud-based evidence in courts of law.

6.0. CONCLUSION

This work has provided insight on the legal process for cloud forensic investigations. This process includes the constitutional and statutory limitations determine level of protection provided, and the level of warrant or subpoena that may be necessary to conduct an investigation. A key focus was on the terms of SLAs regarding access to data granted by the user to the provider. The admissibility process, following actual production, includes the legal requirements necessary to ensure evidence obtained from the cloud passes admissibility, particularly authenticity. From the proceeding summary of insights, it is possible to develop a set of requirements that can be incorporated into system design that will render cloud-computing environments forensically ready—prepared to collect admissible evidence that will survive technical challenges. In the cloud environment, with little ability of the user to control forensic readiness, aside from contractually, this takes the form of contractual obligations demanded by users of their cloud provider, audit certifications from cloud providers documenting the validity of their forensic readiness program and procedures and storage on the part of users who will need to retrieve this evidence on demand. The authors expect that this set of processes and requirements can be reduced to a series of technical requirements that will "bake-in" the qualities of forensic readiness and render more likely the ability of users to rely on cloud providers to collect and store valid and admissible evidence.

REFERENCES

18U.S.C. §§ 2510-22 (2000).

18U.S.C. §§ 2510(15) (2000).

18U.S.C. § 2511(1) (2000).

18U.S.C. § 2701-09 (2000).

18U.S.C.A. § 2510 (West) (2000).

18U.S.C.A. § 2511(c) (2004).

18U.S.C.A. §§ 2701-12 (2004).

18U.S.C.A. §§ 2701(a)(1) & (2) (2004).

18U.S.C.A. § 2702 (West) (2004).

18U.S.C.A. § 2703(b) (2004).

18U.S.C.A. § 2707(e) (2004)

18U.S.C.A. § 2708 (2004).

18U.S.C.A. § 2711 (West) (2004).

18U.S.C.A. § 2711(2) (2004).

42U.S.C. § 13032(b)(1), since recodified in 18 U.S.C. § 2258A (2010).

Alva, A., & Endicott-Popovsky, B. (2012). *Digital evidence education in schools of law*. Paper presented at the ADFSL Conference on Digital Forensics, Security and Law. Richmond, VA.

Biggs, S., & Vidalis, S. (2009). Cloud computing: The impact on digital forensic investigations. In *Proceedings of the International Conference for Internet Technology and Secured Transactions, 2009, ICITST 2009*, (pp. 1–6). ICITST.

Birk, D., & Wegener, C. (2011). Technical issues of forensic investigations in cloud computing environments. In *Proceedings of the 2011 IEEE Sixth International Workshop on Systematic Approaches to Digital Forensic Engineering (SADFE)*, (pp. 1–10). IEEE Press.

Bond v. United States, 529 U.S. 334, 120 S.Ct. 1462, 146 L.Ed.2d 365 (2000).

Broadhurst, R. (2006). Developments in the global law enforcement of cyber-crime. *Policing: An International Journal of Police Strategies & Management*, *29*(3), 408–433. doi:10.1108/13639510610684674

Cable Privacy Act, 47 U.S.C. § 551 (2000).

CAL. PENAL CODE § 1524.2 (West) (2000).

California v. Greenwood, 486 U.S. 35, 39, 108 S.Ct. 1625, 100 L.Ed.2d 30 (1988).

Christiansen, J. (2010). Discovery and admission of electronic information as evidence. In Sullivan, J. (Ed.), *E-Health Business and Transactional Law* (pp. 427–452). Arlington, VA: BNA Books.

City of Ontario, Cal. v. Quon, 130 S. Ct. 2619, 177 L. Ed. 2d 216 (U.S. 2010) (2010).

Commonwealth v. Sbordone, 424 Mass. 802, 678 N.E.2d 1184, 1190, n. 11 (1997).

U.S. Const. amend. IV. (1791).

Convery, N. (2010). Cloud computing toolkit: Guidance for outsourcing information storage to the cloud. *Aberystwyth University*. Retrieved July 22, 2012, from http://www.archives.org.uk/images/documents/Cloud_Computing_Toolkit-2.pdf

Couch v. U.S., 409 U.S. 322, 335-36, 93 S.Ct.611, 34 L.Ed.2d 548 (1973).

Couillard, D. A. (2009). Defogging the cloud: Applying fourth amendment principles to evolving privacy expectations in cloud computing. *Minnesota Law Review*, *93*, 2205–2216.

Daubert v. Merrell Dow Pharmaceuticals, 509 U.S. 579, 113 S. Ct. 2786, 125 L. Ed. 2d 469 (1993).

Davis v. Gracey 111 F.3d 1472, 1484 (10th Cir. 1997) (1997).

Department of Justice. (2012). *Treaty requests*. Retrieved frm http://www.justice.gov/usao/eousa/foia_reading_room/usam/title9/crm00276.htm

Dykstra, J., & Sherman, A. T. (2011). *Acquiring forensic evidence from infrastructure as a service cloud computing: Exploring and evaluating tools, trust, and techniques*. Paper presented at the DFRWS Conference. New Orleans, LA.

Endicott-Popovsky, B., & Horowitz, D. (2012). Unintended consequences: Digital evidence in our legal system. *IEEE Security & Privacy Magazine*, *10*(2), 80–83. doi:10.1109/MSP.2012.54

Fed. R. Evid 104(a) and (b) (1997).

Fed. R. Evid. 401 (1997).

Fed. R. Evid. 801(a) (1997).

Fed. R. Evid 803(6)(E) (1997).

Fed. R. Evid. 901. (1997).

Florida v. Wells, 539 So.2d 464 (Fla. 1989), aff'd, 495 U.S. 1 (1990).

Freedman v. America Online, Inc., 303 F.Supp.2d 121 (D.Conn., 2004) (2004).

Grobauer, B., & Schreck, T. (2010). Towards incident handling in the cloud: Challenges and approaches. In *Proceedings of the 2010 ACM Workshop on Cloud Computing Security Workshop*, (pp. 77–86). ACM Press.

Hale v. Henkel, 201 U.S. 43, 76, 26 S.Ct. 370, 50 L.Ed. 652 (1906).

Harris v. State, 260 Ga. 860, 401 S.E.2d 263, 266 (1991).

Hester v. United States, 265 U.S. 57, 58, 44 S.Ct. 445, 68 L.Ed 898 (1924).

Illinois v. Krull, 480 U.S. 340, 348, 107 S.Ct. 1160, 94 L.Ed.2d 364 (1987).

In re Grand Jury Proceedings Involving Vickers, 38 F. Supp. 2d 159, 162 (D.N.H. 1998) (1998).

In re U.S. for an Order Authorizing the Release of Historical Cell-Site Info., 809 F. Supp. 2d 113, 125 (E.D.N.Y. 2011) (2011).

Jarrett, H. M., Bailie, M. W., Hagen, E., & Judish, N. (2009). *Searching and seizing computers and obtaining electronic evidence in criminal investigations*. Retrieved from http://www.justice.gov/criminal/cybercrime/docs/ssmanual2009.pdf

K&L Gates. (2006). E-discovery amendments to the federal rules of civil procedure go into effect today. *K&L Gates*. Retrieved from http://www.ediscoverylaw.com/2006/12/articles/news-updates/ediscovery-amendments-to-the-federal-rules-of-civil-procedure-go-into-effect-today/

Katz v. United States 389 U.S. 347, 357, 104 S.Ct. 2091, 80 L.Ed.2d 732 (1984).

Kerr, O. (2012). *Does the fourth amendment allow extraterritorial state search warrants*. Retrieved from http://www.volokh.com/2010/01/08/does-the-fourth-amendment-allow-extraterritorial-state-search-warrants/

Kerr, O. S. (2009). The case for the third-party doctrine. *Michigan Law Review*, *107*, 561–590.

Kerr, O. S. (2010). Applying the fourth amendment to the internet: A general approach. *Stanford Law Review*, *62*, 1005–1038.

Kumho Tire Co., Ltd. v. Carmichael, 526 U.S. 137, 119 S.Ct. 1167, 143, 150 L.Ed. 2d 238 (1999).

Kuntze, N., Rudolph, C., Alva, A., Endicott-Popovsky, B., Christiansen, J. R., & Kemmerich, T. (2012). On the creation of reliable digital evidence. In Shenoi, S. (Ed.), *Advances in Digital Forensics VIII*. Heidelberg, Germany: Springer.

LaFave, W. R. (2009). *Search and seizure: A treatise on the fourth amendment § 2.1(b), at n. 82.1* (2004th ed., pp. 2008–2009). Supp.

Liles, S., Rogers, M., & Hoebich, M. (2009). A survey of the legal issues facing digital forensic experts. In *Advances in Digital Forensics V* (pp. 267–276). Berlin, Germany: Springer. doi:10.1007/978-3-642-04155-6_20

Lorraine v. Markel American Insurance Company, 241 F.R.D. 534, 538, 539, 541-542, 545-546, 553, 562-565, 584 (D.Md. 2007) (2007).

Losavio, M. (2005). The law of possession of digital objects: Dominion and control issues for digital forensics investigations and prosecutions. In *Proceedings of the First International Workshop on Systematic Approaches to Digital Forensic Engineering, 2005,* (pp. 177–183). IEEE.

Maryland v. Garrison, 480 U.S. 79, 84, 107 S.Ct. 1013, 94 L.Ed.2d 72 (1987).

Mason v. Pulliam, 557 F.2d 426 (5th Cir. 1977) (1977).

McVeigh v. Cohen, 983 F. Supp. 215 (D.D.C. 1998) (1998).

Mell, P., & Grance, T. (2011). *Definition of cloud computing: NIST special publication 800-145*. Gaithersburg, MD: National Institute of Standards and Technology. Retrieved from http://csrc.nist.gov/publications/nistpubs/800-145/SP800-145.pdf

Model Code of Pre-Arraignment Procedure § SS 240.3 (1975).

New York v O'Neill, 359 US 1, 79 S.Ct. 564, 3 L.Ed.2d 585 (1959).

N.J. v. Mollica, 554 A.2d 1315, 1324 (N.J. 1989) (1989).

O'Connor v. Ortega, 480 U.S. 709, 715, 107 S.Ct. 1492, 94 L.Ed.2d 714 (1987).

Penn. (1936). *Uniform act to secure the attendance of witnesses from without a state in criminal proceedings*. Paper presented at the 41st Annual Conference of the National Conference of Commissioners on Uniform State Laws. Atlantic City, NJ. Retrieved from https://www.law.upenn.edu/library/archives/ulc/fnact99/1920_69/uasaw36.pdf

People v. Mason, 989 P.2d 757, 761 (Colo. 1999) (1999).

People v. Watson, 214 Ill. 2d 271, 825 N.E.2d 257 (2005).

Pollitt, M., Caloyannides, M., Novotny, J., & Shenoi, S. (2004). Digital forensics: Operational, legal and research issues. *Data and Applications Security*, *17*, 393–403.

Quon v. Arch Wireless Operating Co., Inc., 529 F.3d 892 (9th Cir. 2008) (2008).

Re, E. D. (1975). Stare decisis. In *Proceedings of the Seminar for Federal Appellate Judges sponsored by the Federal Judicial Center*, (pp. 1-21). Retrieved from http://www.fjc.gov/public/pdf.nsf/lookup/staredec.pdf/$file/staredec.pdf

Rice, P. (2005). *Electronic evidence: Law and practice*. New York, NY: ABA Publishing.

Richman, W. M., & Reynolds, W. L. (2002). *Understanding conflict of laws*. New York, NY: Matthew Bender.

Right to Financial Privacy Act, 12 U.S.C. §§ 3401-22 (2000).

Robison, W. J. (2010). Free at what cost? Cloud computing privacy under the stored communications act. *The Georgetown Law Journal*, *98*, 1195–1213.

Rodriques v. Furtado, 410 Mass. 878, 575 N.E.2d 1124 (1991).

Ruan, K., Carthy, J., Kechadi, M. T., & Crosbie, M. (2011b). Cloud forensics. In *Proceedings of the IFIP International Conference on Digital Forensics, IFIP Advances in Information and Communication Technology*, (pp. 35–46). IFIP.

Ruan, K., Carthy, J., & Kechadi, T. (2011a). *Survey on cloud forensics and critical criteria for cloud forensic capability: A preliminary analysis*. Paper presented at the 6th Annual Conference of the ADFSL Conference on Digital Forensics, Security and Law. Richmond, VA.

Schalk v. State, 767 S.W.2d 441, 454 (Tex.App. 1988), cert. denied, 503 U.S. 1006, 112 S.Ct. 1763, 118 L.Ed.2d 425 (1992).

Schneckloth v. Bustamonte, 412 U.S. 218, 219, 93 S.Ct. 2041, 36 L.Ed.2d 854 (1973).

Schroeder, S. (2011). *The lure*. New York, NY: Cengage Learning.

Smith v. Maryland, 442 U.S. 735, 743-44, 99 S.Ct. 2577, 61 L.Ed.2d 220 (1979).

Spyridopoulos, T., & Katos, V. (2011). Requirements for a forensically ready cloud storage service. *International Journal of Digital Crime and Forensics*, *3*(3), 19–36. doi:10.4018/jdcf.2011070102

St. Clair v. Johnny's Oyster & Shrimp, Inc., 76 F. Supp. 2d 773, 774 (S.D. Tex. 1999) (1999).

State v. Afana, 233 P.3d 879 (Wash., 2010) (2010).

State v. Bellar, 231 Or. App. 80, 217 P.3d 1094 (2009).

State v. Kern, 81 Wash.App. 308, 914 P.2d 114, 117–18 (1996).

State v. Mathe, 688 P.2d 859 (Wash. 1984) (1984).

State v. Miles, 160 Wash. 2d 236, 156 P.3d 864 (2007).

State v. Moore, 871 P.2d 1086 (Wash. App. 1994) (1994).

State v. Morse, 123 P.3d 832 (Wash. 2005) (2005).

State v. Nordlund, 53 P.3d 520, 525 (Wash. App. 2002), *petition for review denied,* 70 P.3d 964 (Wash. 2003) (2003).

States v. Kassimu, 188 Fed. Appx. 264, 2006 WL 1880335 (5th Cir. 2006) (2006).

Taylor, M., Haggerty, J., Gresty, D., & Hegarty, R. (2010). Digital evidence in cloud computing systems. *Computer Law & Security Report*, *26*(3), 304–308. doi:10.1016/j.clsr.2010.03.002

Taylor, M., Haggerty, J., Gresty, D., & Lamb, D. (2011). Forensic investigation of cloud computing systems. *Network Security*, *3*, 4–10. doi:10.1016/S1353-4858(11)70024-1

Truloch v. Freeh, 275 F.3d 391, 403 (4th Cir. 2001) (2001).

Tucker v. Waddell, 83 F.3d 688 (4th Cir. 1996) (1996).

United States v. Andrus, 483 F.3d 711, 718 (10th Cir.2007), cert. denied, 522 U.S. 12997, 128 S.Ct 1738. 170 L.Ed.2d 542 (2008).

United States v. Bach, 310 F.3d 1063, 1067 (8th Cir. 2002) (2002).

United States v. Calandra, 414 U.S. 338, 346, 94 S.Ct. 613, 38 L.Ed.2d 561 (1974).

United States v. Cameron 762 F.Supp.2d 152, 158-159 (D. Maine 2011) (2011).

United States v. Falcon 766 F.2d 1469, 1476 (10th Cir. 1985) (1985).

United States v. Gorshkov, CR00-550C, 2001 WL 1024026, 3-4 (W.D. Wash. May 23, 2001) (2001).

United States v. Graham CRIM. RDB-11-0094, 2012 WL 691531 (D. Md. Mar. 1, 2012) (2012).

United States v. James 353 F.3d 606 (8th Cir. 2003) (2003).

United States v. Leon, 468 U.S. 897, 916, 104 S.Ct. 3405, 82 L.Ed.2d. 677 (1984).

United States v. Miller, 994 F.2d 441 (8th Cir. 1993) (1993).

United States v. Nafzger, 965 F.2d 213 (7th Cir.1992) (1992).

United States v. Presler, 610 F.2d 1206, 1213-14 (4th Cir. 1979) (1979).

United States v. Richardson, 607 F.3d 357, 363 (4th Cir. 2010) cert. denied, 131 S. Ct. 427, 178 L. Ed. 2d 324 (U.S. 2010) (2010).

United States v. Stephens, 206 F.3rd 914, 917 (9th Cir. 2000) (2000).

United States v. Turner, 770 F.2d 1508 (9th Cir.1985) (1985).

United States v. Ward, 576 F.2d 243, 244-45 (9th Cir.1978) (1978).

United States v. Ziegler, 474 F.3d 1184, 1189 (9th Cir. 2007) (2007).

U.S. v. Brown, 52 F.3d 415, 421 (2d Cir. 1995), *cert. denied*, 516 U.S. 1068 (1996).

U.S. v. Buckner, 473 F.3d 551, 555 (4th Cir. 2007) (2007).

U.S. v. Dawkins, 17 F.3d 399, 405 (D.C. Cir. 1994) (1994).

U.S. v. Friere, 710 F.2d 1515, 1519 (11th Cir. 1983) (1983).

U.S. v. Khorozian 333 F.3d 498, 61 Fed. R. Evid. Serv. 980, (2003).

U.S. v. Ladell, 127 F.3d 622, 624 (7th Cir. 1997) (1997).

U.S. v. Matlock, 415 U.S. 164, 171 (1974).

U.S. v. Miller, U. S. 425 U.S. 435, 442-43, 96 S.Ct.1619, 48 L.Ed.2d 71 (1976).

U.S. v. Morning, 64 F.3d 531, 536 (9th Cir. 1995), cert. denied, 516 U.S. 1152 (1996).

U.S. v. Rico, 51 F.3d 495, 501 (5th Cir.), cert. denied, 516 U.S. 883 (1995).

U.S. v. Rith, 164 F.3d 1323 (10th Cir.), cert. denied, 528 U.S. 827 (1999).

U.S. v. Smith, 27 F. Supp. 2d 1111 (C.D. Ill. 1998) (1998).

USA PATRIOT Act Pub. L. No. 107-56, 115 Stat. 272 (2001).

Video Privacy Protection Act, 18 U.S.C. §§ 2710-12 (2000).

Warshak v. United States, 490 F.3d 455, 470 (6th Cir. 2007), vacated 532 F.3d 521 (6th Cir. 2008) (2008).

Warshak v. United States, 631 F.3d 266, 286 (6th Cir. 2010) (2010).

Weinstein, J. B., & Berger, M. A. (1995). *Weinstein's evidence: Commentary on rules of evidence for the United States courts and magistrates*. New York, NY: M. Bender.

Welsh v. Wisconsin, 466 U.S. 740, 748, 104 S.Ct. 2091, 80 L.Ed.2d 732 (1984).

Wolf v. Colorado 338 U.S. 25, 69 S.Ct. 1359, 93 L.Ed. 1782 (1949).

Wolthusen, S. D. (2009). Overcast: Forensic discovery in cloud environments. In *Proceedings of the Fifth International Conference on IT Security Incident Management and IT Forensics, 2009, IMF 2009*, (pp. 3-9). IMF.

Yan, C. (2011). Cybercrime forensic system in cloud computing. In *Proceedings of the 2011 International Conference on Image Analysis and Signal Processing (IASP)*, (pp. 612-615). IASP.

ENDNOTES

1 The decision to limit the discussion regarding methods of commanding production to criminal investigations flows primarily from two differences between criminal and civil practice: First, there are constitutional limits on the acquisition of evidence in criminal investigations that are not applicable to civil investigations.
Second, in general, the investigative stage of a criminal case is largely complete by the time the case is filed. "Discovery" obligations in criminal cases largely refer to the constitutional and statute/rule based obligations of the parties to disclose their evidence to the other side.
In contrast, the investigative stage frequently only starts when a civil case has been filed. Discovery is an affirmative and aggressive process, continuing from when a case is filed to trial or any earlier discovery cutoff date. We felt that covering the acquisition of cloud data in the civil context would expand the discussion so as to make it unmanageable as a chapter in book.

2 Limits can also be imposed by court rule or the magistrate issuing a warrant. These are not discussed as they have only limited unique applicability to cloud stored data.

3 .*Id.* at 351.

4 If the answer is that the very act of storing ones data on the hard drive of another party vitiates any reasonable expectation of privacy, then no further discussion is needed because such storage-with-third-parties is at the core of cloud storage. It is likely, however, as with many things legal, that the answer will not be so absolute, and a more refined analysis is needed.

5 *Id.*

6 However, even a prolonged period of inactivity might not be indicative of abandonment where the cloud is being used solely as a static backup of fixed data like heirloom photographs or video.

7 *In re U.S. for an Order Authorizing the Release of Historical Cell-Site Info.,* 809 F. Supp. 2d 113, 125 (E.D.N.Y. 2011) ("(T)he 'without needing to access or analyze those communications' caveat appears too narrow to accommodate current case law and the realities of current technology. For example, would the third-party doctrine remove the reasonable expectation of privacy over the contents of emails sent on Gmail, or similar email providers, that use computers to access and analyze the contents of email communications in order to display advertisements? While the court need not answer the question here, it appears that such a technology-specific definition of third-party disclosure would fail to take into account the importance of the information disclosed or the intrusive nature of disclosing such information.")

8 *Warshak,* 631 F.3d at 286

9 See *Warshak v. United States,* 490 F.3d 455, 470 (6th Cir. 2007), *vacated* 532 F.3d 521 (6th Cir. 2008) (the provisions of the decision relevant to the text were reinstated in 631 F.3d 266 (6th Cir. 2010)), *Quon v. Arch Wireless Operating Co., Inc.*, 529 F.3d 892 (9th Cir. 2008) *rev'd and remanded sub nom. City of Ontario, Cal. v. Quon*, 130 S. Ct. 2619, 177 L. Ed. 2d 216 (U.S. 2010), and *State v. Bellar*, 231 Or. App. 80, 217 P.3d 1094 (2009). Although the privacy issue was not reached by the Supreme Court in *Quon,* and the relevant discussion in *Bellar* was in a dissent), the logic of the decisions remain.

10 Kerr at footnote 45, *supra*, and David A. Couillard, *Defogging the Cloud: Applying Fourth Amendment Principles to Evolving Privacy Expectations in Cloud Computing, 93 MINN. L. REV. 2205, 2216 (2009).*

11 42 U.S.C. § 13032(b)(1), since recodified in 18 U.S.C. § 2258A.

12 As noted earlier, the absence of constitutional or statutory protections does not mean the cloud provider *must* provide any requested data. Absent voluntary compliance, enforceable directives would still be needed to compel production.

13 *U.S. v. Miller*, 425 U.S. 435.

14 18 U.S.C. § 2701-09 (2000).

15 18 U.S.C. §§ 2510-22 (2000).

16 18 U.S.C.A. §§ 2701-12 (2004).

17 Keystroke monitoring and other real-time monitoring of electronic communications is covered by the wiretap statute, 18 U.S.C. § 2511(1) (2000).

18 Id. § 2510(15).

19 *Id.*

20 18 U.S.C.A. § 2703(b) (2004).

21 *Id.* § 2711(2).

22 .18 U.S.C.A. § 2703(b) (2004).

23 .Id. § 2703(b).

24 The initial Warshak Circuit opinion held that all unopened email, regardless of the length of time it had been held by the cloud provider, requires a warrant. That opinion was later vacated because the issue was not ripe for consideration. The portions of the decision relating to the necessity for a warrant was reinstated in the substantive appeal of the case. See footnote 50 *supra* for citations.

25 .*See Id.* § 2703(b).

26 .See 18 U.S.C.A. § 2511(c) (2004).

27 18 U.S.C.A. §§ 2701(a)(1) & (2) (2004).

28 18 U.S.C.A. § 2708 (2004).

29 425 U.S. 435.

30 .Id. § 2707(e).

31 111 F.3d 1472 (10th Cir. 1997).

32 *Id.* at 1484.

33 18 U.S.C.A. § 2510 (West)

34 *Id.*

35 18 U.S.C.A. § 2711 (West)

36 18 U.S.C.A. § 2702 (West)

37 "(R)ecognizing the historical function of the grand jury as an independent investigatory body which acts as a buffer between the citizenry and government, the Court has been reluctant to measure the enforceability of grand jury subpoenas against the same standards applicable to search warrants. *See*, e.g., *Hale v. Henkel,* 201 U.S. 43, 76, 26 S.Ct. 370, 50 L.Ed. 652 (1906) (holding that while a grand jury subpoena for the production of books and papers may implicate the Fourth Amendment, when presented with a challenge to such a subpoena a court need only determine whether the request is "far too sweeping in its terms to be regarded as reasonable."); *United States v. Calandra,* 414 U.S. 338, 346, 94 S.Ct. 613, 38 L.Ed.2d 561 (1974) (quoting *Henkel* and again suggesting that Fourth Amendment rights are adequately protected when grand jury subpoenas are subjected to court review for reasonableness, but not for "probable cause"). *In re Grand Jury Proceedings Involving Vickers,* 38 F. Supp. 2d 159, 162 (D.N.H. 1998)

38 *Id.*

39 In State *v. Nordlund,* 53 P.3d 520 (Wash. App. 2002), *petition for review denied,* 70 P.3d 964 (Wash. 2003), the police were investigating several instances of attacks against young girls and sought to search the suspect's computer. The pertinent part of the affidavit said: "(Nordlund) used a computer at this residence to access pornography and to communicate with others via E-mail. Therefore, the computer and any electronic storage media could likely be important evidence in this case regarding intent, dates and locations." Id at 525. The court noted there was no nexus between the alleged crimes and Nordlund's use of the computer to access pornography and send e-mails. "Rather, it appears that the State was fishing for some incriminating document which is precisely what the first and fourth amendment prohibit." *Id.*

40 In Washington State, a district court commissioner was found to lack the authority to issue search warrants when the office of district court commissioner was not properly created. *State v. Moore,* 871 P.2d 1086 (Wash. App. 1994).

41 The Eighth Circuit addressed this issue in a circuitous way in the *Bach* case discussed in footnote 96, *supra.* The Court reversed a decision of the trial court suppressing evidence obtained from Yahoo by a search warrant issued by a state court in Minnesota. The warrant was faxed to Yahoo who complied by sending the requested information to the Minnesota authorities.

42 See, e.g., CAL. PENAL CODE § 1524.2 (West 2000) (requiring out-of-state corporations qualified to do business in California to accept service of, and comply with, California search warrants). Washington, Minnesota, and Florida have similar provisions.

43 "Uniform Act to Secure the Attendance of Witnesses from without a State in Criminal Proceedings." Paper drafted at the 41st Annual Conference of the National Conference of Commissioners on Uniform State Laws. Atlantic City, NJ. (1936) https://www.law.upenn.edu/library/archives/ulc/fnact99/1920_69/uasaw36.pdf

44 See generally "Treaty Requests" in *United States Attorneys' Manual*, last viewed August 12, 2012, http://www.justice.gov/

usao/eousa/foia_reading_room/usam/title9/crm00276.htm.

45 See *Searching and Seizing Computers and Obtaining Electronic Evidence in Criminal Investigations,* Office of Legal Education Executive Office for United States Attorneys (2009) at pp. 84-86 for examples of advice given for searches of computers located in multiple jurisdictions, including out-of-country locations.

46 *Searching and Seizing Computers, supra.*

47 The Manual does, at pp. 84-86, discuss the jurisdictional issue (discussed above in this paper) but only in the context of determining in which judicial district a warrant should be sought.

48 U.S. Const. amend. IV.

49 One of the authors, a former prosecutor, had an experience where a Washington warrant was served on a California Internet Service Provider. The California ISP insisted upon notifying the person whose records were being sought, to give them an opportunity to object, citing California law. The issue was ultimately resolved by obtaining a California warrant under the process referred to earlier as "domesticating the warrant," but the process took several months.

50 As noted earlier, the determination of whether there is a reasonable expectation of privacy in documents shared with third parties involves many of the same issues involved in a consent exception discussion.

51 In a very fact specific ruling the court in *U.S. v. Smith,* 27 F. Supp. 2d 1111 (C.D. Ill. 1998) allowed evidence obtained from a computer under a third party consent, noting that there was no evidence the defendant had password-protected the material seized.
The Fourth Circuit held that a search of an individual's password-protected computer files is an illegal search in violation of the Fourth Amendment when consent to the search was given by another individual who had joint access to the computer but did not know the passwords and therefore did not have authority to grant access to the files. *Truloch v. Freeh,* 275 F.3d 391, 403 (4th Cir. 2001).

52 353 F.3d 606 (8th Cir. 2003).

53 766 F.2d 1469 (10th Cir. 1985).

54 *Id.* at 1476.

55 *See* Model Code of Pre-Arraignment Procedure § SS 240.3 (1975) (a consent search "shall not exceed, in duration or physical scope, the limits of the consent given"); *Mason v. Pulliam,* 557 F.2d 426 (5th Cir. 1977).

56 *See U.S. v. Brown,* 52 F.3d 415, 421 (2d Cir. 1995), *cert. denied,* 516 U.S. 1068 (1996) ("Our court has looked to six touchstones for determining the existence of exigent circumstances. Those are: '(1) the gravity or violent nature of the offense with which the suspect is to be charged; (2) whether the suspect is reasonably believed to be armed; (3) a clear showing of probable cause ... to believe that the suspect committed the crime; (4) strong reason to believe that the suspect is in the premises being entered; (5) a likelihood that the suspect will escape if not swiftly apprehended; and (6) the peaceful circumstances of the entry.' Those factors are 'merely illustrative, not exhaustive, and the presence or absence of any one factor is not conclusive.'" (citations omitted)).
U.S. v. Rico, 51 F.3d 495, 501 (5th Cir.), *cert. denied,* 516 U.S. 883 (1995) ("In evaluating whether exigent circumstances existed, we have found relevant the following factors: (1) the degree of urgency involved and amount of time necessary to obtain a warrant; (2) (the) reasonable belief that contraband is about to be removed; (3) the possibility of danger to the police officers guarding the site of contraband while a search warrant is sought; (4) information indicating the possessors of the contraband are aware

that the police are on their trail; and (5) the ready destructibility of the contraband and the knowledge 'that efforts to dispose of narcotics and to escape are characteristic behavior of persons engaged in the narcotics traffic.'" (citations omitted)).

57 *Id.* at 3-4.

58 *Lorraine,* 241 F.R.D. 534.

59 Two major differences between civil admissibility and criminal admissibility relate to the constitutional privilege against self incrimination and the constitutional right by the accused to confront accusatory witnesses. U.S. CONST. amends. V and VI. While these differences can be significant, the differences are generally not unique to cloud computing and are not discussed further other than noting their existence.

60 *Lorraine,* 241 F.R.D. at 553

61 Alas, there is a further complexity. This is explained in more detail by Judge Grimm in *Lorraine,* 241. F.R.D. at 539., The simplest explanation is that because of the interplay between Fed. R. Evid 104(a) and (b), in addition to the judge, the jury must be persuaded as to the authenticity of an exhibit.

62 *Lorraine,* 241. F.R.D. at 538.

63 Fed. R. Evid. 401

64 *Id.*

65 *Lorraine,* 241. F.R.D. at 541, citing Fed. R. Evid. 401

66 Relevance can be an issue in resolving a hearsay objection. For example in a personal injury traffic accident case offer the issue of whether the defendant ran a red light might be relevant. If the plaintiff's attorney seeks to admit a letter from a third party containing that party's statement that the defendant ran a red light, the proper objection is "hearsay" because the third party is not present to be cross examined. If the proponent's response is that the letter is not being offered for the truth of its contents (and thus is not hearsay), the proper objection is not hearsay, but relevance. The letter itself, without regard to the truth of its contents is simply not relevant and thus inadmissible.

67 *Lorraine,* 241. F.R.D. at 541-42.

68 *Fed. R. Evid. 901.*

69 WEINSTEIN at § 901.03(2)

70 *Lorraine,* 241 F.R.D. *at 545-46.*

71 *Daubert v. Merrell Dow Pharmaceuticals,* 509 U.S. 579, 113 S. Ct. 2786, 125 L. Ed. 2d 469 (1993). *Daubert* applied to scientific evidence. A subsequent case, *Kumho Tire Co., Ltd. v. Carmichael,* 526 U.S. 137, 119 S.Ct. 1167, 143 L.Ed. 2d 238 (1999), expanded this to include to areas of technical or specialized knowledge, and made it clear the test was flexible.

72 *Kumho Tire,*526 U.S. at 150, n. 25.

73 Lorraine, 241 F.R.D. at 562, *et. seq.*

74 *Id* at 562-63.

75 *Lorraine,* 241 F.R.D. at 564*; U.S. v. Khorozian* 333 F.3d 498, 61 Fed. R. Evid. Serv. 980, 2003.

76 Fed. R. Evid. 801(a)

77 *Lorraine,* 241 F.R.D. at 564-65.

78 Fed. R. Evid 803(6)(E)

79 *Lorraine,* 241 F.R.D. at 584.

80 *Lorraine, 241 F.R.D* at 542.

81 *Bach,* 310 F.2d 1063,

82 Fed. R. Evid. 901

83 *Daubert, 509 U.S. 579.*

84 *Bach,* 310 F.2d 1063, for example.

Chapter 9
Compliance in the Cloud and the Implications on Electronic Discovery

Dean Gonsowski
Symantec Corporation, USA

ABSTRACT

Cloud Computing will be a disruptive technology that will ultimately change the face of computing with a market approaching $300 billion over the next five years, according to recent study from the Market Intel Group (Mathews, 2010). The unstoppable migration of data to the Cloud is undoubtedly due to numerous financial benefits, particularly for small and medium-sized companies, which historically do not have the same capital budgets as larger enterprises. However, this boundless upside is not without risks from a legal and compliance perspective, making it all that more important for entities to look before they leap. Today, nearly every corporation is required to preserve and produce Electronically Stored Information (ESI), such as emails and other electronic documents, as part of their response to litigation, regulatory inquiries, and subpoenas. When the subject ESI happens to be stored in the Cloud, there are a handful of potential obstacles that serve to complicate the eDiscovery process. For some, this leads to sanctions and increased compliance risks. In order to navigate these potentially treacherous waters, organizations need to be proactive and follow a "measure twice, cut once" approach. This chapter will discuss the basics of eDiscovery and explore ways to minimize potential compliance hurdles when migrating significant data stores to/from the Cloud.

BACKGROUND

Navigating the complex issues surrounding eDiscovery in a cloud environment requires, at a minimum, incorporating both legal and technical viewpoints, while also considering related corporate functions such as information security, records management, risk, and compliance. Once these constituents are brought into the fold the groups must inherently consult applicable regulations, emerging case law and industry best practices. To this end, standards bodies like the EDRM and Sedona Conference Working Group on Electronic Document Retention and Production

DOI: 10.4018/978-1-4666-2662-1.ch009

Copyright © 2013, IGI Global. Copying or distributing in print or electronic forms without written permission of IGI Global is prohibited.

will be referenced to augment relevant case law and statutes such as the Federal Rules of Civil Procedure (FRCP).

The goal of this chapter is not to delve into basic cloud characteristics (e.g., on-demand, self-service, broad network access, resource pooling, or rapid elasticity) or delivery models (e.g., Software-as-a-Service, Platform-as-a-Service, or Infrastructure-as-a-Service). The various deployment models (private, public, hybrid, etc.) will be discussed with a particular focus on public clouds since private cloud environments tend to look very similar to on-premise IT environments. Finally, specific tools, techniques, and methodologies will not be discussed in this chapter since most applicable case law and regulations do not articulate set standards or deployment methods. Instead, the focus will be on the strategic considerations, as well as any risks attendant with conducting alternative approaches.1

EDISCOVERY IN THE CLOUD

It's All the Same, Just Different

Computer forensic experts, judges, lawyers, and eDiscovery practitioners alike are all facing the next big challenge when dealing with ESI. On one level, the new cloud infrastructure seems to hold a dizzying array of both promise and risks. On the other hand, some will argue that the cloud paradigm really does not change anything at all. In the end, both opinions are somewhat correct: eDiscovery and regulatory compliance issues are all fundamentally the same, but the cloud medium does threaten to pose a range of tactical and strategic challenges.

There is an issue that's looming that hasn't really been discussed or addressed yet. That is the role of governance for companies that are consuming the services versus the role of governance for companies that are providing the services. —Joe McKendrick, Independent Analyst and ZDNet Blogger (Gardner, 2009)

Before diving right into the details surrounding cloud computing and the associated electronic challenges, it is worthwhile to examine where this relatively new discipline fits into the larger information governance infrastructure, as a discipline. While many of these definitions are still evolving, Gartner proffers the following definition regarding information governance:

Information governance is the specification of decision rights and an accountability framework to encourage desirable behavior in the valuation, creation, storage, use, archival and deletion of information. It includes the processes, roles, standards and metrics that ensure the effective and efficient use of information in enabling an organization to achieve its goals (Gartner, 2009).

Similarly, the EDRM organization has attempted to abstract upwards to include notions of governance into their newly promulgated Information Governance Reference Model (IGRM) as shown in Figure 1, which purports to tie various legal duties to the underlying data assets (EDRM, 2011). The purpose is not to conduct a deep dive surrounding the IGRM but to show electronic discovery's place in the larger landscape.

Regardless of which larger information governance umbrella is selected, there are a wide range of applicable Records and Information Management (RIM) regimes that may apply to a given organization, depending on size, location, vertical orientation, and regulatory posture. These RIM imperatives include SEC Rule 17a-4, FINRA, Sarbanes-Oxley, HIPAA/HITECH, EU Data Protection Act, Stored Communications Act, State Privacy Protection Laws, Gramm-Leach-Bliley Act, Safe Harbor Rules, Dodd-Frank, etc. Beyond the above list there may ultimately be thousands of discrete mandates (at the local, state, and federal level) that govern how ESI must be retained

Figure 1. Information governance reference model (IGRM)[2]

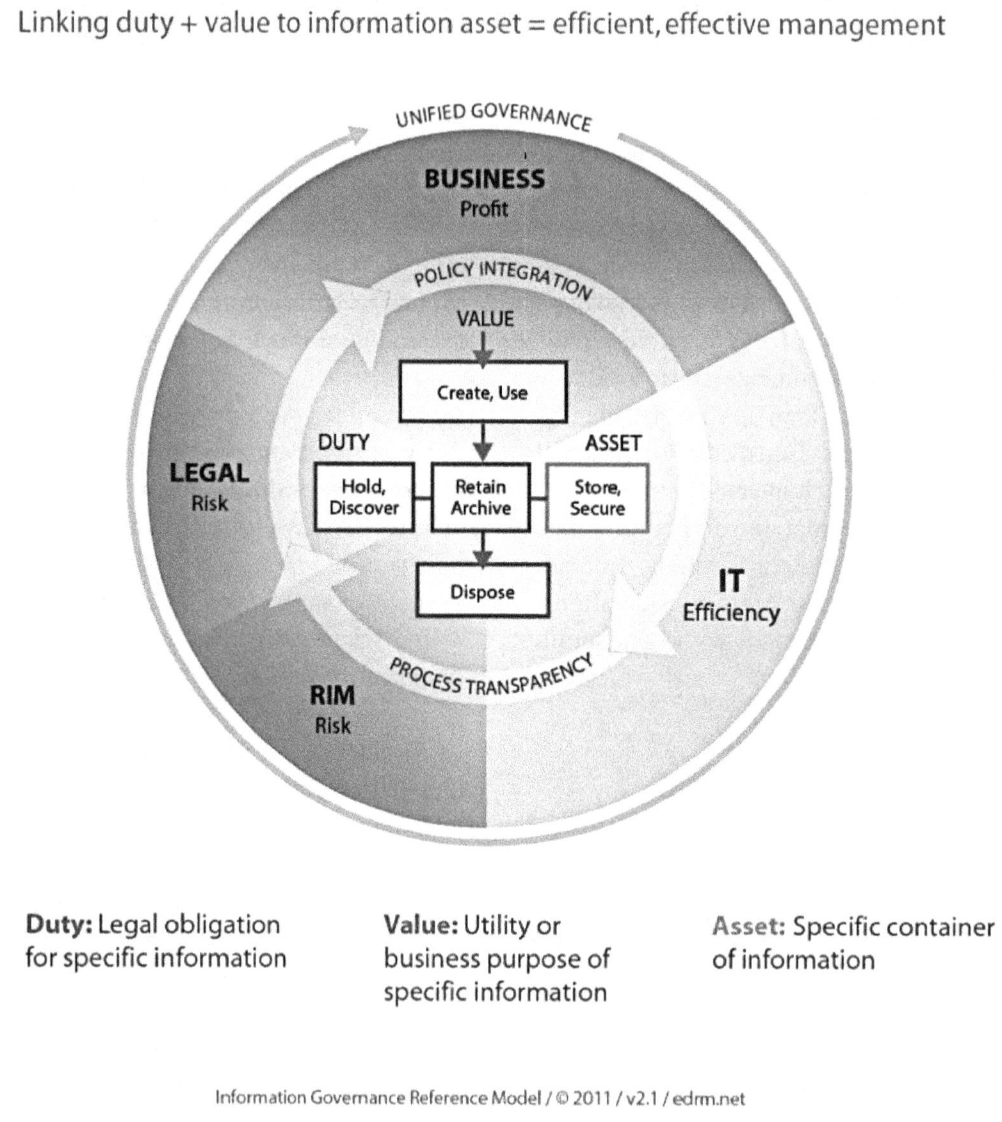

and if and when it may be destroyed. Similar to electronic discovery, records management protocols are media independent and will almost universally apply to the content of the data asset, but not the media format or location.

Within this much larger information governance ecosystem, there exists the relatively new discipline of eDiscovery. Similar to the above discussion, the cloud storage paradigm does not fundamentally alter any obligations surrounding the legal duties, obligations, and requirements, but it may impact the tactics, costs, and speed at which such obligations can be met.

General Discovery Obligations

As a starting place, eDiscovery is merely the digital equivalent of the paper-based version utilized in the judicial system for decades. Under American jurisprudence, discovery is the pre-trial phase of a lawsuit in which each party can seek information from the opposition to support their case. Rules dictating allowable methods of discovery have been set up by Congress (for federal courts) and by state legislatures (for state courts). Under formal civil procedure rules, a party can obtain evidence from the opposing party by a range of discovery devices including:

- **Deposition:** A proceeding in which a witness or party is asked to answer questions orally under oath before a court reporter.
- **Interrogatories:** Written questions sent by one party to the other party for the latter to answer in writing under oath.
- **Request for Admission:** A request to a party that he admit certain facts.
- **Request for Production of Documents:** A request to a party to hand over certain defined documents.
- **Request for Inspection:** A request by a party to look at tangible items (other than writings) in the possession or control of the other party.

In terms of eDiscovery, the most important discovery device is the request for production of documents, since that is the vehicle most often used to petition the opposition for ESI, including things like email, Microsoft Office documents, blogs, wikis, etc. Even the data about ESI (know as metadata) is discoverable. Beyond just creation and modification data, metadata may include stored revisions and even prior drafts (Favro, 2007).

From a scope perspective, one significant challenge is that in the United States, civil discovery (electronic or otherwise) is extremely broad and can involve any material that is "reasonably calculated to lead to admissible evidence." While this exploratory mission is often wide ranging, there are a handful of objections that allow a producing party to withhold providing information that meets the broad guidelines, including a range of attorney-client and work-product "privileges."

- **Attorney-Client Privilege:** A legal concept that protects communications between a client and his or her attorney and keeps those communications confidential.
- **Work-Product "Privilege" (really a doctrine):** Protects materials prepared in "anticipation" of litigation from discovery by opposing counsel.

In many instances, these privileges may be waived if the confidential communication is disclosed to a third party, called "inadvertent disclosure." In many instances, this inadvertent disclosure event will turn the tide of a given lawsuit, and because of the gravity of the error, it has been called the "third rail" of electronic discovery. The cloud paradigm does not change this dynamic per se, but exists as another potential landmine.

eDiscovery

In the early days of eDiscovery the industry was devoid of best practices and applicable case law. To fill that void, the EDRM came into existence in 2005 with a model to describe the process flow of a typical eDiscovery process. "The EDRM develops guidelines, sets standards and delivers resources to help e-discovery consumers and providers improve quality and reduce costs associated with e-discovery" (EDRM, 2005). As part of this initiative the EDRM developed a workflow diagram (amongst other best practices content) to describe the granular eDiscovery process as shown in Figure 2. While this model has been refined over the years, the main process steps have largely remained constant, starting with *Information Management* on the left hand side and then moving to *Identification*, *Preservation*, *Collection*, *Processing*, *Analysis*, *Review*, and *Production*. The process flow then ends with *Presentation*, but in reality, this last step often gets short shrift compared to the others.

Figure 2. Electronic discovery reference model[3]

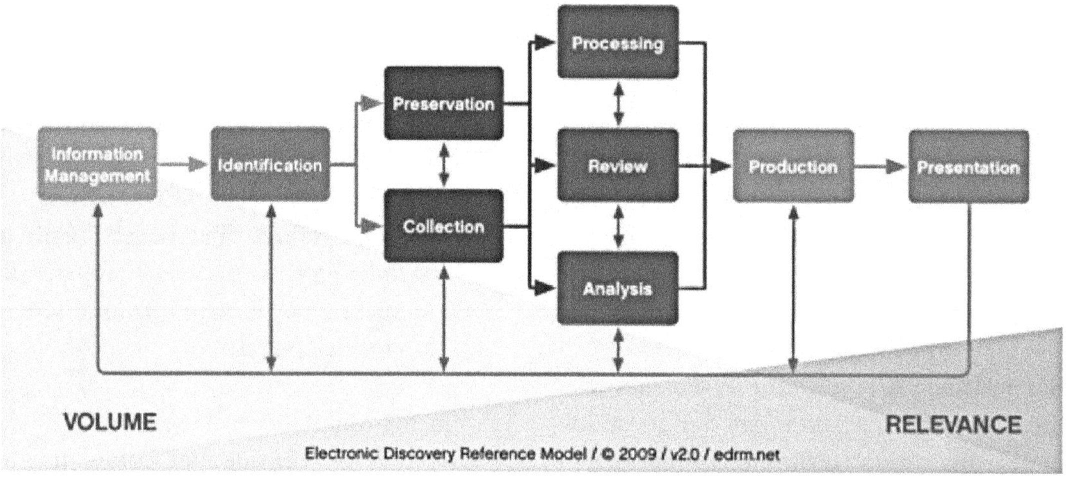

EDRM Phases

Instead of trying to tackle the EDRM landscape in one fell swoop, there are a number of advantages to examining each process step in sequential order. The goal of this chapter will be to focus on the areas where the cloud paradigm manifests material differences in either the strategy or tactics of electronic discovery. In addition, while the stages look to move left to right in a very linear fashion, the reality is that many stages cycle back on one another in an iterative fashion. "The grey arrows, such as the arrow from Identification to Information Management, show that the e-discovery process often is iterative" (EDRM, 2009).

Information Management

Pursuant to the EDRM model, the *Information Management* chevron is the literal start of the eDiscovery process. But, similar to the earlier analysis, it also threatens to subsume the entire workflow discussion due to its scope and relationship to the larger information governance umbrella. While it may seem axiomatic, good information management inherently results in a smoother, more efficient, less costly downstream eDiscovery process. This is particularly true with data volume rates growing at an exponential pace (doubling every 18 months) and given that many organizations are not able to stem the tide by deleting (when appropriate) any organizational content. Unfortunately, while bad information management hygiene is not terribly expensive at the time, massive data proliferation problems come home to roost when an enterprise has to process and review terabytes of ESI for a single matter. Most will focus on the initial eDiscovery processing costs, but the reality is that 60-70% of the typical costs are for the eyes-on attorney review process. Anything that can be done to reduce digital clutter will save money and time downstream in the process.

For most organizations, the *Information Management* process phase is a holistic one that isn't really impacted by discrete, reactive events. The framework at this stage is in contrast to the other (subsequent) EDRM process phases, which are typically tied to a specific, reactive event such as litigation or governmental investigation.

Movement of ESI to the Cloud has at least the potential to make some information management/governance tasks a bit easier. While perhaps not viable at the present time, cloud providers have the conceivable ability to layer onto the ESI under management, governance regimes that could apply to the retention and destruction of media. As an example, it would be possible for a cloud provider to require ingestion of metadata ("information describing the history, tracking, and/or management of an electronic document") upon migration into to the cloud, and it could thereby concurrently set retention and destruction dates.

Deployment with the consolidation of data into a singular system makes it easier to maintain data security if for no other reason than the simplicity of deploying process controls in the Cloud to monitor access, deletion, and the like. Given purported data redundancies that should come as standard with any enterprise class cloud system, it is also then less likely that data would be accidentally lost, overwritten, or destroyed. This type of redundancy is particularly useful to obviate any spoliation sanctions that typically arise out of lost data (as discussed below). Similarly, the cloud environment does permit for stronger tracking and auditing mechanisms, which means that access and control protocols should be easier to deploy.

That being said, these potential benefits assume a level of competency and accountability that is not always uniformly in place. As will be discussed in more detail in section 6 and 7, the key will be for a given consumer to ensure that they have the requisite Service Level Agreements (SLAs) in place to guarantee (at least contractually) that they are able to actually achieve many of the potential benefits.

Identification

Moving right along the EDRM spectrum (from the broader *Information Management* phase) the first reactive step in the overall eDiscovery process is *Identification*. The need to identify ESI is not usually done in the abstract. Instead, the requirement to identify ESI is typically triggered when a given litigation or investigation event becomes "reasonably likely." This trigger gives rise to a number of discrete duties including the inextricably intertwined *Preservation* step.

Proactive Data Mapping

In some instances, organizations can prepare for downstream reactive events by proactively creating a "data map" ahead of time. While this step is not universally undertaken by enterprises, it does make the reactive eDiscovery process that much more efficiently. According to the Global Professional of Information Professionals (AIIM)4, "the community that provides education, research, and best practices to help organizations find, control, and optimize their information," the form and format of data maps differ widely by industry type, organizational size, geography, regulatory environment, business processes, and more. While each organization's data map may look different, there are several key elements essential to any good data map:

- **Looks Matter:** A good data map will be organized either functionally or hierarchically with various data points organized around key subject lines. Typically, it would consist of rows of data with columns of attributes for each data set. The size of the map is entirely dependent upon the organization, but at a minimum, each one should contain information about process, systems, and people.
- **Support Change:** Data maps are subject to frequent change and thus choosing a format that allows updates to be made in a painless manner is critical. In the initial stages significant volumes of data need to be entered, so start with a format that supports quick data entry, such as Excel, and subsequently migrate to a longer-term format that supports searching, reporting, and quick retrieval, such as a database. Do not overcomplicate either the form or the format. The bottom line is "Keep it Simple."

- **Quality Content:** Data map designers tend to "over engineer" the document and set themselves up for a process that involves gathering numerous data values for each entry in the map. Instead, by honing in on only those columns that truly add value to the document, the process of collecting, collating, and organizing the information for it becomes more manageable. For each column in the data map, collect as much accurate information as possible.
- **Access and Storage:** Unless explicitly prohibited, access to the data map can be granted to various groups and roles within an organization. The rationale is that the data map contains critical information that should be accessible broadly rather than available only to some individuals. Most of these individuals, however, would get "read-only" access to it. Accordingly, a view of the data map should be placed on a more widely accessible storage location while the data map itself can be controlled via the appropriate database or file system controls.
- **Maintenance:** Ensuring that the data map stays accurate is vital to the relevance and long-term viability of it. A cross-functional team comprised of business, IT, and compliance that is sponsored by legal should be setup to maintain it. A data map administrator who performs the edits and controls access should also be established, and an appropriate chain of custody should be established such that when the data map administrator leaves the organization, the right handoffs take place.

Despite the utility of creating a proactive data map, most organizations do not devote the time to create one in the first place or, if they do, they often do not keep such maps current. In either case, the reactive process of *Identification* still needs to occur regardless of any proactive efforts the enterprise may have taken to date. Given that the *Identification* phase is most often triggered by the duty to preserve ESI, these two phases really do go hand in glove. In many cases, the duty to preserve ESI is what triggers the need for ESI *Identification*, despite the fact that such step occurs to the left in the EDRM workflow.

Preservation

The duty to preserve ESI typically arises from the common law duty to avoid spoliation of relevant evidence for use at trial, the inherent power of courts and court rules governing the imposition of sanctions. "The obligation to preserve evidence arises when the party has notice that the evidence is relevant to litigation or when a party should have known that the evidence may be relevant to future litigation" (Zubulake v. UBS Warburg LLC, 2003). Failure to respect to this duty can also have drastic consequences. In Silvestri v. General Motors (2001) the court dismissed the plaintiff's entire action as a sanction for failure to preserve key evidence.

The Sedona Conference, another very influential standards body, has issued a number of best practices for various areas within the eDiscovery space. They state that the "duty to preserve relevant information is certainly triggered when a complaint is served, a governmental proceeding is initiated, or a subpoena is received. However, the duty to preserve could well arise before a complaint is served or a subpoena is received and regardless of whether the organization is bringing the action, is the target of the action or is a third party possessing relevant evidence. The touchstone is 'reasonable anticipation'" (The Sedona Conference, 2010).

Preservation Triggers

Potential triggering events include an EEOC claim, litigation surrounding a relevant industry specific event, a preservation letter from opposing counsel (or the government), and of course the filing of a complaint, which will certainly be an unambiguous triggering event.

The significance of the duty to preserve is typically not lost on legal counsel since a breach of this duty (once triggered) may result in the imposition of a range of sanctions—everything from the complete dismissal of claims to monetary fines, spoliation inferences, evidence preclusion, witness preclusion, disallowance of certain defenses, reduced burden of proof, removal of jury challenges, limiting closing statements and supplemental discovery (Gonsowski, 2004). Judges typically have wide latitude to sanction offending parties, either under their inherent authority to manage cases or under FRCP 37 (in Federal court cases). The severity of the spoliation penalty often is linked to the culpability of the conduct with intentional acts, not surprisingly, faring worse than merely negligent or reckless conduct.

Given that failure in the early stages of the eDiscovery process (i.e., Preservation) can lead to the outright loss of a lawsuit, the business driver in the first several phases is risk mitigation, pure and simple. Performing eDiscovery within the Cloud will not be a task that many litigators can master the first time; but novelty will not likely be a viable excuse to prevent sanctions. Instead, courts will look to the "reasonableness" of the conduct to determine if any transgressions were excusable. Given the high stakes nature of the sanctions game, counsel would be wise to prepare for the inevitable eDiscovery gambit ahead of time by getting a handle on the necessary cloud related tasks, versus hoping for the best once a lawsuit hits.

Since the trigger of the duty to preserve is almost entirely a legal judgment call, the tactical step of how that duty will be fulfilled bears more attention. Scoping the *Preservation* obligation is the next phase and the cloud paradigm certainly makes this risk-laden task more complex.

Preservation Scoping

Once the *Preservation* duty is triggered (i.e., when litigation is "reasonably likely"), the next task is defining the universe of potentially responsive data and then determining the scope of what will ultimately be responsive. This is another practical instance, on a matter specific basis, where the cloud storage of ESI becomes a potentially thorny issue. According to Sedona (2010):

Once the duty to preserve information arises, an organization must decide what to preserve and how to do it. In some circumstances, the duty to preserve requires only locating and preserving a limited number of documents. In other circumstances, the scope of the information is larger and the sources of the information may not be known to counsel... identifying and preserving potentially relevant information can be complex and may require trained people, process, and technology, particularly when ESI is at issue.

While this initial mission is complex and broad, particularly when dealing with cloud data, it is not without boundaries. When implementing a legal hold, it is important to recognize that the duty to preserve extends only to "relevant" information. While relevance is broadly defined under the Federal Rules of Civil Procedure, it too is not without limits. Rule 401 of the Federal Rules of Evidence (2011) defines relevant evidence as: "(e)vidence having any tendency to make the existence of any fact that is of consequence to the determination of the action more probable or less probable than it would be without the evidence."

In defining the scope of the *Preservation* effort, the nexus with *Identification* becomes mission critical. According to EDRM (2010):

Identification is used to identify potential sources of relevant information. These sources may include business units, people, IT systems, and paper files. Learning the location of potentially discover-

able data is necessary to issue an effective legal hold. Identification should be as thorough and comprehensive as possible. Conduct interviews with key players to identify what type of records they have that may be relevant. Interviews with IT and records management personnel may be used to identify how and where the relevant data is stored, retention policies, inaccessible data, and what tools are available to assist in the identification process.

Counsel must first determine the scope of information that must be preserved. For many organizations, the best way to initially scope a matter is by defining "key custodians" that may be relevant to the subject litigation or investigation. Often these key custodians can be identified from analysis of the complaint or by interviewing witnesses. Once the key custodians are determined, then they must be linked with sites of potentially relevant information, such as hard drives, network shared drives, backup tapes, personal digital assistants, and loose media. Now, with the advent of cloud data storage and the use of hosted applications, it is critically important to figure out if a given custodian has any data relevant to the matter stored in a cloud environment.

To manage the linking of key custodians to data sources effectively, counsel must become familiar with their client's IT infrastructure and all applicable document retention policies. Increasingly counsel will look to available data maps and if those are not in place, they will have to interview appropriate IT professionals and relevant business unit personnel who may have knowledge of the incident.

One of the primary pain points when trying to master the specific, reactive *Identification* process regarding cloud data is that an enterprise's data may be commingled with numerous other companies' information – particularly in a setting that is more focused on cost savings instead of compliance. This multi-tenant architecture is considered inherent to the economies of scale for basic cloud computing. The use of private (single tenant) versus public (multiple tenants) cloud environments has tremendous impact on the eDiscovery discussion. If an organization creates and manages their ESI in a private cloud, then there should not be any additional hurdles associated with the management and control over their data since this deployment will inherently look very similar to an on-premise deployment with all the requisite elements of access and control. However, if an enterprise is utilizing a public cloud, then the practical and conceptual analogies vis-à-vis an on-premise application does not apply.

For the sake of discussion, we will assume that most enterprises utilizing a public cloud model have some level of multi-tenancy. Where this is the case, the challenge is to triangulate from a custodian-based, data storage paradigm to a cloud environment that may or may not pair given users with their own files. Given that the *Identification* task is often based upon "key players" (aka custodians) the cloud paradigm may make it virtually impossible to make the requisite linkage that would apply with a traditional (on-premise) eDiscovery process. For many enterprises that have moved data to the cloud, the lack of a custodian–data linkage may not have come up in the usual course of evaluating the business decision to move ESI to the cloud. However, it certainly may become a larger issue once a reactive eDiscovery event is at hand.

To some extent, however, this challenge is not entirely new to the traditional eDiscovery process. There can be analogous challenges associated with identifying data on network-shared drives, even when that data is stored on the entity's premises. While there are challenges in this on-premise context, particularly sorting through huge volumes of data, at least the organization has control over the infrastructure and is able to deploy software tools to index and search the corpus of ESI for responsive data. In this scenario, full data indexes (as well as partial metadata indexes) can be used to facilitate a search process to find relevant information for an investigation or litigation event.

While this challenge is not atypical in a "behind the firewall" type of deployment, it does not mean that it will be easy to navigate via a cloud provider once a litigation event rears its ugly head. Even well meaning and cooperative cloud providers may have limitations regarding how they can search across their storage layers to locate responsive data. In particular, they may not have run indexing software across data elements at the time of ingestion. If this step was not taken, which would not be surprising, and then it may be prohibitively expensive and time consuming to index large amounts of data reactively, for one specific client. Even if this is technically feasible, the provider may want to charge an exorbitant amount of money for the service, which is probably not on their typical menu of offerings.

Tactically, once the responsive information is located, it will be imperative to let the cloud provider know that they are obligated to sequester the ESI so that it (as well as any metadata) is not lost, altered, overwritten, destroyed, or unknowingly migrated. Here, preventing the ongoing use of the ESI may mean a significant impact to the business user if the data elements are "locked down" to prevent unwanted alteration. This type of "preserve in place" methodology is technically feasible depending on the software deployed by the cloud provider, but is still fraught with complications and potential risk.

The ongoing migration of ESI is often a common fact of life for many cloud providers given the inherent multi-tenancy and the commingling of data on a wide range of servers/storage devices. While data stored in a public cloud resides on a particular server, the third-party service provider generally may have the right to move data to maximize storage concerns and minimize costs. It is not uncommon for third-party providers to store one company's data at a location where many other companies' data is also stored. This physical location issue may raise downstream data privacy issues where the ESI is moved across international borders (discussed below). Regardless, the cloud provider's ability to execute a client's litigation holds request will bear upon the reasonableness of the data owner in response to the duty to preserve. If the cloud provider loses or alters data that is duly requested to be preserved, this calamity could pose an interesting liability battle with significant finger pointing. In the end, the data owner (versus not the cloud hosting entity) will likely be held to have sufficient legal control under the FRCP and will have a difficult time avoiding spoliation sanctions.

Preservation: Issuing the Legal Hold

Counsel must issue a "litigation hold" at the onset of litigation or whenever litigation is reasonably anticipated. There are a number of traditional participants within an organization who should be notified. Initially, key custodians must be made aware of the hold process. This hold should be periodically re-issued/refreshed so that new employees are aware of it and senior employees are reminded of their obligations.

Next, IT departments and other parties in control of ESI should be notified as well so that data is not inadvertently lost, deleted, recycled, or overwritten. As part of this discussion, counsel will inform the IT representative about procedures that need to be put in place to preserve this potentially responsive ESI. Historically, this was an area where many organizations failed to take adequate precautions since IT systems can easily be set to automatically over-write information. This scenario has been very common with the use of backup tapes and many of the early eDiscovery cases (such as *Zubulake*) involved the involuntary deletion of backup information.

This situation became so commonplace that the Federal Rules of Civil Procedure were amended in 2006 to create a "safe harbor" that insulated organizations from sanctions when these types of systems automatically overwrote information.

FRCP 37(e) explicitly states that "(a)bsent exceptional circumstances, a court may not impose sanctions under these rules on a party for failing to provide electronically stored information lost as a result of the routine, good-faith operation of an electronic information system." By way of example, defendants successfully invoked the safe harbor in *Kermode v. University of Mississippi Medical Center* (2011), where ESI was deleted pursuant to a clear retention policy before the duty to preserve was triggered. In *Grabenstein v. Arrow Electronics, Inc.* (2012), the defendant was protected for deleting emails as part of a normal business process even though an ancillary duty to retain under specialized employment regulations was violated. Nonetheless, the majority of 37(e) case law is of recent vintage so their precedential value is yet to be seen. Nonetheless, FRCP 37(e) is poised to come into play when the loss of cloud data happens after the owner duly informs its cloud provider and data is nevertheless lost. The lack of control over the cloud infrastructure, meaning how data is stored, backed up, deleted, etc., means that the party responsible for the litigation hold must inherently vest some measure of control with the third-party, while potentially suffering the consequences if data is lost. This risk chasm has forced some entities to retreat from initial cloud data migrations.

This legal hold communication may need to be expanded beyond key players to adequately cover cloud data hosting companies. As with key players and internal IT professionals, the legal hold must be adequately communicated with the cloud provider(s) so that they understand the importance of the hold process, the timelines, and the consequences of failing to execute the hold plan. It is likely that counsel will need to be intimately involved with this discussion and just like conversations with key players; the cloud provider will need to be reminded of their ongoing preservation obligation periodically.

There are other considerations at this *Preservation* stage as well, including the auditing, tracking and reporting issues that may be necessary to document the reasonableness of the preservation effort. In some instances, the *Preservation* phase may go on for years and because of the length of the underlying legal process, continuity with legal hold efforts is a necessity. Since the data owner will likely need to cede control of these tasks to the cloud entity, it will be important to understand how to trigger, monitor, and tweak the legal hold tasks over time. One very common example is how to deal with ESI for custodians who have left the company. Similarly, in a cloud context, what happens when information is migrated (due to an upgrade for example) from one system to another? At every stage of such a migration, the ESI must be tracked and the core contents preserved along with the original metadata.

Finally, there is the scenario where a legal hold is in place and the company wants to move data to the Cloud while under this obligation. This ESI migration, while not verboten per se, certainly should be handled with significant care and pursuant to the input of counsel. The main concern is that the migration would be seen as somehow "degrading" the underlying data and then the requesting party could claim that some type of spoliation occurred.

Collection

Having successfully managed the *Identification* and *Preservation* phases, the next step in the EDRM workflow is *Collection*. EDRM defines collection as:

The acquisition of potentially relevant Electronically Stored Information (ESI) as defined in the identification phase of the Electronic Discovery process. The exigencies of litigation, governmental inquiries, and internal investigations generally require that electronically stored information and its associated metadata should be collected in a manner that is legally defensible, proportionate, efficient, auditable, and targeted. The process of collecting electronically stored information will generally provide feedback to the identification function which may impact and expand the scope of the overall Electronic Discovery process (EDRM, 2012, para. 1).

The core element underpinning a successful collection of ESI is the ability to maintain the requisite level of admissibility, since the ability to use data in court or at trial is the sine qua non for conducting the eDiscovery process in the first place. While a deep dive into the admissibility requirements of cloud ESI may seem like a digression, parties producing this type of information or requesting this type of data would be wise to be overly cautious since this area may be one of first impression in many courts.

Collection: Admissibility

In the seminal case on the admissibility topic, *Lorraine v. Markel American Insurance* Co. (2007), United States Magistrate Judge Paul W. Grimm noted that "(v)ery little has been written, however, about what is required to insure that ESI obtained during discovery is admissible into evidence at trial." He went on to note that "(t)his is unfortunate, because considering the significant costs associated with discovery of ESI, it makes little sense to go to all the bother and expense to get electronic information only to have it excluded from evidence or rejected from consideration during summary judgment because the proponent cannot lay a sufficient foundation to get it admitted." Even in 2007 courts were already struggling with the fact that ESI came in "multiple evidentiary 'flavors,' including e-mail, website ESI, Internet postings, digital photographs, and computer-generated documents and data files" (Lorraine v. Markel American Insurance Co., 2007).

With wikis, blogs, social media content, and cloud data this admissibility issue threatens to become even more vexing for litigants attempting to collect and produce ESI for use in court. In *Lorraine* (2007), Judge Grimm started the discussion by noting that the existing evidentiary and procedural rules work for ESI given the inherent flexibility of the existing paradigms. With that said, the admissibility discussion for cloud data is nevertheless nuanced, at best.

Whenever ESI is offered as evidence, the following evidentiary rules must be followed in order for said ESI to be deemed admissible in a legal proceeding. There are five issues that must be addressed when determining admissibility: relevance, authenticity, hearsay, original or duplicate documentation, and unfair prejudice. For the purposes of this chapter we will focus on the first two elements: relevance and authenticity.

Relevance

A starting point to determine ESI's relevance, according to Rule 401, is to ask whether the information has any tendency to make some fact that is of consequence to the litigation more or less probable than it otherwise would be? Essentially, does this information make something relevant to the litigation more likely? While this is an important concept generally, it often does not have a significant impact upon the eDiscovery process. The authentication requirement is more significant. Once evidence has been shown to meet the low threshold of relevance, it is presumptively admissible unless the Constitution, a statute, rule of evidence or procedure, or case law requires that it be excluded. Thus, the function of all the rules of evidence other than Rule 401 is to help determine whether evidence, which in fact is relevant, should nonetheless be excluded.

Authenticity

Authenticity simply means that a document or ESI is indeed what it is represented to be. At a minimum threshold, the party putting forth the document or ESI has to provide sufficient evidence such that, "(t)he Court need not find that the evidence is necessarily what the proponent claims, but only that there is sufficient evidence that the jury ultimately might do so" (United States v. Safavian, 2006; as quoted in Lorraine v. Markel, 2007). In other words, the proponent needs to establish the overwhelming likelihood that a document is what it is supposed to be, but is not required to establish its authenticity beyond a shadow of a doubt.

Establishing authenticity seems straightforward, but the legal rules and protocols surrounding it are involved and complex. Although courts have recognized that authentication of ESI may require greater scrutiny than that required for the authentication of "hard copy" documents, they have been quick to reject calls to abandon the existing rules of evidence when doing so.

In general, the Federal Rules of Evidence apply to computerized data as they do to other types of evidence. Computerized data, however, raise unique issues concerning accuracy and authenticity. Accuracy may be impaired by incomplete data entry, mistakes in output instructions, programming errors, damage, and contamination of storage media, power outages, and equipment malfunctions. The integrity of data may also be compromised in the course of discovery by improper search and retrieval techniques, data conversion, or mishandling. The proponent of computerized evidence has the burden of laying a proper foundation by establishing its accuracy. The judge should therefore consider the accuracy and reliability of computerized evidence, including any necessary discovery during pretrial proceedings, so that challenges to the evidence are not made for the first time at trial (Federal Judicial Center, 2004, p. 82).

As such, courts increasingly are demanding that proponents using ESI evidence pay more attention to the foundational requirements than has been customary for introducing traditional hard evidence. Courts considering admissibility of ESI have acknowledged that a witness with personal knowledge may authenticate it. However, the witness does not need to be the one to have created the ESI or have personal knowledge of the ESI's accuracy. An appellate court held that copies of a post office's computer records could be authenticated by a custodian or other qualified witness with personal knowledge of the procedure that generated the records (United States v. Kassimu, 2006). It is necessary that the authenticating witness provide factual specificity about the process by which the ESI is created, acquired, maintained, and preserved without alteration or change, or the process by which it is produced if the result of a system or process that does so.

One other method of authenticating electronic evidence (under Rule 901(b)(4)) is the use of "hash values" when making documents. Appendix F to The Sedona Guidelines: Best Practice Guidelines and Commentary for Managing Information and Records in the Electronic Age (2005) defines metadata as "information about a particular data set which describes how, when and by whom it was collected, created, accessed, or modified and how it is formatted (including data demographics such as size, location, storage requirements and media information)." Because metadata shows the date, time, and identity of the creator of an electronic record, as well as all changes made to it, metadata is a distinctive characteristic of all ESI that can be used to authenticate it under Rule 901(b)(4).

Unfortunately, in the Cloud context, the use of metadata (as an authentication method) may be in peril since common fields (such as creation date, last modified date, last accessed date, etc.) may be changed as the data is migrated to and within the Cloud. Metadata may also be changed during the collection process as well, giving rise to both authentication challenges and spoliation worries. Entities that maintain information in the Cloud should consider the impact of the cloud on metadata, and understand what metadata the cloud provider preserves and whether it can be readily accessed for e-discovery purposes.

Collection Tactics

The collection paradigm for cloud data is inherently a different ball game since the data owner likely will not have the ability to select the method of collection, the personnel doing the work or the tools to actually manage the process. On one end of the spectrum, a traditional eDiscovery collection process could range from a forensic bit-for-bit image of a given hard drive (typically laptops or desktops) all the way to simple, active file collection.

Forensic Collection

With the foregoing relevance and authentication discussion as a background, we now turn to the tactics of evidence collection—with particular attention to securing information that will be admissible later in the litigation process. Collection via forensic imaging provides the most detail and is the only approach for retrieving deleted or fragmented files from computer systems. However, it often requires an expert to operate purpose built forensic tools and is the most expensive and time-consuming approach. In order to collect forensic images the expert would typically need physical access to the subject information systems. While this is usually feasible for individual systems, it is much more logistically challenging for larger systems such as servers, proprietary databases, and storage systems (like storage area networks). Fortunately, Sedona Principle 9 holds that forensic collections are unnecessary for most basic eDiscovery scenarios: "Absent a showing of special need and relevance, a responding party should not be required to preserve, review, or produce deleted, shadowed, fragmented, or residual electronically stored information" (Sedona, 2007, p. ii).

Active File Collection

Active files are generally easy to access and collect, particularly from an on-premise environment. Most of the challenges involve scale and volume issues. Likely in response to guidelines like Sedona Principle 9, most requests for production ask for active files, which are "documents" that "actively" reside on the custodian's computer hard drive or other storage device. Active documents are generally those that you can see in a file manager or file explorer type of tool. Examples include e-mail and standard Microsoft Office files like word processing documents and spreadsheets.

Given the requirement to have physical access to the information management systems, conducting cloud forensic imaging as a collection method would be fairly unlikely, barring pre-stipulated contractual provisions. There are many factors that would make imaging difficult, if not impossible. For one, in a public could with co-tenancy, the data elements may be comingled, making the forensic collection of any one custodian's "drive" infeasible. Next, the data may be physically spread over a range of geographic locations. Therefore, practically speaking, the difficulty of collecting forensic images will mean that the only viable collection method will be an active file capture conducted by the cloud provider's personnel. If the provider is focused on compliance, then they will likely have a more advanced and streamlined export process.

Processing

The EDRM defines *Processing* as follows: "At a point in the e-discovery lifecycle following preservation, identification and collection it often becomes necessary to 'process' data before it can be moved to the next steps of the Lifecycle. Some primary goals of processing are to discern at an item-level exactly what data is contained in the universe submitted; to record all item-level metadata as it existed prior to processing; and to enable defensible reduction of data by 'selecting' only appropriate items to move forward to review. All of this must happen with strict adherence to process auditing; quality control; analysis and validation, and chain of custody considerations" (EDRM, 2010).

Given that processing engines all differ in terms of the types of formats of ESI they can process, it will be useful to define a *Collection* specification that dictates how files will be collected and the type of metadata that will be included. Additionally, if the data was stored in an encrypted format it will be critical to decrypt all ESI on export from the cloud environment so that ingestion and processing can proceed without delay. Other than the foregoing concerns, it is likely that most phases after *Collection*, including *Processing*, will need to be done using a third party software application that processes data for the subsequent, downstream phases. Therefore, the *Analysis, Review and Production* pieces will likely look very traditional since the ingestion of cloud ESI may be done on-premise or in a software as a service setting. In either event, the cloud paradigm will have little impact once the data is exported.

A further reason for conducting the *Processing*, *Analysis*, and *Review* stages outside of the cloud environment is that most cloud providers have not built out functionality for these highly specialized, legally oriented tasks. Certainly, it is feasible that one day these tasks could be conducted within the Cloud, but for the time being, the best practice is to export ESI into purpose-built eDiscovery applications.

Custody vs. Control

At first blush, the cloud paradigm would seem to frustrate the ability of one party to seek discovery from another since the underlying data is not in the producing party's possession. Yet, the discovery rules have taken this third-party scenario into account for a variety of other analogous situations, such as areas involving partners controlling or storing information. For good or ill, courts do not currently make any material distinction between data that resides behind an enterprise firewall and that may be in a shared (public or private) cloud. Under Rule 34 of the FRCP, a party may serve on any other party a request to produce data in the responding party's "possession, custody, or control." In addition, while there are not any "on point" decisions yet regarding cloud eDiscovery nuances, it's pretty clear from analogous circumstances that the "custody" or "possession" of data won't be a determining factor if the entity has the legal rights to "control" the information. The closest, current analogy under existing case law is seen in other circumstances where a third party holds data that the responding entity needs to preserve and produce. For example, in Tomlinson v. El Paso Corp. (2007) the court found that the defendants could not delegate their obligations to preserve and maintain data where a third party vendor had possession of their electronic information. Similarly, in Rosenthal Collins Group, LLC v. Trading Technologies International, (2011) the court addressed whether a responding party could legally distance itself from the actions of a third party consultant who had control of relevant data and altered it, despite being notified of his preservation duty. The Rosenthal court cited Cyntegra, Inc. v. Idexx Laboratories, Inc. (2007) when issuing terminating sanctions, noting that "courts have extended the affirmative duty to preserve evidence to instances when that evidence is not directly within the party's custody or control so long as the party has access to, or indirect control over, such evidence" (Rosenthal Collins Group, LLC v. Trading Technologies International, 2011, p. 38).

The challenge then posed by ESI in a cloud environment is the control continuum, which starts with actual control on one end and continues to the far end of the spectrum where there is just the perception of the ability to control information. We will discuss SLAs below, but a danger zone likely exists where there is a gap between the actual control a party may have over their cloud provider (and the hosted ESI stored therein) and what a court may consider as a reasonable level of control that the party should have (i.e., does the producing party have the right, authority, or practical ability to obtain the documents from a non-party?).

Instead of the traditional "custody" that a party has with its on-premise data sources, where discovery is mandatory, some might argue that neither "control" nor "possession" are present. While there is a paucity of case law regarding eDiscovery and cloud data, it is relatively clear that the courts would look to the "control" aspect of the hosted ESI and would presume that the party "owning" the underlying data would have the contractual rights to possess and control it, for purposes of litigation or governmental investigation.

One potential avenue to avoid production of electronically stored information would be to try to leverage FRCP 26. Rule 26(b)(2) (2011), which places specific limitations on producing ESI when an "undue burden" exists, states that:

(a) party need not provide discovery of electronically stored information from sources that the party identifies as not reasonably accessible because of undue burden or cost. On a motion to compel discovery or for a protective order, the party from whom discovery is sought must show that the information is not reasonably accessible because of undue burden or cost. If that showing is made, the court may nonetheless order discovery from such sources if the requesting party shows good cause, considering the limitations of Rule 26(b)(2)(C). The court may specify conditions for the discovery.

This scenario could play itself out where the cloud provider attempts to extort the data owner for exorbitant sums to conduct the requisite eDiscovery. Alternatively, there could also be a scenario where the cloud provider has gone out of business, making extraction difficult without working through the bankruptcy courts. In either case, it is likely that the courts would not be terribly sympathetic given the fact that the data owner was responsible for migrating responsive data to the Cloud in the first instance. Presumably, they also had the ability to set up the requisite SLA and vet different vendors. Assuming that the cloud provider is willing (and able) to help the data owner preserve and produce ESI per request, even the formatting of export sets may be an issue. Here, the downstream admissibility of ESI comes into consideration, and notions surrounding authentication, chain of custody, and metadata handling may all affect how willing the court (or requesting party) is to accept the data. Accordingly, it is not just a question of "if" data can be exported out of the Cloud, but more often "how" (and sometimes "when").

Cross Border Concerns

Cloud computing can certainly run afoul of data protection directives if data is physically housed in a region that technically restricts migration, processing, or export. Under the EU Data Protection Directive, unless they take certain steps, organizations are prohibited from transferring personal information to countries that do not provide the same level of protection with respect to personal information of EU residents (the United States is one such country for example). The challenge for many cloud customers is that they may not actually know where their data is located. While the cloud provider may optimize the data's physical location for performance reasons, bandwidth prices, or simply other idiosyncratic business reasons, these decisions may have tremendous downstream consequences for the data owner.

The Sedona Conference (2008) states that:

Cross-border discovery represents a "Catch-22" situation in which the need to gather relevant information from foreign jurisdictions often squarely conflicts with blocking statutes and data privacy regulations that prohibit or restrict such discovery—often upon threat of severe civil and criminal sanctions. U.S. courts often have very little familiarity with foreign data privacy and protection regulations and often are skepti-

cal of efforts to restrict the discovery of relevant information from a European parent or affiliate organization. Cross-border discovery has become a major source of international legal conflict, and there is no clear, safe way forward. At the heart of these conflicts are vastly differing notions of discovery and data privacy and protection, and the frequency and intensity of these conflicts is heightened by an expanding global marketplace and the unabated proliferation of electronically stored information (p. 1).

Accordingly, if an entity has the contractual rights to control their data, the fact that the ESI is not in their possession will not normally obviate their duty to produce it. As such, it is unlikely a company could claim that something like the EU Data Protection Directive would provide a shield against requesting parties. Given the complexities of moving data across international borders, it is imperative that an entity has some insight and choice over where their data is physically stored. As such, while this will be discussed in the subsequent section on SLA, it likely makes sense to consider contractually stipulating where the cloud data must physically reside. They could mandate that ESI be stored in the United States, for example. This approach is probably the safest and may be a good starting place for most entities that do not want to take any unnecessary data migration risks.

In either instance, data privacy issues are highly complex and in most instances an entity should consult with counsel to determine whether cloud storage in a country will restrict downstream movement. There is also a safe harbor provision, which was established in 2000. This provision allows United States companies and organizations to safely migrate data pursuant to rules crafted by the EU and the United States. US companies can opt into the program as long as they adhere to the 7 principles outlined in the Directive:

- **Notice:** Individuals must be informed that their data is being collected and about how it will be used.
- **Choice**: Individuals must have the ability to opt out of the collection and forward transfer of the data to third parties.
- **Onward Transfer:** Transfers of data to third parties may only occur to other organizations that follow adequate data protection principles.
- **Security:** Reasonable efforts must be made to prevent loss of collected information.
- **Data Integrity:** Data must be relevant and reliable for the purpose it was collected for.
- **Access:** Individuals must be able to access information held about them, and correct or delete it if it is inaccurate.
- **Enforcement:** There must be effective means of enforcing these rules.

SERVICE LEVEL AGREEMENTS

During the foregoing discussion, there have been several intersection points where the contract terms negotiated between the parties have been critical in determining the direction of any outcome. This discussion has several dimensions. The first is the practical reality that the service level terms will dictate a number of key variables along the eDiscovery spectrum—including price, availability, data location storage, and the like. In contrast to the actual terms, there likely exists a parallel reality where a reviewing court (or investigating entity) will presume a reasonable level of service level terms. In other words, it is incumbent upon a party utilizing a cloud provider to negotiate terms that not only work for their organization, but which will also be viewed as subsequently reasonable by a reviewing party. For example, selecting a bare bones SLA that does not make mention of data storage locations may make it difficult to later claim that the data owner cannot move ESI across borders due to regional data protection issues.

Given the foregoing host of potential issues, it is clear that a party with legal (but not physical) control over their data is at the mercy of the underlying contractual rights. These rights will in most cases be defined by the SLA of the cloud provider. In addition, in some instances, the cloud provider may simply proffer a one-sided, adhesion contract. While this will certainly be the case in a standard consumer context (say, with Google Docs), most enterprises should wield enough power to meaningfully negotiate the terms and conditions applicable to their data stored in the Cloud.

To that end, there are a number of things to consider when negotiating a SLA for the provision of cloud services:

- **Physical Location of Data:** From an individual user's perspective, the on-demand nature of the Cloud often renders the physical location of the actual data meaningless. However, given the complications of moving data across international borders, it is wise to specify where data will physically reside, particularly avoiding countries with more restrictive data protection regimes. Here, it would be useful to either create an inclusive list (defining countries where data could be physically located) or an exclusive list (defining countries where data would definitively not be physically located). If there are premiums associated with certain jurisdictions then it would be wise to consult local counsel to understand the nuances of data migration out of the specific country to evaluate the risk/reward value proposition.
- **Access Rights:** As discussed previously in this chapter, there are a number of scenarios where a legal hold, identification, search, and extraction of ESI may be required from a cloud environment. In order to understand the cost implications, turnaround times and feature functionality, it will be helpful to prepare for these potential access issues well ahead of time, ideally locking in answers during the contractual process. Failure to do so proactively may mean that a party will not be able to comply with judicial deadlines and could result in fines and sanctions.
- **Ownership:** While it seems self-evident that the user of cloud services should still "own" the stored data, it is wise to call out any anticipated issues surrounding downstream ownership. For example, what happens to the stored data if the customer does not pay its bills? What happens if the cloud provider goes bankrupt? There is certainly a scenario here where a cloud provider might have to auction off its assets (e.g., client data) and this could both keep the stored ESI in limbo and conceivably threaten to release proprietary and confidential information.
- **Notification:** Given that the cloud hosting provider can be subpoenaed directly (by a litigant or governmental agency), companies need to know what type of notification their providers will give about third party requests for information. It is prudent to define whether the movement, migration, or co-mingling of data requires advanced notice or permission. The safest course would be to have the cloud provider give substantial notice before compliance so that the data owner could file an action to either prevent the data disclosure generally or dictate terms for the provision of ESI.
- **Security:** It may seem like a no brainer, but the encryption and general security of stored data needs to be clearly outlined in the applicable SLA. The export of data out of the cloud would surely be a scenario where encryption should be considered mandatory. Sensitive proprietary data may warrant additional protections beyond en-

cryption, where it may be valuable to have role based access rights.

CONCLUSION

Cloud technology clearly offers businesses effective cost-cutting storage options, but is not without legal risk. Before committing to a cloud program, firms should take stock of their business needs, potential litigation claims, and anticipate some worst-case scenarios. Courts, historically regarded as lagging behind the technology curve, are rapidly catching up. Ignorance of technology is no longer a valid excuse and courts will hold a litigant responsible for their cloudy decisions.

The EDRM stages described in this chapter provide defensible guideposts for navigating each of the discrete steps, but cannot anticipate every nuance. It is up to savvy entities to integrate the foresight provided here in relation to their reasonable data management, as it suits their litigation profile and regulatory context. Each enterprise is different, and the law in regards to many of the eDiscovery practices discussed hinges on what is "reasonable," a term grounded in factual context and evolving case law.

As the cloud paradigm gains momentum the services provided will inherently mature, often adding significant functionality in specialized industry vertical niches—as is increasingly seen with compliance, eDiscovery, and information governance. It is very important to test any proposed vendor to make sure that their solutions have been vetted, their functionality can be deployed as stated, and they have referenceable customers. Anything less is certainly a recipe for disaster.

ACKNOWLEDGMENT

Adam Kuhn, Editorial Intern (Symantec), helped with formatting and editing the references for the chapter.

REFERENCES

AIIM. (2009). *The quest for ediscovery: Creating a data map*. Retrieved from www.aiim.org/Resources/Archive/Magazine/2009-Nov-Dec/37867

Cyntegra, Inc. v. Idexx Laboratories, Inc., 2007 WL 5193736 (C.D. Cal. 2007) (2007).

Electronic Discovery Reference Model. (2005). *Projects*. Retrieved from http://www.edrm.net/projects

Electronic Discovery Reference Model. (2009a). (Graphical illustration of the electronic discovery stages). *Electronic Discovery Reference Model*. Retrieved from http://www.edrm.net/resources/edrm-stages-explained

Electronic Discovery Reference Model. (2009b). *EDRM diagram elements*. Retrieved from http://www.edrm.net/resources/diagram-elements

Electronic Discovery Reference Model. (2010). *Identification guide*. Retrieved from http://www.edrm.net/resources/guides/edrm-framework-guides/identification

Electronic Discovery Reference Model. (2010). *Processing*. Retrieved from http://www.edrm.net/resources/guides/edrm-framework-guides/processing

Electronic Discovery Reference Model. (2011). (Graphical illustration of the information governance process). *Information Governance Reference Model*. Retrieved from http://www.edrm.net/projects/igrm

Electronic Discovery Reference Model. (2012). *Collection guide*. Retrieved from http://www.edrm.net/resources/guides/edrm-framework-guides/collection

Favro, P. (2007). A new frontier in electronic discovery: Preserving and obtaining metadata. *Boston University Journal of Science and Technology Law*, *13*, 1–24.

Federal Judicial Center. (2004). *Manual for complex litigation* (4th ed). Retrieved from http://www.fjc.gov/public/pdf.nsf/lookup/mcl4.pdf/$file/mcl4.pdf

Federal Rules of Civil Procedure. (2011). *Website*. Retrieved from http://www.uscourts.gov/uscourts/RulesAndPolicies/rules/2011%20Rules/Civil%20Procedure.pdf

Federal Rules of Evidence. (2011). *Website*. Retrieved from http://www.uscourts.gov/uscourts/RulesAndPolicies/rules/2011%20Rules/Evidence%20Procedure.pdf

Gardner, D. (2009). *Analysts define growing requirements for how governance supports corporate cloud computing*. Retrieved from http://www.zdnet.com/blog/gardner/analysts-define-growing-requirements-for-how-governance-supports-corporate-cloud-computing/2988

Gartner. (2012). Information/data governance. *Gartner IT Glossary*. Retrieved from http://www.gartner.com/it-glossary/informationdata-governance/

Gonsowski, D. (2004). *The negligent spoliation of electronic information: Practical advice for successfully preserving digital data*. Retrieved from http://www.legaltechcenter.net/affiliate/Shared Documents/fios.pdf

Grabenstein v. Arrow Electronics, Inc., 2012 WL 1388595 (D. Colo. 2012) (2012).

Kermode v. University of Mississippi Medical Center, 2011 WL 4351340 (S.D. Miss. 2011) (2011).

Lorraine v. Markel American Insurance Co., 241 F.R.D. 534 (D. Md. 2007) (2007).

Mathews, J. (2010). *The future of virtualization, cloud computing & green IT – Global technologies & markets outlook – 2011-2016*. Colorado Springs, CO: Market Info Group LLC.

NARA Electronic Records Management Definitions, 36 C.F.R. § 1236.2 (2009)

Rosenthal Collins Group, LLC v. Trading Technologies International, 2011 U.S. Dist. LEXIS 17623 (N.D. Ill. 2011) (2011).

Sedona Conference. (2005). *The Sedona guidelines: Best practice guidelines & commentary for managing information & records in the electronic age*. Retrieved from https://thesedonaconference.org/download-pub/90

Sedona Conference. (2007). *The Sedona principles* (2nd ed). Retrieved from https://thesedonaconference.org/download-pub/81

Sedona Conference. (2008). *Framework for analysis of cross-border discovery conflicts: A practical guide to navigating the competing currents of international data privacy and e-discovery*. Retrieved from https://thesedonaconference.org/publication/Framework%20for%20Analysis%20of%20Cross-Border%20Discovery%20Conflicts

Sedona Conference. (2010). *Commentary on legal holds*. Retrieved from https://thesedonaconference.org/download-pub/470

Silvestri v. General Motors, 271 F.3d 583 (4th Cir. 2001) (2001).

Tomlinson v. El Paso Corp., 245 F.R.D. 474 (D. Colo. 2007) (2007).

United States v. Kassimu, 2006 WL 1880335 (5th Cir. 2006) (2006).

Wood, L. (2009). *Cloud computing and compliance: Be careful up there*. Retrieved from http://www.computerworld.com/s/article/9126934/Cloud_computing_and_compliance_Be_careful_up_there

Zubulake v. UBS Warburg LLC, 220 F.R.D. 212 (S.D.N.Y. 2003) (2003).

ENDNOTES

1 Please note several caveats. One, the author is not rendering any substantive legal advice. Next, it is critical that practitioners take note of any local, state, or federal legal developments that may have changed the landscape since publication of this chapter. Since this space is evolving quickly, both in terms of the technology and case law, it is likely that disruptive events could and will occur to make items in the following discussion either obsolete or outdated.

2 Retrieved from http://www.edrm.net/resources/guides/igrm

3 Retrieved from http://www.edrm.net/resources/edrm-stages-explained

4 AIIM: *The Global Community of Information Professionals*. Retrieved from http://www.aiim.org/

Chapter 10
Data Recovery Strategies for Cloud Environments

Theodoros Spyridopoulos
University of Bristol, UK

Vasilios Katos
Democritus University of Thrace, Greece

ABSTRACT

Data acquisition and data recovery are essential to any e-discovery or digital forensic process. However, these two aspects seem to be considerably difficult in a cloud-computing environment. The very nature of the Cloud raises a number of technical and organizational challenges, which renders traditional approaches and tools inapplicable. Resource pooling, rapid elasticity, and geographical distribution of data are only a small part of the Cloud's features that hinder the forensic investigation. At the same time, there is significant absence of forensic readiness in cloud computing policy framework. In this chapter, the authors discuss the challenges pertaining to data acquisition in a cloud environment and discuss possible directions for meeting these challenges by presenting representative cases and sketching acquisition process and scenarios.

INTRODUCTION

The increasing technical and legislative complexity of cloud computing systems has made traditional data acquisition infeasible in principle. Traditional acquisition tools and processes have become inapplicable due to resource sharing among multiple tenants and distributed data in multiple jurisdictions. The very nature of cloud computing is highly coupled with networking operations, thus cloud activities are reflected to network activities and the data identification process requires network-type metadata, however, additional changes might also need to be introduced in the current cloud infrastructure to facilitate data acquisition procedure.

DOI: 10.4018/978-1-4666-2662-1.ch010

Copyright © 2013, IGI Global. Copying or distributing in print or electronic forms without written permission of IGI Global is prohibited.

In this chapter, we first highlight the inapplicability of the traditional acquisition tools base on the premise that data acquisition in cloud computing environments must follow live forensics practice. We then move on to discuss acquisition and recovery scenarios.

LIVE ACQUISITION IN THE CLOUD

Traditional forensic acquisition often follows the well established 'dead forensics' practices. A number of hard disks and other digital storage media are seized and their images are acquired using imaging software and/or hardware. Prior to the seizure of the suspect's equipment, a search warrant is issued (in most countries) and this warrant must identify a unique physical address. The seized equipment is also tied to the suspect, or at least is demonstrated to have been a part of the alleged offense.

Upon acquisition, the digital artifacts are self-sufficient in that they can be examined and analyzed independently. Although in some cases correlation between the different pieces of evidence is necessary in later stage of the analysis, the examiner can relatively easily interpret the artifacts found on the storage device at the initial stage of the analysis. We take a domestic hard disk as an example. All metadata are contained in the disk, including the partitions and file systems that determine the structure and representation of data in this disk. If this disk contains a virtual system or logical volume arrangements for redundancy and better manageability of the storage resources, the underlying structures are still available in the local system. Finally, the user's presence is normally local. Even when remote access is involved, the network activity metadata and logs are still maintained locally.

However, in a cloud-based storage system most of the assumptions above do not hold. Firstly, it is unlikely that the user will access a cloud storage service locally. Internetworking[1] is a critical enabler for cloud services and this alone is sufficient to put forth the need for live forensics. With respect to the cloud storage itself, metadata plays a crucial role not only in tracking down the evidence but also in protecting the legitimate users' privacy. Without metadata, the cloud storage can be seen as a well-stirred soup of data, thus entropy (uncertainty) will be very high, and the lack of context will make it impossible to associate data and stored objects with users, owners, and underlying activities. In a cloud storage environment, file structure is enforced by the master servers, which orchestrate the distribution, movement, and replication of files on the storage (or chunk) nodes. Similar to the users, master servers are entities different from the chunk nodes. The nodes and the master servers exchange command and control information as well as metadata through the network. Therefore local file system metadata are not sufficient for representing the whole picture of the states, ownership, and history of a data object.

Let us take a typical user activity scenario on a local desktop as an example. The information stored on the hard disk is normally sufficient to answer questions related to the user creating, moving and deleting files, attaching and removing storage devices, installing and removing software, etc. Most of this information is revealed by examining the user or system files such as the registry in Microsoft Windows and various log files. Tools like EnCase and Aftertime are very efficient in creating timelines of the user activity as reflected in the acquired disk images. In order to conduct the same exercise on a cloud storage setting, there is a need for further correlation between the participating entities. These entities are the user's computer, the cloud storage master server, the chunk nodes, and depending on the cloud service model used there may be more entities required as we will explain in the following sections.

Data recovery is one of the most important steps in the forensic process as it takes place in the beginning of the forensic process and heavily affects the quality and effectiveness of all forensic phases in later stage, especially forensic analysis. Although data resilience is one of the main drivers for cloud adoption, the absence of standards and guidelines for forensic acquisition poses significant challenges when it comes to the admissibility of the evidence.

Data are unlikely to get completely lost in a cloud storage environment as recovery processes for unintentional deletion, backups and redundant data provide the user with the necessary assurance of data availability and integrity. Some cloud offerings, such as Amazon's Simple Storage Service (S3) service, even support version control[2] called *Versioning,* which allows the user to create a timeline of a file. However, when it comes to acquiring the data for use in a court, the benefits and features above appear to be a double-edged sword. On one hand, rich metadata provided by Versioning may generate additional information of the user's actions to reveal his/her modus operandi. On the other hand, the complexity of the situations may make it impossible to demonstrate a reliable reconstruction of events and therefore allow the defendant to challenge the forensic acquisition process. In addition, the acquisition process will involve queries to live systems such as master servers that cannot be taken off line, imaged, and cryptographically hashed. As a result, preservation requirements described in standards and good practice guides such as the ACPO[3] guidelines cannot be met.

From the discussions above, we conclude that data acquisition process in the cloud heavily involves live forensics, and the traditional data acquisition tools have become inapplicable for cloud-based storage due to the increasing complexity of the underlying infrastructure.

An accurate capture of the limitations, constraints, and characteristics of the operating environment and application domain in general is a critical step to the requirement analysis and specification of any software application or tool. However, cloud-computing environments often encompass social, legal, and technical complications that are incompatible due to conflicting priorities and agendas. Therefore, any requirements specification may only be able to capture a fraction of the whole picture. We made an attempt to capture a fraction of the complexity and dynamics of the cloud ecosystem as shown in Figure 1. In this chapter, we will discuss some acquisition scenarios and process, considering some of the major technical, economic and legal constrains.

OVERVIEW OF ACQUISITION CHALLENGES

Cloud forensics requires alternative or novel approaches compare to traditional digital forensic investigations, especially in the evidence collection phase when data needs to be recovered from different parts of the Cloud while ensuring sufficient level of forensic soundness. In a traditional single-user computing environment, where data are often associated with a single user (the owner of the device), the recovery process is conducted by using a combination of hardware (e.g. write blocker imaging devices), and software tools (e.g. Encase) to extract and analyze forensic artifacts collected from the suspect's machine.

However, as described earlier, data recovery in cloud computing systems introduces a number of technical and organizational challenges, which can affect the entire acquisition process. These challenges and their consequences, as depicted in Table 1, are discussed in detail in this section.

Network-Type Metadata

Due to the decoupling between cloud user credentials and physical users, network-type metadata play a significant role in the data acquisition process. This stems from the fact that network-type metadata, such as the IP address, time of access, etc., can bind a cloud-username with a physical entity in order to prove the physical ownership of the data attributed to a cloud username.

Figure 1. The complexity and dynamics of the cloud ecosystem

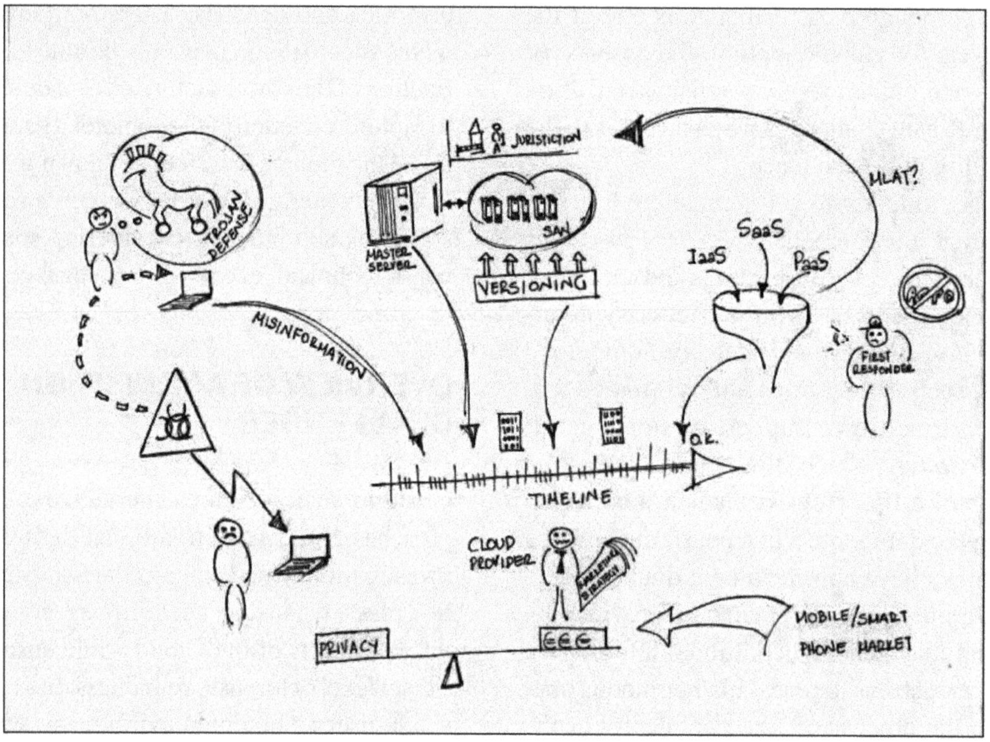

However, network-type metadata not only can be used to identify the relationship between the Cloud and the user/client but also can be used to understand the data that reside inside the Cloud. The very nature of the Cloud is highly coupled with networking operations thus cloud activities will always involve network activities and the data identification process will require network type metadata. For instance, since a cloud system consists of many servers geographically distributed and connected to each other through the Internet, network metadata can provide information regarding data transfers inside the Cloud between the servers or point to places in the Cloud that potential evidence might reside. Network-type metadata might also be the answer to the problem of deleted data recovery mentioned earlier. For example, the Google File System (GFS), the distributed parallel fault tolerant file system that Google uses to store data in the Cloud (Ghemawat, et al., 2003), consists of two basic entities, the *master server*, which is the server that maintains the metadata of cloud data and the *chunk servers* where the actual data are located according to each chunk server's local file system. In a forensic investigation in order to collect data from the Cloud, the first step has to be the examination of the master server in order to obtain the location of the data in the Cloud. This examination actually refers to the metadata that is stored on the master server, which is nothing more than IP addresses pointing to certain chunk servers. In the scenario of data deletion, these pieces of information, if available, could be used to retrieve deleted data without violating other clients' privacy (Spyridopoulos & Katos, 2011).

Resources Sharing

Multi-tenancy, as one of the key features of cloud computing, is one of the most important factors that affect the data acquisition process in a cloud

Table 1. Data acquisition in cloud environments: overview of challenges and consequences

Challenges	Consequences
Resources Sharing Cloud Elasticity Geographical Distribution Multiple Jurisdiction Areas Decoupling of Cloud-user-names (Online Users) and Physical Users Network-type Metadata Preservation/Integrity Timelines and Correlation Balancing Forensic Capabilities and Commercial Success	Privacy Violation Lost Data Inaccessible Data No Physical Access to Data Impossible User Identification Admissibility issues Cloud Service Continuity

system. According to the NIST Definition of Cloud Computing (Mell & Grance 2011), cloud computing is a model for enabling ubiquitous, convenient, on-demand access to a shared pool of resources that can be rapidly provisioned and released with minimal management effort or service provider interaction. Sources like applications, servers, network and storage, can be simultaneously allocated by multiple users following a multi-tenant cloud architecture. The fact that the same sources are shared amongst multiple users can lead to privacy violations during a forensic data acquisition in the Cloud. Cloud providers, in most cases, are not data owners (Kroll, 2011), and due to the multi-tenancy nature of the Cloud, forensic data recovery might lead to the acquisition of data whose ownership may be ambiguous or deceptive. In the worst scenario, since the same space on the disk can be used by multiple clients, deleted data from a third client may be recovered during the acquisition process resulting in privacy violation.

Another problem as a result of sharing the same sources among multiple tenants is that the Cloud cannot cease its operation since it will create devastating consequences for the clients' business continuity. In other words, data recovery has to be conducted on a running machine rather than a switched-off computer. This introduces challenges in collecting all the possible evidence, since data may be changing during the acquisition process in a live system; in such case the data change might result in the corruption of potential evidence. In order to overcome these implications the investigation process has to encompass a live correlation step where information gathered from more than one sources are correlated while being acquired in order to draw as much valuable information as possible.

Cloud Elasticity

Another essential feature of cloud computing systems that can hinder the data acquisition process in a forensic investigation is its inherent elasticity. As mentioned by Scott and Dominick (2011), "this elasticity poses a challenge to the forensics investigator due to resources such as disk space and memory allocated today that is gone and overwritten tomorrow." In traditional computing environments, data can still be recovered even if they are deleted from the disk. However, in cloud environments, the characteristics of volatility and elasticity make the recovery of deleted data a very challenging process (Grispos, 2011). The inherent mechanism of the Cloud that enables the quick provision and release of resources introduces a major obstacle in the data recovery process. The fact that the suspect's resources, and more specifically, the storage area can be quickly released and provisioned by another client combined with the multi-tenancy feature means that the suspect's data reside on a part of the disk can be now used by another client. According to Google security whitepaper (2010), after a user deleting data form a Google service, the data are no longer accessible from the user's Google Apps interface and eventually they are deleted from both active and replication chunk servers. Pointers to the data on Google's active and replication chunk servers are also removed making the recover process almost impossible. To make things worse the space on the disk where these data used to reside is now considered as free and can be overwritten by other customers' data over time. This situation can result in two different scenarios. In the first scenario the suspect's data are considered as lost, even though they might be somewhere in the cloud system, thus the investigator cannot carry out the data acquisition process. In this scenario, no evidence can be extracted from the Cloud. In the second scenario, the investigator recovers the deleted data by taking the risk to violate the privacy of other clients' data. As a result, more sophisticated recovery tools are needed to distinguish the owner of the data on the disk prior to recovery and collect the suspect's deleted data without violating other users' privacy. Such tools should perform low-level activities including examination of the disk's local file system, have access to higher-level feedback from the master server, link data on the disk with ownership metadata and timestamps, and eventually perform the data extraction based on ownership information.

Geographical Distribution

Data servers in a cloud environment can be geographically dispersed, especially in a public cloud service where servers can span all over the world, which leads to a geographical distribution of data. This means a client's data can be found in more than one country around the world, and in a cloud forensic investigation the suspect's data to be seized and acquired might require data recovery from multiple servers reside in more than one country. Such a distributed data recovery process can be a rather time-and-effort-consuming process compare to traditional forensic investigation on a single user computer. Data needs to be recovered from each and every cloud server involved in the investigation around the world.

Another disadvantage of the geographical distribution of the servers in a Cloud is the lack of real time synchronization between them. It is not feasible to synchronize terabytes of data on disk and physical memory between geographically distributed servers across WAN links in real time. Thus, there can be different versions of the client's data in the cloud system, i.e., old versions of a file may co-exist along with newer versions of the same file. This can lead to the inaccurate event reconstruction in cloud environments.

Multiple Jurisdictions

Distributed data not only leads to a distributed data acquisition model but also introduces legal implications to the entire forensic process. Since data can be geographically distributed, they can be found under different jurisdictions. Every jurisdiction has its own legislation and compliance requirements. This means that data acquisition process might have to deal with different data privacy legislations and recovery rules in different jurisdictions. For example, Amazon stores data from customers in the European Union (EU) in its cloud services in the Republic of Ireland (Grispos, 2011). This means that in the case of a forensic investigation the seizure and examination of the suspect's data must be done in accordance to the local legislation and in cooperation with the local authorities. However, such process is rather time consuming and therefore can lead to loss of data/evidence either deliberately when deleted by the suspect, or inadvertently when deleted by the cloud system. Moreover, in some cases the investigator might not even be able to access the data because of a country's strict privacy rules. For example, the EU Data Protection Directive[4] prohibits the transfer of data from EU members to countries with inadequate data protection laws (Deyrup, et al., 2010). In order for these data transfers to be accomplished, bilateral cooperation framework agreements have been developed between EU and certain countries, which provide principles that an entity can adhere to in order to collect data from EU members. Lastly, jurisdictional issues might also arise due to the relevant legislation in the provider's or the client's/suspect's location.

In short, the absence of universal legal standards with regards to forensic data collection from a cloud system, can easily lead to the violation of foreign laws if the investigator is not careful enough.

Virtualization

Virtualization enables the elasticity of the Cloud. It brings both challenges and opportunities to the data acquisition process. In general, virtualization makes it even more difficult to extract data from the Cloud as it exacerbates the problems of not having physical access to distributed data. Virtualization adds another layer of file system and data; data now "live" in a virtualized environment. Mapping is required between data in the local file system of the virtual machine and its location in the local file system of the cloud server (chunk server). As a result, more complex techniques are required to retrieve data in virtualization layer.

On the other hand, virtualization is implemented via virtual images. This means that every client's instance in the Cloud is essentially a file, thus theoretically, the only thing needed is to obtain a copy of the client's virtual disk is to make an exact copy of this file. However, in practice it is not as simple. Firstly, this approach can only be applied in IaaS service model. Secondly, when taking only this image into consideration the investigator might lose valuable data that the client managed to get rid of by using the elasticity feature of the Cloud. Lastly, examining this image might violate other tenants' privacy because the same space on the disk where the data of the image resides might have been used previously by other tenants sharing the cloud environment. As a result, the image might contain other tenants' data in deleted form that will also be recovered in a forensic investigation as described earlier.

Decoupling of Cloud User Credentials (Online Users) and Physical Users

Another major challenge for cloud forensic data acquisition is the existence of many users in conjunction with the decoupling of their cloud user credentials (online users) and the actual physical users. In a typical acquisition scenario, a computer or host may involve a single user, or in the case of a "traditional" seizure warrant, the court order is coupled to an address. Such a scenario is often not possible in the cloud environment and thus creating an obstacle for the underlying acquisition processes. Online usernames (the usernames that cloud clients use) have to somehow be mapped to their owners, i.e., the physical users; otherwise, data in the Cloud to be acquired in a forensic investigation might not be able to be attributed to a physical user. In general, data identification requires a sophisticated metadata management mechanism and the quality and repeatability of the forensic acquisition process are heavily depend on these metadata.

Preservation/Integrity

The main purpose of a digital forensic investigation is to collect evidence of a crime or an illicit act in a way that it can be presented to the court with proven integrity and validity, i.e., the evidence must be admissible. There must be a way to ensure that data extracted from the source have not been tampered throughout the whole investigation process, preserving thereby the digital chain of custody. Therefore, activities prior to data collection have to take place that can guarantee the integrity of the data throughout the whole procedure. Preservation mainly refers to "the preservation of original artifacts in a way that is reliable, complete, accurate and verifiable" (Scott & Dominick, 2011). The ACPO Good Practice Guide (ACPO, 2008) proposes certain techniques and processes that can assure the chain of custody.

In traditional digital forensics, preservation is accomplished by imaging the data source through write blocking devices and special software toolkits that prevent data alteration and guarantee data authenticity. These software toolkits utilize certain algorithms (such as the MD5 and SHA-* cryptographic hash functions) and calculate fixed length numerical values, known as hash values, based on the exact data that compose the evidence.

A hash value is the identity of the evidence and can verify that the evidence or copies of it have not been altered since acquisition, maintaining thereby a valid chain of custody. After duplication via bit-stream imaging, the digital evidence is authenticated and verified, and then the investigator mounts the image as a read-only disk in order to examine its contents without altering any of the evidence.

However, in cloud environments, collecting evidence from the Cloud using write blocking devices is at the moment impossible since the investigator might not have physical access to the cloud servers. Moreover, even if the investigator had access to each server of the Cloud, imaging using write-blocking devices, in other words, "freezing" the Cloud, would result in the interruption of the provider's service continuity, which consequently leads to the interruption of clients' business continuity. The whole situation ends up in a loop since imaging all evidence in the Cloud is impractical while partial imaging may have legal implication in the presentation to the court. This leads to the suggestion that forensic acquisition processes and tools should be an integrated part of the cloud functionality, instead of a bolt-on service. Furthermore, due to the elasticity of the Cloud, the release of storage sources that elasticity offers during the acquisition operation can have destructive consequences to the integrity of the acquired image.

Timelines and Correlation

During the examination, the investigator has to collect all the evidence and use them in order to reconstruct the digital crime scene. The investigator has to construct a narrative report supported by the evidence in order to explain if and how the offense was committed. As a result, system timestamps in system log files and other time-relevant metadata such as the creation, access and deletion times of files are of vital importance for reconstructing the timeline of events that took place and correlating incidents.

However, time synchronization in the Cloud faces various challenges. Firstly, due to the distributive nature of cloud computing, perfect time synchronization between all servers is almost impossible. As a result, the time of an incident may differ from server to server. For example, if a file was created at time t_1 its various replications in the cloud servers might indicate different creation times. Thus, timestamps from the local file system of every server in the Cloud can be misleading or deceptive. It would be preferable if the master server (the server that keeps the metadata of cloud's data) set a reference time in the Cloud and used time synchronization protocols. However, this means that every data extraction from the Cloud for forensic purposes can only be done with granted access to the master server. In addition, another time mismatch can occur between the master server and the client's (suspect's) computer; only examination of network metadata can solve this problem. Nevertheless, it is possible for the cloud system to track every change that happens to the client's data and keep different versions of them via features such as Versioning. However, such feature is not yet supported by all cloud providers.

Balancing Forensic Capabilities and Commercial Success

The unprecedented popularity of cloud service models has been reflected in the plethora of campaigns, white papers, press releases and other marketing activities led by a number of reputable companies. Many believe that cloud computing is a big step towards computing as a utility. However, once cloud computing becomes a utility it also essentially becomes a part of our critical infrastructure. In terms of security, cloud computing did not follow the mistakes of the past. In the early days of the Internet, security was not a priority in its development agenda. Security considerations moved to the foreground only after the Morris worm incident in 1988, and systematic development of security started when firms began to realize the commercial added value of the Internet. Understanding that security is an important factor for the commercial success of an emerging technology, cloud solutions integrated security considerations right from the beginning. Security is not considered to be an overhead but rather a business enabler. Unfortunately, at the time of this writing, forensic readiness in the Cloud does not seem to follow the same fate. This is mainly due to the following two reasons.

First, system failures can fall into two general categories, namely technical security failures, and business logic failures. The technical security failures refer to the well-known confidentiality, integrity, or availability failures. The business logic failures refer to a wider spectrum uncovered by the technical security failures which includes the societal and legal consequences of rapid adoption of cloud computing. Cloud can be the object of a crime, or the tool of a crime. In a Denial of Service (DoS) attempt, for example, the Cloud is the object of the crime, whereas distributing illicit material through the Cloud is using Cloud as tool of the crime. Current security control families do not address the situation of the later.

Secondly, the global and cross-border nature of the Cloud, the different jurisdictions, social and legal frameworks seem to raise the resistance in defining good and acceptable forensic readiness practices. As long as there is no legislation to enforce forensic readiness in cloud computing, forensics will always be an after-thought and the first responder's investigations will remain ad-hoc.

CLOUD ACQUISITION PROCESS

Correlation Right from the Beginning

In digital forensics, correlation of evidence is typically performed during the analysis phase. The digital artifacts are mined for circumstantial and "smoking gun" evidence. In the case of the latter, investigation normally concludes with the investigator being able to prove the allegation and the expert witness report is fairly straightforward. However, in the absence of "smoking gun" evidence, the analyst needs to capture all circumstantial or potentially exculpatory evidence and align them in a way to construct plausible scenarios that will prove or disprove the allegation. This process is known as correlation.

In the case of cloud storage forensics, correlation is a vital and mandatory process during the acquisition stage. Identification of the digital artifacts is a challenging and non-trivial exercise, and the first responder will need to correlate among artifacts gathered from various cloud components in order to examine and analyze these artifacts and produce evidence at later stage. Depending on the deployment model, context of the case and technologies involved, the emphasis and strategy for correlation will be different. In Table 2, we summarize some of the data sources and correlation needs for a number of different cases. It should be noted that this list can be further extended.

Normally, most of digital artifacts are located in storage devices but ownership information of these artifacts can only be determined by linking

Table 2. Evidence sources and correlation needs

Source	Evidence type
Cloud storage node	Files
User's PC	User activity files, network identification, location services, local files, cache
Master Server	File chunk locations, file metadata, node arrangement
Network logs	Network activity, connection transcripts
Cloud Authentication, Authorization, Accountability (AAA) services	User activity
Versioning	Version control logs and information

the storage node to the master server and AAA (Authentication, Authorization, Accountability) logs. In more complex cases memory acquisition of a user's device might be required, for example, when a user claims a Trojan Defense.

From above we conclude that forensic acquisition from cloud storage is extremely sophisticated and costly. Improving forensic readiness may significantly decrease the cost of acquisition, but this could only happen from the cloud provider's side and users at the moment do not have rights or even awareness to interfere.

Cloud Forensic Readiness

Information assurance in the Cloud should include forensic readiness considerations. Developing forensic readiness can be financially beneficial for cloud providers. As discussed before, forensic acquisition from cloud storage can be a very costly process, especially when a cloud provider is required to provide logs and forensic artifacts under the request from law enforcement. Forensic readiness can place structures and add additional information that can support the first responder to make informed decisions on identifying the digital artifacts. A complete readiness solution could offer accountability, first responder activity logging, as well as privacy protection mechanisms to enhance trust of the cloud infrastructure.

A forensic readiness solution should consider all evidence sources reside on the cloud provider premise as identified in Table 2 and ideally include the user's domain as well. Realistically though, the latter might not be feasible. Logging should take places on different components in the Cloud and can be used for auditing and coordinating forensic acquisition process.

Apart from bringing new technical functionality, the cloud paradigm is also encouraging a new way of thinking and a wave of innovation of business model. This provides an avenue for developing new attack vectors, thus trust and reliability of the Cloud must not be neglected. Cyber crime involving cloud computing environments and their functionality is inevitable. Forensic readiness in cloud environment is a critical capability and we also call for legislations to catch up as soon as possible.

Identification of Evidence Sources

As discussed earlier, traditional forensic investigation processes and tools can hardly be applicable in the Cloud. New processes and tools have to be developed and implemented to address forensic challenges posed by cloud computing. A proposed acquisition process is presented in Figure 2.

In general, based on the cloud service model, the acquisition process is required from both provider and suspect. Locating relevant storage locations in a cloud infrastructure prior to performing the acquisition requires a service-model based strategy. Understanding the particular technical and practical requirements for the underlying service model is a mandatory trait of the first responder. This is also in line with Principle 2 of the ACPO guide (2008):

In circumstances where a person finds it necessary to access original data held on a computer or on storage media, that person must be competent to do so and be able to give evidence explaining the relevance and the implications of their actions.

In other words, the first responder who will be handling the acquisition needs to have expertise about cloud technology in general and the particular service model being handled. If the cloud service model is *Infrastructure as a Service* (IaaS) or *Storage as a Service*, for example, the investigator can recover data that the suspect saved in the Cloud, while in *Platform as a Service* (PaaS) and *Software as a Service* (SaaS) the only data that the investigator can collect are network logs and cloud logs (from Cloud Authentication, Authorization, Accountability services) and data that can be found in the suspect's machine.

Figure 2. Cloud acquisition process

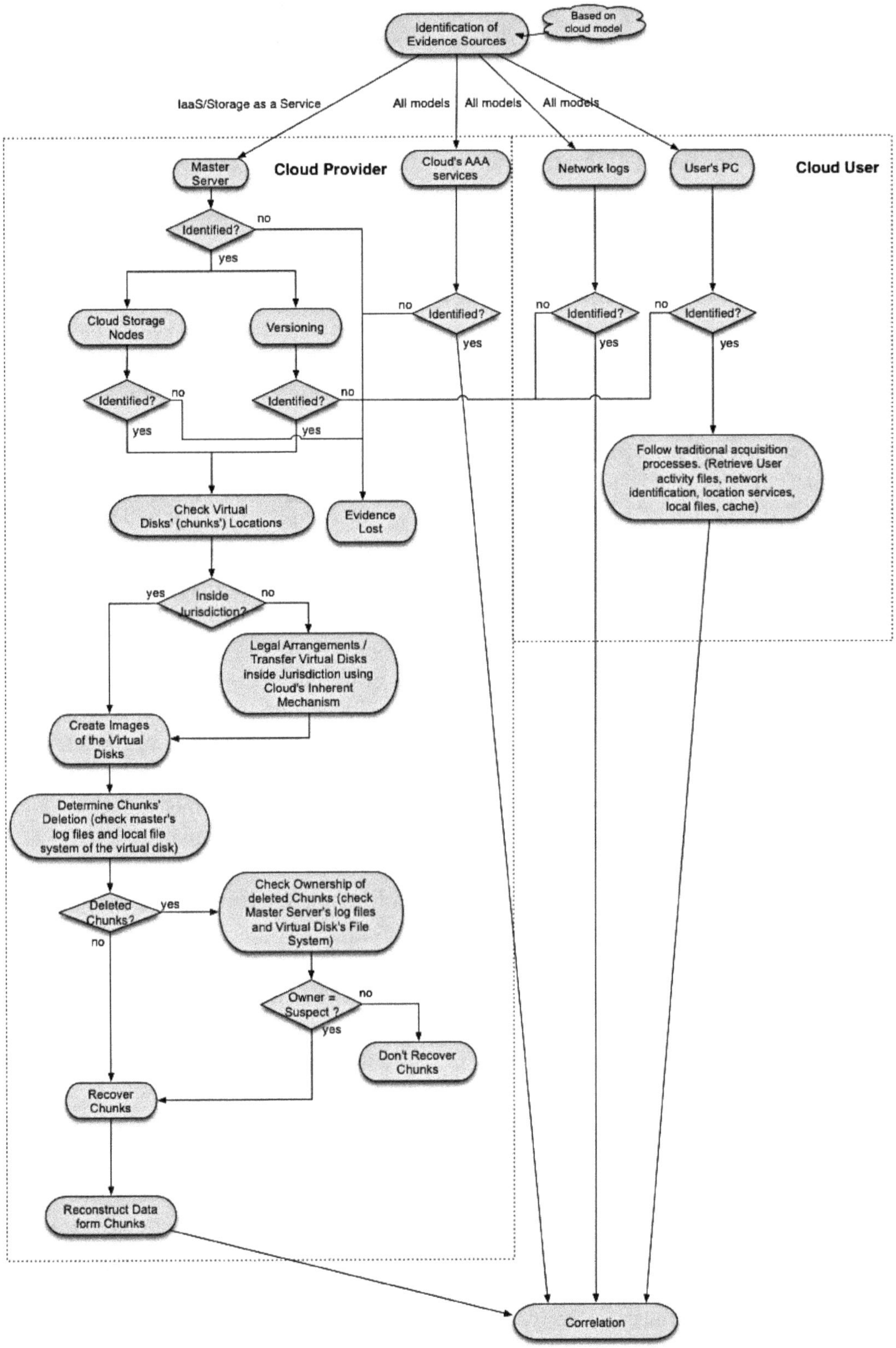

More specifically, the first step of the acquisition process includes the identification of evidence sources. In this phase, the investigator has to collect all the valuable artifacts from all evidence sources that are identified and available during the acquisition process. The suspect's PC, network logs and cloud AAA (Authentication, Authorization, and Accountability) services are evidence sources that can be found in all cloud models. After they are identified, traditional digital forensic processes can take place in order to recover, examine, and record the evidence they convey. In the next step, data recovered from the suspect's PC, such as user-activity files, network identification, location services, local files and cache memory, can later be correlated with other pieces of artifacts to draw conclusions about the suspect's activities and generate evidence.

When the crime scene involves IaaS or PaaS cloud model, then the recovery of evidence can be more complicated. More specifically, IaaS providers offer both computing power and storage capacity to its client through virtualization. Client can choose its own Operating Systems (OS), and use storage space provided in the form of virtual disks. For example, Amazon's Elastic Compute Cloud (EC2) is a Web service that provides elastic computing capacity and is a leading IaaS offering. All volatile data will be lost when a client's instance in EC2 reboots or is shutdown. However, Amazon keeps persistent data in virtual storage systems such as S3. This means that forensic artifacts can not only be found in logs, but also in the data saved in the Cloud by the suspect. These artifacts can theoretically be relatively easily extracted since they are located on the virtual disk.

The first step of identification of evidence sources is the identification of the master server because it carries all the valuable metadata for locating and collecting the suspect's actual data; no data can be retrieved without identifying the master server. After the master server is identified, the acquisition process continues to the identification of the cloud storage nodes, i.e., chunk servers, where the suspect's data resides. Considering a hard disk bit-stream copy for example, traditional tools see ones and zeroes, copy them indiscriminately and offer a reliable and verbatim representation of the state of the suspect's disk. During the analysis phase, analysis tools provide functionalities to create a timeline of activities. This process can involve file recovery and data carving as well. The process can be done this way because there is a relatively low ambiguity once the disk is in the possession of the forensic analyst. However, this approach cannot be followed in a cloud environment.

Features such as Versioning are functionalities that provides added value both to the end user and the forensic investigator, but it can also create new attack vectors. Take a cloud storage service (e.g. Dropbox) with local folder synchronization and version control as an example; a malicious employee can exploit this functionality to perform exhilaration by copying files onto the cloud folder followed by a delete operation. After the deletion, the local folder will appear empty, but the employee can recover the purposefully deleted files from another location. In this case acquisition tools will need to interact with the Versioning mechanism to present a timeline which reflects accurately the suspect's modus operandi.

Evidence Collection

After identifying evidence sources, the acquisition process continues to evidence collection. Various issues and challenges arise and need to be addressed in the evidence collection phase in the cloud environment.

First of all, due to the fact that most of cloud environments operate in multiple jurisdictions and regulatory, privacy and legal requirements vary in these different jurisdictions, the investigator might not be able to access forensic artifacts that are physically located outside the jurisdiction of the investigator. Thus, legal arrangements such as the Mutual Legal Assistance Treaty (MLAT) have to be established between the countries involved in such potential incidents to allow access of servers for lawful investigation.

In order to speed up the process of data acquisition, the investigator could also leverage the inherent data redundancy of the Cloud to transfer the suspect's data into a chunk server that resides inside the jurisdiction area of the investigator (Spyridopoulos & Katos, 2011). In order to do so, the investigator needs access to the master server which regulates the data flow and storage inside the cloud system, then utilize the mechanism of redundancy and insert "fake" information (metadata) of deleted or corrupted copies of the suspect's data to the master server's system. A forensic tool with the ability to insert false information (metadata) of deleted or corrupted copies to the master server's system would trigger the master server to activate its mechanism of redundancy to make a new copy of those files. By explicitly indicating the master server where the new copy shall be created can result in transferring the suspect's data into a server inside the investigator's jurisdiction. In order to avoid legal complications from altering metadata in the cloud system, the tool should be able to log all of its actions and keep copies of the original metadata. According to ACPO Principle 2, system and original data alteration in live forensics is an acceptable practice provided that the person performing the alteration is a fully qualified expert and can justify that action was a conscious decision with valid motives in a court of law. The automation of this process can also help improve efficiency for evidence collection.

Creating Virtual Image

The next phase of the acquisition process is the creation of an image of the virtual disk where the suspect's data resides. This is in theory a relatively easy process because a virtual disk is essentially a file. However, due to the multi-tenant nature of the cloud system, the virtual image might include other tenant's data as well. This can made the acquisition process very tricky, especially when recovering deleted files. In this case, we discuss two scenarios as follows:

Scenario 1: File Not Overwritten

In this scenario, the suspect's deleted file has not been overwritten by any other file thus there is no additional challenge in the acquisition process. If the blocks that construct the chunks of file on the file system of the virtual disk have not been used by other chunks, the file can be retrieved without any privacy violation issues. However, it can be rather difficult to determine the ownership of the chunks, particularly when there is a chance that they have been overwritten.

Scenario 2: File Overwritten

In this scenario, the suspect's file has been overwritten by another file and the recovery of the suspect's data are nearly impossible. Some or all of the blocks that construct the chunks of the deleted file may have been overwritten and the investigator may unintentionally recover data that belong to another user (assume client B) thus violating client B's privacy. At this point two sub-scenarios emerge:

Sub-Scenario 1: Client B's File Not Deleted

In this sub-scenario client B's file (more specifically the file chunks) overwrite the suspect's file and remains in the system (client B's file is not deleted). In this case, since the investigator anticipates that another file resides in an area where the suspect's file used to reside the investigator assumes that the owner of this file is not the suspect. However, in order to fully support the hypothesis the investigator has to conduct a further investigation. Therefore, the investigator can check the master server's memory to determine the ownership of those chunks. In the master server's memory information can be retrieved to prove that the chunks in this particular area are owned by client B and not the suspect.

Sub-Scenario 2: Client B's File Has Been Deleted

In this sub-scenario, client B's file had firstly overwritten the suspect's file and then after some time intervals it was deleted. So the data resides in the area where chunks of the suspect's file used to "live" belongs to client B. However, since the master server deletes all metadata of the file from its memory and logs on the disk all metadata about the file except for the chunks' locations on the system (that is the location of the chunks on the servers that keep the chunks that construct the deleted file) after the deletion (Ghemawat, et al., 2003), there is no information to indicate that deleted chunks do not belong to the suspect. As a result, in order to safely recover only the suspect's files from the image, the master server has to permanently keep the location of the chunks in the cloud system (Spyridopoulos & Katos, 2011) otherwise it would be impossible to determine the ownership of the deleted data.

To summerize, in order to avoid potential privacy violation when recovering deleted data, the investigator needs to:

1. Check the local file system of the virtual disk referring to master server's logs for deleted files.
2. Deleted file identification.
3. Check master server's memory
    a. If another tenant's file chunks have overwritten the chunks of the suspect's file then do not retrieve the file.
    b. If there is no information on the ownership of these chunks on the disk then check master server's logs in order to determine if other users deleted chunks have overwritten the chunks of the suspect's file (modifications to the logging mechanism need to be made). This process can be conducted by comparing the deletion times of the chunks that used to reside in the same areas of the disk.

It is obvious that in order to safely extract all the valuable data of the suspect, whether deleted or not, certain changes will need to be made to the master server's log mechanism, and in order to accomplish the task of data recovery, the investigator has to have access to all cloud components to avoid privacy violation incidents. Lastly, in order to construct a timeline of actions from the suspect associated with results of these actions, a correlation of the all pieces of evidence found in the Cloud and the suspect's machine needs to be performed; this correlation may lead to more accurate conclusions on the suspect's actions.

CONCLUSION

Traditional forensic tools and procedures have become inapplicable due to rapid cloud adoption and the complexity of the underlying cloud infrastructure. In cloud computing environments, data acquisition has to take place from both provider and client side. In this chapter, we presented challenges for data recovery and forensic acquisition in cloud computing environments. We discussed various recovery scenarios for the Cloud. The proposed recovery process flow is by no means comprehensive and needs to be further implemented and tested. However, we believe this is a step forward to understand the issues of data acquisition and recovery in the Cloud in order to direct tools and solutions to be developed and implemented in the cloud environment. It is financially beneficial for the cloud providers to be equipped with such solutions to meet the increasing need for e-discovery in the Cloud. We also concluded that the first responder must acquire knowledge and skill sets to meet the investigative needs of cloud crimes.

REFERENCES

Association of Chief Police Officers. (2008). Good practice guide for computer-based electronic evidence official release version. *Director (Cincinnati, Ohio)*, *67*(5), 72.

Deyrup, I., Matthews, S., Iqbal, A., Black, B., Fisher, C., Cella, J., et al. (2010). *Cloud computing & national security law*. Unpublished.

Ghemawat, S., Gobioff, H., & Leung, S.-T. (2003). The Google file system. *ACM SIGOPS Operating Systems Review*, *37*(5), 29. doi:10.1145/1165389.945450

Google. (2010). Security whitepaper: Google apps messaging and collaboration products. *Security, 745*.

Grispos, G. (2011). *Calm before the storm: The emerging challenges of cloud computing in digital forensics*. Retrieved from http://www.dcs.gla.ac.uk/~tws/papers/grispos11calm-rev2425.pdf

Krollontrack. (2011). *Capturing the cloud – Computer forensics and cloud computing*. Retrieved from http://www.krollontrack.com/blog/post/2011/04/19/Capturing-the-Cloud-e28093-Computer-Forensics-and-Cloud-Computing.aspx

Mell, P., & Grance, T. (2011). *The NIST definition of cloud computing*. Washington, DC: NIST US Department of Commerce.

Scott, Z., & Dominick, G. (2011). Cyber forensics in the cloud. *Technology (Elmsford, N.Y.)*, *14*(1), 1–36.

Spyridopoulos, T., & Katos, V. (2011). Requirements for a forensically ready cloud storage service. *International Journal of Digital Crime and Forensics*, *3*(3), 19–36. doi:10.4018/jdcf.2011070102

ENDNOTES

1 Internetworking is the connection of individual networks in order to create a single larger network.

2 Versioning feature for amazon S3 now available: http://aws.amazon.com/about-aws/whats-new/2010/02/08/Versioning-feature-for-amazon-s3-now-available/

3 ACPO (Association of Chief Police Officers) Good Practice Guide for Computer-Based Electronic Evidence: http://www.7safe.com/electronic_evidence/ACPO_guidelines_computer_evidence.pdf

4 The EU Data Protection Directive: http://eur-lex.europa.eu/LexUriServ/LexUriServ.do?uri=CELEX:31995L0046:en:NOT

Chapter 11
Forensics as a Service

Jon Rav Gagan Shende
EBSL Technologies International, USA

ABSTRACT

In today's dynamic information technology system, one area of tremendous focus and recent growth has been that of the cloud-computing model in its various offerings. With this growth, however, come new challenges within the realms of e-discovery and digital forensics, as we traditionally know it. The rapid growth of cloud-computing services and the rate of acceptance and use by consumers are on the rise. Conversely, both legitimate and illegitimate activates can leverage the resources of the cloud to execute their operations. With the challenges growing to combat computer crime that utilizes the cloud ecosystem and the ease of which a criminal activity may be hidden using a cloud service, it is imperative that a cloud provider dedicate time, training, budget, and other resources to provide the facility for forensic investigators as well as law enforcement to combat this threat. The Cloud-Forensics-as-a-Service (FRaaS) model introduced later in this chapter can provide a comprehensive cloud forensics solution for creating a repeatable system. Such a system could be implemented as a standard forensics operational model for deployment within the cloud ecosystem regardless of environments and client service lines.

INTRODUCTION

This chapter will introduce a process for implementing a living Forensics-as-a-Service (FRaaS) model that could augment a cloud-computing ecosystem to meet the needs of a forensics investigation in this environment.

DOI: 10.4018/978-1-4666-2662-1.ch011

One of the challenges with any cloud-computing ecosystem is the lack of a repeatable environment. This may lead to a deficiency of uniformity when conducting a forensic investigation within multiple cloud ecosystems. If an investigator assumes the challenge of conducting a forensic investigation within the Cloud, there will be a constant volume of information to process, which can overload any one monitoring tool.

Copyright © 2013, IGI Global. Copying or distributing in print or electronic forms without written permission of IGI Global is prohibited.

Within the forensics community, we know that for any digital forensics investigation, the factors of Volume, Evidence, and Time are of importance. We need to be cognizant of the fact that the volume of potential evidence has the potential for any evidence to be contaminated. The time to identify potential criminal activity is also critical. For example, a crime may be ongoing for an extended time unbeknownst to authorities.

Given the rise of cloud computing, we now have to contend with the volume of proportionally increasing data resulting in an increase in processes forensic investigators will have to analyze. As a result, a system needs to be implemented that can store multiple formats of data from numerous sources. Financial considerations of deploying this system as inexpensively as possible should be a priority. This system must be able to provide the option to scale out to meet needs as well as ensure that the processing capacity to support complex data analysis is made available, all within defined processes and budgetary requirements.

Additionally digital evidence must still satisfy the same legal requirements as that in a traditional forensic system. It must be *Authentic–Reliable–Complete–Believable–Admissible (ARCBA).* In this ecosystem, we also have to contend with the challenge of traceability given its assumed "vastness."

How then should we remediate such a situation? An ad-hoc data gathering process will have significant ramifications in the event that evidence retrieved is important to a future litigation process. The FRaaS model and its related tools aims to ensure that relevant evidence collected and presented will follow a defined and repeatable process when gathering, verifying and storing evidence or information.

As we traverse this chapter, we will discuss aspects of the FRaaS model, which will include a process that should be able to amalgamate relevant instance "data points." This process may then enable an investigator to concentrate on critical information that is applicable, actionable, and presentable for use in an e-discovery forum.

This model will provide a real-time tool, which should reduce the time to organize and filter information within the cloud ecosystem in which it is operating. Thus, allowing the investigator to manage instance flow and seamlessly tie relevant event data.

In summary, the FRaaS model aims to establish a cloud forensic investigative process, which can be implemented within a cloud ecosystem, integrated with tools that should ensure relevant information is gathered, verified, and stored in a manner that is forensically sound and legally defensible.

Before proceeding any further with our FRaaS model, a high-level recap on cloud computing follows. What exactly is cloud computing? Is it virtualization? Is it services that we accessed via a Web browser over the years, a new technology, or is it all of these rebranded from a marketing and revenue focused viewpoint? More importantly, how will these diverse components impact and affect a digital forensics investigation as society moves away from traditional infrastructures into a cloud ecosystem?

The industry term "Cloud Computing" started gaining notice when Google and IBM launched a university initiative to address Internet scale computing in 2007 (Google News, 2007). Some of the services that now comprise the cloud-computing ecosystem, have been evolving since the '90s. Some of its predecessors are grid computing and utility computing as well as the Software-as-a-Service offerings established a little over a decade ago.

We should leverage tested forensics methods, processes, and tools that have been in use within the traditional forensics environments where there is an alignment to a cloud system. However, there may be some challenges with this in the form of conformity, repeatability, and seamlessness of processes and techniques.

A cloud service's revenue lifecycle, simply stated, is a pay-as-you-go service. An end user can subscribe for any of the offered cloud services and based on service usage from the provider, will incur usage fees for consuming that particular service or series of services for its time in use. Once this service execution is completed, instances may be deleted with possibly no record kept. This of course will affect a forensic investigation, as there can then be a lack of traceability or evidence to investigate.

The National Institute for Science and Technology (NIST) defines cloud computing as "a pay-per-use model for enabling available, convenient, on-demand network access to a shared pool of configurable computing resources (e.g., networks, servers, storage, applications, services) that could be rapidly provisioned and released with minimal management effort or service provider interaction" (Mell & Grance, 2011).

Cloud Computing Services can be divided into the following three categories:

- **Infrastructure as a Service (IaaS):** (Tier 3 and Amazon EC2) While the subscriber does not control the cloud infrastructure they do have control over select portions of the network, e.g. firewalls, operating system, deployed applications and storage.
- **Platform as a Service (PaaS):** Was referred to in the early '70s as Framework as a Service. What is does is provide different combinations of services to a subscriber supporting an application development life cycle. For example, Google's App Engine, which will let a subscriber run Web applications on Google's infrastructure or Azure. In essence, the subscriber will use programming (e.g., dot Net, Java, python) and tools supplied by the service provider with no underlying responsibility for the cloud-deployed network, servers, operating system and storage, etc.
- **Software as a Service (SaaS):** Facebook and Salesforce.com comprise applications running on a cloud infrastructure that may be accessed via a Web browser interface. If we take into consideration that for a SaaS to exist it has to be run on a service which is built on an infrastructure, we can then draw a relationship between these cloud deployment service models. To illustrate, an Infrastructure-as-a-Service could be looked at as the foundation platform of a cloud computing service. Upon this PaaS and then SaaS is built.

Initially the FRaaS model was proposed for application at the PaaS level within the cloud-computing stack. However it may be applied to collect data across all platforms by the cloud provider.

Each cloud-computing environment will have unique properties and variations, which can affect the investigation whether from the cloud provider or end user interaction, as well as technical and non-technical issues (identified later in this chapter).

Recall that despite the whole cloud ecosystem and the challenges that may be perceived here, this system is still built on hardware and software systems. We should leverage our experience and knowledge of digital forensics within networks by looking at information communication channels and the client browser, as this is the first line of use for interacting with a cloud system. Also by looking within the virtual environments we can utilize information from the Virtual Machines (VMs) and the server applications.

From a real world experience this author saw the use of a third party virtual system Juniper VGW series within a private cloud deployment which provided "hypervisor-based security processing with visibility and comprehensive auditing of inter-VM and intra-VM communications and Netflow-style data collection" (Juniper Networks, 2010).

As cloud technologies evolve and mature, vendors and investigators need methods, tools, processes, and protocols tuned to the cloud ecosystem which may be implemented to assist in identifying relevant events that support the detection and analysis of criminal activity.

The NIST Special Publication 800-145 (Mell & Grance, 2011) identifies two main deployment models: the public and private cloud environments. Public clouds are available to the public who utilize this offering on the "pay-as-you-go model." The infrastructure is owned by the cloud provider offering services to its consumers.

A private cloud is typically exclusively tailored to an organization's needs and may not have the flexibility and scalability as a public cloud provider offering. However, it can be more controlled, this drawing from experience leading a security assessment for a client's private cloud environment. As a security practitioner, it is easier to conduct an investigation given a defined and repeatable infrastructure; this could be exploited within any environment that required digital forensics interactions.

Standardizing the design of a cloud infrastructure will contribute to the development of tools and processes that will lend to an easier digital forensics investigative process within the cloud-computing environment.

As of this writing, there is one private cloud model that has been designed and implemented to create a private cloud environment; this is the collaboration between VMware, Cisco, and EMC in the form of the VCE model (The Virtual Computing Environment Company).

A 2010 article by Shende mentioned that "within the digital forensic process where there is a no one-size-fits-all solution for a digital forensic examination, all forensic evidence must follow the forensic process of: Collection–Examination–Analysis–Reporting (also despite its environment), forensic evidence must:

- Be relevant to the issue at hand
- Be authentic
- Not be unfairly prejudicial, to not be hearsay or if hearsay, able to meet the requirements for an exception
- Be the original or duplicate of the evidence or able to meet an exception to that rule."

This article went on to discuss the challenge of reciprocity. "Digital forensics within the cloud computing environment can have legal implications within an international jurisdiction which will require collaboration; drawing from established relationships with legal entities in foreign countries and/or the establishment of new ones if possible. Additionally, "as with any live forensic examination another challenge will be the establishing of snapshots of the system in operation" (Shende, 2010).

A pertinent question for cloud vendors is, with regard to the requirements of time stamps for a digital forensics investigation, how will they ensure synchronized clocks across all their systems more so when we are looking at a globally spanning investigation? There is a real possibility that malware can be injected into the kernel space of a system. It is also possible that in turn it could alter software processes to modify data or system functionality to circumvent detection.

This malware may engage a system change to obfuscate evidence or delete pertinent data residues within a set period once certain requirements occur during an investigation. In light of such, we need a process in place in which a forensic examiner may be able to tell a change within an instance occurred. It is possible that a cloud provider could implement a system (protocols, tools, or processes) that may assure that such an event may be mitigated. Wolthusen proposed a theory, which is pertinent to the preceding statement. "Data may be present or available in a given configuration for a limited time or be staged through different levels of storage hierarchies; it is hence important to place bounds on events in question so as to be able to capture events of interest completely" (Wolthusen, 2009).

The Cloud and Data

Despite the technologies, processes, regulatory and other compliance requirements, at the end of the day a major aspect of the Cloud is about data and how interactions with such data occur. When considering the interactions with data, we should take into consideration the following four aspects:

Data at Rest traditionally signified data residing in file systems, distributed desktops, large centralized data stores, and databases with allocated disk space. It can also refer to data being used by the data owner but not moving through a network. When referencing data within the cloud ecosystem we could say that within this medium, data at rest refers to data stored within the distributed datacenters cloud providers rely on to manage their consumer data. This data can be directly managed by the cloud provider or housed for client interaction dependent on the cloud computing service in use.

Data in Motion historically implied data moving from one point to another such as through a network to an external point via email, instant messaging, Peer-to-Peer (P2P), FTP, VPN, and other communication methods.

In the traditional network this process is typically secured, however it may rely on multiple vendor products. Both communicating parties are said to be protecting the data once a third party is unable to eavesdrop on the ongoing communication. The result of this amalgamation is a complex and costly infrastructure that poses management and ongoing multiple challenges for end user training within IT departments.

Within the cloud ecosystem, there is a need for tools to secure communication within the cloud that can provide a defined and repeatable system that is secure, auditable, and compliant. This system should have centralized control, tracking and reporting modules. There should be a defined architecture and authentication process as well as a repeatable platform for all services.

Data in Execution refers to data that is loaded into memory and executed. Hejaz, Talh, and Debbabi (2009) presented a new technique for extracting information from windows physical memory, "the technique is based on analyzing the call stack and the security sensitive APIs. It allows extracting sensitive information that cannot be extracted by string matching-based techniques. In addition, the chapter leverages string matching to get a more reliable technique for analyzing and extracting what we called "application/protocol fingerprints." The technique detailed in this chapter aims to present a template for a future process that can be leveraged within the cloud ecosystem.

Data Storage and Disposition: One aspect of the Data Management Life Cycle (DMLC) which has an impact on a forensics examination is that of data storage and disposition. This is one area of the DMLC that does not get is just amount of attention within the corporate world. Storage and Disposition processes are often ill-defined or vague and if present in a policy, may not be effectively managed or have a quantified time period for storage prior to disposition based on criticality of data. Another drawback here is that there may not be an individual, group or third party with defined responsibilities on how to manage this disposition process. Therefore, assigning accountability in the event of an adverse incident poses a problem. As such we face the possibility of data held in this area being mis-handled and possibly having its integrity compromised by an inefficient process, individual or policy. This of course will have a negative impact if the need for a forensic investigation arises.

As mentioned earlier, if within the cloud ecosystem there is no need for an instance or the functions that were being executed in the instances are completed, it is quite possible that the instance will be deleted by the user. The potential for finding evidence in this sceanario is limited and will pose a challenge to an investigator. The FRaaS model addresses this drawback and is discussed in detail later in the chapter.

BACKGROUND

Researchers Birk and Wegener (2011) pointedly summarize the challenge of digital forensics within the cloud-computing ecosystem, "Cloud forensics constitutes a new and disruptive challenge for investigators."

The aim of this chapter is to present a model for a Cloud Forensics as a Service (FRaaS) offering that may be implemented in a cloud computing ecosystem be it from that of a cloud provider or within a private cloud environment. Of importance was a need to ensure that this model could meet the needs of "discoverable information."

Looking at e-discovery, we have been seeing corporate retention policies that direct to a process which state "retain all." However, there is a marked lack of proper data classification and ownership assignment. There can also be the scenario where within any system improper deletion occurs. This adds to operational cost and leads to unnecessary legal risk.

With the capacity and processing power available in the Cloud augmented by the ability to create, execute, and delete instances as needed, there is a heightened need to ensure that there are policies, processes and procedures in place to safeguard the legal and retention aspects of the e-discovery process. Such items could mitigate the potential for costly litigation, fines, losses, and other sanctions.

The proposed FRaaS model presents a process to ensure that instances within the cloud environment are authentic, accurate, and complete. With this model, we will utilize information extracted or stored by the FRaaS system, which should meet most e-discovery requirements.

In the current cloud environments, there are areas of concerns that need assurance from cloud provider and private cloud infrastructures.

Examples of such follows:

1. How will the confidentiality of consumer sensitive data which fall under the general areas of IT Security and Compliance have an impact on data held in a cloud environment and subsequently a forensics investigation?
2. The probability that there will be authorized instance deletion within the cloud ecosystem once an end-user no longer needs a service. Additionally, if existent, a Service Level Agreement (SLA), which may state the retention of data for a defined time may not add that instance storage is required or that dedicated instance storage after this period expires, is still required. Traditionally we define this for example a policy will state that firewall and Snort logs must be preserved for one year or router logs preserved for 6 months. Whilst with a private cloud ecosystem we could assemble an image of this traditional data, can we expect similar results taken from a cloud provider providing a public cloud service with numerous consumers?
3. Data may be destroyed according to a defined policy. This will most likely negate any future discovery related to evidence held within that particular instance.
4. The absence of clearly defined and repeatable processes that will ensure the integrity of consumer data at rest; this in the event of a subpoena for access to this data for an investigation (Shende, 2011).

When we consider a traditional digital forensic investigation, we are considering tangible, defined, and accessible resources for an investigator. With the cloud ecosystem, we are no longer running with a traditionally defined security perimeter. In addition, the cloud security perimeter is malleable, living and is impacted by devices at any place, on any device, where people will access an enterprise provided network, resources, and systems.

With connection occurring via the Internet in order to access data or services housed and interacted with from multiple systems and devices, a digital forensics investigator will now have to contend with data accessed via a Web browser for SaaS environment. These interactions may now cross international borders and may pose physical, legal, and technical challenges that could complicate an investigation.

With a traditional network forensics process, packet capture and analysis is important. Within the cloud ecosystem, an investigator will encounter an increased volume of data to process. This volume, which has the potential for exponential growth, will pose both physical and technical challenges for a forensics investigator or a forensics investigation team.

This increased volume can be a time and resource intensive process for a digital forensics investigation. Added to this are time and financial constraints. The added potential for error exists if a forensic investigator does not completely understand the cloud architecture affecting the current investigation. This includes areas such as complex linkages that bridge cloud services with an enterprise's system. Additionally, the investigator will also have to contend with how these systems impact an enterprise in terms of potential ingress points which leads to systems compromise.

A concern when faced with the task of conducting a forensic investigation within a virtualized system is that potential loss of data relevant to an investigation will occur once an image stops or a virtualized server shuts down. In this case, there may be a reduced chance of retrieving a specific image from its virtualized server. Grobauer and Schreck (2010) identified the following forensic challenges within the cloud-computing environment:

1. Separation of customer's data sources during evidence collection
2. Adapting forensic analysis methods to the cloud
3. Improving live analysis techniques
4. Improving log generation and analysis techniques.

To these, I would add:

- It is paramount that early dialogue, expectations, and cooperation from the cloud providers are established. This reduces the strain that will impact a chain of custody process for evidence within the cloud ecosystem.
- An investigator will face challenges in acquiring forensic data.
- We need to see more research and development for forensic tools needed to process data retrieved from the cloud ecosystem.
- There is the real chance the segmented cloud data extracted for investigation may lack key forensic metadata.

Having touched on the volume of data within the Cloud and its accompanying challenges with processing, I would argue that there is an advantage to using the cloud's processing and capacity to our benefits. Could a forensic investigator realize an advantage with the existence of instances within the cloud ecosystem?

An investigator would be able to take advantage of the potential for a repeatable process for data duplication and streamlined logging - more so with an automated centralized logging system in place that is capable of capturing data from existing system images. A real world argument is that of the criminal mind and the advantage the cloud could provide for exploiting malware or other criminal activities. For example, with as little as $50 a cloud environment could be established to execute a service or other activity, which may then be used to commit a crime.

Product offerings such as Amazon Web Services (AWS), an Amazon Machine Image (AMI) (either Linux or Windows) may be set up and processes executed to do whatever a user envisions within the confines of the virtualized world.

The cloud provider may not know that such an act is being committed until it is too late. An example of such an incident was the major hack of Sony's PlayStation Network that reportedly came via Amazon's Elastic Compute Cloud (EC2) service (Galante, Kharif, & Alpeyev, 2011). The attacker may own this type of attack environment potentially from the operating system up. With an IaaS, however, other hardware systems (IDS/IPS and firewalls) remain under the control of and belong to the cloud provider.

Within the cloud ecosystem (as demonstrated above) any tech savvy individual has the opportunity to access a collection of servers in geographically dispersed locations. These servers, easily provisioned with a few scripts, can be initiated with total anonymity for the user and maintained by utilizing false or stolen identity and financial tools.

Another factor now is the use of cloud *Application Programming Interface* (API) that can allow for "mobility" of a criminal operation executed by a handful of scheduled script calls or on alert of movement from law enforcement. If we take into consideration already existing evasion techniques such as Fast Flux DNS, leveraging cloud services for a criminal activity may pose a challenge in capturing and successfully prosecuting criminals.

One issue impacting an investigation within the Cloud identified by Garfinkel is that the "Use of the "Cloud" for remote processing and storage, and to split a single data structure into elements, means that frequently data or code cannot even be found" (Garfinkel, 2010).

One might argue that there are advantages for the case to adopt a cloud service; however, from a digital forensics point of view an understanding of the inherent limitations of such a system needs to be clearly mapped, properly reviewed and scoped by an enterprise's IT Security team.

This system then needs to be aligned with security and forensic policies with a process demonstrating how such an implementation will adapt and integrate with a current security model. Metrics gained from such a deployment may vary based on the selected cloud provider the enterprise chooses.

Gathered data then assists the enterprise security on how to mitigate the potential for compromise and other risk that can affect the enterprises operations stemming from this added environment. In turn then, the potentially exists to alleviate some of the pain points of a digital forensics investigation within the cloud computing ecosystem. We can further expand on this to address the place of a digital forensics policy specific to the cloud-computing environment as well as suggest processes to mitigate the shortcomings of remote forensic tools applied within this environment.

Keep in mind that a major challenge within the cloud-computing ecosystem is that local processing tools of cloud-stored data were not designed to process the format of data living within this environment. To illustrate, a digital forensic investigation within an IaaS should start with the virtual machine and its instances.

Over the last several years, there has been numerous digital forensics investigation frameworks presented for field applications (e.g. Selamer, Yusof, & Sahib, 2008). Developing on these, some areas for consideration as we evolve within the cloud ecosystem should be creating and defining a repeatable and industry standard for a Cloud Forensics Management System (CFMS) as well as a cloud forensic strategy. This strategy should be a subset of an IT Security strategy that is in turn part of a broader IT business operations strategy.

Additionally, we can now take into consideration the complexity and possible forensic roadblocks as well as the ever expanding IT Security concerns, which an investigator may encounter. For instance, a service such as Microsoft's new Azure offering, which includes mesh networking capabilities, might transform an end user's computer into a router. With this new offering, processing is split between the end-users local machine and Microsoft's servers. The location of processing volumes handled is dependent on the service application programmer (Windows Azure).

This chapter presents a Forensics-as-a-Service living model detailed in segments that can be integrated within a cloud computing environment and one, which will be able to assist with a forensic investigation once properly configured and deployed.

Issues, Controversies, Problems

As stated earlier there should be a connection between IT Security processes within the cloud environment and digital forensics. However, there must also be awareness and training programs for both end users in addition to the cloud providers. This should reference operational, industry compliance and regulatory impacts when running workloads in the Cloud.

Some areas of concern that impact conformity, repeatability and seamlessness as identified earlier are not clear definitions as of this writing; as are factors like cloud specific laws, court-approved methods geared to the cloud ecosystem, a repeatable operating procedure for investigations in the Cloud, and the part of the cloud provider operational processes that will impact a forensic examination. What is clear when looking at conducting an investigation within the cloud ecosystem is that the currently applied rules of investigation may not necessarily apply within this new environment.The FRaaS model aims to address some of these concerns.

Other challenges pertaining to the non technical aspect of a digital forensic investigation within the Cloud are "discovery of computation structure… attribution of data…stability of evidence…(and) presentation and visualization of evidence" as has been identified by Wolthusen (2009). Adding to the non-technical aspects of the investigation are jurisdictional and legal ramifications as it relates to the physical location of the cloud provider's servers that hold data pertinent to an investigation.

One question with regard to a cloud provider holding data as stated in the previous sentence is how can an investigator identify and track data that has geographic spread? One proposal, in the form of provenance is to look at identity authorizations in the Cloud pertaining to the issue of anonymous authentication and how it can impact a digital forensic investigation.

Clifford A. Lynch references provenance in his *When Documents Deceive* article (2001), Lynch proposed utilizing tools that lent to the determination of the source of identity of an individual or organization. The premise of this stood behind a metadata assertion, giving allowance for the development of trust in an individual or organizational entity's identity.

An article published by Foster, Zhao, Raicu, and Lu (2008) stated their opinion of provenance, which points out any data product's derivation history. They state that provenance includes "all the data sources, intermediate data products and the procedures that were applied to produce the data product. From a security assessment or investigation, we can see a parallel to that of an "audit trail."

Cloud consumers must open dialogue with their vendor regarding processes and protocols for successfully handling and managing of incidents. The processes and protocols need to be clearly established within the requirements portion when drafting their SLA.

Foster et al. (2008) also stated that with regard to the cloud there is the potential for existential challenges with an audit trail stemming from "issues such as tracking data production across different service providers (with different platform visibility and access policies) and across different software and hardware abstraction layers within one provider."

Researchers Lu, Lin, Liang, and Shen took the process of provenance as suggested by Lynch a step further and proposed that cloud computing should provide provenance "to record ownership and process history of data objects in the Cloud (on the assumption that) given its provenance, a data object can report who created and who modified its contents" (Lu, Lin, Liang, & Shen, 2010).

This of course will greatly affect the outcome of a digital forensic investigation in progress by providing some sort of accountability and a potential best-case process and user-related footprint. They also stressed in order to ensure the integrity of data; the data should be secured via a secure provenance method.

As such we could theorize that the concept of "secure provenance" should satisfy requirements of Unforgeability and Conditional privacy preservation where only a trusted authority has the ability to reveal the real identity recorded in the provenance.

Another challenge lies with that of reciprocity. Digital forensics within the cloud-computing environment can have legal implications within an international jurisdiction that will require cooperation from established relationships with legal entities in foreign countries and/or the establishment of new ones if possible.

Perhaps, one question we can ponder is whether or not there exists a necessity for establishing snapshots of systems in operation. In this case, one could question if utilizing a system that capitalizes on snapshots for such a globally distributed ecosystem may be a move toward a defined forensics system for the cloud-computing environment. This theory is used to map out the FRaaS model that can be further developed as cloud services mature and digital forensics tools in this area improve.

Shende (2010) identified some issues, which could affect evidence garnered from a digital forensic investigation conducted within a cloud service:

- A network forensics investigator is limited to tools on the box rather than the entire network; however, if a proper ISO is made of the machine image, then all the standard information in the machine image's ISO should be available as it would with any other server in a data center.
- Lack of access to network routers, load balancers and other networked components.
- No access to large firewall installations.
- There are challenges in mapping known hops from instance to instance which will remain static across the cloud-routing schema.
- System Administrators can build and tear down Virtual Machines (VMs) at will. This could influence an enterprises security policy and plans as new rules and regulations will require implementation as we work with cloud servers and services that are suspected of being compromised.
- An enterprises threat environment should be treated with the same mindset for the cloud ecosystem as it would for any exposed service that is offered across the Internet.
- With the cloud ecosystem, an advantage to forensics is the ability for a digital investigator to store extensive log files on a storage instance or in a very large database for easy data retrieval and discovery.
- An enterprise has to be open to the fact that there will be a risk of data being damaged, accessed, altered, or denied by the cloud provider.
- Routing information that is not already on "the box" will be difficult to obtain within this ecosystem.
- For encrypted disks, it would be feasible to spin up "n" cloud instances to help crack the encryption?

As stated earlier, regarding running time and capacity intensive workloads in the Cloud, we are challenged by budget, time, and resources. However, when we consider the fact that a majority of the processes involved in a digital forensics investigation may leverage a large-scale computing environment, a system that could efficiently and effectively leverage cloud resources can be advantageous to any one investigator. For example, a Hadoop on demand (Elastic Map/Reduce) platform (Foundation) can be utilized to analyze and correlate potential evidence contained within several terabytes (TB) of "potential evidence" (e.g. log files). This Hadoop cluster may be utilized in a time and investigation use specific period without the forensic investigator having to be overly concerned about budgeting constraints for associated hardware and software.

The advantage of processing power can be seen in the instance of having to crack an encryption algorithm as well. For example, High Performance Computing (HPC) on Amazon Web Service (AWS) could provide a digital forensic investigator a specifically configured system that is designed for conducting a forensic investigation by providing the requisite processing power in a cost-effective manner.

As a final point, within a cloud FRaaS system, an investigator can leverage the sheer volume of this environment to scale processes across numerous machines in lieu of having to queue for the limited available local platforms to process data as per the traditional digital forensics systems.

Since the cloud ecosystem will most likely span international borders at different times there needs to be a familiarity with cross border regulatory compliance, as well as, local and international regulations and laws. There should also be a defined process that both parties conform to and provides guidance on how to investigations, liability, and affected business processes are managed. These processes may also segway into the realms of risk assessments, risk management and risk mitigation or controls, which fall within the realm of another topic.

Solution: The Forensics-as-a-Service Model (FRaaS) Summary

While the FRaaS model is not all encompassing and able to address every aspect of conducting an investigation within the cloud-computing environment presently, the model does address several of the major concerns identified within this chapter.

As the discussion thus far has indicated, FRaaS model that is proposed will impact digital forensics and data integrity within the cloud ecosystem.

Within the branches of IT Security, when it comes to data, there is a growing awareness of an entity's ability to assess, classify, define and assign ownership for specific volumes of data in any environment. Capitalizing on this momentum to create a "forensic parallel path" for data investigation and utilize cloud-computing resources to gain processing capacity and benefits of scale is advantageous.

This FRaaS model should easily integrate with a cloud providers security processes since these processes are configured to collect, classify, and correlate large volumes of security related data. Said data may include data imported automated scanning tools, honeypot systems, security analysts and clients. The "forensic parallel path" can then be utilized solely for forensic purposes and follow on the same security mind-set but in a forensics investigation light.

For data classified as critical to operations, which play an important part in the event of an incident, it will be necessary to have a system, which has the ability to set and leverage benchmarks. On another level, this system should have the ability to analyze large volumes of log data obtained from access logs, system logs, infrastructure updates or modifications and service implementation changes. Access security levels and privileges within the model will have to be defined within an SLA and conform to mutually agreed upon policies and defined metrics.

When we start delving into the areas of remote forensics with the chance that we will possibly cross borders then it is important that the cloud provider client's management team as well as legal counsel promote privacy awareness within the enterprise. This must include an education program that covers conformity with privacy laws in jurisdictions where there will be cause for investigation coupled with relevant processes to be implemented or impacted if in place. Based on the FRaaS model, a cloud provider should execute this process in-house or allow a client's forensics team the option to executive the model remotely via a secured connection.

Another important factor is how a cloud provider designs, tests and implements their incident response strategy. This is of importance to any client, as such a strategy should address identification and notification with options for remediating any issues resulting from unauthorized access to data and alerting. The manner with which an investigation is initiated should also be considered. The FRaaS will provide multiple opportunities for notifications that may be configured based on cloud provider, client or both cloud provider and client policies and requirements. Clear definitions of what clients categorize as incidents and questionable activity are included

After an investigator logs into the FRaaS, any data tagged for investigation can be easily integrated into internal monitoring tools. The aim is to prevent data silos and unnecessary complexity in a cloud forensics investigation. This will enable an investigator to maintain a streamlined and simple reporting system. Such a system should be compliant with forensics, legal, and compliance requirements that can be drawn and integrated from a centralized dashboard system.

To summarize the argument for this model, based on some challenges and concerns identified earlier, it could be stated that:

- With the cloud ecosystem, forensic investigators can ease the facilitation of a forensic examination via the promise of data consolidation and additionally capitalize on the processing and scalability of cloud services.
- An investigator should work with a cloud provider to gain access to and leverage dedicated cloud storage, to overcome storage, and if needed archival capabilities, to preserve the integrity of metadata.
- Cloud providers should be proactive in combating computer crimes and dedicate a defined set of resources for forensic purposes solely within their ecosystem.
- As part of an offering, a cloud provider should offer instance snapshots at defined and agreed upon time frames (per an SLA and policies).
- There ought to be a process to verify instances as free from defect. Once this is accomplished there should be an agreed upon time period to retain and retire these instances as the volume grows per a Cloud Security Policy requirement.
- As a verification point, it is advisable that a process exists to retain sampling of instance snapshots as volume grows.
- There must be a cloud forensic policy that defines processes and methods for evaluating these samples for integrity prior to selection for archiving by the cloud provider.
- One major non-technical challenge within a cloud environment and the forensics process is that of maintaining a proper chain of custody. Due to the FRaaS model process oriented and modular design, combined with the items listed above (instance collection process, repository for instances, etc.) this system will allow automated and easier tracking of information as it traverses the gather, analyze and report phases during an investigation.

However, before we proceed, Pollitt (McKemmish, et al., 2008) said the following (which every investigator should always keep in mind), "Despite the application of sophisticated tools, the forensic process still relies on the examiner's knowledge of the technical aspects of the specimen and understanding of the case and the law."

When this FRaaS model was designed the following items were considered:

- A potential lack of access to network routers, load balancers and other networked components and/or large firewall installations by the digital forensic investigator(s).
- Challenges from mapping known hops within instances with respect to the cloud-routing schema.
- The maturity of an enterprise's security policy and how it addresses cloud security requirements.
- Technical and non-technical data risks, e.g. data damaged, accessed, altered or denied access to by the cloud provider.
- Data that fail to replicate across instances by some means.
- Being able to capture snapshots of a cloud consumer's virtual instance for offline analysis.
- An ability to interface with multitenant incident response tools (application-level firewalls, proxies, and centralized logging systems).

An important consideration was to ensure that this system could be deployed in any cloud environment regardless of systems in place. The model's design takes into consideration the potential for compatibility with relevant incident detection and analysis tools, which can be employed by both cloud provider and clients. However in the case of a SaaS system, we need to establish a definitive process for instance benchmarking and retiring, giving consideration to the state of instance flux that we may encounter within this environment.

In designing this model, one premise was that a cloud forensic lifecycle for any investigation should mirror that of a traditional system as close as possible. Within this ecosystem however it is suggested that two new phases (Alert and Security) as possible add-ons be included:

Identify, Collect, Sample, Verify, Alert/Security, Preserve, Analyze, Present; the Alerting segment and a Security segment should be integrated where Alerting is aligned with the Security segment. For the FRaaS to be successfully implemented there must be a connection with cloud security and change management processes and personnel.

One of the motivations behind the design of this model was considering the reality of structural differences between physical and virtual environments, which comprises the cloud-computing ecosystem. From a digital forensics view, one much touted concern is compromising the integrity of evidence with the likelihood that instance snapshots can be copied or moved with limited detection. Another is constraint oversight when it comes to user access and constraints impacting data within instances.

This model is designed to address a majority of the concerns identified throughout this chapter. Of note is that this is a living model and once deployed first in a test environment will be subject to modifications and updates. The initial environment for such a tool will be within a cloud provider environment; it is best served with a dedicated forensics segment. The cloud provider has the resources, bandwidth, and capacity to implement a test and subsequently a full production environment for the FRaaS system.

Investigator authentication will occur at the juncture of the FRaaS service held within the cloud provider's dedicated forensics environment. However, there can be an additional module for an experienced cloud provider client forensics team to remotely access forensics servers held within the cloud provider environment.

The FRaaS model initializes with a proprietary Instance Gathering Process (IGP) that will start the IGP system and the instance benchmark and verification system in two scenarios. The first will be that of a client requesting this FRaaS service as part of their service contract; the second being the cloud provider offers the FRaaS as an add-on service for clients.

In both scenarios there must be a defined, tested and implemented cloud forensic policy and SLA in place with plans for compliance testing schedules, whether set or random and per SLA terms.

With either scenario, each client is given a unique FRaaS identifier for future reference. Once the unique FRaaS client identifier is assigned, the benchmark system can be initialized upon client signup completion and verification. After this is completed, a "ground zero" snapshot is created to act as the initial benchmark. The IGP will have granular access controls in place and metrics that will make reporting an easy process.

To make compliance reporting simple and foolproof, one needs to monitor internal enterprise applications and SaaS applications side-by-side, from a centralized dashboard. As shown in the following sections, the complete model displayed in Figure 1 is broken up into 6 segments to better demonstrate its flow and usage. A detailed walk-through is also included for clarity.

The FRaaS: A Breakdown

This model starts with an Instance Gathering Process (IGP) (see Figure 1). This system includes securely developed and tested software environments to effectively manage and prevent information leakage. The IGP at will have built in modules to address timestamps, hashing tools, tools for aggregating Access Control and centralized log monitoring records.

With regards to timestamps, the system could use The Network Time Protocol (NTP)[1] with main

Figure 1. Forensics as a service (FRaaS) model

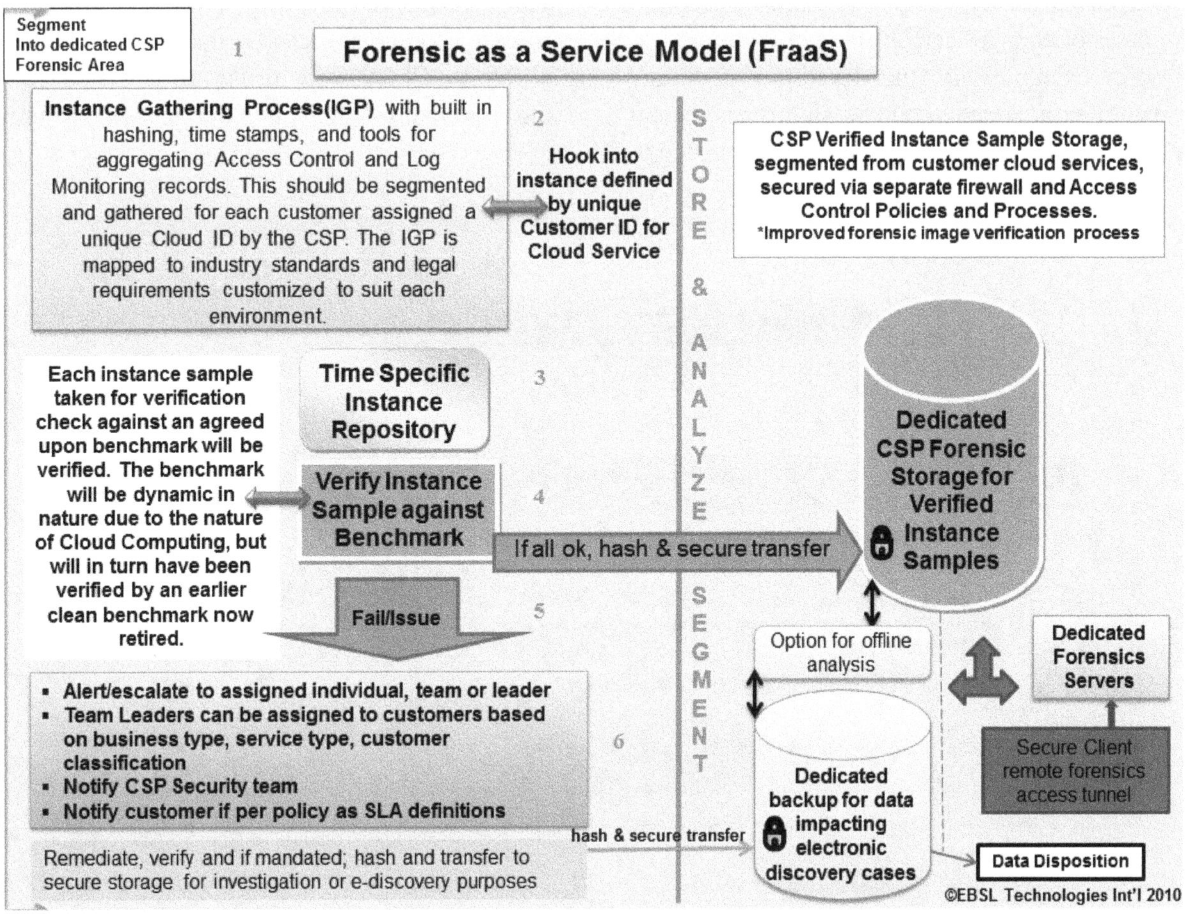

and relay servers. Any system that will touch evidence will be configured to this system to ensure accurate time stamping as we engage in an investigation. The cloud provider should also use the same system to ensure seamless time configurations across all systems and security logs (Net-Flow, Web, centralized logging systems, etc.).

Of importance is the fact that the IGP does not rely on host operating system but rather runs on a separate OS within the segregated FRaaS system. With the option of a smart connector, an investigator can bypass the cloud provider operating system upon which the virtual environment is built and conduct a reading of the physical disk. The software development cycle follows a strict software development process, with security and testing consideration having strong input. This segment followed a strict security process where Development, QA, and production environments are configured in a manner that allows seamless updates or changes across all environments.

For example with the development of any custom authentication and session management schemes processes are documented and tested to ensure that proper attention is given to potential flaws in areas such as logout, timeouts and password management (see Figure 2 for an overview of the FRaaS platform and the authentication mechanism).

The FRaaS platform depicts at a high level how the system will function with the Application Programming Interface (API)/Graphical User Interfaces (GUI) components at the top layer. This is supported by the second layer services segments where we have policies, security mapping metrics and calculated risk value data.

Due to the ever-growing volumes and types of data, the author believes that we will need to filter data based on large file types in certain circumstances to make the analysis more manageable and specific to an investigation.

Following on the second layer, we have the Cloud Forensics Operational Platform (CFOP), which contains the various import, analysis, process, storage and case management engines. Within the CFOP, we will also see a defined Case and Forensics Lifecycle management system

Figure 2. The FRaaS platform

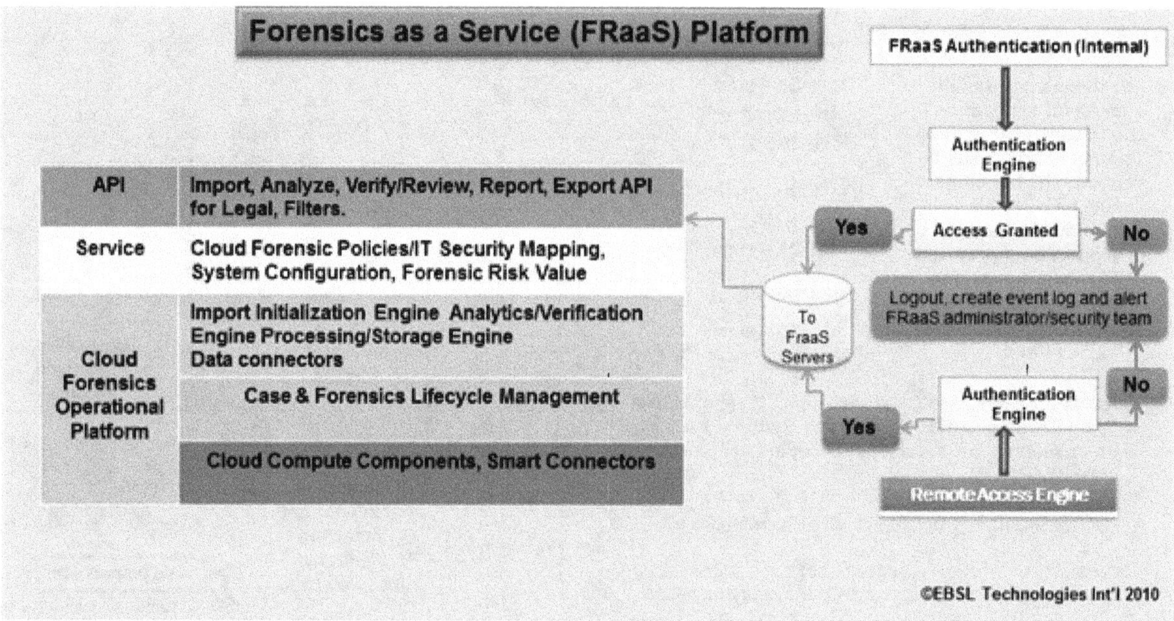

augmenting accountability, transparency, and the automation of the cloud forensics process.

Closing out this platform, we have the hardware and software systems that contribute to the FRaaS with smart connectors, which can allow automated or integrated interaction, e.g. (importing log data) with security, legal, e-discovery, and risk components.

The FRaaS application manages data movement from the time of initiating a connection into the instance to migrating into the verification module. Built in automation will ensure transparency in terms of what data sources are been queried. In addition, once there is a need for a pipeline to transmit data the transport functions are configured to protect traffic across all "data in motion" areas by continuously maintaining SSL/TLS protocols.

The emphasis on security as touched on above is to demonstrate that when developing this model the development team works closely with IT Security teams to ensure the integrity of data that will be used in an investigation.

With regard to authorizations into this system, we created two primary user types and one secondary user type with restricted access. Authentication credentials for both types are separated via a logical firewall as well as stored physically, from each other.

Of the primary user type, there is a further subdivision as follows. The first is an administrator who has root access, the ability to add or delete a user and can track access, usage, and time spent within the FRaaS modules. The other will be an investigator who has full control of the system except those functions configured for the administrator.

Both primary users will have clearly defined roles and privileges integrated with role-based encryption polices. For security purposes, the author recommends two unique administrators. This in the event that a client FRaaS administrator get locked out of the system via remote access the other administrator can reset the password.

Finally, we have the secondary user type that can be created for an analyst, remote for law enforcement personnel on approval from a cloud provider client, or other supportive roles reporting to the primary investigator.

As stated earlier, each client will have a unique FRaaS identifier and that there will be a separate and secured storage area as shown in Figure 1. In order to ensure the security of storage encryption keys within the FRaaS each unique identifier and its related storage key will be stored in an encrypted area within the FRaaS infrastructure. It will reside in an encrypted state and governed by the FRaaS administrator. This step will augment access control in that only an administrator will be able to access the instances stored within the secured storage area.

For example if the client decided to utilized the system via remote access then the cloud provider FRaaS administrators will not be able to access areas secured by the client's FRaaS administrator without first knowing the administrator password.

Another built in security feature of the IGP is a smart filter that is configured detects and block any attempts to initiate an unauthorized session with the IGP. This filter will log any attempt to access or change the functionality of the IGP and if a session is not in operation a shutdown sequence will initiate with an automated alert sent to the FRaaS administrator and/or designated security personnel.

Of note within the area of Access Control, until recently Access-Control-as-a-Service for the cloud ecosystem posed a significant challenge; however, with the advent of Microsoft's Windows Azure Active Directory (Microsoft, 2010), we should expect to see improved control and reporting for Access Control within the Cloud.

It has been argued that a significant risk to a cloud system may result from flaws within the cloud architecture, system, or operator errors made during system hardening procedures or other functional oversights.

With the IGP and the dedicated segment for storage and analysis of data for digital forensics purpose, these concerns can be recognized, managed, and controlled. While there may be operational errors as stated, clearly documented cloud security policies and tested processes could contribute to the integrity of the initial forensic instance benchmark. Any event that may impact the cloud ecosystem one in client execution can be expected to have minimal adverse events on the FRaaS segment as the FRaaS will be independent of the end-user (client) cloud computing operational ecosystem.

Within this first module relevant cloud consumer information may be imported from the cloud provider customer database on account sign up. This process may be configured to auto populate once the consumer's information is verified by the cloud provider to save on time and resources. Each consumer will then be assigned a unique cloud forensic ID based on their customer ID provided by the cloud provider and a ranking of forensic risk assigned based on data or actions being executed within the cloud provider's cloud.

Once the IGP process initiates and integrates into its assigned customer instance with the unique forensic identifier, criterion that will be met such as forensic risk value as well as level of service must conform to that defined in an applicable forensics policy, regulations, and compliance metrics that are specific to each consumer as defined in a SLA. The IGP also includes secure add-ons that are designed to be easily configurable for monitoring and reporting that comply with data privacy and industry regulatory compliance requirements as well.

After the IGP completes its primary function, a FRaaS pre-configured automation process goes on to capture target instances and transfer then to a time specific repository where a verification process is initiated.

This storage area is a temporary holding point for the captured data that is held untouched by any other mechanism as it passes onto to the verification process. Instances are held here and sent out to the verification module in a first in first out process for tracking and tagging purposes.

Once this verification is completed a hash is taken and logged. Although cloud storage will allow for the opportunity of storage scaling, any one investigation will only require specific or finite data for presentation in a court of law as evidence. With this in light, the author decided to perceive storage as within this stage of the FRaaS. In light of this, a benchmarking process becomes important in managing, storing, and analyzing potential evidence gleaned from the instances gathered.

To further expand on this argument we could assume that within this phase storage requisites required to store instances can grow in volume, becoming unmanageable after some time collecting instances. By leveraging the FRaaS benchmarking process to verify instances as uncorrupted and retire them after a set time period. The retired instances will be replaced by more current and verified instances based on prior benchmarking data, which in turn will be retired and replace in an Instance Benchmarking Verification Lifecycle (IBVL).

This process will reduce the amount instances that an investigator may have to analyze and the length of time he/she will have to go back in time to search for anomalies or hints at a potential malicious activity commencing.

By implementing the IBVL then, an investigator can be assured that the integrity of retired instances meets legal, regulatory, compliance, content and business metrics. The investigator may then focus on those instances that cause alerts or fail responses within the FRaaS verification process; those instances that have been flagged, tagged securely transferred and stored in an encrypted state in a dedicated storage per a predefined forensics policy.

On a side note: It is quite probable that the cloud provider's internal security and forensics team may have already initiated and completed an investigation on these rogue instances and may have 1) cleared them as false positives or 2) completed other security and forensics actions as warranted and documented results in a findings report (see Figure 3).

Once instances have been verified based on set parameters and criteria they will be transferred to a cloud provider storage area set aside specifically computer crime investigations. Transmission to storage will be encrypted in motion and any data held in storage or at rest, will be held in an encrypted state. One process the FRaaS will use within the storage segment is metadata tagging which will help in classification as mentioned earlier.

For additional security and as a step to maintain the integrity of any data in this process, the encryption keys will be stored separately as mentioned earlier.

Once an instance sample is verified and prior to storage, it will be hashed then sent to storage.

If however the instance exhibits any variation from a benchmark it is being verified against the system will hold it for further investigation and an automated alert sent out to IT Security, Forensics and the Legal teams.

The FRaaS will incorporate an incident ticketing integration system to track this alert as well as seamlessly exchange alert data between the FRaaS alert and the cloud provider Security and Monitoring system. This can also be configured to update an automated change management system if the alert is valid. The cloud provider's security and risk management team should take corrective action as needed; however, the FRaaS log will establish a unique identifier that will provide a point of reference between systems. This will provided a baseline for synchronizing any ticketing systems managed by the cloud provider, allow seamless data processing and tracking for reporting purposes.

This area will also be segmented from the "regular" cloud environments and will include additional security (physical and logical) and access control policies and processes to enhance it safety. There will also be an automated process with manual oversight if needed to retire instances base to a specifically set time criteria under a data disposition operational module.

In designing a tool deployed within a browser for gathering and analysis, a REST-compliant API (Fielding, 2000) may be leveraged in tandem with policies and technologies designed to meet privacy, security, regulatory and compliance metrics. This segment could be aligned within the service layer of the FRaaS platform as depicted in Figure 2.

Although one can argue the challenges of security with REST (as with any Web-service it is

Figure 3. FRaaS-time specific repository

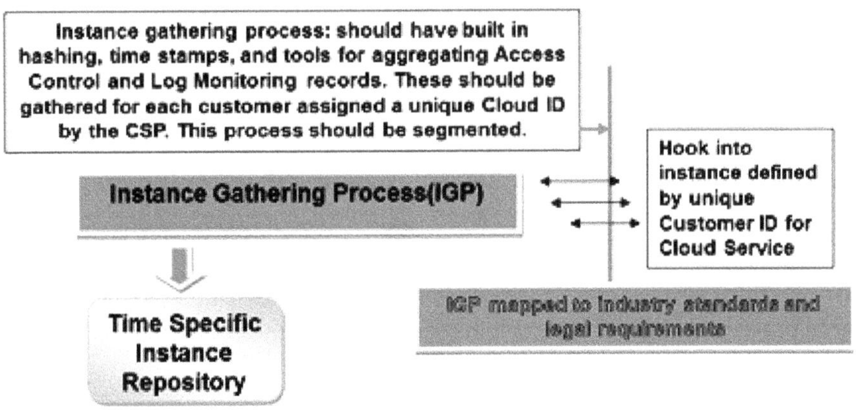

vulnerable to the same attack vectors as standard Web applications, such as injection attacks, Cross-Site Scripting (XSS), broken authentication, and cross-site request forgery attacks).

However, API security and secure design methodologies are a key step in the software design process for all software modules within the FRaaS. In light of this one step taken to ensure secure transfer and instance or other data integrity lies within the communication between the FRaaS modular applications and a Web Services REST API server through Secure Sockets Layer (SSL) encryption (see Figure 4).

Protection against any unauthorized operations is augments with the utilization of a FRaaS user account-specific token. There are detailed processes that demonstrate the set-up, configuration and management of this process; however it is not within the scope of this discussion.

The processes suggested when designing security for REST APIs were based off OWASP recommendations and can be summarized by the following quote from Reese (2009):

1. All REST API calls must take place over HTTPS with a certificate signed by a trusted CA. All clients must validate the certificate before interacting with the server.
2. All REST API calls should occur through dedicated API keys consisting of an identifying component and a shared, private secret. Systems must allow a given customer to have multiple active API keys and de-activate individual keys easily.
3. All REST queries must be authenticated by signing the query parameters sorted in lower-case, alphabetical order using the private credential as the signing token. Signing should occur before URL encoding the query string.

Both storage types in the model are encrypted and follow a strict access control policy. Regarding storing user names and passwords as has been mentioned earlier one encryption system considered was the OWASP—Salted Hash Password Technique to store usernames and passwords in a file (IBM Developerworks, 2010), which was then stored in an encrypted state in a secured location.While this technique is good within the test environment we are considering a multipart autentication process to replace this mechanism in the near future. This segment of the FRaaS will also offer a module to exfiltrate data for offline analysis.

Due to the potential volumes within the cloud computing ecosystem and the growth of big data the storage aspects of this model may be best served by building on Hadoop.

One of the more appealing features of a Hadoop system for deployment within the FRaaS storage aspect is that both HDFS and MapReduce are designed to continue to work in the face of system failures.

Historically there have been causes for concern when using Hadoop within a cloud storage setting. An example of such is the potential for a high machine failure rate and an impact on availability. To discuss the process to remediate this is beyond the scope of this chapter and "a metadata replication based solution to enable high availability," has been presented by Feng Wang et al. (2009).

Once the information stored is no longer needed whetherr they are, expired per SLA metrics or retired on instruction from the client or a forensics investigator, it is up to the client to instruct the cloud provider on disposition. This however could be an automated process managed directly by the cloud provider it a disposition clause is written to a cloud forensic policy and or a specific SLA.

The FRaaS will have a module that will allow for a simple and transparent data disposition module that could be managed by an API and completed in a managed time period dependant on the volume of data to be disposed.

Figure 4. FRaaS-transfer to dedicated secured storage if sample ok

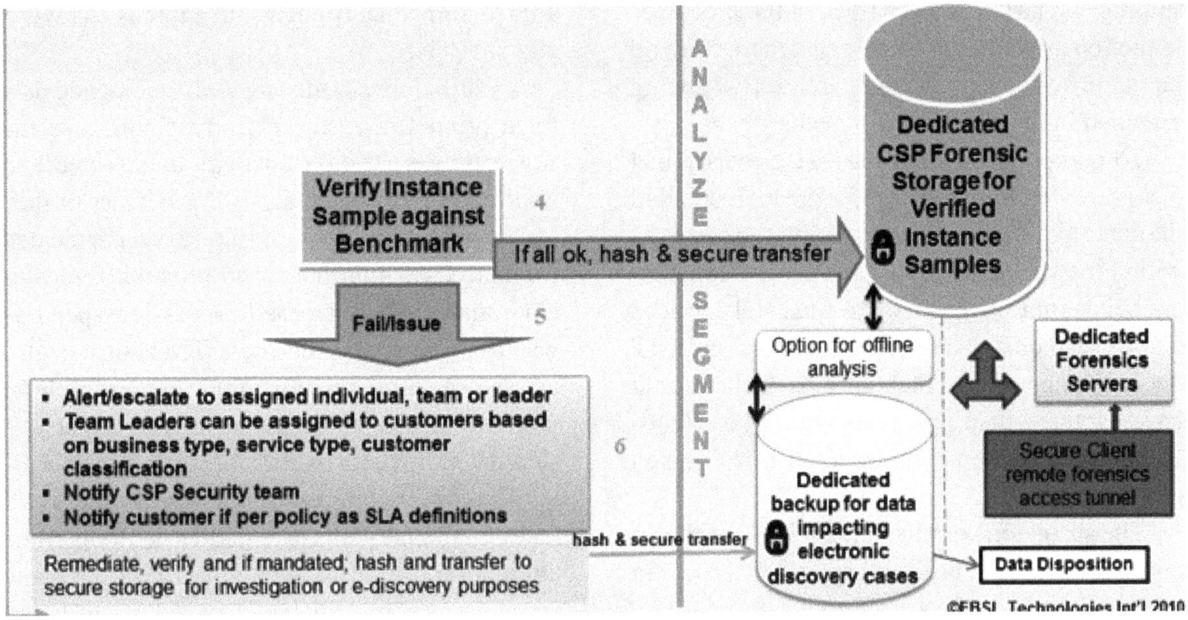

FRaaS Case Study

Company Background

EBSL Global Services is a fictional global services organization that specializes in financial services, and consumer financial information management. The corporation utilizes proprietary algorithms to gather, analyze, and deliver key financial data that clients utilize for mergers and acquisitions, investments and for financial risk valuations on both corporate and private citizens.

The company employs cutting edge technologies, policies and procedures to ensure that it assures the security, integrity and availability of critical l information it processes on a daily basis. Due to its ever-increasing needs for processing power and capacity in order to meet these and its business and budgetary requirements the company decided to move some services to the cloud.

EBSL Global Service closed a SLA for both Infrastructure and limited Software-as-a-Service, services with a Cloud provider six months ago. Part of what was attractive about this cloud provider was their availability of datacenter both in the US and the UK and their knowledge of US-EU Safe Harbour and the EU Directive as EBSL Global processes large amount of data that is considered *Personally Identifiable Information* (PII).

Business Situation

With a large number of instances in use, it was a challenge for the EBSL Global Services security team to get assurance that systems were kept up to date as well as configured properly. Although the cloud provider had a defined cloud security policy and possessed an ISO 27001 certification one concern was that in the event of some malicious event occurring, e.g. injecting a root kit to monitor or capture sensitive information executing within the cloud environment the security engineers at EBSL Global Services needed to keep track of which changes had been made, when and by whom and ensure that internal provided attestation that all was in accordance with corporate policy. As the volume of instances grew or instances were simply deleted to better utilize the cloud services, the CISO found it was becoming very time consuming and harder to keep track of the processes in motion as well as to be sure that there were no human errors or potential malicious activity being executed in his cloud environments.

To compound his concern, IT Security had just presented him with a report, which detailed the outcome of consumer complaints the occurred within the last ten days, around private consumers being shut off from some financial services due to suspicious activity on their accounts. IT Security reported a potential breach that could have captured data processes within the cloud-computing environment and zeroed in on one area of service therein.

The suspicion was that a malicious insider or outsider may have utilized aspects of the cloud service to execute their crime.

The CISO who had been notified of a pilot program at the cloud provider for a Forensics-as-a-Service, add on service had signed a SLA specific to this feature, due to the sensitive and mission critical nature of the business.

Solution

By leveraging the FRaaS residing in a segmented and dedicated environment when a request came in from the CISO of EBSL Global the cloud provider's forensics team should be able to leverage real-time instance gathering capabilities and its forensics analysis features. Due to its intuitive user interface the cloud provider's forensics team can review the automated tracking and verification process and provide the EBSL Global Service forensics team with an initial report that follows a chain of command and defined and authenticated tracking process. If needed, the cloud provider security team can provide remote access to a dedicated storage area where encrypted instances that either failed the automated verification process or violated an element of the cloud forensics policy and was placed for manual review. Due to the presence of this storage area, the team should be able to immediately engage in a forensics review and analysis.

By utilizing the filtering tool, the flagged data for a pre-defined time period (in this case the suggestion is 30 days out) can be selected and imported for offline analysis if necessary or they can simply utilize the forensics servers dedicated for analysis within the cloud provider forensics environment for increased processing speed as well as lower operational cost. The team can also use the same process for importing a sample of verified data for the same time period that was stored within the repository for verified instances.

The concern that any digital forensic team will face a challenge with current forensics tools when attempting to process data dispersed over many storage systems, can be managed by utilizing the verification/benchmark and alert/fail utilities built into the FRaaS model. This will allow an investigator to access a defined and finite subset of data with which to commence an investigation. Data stored in an encrypted state and any access in this state verified at a granular level, with data verified or flagged from any location and stored centrally. Also within the FRaaS Instance Gathering Process (IGP) is module that focused solely on log data and on cloud provider client instance activation and usage; can import data from a centralized logging station, cloud provider access logs, cloud provider NetFlow logs, and the Web server virtual machine.

Given the proposed design of the FRaaS with its transparent, automated, secure authentication and encrypted environments the following concerns raised by the legal team can be allayed. Due to the automated IGP, analysis and processing modules, a pattern for an electronic chain of custody can be established throughout the FRaaS model *(The cloud provider was chosen because it housed data enters both in the US and the UK the concern of jurisdiction and conformity with regulatory and privacy concerns were not an issue.).*

- Can we verify that the cloud provider provided a complete and authentic forensic copy of the data requested?
- Is there a defined and repeatable process that can assure the authenticity and integrity of the data and can this process be trusted?
- What assurance do we have that the cloud provider's forensic analyst/technician and the tools used to gather data is trusted?
- Can the cloud provider provide us with a record of who had access to our data, and how access control was enforced?
- How does the cloud provider provide assurance on timestamps consistently across any system involved in this investigation?

Benefits

- Manageable costs during the entire forensics process due to the presence of the implemented FRaaS system.
- Any access to instances/data stored or processed within the FRaaS involves defined user authentication and authorization and a record of access kept in a hashed log.
    - The FRaaS model requires segregated key management and role based policies, to ensure separation of duties between cloud provider administrators, client administrators and users as well as any third party authorized individuals such as law enforcement.
- The presence of the forensics policies and the ability to configure, monitor, and update modules, processes, and policies with the help of automation provides assurance that the cloud provider with its FRaaS system will provide time conscious support during an investigation. This can address no technical legal concerns.
- The instance gathering process and benchmarking process will be able to reduce the time spent by the investigator who was able to concentrate of those instances that causes and alert or failed a benchmark approval.
- EBSL Global internal forensic analyst should be able to utilize the secured remote application authenticate within the cloud services and gain direct access into the FRaaS system. Once remotely in, the investigator was able to leverage the built-in reporting and analytic tools for parsing, searching and extracting information stored within the dedicated storage for instances that caused an alert without interrupting or having to touch their running cloud services.
- The concerns of forensic metadata from the cloud provider environment can be allayed by the module that implements "the instance verification against an established sample" process, which is then securely transmitted and stored in an encrypted form. Access control to this stored data is heavily monitored and controlled. The argument here is that verified instances stored securely without evidence of a crime can be used to support a forensic investigation, once it has been established a crime has been committed.

FUTURE WORK

The author is currently working on additional stages of the FRaaS with EBSL Technologies develop this model into a system that can be deployed into a cloud provider environment.

Within the SaaS ecosystem we see a challenge with the dynamic nature of instances within this environment which will differ from instances used within other environments. A potential study can be done to analyze this ecosystem and provide metrics to measure the rate of change of instances in comparision to other environments e.g. IaaS.

CONCLUSION

With the advent and growth potential of cloud computing services compounded by the rate of acceptance and use by consumers, cloud providers and forensics investigators need to subscribe to a defined and repeatable process. Such a process should augment an investigation within the Cloud as well as be able to identify, extract, and process irrefutable evidence that can be presented in a court of law. In light of this, such a process must be able to leverage the resources of the Cloud to execute their operations and dedicate resources to facilitate a forensics investigation within this environment.

Additionally, the growing challenge to combat computer crime that utilizes the cloud ecosystem is compounded by the ease which criminal activity may be hidden using a cloud service. It is imperative that cloud providers take a proactive stance and dedicate time, training, budget with necessary resources to provide the facility for forensic investigators as well as law enforcement to combat this threat.

The FRaaS model correctly implemented has the potential to provide a comprehensive cloud forensics solution, creating a repeatable system that can be deployed within the cloud-computing ecosystem. Such a system should be implemented as a standard forensics operational model for deployment within the cloud ecosystem regardless of environments and client service lines. The model as depicted above while by no means a final product is a system that any cloud provider can implement within their cloud environment. This model may be deployed as a dedicated offering in its service offerings for its consumers. Having such a model will only serve to enhance investigation times, reduce the impact on the cloud provider assets, personnel that will need to be engaged to respond to a court order and with a proper service metric implementation ensure a quick Return on Investment (ROI) for the cloud provider. Such a system will also provide assurance to consumers of an additional process in place, which will augment a potential investigation into a suspected crime that may affect their business operations.

In summary, the FRaaS can also be looked at technically as, a dedicated resource to assist the forensics and legal community in investigating, gathering evidence, and prosecuting computer crimes. From a business vantage, it will provide assurance that the cloud provider is investing in processes to ensure that in the event of an incident, cloud providers are proactively taking steps to expedite an investigation and reduce the financial and reputational impact on their client operations.

REFERENCES

Amazon Web Services. (2012). *High performance computing (HPC) on AWS*. Retrieved from http://aws.amazon.com/hpc-applications/

Birk, D., & Wegener, C. (2011). *Technical issues of forensic investigations in cloud computing environments*. Retrieved May 2012, from http://code-foundation.de/stuff/2011-birk-cloud-forensics.pdf

Council, P. S. (2012). *PCI SSC data security standards overview*. Retrieved from https://www.pcisecuritystandards.org/security_standards/

European Union Law. (1995). *Data protection*. Retrieved from http://eur-lex.europa.eu/LexUriServ/LexUriServ.do?uri=CELEX:31995L0046:en:NOT

Fielding, R. T. (2000). *Architectural styles and the design of network-based software architectures*. (Unpublished Doctoral Dissertation). University of California. Irvine, CA.

Foster, I., Zhao, Y., Raicu, I., & Lu, S. (2008). Cloud computing and grid computing 360-degree compared. In *Proceedings of Grid Computing Environments Workshop*, (pp. 1-10). Chicago, IL: IEEE Grid Computing Environments.

Foundation, T. A. (2012). *Hadoop map reduce*. Retrieved from http://hadoop.apache.org/mapreduce/

Galante, J., Kharif, O., & Alpeyev, P. (2011). Sony network breach shows Amazon cloud's appeal for hackers. *Bloomberg News*. Retrieved from http://www.bloomberg.com/news/2011-05-15/sony-attack-shows-amazon-s-cloud-service-lures-hackers-at-pennies-an-hour.html

Garfinkel, S. (2010). *Digital forensics research: The next 10 years*. London, UK: Elsevier. doi:10.1016/j.diin.2010.05.009

Google News. (2007). *Google and IBM announce university initiative to address internet-scale computing challenges*. Retrieved from http://www.google.com/intl/en/press/pressrel/20071008_ibm_univ.html

Grobauer, B., & Schreck, T. (2010). Towards incident handling in the cloud: Challenges and approaches. In *Proceedings of the 2010 ACM Workshop on Cloud Computing Security Workshop CCSW 2010,* (pp. 77-86). New York, NY: ACM Press.

Hejaz, S., Talh, C., & Abbabi, M. (2009). Extraction of forensically sensitive information from windows physical memory. *Digital Investigation*, *6*, 121–131. doi:10.1016/j.diin.2009.06.003

IBM. (2010). *OWASP - Salted hash password technique*. Retrieved from https://www.ibm.com/developerworks/mydeveloperworks/wikis/home/wiki/W3411066dca35_46c6_b97f_c3b-5a2ca5180/page/OWASP%20-%20Salted%20Hash%20Password%20Technique?lang=en

Juniper Networks. (2010). *Juniper networks VGW series*. Retrieved from http://www.juniper.net/us/en/products-services/software/security/vgw-series/#overview

Lu, R., Lin, X., Liang, X., & Shen, X. (2010). Secure provenance: The essential of bread and butter of data forensics in cloud computing. In *Proceedings of the 5th ACM Symposium on Information, Computer and Communications Security,* (pp. 282-292). New York, NY: ACM.

Lynch, C. A. (2001). When documents deceive: Trust and provenance as new factors for information retrieval in a tangled web. *Journal of the American Society for Information Science and Technology*, *52*, 12–17. doi:10.1002/1532-2890(2000)52:1<12::AID-ASI1062>3.0.CO;2-V

McKemmish, R., Pollitt, M., Cohen, F., Preston, C., Pavlic, T., & Slay, J. … Marberry, C. (2008). *Advances in digital forensics IV*. New York, NY: Springer.

Mell, P., & Timothy, G. (2011). *The NIST definition of cloud computing*. Gaithersburg, MD: NIST.

Microsoft. (2010). *Windows Azure active directory*. Retrieved from http://www.windowsazure.com/en-us/home/features/access-control/

Reese, G. (2009). *Principles for standardized REST authentication*. Retrieved from http://broadcast.oreilly.com/2009/12/principles-for-standardized-rest-authentication.html

Selamer, S., Yusof, R., & Sahib, S. (2008). Mapping process of digital forensic investigation framework. *International Journal of Computer Science and Network Security*, *8*(10), 163–169.

Services, U. H. (2012). *Health insurance portability and accountability act*. Retrieved from www.hhs.gov/ocr/hipaa/

Shende, J. G. (2010). *The Impact of the cloud on digital forensics part 1*. Retrieved from http://jonshende.sys-con.com/node/1624576

Shende, J. R. (2010). *Digital forensic challenges within cloud computing*. Retrieved from http://jonshende.sys-con.com/node/1576458

Shende, J. R. (2011). *The impact of the cloud on digital forensics*. Retrieved from http://www.dfinews.com/article/impact-cloud-digital-forensics-part-1?page=0,2

Virtual Computing Environment Company. (2012). *VCE company LLC*. Retrieved from http://www.vce.com/

Wang, F., Qiu, J., Yang, J., Dong, B., Li, X., & Li, Y. (2009). *Hadoop high availability through metadata replication*. Shanghai, China: IBM.

WindowsAzure. (2012). *Website*. Retrieved from http://www.windowsazure.com/en-us/home/features/overview/

Wolthusen, S. (2009). *Overcast: Forensic discovery in cloud environments*. Paper presented at the 2009 Fifth International Conference on IT Security Incident Management and IT Forensics. Stuttgart, Germany.

ENDNOTES

1 More on NTP configuration is detailed here http://www.ntp.org/.

Chapter 12
Forensics as a Service

Dener Didoné
Universidade Federal de Pernambuco (UFPE), Brazil

Ruy J. G. B. de Queiroz
Universidade Federal de Pernambuco (UFPE), Brazil

ABSTRACT

Cloud computing as a paradigm shift is transforming how services are being delivered. In this chapter, the authors present a Forensics as a Service (FaaS) model using cloud computing to deliver forensic services. This model leverages the flexibility, elasticity, and dynamics of cloud computing, and is affordable for business, government, or individuals in need, due to its reduced cost. It also addresses the challenge of processing a large volume of forensic data by using MapReduce and distributed computing.

INTRODUCTION

According to the report by Anderson and Rainie (2010), 71% of interviewed people agreed with the statement:

By 2020, most people won't do their work with software running on a general-purpose PC. Instead, they will work in Internet-based applications such as Google Docs, and in applications run from Smartphones. Aspiring application developers will develop for Smartphone vendors and companies that provide Internet-based applications, because most innovative work will be done in that domain, instead of designing applications that run on a PC operating system.

This report shows the growing trend of using elastic computing power offered by the Cloud provided as a commodity.

Garfinkel (2010) states that "the growing size of storage devices means that there is frequently insufficient time to create a forensic image of a subject device, or to process all of the data once it is found," which he has listed as one of the key challenges for computer forensics today. This chapter aims to propose a *Forensic as a Service*

DOI: 10.4018/978-1-4666-2662-1.ch012

Copyright © 2013, IGI Global. Copying or distributing in print or electronic forms without written permission of IGI Global is prohibited.

(FaaS) model to address this challenge using the cloud computing infrastructure. Our model of FaaS shows how to use the MapReduce computation model for solving everyday forensics tasks, delivered through the Cloud. Our settings allow the use of public or private clouds to perform these tasks.

In this chapter, we will first briefly discuss *MapReduce* programming model and Forensics as a Service. We will then present our FaaS model with evaluation and validation, followed by discussions on the security, legal, economic and governmental implications of this proposed model.

BACKGROUND

MapReduce

MapReduce is a distributed programming paradigm, developed by *Google* to simplify the development of scalable, massive parallel applications that process terabytes of data on large commodity clusters.

Programs written in this functional style are automatically parallelized and executed on a large cluster of commodity machines. The run-time system takes care of the details of partitioning the input data, scheduling the program's execution across a set of machines, handling machine failures, and managing the required inter-machine communication. This allows programmers without any experience with parallel and distributed systems to easily utilize the resources of a large distributed system. (Dean & Ghemawat, 2004)

Users specify a map function that processes a *key/value* pair to generate a set of intermediate key/value pairs, and a reduce function that merges all intermediate values associated with the same intermediate key. Many real world tasks are expressible in this model, including forensics tasks (string operations, image processing, statistical analysis, etc.) (Roussev, Wang, Richard III, & Marziale, 2009).

The canonical example application of MapReduce is a process to count the appearances of each different word in a set of documents (see Algorithm 1).

In this example retrieved from Dean and Ghemawat (2004), each document is split into words, and each word is counted initially with a "1" value by the Map function, using the word as the result key. The framework puts together all the pairs with the same key and feeds them to the same call to *Reduce*, thus this function just needs

Algorithm 1. Canonical example application of MapReduce

```
void map(String name, String document):
  // name: document name
  // document: document contents
  for each word w in document:
    EmitIntermediate(w, "1");
void reduce(String word, Iterator partialCounts):
  // word: a word
  // partialCounts: a list of aggregated partial counts
  int result = 0;
  for each pc in partialCounts:
    result += ParseInt(pc);
  Emit(AsString(result));
```

to sum all of its input values to find the total appearances of that word.

Hadoop was developed as an open-source implementation of the MapReduce programming model. This is a top-level Apache project being built and used by a global community of contributors, using the Java programming language. *Yahoo!* has been the largest contributor to the project, using Hadoop extensively across its businesses (Wikipedia, 2011).

Its architecture is composed by Hadoop Common, which contains the files needed to run Hadoop and support for the Hadoop's subprojects—Hadoop Distributed File System (HDFS) and MapReduce.

According with Apache Hadoop—HDFS Architecture Guide (2010), the HDFS is a distributed file system designed to run on commodity hardware, being highly fault-tolerant and designed to be deployed on low-cost hardware, providing high throughput access to application data and is suitable for applications that have large data sets.

Apache Hadoop—MapReduce Tutorial (2010) says that a MapReduce job usually splits the input dataset into independent chunks which are processed by the map tasks in a completely parallel manner. The framework sorts the outputs of the maps, which are then input to the reduce tasks. Typically, both the input and the output of the job are stored in a file-system. The framework takes care of scheduling tasks, monitoring them and re-executes the failed tasks.

The MapReduce framework consists of a single master *JobTracker* and one slave *TaskTracker* per cluster-node. The master is responsible for scheduling the jobs' component tasks on the slaves, monitoring them, and re-executing the failed tasks. The slaves execute the tasks as directed by the master. The visual description of MapReduce can be found in Figure 1, adapted from Mallassi (2010).

Minimally, applications specify the input/output locations and supply map and reduce functions via implementations of appropriate interfaces and/or abstract-classes. These, and other job parameters, comprise the job configuration. The Hadoop job client then submits the job (jar/executable, etc.) and configuration to the *JobTracker* which then assumes the responsibility of distributing the software/configuration to the slaves, scheduling tasks and monitoring them, providing status and diagnostic information to the job-client.

Although the Hadoop framework is implemented in Java, MapReduce applications need not be written in Java. Hadoop Streaming is a utility which allows users to create and run jobs with any executables (e.g. shell utilities) as the mapper, and/or reduce and Hadoop Pipes is a SWIG - compatible C++ API to implement MapReduce applications (non JNITM based).

Figure 1. Visual description of MapReduce (Mallassi, 2010)

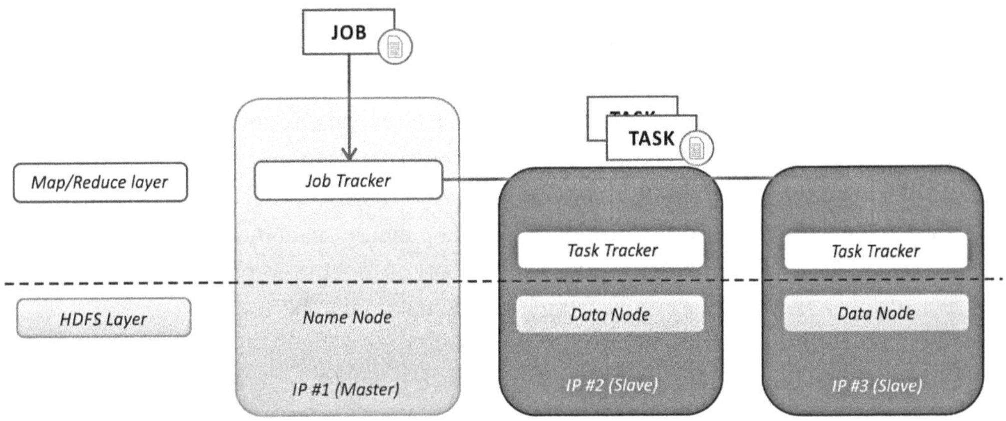

Forensics as a Service (FAAS)

The idea of FaaS was born to address one of the problems faced by digital forensics today as anticipated by Garfinkel (2010), i.e., the growing size of storage devices, which means that there is frequently insufficient time to create a forensic image of a subject device, or to process all the data once it is found. The increasing volume of devices coupled with the growth of storage space and the reduced cost of storage can easily generate terabytes of data to be analyzed in digital investigations. Nance, Hay and Bishop (2009) also identified six categories for digital forensic research, and "Data Volume" is one of the six where authors believe that parallelization of data processing could provide benefits to the area.

Roussev and Richard III (2004) demonstrated through an early prototype that utilizing large-scale distributed clusters can efficiently speed up typical forensic functions. Authors also emphasize the need for more sophisticated forensic analysis techniques, which may be enabled by the transition of current tools for distributed tools.

Tang and Daniels (2005) created a simple framework for network forensics based on the distributed techniques providing an integrated platform for automatic forensics evidence collection and storage, including a mechanism for generating attack graphs to illustrate hacking procedures. Another model is the ForNet presented in Shanmugasundaram, Memon, Savant, and Bronnimann (2009), aimed at using distributed forensics for evidence collection and network query.

More recently, Roussev et al. (2009) describe a new implementation of the MapReduce processing model, which significantly outperforms prior work on typical forensic tasks in large datasets, demonstrating linear scaling for CPU-intensive processing and even super-linear scaling for indexing-related workloads. Roussev et al. (2009) use an approach to accommodate more processing in the same amount of time, optimizing the utilization of more hardware resources. The purpose of this is to support the use of distributed computational resources to improve the turnaround time of forensic investigations.

Besides these studies, commercial tools such as Forensics Toolkit (FTK) from AccessData, now include support for multi-core processors, and distribution of processing, but with limited distribution (limited to four machines).

OVERVIEW OF THE FAAS MODEL

We build our FaaS model with MapReduce and Hadoop. By leveraging the elasticity of cloud computing platforms as well as its "unlimited" storage and processing power, our FaaS model is more affordable and flexible for businesses, governments or individuals in need.

Although the MapReduce programming model does not solve all the problems of distribution of processing, so far it has demonstrated great ability in handling forensic tasks such as string operations, image processing, statistical analysis, etc.

Figure 2 illustrates the scenario of our model, where users can use any devices (the most common are computers and laptops) to access servers through the Cloud and then perform forensics tasks, taking advantage of functions implemented by Hadoop MapReduce.

At the beginning of computing, programs were written serially, i.e., consisted of a sequence of instructions being executed one after another. Parallel programming has been developed to improve performance and efficiency of programs, because in this type of programming the processing is broken into several parts where each one can be executed concurrently. In parallel programming instructions, each part is executed simultaneously on different CPUs, may be multiple CPUs on a single machine, or multiple computers networked together. Apart from being more efficient, they can also be used to solve problems in large data sets using non-local resources. When you have a set of networked computers, in our case

Figure 2. Proposed model for delivery of forensic as a service (FaaS)

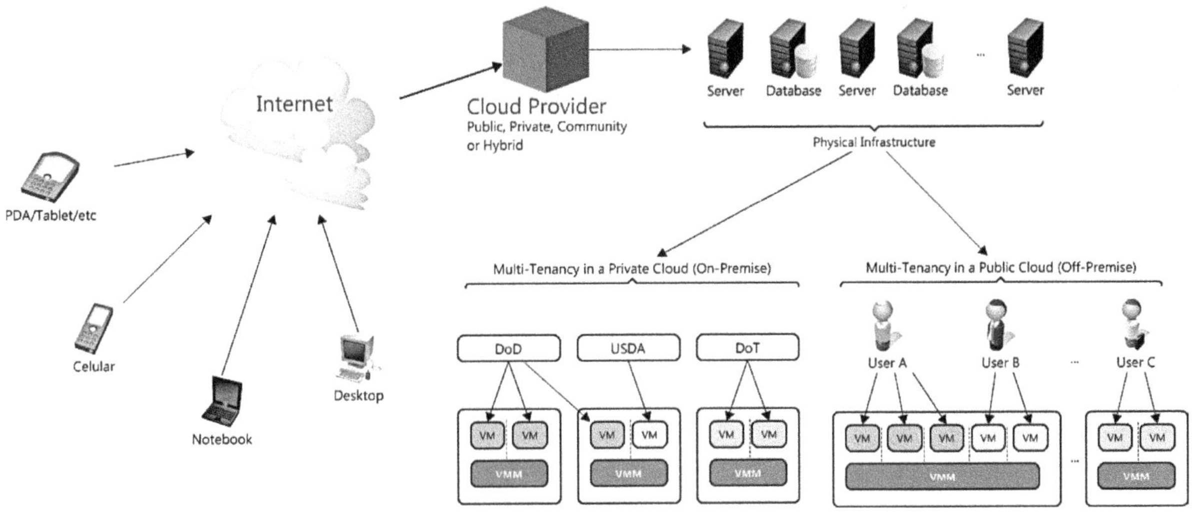

the Cloud, we have a large computational power at hand; we can make use of distributed processing and parallel programming using MapReduce to solve the problems involving large data sets.

In our model of parallel and distributed programming using the Cloud and MapReduce, the user specifies a mapping function (map) and a function of reduction (reduce). Many forensic functions can be specified in this model, the *grep* command is such an example. This command is used to perform searches in the content of files (input data) searching for lines that meet a given regular expression, and all lines found are sent to an output.

According to Dean and Ghemawat (2004), the mapping function emits a line if it matches the regular expression passed, and the reduction function only copies the intermediate pair provided by the map function for the output, as described in Algorithm 2.

Algorithm 2. Pseudo-code

```
if match (value, pattern)
  emit (value, 1)
```

This is just another example of use of MapReduce tasks in conducting typical forensic work. We can find more examples in the work of Roussev et al. (2009), such as, for example, *bloomfilter*, which is a probabilistic data structure used to test whether an element is member of a set or not, false positives are possible, but not false negatives.

We emphasize here the need for discussion and future research for the development and creation of tools that use MapReduce programming model for forensic examination. Rethinking tools and re-write code is one way to contribute to the evolution of the forensic discipline, because according to Garfinkel (2010), the established progress by computer forensics in the last 10 years has become irrelevant, which means that we are likely to be facing a crisis.

The model can be deployed in either public or private cloud, depending on the specific security, ownership, and access requirements of the users. In the public deployment model, applications will run off-premise and hosted by the cloud provider. In the private deployment model, they are physically hosted on-premise by the company. In the next sections we will present the two deployment models for FaaS.

Implementation of the Proposed Model in Public Cloud

We choose Amazon Elastic MapReduce[1], a service offered by Amazon Web Service (AWS) for our public cloud deployment. Amazon Elastic MapReduce utilizes a hosted Hadoop framework running on the Web-scale infrastructure of Amazon Elastic Compute Cloud (EC2)[2] and Amazon Simple Storage Service (S3)[3]. (Amazon Web Services, 2011) It enables businesses, researchers, data analysts, and developers to easily and cost-effectively process vast amounts of data.

Utilization of this service is simple through the AWS Management Console. In this console, you have full control of Jobs being executed or finalized. EC2 offers four types of instances:

- Standard instances, suited for most applications.
- Instances with large memory sizes for high throughput applications, including database and memory caching applications.
- Instances with more CPU resources than memory (RAM) and are well suited for compute-intensive applications.
- High Performance Instances combine large memory sizes and high CPU resources with 10 Gbps networking. They are well-suited for high performance, I/O intensive applications, such as mapping genomes for scientific research, simulating aerospace and automotive designs for engineering activities, and mining data for business intelligence.

According to the Amazon, One EC2 Compute Unit (ECU) provides the equivalent CPU capacity of a 1.0-1.2 GHz 2007 Opteron or 2007 Xeon processor. For the use of more than 20 instances, it is necessary to complete the Amazon EC2 instance request form.

The prices of instances to be started to do their jobs will depend on which region they are physically located, the amount and type of the instance. The premises made available by Amazon include two in the United States (N. Virginia, N. California) and one in the European Union (Ireland) [4] (see Tables 1 and 2).

Prices for N. Virginia e N. California are the same, so we provide just the prices of one of them, considering that the price of N. Virginia is valid for N. California. We have to pay attention to a detail, i.e., the option of Cluster GPU On-Demand Instances and Cluster Compute On-Demand Instances are just available on N. Virginia.

To use MapReduce, you must also use the storage service for the inputs and outputs of your computations. Amazon offers a service called Simple Storage Service (S3). This service provides a simple Web services interface that can be used to store and retrieve any amount of data, at any time, from anywhere on the Web.

The S3 service was built to be simple, so it has a minimal set of features that include some features listed below:

- Write, read, and delete objects containing from 1 byte to 5 Terabytes of data each. The number of objects you can store is unlimited.
- Each object is stored in a bucket and retrieved via a unique, developer-assigned key.
- A bucket can be stored in one of several Regions. You can choose a Region to optimize for latency, minimize costs, or address regulatory requirements. Objects stored in a Region never leave the Region unless you transfer them out.
- Authentication mechanisms are provided to ensure that data is kept secure from unauthorized access. Objects can be made private or public, and rights can be granted to specific users.

The Amazon S3 Service Level Agreement (SLA) is the only legally binding document be-

Table 1. Amazon EC2 and MapReduce prices on N. Virginia – US

US – N. Virginia Standard On-Demand Instances	Amazon EC2 (On-Demand Instances)	Amazon Elastic MapReduce
Small (Default)	$0.085 per hour	$0.015 per hour
Large	$0.34 per hour	$0.06 per hour
Extra Large	$0.68 per hour	$0.12 per hour
High-Memory On-Demand Instances		
Extra Large	$0.50 per hour	$0.09 per hour
Double Extra Large	$1.00 per hour	$0.21 per hour
Quadruple Extra Large	$2.00 per hour	$0.42 per hour
High-CPU On-Demand Instances		
Medium	$0.17 per hour	$0.03 per hour
Extra Large	$0.68 per hour	$0.12 per hour
Cluster Compute On-Demand Instances		
Quadruple Extra Large	$1.60 per hour	$0.33 per hour
Cluster GPU On-Demand Instances		
Quadruple Extra Large	$2.10 per hour	$0.42 per hour

tween the cloud provider and cloud user defining the service level. This contract states that Amazon will be reasonable for a service uptime of 99.9% during the monthly billing cycle. Apart from this SLA for S3, all services used, i.e., S3, Amazon Elastic MapReduce and the EC2 are subject to the Amazon Web Services Customer Agreement[5].

The prices charged by Amazon S3 on, both for data storage and data transfer and requests are available on the service and vary according to the chosen region, and 4 options for the region, two in USA (N. Virginia, N. California) in a U.S. (Ireland) and one in APAC (Singapore)[6]. We calculated the cost of services used in our model through a Web service called AWS Simple Monthly Calculator[7].

Implementation of the Proposed Model in Private Cloud

We use Eucalyptus (Elastic Utility Computing Architecture Linking Your Programs to Useful Systems) for the private deployment model of FaaS. Eucalyptus is an open source software infrastructure for implementing on-premise Clouds built on top of existing Enterprise IT and service provider infrastructure. Thus, with a Eucalyptus private cloud, sensitive data remains secure from external intrusion behind the enterprise firewall.

Eucalyptus (2009) was designed to ensure its compatibility with existing Linux-based data center installations, and can be deployed without modification on all major Linux OS distributions (Ubuntu, RHEL/CentOS, openSUSE, and Debian). The software framework is a highly modular cooperative set of Web services that interoperate based on standard communication protocols. Through this framework, virtual machines and storage resources are interconnected on an isolated layer-2 network (Nurmi, et al., 2008).

The conceptual representation of the Eucalyptus Cloud is presented in Figure 3. It includes the following components: Cloud Controller (CLC), Cluster Controller (CC), Node Controller (NC), Storage Controller (SC), Walrus, and a Management Platform. The document provided by Euca-

Table 2. Amazon EC2 and MapReduce prices on Ireland – EU

EU – Ireland Standard On-Demand Instances	Amazon EC2 (On-Demand Instances)	Amazon Elastic MapReduce
Small (Default)	$0.095 per hour	$0.015 per hour
Large	$0.38 per hour	$0.06 per hour
Extra Large	$0.76 per hour	$0.12 per hour
High-Memory On-Demand Instances		
Extra Large	$0.57 per hour	$0.09 per hour
Double Extra Large	$1.14 per hour	$0.21 per hour
Quadruple Extra Large	$2.28 per hour	$0.42 per hour
High-CPU On-Demand Instances		
Medium	$0.19 per hour	$0.03 per hour
Extra Large	$0.76 per hour	$0.12 per hour

lyptus Systems (2009) gives an overview of the structure of Eucalyptus briefly presented below:

CLC is the entry-point into the Cloud for administrators, developers, project managers, and end-users. The CLC is responsible for querying the node managers for information about resources, making high-level scheduling decisions, and implementing them by making requests to cluster controllers. The CLC, as shown in Figure 3, is also the interface to the management platform. In essence, the CLC is responsible for exposing and managing the underlying virtualized resources (servers, network, and storage) via a well-defined industry standard API (Amazon EC2) and a Web-based user interface.

CCs generally execute on a cluster front-end machine, or any machine that has network connectivity to both the nodes running NCs and to the machine running the CLC. CCs gather information about a set of VMs and schedules VM execution on specific NCs. The CC also manages the virtual instance network and participates in the enforcement of SLAs as directed by the CLC. All nodes served by a single CC must be in the same broadcast domain (Ethernet).

NCs are the machines on which virtual machine instances run. Node Controller (NC) is executed on every node that is designated for hosting VM instances. NCs control the execution, inspection, and termination of VM instances on the host where it runs, fetches and cleans up local copies of instance images (the kernel, the root file system, and the ramdisk image), and queries and controls the system software on its node (host OS and the hypervisor) in response to queries and control requests from the cluster controller. The Node controller is also responsible for the management of the virtual network endpoint.

SC provides block storage service (similar to Amazon Elastic Block Storage, i.e., EBS) while the Walrus storage system spans the entire cloud and is similar to the Amazon S3 in functionality. Storage Controller (SC) implements block-accessed network storage (e.g. Amazon EBS) and is capable of interfacing with various storage systems (NFS, iSCSI, etc.). An elastic block store is a Linux block device that can be attached to a virtual machine but sends disk traffic across the locally attached network to a remote storage location. An EBS volume cannot be shared across instances but does allow a snapshot to be created and stored in a central storage system such as Walrus, the Eucalyptus storage service.

Walrus (*put/get* storage) allows users to store persistent data, organized as consistent buckets and objects. It allows users to create, delete, list

Figure 3. Conceptual representation of the eucalyptus cloud (Eucalyptus System, 2009)

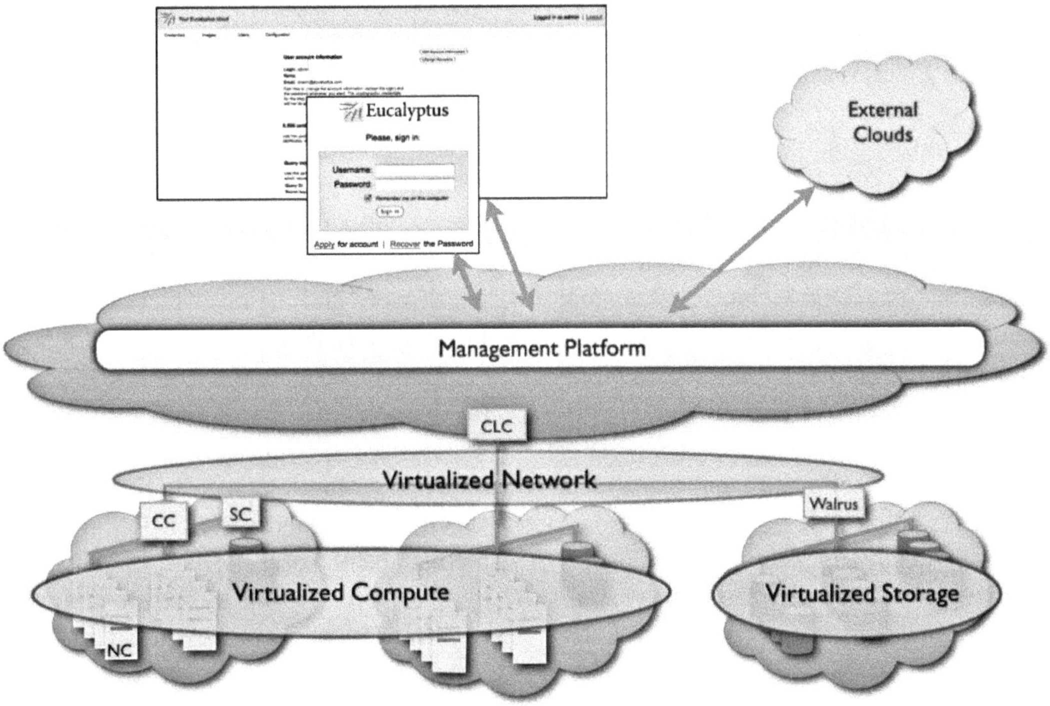

buckets, put, get, delete objects, and set access control policies. Walrus is interface compatible with Amazon's S3, and supports the Amazon Machine Image (AMI) image-management interface, thus providing a mechanism for storing and accessing both the virtual machine images and user data.

A Management Platform provides a one-stop console for the cloud administrator to configure and manage the Cloud. The Management Platform also exports various interfaces for the administrator, project manager, developer, and other users, with customizable levels of access and privileges. Management Platform provides an interface to various Eucalyptus services and modules. These features can include VM management, storage management, user/group management, accounting, monitoring, SLA definition and enforcement, cloud-bursting, provisioning, etc.

To use Hadoop in your private cloud managed by Eucalyptus, you should use an image that contains pre-installed Hadoop. There are some public images containing everything that you need to perform their tasks in your private cloud. These images have a virtual machine format AMI, due to the interoperability between Eucalyptus and Amazon.

There are links in Eucalyptus for pre-packaged virtual machines that are ready to run in your Eucalyptus Cloud. Clicking on the link you can download a package that contains a VM image (*.img*), a Xen compatible *kernel/ramdisk* pair (*xen-kernel/vmlinuz** and *xen-kernel/initrd**) and a KVM compatible *kernel/ramdisk* pair (*kvm-kernel/vmlinuz** and *kvm-kernel/initrd**). Eucalyptus is compatible with and packaged for multiple distributions of Linux including Ubuntu, RHEL, OpenSuse, Debian, Fedora, and CentOS and will work with a variety of hypervisors and virtualization technologies. Moreover, Eucalyptus provides an official guide to create images, use, and/or distribute them.

According to Wardley, Goyer, and Barcet (2009), Ubuntu distributions now include the Eucalyptus software core as the key component of the Ubuntu Enterprise Cloud (UEC), bringing Amazon EC2-like infrastructure capabilities inside the firewall.

Eucalyptus is an open source implementation for the emerging standard of the EC2 API, designed to simplify the process of building and managing an internal cloud for businesses of any size, thereby enabling companies to create their own self-service infrastructure. As the technology is open source, it requires no license fees or subscription for use, experimentation, or deployment. Updates are provided freely and support contracts can be purchased directly from Canonical[8].

UEC is specifically targeted at those companies wishing to gain the benefits of self-service IT within the confines of the corporate data center whilst avoiding either lock-in to a specific vendor, expensive re-occurring product licenses, or the use of non-standard tools that are not supported by public providers.

From there, the execution of jobs on Hadoop through Eucalyptus becomes a simple task that does not require sophisticated technical expertise.

Private cloud deployment of our proposed model is not limited only to the Eucalyptus platform. In addition to Eucalyptus, another service offered by Amazon, called Virtual Private Cloud (VPC) has drawn our attention, and can also be a solution for implementing the proposed model. Amazon VPC allows you to connect an existing structure along with an isolated set of features offered by Amazon, as well as using Amazon EC2 instances, S3 Storage and MapReduce via Virtual Private Network (VPN).

PUBLIC CLOUD DEPLOYMENT TESTING AND PERFORMANCE

In this section, we discuss the performance of our proposed FaaS model deployed in a public cloud, using AWS EC2, S3, and Elastic MapReduce. We use two Hadoop examples, i.e., *wordcount* and *grep*, to compare execution times on a single machine and in the Cloud. These same examples were used by Roussev et al. (2009) to conduct typical forensics tasks.

The first example, *wordcount*, calculates the number of occurrences number of each word in a given input (text files normally), and returns a list of word and the occurrences of these words in the specified input.

The second example, *grep*, performs a search on the contents of text files locating lines that match with a given regular expression, storing them, or writing on the specified output.

Grep command used on Hadoop is less effective than the original algorithm used in Linux systems, because it only returns the number of occurrences for regular expression given. In the Linux version of *grep* command, the output of the command results in the list of matching lines.

Instance configuration to be used in Amazon's EC2 service was determined empirically, using instances with high memory, named by Amazon as "High-Memory Extra Large Instance" (m2-xlarge), with following settings:

- 17.1 GB of memory;
- 6.5 EC2 Compute Unit (2 virtual cores with 3.25 EC2 Compute Units each);
- 420 GB of local instance storage;
- 64-bit platform.

We used two instances with this configuration. It is good to know that one EC2 Compute Unit (ECU) provides the equivalent CPU capacity of a 1.0-1.2 GHz 2007 Opteron or 2007 Xeon processor.

Tests were performed in 5 files of different sizes: 10, 100, 1024, 2048, and 3072 MB each, containing random text generated by the Lorem Ipsum Generator Service (http://www.lipsum.com/).

Tests with *wordcount* were performed in these data sets with the instances configuration presented before, they returned the results as shown in Figure 4.

Tests carried out with *grep* in the same data sets and instance configuration using the term "lacinia" as a key search returned the results as shown in Figure 5.

We used a single workstation to implement the *grep* and *wordcount* algorithms and obtain the results in order to compare results with the MapReduce model in cloud computing and single station. The results are shown in Figures 6 and 7.

Single station used is a notebook Dell, with an Intel Core 2 Duo T7250 – 2 GHz, 2 GB of memory, and operating system Windows 7 Professional in a 32-bit platform.

Figures 8 and 9 aggregate times obtained from Amazon and single station for both algorithms on all datasets.

As we can see from Figure 8, the results were satisfactory to *wordcount* algorithm, comparing the results obtained from Amazon and single station. We can observe from Figure 8 that the execution times decrease when data sets are bigger than 2 GB.

According to Figure 9, in the *grep* execution, the results were insignificant for the analyzed data set, but we believe that with files of 3 GB or more, there is a possible reduction in execution times in the Cloud.

Reduction

Traditional computer forensics tools often involve having forensic practitioner manually analyze data fragments recovered by automated forensic tools. Our proposed model provides a substantial reduction in the quantity of data that need to be analyzed by the forensics practitioner, as well as reduces the execution times to perform forensic tasks.

In tests performed with *wordcount* algorithm, the reduction was 99.9% for those data sets, resulting in files of 2.52 KB. It is noteworthy that the reduction of the data sets obtained varies considerably on the size of the vocabulary used. The dataset of this experiment also showed a

Figure 4. Results execution from the wordcount algorithm in the cloud

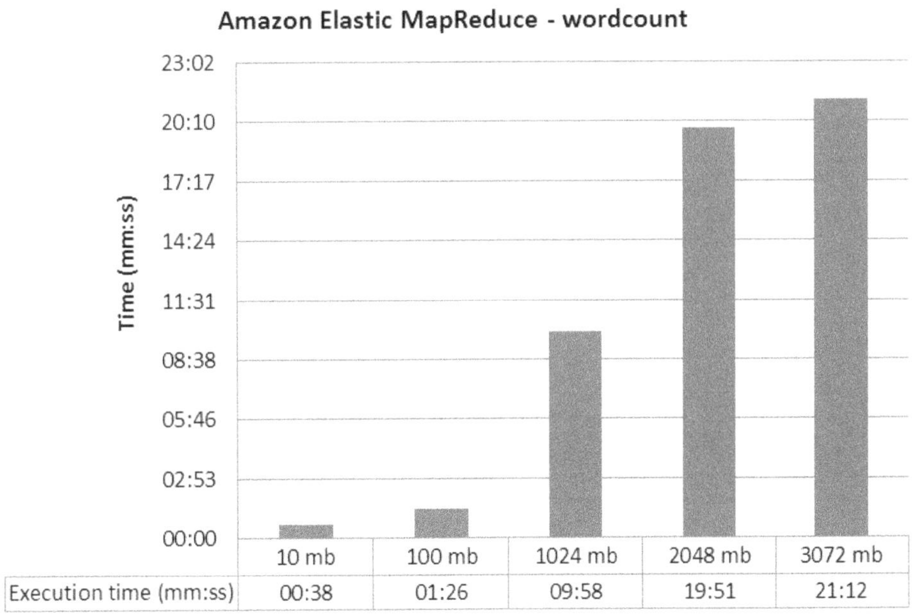

Figure 5. Results execution from the grep algorithm in the cloud

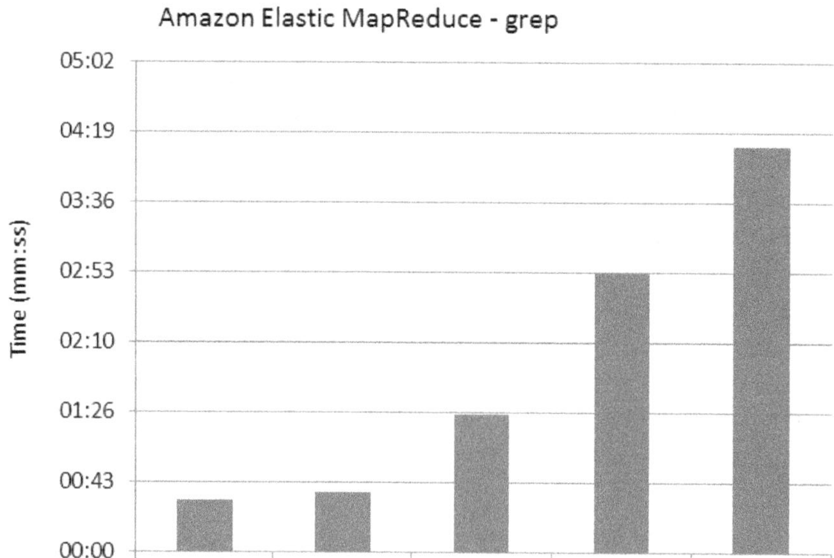

	10 mb	100 Mb	1 Gb	2 Gb	3 Gb
Execution time (mm:ss)	00:32	00:37	01:25	02:52	04:11

Figure 6. Execution results from the wordcount algorithm in a single station

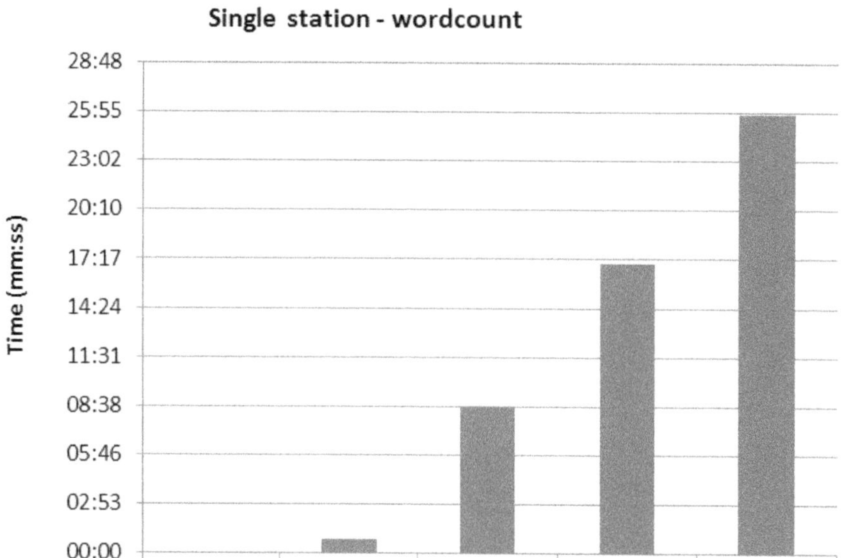

	10 mb	100 Mb	1 Gb	2 Gb	3 Gb
Execution time (mm:ss)	00:05	00:50	08:33	17:04	25:47

Figure 7. Execution results from the grep algorithm in a single station

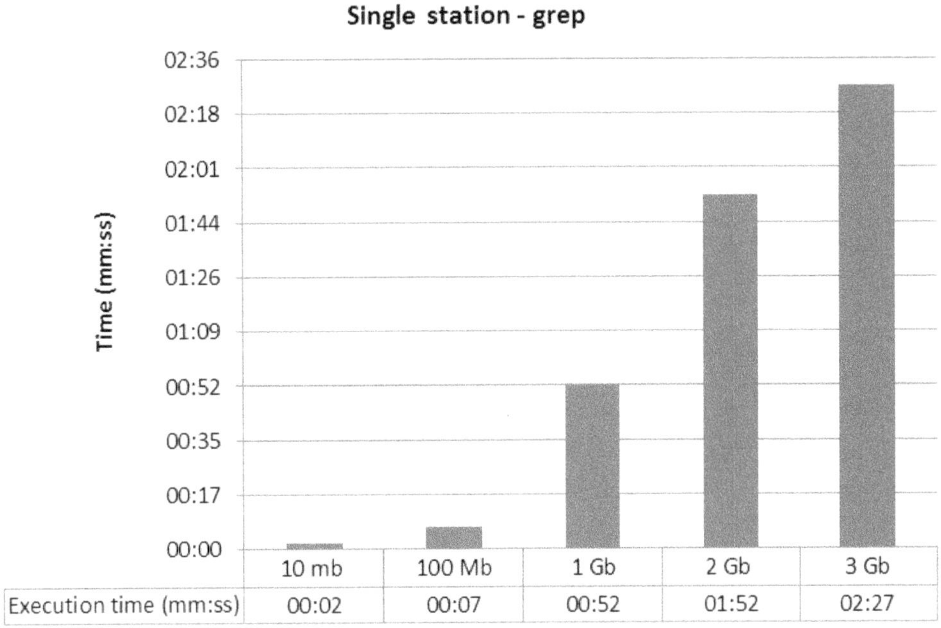

Figure 8. Comparison of execution times from the wordcount algorithm—Amazon vs. single station

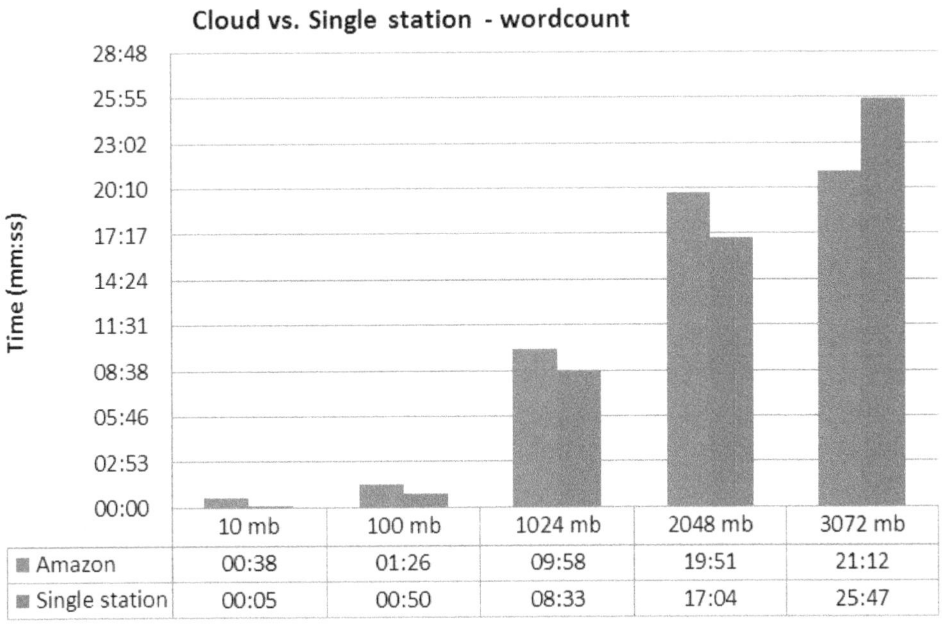

Figure 9. Comparison of execution times from the grep algorithm—Amazon vs. single station

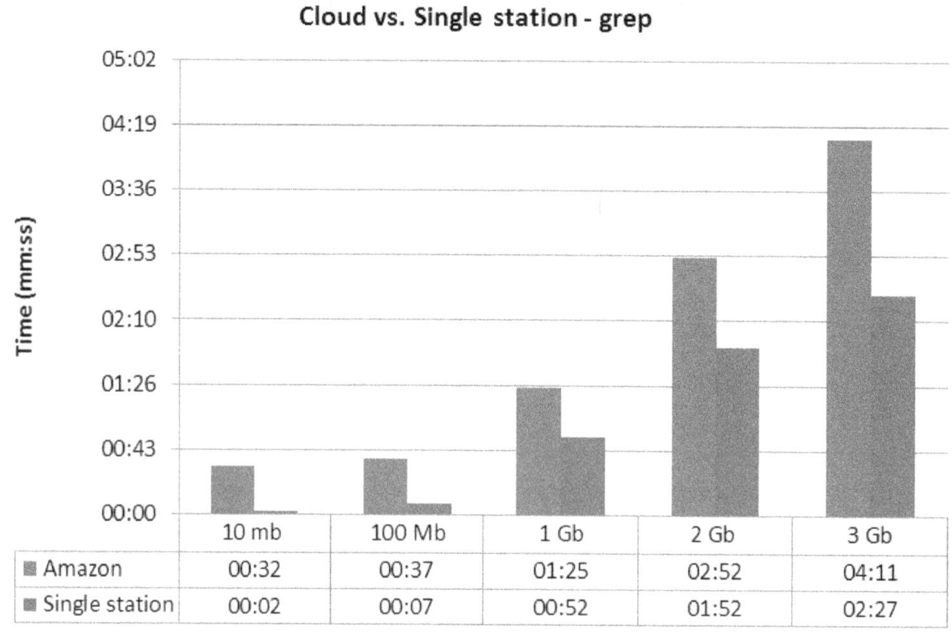

significant decrease due to the limited vocabulary used in the data set, from A to V.

In the case of *grep* algorithm, the execution returned the word and the number of occurrences, if found. If no results were returned, forensic practitioner would not lose time analyzing one data set in particular.

Economics

The amount spent by the tests in each data set was $ 1.32, where $ 1.14 cents for each EC2 instance, and $ 0.18 cents for the use of Elastic MapReduce.

If the experiments were conducted in a private cloud, spending would be null, because with an already established infrastructure there is no cost for initial deployment, neither for use of Eucalyptus nor Hadoop.

The experiments performed with Hadoop MapReduce on a single station did not result in expenditures, since Hadoop is distributed under open source license, and we already have the equipment.

Limitations

The major limitation evident in the tests was uploading big data sets of 3 GB or more to Amazon S3 storage. This was expected, and was also noted by Hawthorn (2009), highlighting issues of latency and bandwidth. This issue occurs regardless of cloud type adopted but is particularly evident in public models. In case of forensic in systems already running on Clouds, this limitation of uploading large data sets will not be such an issue.

When using the Amazon Elastic MapReduce service, there is an overhead in two occasions. The first occurs on Amazon EC2 instances from its initialization to finalization, and the moment is the startup and configuration period of Hadoop for utilization of the instances.

Although the MapReduce programming model simplifies the utilization of distributed and parallel processing, it is still necessary advances in functional programming, modeling forensic tasks using this paradigm.

The creation of parallel and distributed tools to contribute to the achievement of forensics is described by Roussev et al. (2009) as one of necessary advances in this area, which is in line with the findings from this work.

We used data sets created by Lorem Ipsum Generator, but standardized data sets as described by Garfinkel (2010) can be used to increase scientific assessment of forensic methods. Furthermore, using standard data sets can allow a direct comparison among different approaches and tools. NIST also is working on providing researchers documented data sets of simulated digital evidence for examination. Researchers can also use these data sets for validation of tools used in investigations, verification of equipment, training of researchers and even proficiency of researchers as part of certification of laboratories. NIST provides a site (http://www.cfreds.nist.gov/) that is a repository of images, some produced by the NIST and others are contributions from various organizations.

DISCUSSIONS ON SECURITY ISSUES OF THE MODEL

In this section, we present the discussions related to our proposed model including security issues when implementing in public and private clouds with details of choice of suppliers, management, interoperability, privacy, legal, as well as economic considerations.

Presented as one of the key aspects for the adoption of cloud computing, security has been widely discussed among industries and governments in search of standards for the use of cloud computing that provides information security, including privacy protection, safeguarding the security interests, whether national, in the case of governments, or internal, in the case of industries (Kundra, 2010). Confidentiality, privacy, integrity, and auditability are still under-addressed issues, and need to be taken in to consideration when implementing Forensic as a Service. However, the use of cloud computing today is a matter of trust, and studies such as Lillard et al. (2010) show that cloud computing will reach a mature level, ensuring better data security.

Some solutions that aim to provide confidentiality and security can already be adopted, such as data encryption for transmission to the Cloud, the use of encrypted storage disks, VLANs, etc. However, one unresolved obstacle is the lack of law and regulation. An example is the request of some countries to SaaS providers that keep users' data and copyrighted materials within their borders.

The decision as to whether or not to adopt cloud computing is based on risk, not technology, since the Cloud assumes multiple levels of security in information systems, depending on the cloud-sourcing (the supply of resources needed by the business process) model used. Figure 10 illustrates these models, being possible to replace the idea of using government for corporate use.

The proposed FaaS model as any type of cloud adoption involves security-related issues, which vary according to the deployment model due to their specific security levels.

Public Clouds

The public clouds are faced with security and legal complications. Since you decide for adoption of cloud, is necessary a starting point for evaluating any cloud service, Damoulakis (2010) suggests the following key issues:

Where are my data? Your data is logically stored in the cloud, but may be physically stored in one or more countries, including overcoming state and international barriers. You should think about legal issues (jurisdiction, compliance) and availability issues. Once the forensic data are handled by a third part, we must have full knowledge of where and who they are, even to meet the requirements of chain of custody. Amazon offers a choice of local storage and processing of data, being dependent on the local service type. Among

Figure 10. Cloud sourcing models (Kundra, 2010)

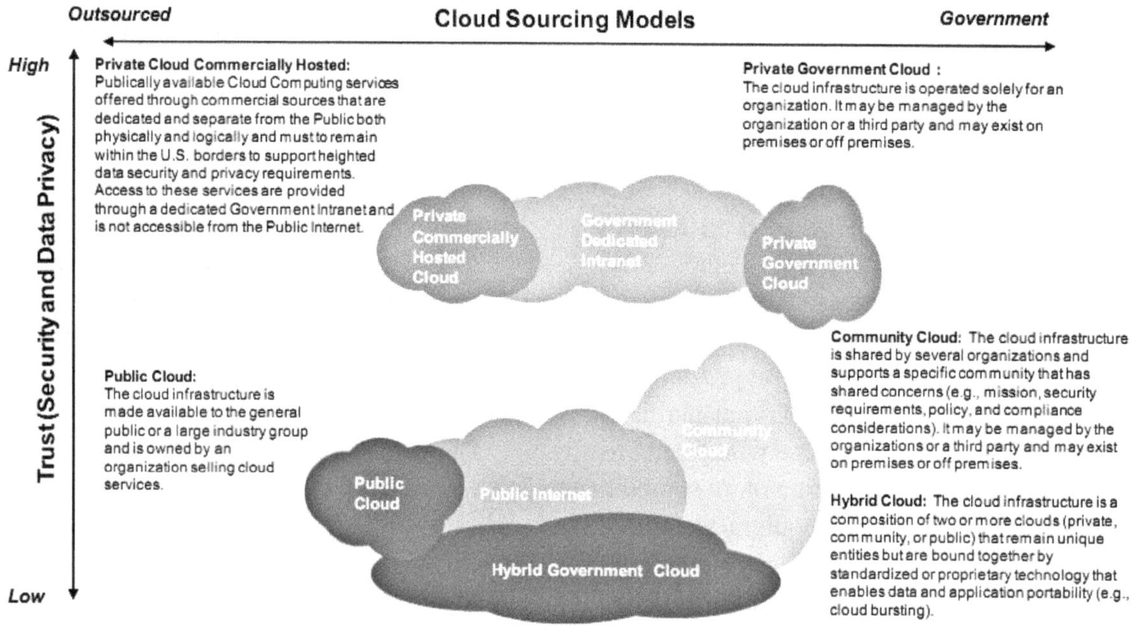

the places offered are the United States, European Union, and Asia-Pacific.

How are my data being protected? You need to know if data is being mirrored, replicated, backed up and checksummed to thus establish the integrity of stored data. A significant advance in helping the integrity of the data is offered by Amazon in its S3 service, using a combination of MD5 checksums and Cyclic Redundancy Check (CRC) to detect corrupted data. In addition, the service calculates sums of all network traffic to detect corruption of data packets to store or retrieve data.

Who can access or view my data? Since cloud servers use the model of multi-tenancy (data from several companies sharing the same database), it is important to know how issues of access and visibility are being managed and what steps are taken to ensure security and confidentiality of data. This can be extended to employees of the Cloud providers upon who may or may not have access to details of my organization (whether public or private) and what they can see. This is a very delicate issue, due the sensitive classification of forensic data.

Besides this obvious question, Iball (2010) suggests a few more questions: How is the facility secured both physically and digitally? How often they conduct routine checks and audit access to restricted areas by system administrators? What industry standards do your services met?

In the case of industry standards, Amazon has achieved in 2010, the ISO 27001 certification of the Information Security Management System (ISMS) covering infrastructure, data centers, and services including Amazon Elastic Compute Cloud (Amazon EC2), Amazon Simple Storage Service (Amazon S3) and Amazon Virtual Private Cloud (Amazon VPC). ISO 27001/27002 is a widely adopted global security standard that sets out requirements and best practices for a systematic approach to managing company and customer information that is based on periodic risk assessments appropriate to ever-changing threat scenarios. AWS's ISO 27001 certification includes all AWS data centers in all regions worldwide and AWS has established a formal program to maintain the certification.

Another certification includes the Statement on Auditing Standards No. 70 (SAS70) Type II Audit. SAS70 certifies that a service organization has had an in-depth audit of its controls (including control objectives and control activities), which in the case of AWS relates to operational performance and security to safeguard customer data.

Iball (2010) also adds that the more questions are raised, the smaller the chances of your data being exposed to unnecessary risks, and more, having the right Service Level Agreement (SLA) is also key to a successful and long-term relationship with a service provider. SLAs makes the trust between the parties (customers and providers) fortified, which is important because from the SLAs the crucial details will be defined for the implementation of the proposal, personalizing all requirements for security. Damoulakis (2010) mentions that it is additionally recommended to understand the capabilities related to common concerns, such as intrusion detection, hacker attack or post attack containment.

To complement your reading, see the articles published by Everett (2009) and Hawthorn (2009) available in the additional reading section.

Beyond the issues raised by the authors, the Cloud Security Alliance (CSA) launched a guide to assist in the adoption of cloud computing, leading to a better understanding of the issues that must be asked, the currently recommended practices and pitfalls to be avoided (CSA, 2009). The Jericho Forum has also released a document which aims to enable stakeholders and business decision-makers to appreciate the key considerations that need to be taken into account when deciding which parts of their business could be operated in which of the available cloud formations (Jericho, 2009).

Before you set your provider and where your instance runs, you need to focus on the jurisdiction and compliance issues. For example, in the EU the security is treated by law, e.g. European data protection law stipulates that the company, as data controller, is entirely responsible for the security of its own data. The UK's Data Protection Act of 1998 requires that data controllers incorporate security requirement into their contracts with data processors. This means that the onus is on the Small to Medium Size Enterprises (SMEs) to ensure that the Cloud computing provider offers the appropriate levels of data security. With UK only data centers, business can be confident of stringent data security practices, covered by UK laws.

Private Clouds

The private clouds have higher security assurance compare to public clouds. Some issues related to jurisdiction and security mechanisms are already widely understood, since Clouds using the private data centers already established in the organizations, running behind your own firewall, which can be managed by the organization itself (which is more secure) or outsourced.

Private cloud gives user more control over the issues raised previously in the case of public clouds. Private cloud can provide the exact location of where the data is being stored, who are responsible about them, and who has access and all issues of digital or physical protection.

According to Harris and Alter (2010), public cloud is more common today, however, the industry will see more investment in private clouds because organizations today still own a large number of servers, which can be used to host private clouds, or hybrid solutions in conjunction with public clouds. According to the report by the end of 2012, the use of private cloud will permeate 77% of companies.

Private cloud is operated by only one organization. It can be managed by the organization itself or outsourced, and can exist as on-premise and off-premise. Our model uses on-premise model, which means that the software is installed and run on computers on the premises (in the building) of the organization or person using the software. In a private cloud the owner-user has, in principle, full control over the feature set of the Cloud implementation, however there are costs, which cannot be shared with other customers associated with this increase in control.

Interoperability

Both for users of public and private cloud the issue of interoperability between service providers still causes concern. If there is a change between public cloud providers, private to public or any other setting changes, there are no assurances that the technologies will be compatible and will enjoy the features of the principle of interoperability. To address these issues, a forum was created entitled Cloud Computing Interoperability Forum – CCIF (www.cloudforum.org/). A key focus will be placed on the creation of a common agreed upon framework/ontology that enables the ability of two or more cloud platforms to exchange information in a unified way.

Our private cloud deployment used Eucalyptus, which is interoperable with our public cloud deployment using Amazon. Eucalyptus supports the popular AWS cloud interface allowing these on-premise clouds to interact with public clouds using a common programming interface (Eucalyptus System, 2009).

Governmental Use

According to the Federal Chief Information Officer of USA, Vivek Kundra (2010), the USA Government is the world's largest consumer of IT, spending over $76 billion annually on more than 10,000 different systems and in 2009 they announced the Federal Government's Cloud Computing Initiative, demonstrating the potential to greatly reduce waste, increase data center efficiency and utilization rates and lower operating costs. Kundra (2010) says that moving to the Cloud supposed to include standards for a cloud-computing environment, providing security, protecting privacy and safeguarding the national security interests. The report concludes with 30 illustrative case studies at the Federal, state and local government levels. These case studies reflect the growing movement across the public sector to leverage cloud-computing technologies.

At the mean time, in a recent paper published by Paquette, Jaeger and Wilson (2010), the security risks associated with governmental use of cloud are identified and discussed, dealing with the current use of technology in government agencies and presenting the risks associated with its use by analyzing specific cases. The discussion is expanded by exploiting the level of understanding of the risks to which agencies and departments are submitted.

Based on the definition of risk, cloud computing and government use of cloud, the authors reported five types of risks associated with the use of technology, they are: tangible/known risks (access, availability, infrastructure, and integrity) and intangible/unknown risks.

The tangible risks initially start with access, where Paquette et al. (2010) says that all private data must be secured to ensure that only authenticated users are allowed the access authorized by the customer (federal agency), and that any unwanted or outside access requests are denied.

FUTURE WORK

Based on the proposed model, we identify the following future research directions:

- Development of security, privacy and legal frameworks for using cloud computing as a trusted platform for delivering forensic services.
- Ensuring data integrity and evidence preservation while being handled in a cloud computing platform so that evidence can be admissible to court.
- Implementing and testing FaaS in real-world cases.

CONCLUSION

The proposed Forensics as a Service model in this chapter aims to address the challenge of processing growing size of storage devices in digital investigation. This model uses MapReduce and can be deployed in public or private cloud. Our results show cost savings through the use of public clouds, and a significant reduction of size in data sets analyzed, but it is necessary to carry out more research and some new tests to prove efficiency and accuracy of this model.

We also discussed security and legal issues when implementing this model. The proposed model and the application of cloud computing to solve forensic challenges is just one approach to many challenges faced by the digital forensic community today. Other novel approaches need to be explored in order to leverage the opportunities brought by this rapidly emerging technology.

REFERENCES

Amazon Web Services. (2011). *Amazon elastic MapReduce.* Retrieved January 6, 2011, from http://aws.amazon.com/elasticmapreduce/

Anderson, J., & Rainie, L. (2010). The future of cloud computing. *Pew Research Center's Internet & American Life Project.* Retrieved February 23, 2011 from http://pewInternet.org/Reports/2010/The-future-of-cloud-computing.aspx

Apache. (2010a) *MapReduce tutorial.* Retrieved February 11, 2011, from http://hadoop.apache.org/mapreduce/docs/current/mapred_tutorial.html

Apache. (2010b). *HDFS architecture guide.* Retrieved February 11, 2011, from http://hadoop.apache.org/hdfs/docs/current/hdfs_design.html

Cloud Security Alliance. (2009). *Security guidance for critical areas of focus in cloud computing V2.1.* Washington, DC: Cloud Security Alliance.

Damoulakis, J. (2010). In clouds we trust. *IT Now, 52*(2), 11–12.

Dean, J., & Ghemawat, S. (2004). MapReduce: Simplified data processing on large clusters. In *Proceedings of the Sixth Symposium on Operating System Design and Implementation – OSDI.* New York, NY: Google Inc.

Eucalyptus System. (2009). *Eucalyptus open-source cloud computing infrastructure - An overview.* Retrieved February 5, 2011, from http://www.eucalyptus.com/pdf/whitepapers/Eucalyptus_Overview.pdf

Everett, C. (2009). Cloud computing – A question of trust. *Computer Fraud & Security, 6,* 5–7. doi:10.1016/S1361-3723(09)70071-5

Garfinkel, S. (2010). Digital forensics research: The next 10 years. In *Proceedings of the Digital Forensics Research Workshop (DFRWS).* DFRWS.

Harris, J. G., & Alter, A. E. (2010). *Cloudrise: Rewards and risks at the dawn of cloud computing.* Retrieved February 23, 2011, from http://www.accenture.com/SiteCollectionDocuments/PDF/Cloudrise_Rewards_and_Risks_at_the_Dawn_of_Cloud_Computing.pdf

Hawthorn, N. (2009). Finding security in the cloud. *Computer Fraud & Security, 10,* 19–20. doi:10.1016/S1361-3723(09)70131-9

Iball, J. (2010). Don't cloud data security. *IT Now, 52*(2), 14–15.

Jericho Forum. (2009). *Cloud cube model: Selecting cloud formations for secure collaboration.* Retrieved February 6, 2011 from http://www.opengroup.org/jericho/cloud_cube_model_v1.0.pdf

Kundra, V. (2010). *State of public sector cloud computing.* Retrieved from http://cloudcomputing.sys-con.com/node/1408645

Lillard, T. (2010). *Digital forensics for network, internet, and cloud computing: A forensic evidence guide for moving targets and data*. New York, NY: Elsevier.

Mallassi, O. (2010). *How to "crunch" your data stored in HDFS?* Retrieved July 5, 2011 from http://blog.octo.com/en/how-to-crunch-your-data-stored-in-hdfs/

Nance, K., Hay, B., & Bishop, M. (2009). Digital forensics: Defining a research agenda. In *Proceedings of the 42nd Hawaii International Conference on System Sciences*. IEEE.

Nurmi, D., Wolski, R., Grzegorczyk, C., & Obertelli, G. Soman, Youseff, L., & Zagorodnov, D. (2008). The eucalyptus open-source cloud-computing system. In *Proceedings of Cloud Computing and Its Application*, (pp. 124-131). IEEE.

Paquette, S., Jaeger, P., & Wilson, S. (2010). Identifying the security risks associated with governmental use of cloud computing. *Government Information Quarterly*, *27*, 245–253. doi:10.1016/j.giq.2010.01.002

Roussev, V., & Richard, G., III. (2004). Breaking the performance wall: The case for distributed digital forensics. In *Proceedings of the Digital Forensics Research Workshop (DFRWS)*. DFRWS.

Roussev, V., Wang, L., Richard, G., III, & Marziale, L. (2009). MMR: A platform for large-scale forensic computing. In *Proceedings of the Fifth Annual IFIP WG 11.9 International Conference on Digital Forensics*. IFIP.

Shanmugasundaram, K., Memon, N., Savant, A., & Bronnimann, H. (2012). ForNet: A distributed forensics network. In *Proceedings of the Second International Workshop on Mathematical Methods, Models and Architectures for Computer Networks Security*. IEEE.

Tang, Y., & Daniels, T. (2005). A simple framework for distributed forensics. In *Proceedings of the Second International Workshop on Security in Distributed Computing Systems (SDCS - ICDCSW)*, (pp. 163-169). ICDCSW.

Wikipedia. (2011). *Cloud computing*. Retrieved January 10, 2011, from http://en.wikipedia.org/wiki/Cloud_computing

ADDITIONAL READING

Accenture. (2010). Cloudrise: Rewards and risks at the dawn of cloud computing. *High Performance Institute*. Retrieved February 3, 2011, from http://nstore.accenture.com/acn_com/PDF/Accenture_Chinas_ Pragmatic_Path_to_Cloud_Computing.pdf

Altheide, C., & Carvey, H. (2011). *Digital forensics with open source tools*. New York, NY: Syngress.

Anastasi, J. (2003). *The new forensics: Investigating corporate fraud and the theft of intellectual property*. New York, NY: Wiley.

Armbrust, M., Fox, A., Griffith, R., Joseph, A., Katz, R., & Konwinski, A. … Zaharia, M. (2009). Above the clouds: A Berkeley view of cloud computing. In *Proceedings of IFIP Advances in Information and Communication Technology*. IFIP.

Bauchner, E. (2005). *Computer investigation (forensics: the science of crime-solving)*. New York, NY: Mason Crest.

Benton, D., & Grindstaff, F. (2006). *Practical guide to computer forensics*. New York, NY: BookSurge Publishing.

Branigan, S. (2004). *High-tech crimes revealed: Cyberwar stories from the digital front*. Reading, MA: Addison-Wesley.

Brits, M. (2003). *Computer forensics and cyber crime*. Upper Saddle River, NJ: Pearson.

Brown, C. (2005). *Computer evidence: Collection and preservation*. New York, NY: Charles River Media.

Bunting, S. (2011). *Encase computer forensics*. New York, NY: John Wiley & Sons.

Bunting, S., & Anson, S. (2007). *Mastering windows network forensics and investigation*. New York, NY: Sybex.

Buyya, R., Yeo, C., & Venugopal, S. (2008). Market-oriented cloud computing: Vision, hype, and reality for delivering IT services as computing utilities. In *Proceedings of the 10th IEEE International Conference on High Performance Computing and Communications*, (pp. 5-13). IEEE Press.

Carrier, B. (2005). *File system forensic analysis*. Reading, MA: Addison-Wesley Professional.

Carvey, H. (2009). *Windows forensic analysis DVD toolkit* (2nd ed.). New York, NY: Syngress.

Casey, E. (2011). *Digital evidence and computer crime: Forensic science, computers, and the internet* (3rd ed.). New York, NY: Academic Press.

Casey, E., & Ferraro, M. (2004). *Investigating child exploitation and pornography: The internet, law and forensic science*. New York, NY: Academic Press.

Cloyannides, M. (2004). *Privacy protection and computer forensics* (2nd ed.). New York, NY: Artech House Publishers.

Crowley, P., & Kleiman, D. (2007). *CD and DVD forensics*. New York, NY: Syngress.

Farmer, D., & Venema, W. (2005). *Forensic discovery*. Reading, MA: Addison-Wesley Professional.

Gellman, R. (2009). Privacy in the clouds: Risks to privacy and confidentiality from cloud computing. *World Privacy Forum*. Retrieved February 22, 2011 from http://www.worldprivacyforum.org/pdf/WPF_Cloud_Privacy_Report.pdf

Horigan, J. (2008). Cloud computing gains in currency. *Pew Internet & American Life Project*. Retrieved February 21, 2011, from http://pewresearch.org/pubs/948/cloud-computing-gains-in-currency

Iball, J. (2010). Don't cloud data security. *IT Now*, *52*(2), 14–15.

Lee, H., Palmbach, T., & Miller, M. (2001). *Henry Lee's crime scene handbook*. London, UK: Academic Press.

Marins, C. E. (2001). Desafios da informática forense no cenário de cloud computing. In *Proceedings of the Fourth International Conference of Computer Science*. IEEE.

Marshall, A. (2009). *Digital forensics: Digital evidence in criminal investigations*. New York, NY: Wiley.

Maturo, J., Saraiva, J., & Terzian, F. (2006). Especial: Crimes digitais. *Safernet*. Retrieved January 5, 2011, from http://www.safernet.org.br/site/noticias/especial-crimes-digitais

Mell, P., & Grance, T. (2009). *The NIST definition of cloud computing*. Washington, DC: National Institute of Standards and Technology.

Peisert, S., Bishop, M., & Marzullo, K. (2008). Computer forensics in forensis. In *Proceedings of the Third International Workshop on Systematic Approaches to Digital Forensic Engineering – SADFE,* (pp. 102 – 122). SADFE.

RCFL. (2010). *Annual report for fiscal year 2010*. Quantico, VA: Federal Bureau of Investigation.

Regional Computer Forensics Laboratory. (2009). *Annual report for fiscal year 2009*. Quantico, VA: Federal Bureau of Investigation.

Steel, C. (2006). *Windows forensics: The field guide for corporate computer investigations*. New York, NY: Wiley.

Vaquero, L. M., Rodero-Merino, L., Caceres, J., & Lindner, M. (2009). A break in the clouds: Towards a cloud definition. *ACM – SIGCOMM. Computer Communication Review*, *39*(1), 78–85.

Wardley, S., Goyer, E., & Barcet, N. (2009). *Ubuntu enterprise cloud architecture*. Retrieved January 10, 2011, from http://www.canonical.com/sites/default/files/active/Whitepaper-UbuntuEnterpriseCloudArchitecture-v1.pdf

Yahoo, Inc. (2011). *Yahoo! Hadoop tutorial*. Retrieved February 23, 2011 from http://developer.yahoo.com/hadoop/tutorial/module4.html#tolerence

KEY TERMS AND DEFINITIONS

Amazon Web Services (AWS): The largest and best known provider of cloud computing market.

Cloud Computing: Describes the delivery of computing as a service via Internet. Therefore, you can use large computational power at low cost.

Distributed Forensics: Is the use of distributed computing to perform forensic tasks.

Eucalyptus: Eucalyptus is infrastructure software used for implementation of private and hybrid clouds on computer clusters.

Forensic as a Service: A new way to perform forensics tasks in large data sets. It is the delivery of Forensic as s Service as combining the advantages of using cloud computing and distributed computing through the MapReduce programming model.

Forensics Computing: It is an evolution of techniques for data recovery, which aims to search and analysis of evidence found in electronic devices, typically used to solve cybercrimes. These crimes often use computers, but also can use Smartphones, Cell Phones, Tablets, PDAs, among others.

Hadoop: The free implementation of MapReduce model, supported by Apache.

MapReduce: Introduced by Google, this is a programming model used for support distributed computing on large data sets on clusters of computers.

ENDNOTES

1 http://aws.amazon.com/elasticmapreduce

2 http://aws.amazon.com/ec2

3 http://aws.amazon.com/s3

4 Information provided about configuration and pricing of instances were retrieved from Amazon in February 2011, and can be found in the page of service provided by Amazon, Elastic MapReduce (http://aws.amazon.com/elasticmapreduce/).

5 http://aws.amazon.com/agreement

6 Information on the S3 was retrieved in February 2011 and is subject to change.

7 http://aws.amazon.com/calculator

8 http://www.canonical.com

Chapter 13
A Forensic-as-a-Service Delivery Platform for Law Enforcement Agencies

Fabio Marturana
University of Rome "Tor Vergata", Italy

Simone Tacconi
Postal and Communications Police, Italy

Giuseppe F. Italiano
University of Rome "Tor Vergata", Italy

ABSTRACT

With the global diffusion of cybercrime, the ever-growing market penetration of high-performance and low-cost personal digital devices, and the commercial success of cloud computing, the area of digital forensics is faced with various new challenges that must be taken seriously. In this chapter, the authors describe a novel approach to digital investigations based on the emerging "Forensics as a Service" (FaaS) model. This model attempts to optimize Law Enforcement Agency's (LEA) forensic procedures, reduce complexity, and save operational costs. Inspired by previous work on distributed computing for forensic analysis, this chapter provides the reader with design guidelines of a FaaS platform for secure service delivery. The proposed FaaS platform should be able to support investigators and practitioners in their daily tasks (e.g. digital evidence examination, analysis, and reporting) once implemented by a cloud forensic provider or internally by a LEA. In this chapter, the authors also present the architecture components, interfaces, communication protocols, functional and non-functional requirements, as well as security specifications of the proposed framework in detail.

DOI: 10.4018/978-1-4666-2662-1.ch013

Copyright © 2013, IGI Global. Copying or distributing in print or electronic forms without written permission of IGI Global is prohibited.

INTRODUCTION

The pervasiveness of the Internet and the large availability of low-cost, sophisticated and heterogeneous digital devices (i.e. PDAs, laptops, tablets, mobiles, and smartphones, etc.) characterized by large storage capacity and broadband network connections have contributed to the global diffusion of cyber threats and cybercrimes.

As technology penetrating to all works of life, cybercrime is also evolving at an astonishing pace. Whilst society is inventing and evolving, at the same time, criminals are deploying a remarkable adaptability in order to derive the greatest benefit from it (National Gendarmerie, 2011). According to McAfee (2012), the first part of 2012 has seen an impressive increase of cyber threats and malware. According to Federal Bureau of Investigation (FBI) 2008 statistics, in the United States, the size of the average digital forensic case is growing at the rate of 35% per year—from 83 GB in 2003 to 277 GB in 2007. With storage capacity growth outpacing network bandwidth and latency improvements, forensic data is not only getting bigger, but is also growing significantly larger relative to the ability to process them in a timely manner (Roussev, et al., 2009).

Under such circumstances, we believe that ever-growing amount of disk storage and bandwidth available to ordinary computer users will soon overwhelm forensics practitioners accustomed to handle digital evidence on a stand-alone workstation. Performing simple preprocessing operations, such as keywords indexing and image thumbnail generation, against a captured image will therefore consume vast amount of time before an investigation can even begin. Non-indexed "live" searches, such as those involving regular expressions, are already time-consuming and will become completely infeasible. Even worse, it will be impossible to raise the level of sophistication of digital forensics analysis because single forensics workstations will simply not be up to the task. As a consequence, forensic investigation tools will have to employ a pool of distributed resources in order to make investigations manageable (Roussev & Richard, 2004).

The Digital Forensic Research Workshop (DFRWS) has defined digital forensics as "the application of scientifically derived and proven methods aiming at preservation, collection, validation, identification, analysis, interpretation, documentation and presentation of digital evidence extracted from high-tech devices, maintaining a documented chain of evidence, for presentation in courts" (Digital Forensic Research Workshop, 2001). Huge efforts have been made in the last decade to improve digital forensic techniques and capabilities in order to develop new tools and procedures to support LEAs investigations. Following this trend, practitioners and researchers have developed new ideas and methods for retrieving evidence more effectively as it happened in the field of digital triage and machine learning-based automated analysis of evidence (Marturana, et al., 2012a, 2012b).

According to NIST (Mell & Grance, 2009), cloud computing as "a model for enabling ubiquitous, convenient, on-demand network access to a shared pool of configurable computing resources (e.g., networks, servers, storage, applications, and services) that can be rapidly provisioned and released with minimum management effort or service provider interaction." Cloud computing has four deployment models (i.e. public, private, hybrid and community cloud) and three service models, i.e., Infrastructure-as-a-Service (IaaS), Platform-as-a-Service (PaaS), and Software-as-a-Service (SaaS).

Cloud computing is radically changing the way information technology services are created, delivered, accessed, and managed. Cloud computing is bringing a new wave of innovation, and enabling tasks formerly carried out by well-rounded computers and servers to be performed on a pocket device such as a smartphone. According to Perry et al. (2009), this new service delivery paradigm has the potential to become one of the most transformative developments in the history of computing, following the footsteps of mainframes, minicomputers, PCs (Personal Computers), and smart phones.

Cloud-based document and photo sharing, calendar and address book synchronization, image and word processors are scalable, platform-independent, and accessible from anywhere on demand. Cloud computing benefits also include greater data availability (i.e. the theft of a device leaves the data still available in the cloud), logical security and lower storage and processing hardware costs (Lillard, et al., 2010). Based on this virtually unlimited, on-demand, self-service, and elastic cloud computing service delivery model, several researchers (Roussev, et al., 2009; Didoné & de Queiroz, 2011) started discussing the possibility of adopting the service paradigm or even extend it to define a new FaaS platform which allows LEAs or external Forensic Service Providers (FSP) and contractors to perform forensic tasks "as a Service."

In this chapter, we first review literature on distributed and FaaS models, then describe the steps required to implement a FaaS platform to support LEA investigation and generate admissible evidence on the scene or in lab. We further elaborate on the design principles, specific functional and non-functional requirements, a communication protocol among the involved entities, as well as a security framework assuring access control, confidentiality, integrity of data, non-repudiation, availability, and secure logging. Future research directions and conclusions are covered in the last two sections of the chapter.

BACKGROUND

The Evolution of Digital Forensics

According to Garfinkel (2010), the field of digital forensic analysis is undergoing a rapid maturation to maintain pace with technological changes in the computer industry and to overcome difficulty in defining standard methodologies and tools for forensic analysis, which risk to nullify the results achieved over the last decade. Several critical issues concerning digital investigations are the growing size of storage devices causing delays in the process of creating forensic images and processing extracted data, the diffusion of embedded flash storage and hardware interfaces resulting in storage drives that can no longer be readily removed or imaged, and the proliferation of heterogeneous digital devices, Operating Systems (OSs), and file formats which dramatically increases the complexity and costs of data extraction and analysis tools.

Though in the last decade most cases were already complex due to large distributed networks and removable storage devices (diskettes, zip disks, etc.), the rapid diffusion of mobile phones, smartphones, and tablets in the marketplace have caused a deep change to the landscape as today's cases are far more complex and require the analysis of multiple, heterogeneous digital artifacts (e.g. solid state disk drives, thumb drives, iPods, cell phones, mobile handsets, PDAs, tablets, etc.), followed by manifold evidence correlations. The situation outlined above is worsened by pervasive encryption because, much more frequently, recovered data cannot be processed without previously being decrypted with sufficient time, luck and expensive RAM forensics techniques (Casey & Stellatos, 2008).

The Expanding Field of Mobile Forensics

The reduced cost and ever-growing storage capacity and supported features have enabled the proliferation of mobile devices (i.e., smart phones, tablets, iPads, etc.) around the world. The International Telecommunication Union (ITU, 2010) reported that cell phone global market penetration rate is above 50% in general and almost 100% in most developed countries (ITU, 2010) with five main operating systems (i.e. Android, Apple, Blackberry, Windows Mobile, Symbian, etc.) fighting to gain market share and hundreds of thousands of downloadable applications already available in the app store marketplace. However, these mobile devices are also primary tools for criminals and terrorists to communicate with each other. NIST defines mobile forensics as "the science of recovering digital evidence from a mobile phone under forensically sound conditions using accepted methods" (Jansen & Ayers, 2007). Marturana et al. (2011a, 2011b) has proposed a new approach to mobile forensics recently, introducing the "triage" concept to mobile forensic extraction capabilities based on machine learning classification algorithms. This approach can provide an automated categorization of mobile artifacts based on the material extracted from mobile artifacts.

The Investigative Domain of Cloud Computing

Ruan et al. (2011) conclude that the birth of cloud computing not only has exacerbated the problem of scale for digital investigations, but also created a brand new front for cybercrime investigation with various challenges. Access to the case data might be denied and it might be impossible to perform data preservation and isolation on systems of forensic interest as critical information is stored in unidentified servers "somewhere in the cloud." Frequently, evidentiary data or code cannot even be found as single data structures are split into many virtual elements distributed in the "Cloud" (Garfinkel, 2010).

Digital forensics knowledge and tools need to be extended into cloud computing environments to help cloud organizations, cloud providers and their customers, to establish forensic capabilities in order to reduce cloud security risks (Ruan, et al., 2011). Ruan et al. (2011) also proposed a new model of role-based interaction among cloud organizations, cloud providers, LEAs, academia and third parties to carry out investigations on critical incidents happened in the cloud such as criminal intrusions and major policy violations, as well as collaborating in cases of resource confiscation. On the one hand, novel forensic service models can also be developed to support digital investigations leveraging the cloud computing paradigm shift.

An Example of Cloud Computing Platform

To address the challenges outlined in the previous section, a number of commercial organizations, including Google, Amazon, Yahoo, and Microsoft have applied cloud-computing concepts in building large systems from commodity computers, disks, and networks, and creating software to make this hardware easier to program and manage (NSA, 2012).

Google, for example, has developed a cloud-based computing infrastructure based on its original design philosophy. Rather than building a system from a moderate number of high-performance computers, assuming that hardware will fail regularly, and designing software to deal with that fact, Google has built its cloud infrastructure as a cluster containing a much larger number of commodity computers. Since Google is not using state-of-the-art and expensive hardware, it can optimize costs, power consumption, and space needs by making appropriate tradeoffs.

Cloud-based solutions have led to some significant software challenges because writing distributed software that can take full advantage of the aggregated computing power of many entry-level machines is far more difficult than writing software for a centralized enterprise-class server farm. To solve the problem, Google has implemented an original design philosophy by optimizing system software for the specific application planned to run on it through the foundation of its cloud software stack architecture: the Google File System (GFS). GFS is a scalable distributed file system for large data-intensive applications. GFS is optimized for storing very large files (>1GB) using a 64 MB block size (called chunk). It is also optimized to improve I/O performance by supporting appended operations since Google's applications typically write files sequentially once and read them many times. These appended chunks that constitute a single file do not need to reside on the same disk and are allocated across all of the machines in the Cloud. Doing chunk allocation in this manner also provides the architectural underpinnings for GFS fault tolerance, as GFS doesn't adopt fault-tolerance techniques used in enterprise class servers such as Redundant Arrays of Inexpensive Disks (RAID) (Ghemawat, et al., 2003).

Built on top of GFS, Google's MapReduce framework is the heart of this cloud-based computational model. The basic idea behind this model is that programs can be written containing two simple functions Map and Reduce to process a collection of data, in order to leverage the parallel computing power of the Cloud. The underlying runtime system then divides the program into many small tasks and takes care of their executions. The runtime system also ensures that the correct subset of data is delivered to each task and collects results. The MapReduce model is interesting from a number of perspectives. Decades of high-performance computing has demonstrated the difficulty of writing software that takes full advantage of the processing power provided by a parallel or distributed system, the MapReduce runtime system however, is able to automatically partition a computation and run the individual parts on many different machines, achieving substantial performance improvement. Moreover, because most of the details of task scheduling and file management are hidden in the MapReduce and GFS runtime system, it is relatively easy to develop new applications on top of it (Dean & Ghemawat, 2008).

Finally, designed to store very large quantities of data, the Bigtable data storage system is the last major component of Google's approach to cloud computing. Bigtable horizontally partitions an individual table by grouping sets of rows into tablets, which are managed by different machines in a Google cloud. Google claims that Bigtable can store petabytes of data across thousands of servers (Chang, et al., 2008).

Implementing Forensic Processing through Distributed Computing

Roussev and Richard (2004) argue that implementations of digital forensics tools relying on single-machine processing are incapable of performing the analysis of even modest forensic targets at interactive rates and this problem will only get worse with the explosive growth of data volumes. Based on this reasoning, they proposed the Distributed Digital Forensic (DDF) proof-of-concept as a concrete solution to the issues outlined above.

Several researchers have proposed models for distributed forensic services inspired by large-scale distributed computing and the cloud computing paradigm. Roussev et al. (2009) proposed the MPI MapReduce (MMR) framework. It is an open implementation of Google's MapReduce for optimizing forensic computing. Didoné and de Queiroz (2011) also proposed a FaaS service implementation inspired by Roussev et al. and it is also developed based on MapReduce.

Drawing inspiration from Google's design concepts and MapReduce framework, Roussev et al. have explored the possibility of developing scalable forensic computing solutions to match the ever-growing size of forensic collection. There are three mutually independent approaches to solve scalability issues and improving processing performance, i.e., improving algorithms and tools, using additional hardware resources and facilitating human collaboration. Roussev et al. followed the second approach and used commodity distributed computational resources as a solution to speedup forensic investigations. They stated that forensic tools generally perform functions such as hashing, indexing and feature extraction in a serial manner resulting in processing time growing linearly with the size of the forensic collection. Another approach requires additional computational resources to maintain the cost of the expansion constant over time. The main challenge of this approach is the lack of a software platform that enables forensic processing to be scaled seamlessly to the available computing resources.

Finally, ForNet proposed by Shanmugasundaram et al. (2003) is also a well-known project in the area of distributed forensics, and it focuses on the distributed collection and search of network evidence.

THE FORENSICS AS A SERVICE PLATFORM

Motivation

A digital investigation is an interactive process in which analysts issue queries, perform hashing, indexing, feature extraction and correlation tasks against the target datasets, and based on the results perform a deeper search to build a clearer picture of the case. Investigation complexity and the amount of available forensic artifacts permit; these operations have been traditionally carried out by forensic practitioners in a sequence on stand-alone forensic workstations. However as mentioned earlier, the growing size of storage devices and proliferation of multi-vendor handsets and OSs are causing delays and increasing complexity in the investigative process. Novel approaches need to be developed to solve this problem.

In this section, we propose a FaaS platform to address this need. The FaaS platform includes the following main components: the communication interfaces between cloud provider and LEA and internal to the cloud provider, the architecture and functional model, as well as the functional and non-functional security requirements. The proposed framework is designed to be compatible with different service implementations.

Overview of the Proposed Solution

To provide a viable solution to the issues outlined in the previous section, we have defined an investigative framework for distributed forensic data processing, called FaaS platform. It is inspired by the DDF toolkit developed by Roussev and Richard (2004) and the prototype proposed by Roussev et al. (2009) based on Google's cloud implementation and the MapReduce distributed programming paradigm) leveraging the opportunities offered by cloud computing.

The proposed solution is based on the assumption that, based on the file type, forensic practitioners generally perform operations such as indexing, keyword searching or image analysis on a list of files mostly extracted from a captured image. To get the result in the distributed scenario, we may run a set of remote processes on many commodity servers capable of caching files or fragments in RAM and executing a set of operations on them. As a result, data may remain cached during the entire process, allowing complex operations to be performed quickly.

We therefore decided to use a forensic image as the natural unit of distribution so that independent file operations such as keyword searching may be split and performed in parallel on different servers. In this scenario few dependencies place constraints on the distribution of files or file fragment data or require complex distributed synchronization. This is in sharp contrast to distributed problems like multiplication of large matrices, where dependencies are numerous and there is no single correct answer to the problem of optimal data distribution, as stated by Roussev and Richard (2004).

Similarly, we can argue that the same applies for captured image uploaded to the FaaS platform, as it may be divided in advance by the client into fragments of smaller size that may be sent in parallel to the cloud provider after generating the correspondent hash value, resulting in more efficient uploads. The cloud provider will be responsible for verifying hash correctness and acknowledging each independent fragment and forwarding it to one or more remote processes. It is possible to rebuild the complete captured image on one or more servers by making use of the distributed file systems capability of replicating files, so that at a certain time more than a server actually stores the complete image.

In the distributed scenario where few dependencies place constraints on the distribution of files and image fragments or require complex distributed synchronization, it might be quite easy to reduce delays and increase efficiency by simply caching the whole dataset assigned to each subtasks in a remote server's RAM as long as the subtask is up and running. The cloud management software will take the responsibility to activate remote processing tasks and collect partial results, at the same time, allowing complex operations to be performed quickly.

Service Architecture, Functional Model, and Interfaces

In this section, we present the following:

1. The architectural components of the FaaS platform
2. The functional FaaS model
3. A communication interface (CSP-LEA) between a cloud provider and a LEA for service request and result delivery
4. An internal interface (O-FP) for data exchange among the cloud provider cloud servers.

The main architectural components as depicted in Figure 1 is composed of a central process, called Orchestrator (O) and a number of remote Forensic Processes (FP).

The Orchestrator is responsible for the following functions via the CSP-LEA interface:

- Accepting incoming communications.
- Initiating outgoing communications.
- Aggregating and delivering results.

The Orchestrator is responsible for the following functions via the O-FP interface:

- Distributing captured image fragments once they are uploaded among available remote forensic processes.
- Keeping trace of captured images retained by each remote forensic process.
- Distributing processing tasks among available remote forensic processes with regards to retained images.

Figure 1. Functional model

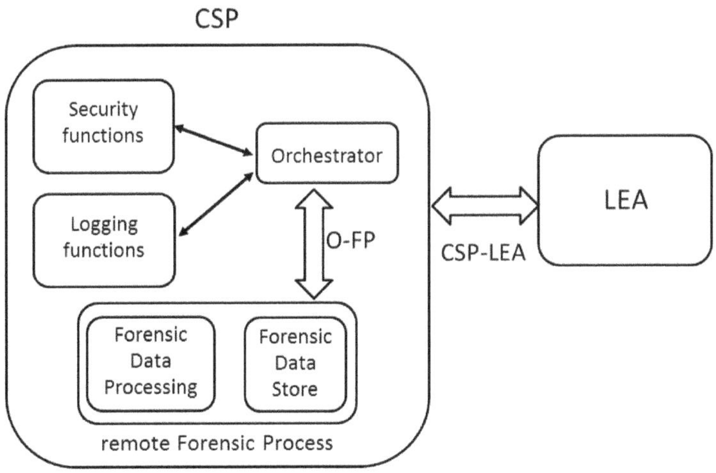

- Sending flush command to the remote forensic processes for deleting retained forensic data when needed.

The Remote Forensic Processes (RFP) is in charge of:

- Receiving, acknowledging and storing captured image fragments.
- Processing captured images.
- Deleting retained images and forensic data upon Orchestrator request.
- Delivering results to the Orchestrator.

Functional Requirements

A minimal set of forensic processing capabilities that should be supported by the proposed FaaS platform is described as follows:

1. Upload of a "live" digital media logical acquisition to the cloud provider.

We consider here a live forensic scenario in which LEA professionals should identify and make a logical copy of all the powered-on digital devices (i.e. computers, tablets, mobile phones, smartphones, PDAs, etc.) found at the crime scene, and inspect them to find volatile evidence that would vanish upon power-off. At the end of the image creation process, investigators should upload such images without delay to the FaaS platform. To do so, any secure connection available at the crime scene (e.g. a secure VPN tunnel upon a Wi-Fi or a 3G data link) should be used by investigators to upload images to the platform. Alternative data transfer procedures should be considered in case the crime scene is not under network coverage, such as the acquisition of a forensic images at the scene and upload once back at the forensic lab.

2. Upload of a "post mortem" digital media logical or physical acquisition to the cloud provider.

In this scenario, a post-mortem investigation on digital artifacts is conducted in a forensic lab. Physical and logical content of such digital artifacts should be acquired and uploaded to the server-side platform. A secure network connection available at the lab should be used to upload images. Once uploaded, data should be retained by the platform for the whole duration of the investigation and may be queried at any time.

3. Generic file upload to the cloud provider.

It should be possible anytime to upload generic support files (e.g. pictures, video recordings notes taken at the crime scene or at lab during a post-mortem analysis, etc.) that may be useful for investigators to the FaaS platform.

4. On-demand analysis of the information uploaded to the cloud provider.

Once uploaded and rebuilt on more than one server in the forensic cloud, it should be possible to process and query on a captured image in parallel from different servers. This feature should reduce response time and optimize available resources. The following is a list of possible operations that a LEA practitioner should be able to execute:

- **OS Information Retrieval:** It should be possible to garner OS information on which the forensic artifact resides.
- **Deleted File Retrieval:** It should be possible to use carving tools to extract the list of deleted files from unallocated space and slack space.
- **File Classification by Category or Extension:** It should be possible to classify the content of the analyzed image on the basis of statistics on file type, metadata, extension, average dimension, etc.
- **Installed Application Software List Retrieval:** It should be possible to retrieve the list of installed software.

- **Web Browsing Cache, Cookies and History Repository Analysis:** It should be possible to extract Web-browsing artifacts including navigation cache, history, the list of stored cookies, as well as additional browser-specific artifacts (e.g. Internet Explorer, Firefox, Chrome, Opera, Safari, etc.).
- **Saved Skype Call History, Chat and Instant Messaging Communication Retrieval:** It should be possible to retrieve artifacts including Skype call history, chat and instant messaging sessions when available.
- **Local Email Database Extraction:** It should be possible to retrieve email databases and extract relevant artifacts from e-mails.
- **Digital Timeline Creation:** It should be possible to rebuild the sequence of events and actions happened in a specific timeframe.
- **Encrypted File Retrieval:** It should be possible to extract encrypted files.
- **Content-Based Indexing:** It should be possible to index image content to optimize queries.
- **Cryptographic Hash Calculation:** It should be possible to calculate or verify files' digest.
- **Keyword Searching:** It should be possible to search for keywords.

Non-Functional Requirements

The following non-functional requirements are also part of the proposed platform:

1. **Platform-Independence:** The outlined requirements should be met regardless of the machine architecture and OS.
2. **Scalability:** The platform should be able to scale horizontally and the addition of more distributed machines should lead to proportional improvement on forensic tasks execution time.
3. **Efficiency:** The extra work performed by the platform to distribute data and queries among its nodes, as well as to collect results, should be negligible compared to the total execution time.
4. **Robustness:** In a distributed system, the service delivery platform includes many components that can potentially fail at any time. The platform should be able to detect and recover from such exceptional conditions and ensure the same level of confidence in the end result as in normal cases.
5. **Extensibility:** It should be easy to add a new function as a building block to the FaaS platform or replace an existing one. Therefore, writing a processing function from scratch to meet a new requirement should be compliant to the proposed model.
6. **Interactivity:** To improve the user-interactive experience in such a distributed solution, it should be possible to perform the time-consuming processing in the background (on cloud machines) while allowing operators to issue queries and to view partial results as soon as they become available.
7. **Ease of Administration:** It should be easy for administrators to operate the distributed platform with little interaction with the underlying infrastructure.

Message Flows and Communication Protocol

In this section, we will use the following pseudo code to describe the message flows between the LEA and the cloud provider (via the CSP-LEA interface) as well as between the Orchestrator and the remote forensic processes (via the O-FP interface):

Interface:Request_
source:Command(parameters)

- Interface is the interface on which the message flow is processed.
- Request_source is the message originator.
- Command is the type of request to be processed by the end-point.
- parameters (optional) is the aggregated list of data and flags to be processed by the end-point.

Message Flow for Forensic Image Upload

The following stages as presented in Figure 2 and Figure 3 describe the message flow when a LEA operator uploads a forensic image to the cloud provider:

- LEA-cloud provider:LEA:Req_upload
  The LEA sends a request to update a forensic image to the Orchestrator
- O-FP:O:Req_upload
  The Orchestrator identifies the set of available remote forensic processes that can store fragments of the uploaded forensic image and sends multiple requests to these remote forensic processes
- O-FP:FP:Req_upload(ack)
  Each remote forensic process acknowledges the request upon receiving the aforementioned request without delay
- LEA-cloud provider:cloud provider:Req_upload(ack)
  The Orchestrator acknowledges the LEA upon receiving the upload request. The cloud provider is now ready to process the upload request
- LEA-cloud provider:LEA:Send(fragment)
  The LEA breaks the message into fragments and sends them in parallel upon receiving the acknowledgement from the Orchestrator
- O-FP:O:Send(fragment)

Figure 2. Message flow for forensic image upload

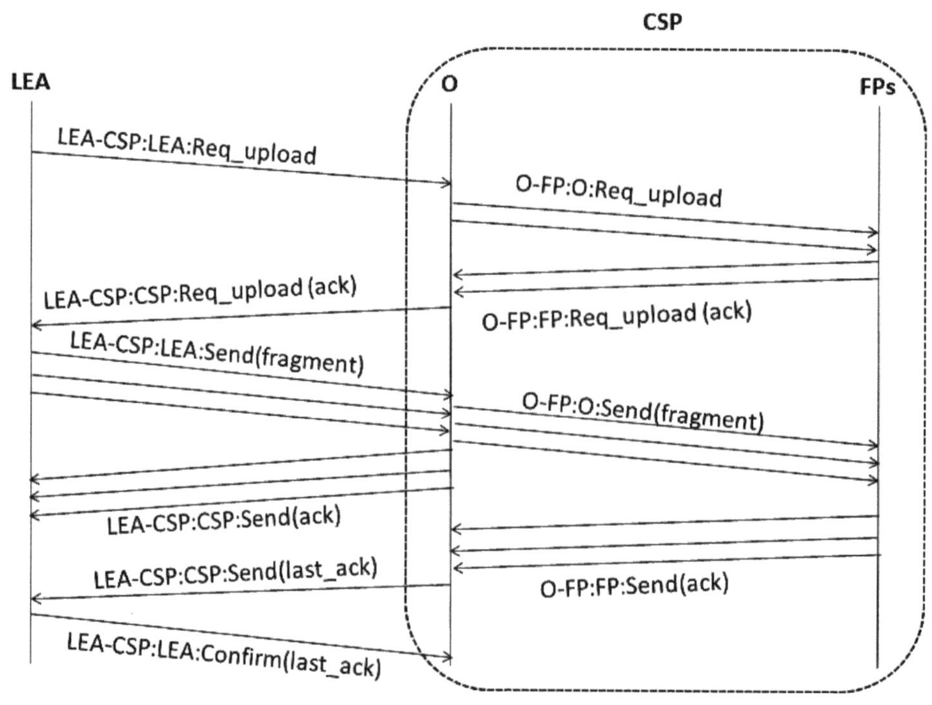

The Orchestrator forwards the fragments to selected remote forensic process (i.e. pipeline) upon receiving them without delay, and keeps a log trace of each process ID (i.e. logging function). The distributed file system should be able to replicate missing fragments from selected processes to rebuild the complete image in more than one server

- LEA-cloud provider:cloud provider:Send(ack)
  The Orchestrator acknowledges the LEA upon receiving all fragments without delay
- O-FP:FP:Send(ack)
  Each remote forensic process acknowledges the Orchestrator upon receiving a fragment without delay
- LEA-cloud provider:cloud provider:Send(final_ack)
  The Orchestrator acknowledges the LEA in return upon receiving the final acknowledgement
- LEA-cloud provider:LEA:Confirm(final_ack)
  The LEA acknowledges the Orchestrator in return and the processing of the upload request is completed upon receiving this final acknowledgement

Message Flow for Generic Processing Request

The following stages as presented in Figure 4 and Figure 5 describe the message flow when a LEA operator requires the cloud provider to perform a forensic task, such as keyword searching, indexing, hashing, feature extraction or correlation, where each task is targeted to a specific forensic image retained by the cloud provider:

- LEA-cloud provider:LEA:Req_proc(attrib)

Figure 3. Sequence diagram for forensic image upload

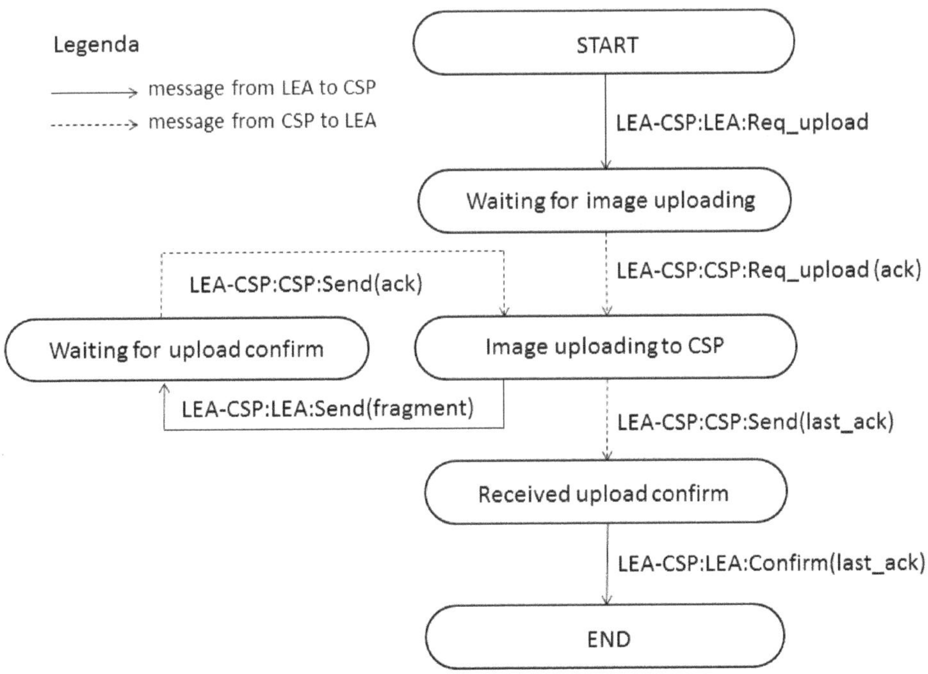

Figure 4. Message flow for generic processing request

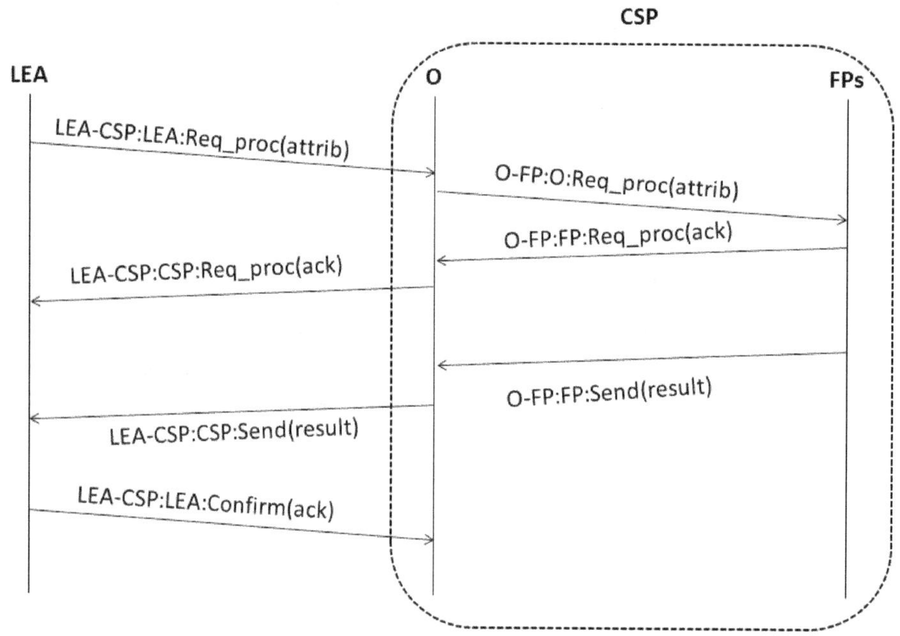

Figure 5. Sequence diagram for generic processing request

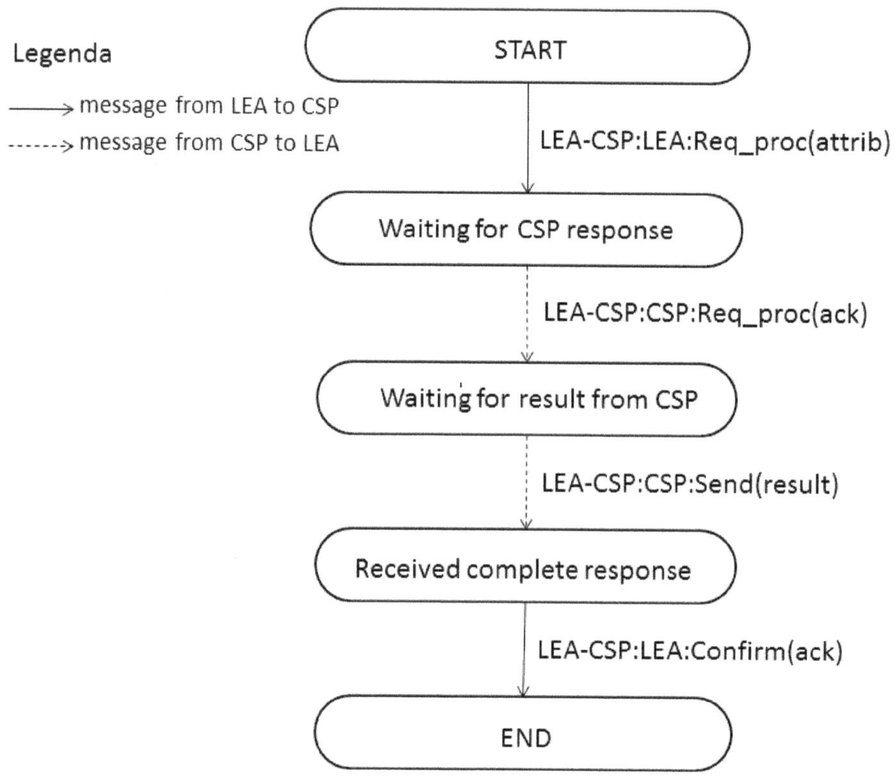

The LEA sends a processing request to the Orchestrator, including the name of the image file to process, the type of processing request and parameters in attrib

- O-FP:O:Req_proc(attrib)
  The Orchestrator queries the logging server for remote forensic processes handling the correspondent image file and forward them the request upon receiving a processing request from the LEA
- O-FP:FP:Req_proc(ack)
  Each remote forensic process acknowledges the Orchestrator and starts processing the request upon receiving a Req_proc(attrib)
- LEA-cloud provider:cloud provider: Req_proc(ack)
  The Orchestrator acknowledges in return that it has received a processing request message from the LEA it is being processed upon receiving an acknowledgement from each remote forensic process. The cloud provider is now ready to process the given request
- O-FP:FP:Send(result)
  Each remote forensic process sends results to the Orchestrator when they are available without delay
- LEA-cloud provider:cloud provider:Send(result)
  The Orchestrator collects partial results from remote forensic processes, prepares the response that fully meets its processing requirement and sends it to the LEA
- LEA-cloud provider:LEA:Confirm(ack)
  The LEA acknowledges it has received the response from the cloud provider without delay. The cloud provider is now no longer required to do further work on the given request and the request is closed.

Presentation-Layer Communication Protocol

HTTPS, the SSL/TLS-based secure version of HTTP, is the presentation-layer protocol used to support service requests and result delivery generated by the message flows outlined in the previous section. HTTPS works on top of the TCP/IP stack in a geographic Wide Area Network (WAN); it overcomes the limitation of the simple text-based message protocol of the DDF toolkit developed by Roussev and Richard (2004) which was optimized to work in a private Gigabit Ethernet LAN (Local Area Network).

HTTPS protocol adopts a Web-based client/server configuration in which data exchange is initiated from the LEA side by using a HTTPS client to invoke the cloud provider's HTTPS server.

To overcome potential protocol-dependent security issues, the following settings should be considered:

- The POST method should be used for all requests.
- Proxies can be used but content caching should not be used, which can be ensured by using the header "cache-control: no store." Special care should be taken for the logs kept by proxy servers.

HTTPS status codes cannot be used as a substitute for CSP-LEA messages, e.g., a LEA should not consider a blank HTTPS 200 (OK) as an Acknowledgement to a processing request message as it must also carry a full and well-formed LEA-cloud provider:cloud provider:Req_proc(ack) message at its payload.

In order to improve protocol performance:

- Cloud provider and LEA should not send header fields unless there is a clear need. Some HTTPS header fields (e.g. negotiation of content or language, range-limiting of requests, cache control, etc.) should be avoided as they may be useless or complicate the handover protocol, without adding benefits.
- The use of compression software (e.g. gzip) is recommended.

Security Requirements

In this section, we describe the requirements to allow secure data exchange at low cost with reliability and accuracy using standard procedures. The proposed model aims to guarantee security in aspects of access control, confidentiality, integrity, non-repudiation, and availability as well as secure logging of cloud provider's operations (e.g. between Orchestrator and remote forensic processes) and data delivery to LEAs. In order to achieve a desirable level of security, we recommend the following measures.

Access Control

The FaaS platform team personnel should be able to access the infrastructure based on well-defined authorization criteria after successful identification, authentication, and authorization of the identity of the personnel. It is strictly forbidden to access the system by using the identity of someone else. Therefore, the system should have state-of-the-art measures to prevent the use of the account of someone else (e.g. with secure authentication devices). In particular:

1. A strong cryptographic authentication mechanism is recommended to be used by the FaaS platform for either local or remote users (LEAs). It is recommended to use a combination of two or three factors such as a password, a cryptographic key and secure smart cards or token devices or biometrics.
2. The information of the identities of the people authorized to access the system and their respective accounts is securely stored and classified. This information is recommended to be kept for the entire life of the system. The use of this information is restricted to the investigation of malicious actions in the system by lawful authorities.
3. Successful or unsuccessful access attempts to the FaaS platform infrastructure should be securely logged.
4. The number of failed login attempts is recommended to be limited to a specified number (e.g. three attempts). Exceeding that number of failed login attempts will trigger the pertinent procedure for handling security alerting events.
5. A Regulatory authority should regularly perform an audit on the access control security policy and its enforcement.

Confidentiality of Data at Rest

The privacy of sensitive information involved in FaaS sessions should be protected when at rest by using appropriate mechanisms such as encryption; only standardized and well-known encryption algorithms such as the Advanced Encryption Standard (AES) are recommended. The key length of the related encryption keys should provide adequate protection from exhaustive attacks; the cryptographic key should be securely managed from its generation, use, and storage to destruction.

FaaS platform data that are stored within storing devices requires high protection in terms of confidentiality. Hence, the retained data, the session execution data, and related log data that the cloud provider network produces and stores are recommended to be kept encrypted during their entire retention period within storage devices. Key management procedures, necessary for succeeding any encryption procedures, is recommended to be also taken into consideration. Each encryption key should have retention period equal to the retention period of the stored data that encrypts and then it should be removed together with the data that normally encrypts.

Confidentiality of Data in Transit

The privacy of sensitive information involved in FaaS sessions should be protected when in transit by using appropriate cryptographic mechanisms similar to those outlined in the previous section.

Additionally, the following requirements should be applied:

1. On the O-FP interface: user data are uploaded to the cloud provider and stored by remote forensic processes. These data should be collected by the Orchestrator in a secure manner. Hence, all the user data should be routed through the cloud provider internal network separate from other traffic so that it is possible to forward these data over secured network links. Alternatively, users are recommended to encrypt sensitive data before uploading to the platform.
2. On the LEA-cloud provider interface: confidentiality of data in transit through the external communication interfaces is recommended to use strong encryption (at least 128 bits). Connection level security methods, such as IPSec or TLS, are also encouraged.

Integrity of Data at Rest and In Transit

Any system that is used to storage artifacts of FaaS platform should ensure the integrity of data at rest by using hashing algorithms and digital signatures.

The following is a list of requirements that should be applied to protect integrity of data in transit:

- **O-FP Interface:** Orchestrator and remote forensic processes should perform cryptographic message integrity checks. Hashing the transmitted packets and adding the hash checksums to the transmitted information wherever this is possible is a recommended method,
- **LEA-Cloud Provider Interface:** The integrity data in transit should be protected through hashing or HMAC algorithms; when uploading data and processing requests, data integrity can be guaranteed by applying security measures to application level.

In particular:

1. The LEA should apply data integrity protection by computing a hash over the entire set of fields in the service request (including the timestamp), and then the hash should be digitally signed with the entity's private key. This signed hash and the entity's certificate (to validate its public key) should be enclosed in the request sent to the cloud provider. The cloud provider may choose to validate the request by computing the request's hash and verifying that it matches the one signed by the LEA. The cloud provider may choose to validate the certificate as well,
2. The cloud provider should similarly compute a hash of each required response, sign the hash value of the entire set of fields (including the timestamp) and send to the LEA the signed hash and its certificate (validating this public key) along with the set of fields.

Non-Repudiation

The service origin (e.g. an authorized LEA officer) makes the request and awaits response from cloud provider. In both ways the same methodology as described in the last section can be used to ensure non-repudiation, i.e., to use the private key and digitally sign the hashed data of the entire request or response message. Following the entire block of information (the data of the request or response, the signed hash and the entity's certificate) is sent towards the correct destination.

Availability

The operating systems should be up-to-date and all the state-of-the-art security applications need to be installed to detect and protect the system against malicious code, intrusions, and any other threats. All users, services, applications, ports and addresses of the system not strictly needed should be properly disabled, locked, or removed. Physical premises of the systems should implement strict access control and monitoring.

Secure Logging

Secure and effective log management is important. Correlated logs are used during scheduled security audits to assure intended technical measures are in place and that the security policies and procedures are implemented. These logs are also analyzed during non-scheduled security audits to discover the cause of incidents such as lack of security measures, non-conformance with security procedures or system misconfigurations. Hence, a secure log management framework is recommended to be implemented and maintained by the forensic provider.

FUTURE RESEARCH DIRECTIONS

Some of the possible future research areas on FaaS may be:

1. Designing and implementing a thin-client-side application for the FaaS platform, which should run on a smartphone or tablet with iOS or Android. Such device should allow the collection and processing of evidentiary data (e.g. RAM acquisition, keyword searching of RAM, Registry, active processes, network connections, file classification by category or extension) directly at the crime scene, along with other generic material about the case under investigation, such as notes, pictures and video recordings. The client-side software, running on investigator's mobile device, should acquire forensic images of each digital device found at the scene via USB interface, upload such images on demand to the FaaS platform and send requests for remote data processing. As an alternative to improve upload efficiency, the client-side software could acquire data on a local storage, process them, and send results to the forensic platform, uploading the reminder files (e.g. forensic images) once back at the lab. It should be possible to create supporting files that may be uploaded on demand to the case folder using the FaaS platform.
2. Extending client side capabilities to include a secure terminal server for on-demand remote support to LEA's personnel on the crime scene (e.g. defining a mutual client/server communication protocol configuration).
3. Extending the proposed service delivery model to allow LEAs to implement the service internally with a private cloud infrastructure and have complete control of the retained data. This is a critical aspect that needs to be addressed separately and relatively soon as there will be reluctance on the part of LEAs to have evidence scattered in the Cloud, not to mention outside their jurisdictional areas, despite the low cost advantage of public cloud offerings.
4. Performing and evaluating benchmarks to compare advantages and challenges of delivering forensic support services in house or outsourcing to a specialized third party.

CONCLUSION

In this chapter, we proposed a cloud-based Forensics as a Service (FaaS) platform to address the pressing need of finding alternative solutions to handle large volume of digital forensic artifacts.

The proposed solution is based on the assumption that it is possible to break forensic tasks into independent subtasks to run on remote processes in the Cloud.

We also discussed in this chapter design guidelines of a FaaS platform for forensic-oriented and secure service delivery, which once implemented by a Forensic Service Providers (FSP) or a LEA should support investigators in their daily tasks (e.g. digital evidence examination, analysis, and reporting).

Architecture components, interfaces, communication protocols, functional and non-functional requirements, and security specifications of the proposed platform have also been discussed in detail to provide the reader with implementation guidelines.

We believe adopting distributed forensic delivery solutions is a solution to avoid backlogs, thus improving investigation effectiveness, and reduce operational costs and capital investments for LEAs.

REFERENCES

Casey, E., & Stellatos, G. J. (2008). The impact of full disk encryption on digital forensics. *Operating System Review*, *42*(3), 93–98. doi:10.1145/1368506.1368519

Chang, F., Dean, J., Ghemawat, S., Hsieh, W. C., Wallach, D. A., & Burrows, M. … Gruber, R. E. (2008). *Bigtable: A distributed storage system for structured data*. Retrieved from http://static.usenix.org/event/osdi06/tech/chang/chang.pdf

Dean, J., & Ghemawat, S. (2008). MapReduce: Simplified data processing on large clusters. *Communications of the ACM*, *51*(1), 107–113. doi:10.1145/1327452.1327492

Didoné, D., & De Queiroz, R. J. G. B. (2011). Forensic as a service – FaaS. In *Proceedings of the 6th International Conference on Forensic Computer Science*, (pp. 202-210). IEEE.

Digital Forensic Research Workshop. (2001). *A roadmap for digital forensic research*. Retrieved April 20, 2012, from http://www.dfrws.org/dfrws-rm-final.pdf

Garfinkel, S. L. (2010). Digital forensics research: The next 10 years. *Digital Investigation*, *7*, S64–S73. doi:10.1016/j.diin.2010.05.009

Ghemawat, S., Gobioff, H., & Leung, S. (2003). The Google file system. In *Proceedings of the 19th ACM Symposium on Operating Systems Principles*. Lake George, NY: ACM Press.

International Telecommunication Union. (2010). *Measuring the information society*. Retrieved from http://www.itu.int

Jansen, W., & Ayers, R. (2007). *Guidelines on cell phone forensics*. Washington, DC: National Institute of Standard and Technology.

Lillard, T. V., Garrison, C. P., Schiller, C. A., & Steele, J. (2010). *Digital forensics for network, internet, and cloud computing*. Burlington, MA: Syngress Publishing.

Marturana, F., Bertè, R., Me, G., & Tacconi, S. (2011a). Mobile forensics "triaging": New directions for methodology. In *Proceedings of the 8th Conference of the Italian Chapter of AIS (ITAIS 2011)*. ITAIS.

Marturana, F., Bertè, R., Me, G., & Tacconi, S. (2011b). A quantitative approach to triaging in mobile forensics. In *Proceedings of International Joint Conference of IEEE TrustCom-11/IEEE ICESS-11/FCST-11, (TRUSTCOM 2011)*, (pp. 582-588). IEEE Press.

Marturana, F., Bertè, R., Me, G., & Tacconi, S. (2012a). Data mining based crime-dependent triage in digital forensics analysis. *IERI Lecture Notes in Information Technology*, *10*, 101–106.

Marturana, F., Bertè, R., Me, G., & Tacconi, S. (2012b). Triage-based automated analysis of evidence in court cases of copyright infringement. In *Proceedings of the 1st IEEE International Workshop on Security and Forensics in Communication Systems (SFCS 2012)*. IEEE Press.

McAfee. (2012). *Threats report, first quarter 2012*. Retrieved June 20, 2012, from http://www.mcafee.com/us/resources/reports/rp-quarterly-threat-q1-2012.pdf

Mell, J. P., & Grance, T. (2011). *The NIST definition of cloud computing*. Washington, DC: National Institute of Standard and Technology.

National Gendarmerie. (2011). *Prospective analysis on trends in cybercrime from 2011 to 2020*. Retrieved from http://www.mcafee.com/us/resources/white-papers/wp-trends-in-cyber-crime-2011-2020.pdf

National Security Agency. (2012). *An overview of cloud computing*. Retrieved June 17, 2012, from http://www.nsa.gov/research/_files/publications/cloud_computing_overview.pdf

Perry, R., Hatcher, E., Mahowald, R. P., & Hendrick, S. D. (2009). *Force.com cloud platform drives huge time to market and cost savings*. Retrieved June 22, 2012, from http://www.salesforce.com/fr/assets/pdf/whitepapers/whitepaper-idc-force-roi-study.pdf

Roussev, V., & Richard, G. (2004). Breaking the performance wall: The case for distributed digital forensics. In *Proceedings of the Annual Digital Forensics Research Workshop - DFRWS*. DFRWS.

Roussev, V., Wang, L., Richard, G., & Marziale, L. (2009). A cloud computing platform for large-scale forensic computing. In *Proceedings of the 5th IFIP International Conference on Digital Forensics, Advances in Digital Forensics*, (pp. 201-215). IFIP.

Ruan, K., Carthy, J., Kechadi, T., & Crosbie, M. (2011). Cloud forensics: An overview. In *Proceedings of the 7th IFIP International Conference on Digital Forensics, Advances in Digital Forensics*. Berlin, Germany: Springer.

Shanmugasundaram, K., Memon, N., Savant, A., & Bronnimann, H. (2003). ForNet: A distributed forensics network. In *Proceedings of the 2nd International Workshop on Mathematical Methods, Models and Architecture for Computer Network Security*, (pp. 1-16). IEEE.

Key Terms AND Definitions

Cloud Computing: Comparable to distributed computing, is a type of Internet-based computing, where different computing services, such as servers, storage and applications, are delivered to computers or digital devices through the Internet.

Cloud Provider: An organization who delivers computing services, such as servers, storage and applications, to its customers through the Internet, according to the Cloud Computing paradigm.

Digital Forensics: A multidisciplinary science that applies investigative techniques and forensically sound methods to retrieve and analyze evidences from digital artifacts.

Distributed Computing: Any computing that involves multiple remote computers each having a role in a computation problem or information processing.

Forensic-as-a-Service: Based on cloud computing service model, is the use of distributed computing for conducting forensic tasks.

Law Enforcement Agency: An investigative Police service empowered to enforce laws in different jurisdictions (i.e. national, international, multinational, federal, etc.).

Service Delivery Platform: A framework, including requirements, architecture, interfaces and communication protocols, designed to deliver a generic service through the Internet.

Chapter 14
Designing a Forensic-Enabling Cloud Ecosystem

Keyun Ruan
University College Dublin, Ireland

ABSTRACT

Cloud computing is a major transition, and it comes at a unique historical and strategic time for applying foundational design thinking to secure the next-generation computing infrastructure and enable waves of business and technological innovation. In this chapter, the researcher summarizes six key research and development areas for designing a forensic-enabling cloud ecosystem, including architecture and matrix, standardization and strategy, evidence segregation, security and forensic integration, legal framework, and privacy.

INTRODUCTION

Cloud computing is like a supercomputer split among cloud actors connected and delivered via networks. The split of technical infrastructure as an evolutionary computing service delivery model provides massive cost reduction and increases resource utilization. The split among cloud actors, on the other hand, requires new interfaces, trust and transparency, as well as legal framework to ensure smooth and secure service delivery with clearly defined segregation of duties for all cloud actors to implement relevant technical, organizational, and legal controls and mechanisms. Foundational thinking for designing standards, system architecture, and research roadmaps are needed at the current stage of cloud development. In this chapter, the researcher discusses the importance and strategies for designing a forensic-enabling cloud ecosystem.

With the ever-rising cyber crime and the rapid emergence of cloud computing, digital investigations are faced with significant challenges. While data are being migrated to cloud computing environments, so does digital evidence. In 2011, hackers rented Amazon servers and triggered the second-largest online data breach in U.S. history

DOI: 10.4018/978-1-4666-2662-1.ch014

Copyright © 2013, IGI Global. Copying or distributing in print or electronic forms without written permission of IGI Global is prohibited.

(Galante, et al., 2011). Cases as such cannot be handled by traditional digital forensic tools and procedures due to cloud forensic challenges outlined by pioneering researchers in Spyridopoulos and Katos (2011), Birk and Wegener (2011), Biggs and Vidalis (2009), Ruan et al. (2011a). At the meantime, global cybercrime is growing at an astonishing rate causing devastating financial losses. Annual loss caused by cyber crime in Europe alone is estimated to be 750 billion Euros (Cheslow, 2012). Designing a forensic-enabling cloud ecosystem is thus of high importance in order to prevent explosive growth of cybercrime in cloud environments due to lack of forensic considerations during cloud adoption.

The Information Society Alliance published a report (ISA, 2010), and it argues that the solution to current cyber security challenge is a fundamental change in market behavior so that the complex IT systems, on which society increasingly depends, have security embedded from the start rather than added as an afterthought. This did not happen in the history of the computer era. Even though John von Neumann designed the first theoretical computer virus (Neumann, 1949), he did not include security design in his own computer architecture known as the von Neumann Architecture (Neumann, 1945). Gartner (2012) estimates that personal cloud will replace personal computer by 2014, however, study shows security still is an afterthought during cloud adoption (Ernst & Young, 2011). Compare to security, forensic implementations have been an "after-after-thought." Anderson et al. (2012) carried out a research aimed to scientifically estimate the cost of cyber crime, and it concludes that "we should spend less in anticipation of cybercrime (on antivirus, firewalls, etc.) and more in response, i.e., the prosaic business of hunting down cyber criminals and throwing them in jail." The good news is that cloud computing is still at early stage of development and it is expected to reach maturity in another 10 years (Thomason, 2010, CSA & ISACA, 2012). According to CIO and CAOC (2012), cloud computing represents a paradigm shift that is larger than IT. This new paradigm requires agencies to re-think not only the way they acquire IT services in the context of deployment, but also how the IT services they consume provide mission and support functions on a shared basis. Researcher believes that now is a historically unique timing for including security and forensic implementations by design into cloud architecture iterations, and it might not be too late to change the game.

The cost of litigation and investigation in a cloud ecosystem without forensics by design can be very high. For example, the court in *In Re Fannie Mae Securities*, held an agency in contempt for failing to meet discovery deadlines even though the agency had already spent 6 million USD (9% of its total budget) on discovery. Using e-discovery tools to streamline search, collection, and processing could help Federal agencies avoid great cost in litigations, congressional requests, investigation, and other types of data requites. Federal agencies should inquire if there is an option or offering for e-discovery capabilities as part of the cloud service provided. If the right e-discovery functionality and tools are incorporated into an agency's CSP environment, there may be a potential for additional and significant cost avoidance and IT efficiencies (CIO & CAOC, 2012).

In this chapter, six strategic areas and directions for designing a forensic-enabling cloud ecosystem are discussed as follows:

1. **Architecture/matrix:** The need for cloud forensic reference architecture and control matrix.
2. **Standardization/strategy:** The need for considering forensic aspects in cloud standardization efforts as well as national cloud strategies.
3. **Evidence segregation:** The need for designing a data segregation strategy for multi-tenant cloud ecosystem enabled by virtualization technologies.

4. **Security and forensics integration:** The need for further integrating forensic design into security architectures.
5. **Legal framework:** The need for designing a legal framework to secure cross-border data transfer and facilitate international collaboration on digital investigations.
6. **Privacy:** The need for ensuring privacy protection when designing forensic implementations for the cloud ecosystem.

CLOUD FORENSIC REFERENCE ARCHITECTURE (CFRA) AND MATRIX

Traditional digital forensic processes and procedures are inadequate in handling cloud cases. According to the survey result (Ruan, et al., 2011b), 89% of the respondents agree or strongly agree that "designing forensic architectures for the cloud" is valuable research direction for cloud forensics. Such forensic reference architecture cannot be built without referring to the reference architectures for cloud computing and cloud security.

Several organizations are leading international efforts to provide reference architectures for cloud computing and cloud security, including the NIST Cloud Computing Reference Architecture (Liu, et al., 2012), the NIST Cloud Computing Security Reference Architecture (DRAFT)[1], the Cloud Security Alliance Trusted Cloud Initiative (TCI) Reference Architecture[2], and the Cloud Security Alliance Cloud Control Matrix[3].

A high level Cloud Forensic Reference Architecture (CFRA) should meet the following requirements:

- To serve as a foundation for cloud forensic terminology.
- To serve as a framework for generating processes and procedures for forensic investigations in different cloud investigative scenarios under specific cloud offering (e.g., different cloud deployment model, cloud service model, etc.).
- To be developed based on specific use cases.
- To help specify a list of forensic capabilities for cloud actors, and the segregation of duties among these cloud actors to deliver these capabilities.
- To help generate forensic-related terms for cloud contracts and Service Level Agreements (SLA).
- To reflect the relation between pre-incident security prevention and post-incident forensic investigation on an architectural level on all cloud system layers, i.e., physical, abstraction, and service layer.
- To provide input for forensic standardization gap analysis.

Ruan and Carthy (2012b) introduces the Cloud Forensic Maturity Model (CFMM) in order to assess and develop forensic capabilities for all actors in the cloud ecosystem. The CFMM has two inter-related components, i.e., the Cloud Forensic Investigative Architecture (CFIA) and the Cloud Forensic Capability Matrix (CFCM).

The CFIA as shown in Figure 1 is composed of four categories of capabilities.

1. **Pre-investigative capabilities:** Capabilities in preparation for both internal and external investigations including event management, identity management, encryption management, and interoperability.
2. **Investigative capabilities:** Capabilities required in the core investigative process including pro-active data collection, reactive data collection (hybrid acquisition), examination, and analysis.
3. **Supportive capabilities:** Capabilities required to support and complete the investigation case including evidence management, case management, multi-jurisdiction, and multi-tenancy.

Figure 1. Cloud forensic investigative architecture (Ruan & Carthy, 2012b)

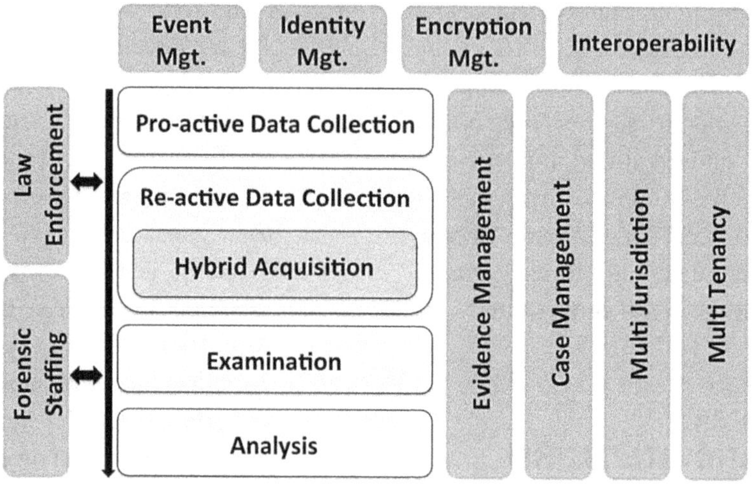

4. **Interfacing capabilities:** Capabilities dealing with the internal and external interface between the cloud system environment and investigative parties involved in cloud investigations, e.g., internal forensic team or external law enforcement agencies.

A list of sub capabilities with a set of key criteria in organizational, legal and technical dimensions is defined under each key capability. For example, under *Encryption Management* key capability, there are four sub capabilities, i.e., acquisition in transit, acquisition at rest, key management and evidence decryption. Various forensic processes can be generated from combining necessary capabilities required in a specific cloud scenario.

Based on these key capabilities and sub-capabilities, the CFCM is created to assess and develop forensic capabilities for all cloud actors. CFCM borrowed the concept from the Software Capability Maturity Model (CMM) and is divided into 6 levels of maturity. An example section of CFCM is shown in Table 1.

The CFMM is only one initial step towards cloud forensic capability assessment and development, and the researcher is still actively collecting use cases to refine and validate the CFMM. However, the researcher believe a Cloud Forensic Reference Architecture can be built based on some of the ideas and input from CFMM, along with comprehensive mapping and analysis referring to the cloud security reference architectures.

STRATEGIES AND STANDARDIZATION

According to survey results presented in Ruan et al. (2011b), 60% of the respondents agree or strongly agree that "establishment of a foundation of standards and policies for forensics that will evolve together with the technology" is an opportunity of cloud forensics. Cloud computing and its standardization have become a focus area for digital strategies of world's leading economies. In this section, the researcher first summarizes the current national/international strategies and cloud standardization progress of leading Standards Developing Organizations (SDO), and then provide recommendations on aspects related to digital investigation to be considered for such strategies and standardization efforts.

The United States Federal Government has adopted the "Cloud First" strategy to accelerate

Table 1. Pre-investigative capability matrix for cloud consumer, cloud provider, cloud auditor, and law enforcement (reference)

	Consumer						Provider						Auditor						Law Enforcement					
	1	2	3	4	5	6	1	2	3	4	5	6	1	2	3	4	5	6	1	2	3	4	5	6
Pre-investigative capabilities																								
Identity management																								
Authorization	X	X	X	X	X	**X**	X	X	X	X	X	**X**	X	X	X	X	X	**X**						
Authentication	X	X	X	X	X	**X**	X	X	X	X	X	**X**	X	X	X	X	X	**X**						
Role management	X	X	X	X	X	**X**	X	X	X	X	X	**X**	X	X	X	X	X	**X**						
Anonymity management				X	X	**X**			X	X	X	**X**			X	X	X	**X**					X	**X**
Event management																								
Event construction					X	**X**				X	X	**X**				X	X	**X**						
Event freezing					X	**X**					X	**X**					X	**X**					X	**X**
Event traceability					X	**X**				X	X	**X**				X	X	**X**				X	X	**X**
Time sequence				X	X	**X**			X	X	X	**X**			X	X	X	**X**						
Event reconstruction				X	X	**X**			X	X	X	**X**			X	X	X	**X**			X	X	X	**X**
Encryption management																								
Acquisition in transit					X	**X**				X	X	**X**				X	X	**X**					X	**X**
Acquisition at rest				X	X	**X**			X	X	X	**X**			X	X	X	**X**				X	X	**X**
Key management		X	X	X	X	**X**		X	X	X	X	**X**	X	X	X	X	X	**X**						
Evidence decryption				X	X	**X**			X	X	X	**X**			X	X	X	**X**				X	X	**X**
Interoperability																								
Dependency					X	**X**					X	**X**					X	**X**					X	**X**
Migration					X	**X**					X	**X**					X	**X**					X	**X**

cloud adoption. In the Federal Cloud Computing Strategy (Kundra, 2011), cloud computing has been recognized as a fundamental shift in IT, and can significantly improve public sector IT. The FedRAMP (Federal Risk and Authorization Management Program) is responsible for defining requirements for cloud computing security controls, including vulnerability scanning, and incident monitoring, logging, and reporting. The Federal Cloud Strategy has identified the following potential security benefits of cloud computing:

- The ability to focus resources.
- Potential platform strength.
- Improved resource availability.
- Improved backup and recovery.
- Ability to leverage alternate cloud services.

And the additional potential vulnerabilities:

- The inherent system complexity.
- The dependency on the service provider to maintain logical separation in a multi-tenant environment.
- The need to ensure that the organization retains an appropriate level of control.

As well as key security considerations include the need to:

- Carefully define security and privacy requirements.
- Determine the extent to which negotiated service agreements are required.
- Assess the extent to which the server and client-side computing environment meets organizational security and privacy requirements.
- Continue to maintain security management.

Forensics is one of the seven key security areas need to be addressed when Federal agencies consider implementing a cloud computing solution according to FedRAMP.

NIST (National Institute of Science the Technology) is responsible for leading cloud standardization and specifying security requirements for Federal Government cloud adoption under the NIST Cloud Computing Program[4].

In order to accomplish the DoD Cloud Computing Goal, i.e., "implementing cloud computing as the means to deliver the most innovative, efficient, and secure information and IT services in support of the Department's mission, anywhere, anytime, on any authorized device," the US DoD (Department of Defense) cloud computing strategy (DoD 2012) has identified four concurrent steps that enable a phased implementation of the DoD Enterprise Cloud Environment:

Step 1: Foster Adoption of Cloud computing.
Step 2: Optimize Data center Consolidation.
Step 3: Establish the DoD Enterprise Cloud Infrastructure.
Step 4: Deliver Cloud Services.

Five key e-discovery areas have been identified for Federal agencies to consider when implementing cloud solutions: information management, locating relevant documents, preservation of data, movement of documents, and potential cost avoidance through the incorporation of e-discovery tools in CSP environments (CIO & CAOC, 2012). E-discovery requirement has been identified as one of the ten focus areas for improved collaboration and alignment during the contract when acquiring cloud computing services: "federal agencies must ensure that all data stored in a CSP environment is available for legal discovery by allowing all data to be located, preserved, collected, processed, reviewed, and produced."

In 2012, the European Commission released its cloud computing strategy (EC, 2012) and it recognize the strategic importance of cloud computing by stating that "the commission aims at enabling and facilitating faster adoption of cloud computing throughout all sectors of the economy which can cut ICT costs, and when combined with new digital business practices, can boost productivity, growth and jobs…it represents a political commitment of the Commission and serves as a call on all stakeholders to participate in the implementation of these actions, which could mean an additional EUR 45 billion of direct spend on Cloud Computing in the EU in 2020 as well as an overall cumulative impact on GDP of EUR 957 billion, and 3.8 million jobs, by 2020." The EU cloud strategy has specified the following three key actions:

Key Action 1: Cutting through the Jungle of Standards.
Key Action 2: Safe and Fair Contract Terms and Conditions.
Key Action 3: Establishing a European Cloud Partnership to drive innovation and growth from the public sector.

And the outcome of reinforcing the actions above is expected to be laying the foundation for Europe to become a world cloud computing powerhouse, and a stable basis for a rapid take-off phase from 2014-2020 during which use of publically available cloud computing offerings cloud achieve a 38% compound annual growth rate that would be achieved if the decisive policy steps are not implemented.

ETSI (The European Telecommunications Standards Institute) is the standardization body responsible for leading standardization efforts under the European Commission, and especially to address general cyber security challenges for cloud computing through standardization. ETSI launched its Cloud Standard Coordination Program in December 2012[5]. The EU cloud strategy also emphasized on a reinforced international dialogue on safe and seamless cross-border use of cloud computing.

The United Kingdom has launched its Government G-Cloud Programme[6] as part of its cloud computing strategy. In the Government Cloud Strategy released in March 2011[7], it states that "the government will push ahead with its agenda for data centre, network, software and asset consolidation and the shift towards cloud computing. It will mandate the reuse of proven, common application solutions and policies. These solutions much balance the need to be open, accessible and usable with the growing cyber-security threat and the need to handle sensitive information with due care."

Leading SDOs active in cloud computing and security standardization include:

- **ISO/IEC JTC 1/SC 27 and SC 38:** ISO/IEC JTC 1 is Joint Technical Committee 1 of the International Organization for Standardization (ISO) and the International Electrotechnical Commission (IEC). It deals with all matters of information technology. SC 27 looks after IT Security techniques, and SC 38 is responsible for Distributed Application Platform and Services (DAPS) under which WG3 is dealing with Cloud Computing.
- **ITU-T SG 17 and 13 X.ccsec, X.gpim:** ITU (International Telecommunication Union) is the United Nations specialized agency for Information and Communication Technologies – ICTs. X.ccsec is a high-level security framework for cloud computing. This recommendation provides a high-level security framework for cloud computing based on the analysis of cloud security threats, security requirements, and security areas. This security framework provides the methodology for identifying the security functions that are required with each functional block of the reference architecture of cloud computing. This can then be used to guide the development of security controls, policies, and procedures for the specific cloud service models. ITU-T X.gpim is a guideline for management of personally identifiable information for telecommunication organizations.
- **NIST Cloud Computing Program[8]:** Various
- **BS 10012:** BS 10012 Data Protection Demystified – Acting to Protect Personal Information, is a British legal standard created to maintain the privacy of all sensitive personal information held by companies. BSI (Business Standards Company) is the UK's National Standards Body (NSB) and were the first national standards body.
- **Cloud Security Alliance:** Various
- **OASIS (Organization for the Advancement of Structured Information Standards):** Cloud-Specific or Extended Technical Committees
- **DMTF:** Cloud Management
- **ODCA:** Cloud Contracts
- **AICPA Service Organization Control (SOC) Reports SOC 1, SOC 2, SOC3:** Service Organization Control (SOC) Reports, effectively known as SOC 1, SOC

2, and SOC 3 Reports, is a comprehensive framework put forth by the American Institute of Certified Public Accountants (AICPA) geared towards reporting on controls at service organizations.

The following aspects need to be considered and integrated into cloud standardization for enabling digital investigations.

- **Interfaces:** Interfaces between cloud actors for exchanging forensic data when internal investigations are needed; interfaces between the cloud ecosystem and external investigative parties such as law enforcement agencies when external investigations are needed.
- **Interoperability and Portability:** The interoperability and portability of forensic data across different cloud platforms.
- **Data integrity:** Data integrity on all cloud system layers including physical layer, abstraction layer, service layer, and during all data transfer internationally.
- **Service template:** Security and forensic pattern integration into cloud service templates as cloud service templates are fundamental components for all services created from computing resources in the cloud.

EVIDENCE SEGREGATION

Multi-tenancy and virtualization are two key features of cloud computing. While multi-tenancy and virtualization can bring major benefits such as parallelism and optimal resource utilization, which lead to reduced overhead, efficiency, and availability of resources and applications, they also lead to the aggregation of heterogeneous data. A dilemma between data aggregation and data segregation is thus created when it comes to cloud forensics, as suspect data needs to be properly segregated from other co-tenants sharing the same computing infrastructure during a digital investigation. In this section, the researcher discusses data aggregation scenarios and data segregation strategies.

Data Aggregation in Virtual Environments

Virtualization is an enabling technology for cloud computing. It creates an "illusion" that the user is operating on a complete machine, while on the objective physical layer, it is merely a set of files. Virtualization plays a critical role on the abstraction layer of cloud architecture, where both virtual hardware and software resources are created from the physical cloud infrastructure. Different types of virtualization include hardware, desktop, software, memory, storage, data and network virtualization, which involves different levels of data aggregation on the actual resources being virtualized. For example, there are three different types of hardware virtualization, i.e., full virtualization, partial virtualization and para-virtualization. Full virtualization is an almost complete simulation of the actual hardware. Partial virtualization simulate some but not all of the target environment. Paravirtualization does not simulate the hardware environment; however, the guest programs are executed in their own isolated domains, as if they are running on a separate system. How exactly data are being aggregated on the host machine in these three types of hardware virtualization need to be clearly understood for the development of data segregation strategies and procedures.

Data Aggregation in Multi-Tenant Environments

Multi-tenancy is a separate concept from virtualization, though it is often enabled by virtualization. Multi-tenancy refers to a principle in software architecture where a single instance of the software runs on a server, serving multiple client organizations (tenants). With a multitenant architecture, a software application is designed to virtually partition its data and configuration, and each client organization works with a customized virtual application instance. Multi-tenancy brings inherent data aggregation benefits, i.e., running queries across customer, mining data, and looking for trends is much simpler.

Investigating multi-tenant cloud environments and investigating multi-user computer environments are comparable but very different scenarios. The two scenarios both involve sharing the same physical infrastructure, however the in the later multiple software instances (or hardware systems) are set up for different users, while multi-tenancy is created from the same software or hardware resources via virtualization.

Microsoft outlined three types of data architecture[9] for multi-tenant environment as follows:

1. **Separate database:** Data is isolated because tenant data are stored in separate databases
2. **Shared database, separate schemas:** Each tenant have its own set of tables that are grouped into a schema created specifically for the tenant, and multiple tenants share the same database
3. **Shared database, shared schema:** Multiple tenants' data are hosted using the same database and the same set of tables.

Data segregation strategies and procedures, for example, are needed for each data architecture listed above.

Evidence Segregation Strategies and Requirements

Evidence segregation for the purpose of digital investigation can take place before, during, and after forensic data collection. Different segregation strategies are needed for these three different stages.

1. Data segregation before forensic data collection involves the following aspects:
   a. Designing a data segregation architecture taking into considerations various levels of data aggregation as a result of virtualization and multi-tenancy.
   b. Designing data identification, classification and labeling mechanisms that can facilitate data segregation processes.
2. Data segregation during forensic data collection often involves live segregation based on analysis of network traffic, transactions, and metadata.
3. Data segregation after forensic data collection involves the examination of collected forensic data and "flipping through" aggregated datasets with adequate protection on co-tenants privacy.

Sufficient evidence segregation strategies need to meet the following requirement:

- Identification of data ownership while provisioning and deprovisioning.
- Preservation of data integrity throughout segregation processes.
- Privacy protection of co-tenants.
- Acceptable cost: the cost of data segregation cannot be too high to make the cost savings brought by data aggregation senseless.

SECURITY AND FORENSIC INTEGRATION

One of the widely adopted definitions of digital forensics was created at the 1st Digital Forensic Research Workshop (DFRWS) in 2001 and it defines digital forensics as:

The use of scientifically derived and proven methods toward the preservation, collection, validation, identification, analysis, interpretation, documentation, and preservation of digital evidence derived from digital sources for the purpose of facilitating or furthering the reconstruction of events found to be criminal, or helping to anticipate unauthorized actions shown to be disruptive to planned operations (DFRWS, 2001).

This definition implies that two groups of professionals are involved for digital forensic cases, i.e., law enforcement agencies in cases of criminal offense, and security professionals in cases of disrupted operations. In this section, the researcher discusses forensic and security integration and its implications in cloud computing environments.

Digital forensics is traditionally seen as a component of incident response for the purpose of post-incident investigations in security architectures. NIST SP 800-86 (Kent, et al., 2006) is one of the most comprehensive existing guidelines for integrating forensics into incident response for traditional computing environments. However, this level of integration is not enough. During the incident response phase, digital forensic investigators collect and work with forensic data generated from the system's security implementations on all operational layers, which means preserving potential forensic artifacts, constructing system incidents and events in a way that they can be easier "re-constructed," etc., have to be an integrated part of security architectural design. On the other hand, a digital investigation can provide extremely valuable feedback for security implementations by reconstructing the "who," "why," "how," "what," and "when" of a system event or incident. There needs to be an integrated mechanism or procedure for receiving and upgrading from such feedback.

The limited level of integration of digital forensics in security architectural design is one of the reasons why it is faced with significant challenges today, and is also one of the key areas that need to be strengthened when designing a forensic-enabling cloud ecosystem. According to Ruan et al. (2011b), 54% of the respondents agree or strongly agree that "dedicated forensic implementations are more cost-effective when applied on a larger scale and offered as part of the cloud infrastructure." Ideally, on an architectural level, the cloud computing security architecture and forensic architecture should mirror each other from service level, abstraction level to physical level. For each architectural component, a detailed analysis on the segregation of duties for all actors involved in the cloud architecture must be made. Security architecture for pre-incident prevention, and forensic architecture for post-incident investigation should overlap at incident response/management.

Continuous monitoring is another domain for security and forensic integration. Both EU and US standardization groups have emphasized the importance of continuous monitoring in the cloud ecosystem, as a means to ensure transparency, trust, accountability, and enable auditing on the service levels and cloud contracts. Essentially, effective continuous monitoring requires investigative techniques and mechanisms, i.e., to be able to understand at any given time (including real-time) or period of time, what is happening or has happened in the cloud environment where control of the system is split among various cloud actors. Forensic mechanisms are also needed in cloud auditing to help prove and provide audit trails.

The intersection between security intelligence and big data analytics introduces the third domain for security and forensic integration. "Large enterprise now regularly collect gigabytes or even terabytes of data for security intelligence, investigations, and forensics. Many existing tools can't meet these scalability needs."[10] Real-time investigations might be required for threat and vulnerability identification, which involves analyzing extra large amount of live transactions and large-scale datasets, thus forensic-enabling capabilities must be taken into considerations when designing security patterns (Schumacher, et al., 2006).

LEGAL AND REGULATORY FRAMEWORK

Both EU and Federal Cloud Strategies have emphasized the "global nature" of cloud computing and the importance of having an international legal, regulatory, or governance framework. Some of major bills and proposals in relation to creating such frameworks are listed as follows:

- Freedom of Information Act (FOIA)
- Federal Records Act (FRA)
- Cloud Computing Act of 2012
- Electronic Communication Privacy Act Modernization Act of 2012
- Proposal for a Regulation of the European Parliament and of the Council on the Protection of Individuals with regard to the Processing of Personal Data and on the Free Movement of Such Data (General Data Protection Regulation), 25.1. 2012
- Article 29 Data Protection Working Party, WP196 – Opinion 05/2012 on Cloud Computing, adopted July 1st 2012
- EU Data Protection Directive[11]

Key areas in relation to forensic investigation that need to be considered in the discussions for creating such frameworks are:

- **Identity management:** How to map virtual identity with physical identity for persons and hardware resources.
- **Log and record management:** How to design sufficient log and record management systems to collect data that can be used in real-time or post-incident investigations.
- **Evidence management:** How to preserve data integrity and chain of custody throughout evidence life cycle.
- **Data location:** How to precisely locate data and create data profiles for individuals and organizations.
- **Incident response:** How to coordinate and facilitate incident response when cross border investigations are required (and often as default scenarios in cloud environments).

PRIVACY VS. MONITORING

Another dilemma for digital investigation in the cloud is to draw a fine line between privacy protection and adequate mechanisms to track down malicious users and cyber criminals.

Microsoft, for example, has admitted that Patriot Act[12] can access EU-based cloud data[13]. However, the ETST also released a new draft standard on Lawful Interception (LI) of Cloud/Virtual Services[14], which states that "to facilitate monitoring nomadic access and surveillance of an individual whether they go online from their home computer, mobile or an Internet café, service providers must implement a Cloud Lawful Interception Function that could mean the installation of a new monitoring interface or more likely ensuring presentation of information in a format recognizable to interception mechanisms."

Personal Identifiable Information (PII) is defined by OMB (Office Management and Budget) as "information which can be used to distinguish or trace an individual's identity, such as their name, social security number, biometric records, etc., alone or when combined with other personal or identifying information which is linked or linkable to a specific individual, such as date and place of birth, mother's maiden name, etc."[15]

According to CIO and CAOC (2012), five areas identified as key factors for agencies to consider when PII is or could be a part of the data moved to the cloud environment are:

- Compliance with the Privacy Act of 1974 and related PII requirements
- Privacy Impact Assessments (PIAs)
- Privacy training
- Data location
- How a CSP responds to a breach

Important cloud privacy related regulations, policies, and initiatives are listed below:

- OBM Privacy Act 1975
- OMB FY 2010 Reporting Instructions for the Federal Information Security Management Act and Agency Privacy Management
- Privacy: Stored Communications Act[16]
- OBM 2006 Reporting Incidents Involving Personally Identifiable Information and Incorporating the Cost for Security in Agency Information Technology Investments
- OMB 2003 Guidance for Implementing the Privacy Provisions of the E-Government Act of 2002[17]
- Directive 95/46/EC of the European Parliament and of the Council of 24 October 1995 on the protection of individuals with regard to the processing of personal data and on the free movement of such data[18]
- EU Concerning the processing of personal data and the protection of privacy in the electronic communications sector 2002[19]
- Canada: Personal Information Protection and Electronic Documents Act 2012
- Cloud Security Alliance Privacy Level Agreement (PLA)

On the other hand, anonymity in cloud environment is a major threat to cloud security. Similar to airport security, passengers cannot expect to remain entirely anonymous while passing the terminals, and are required to prove their identity to ensure public security. As computing infrastructure becoming part of our critical infrastructure, it is equally important to implement adequate mechanisms to enable tracking and tracing potential malicious users in protection of public security. Such implementations and mechanisms must carefully draw boundaries for dealing with PII of non-suspects.

CONCLUSION AND FUTURE THOUGHTS

Cloud computing is emerging into the 5th utility (Buyya, et al., 2008), and we are at a time for fundamental design thinking for the next-generation computing infrastructure that is born with a global nature and enable waves of business and technological innovations. We need to leverage this unique transition to look back and learn from past experiences, as well as look forward and envision the future. In this chapter, the researcher summarized six aspects for designing a forensic-enabling cloud ecosystem and is actively working on several of these areas. Hard efforts need to be put into these areas, but there is no reason not to be optimistic and feel fortunate for having the opportunity to lay a foundation for the computing infrastructure of the future.

REFERENCES

Anderson, R., Barton, C., Bohme, R., Clayton, R., van Eeten, M. J. G., & Levi, M. ... Savage, S. (2012). *Measuring the cost of cyber crime.* Retrieved from http://weis2012.econinfosec.org/papers/Anderson_WEIS2012.pdf

Biggs, S., & Vidalis, S. (2009). Cloud computing: The impact on digital forensic investigations. In *Proceedings of the International Conference for Internet Technology and Secured Transactions, 2009.* ICITST.

Birk, D., & Wegener, C. (2011). Technical issues of forensic investigations in cloud computing environments. In *Proceedings of the 2011 IEEE Sixth International Workshop on Systematic Approaches to Digital Forensic Engineering (SADFE),* (pp. 1–10). IEEE Press.

Buyya, R., Shi Yoe, C., Venugopal, S., Broberg, J., & Brandic, I. (2008). Cloud computing and emerging IT platforms: Vision, hype, and reality for delivering computing as the 5th utility. In *Proceedings of Future Generation Computer Systems*. IEEE. doi:10.1016/j.future.2008.12.001

Cheslow, D. (2012). *Interpol to crack down on cybercrime*. Retrieved from http://www.msnbc.msn.com/id/47338831/ns/technology_and_science-tech_and_gadgets/t/interpol-crack-down-cyber-crime/

CIO & CAOC. (2012). *Creating effective cloud computing contracts for the federal government - Best practices for acquiring IT as a service*. Washington, DC: CIO & CAOC.

CSA & ISACA. (2012). *Cloud computing market maturity study results*. Washington, DC: CSA & ISACA.

DFRWS. (2001). *A road map for digital forensic research*. Utica, NY: Digital Forensic Research Workshop.

DoD. (2012). *Cloud computing strategy*. Washington, DC: DoD.

Ernst & Young. (2011). *The Ernst & Young 14th global information security survey*. New York, NY: Ernst & Young.

European Commission. (2012). *Unleashing the potential of cloud computing in Europe*. Brussels, Belgium: European Commission.

Galante, J., Kharif, O., & Alpeyev, P. (2011). *Sony network breach shows Amazon cloud's appeal for hackers*. Retrieved from http://www.bloomberg.com/news/2011-05-15/sony-attack-shows-amazon-s-cloud-service-lures-hackers-at-pennies-an-hour.html

Gartner. (2012). *The new PC era: The personal cloud*. New York, NY: Gartner.

ISA. (2010). *Can society afford to rely on security by afterthought not design?* Washington, DC: ISA.

Kent, K., Chevalier, S., Grance, T., & Dang, H. (2006). *Guide to integrating forensic techniques into incident response. NIST SP 800-86*. Washington, DC: NIST.

Kundra, V. (2011). *Federal cloud computing strategy*. Washington, DC: Federal Government.

Liu, F., Tong, J., Mao, J., Bohn, R., Messina, J., Badger, L., & Leaf, D. (2011). *NIST Cloud computing reference architecture. NIST Special Publication 500-292*. Washington, DC: NIST.

Neumann, J. (1945). *First draft of a report on the EDVAC*. Retrieved from http://qss.stanford.edu/~godfrey/vonNeumann/vnedvac.pdf

Neumann, J. (1949). *Theory of self-reproducing automata*. Retrieved from http://cba.mit.edu/events/03.11.ASE/docs/VonNeumann.pdf

Ruan, K., Baggili, I., Carthy, J., & Kechadi, T. (2011b). *Survey on cloud forensics and critical criteria for cloud forensic capability: A preliminary analysis*. Paper presented at the 6th Annual Conference of the ADFSL Conference on Digital Forensics, Security and Law. Richmond, VA.

Ruan, K., & Carthy, J. (2012b). Cloud forensic maturity model. In *Proceedings of the 4th International Conference on Digital Forensics & Cyber Crime*. Lafayette, IN: IEEE.

Ruan, K., Carthy, J., Kechadi, T., & Crosbie, M. (2011a). Cloud forensics: An overview. *Advances in Digital Forensics, 7*.

Ruan, K., James, J. I., Carthy, J., & Kechadi, T. (2012a). Cloud forensics: Key terms for the service level agreement. *Advances in Digital Forensics, 8*.

Schumacher, M. (2006). *Security patterns: Integrating security and systems engineering*. Hoboken, NJ: Wiley.

Spyridopoulos, T., & Katos, V. (2011). Requirements for a forensically ready cloud storage service. *International Journal of Digital Crime and Forensics*, *3*(3), 19–36. doi:10.4018/jdcf.2011070102

Thomason, I. (2010). *Cloud services a decade away from maturity*. Retrieved from http://www.v3.co.uk/v3-uk/news/1999968/cloud-services-decade-away- maturity

ENDNOTES

1. NIST Cloud Security: http://collaborate.nist.gov/twiki-cloud-computing/bin/view/CloudComputing/CloudSecurity
2. Cloud Security Alliance Trust Cloud Initiative: https://cloudsecurityalliance.org/research/tci/
3. Cloud Security Alliance Cloud Control Matrix: https://cloudsecurityalliance.org/research/ccm/
4. http://www.nist.gov/itl/cloud/
5. http://www.etsi.org/WebSite/NewsandEvents/201212_CLOUDSP.aspx
6. The G-Cloud Programme: http://gcloud.civilservice.gov.uk/
7. HM Government (2011).
8. http://www.nist.gov/itl/cloud/
9. http://msdn.microsoft.com/en-us/library/aa479086.aspx
10. http://www.networkworld.com/community/blog/intersection-security-intelligence-and-big-data-analytics
11. http://eur-lex.europa.eu/LexUriServ/LexUriServ.do?uri=CELEX:31995L0046:en:NOT
12. http://www.gpo.gov/fdsys/pkg/PLAW-107publ56/html/PLAW-107publ56.htm
13. http://www.zdnet.com/blog/igeneration/microsoft-admits-patriot-act-can-access-eu-based-cloud-data/11225
14. ETSI DTR 101 567 V0.0.5 'Lawful Interception (LI); Cloud/Virtual Services (CLI)', April 2012.
15. Safeguarding Against and Responding to the Breach of Personally Identifiable Information, OMB, May 22, 2007.
16. http://ilt.eff.org/index.php/Privacy:_Stored_Communications_Act
17. http://www.whitehouse.gov/omb/memoranda_m03-22/
18. http://eur-lex.europa.eu/LexUriServ/LexUriServ.do?uri=CELEX:31995L0046:EN:HTML
19. http://eur-lex.europa.eu/LexUriServ/LexUriServ.do?uri=CELEX:32002L0058:en:HTML

Compilation of References

18 U.S.C. § 2511(1) (2000).

18 U.S.C. § 2701-09 (2000).

18 U.S.C. §§ 2510(15) (2000).

18 U.S.C. §§ 2510-22 (2000).

18 U.S.C.A. § 2510 (West) (2000).

18 U.S.C.A. § 2511(c) (2004).

18 U.S.C.A. § 2702 (West) (2004).

18 U.S.C.A. § 2703(b) (2004).

18 U.S.C.A. § 2707(e) (2004)

18 U.S.C.A. § 2708 (2004).

18 U.S.C.A. § 2711 (West) (2004).

18 U.S.C.A. § 2711(2) (2004).

18 U.S.C.A. §§ 2701(a)(1) & (2) (2004).

18 U.S.C.A. §§ 2701-12 (2004).

42 U.S.C. § 13032(b)(1), since recodified in 18 U.S.C. § 2258A (2010).

AAB Joint Ventures v. United States, 75 Fed. Cl. 432 (2007).

Adams, K., & Agesen, O. (2012). *A comparison of software and hardware techniques for x86 virtualization.* Retrieved July 30, 2012 from http://www.vmware.com/pdf/asplos235_adams.pdf

Adelstein, F. (2006). Live forensics: Diagnosing your system without killing it first. *Communications of the ACM, 49*(2), 63–66. doi:10.1145/1113034.1113070

ADF. (2011). *ADF solutions.* Retrieved 31 January, 2011, from http://www.adfsolutions.com/

Agarwal, A., Gupta, M., Gupta, S., & Gupta, S. C. (2011). Systematic digital forensic investigation model. *International Journal of Computer Science and Security, 5*(1), 118–130.

AIIM. (2009). *The quest for ediscovery: Creating a data map.* Retrieved from www.aiim.org/Resources/Archive/Magazine/2009-Nov-Dec/37867

Aitken, B., McCann, P., McHugh, A., & Miller, K. (2012). *Digital curation and the cloud. Technical Report.* New York, NY: Digital Curation Centre.

Ali, I., & Meghanathan, N. (2011). Virtual machines and networks - Installation, performance, study, advantages and virtualization options. *International Journal of Network Security & Its Applications, 3*(1), 1–15. doi:10.5121/ijnsa.2011.3101

Alva, A., & Endicott-Popovsky, B. (2012). *Digital evidence education in schools of law.* Paper presented at the ADFSL Conference on Digital Forensics, Security and Law. Richmond, VA.

Amazon. (2011). *Amazon elastic compute cloud (Amazon EC2).* Retrieved 15 February, 2011, from http://aws.amazon.com/ec2/

Amazon Web Services. (2011). *Amazon elastic MapReduce.* Retrieved January 6, 2011, from http://aws.amazon.com/elasticmapreduce/

Amazon Web Services. (2012). *High performance computing (HPC) on AWS.* Retrieved from http://aws.amazon.com/hpc-applications/

Amazon Web Services. (2012a). *AWS customer agreement*. Retrieved from http://aws.amazon.com/agreement/

Amazon Web Services. (2012b). *AWS import/export*. Retrieved from http://aws.amazon.com/importexport/

Anderson, J., & Rainie, L. (2010). The future of cloud computing. *Pew Research Center's Internet & American Life Project*. Retrieved February 23, 2011 from http://pewInternet.org/Reports/2010/The-future-of-cloud-computing.aspx

Anderson, N. (2012). *Mega-victory: Kim dotcom search warrants invalid, mansion raid illegal*. Retrieved 11 July, 2012, from http://arstechnica.com/tech-policy/2012/06/mega-victory-kim-dotcom-search-warrants-invalid-mansion-raid-illegal/

Anderson, R., Barton, C., Bohme, R., Clayton, R., van Eeten, M. J. G., & Levi, M. ... Savage, S. (2012). *Measuring the cost of cyber crime*. Retrieved from http://weis2012.econinfosec.org/papers/Anderson_WEIS2012.pdf

Apache. (2010a) *MapReduce tutorial*. Retrieved February 11, 2011, from http://hadoop.apache.org/mapreduce/docs/current/mapred_tutorial.html

Apache. (2010b). *HDFS architecture guide*. Retrieved February 11, 2011, from http://hadoop.apache.org/hdfs/docs/current/hdfs_design.html

Armbrust, M. (2009). *Above the clouds: A Berkeley view of cloud computing*. Berkeley, CA: University of California.

Armbrust, M. (2010). A view of cloud computing. *Communications of the ACM*, *53*(4), 50–58. doi:10.1145/1721654.1721672

Arms, W. (2000). *Digital libraries*. Retrieved 10 February, 2011, from http://www.cs.cornell.edu/wya/DigLib/MS1999/Glossary.html

Armstrong, C. (2003). Mastering computer forensics. In Irvine, C., & Armstrong, H. (Eds.), *Security Education and Critical Infrastructures*. Dordrecht, The Netherlands: Kluwer Academic Publishers.

Arthur Andersen LLP v. United States, 544 U.S. 696 (2005).

Association of Chief Police Officers. (2008). Good practice guide for computer-based electronic evidence official release version. *Director (Cincinnati, Ohio)*, *67*(5), 72.

Avizzienis, A., Laprie, J.-C., Randell, B., & Landwehr, C. (2004). Basic concepts and taxonomy of dependable and secure computing. *IEEE Transactions on Dependable and Secure Computing*, *1*(1). doi:10.1109/TDSC.2004.2

Bailey, S. (2008). *Managing the crowd: rethinking records management for the web 2.0 world*. London, UK: Facet Publishing.

Balduzzi, M., et al. (2012). A security analysis of amazon's elastic compute cloud service. In *Proceedings of the 27th Annual ACM Symposium on Applied Computing*, (pp. 1427-1434). Trento, Italy: ACM.

Barbara, J. J. (2009). Cloud computing: Another digital forensic challenge. *Forensic Magazine*. Retrieved from http://www.forensicmag.com/article/cloud-computing-another-digital-forensic-challenge

Bares, R. A. (2009). Hiding in a virtual world: Using unconventionally installed operating systems. In *Proceedings of the 2009 IEEE International Conference on Intelligence and Security Informatics*, (pp. 276-284). IEEE Press.

Barnard, A. (2009). Could your phone testify against you? *The New York Times Upfront*, 142.

Barnhill, D. S. (2010). Cloud computing and stored communications: Another look at Quon v. Arch Wireless. *25. Berkeley Technology Law Journal*, *27*, 621–671.

Barrett, D. (2008). How virtualized environments affect computer forensics. In *Proceedings of the Conference on Digital Forensics, Security & Law*, (pp. 39-50). IEEE.

Barrett, D. (2010). Forensic challenges in virtualized environments. *Journal of Advancing Technology*, *10*(2), 15–25.

Barrett, D., & Kipper, G. (2010). *Virtualization and forensics: A digital forensic investigator's guide to virtual environments*. Burlington, MA: Elsevier.

Baryamureeba, V., & Tushabe, F. (2004). *The enhanced digital investigation process model*. Paper presented at the Digital Forensic Research Workshop. New York, NY.

Beebe, N., & Clark, J. (2004). *A hierarchical, objectives-based framework for the digital investigations process*. Paper presented at the Digital Forensics Research Workshop 2004. New York, NY.

Benfell, P. (2007). Great expectations: Heliocentrism, semantics and records management. *Records Management Journal*, *7*(2), 74–81. doi:10.1108/09565690710757878

Biggs, S., & Vidalis, S. (2009). *Cloud computing: The impact on digital forensic investigations*. Washington, DC: IEEE.

Bilby, D. (2006). *Low down and dirty: Anti-forensic rootkits*. Retrieved from http://www.blackhat.com/presentations/bh-jp-06/BH-JP-06-Bilby-up.pdf

Birk, D. (2011). *Technical challenges of forensic investigations in cloud computing environments*. Retrieved July 30, 2012 from http://www.zurich.ibm.com/~cca/csc2011/submissions/birk.pdf

Birk, D., & Wegener, C. (2011). Technical issues of forensic investigations in cloud computing environments. In *Proceedings of the 2011 IEEE Sixth International Workshop on Systematic Approaches to Digital Forensic Engineering (SADFE)*, (pp. 1–10). IEEE Press.

Bloomberg, J. (2011). *Cloud brokering: Building a cloud of clouds*. Retrieved 23 July, 2012, from http://www.zapthink.com/2011/04/19/cloud-brokering-building-a-cloud-of-clouds/

Bond v. United States, 529 U.S. 334, 120 S.Ct. 1462, 146 L.Ed.2d 365 (2000).

Brennels. (2010). *Cloud 101 - Recovery as a service (RaaS) is here!* Retrieved 16 February, 2011, from http://cloudrecovery.info/2010/02/17/cloud-101-%E2%80%93-recovery-as-a-service-raas-is-here/

Brennels. (2010). *Cloud 101 - The four type of cloud services?* Retrieved 14 February, 2011, from http://cloudrecovery.info/2010/02/08/cloud-101-the-four-types-of-cloud-services/

Brezinski, D., & Killalea, T. (2002). *Guidelines for evidence collection and archiving*. Retrieved from http://www.ietf/org/rfc/rfc3227.txt

Bright, P. (2008). Storms in the cloud leave users up creek without a paddle. *Ars Technica*. Retrieved from http://arstechnica.com/microsoft/news/2008/08/storms-in-the-clouds-leave-users-up-creek-without-a-paddle.ars

Broadhurst, R. (2006). Developments in the global law enforcement of cyber-crime. *Policing: An International Journal of Police Strategies & Management*, *29*(3), 408–433. doi:10.1108/13639510610684674

Brown, C. (2006). *Computer evidence: Collection & preservation*. New York, NY: Charles River Media.

Broyles, K. E. (1996). Taking the courtroom into the classroom: A proposal for educating the lay juror in complex litigation cases. *64. The George Washington Law Review*, *714*, 721–722.

Bryan, D. M. N., & Anderson, M. (2010). Cloud computing: A weapon of mass destruction? In *DEFCON 18*. Las Vegas, NV: DEF CON Communications, Inc.

Buckley, D. (2010). *Windows timeline prefetch analysis*. Retrieved July 30, 2012 from http://www.fishnetsecurity.com/Resource_/PageResource/White_Papers/FishNet_Security_WindowsTimelinePrefetchAnalysis.pdf

Buskirk, E. V., & Liu, V. T. (2006). Digital evidence: Challenging the presumption of reliability. *Journal of Digital Forensic Practice*, *1*(1), 19–26. doi:10.1080/15567280500541421

Buyya, R., Shi Yoe, C., Venugopal, S., Broberg, J., & Brandic, I. (2008). Cloud computing and emerging IT platforms: Vision, hype, and reality for delivering computing as the 5th utility. In *Proceedings of Future Generation Computer Systems*. IEEE. doi:10.1016/j.future.2008.12.001

Cable Privacy Act, 47 U.S.C. § 551 (2000).

CAL. PENAL CODE § 1524.2 (West) (2000).

Calhoun, M. C. (2008). Scientific evidence in court: Daubert or Frye, 15 years later. *Legal Backgrounder, 23*(37).

California v. Greenwood, 486 U.S. 35, 39, 108 S.Ct. 1625, 100 L.Ed.2d 30 (1988).

Carbone, J. (2009). *The new second level address translation (SLAT) feature in windows server 2008 R2 hyper-V*. Retrieved July 30, 2012 from http://www.virtualization-admin.com/articles-tutorials/microsoft-hyper-v-articles/general/second-level-address-translation-benefits-hyper-v-r2.html

Carrier, B. D. (2003). Open source digital forensics tools: The legal argument. *@stake Research Report.*

Carrier, B. D. (2006). *A hypothesis-based approach to digital forensic investigations.* (PhD Thesis). Purdue University. West Lafayette, IN.

Carrier, B. D. (2006). *Basic digital forensic investigation concepts.* Retrieved 28 January, 2011, from http://www.digital-evidence.org/di_basics.html

Carrier, B. D. (2008). *A brief introduction to the computer history model.* Retrieved 2 February, 2011, from http://www.digital-evidence.org/hist_model1.html

Carrier, B. D. (2012). *Sleuth kit hadoop.* Retrieved 22 July, 2012, from http://www.sleuthkit.org/tsk_hadoop/

Carrier, B. D. (2006). Risks of live digital forensic analysis. *Communications of the ACM, 49*(2), 56–61. doi:10.1145/1113034.1113069

Carrier, B. D., & Spafford, E. H. (2003). Getting physical with the digital investigation process. *International Journal of Digital Evidence, 2*(2), 1–20.

Carrier, B. D., & Spafford, E. H. (2006). Categories of digital investigation analysis techniques based on the computer history model. *Digital Investigation, 3*, 121–130. doi:10.1016/j.diin.2006.06.011

Casey, E. (2004). *Digital evidence and computer crime.* London, UK: Elsevier Academic Press.

Casey, E. (2009). Investigation delayed is justice denied: proposals for expediting forensic examinations of digital evidence*. *Journal of Forensic Sciences, 54*(6), 1353–1364. doi:10.1111/j.1556-4029.2009.01150.x

Casey, E., & Stellatos, G. J. (2008). The impact of full disk encryption on digital forensics. *Operating System Review, 42*(3), 93–98. doi:10.1145/1368506.1368519

Cecil, J. S., Hans, V., & Wiggins, E. (1991). Citizen comprehension of difficult issues: Lessons from civil jury trials. *40. The American University Law Review*, 727–774. Retrieved from http://www.wcl.american.edu/journal/lawrev/40/cecil.pdf

Censer, M. (2011). Major players zero in on cloud computing market. *The Washington Post.* Retrieved 15 August, 2012 from http://www.washingtonpost.com/business/capitalbusiness/major-players-zero-in-on-cloud-computing-market/2011/04/27/AFN1slTF_story.html

Chang, F., Dean, J., Ghemawat, S., Hsieh, W. C., Wallach, D. A., & Burrows, M. … Gruber, R. E. (2008). *Bigtable: A distributed storage system for structured data.* Retrieved from http://static.usenix.org/event/osdi06/tech/chang/chang.pdf

Cheng, E. (2007). Independent judicial research in the Daubert age. *Duke Law Journal, 56*, 1263–1318.

Cheslow, D. (2012). *Interpol to crack down on cybercrime.* Retrieved from http://www.msnbc.msn.com/id/47338831/ns/technology_and_science-tech_and_gadgets/t/interpol-crack-down-cyber-crime/

Chirgwin, R. (2012). *Megaupload seizures illegal says NZ high court.* Retrieved 24 July, 2012, from http://www.theregister.co.uk/2012/06/28/dotcom_seizures_illegal/

Choo, K. K. R. (2010). Cloud computing: Challenges and future directions. *Trends & Issues in Crime and Criminal Justice, 400*, 381–400.

Christiansen, J. (2010). Discovery and admission of electronic information as evidence. In Sullivan, J. (Ed.), *E-Health Business and Transactional Law* (pp. 427–452). Arlington, VA: BNA Books.

Ciardhuain, S. O. (2004). An extended model of cybercrime investigations. *International Journal of Digital Evidence, 3*(1).

CIO & CAOC. (2012). *Creating effective cloud computing contracts for the federal government - Best practices for acquiring IT as a service.* Washington, DC: CIO & CAOC.

Cisco. (2012). *Cisco visual networking index: Global mobile data traffic forecast update, 2011–2016.* Retrieved 11 July, 2012, from http://www.cisco.com/en/US/solutions/collateral/ns341/ns525/ns537/ns705/ns827/white_paper_c11-520862.html

City of Ontario, Cal. v. Quon, 130 S. Ct. 2619, 177 L. Ed. 2d 216 (U.S. 2010) (2010).

Civie, V., & Civie, R. (1998). Future technologies from trends in computer forensic science. In *Proceedings of Information Technology Conference, 1998.* IEEE Press.

Clanchy, M. T. (1993). *From memory to written record: England 1066-1307*. Oxford, UK: Blackwell Publishing.

Clede, B. (1993). Investigating computer crimes. *Law and Order*, *41*(7), 99–102.

Cloud Security Alliance. (2009). *Security guidance for critical areas of focus in cloud computing V2.1*. Washington, DC: Cloud Security Alliance.

CNN. (2009). *CNN: Her name was Neda*. Retrieved from http://www.youtube.com/watch?v=b5KBrsz1oxs &feature=related

Cohen, F. (2007). *Challenges to digital forensic evidence*. New York, NY: ASP Press.

Cohen, F. (2011). Putting the science in digital forensics. *Journal of Digital Forensics. Security and Law*, *6*(1), 7–14.

Cohen, F. (2012a). *Digital forensic evidence examination* (4th ed.). New York, NY: ASP Press.

Cohen, F. (2012b). *Update on the state of the science of digital evidence examination*. Paper presented at the Conference on Digital Forensics, Security, and Law. New York, NY.

Cohen, F. B. (2010). Fundamentals of digital forensic evidence. *Handbook of Information and Communication Security*. Retrieved from http://all.net/ForensicsPapers/HandbookOfCIS.pdf

Collier, P. A., & Spaul, B. J. (1992a). A forensic methodology for countering computer crime. *Artificial Intelligence Review*, *6*(2), 203–215. doi:10.1007/BF00150234

Collier, P. A., & Spaul, B. J. (1992b). Forensic science against computer crime in the United Kingdom. *Journal - Forensic Science Society*, *32*(1), 27–34. doi:10.1016/S0015-7368(92)73043-6

Columbia Pictures Inc. v. Bunnell, 245 F.R.D. 443 (C.D. Cal 2007) (2007).

Commonwealth v. Sbordone, 424 Mass. 802, 678 N.E.2d 1184, 1190, n. 11 (1997).

Communications Assistance for Law Enforcement Act of 1994, 47 U.S.C. §§ 1001-1010 (1994).

Connery, E. M., & Levy, S. B. (1979). Computer evidence in federal courts. *Commercial Law Journal*, *84*, 266–276.

Contini, S., Steinfeld, R., Pieprzyk, J., & Matusiewicz, K. (2007). *A critical look at cryptographic hash function literature*. Paper presented at ECRYPT Hash Workshop. Sydney, Australia: Macquarie University.

Continuity. (2012). *Oxford dictionary online*. Retrieved August 15, 2012 from http://oxforddictionaries.com/words/about

Convery, N. (2010). Cloud computing report. *Archives and Records Association*. Retrieved 15 August, 2012 from Retrieved 15 August, 2012 from http://www.archives.org.uk/images/documents/Cloud_computing_report_final-1.pdf

Convery, N. (2010). Cloud computing toolkit: Guidance for outsourcing information storage to the cloud. *Aberystwyth University*. Retrieved July 22, 2012, from http://www.archives.org.uk/images/documents/Cloud_Computing_Toolkit-2.pdf

Convery, N., & Ferguson-Boucher, K. (2011). Storing information in the cloud – A research project. *Journal of the Society of Archivists*, *32*(2), 221–239. doi:10.1080/00379816.2011.619693

Cook, T. (2005). Macro-appraisal in theory and practice: origins, characteristics and implementation in Canada, 1950-2000. *Archival Science*, *5*(2-4), 101–161. doi:10.1007/s10502-005-9010-2

Cooney, M. (2012). *Gartner: 10 key IT trends for 2012 virtualization, social media, energy are top issues IT will have to contend with*. Retrieved July 30, 2012 from http://www.networkworld.com/community/blog/gartner-10-key-it-trends-2012

Core-Vent Corp. v. Nobel Industries *AB*, 11 F.3d 1482, 1486 (9th Cir. 1993) (1993).

Couch v. U.S., 409 U.S. 322, 335-36, 93 S.Ct.611, 34 L.Ed.2d 548 (1973).

Couillard, D. A. (2009). Defogging the cloud: Applying fourth amendment principles to evolving privacy expectations in cloud computing. *Minnesota Law Review*, *93*, 2205–2239.

Council, P. S. (2012). *PCI SSC data security standards overview*. Retrieved from https://www.pcisecuritystandards.org/security_standards/

Covad Communs. Co. v. Revonet, Inc., 2009 U.S. Dist. LEXIS 47841 (D.D.C. May 27, 2009) (2009).

CRA. (2003). *Four grand challenges in trustworthy computing*. Retrieved from http://www.cyber.st.dhs.gov/docs/CRA%20Grand%20Challenges%202003.pdf

Craiger, J. P. (2005). *Computer forensic procedures and methods*. Retrieved from http://ncfs.org/craiger.forensics.methods.procedures.final.pdf

Creeger, M. (2010). Moving to the edge: A CTO roundtable on network virtualization. *Communications of the ACM*, *53*(8), 55–62. doi:10.1145/1787234.1787251

CSA & ISACA. (2012). *Cloud computing market maturity study results*. Washington, DC: CSA & ISACA.

Cyntegra, Inc. v. Idexx Laboratories, Inc., 2007 WL 5193736 (C.D. Cal. 2007) (2007).

Damoulakis, J. (2010). In clouds we trust. *IT Now*, *52*(2), 11–12.

Dardick, G. S. (2010). Cyber forensics assurance. In *Proceedings of the 8th Australian Digital Forensics Conference*. Perth, Australia: Edith Cowan University.

Daubert v Merrell Dow Pharmaceuticals Inc 509 US at 579, 113 S.Ct. 2786, 125 L.Ed.2d 469 (1993).

Davis v. Gracey 111 F.3d 1472, 1484 (10th Cir. 1997) (1997).

Dean, J., & Ghemawat, S. (2004). MapReduce: Simplified data processing on large clusters. In *Proceedings of the Sixth Symposium on Operating System Design and Implementation – OSDI*. New York, NY: Google Inc.

Dean, J., & Ghemawat, S. (2008). MapReduce: Simplified data processing on large clusters. *Communications of the ACM*, *51*(1), 107–113. doi:10.1145/1327452.1327492

Decker, M., Kruse, W., Long, B., & Kelley, G. (2011). *Dispelling common myths of "live digital forensics"*. Retrieved July 30, 2012 from http://www.dfcb.org/docs/LiveDigitalForensics-MythVersusReality.pdf

Degnan, D. (2011). Accounting for the costs of electronic discovery. *Minnesota Journal of Law. Science & Technology*, *12*, 151–190.

DeHetre, J. D. (1975). Data processing evidence-Is it different? *Chicago-Kent Law Review*, *52*, 567–599.

Department of Justice. (2012). *Treaty requests*. Retrieved frm http://www.justice.gov/usao/eousa/foia_reading_room/usam/title9/crm00276.htm

Deyrup, I., Matthews, S., Iqbal, A., Black, B., Fisher, C., Cella, J., et al. (2010). *Cloud computing & national security law*. Unpublished.

DFRWS. (2001). *A road map for digital forensic research*. Utica, NY: Digital Forensic Research Workshop.

Didoné, D., & De Queiroz, R. J. G. B. (2011). Forensic as a service – FaaS. In *Proceedings of the 6th International Conference on Forensic Computer Science*, (pp. 202-210). IEEE.

Digi 01. (2001). *A road map for digital forensics research*. Paper presented at the First Digital Forensic Research Workshop. Utica, NY. Retrieved 15 August, 2012 from http://www.dfrws.org/2001/dfrws-rm-final.pdf

Digital Forensic Research Workshop. (2001). *A roadmap for digital forensic research*. Retrieved April 20, 2012, from http://www.dfrws.org/dfrws-rm-final.pdf

Digital Preservation Coalition. (2012). *Website newsroom*. Retrieved 15 August, 2012 from http://www.dpconline.org/newsroom/not-so-new/852-digital-resilience-and-digital-preservation-registration-opens-for-members

DLM Forum Foundation. (2011). *MoReq2010®: Modular requirements for records systems — Volume 1: Core services & plug-in modules*. Retrieved 15 August, 2012 from http://moreq2010.eu/

DoD. (2012). *Cloud computing strategy*. Washington, DC: DoD.

Dropbox. (2012). *Where does Dropbox store everyone's data?* Retrieved from https://www.dropbox.com/help/7

Duffy, J. (2009). *Cisco unveils cloud computing platform for service providers*. Retrieved 10 February, 2011, from http://www.infoworld.com/d/cloud-computing/cisco-unveils-cloud-computing-platform-service-providers-113

Duranti, L. (2008). *It's all about trust: The reliability, accuracy and authenticity of digital records*. Retrieved 15 August, 2012 from http://www.liv.ac.uk/lucas/Archived_News_and _Events.htm

Duranti, L. (2009). From digital diplomatics to digital records forensics. *Archivaria*, *68*, 39–66.

Duranti, L. (2010). Diplomatics. In *Encyclopedia of Library and Information Sciences* (3rd ed.). New York, NY: Taylor & Francis.

Dykstra, J. (2012). *Survey of digital forensics and the law*. Unpublished Raw Data.

Dykstra, J., & Sherman, A. T. (2011). *Acquiring forensic evidence from infrastructure as a service cloud computing: Exploring and evaluating tools, trust, and techniques*. Paper presented at the DFRWS Conference. New Orleans, LA.

Dykstra, J., & Sherman, A. T. (2011). Understanding issues in cloud forensics: Two hypothetical case studies. In *Proceedings of the 2011 ADSFL Conference on Digital Forensics, Security, and Law*, (pp. 191-206). ADSFL.

Dykstra, J., & Sherman, A. T. (2012). Acquiring forensic evidence from infrastructure as a service cloud computing: Exploring and evaluating tools, trust, and techniques. *Digital Investigation*. Retrieved from http://www.csee.umbc.edu/~dykstra/DFRWS_Dykstra.pdf

Edelstein, O., Factor, M., King, R., Risse, T., Salant, E., & Taylor, P. (2011). Evolving domains, problems and solutions for long term digital preservation. In *Proceedings of the 8th International Conference on Preservation of Digital Objects (iPRES 2011)*. Singapore, Singapore: iPRES.

Edmond, G. (2010). Impartiality, efficiency or reliability? A critical response to expert evidence law and procedure in Australia. *The Australian Journal of Forensic Sciences*, *42*, 83–99. doi:10.1080/00450610903258128

Electronic Discovery Reference Model. (2005). *Projects*. Retrieved from http://www.edrm.net/projects

Electronic Discovery Reference Model. (2009a). (Graphical illustration of the electronic discovery stages). *Electronic Discovery Reference Model*. Retrieved from http://www.edrm.net/resources/edrm-stages-explained

Electronic Discovery Reference Model. (2009b). *EDRM diagram elements*. Retrieved from http://www.edrm.net/resources/diagram-elements

Electronic Discovery Reference Model. (2010). *Identification guide*. Retrieved from http://www.edrm.net/resources/guides/edrm-framework-guides/identification

Electronic Discovery Reference Model. (2010). *Processing*. Retrieved from http://www.edrm.net/resources/guides/edrm-framework-guides/processing

Electronic Discovery Reference Model. (2011). (Graphical illustration of the information governance process). *Information Governance Reference Model*. Retrieved from http://www.edrm.net/projects/igrm

Electronic Discovery Reference Model. (2012). *Collection guide*. Retrieved from http://www.edrm.net/resources/guides/edrm-framework-guides/collection

Ellison, L. (2009). *Why Larry Ellison hates cloud computing*. Retrieved from http://techpulse360.com

Endicott-Popovsky, B., & Frincke, D. (2006). Adding the fourth 'R': A systems approach to solving the hacker's arms race. In *Proceedings of the Thirty-Ninth Annual Hawaii International Conference on System Sciences: Symposium: Skilled Human-intelligent Agent Performance: Measurement, Application and Symbiosis*. Kauai, HI: IEEE.

Endicott-Popovsky, B. E., & Frincke, D. A. (2006). Embedding forensic capabilities into networks: Addressing inefficiencies in digital forensics investigations. In *Proceedings of the 7th IEEE Workshop on Information Assurance*. West Point, NY: U.S. Military Academy.

Endicott-Popovsky, B. E., & Frincke, D. A. (2007). Embedding Hercule Poirot in networks: Addressing inefficiencies in digital forensic investigations In *Proceedings of the Human Computer Interact (HCI) Conference*. Beijing, China: HCI.

Endicott-Popovsky, B., & Horowitz, D. (2012). Unintended consequences: Digital evidence in our legal system. *IEEE Security & Privacy Magazine*, *10*(2), 80–83. doi:10.1109/MSP.2012.54

Ernst & Young. (2011). *The Ernst & Young 14th global information security survey*. New York, NY: Ernst & Young.

Eucalyptus. (2010). *Eucalyptus user guide*. New York, NY: Eucalyptus Systems, Inc.

Eucalyptus. (2010). *Resources*. Retrieved 9 February, 2011, from http://www.eucalyptus.com/resources/info/cloud-myths-dispelled - q2

Eucalyptus. (2011). *Eucalyptus: The open source cloud platform*. Retrieved 27 February, 2011, from http://open.eucalyptus.com/

Eucalyptus System. (2009). *Eucalyptus open-source cloud computing infrastructure - An overview*. Retrieved February 5, 2011, from http://www.eucalyptus.com/pdf/whitepapers/Eucalyptus_Overview.pdf

European Commission. (2012). *Unleashing the potential of cloud computing in Europe*. Brussels, Belgium: European Commission.

European Union Law. (1995). *Data protection*. Retrieved from http://eur-lex.europa.eu/LexUriServ/LexUriServ.do?uri=CELEX:31995L0046:en:NOT

Everett, C. (2009). Cloud computing – A question of trust. *Computer Fraud & Security*, *6*, 5–7. doi:10.1016/S1361-3723(09)70071-5

EY. (2011). *Into the cloud, out of the fog: Ernst & Young's 2011 global information security survey: 34*. New York, NY: Ernst & Young.

Farmer, D., & Venema, W. (2005). *Forensic discovery*. Reading, MA: Addison-Wesley.

Farmer, D., & Venema, W. (2012). *Improving the security of your site by breaking into it*. http://www.porcupine.org/satan/demo/docs/admin_guide_to_cracking.html

Favro, P. (2007). A new frontier in electronic discovery: Preserving and obtaining metadata. *Boston University Journal of Science and Technology Law*, *13*, 1–24.

FBI. (2012). *A bibliography related to crime scene interpretation with emphases in forensic geotaphonomic and forensic archaeological field techniques*. Washington, DC: FBI Print Shop.

Fed. R. Evid 104(a) and (b) (1997).

Fed. R. Evid 803(6)(E) (1997).

Fed. R. Evid. 401 (1997).

Fed. R. Evid. 801(a) (1997).

Fed. R. Evid. 901. (1997).

Federal Judicial Center. (2004). *Manual for complex litigation* (4th ed). Retrieved from http://www.fjc.gov/public/pdf.nsf/lookup/mcl4.pdf/$file/mcl4.pdf

Federal Rules of Civil Procedure. (2011). *Website*. Retrieved from http://www.uscourts.gov/uscourts/RulesAndPolicies/rules/2011%20Rules/Civil%20Procedure.pdf

Federal Rules of Evidence. (2011). *Website*. Retrieved from http://www.uscourts.gov/uscourts/RulesAndPolicies/rules/2011%20Rules/Evidence%20Procedure.pdf

Ferguson-Boucher, K. (2007). *ESI: Without a trace: A comparative study of records management and digital forensics*. (Dissertation). Aberystwyth University. Aberystwyth, UK.

Ferguson-Boucher, K. (2011). Cloud computing: A records and information management perspective. *IEEE Security and Privacy*, *9*(6), 63–66. doi:10.1109/MSP.2011.159

Ferguson-Boucher, K., & Endicott-Popovosky, B. (2008). *Digital forensics and records management: What we can learn from the discipline of archiving*. Paper presented at the Security, Compliance and Risk Management Institute Conference: Where Information Technology, Law and Risk Management Converge. Seattle, WA.

Ferrie, P. (2012). Attacks on more virtual machine emulators. *Symantec Advanced Threat Research*. Retrieved from www.symantec.com/avcenter/reference/Virtual_Machine_Threats.pdf

Fielding, R. T. (2000). *Architectural styles and the design of network-based software architectures*. (Unpublished Doctoral Dissertation). University of California. Irvine, CA.

Fiterman, E. M., & Durick, J. D. (2010). Ghost in the machine, forensic evidence collection in the virtual environment. *Digital Forensics Magazine*, *2*, 73–77.

Flagg v. City of Detroit, 252 F.R.D. 346, 353 (E.D. Mich. 2008) (2008).

Florida v. Wells, 539 So.2d 464 (Fla. 1989), aff'd, 495 U.S. 1 (1990).

Foster, I., Zhao, Y., Raicu, I., & Lu, S. (2008). Cloud computing and grid computing 360-degree compared. In *Proceedings of Grid Computing Environments Workshop*, (pp. 1-10). Chicago, IL: IEEE Grid Computing Environments.

Foundation, T. A. (2012). *Hadoop map reduce*. Retrieved from http://hadoop.apache.org/mapreduce/

Fowler, B. (2009). *Securing a virtual environment.* Retrieved from http://www.infosecwriters.com/text_resources/pdf/BFowler_VIrtual_Environment.pdf

Freedman v. America Online, Inc., 303 F.Supp.2d 121 (D.Conn., 2004) (2004).

Frye v. United States, 293 U.S. 1013 (1923). Daubert v. Merrell Dow Pharmaceuticals, 509 U.S. 579 (1993).

Galante, J., Kharif, O., & Alpeyev, P. (2011). Sony network breach shows Amazon cloud's appeal for hackers. *Bloomberg*. Retrieved November 2, 2011, from http://www.bloomberg.com/news/2011-05-15/sony-attack-shows-amazon-s-cloud-service-lures-hackers-at-pennies-an-hour.html

Gallegos, F. (2005). Computer forensics: An overview. *Information Systems Control Journal, 6*, 13–16.

Gardner, D. (2009). *Analysts define growing requirements for how governance supports corporate cloud computing*. Retrieved from http://www.zdnet.com/blog/gardner/analysts-define-growing-requirements-for-how-governance-supports-corporate-cloud-computing/2988

Garfinkel, S. L. (2010). Digital forensics research: The next 10 years. *Digital Investigation, 7*, S64–S73. doi:10.1016/j.diin.2010.05.009

Gartner. (2011). *Gartner reveals top predictions for IT organizations and users for 2012 and beyond: Predictions show IT budgets are moving out of the control of IT departments*. Retrieved July 30, 2012 from http://www.gartner.com/it/page.jsp?id=1862714

Gartner. (2012). *Forecast: Public cloud services, worldwide, 2010-2016, 2Q12 update.* New York, NY: Gartner.

Gartner. (2012). Information/data governance. *Gartner IT Glossary*. Retrieved from http://www.gartner.com/it-glossary/informationdata-governance/

Gartner. (2012). *The new PC era: The personal cloud.* New York, NY: Gartner.

Gellman, R. (2009). *Privacy in the clouds: Risks to privacy and confidentiality from cloud computing*. Paper presented at the World Privacy Forum. Washington, DC.

General Electric Co. v. Joiner, 522 U.S. 136 (1997).

Ghemawat, S., Gobioff, H., & Leung, S. (2003). The Google file system. In *Proceedings of the 19th ACM Symposium on Operating Systems Principles*. Lake George, NY: ACM Press.

Giannelli, P. (2006). *Judicature - Scientific evidence.* Retrieved from http://goextranet.net/Seminars/Ohio06/Tab%2002-Scientific%20Evidence-Gianelli/Judicature%20-%20Scientific%20Evidence.pdf

Giannelli, P. C. (2007). *Scientific evidence* (4th ed.). Newark, NJ: Lexis Law.

Gillespie, A. A. (2012). Jurisdictional issues concerning online child pornography. *International Journal of Law and Information Technology, 20*(3). doi:10.1093/ijlit/eas007

Giobbi, R., & McCormick, J. (2007). *US-CERT vulnerability note VU912593 - Guidance EnCase enterprise uses weak authentication to identify target machines.* Retrieved from http://www.kb.cert.org/vuls/id/912593

Gladyshev, P. (2004). *Formalising event reconstruction in digital investigations.* (PhD Thesis). University College Dublin. Dublin, Ireland.

Gladyshev, P., & Almansoori, A. (2010). Reliable acquisition of RAM dumps from intel-based apple mac computers over firewire. In *Proceedings of the Second International Conference on Digital Forensics and Cyber Crime (ICDF2C)*. Abu Dhabi, UAE: ICST.

Gladyshev, P., & Patel, A. (2004). Finite state machine approach to digital event reconstruction. *Digital Investigation, 1*(2), 130–149. doi:10.1016/j.diin.2004.03.001

Gogolin, G. (2010). The digital crime tsunami. *Digital Investigation, 7*(1-2), 3–8. doi:10.1016/j.diin.2010.07.001

Gonsowski, D. (2004). *The negligent spoliation of electronic information: Practical advice for successfully preserving digital data.* Retrieved from http://www.legaltechcenter.net/affiliate/Shared Documents/fios.pdf

Google. (2010). Security whitepaper: Google apps messaging and collaboration products. *Security, 745.*

Google. (2012). *Google mail - Service details.* Retrieved 24 July, 2012, from http://www.google.com/appsstatus-hl=en&v=issue&ts=1343170799000&iid=ccc3254047e72fb00c9cb8532281e28

Google News. (2007). *Google and IBM announce university initiative to address internet-scale computing challenges*. Retrieved from http://www.google.com/intl/en/press/pressrel/20071008_ibm_univ.html

Gosh, A. (2004a). *Guidelines for the management of IT evidence*. Paper presented at the APEC Telecommunications and Information Working Group. New York, NY.

Gosh, A. (2004b). *HB 231:2004 information security risk management guidelines*. Sydney, Australia: Standards Australia.

Goss, J. (2010). *Forensic triage: Managing the risk*. (Master of Science Thesis). University College Dublin. Dublin, Ireland.

Government, H. M. (2011). *Government cloud strategy*. Retrieved 15 August, 2012 from http://www.cabinetoffice.gov.uk/sites/default/files/resources/government-cloud-strategy_0.pdf

Grabenstein v. Arrow Electronics, Inc., 2012 WL 1388595 (D. Colo. 2012) (2012).

Grant v Marshall FCA 1161 (2003).

Grispos, G. (2011). *Calm before the storm: The emerging challenges of cloud computing in digital forensics*. Retrieved from http://www.dcs.gla.ac.uk/~tws/papers/grispos11calm-rev2425.pdf

Grivas, S. G. (2010). *Cloud broker: Bringing intelligence into the cloud*. Washington, DC: IEEE. doi:10.1109/CLOUD.2010.48

Grobauer, B., & Schreck, T. (2010). Towards incident handling in the cloud: Challenges and approaches. In *Proceedings of the 2010 ACM Workshop on Cloud Computing Security Workshop*, (pp. 77–86). ACM Press.

Guidance Software. (2011). *Leading eDiscovery, forensics, and cybersecurity solutions – Encase*. Retrieved from http://www.guidancesoftware.com

Gutheil, T. G., & Bursztajn, H. J. (2005). Attorney abuses of Daubert hearings: Junk science, junk law, or just plain obstruction? *The Journal of the American Academy of Psychiatry and the Law*, *33*(2), 150–152.

Halderman, J. (2009). Lest we remember: Cold-boot attacks on encryption keys. *Communications of the ACM*, *52*(5), 91–98. doi:10.1145/1506409.1506429

Hale v. Henkel, 201 U.S. 43, 76, 26 S.Ct. 370, 50 L.Ed. 652 (1906).

Haletky, E. (2009). *VMware vSphere and virtual infrastructure security: Securing the virtual environment*. Boston, MA: Pearson.

Hankeln. (2008). *How to read VMFS or any other file system with MOA*. Retrieved July 30, 2012 from http://sanbarrow.com/latest-videoesxi-exe.html

Hannan, M. (2004). *To revisit: What is forensic computing?* Paper presented at the 2nd Australian Computer, Network & Information Forensics Conference. Perth, Australia.

Hargreaves, C. J. (2009). *Assessing the reliability of digital evidence from live investigations*. Cranfield, UK: Cranfield University.

Harris v. State, 260 Ga. 860, 401 S.E.2d 263, 266 (1991).

Harris, J. G., & Alter, A. E. (2010). *Cloudrise: Rewards and risks at the dawn of cloud computing*. Retrieved February 23, 2011, from http://www.accenture.com/SiteCollectionDocuments/PDF/Cloudrise_Rewards_and_Risks_at_the_Dawn_of_Cloud_Computing.pdf

Harris, V. (2000). Law, evidence and electronic records: A strategic perspective from the global periphery. *Comma: International Journal on Archives*, *41*, 29–43.

Hau, W., Araujo, R., Chudgar, V., Hustad, R., & Chaubal, C. (2009). *How virtualization affects PCI DSS: A review of the top five issues*. Retrieved July 30, 2012 from http://whitepapers.techrepublic.com.com/abstract.aspx?docid=1086319

Hawthorn, N. (2009). Finding security in the cloud. *Computer Fraud & Security*, *10*, 19–20. doi:10.1016/S1361-3723(09)70131-9

Hejaz, S., Talh, C., & Abbabi, M. (2009). Extraction of forensically sensitive information from windows physical memory. *Digital Investigation*, *6*, 121–131. doi:10.1016/j.diin.2009.06.003

Hester v. United States, 265 U.S. 57, 58, 44 S.Ct. 445, 68 L.Ed 898 (1924).

Hewlett-Packard. (2011). *Everything as a service*. Retrieved 16 February, 2011, from http://www.hp.com/hpinfo/initiatives/eaas/index.html

Higginbotham, S. (2010). *Ericsson CEO predicts 50 billion internet connected devices by 2020*. Retrieved 27 January, 2011, from http://gigaom.com/2010/04/14/ericsson-sees-the-internet-of-things-by-2020/

Higginbotham, S. (2011). *VMware and Verizon team up for mobile virtualization*. Retrieved July 30, 2012 from http://gigaom.com/2011/10/18/vmware-and-verizon-team-up-for-mobile-virtualization/

Hobson, E. W. (2010). *What is cloud computing?* Retrieved 12 February, 2011, from https://sites.google.com/site/cloudinvestigations/whatis

Hu, Y. J. (2012). *Towards law-aware semantic cloud policies with exceptions for data integration and protection*. New York, NY: ACM. doi:10.1145/2254129.2254162

Hunton, P. (2012). Managing the technical resource capability of cybercrime investigation: A UK law enforcement perspective. *Public Money & Management*, *32*(3), 225–232. doi:10.1080/09540962.2012.676281

Hurley, C. (2011). *Strength below and grace above: the structuration of records*. Retrieved 15 August, 2012 from http://www.infotech.monash.edu.au/research/groups/rcrg/publications/strength-below.pdf

Hutz, R. E. (2012, May 22). E-discovery: The relationship between cloud computing, e-discovery and privilege. *InsideCounsel*.

Iball, J. (2010). Don't cloud data security. *IT Now*, *52*(2), 14–15.

IBM. (2010). *IBM x-force 2010 mid-year trend and risk report*. New York, NY: IBM X-Force.

IBM. (2010). *OWASP - Salted hash password technique*. Retrieved from https://www.ibm.com/developerworks/mydeveloperworks/wikis/home/wiki/W3411066dca35_46c6_b97f_c3b5a2ca5180/page/OWASP%20-%20Salted%20Hash%20Password%20Technique?lang=en

IBTimes. (2010). *Number of internet users in emerging markets to double by 2015: Report*. International Business Times.

IC3. (2011). 2011 internet crime report. *Internet Crime Complaint Center*. Retrieved from http://www.ic3.gov

Illinois v. Krull, 480 U.S. 340, 348, 107 S.Ct. 1160, 94 L.Ed.2d 364 (1987).

In re Grand Jury Proceedings Involving Vickers, 38 F. Supp. 2d 159, 162 (D.N.H. 1998) (1998).

In re U.S. for an Order Authorizing the Release of Historical Cell-Site Info., 809 F. Supp. 2d 113, 125 (E.D.N.Y. 2011) (2011).

Ingthorsson, O. (2010). Cloud computing - Data privacy and compliance. *Cloud Computing Topics*. Retrieved from http://cloudcomputingtopics.com/2010/03/cloud-computing-data-privacy-and-compliance/

International Telecommunication Union. (2010). *Measuring the information society*. Retrieved from http://www.itu.int

Internet World Stats. (2011). *Internet usage statistics: The internet big picture*. Retrieved 11 July, 2012, from http://internetworldstats.com/stats.htm

IOCE. (2002). *Guidelines for best practice in the forensic examination of digital technology*. Retrieved from http://www.ioce.org/fileadmin/user_upload/2002/Guidelines%20for%20Best%20Practices%20in%20Examination%20of%20Digital%20Evid.pdf

Irons, A. (2006). Computer forensics and records management—Compatible disciplines. *Records Management Journal*, *16*(2), 111. doi:10.1108/09565690610677463

ISA. (2010). *Can society afford to rely on security by afterthought not design?* Washington, DC: ISA.

ISO 15489-1:2001. (2001). *Information and documentation: Records management – Part 1: General*. Retrieved from http://www.iso.org

ISO/IEC. (2011). *Draft - Guidelines for identification, collection, acquisition, and preservation of digital evidence, CD 27037: ISO/IEC*. Retrieved from http://www.iso.org

James, J. (2010). Analysis of evidence using formal event reconstruction. *Digital Forensics and Cyber Crime*, *31*, 85–98. doi:10.1007/978-3-642-11534-9_9

James, J. I., & Gladyshev, P. (2010). *2010 report of digital forensic standards, processes and accuracy measurement*. Retrieved 22 December, 2010, from http://www.forensicfocus.com/2010-digital-forensics-standards-processes-accuracy

Jang, Y. (2012). Need of open network approach for cyber security organizational. In *Proceedings of the International Symposium on Cybercrime Response 2012*. Jung-gu, Republic of Korea: Cyber Terror Response Center.

Jansen, W. A. (2011). *Cloud hooks: Security and privacy issues in cloud computing*. Washington, DC: IEEE. doi:10.1109/HICSS.2011.103

Jansen, W., & Ayers, R. (2007). *Guidelines on cell phone forensics*. Washington, DC: National Institute of Standard and Technology.

Jarrett, H. M., Bailie, M. W., Hagen, E., & Judish, N. (2009). *Searching and seizing computers and obtaining electronic evidence in criminal investigations*. Retrieved from http://www.justice.gov/criminal/cybercrime/docs/ssmanual2009.pdf

Jenkins, M. M. (1975). Computer-generated evidence specially prepared for use at trial. *Chicago-Kent Law Review*, *52*, 600–609.

Jericho Forum. (2009). *Cloud cube model: Selecting cloud formations for secure collaboration*. Retrieved February 6, 2011 from http://www.opengroup.org/jericho/cloud_cube_model_v1.0.pdf

Johnson, B. (2008). *Cloud computing is a trap, warns GNU founder Richard Stallman*. Retrieved from http://guardian.co.uk

Jones, K. J., Bejtlich, R., & Rose, C. W. (2006). *Real digital forensics*. Reading, MA: Addison-Wesley.

Jones, N. (2004). Training and accreditation - Who are the experts? *Digital Investigation*, *1*(3), 189–194. doi:10.1016/j.diin.2004.07.009

Jones, R. (2012). *Towards a global criminology?* Edinburgh, UK: Edinburgh School of Law Research.

Jonker, A. (2011). *The past that wasn't*. Paper presented at the International Symposium on the Law of Unintended Consequences: The Right to be Forgotten, the Duty to Remember. Vancouver, Canada. Retrieved 15 August, 2012 from http://www.slais.ubc.ca/people/students/student-groups/aca/symposium2011/index.html

Juniper Networks. (2010). *Juniper networks VGW series*. Retrieved from http://www.juniper.net/us/en/products-services/software/security/vgw-series/#overview

K&L Gates. (2006). E-discovery amendments to the federal rules of civil procedure go into effect today. *K&L Gates*. Retrieved from http://www.ediscoverylaw.com/2006/12/articles/news-updates/ediscovery-amendments-to-the-federal-rules-of-civil-procedure-go-into-effect-today/

Katz v. United States 389 U.S. 347, 357, 104 S.Ct. 2091, 80 L.Ed.2d 732 (1984).

Katz v. United States, 389 U.S. 347 (1967).

Kaufman, L. M. (2009). Data security in the world of cloud computing. *IEEE Security & Privacy*, *7*(4), 61–64. doi:10.1109/MSP.2009.87

Kelman, A., & Sizer, R. (1982). *Computer in court - A guide to computer evidence for lawyers and computing professionals*. London, UK: Gower.

Kenneally, E. E. (2005). Confluence of digital evidence and the law: On the forensic soundness of live-remote digital evidence collection. *UCLA Journal of Law and Technology*, *5*.

Kent, K., Chevalier, S., Grance, T., & Dang, H. (2006). *Guide to integrating forensic techniques into incident response, special publication 800-86*. Gaithersburg, MD: National Institute of Standards and Technology.

Kerbs, B. (2008). *Amazon: Hey spammers, get off my cloud!* Retrieved 27 July, 2012, from http://voices.washingtonpost.com/securityfix/2008/07/amazon_hey_spammers_get_off_my.html

Kermode v. University of Mississippi Medical Center, 2011 WL 4351340 (S.D. Miss. 2011) (2011).

Kerr, O. (2012). *Does the fourth amendment allow extraterritorial state search warrants*. Retrieved from http://www.volokh.com/2010/01/08/does-the-fourth-amendment-allow-extraterritorial-state-search-warrants/

Kerr, O. S. (2005). Searches and seizures in a digital world. *Harvard Law Review*, *119*, 531–585.

Kerr, O. S. (2009). The case for the third-party doctrine. *Michigan Law Review*, *107*, 561–590.

Kerr, O. S. (2010). Applying the fourth amendment to the internet: A general approach. *Stanford Law Review*, *62*, 1005–1038.

Kessler, G. C. (2010). *Judges' awareness, understanding, and application of digital evidence*. Davie, FL: Nova Southeastern University.

Kim, R. (2012). *Vendor lock-in and the challenge to platform as a service*. Retrieved 27 July, 2012, from http://gigaom.com/cloud/vendor-lock-in-and-the-challenge-to-Platform as a Service/

Kirschenbaum, M., Ovenden, R., & Redwine, G. (2010). *Digital forensics and born-digital content in cultural heritage collections*. Washington, DC: Council on library and information resources. Retrieved 15 August, 2012 from http://www.clir.org/pubs/reports/pub149/pub149.pdf

KMPG. (2012*). Government: Exploring the cloud: A global study of government's adoption of the cloud.* Retrieved 15 August, 2012 from http://www.kpmg.com/Global/en/IssuesAndInsights/ArticlesPublications/Documents/exploring-cloud.pdf

Koopmans, M. (2010). *The art of triage with (g)PXE. (Master of Science)*. Dublin, Ireland: University College Dublin.

Kortchinsky, K. (2009). *CLOUDBURST: A VMware guest to host escape story*. Retrieved from http://www.blackhat.com/presentations/bh-usa-09/KORTCHINSKY/BHUSA09-Kortchinsky-Cloudburst-SLIDES.pdf

Kosner, A. W. (2012). *Amazon cloud goes down friday night, taking Netflix, Instagram and Pinterest with it*. Retrieved 24 July, 2012, from http://www.forbes.com/sites/anthonykosner/2012/06/30/amazon-cloud-goes-down-friday-night-taking-netflix-instagram-and-pinterest-with-it/

Kravets, D. (2012). *Feds tell megaupload users to foreget about their data*. Retrieved 22 July, 2012, from http://www.wired.com/threatlevel/2012/06/feds-megaupload-data/

Krollontrack. (2011). *Capturing the cloud – Computer forensics and cloud computing*. Retrieved from http://www.krollontrack.com/blog/post/2011/04/19/Capturing-the-Cloud-e28093-Computer-Forensics-and-Cloud-Computing.aspx

Kruse, W. G., & Heiser, J. G. (2002). *Computer forensics: Incident response essentials*. Reading, MA: Addison Wesley.

Kui, R. (2012). Security challenges for the public cloud. *IEEE Internet Computing*, *16*(1), 69–73. doi:10.1109/MIC.2012.14

Kumho Tire Co. v. Carmichael, 526 U.S. 137 (1999).

Kumho Tire Co., Ltd. v. Carmichael, 526 U.S. 137, 119 S.Ct. 1167, 143, 150 L.Ed. 2d 238 (1999).

Kundra, V. (2010). *State of public sector cloud computing*. Retrieved from http://cloudcomputing.sys-con.com/node/1408645

Kundra, V. (2011). *Federal cloud computing strategy*. Washington, DC: Federal Government.

Kunick, J. (2012, June 15). Technology: The promises and perils of the cloud. *InsideCounsel*.

Kuntze, N., Rudolph, C., Alva, A., Endicott-Popovsky, B., Christiansen, J. R., & Kemmerich, T. (2012). On the creation of reliable digital evidence. In Shenoi, S. (Ed.), *Advances in Digital Forensics VIII*. Heidelberg, Germany: Springer.

Lacovino, L. (2006). *Recordkeeping, ethics and law: Regulatory models, participant relationships and rights and responsibilities in the online world*. Dordrecht, The Netherlands: Springer.

LaFave, W. R. (2009). *Search and seizure: A treatise on the fourth amendment § 2.1(b), at n. 82.1* (2004th ed., pp. 2008–2009). Supp.

Laudon, K. C., & Laudon, J. P. (1999). *Essentials of management information systems*. Englewood Cliffs, NJ: Prentice Hall.

Lemos, R. (2001). *FBI hack raises global security concerns*. Retrieved 11 July, 2012, from http://news.cnet.com/2100-1001-256811.html

Lemos, R. (2010). *Cloud-based denial of serice attacks looming, researchers say*. Retrieved 27 July, 2012, from http://www.darkreading.com/security/news/226500300

Leong, R., & Leung, H. (2007). Deriving cse-specific live forensics investigation procedures from FORZA. In *Proceedings of the 2007 ACM Symposium on Applied Computing*. ACM Press.

Liles, S., Rogers, M., & Hoebich, M. (2009). A survey of the legal issues facing digital forensic experts. In *Advances in Digital Forensics V* (pp. 267–276). Berlin, Germany: Springer. doi:10.1007/978-3-642-04155-6_20

Lillard, T. (2010). *Digital forensics for network, internet, and cloud computing: A forensic evidence guide for moving targets and data*. New York, NY: Elsevier.

Lillard, T. V., Garrison, C. P., Schiller, C. A., & Steele, J. (2010). *Digital forensics for network, internet, and cloud computing*. Burlington, MA: Syngress Publishing.

Lim, K.-S. (2012). On-the-spot digital investigation by means of LDFS: Live data forensic system. *Mathematical and Computer Modelling*, *55*(1), 223–240. doi:10.1016/j.mcm.2011.05.019

Limongelli, V. (2008). Digital evidence: Findings of reliability, not presumptions. *Journal of Digital Forensic Practice*, *2*(1), 13–16. doi:10.1080/15567280701721913

Liu, F., Tong, J., Mao, J., Bohn, R., Messina, J., Badger, L., & Leaf, D. (2011). *NIST Cloud computing reference architecture. NIST Special Publication 500-292*. Washington, DC: NIST.

Lomas, E. (2010). Information governance: information security and access within a UK context. *Records Management Journal*, *20*(2), 182–198. doi:10.1108/09565691011064322

Lorraine v. Markel American Insurance Company, 241 F.R.D. 534, 538, 539, 541-542, 545-546, 553, 562-565, 584 (D.Md. 2007) (2007).

Losavio, M. (2005). The law of possession of digital objects: Dominion and control issues for digital forensics investigations and prosecutions. In *Proceedings of the First International Workshop on Systematic Approaches to Digital Forensic Engineering, 2005,* (pp. 177–183). IEEE.

Lu, R., Lin, X., Liang, X., & Shen, X. (2010). Secure provenance: The essential of bread and butter of data forensics in cloud computing. In *Proceedings of the 5th ACM Symposium on Information, Computer and Communications Security,* (pp. 282-292). New York, NY: ACM.

Lynch, C. A. (2001). When documents deceive: Trust and provenance as new factors for information retrieval in a tangled web. *Journal of the American Society for Information Science and Technology, 52*, 12–17. doi:10.1002/1532-2890(2000)52:1<12::AID-ASI1062>3.0.CO;2-V

Maconachy, W. V., Schou, C. D., Ragsdale, D., & Welch, D. (2001). A model for information assurance: An integrated approach. In *Proceedings of the 2001 IEEE Workshop on Information Assurance and Security,* (pp. 306-310). West Point, NY: United States Military Academy.

Mallassi, O. (2010). *How to "crunch" your data stored in HDFS?* Retrieved July 5, 2011 from http://blog.octo.com/en/how-to-crunch-your-data-stored-in-hdfs/

Mansfield-Devine, S. (2010). Fighting forensics. *Computer Fraud & Security*, *1*, 17–20. doi:10.1016/S1361-3723(10)70112-3

Marcella, A. J., & Menendez, D. (2008). *Cyberforensics: A field manual for collecting, examining and preserving evidence of computer crimes* (2nd ed.). New York, NY: Auerbach Publications.

Martin, A. (2007). *Firewire memory dump of a Windows XP computer: A forensic approach*. Retrieved from http://www.friendsglobal.com/papers/FireWire%20Memory%20Dump%20of%20Windows%20XP.pdf

Marturana, F., Bertè, R., Me, G., & Tacconi, S. (2011a). Mobile forensics "triaging": New directions for methodology. In *Proceedings of the 8th Conference of the Italian Chapter of AIS (ITAIS 2011)*. ITAIS.

Marturana, F., Bertè, R., Me, G., & Tacconi, S. (2011b). A quantitative approach to triaging in mobile forensics. In *Proceedings of International Joint Conference of IEEE TrustCom-11/IEEE ICESS-11/FCST-11, (TRUSTCOM 2011)*, (pp. 582-588). IEEE Press.

Marturana, F., Bertè, R., Me, G., & Tacconi, S. (2012a). Data mining based crime-dependent triage in digital forensics analysis. *IERI Lecture Notes in Information Technology, 10*, 101–106.

Marturana, F., Bertè, R., Me, G., & Tacconi, S. (2012b). Triage-based automated analysis of evidence in court cases of copyright infringement. In *Proceedings of the 1st IEEE International Workshop on Security and Forensics in Communication Systems (SFCS 2012)*. IEEE Press.

Maryland v. Garrison, 480 U.S. 79, 84, 107 S.Ct. 1013, 94 L.Ed.2d 72 (1987).

Mason v. Pulliam, 557 F.2d 426 (5th Cir. 1977) (1977).

Mason, S. (2007). *Electronic evidence: Disclosure, discovery & admissibility*. London, UK: Butterworths.

Mathews, J. (2010). *The future of virtualization, cloud computing & green IT – Global technologies & markets outlook – 2011-2016*. Colorado Springs, CO: Market Info Group LLC.

McAfee. (2010). *A good decade for cybercrime*. Santa Clara, CA: McAfee, Inc.

McAfee. (2012). *Threats report, first quarter 2012*. Retrieved June 20, 2012, from http://www.mcafee.com/us/resources/reports/rp-quarterly-threat-q1-2012.pdf

McCumber, J. (1991). Information systems security: A comprehensive model. In *Proceedings of the 14th National Computer Security Conference*. Baltimore, MD: National Institute of Standards and Technology.

McGuigan, B. (2011). *What is distributed computing?* Retrieved 10 February, 2011, from http://www.wisegeek.com/what-is-distributed-computing.htm

McKemmish, R. (1999). What is forensic computing. *Trends and Issues in Crime and Criminal Justice, 118*.

McKemmish, R. (2008). When is digital evidence forensically sound? In Ray, I., & Shenoi, S. (Eds.), *Advances in Digital Forensics 4*. Berlin, Germany: Springer. doi:10.1007/978-0-387-84927-0_1

McKemmish, R., Pollitt, M., Cohen, F., Preston, C., Pavlic, T., & Slay, J. … Marberry, C. (2008). *Advances in digital forensics IV*. New York, NY: Springer.

McVeigh v. Cohen, 983 F. Supp. 215 (D.D.C. 1998) (1998).

Meadows, R. (2009). *Cisco router and switch forensics: Investigating and analyzing malicious network activity*. Burlington, MA: Elsevier.

Meeker, M. (2012). Internet trends. *D10 Conference*. Retrieved 11 July, 2012, from http://allthingsd.com/20120612/mary-meeker-explains-internet-2012-in-17-minutes-the-full-d10-interview-video/?refcat=d10

Mell, P., & Grance, T. (2011). *Definition of cloud computing: NIST special publication 800-145*. Gaithersburg, MD: National Institute of Standards and Technology. Retrieved from http://csrc.nist.gov/publications/nistpubs/800-145/SP800-145.pdf

Mell, P., & Grance, T. (2011). The NIST definition of cloud computing. *National Institute of Standards and Technology, 7*.

Mell, J. P., & Grance, T. (2011). *The NIST definition of cloud computing*. Washington, DC: National Institute of Standard and Technology.

Messmer, E. (2011). *How one municipality is securing Google apps, docs*. Retrieved from http://csonline.com

Meyers, M., & Rogers, M. (2004). Computer forensics: The need for standardization and certification. *International Journal of Digital Evidence, 3*(2).

Microsoft. (2010). *Computer online forensic evidence extractor (COFEE)*. Retrieved 4 February, 2011, from http://www.microsoft.com/industry/government/solutions/cofee/default.aspx

Microsoft. (2010). *Windows Azure active directory*. Retrieved from http://www.windowsazure.com/en-us/home/features/access-control/

Microsoft. (2011). TrojanDropper:Win32/Bohu.A. *Malware Protection Center*. Retrieved 25 February, 2011, from http://www.microsoft.com/security/portal/Threat/Encyclopedia/Entry.aspx?Name=TrojanDropper%3AWin32%2FBohu.A

Microsoft. (2012). *Microsoft virtualization from the datacenter to the desktop*. Retrieved July 30, 2012 from http://technet.microsoft.com/en-us/virtualserver/bb676673.aspx

Microsoft Corporation. (2010). *Microsoft services agreement*. Retrieved from http://explore.live.com/microsoft-service-agreement

Mislan, R. P. (2010). The growing need for on-scene triage of mobile devices. *Digital Investigation, 6*(3-4), 112–124. doi:10.1016/j.diin.2010.03.001

Model Code of Pre-Arraignment Procedure § SS 240.3 (1975).

Moles, R. N. (2007). *The role and function of the expert witness*. Retrieved from http://netk.net.au/Reports/ExpertWitness.asp

Moreno-Vozmediano, R. (2012). Key challenges in cloud computing to enable the future internet of services. *IEEE Internet Computing*, 99.

Morgester, R. (2006). Search warrant language for cellular phones. *Cyber Crime Newsletter*. Retrieved from http://www.olemiss.edu/depts/ncjrl/pdf/May-June%202006%20Final%20Copy.pdf

Morrison, S. R. (2011). What the cops can't do, internet service providers can: Preserving privacy in email contents. *Virginia Journal of Law & Technology*, *16*, 253–300.

Mullins, R. (2011). *Cisco's virtualization play with windows server 8*. Retrieved July 30, 2012 from http://www.informationweek.com/news/tech-center/storage-virtualization/231602145

Myslewski, R. (2009). *Intel puts cloud on a single megachip*. Retrieved 10 February, 2011, from http://www.theregister.co.uk/2009/12/02/intel_scc/

N.J. v. Mollica, 554 A.2d 1315, 1324 (N.J. 1989) (1989).

Nance, K., Hay, B., & Bishop, M. (2009). Digital forensics: Defining a research agenda. In *Proceedings of the 42nd Hawaii International Conference on System Sciences*. IEEE.

NARA Electronic Records Management Definitions, 36 C.F.R. § 1236.2 (2009)

National Archives. (2011). *Identifying information assets and business requirements*. Retrieved 15 August, 2012 from http://www.nationalarchives.gov.uk/documents/information-management/identify-information-assets.pdf

National Gendarmerie. (2011). *Prospective analysis on trends in cybercrime from 2011 to 2020*. Retrieved from http://www.mcafee.com/us/resources/white-papers/wp-trends-in-cybercrime-2011-2020.pdf

National Institute of Standards and Technology. (2012). *Disk imaging*. Retrieved from http://www.cftt.nist.gov/disk_imaging.htm

National Security Agency. (1999). *National security telecommunication and information systems security instruction no 4009. National Information Systems Security (INFOSEC) Glossary*. Washington, DC: NSA.

National Security Agency. (2012). *An overview of cloud computing*. Retrieved June 17, 2012, from http://www.nsa.gov/research/_files/publications/cloud_computing_overview.pdf

Neumann, J. (1945). *First draft of a report on the EDVAC*. Retrieved from http://qss.stanford.edu/~godfrey/vonNeumann/vnedvac.pdf

Neumann, J. (1949). *Theory of self-reproducing automata*. Retrieved from http://cba.mit.edu/events/03.11.ASE/docs/VonNeumann.pdf

New York v O'Neill, 359 US 1, 79 S.Ct. 564, 3 L.Ed.2d 585 (1959).

Newman, R. C. (2007). *Computer forensics: Evidence collection and management*. London, UK: Auerbach Publications.

Nguyen, L. (2012). *Tori Stafford trial: Cellphone record shows gap during abduction, murder*. Retrieved 13 July, 2012, from http://www.canada.com/life/Tori+Stafford+trial+Cellphone+record+shows+during+abduction+murder/6486178/story.html

Nickkel, B. J. (2006). *The role of digital forensics within a corporate organization*. Paper presented at the Gartner IT Security Summit. London, UK.

NIJ. (2008). *Electronic crime scene investigation: A guide for first responders* (2nd ed). Retrieved 2 February, 2011, from http://www.ojp.usdoj.gov/nij/publications/ecrime-guide-219941/welcome.htm

Norton, Q. (2012). *25 alleged anons arrested in international crackdown*. Retrieved 27 July, 2012, from http://www.wired.com/threatlevel/2012/02/anonymous-arrested-interpol/

Nurmi, D., Wolski, R., Grzegorczyk, C., & Obertelli, G. Soman, Youseff, L., & Zagorodnov, D. (2008). The eucalyptus open-source cloud-computing system. In *Proceedings of Cloud Computing and Its Application*, (pp. 124-131). IEEE.

O'Connor v. Ortega, 480 U.S. 709, 715, 107 S.Ct. 1492, 94 L.Ed.2d 714 (1987).

O'Connor, T. (2010). *Admissibility of scientific evidence under daubert*. Retrieved 26, January, 2011, from http://www.drtomoconnor.com/3210/3210lect01a.htm

Ogloff, J., Clough, J., & Goodman-Delahunty, J. (2006). *The jury project: Stage 1 - A survey of Australian and New Zealand judges*. Melbourne, Australia: Australian Institute of Judicial Administration.

Orakwue, E. (2009). Rise of the virtual machine. *ISSA Journal*. Retrieved from http://www.issa.org/Library/Journals/2009/February/Orakwue-Rise%20of%20the%20Virtual%20Machine.pdf

Palmer, G. (2001). DFRWS technical report: A road map for digital forensic research. In *Digital Forensic Research Workshop*. Utica, NY: G. Palmer.

Paquette, S. (2010). Identifying the security risks associated with governmental use of cloud computing. *Government Information Quarterly*, *27*(3), 245–253. doi:10.1016/j.giq.2010.01.002

Paquette, S., Jaeger, P., & Wilson, S. (2010). Identifying the security risks associated with governmental use of cloud computing. *Government Information Quarterly*, *27*, 245–253. doi:10.1016/j.giq.2010.01.002

Parnell, B.-A. (2012). *Microsoft's Azure cloud down and out for 8 hours*. Retrieved 24 July, 2012, from http://www.theregister.co.uk/2012/02/29/windows_azure_outage/

Paul, W. (2012). Cyber war, formal verification and certified infrastructure. *Verified Software: Theories, Tools, Experiments, 1*(1).

Peisert, S., Bishop, M., & Marzullo, K. (2008). *Computer forensics in forensis*. Paper presented at the Third International Workshop on Systematic Approaches to Digital Forensic Engineering. Oakland, CA.

Penn. (1936). *Uniform act to secure the attendance of witnesses from without a state in criminal proceedings*. Paper presented at the 41st Annual Conference of the National Conference of Commissioners on Uniform State Laws. Atlantic City, NJ. Retrieved from https://www.law.upenn.edu/library/archives/ulc/fnact99/1920_69/uasaw36.pdf

People v. Mason, 989 P.2d 757, 761 (Colo. 1999) (1999).

People v. Watson, 214 Ill. 2d 271, 825 N.E.2d 257 (2005).

Perry, R., Hatcher, E., Mahowald, R. P., & Hendrick, S. D. (2009). *Force.com cloud platform drives huge time to market and cost savings*. Retrieved June 22, 2012, from http://www.salesforce.com/fr/assets/pdf/whitepapers/whitepaper-idc-force-roi-study.pdf

Pettey, C. (2011). *Gartner says 30 percent of midsize companies will use recovery-as-a-service by 2014*. New York, NY: Gartner.

Pew Internet and American Life Project. (2011). *Internet adoption*. Retrieved from http://www.pewinternet.org/Trend-Data/Internet-Adoption.aspx

Phillippi, N. (2010). *The difference between virtualization and cloud computing*. Retrieved July 30, 2012 from http://www.erpsoftwareblog.com/2010/08/the-difference-between-virtualization-and-cloud-computing/

Pollitt, M. (1995). *Principles, practices, and procedures: An approach to standards in computer forensics*. Retrieved from http://www.digitalevidencepro.com/Resources/Principles.pdf

Pollitt, M. (2007). *An ad hoc review of digital forensic models*. Washington, DC: IEEE. doi:10.1109/SADFE.2007.3

Pollitt, M. (2009). The good, the bad and the unaddressed. *Journal of Digital Forensic Practice*, *2*, 172–174. doi:10.1080/15567280902882852

Pollitt, M., Caloyannides, M., Novotny, J., & Shenoi, S. (2004). Digital forensics: Operational, legal and research issues. *Data and Applications Security*, *17*, 393–403.

Polsson, K. (2011). *Chronology of personal computers*. Retrieved 25 January, 2011, from http://www.islandnet.com/~kpolsson/comphist/

Ponemon. (2011). *The security of cloud infrastructure: Survey of U.S. IT and compliance practitioners*. New York, NY: Ponemon Institute.

Popek, G. J., & Goldberg, R. P. (1974). Formal requirements for virtualizable third generation architectures. *Communications of the ACM*, *17*(7), 412–421. doi:10.1145/361011.361073

Purdy, C. (2010). *Industry's first forensic-base critical infrastructure security solution.* Retrieved 29 January, 2011, from https://http://www.guidancesoftware.com/Media/NewsRoom/NewsRoomBlog.aspx?B=BlogContentDetails&Blog_S=NewsRoomMenu&newsroommenu_id=3503&image_id=1000000303&md_id=1000000296&id=1000000267&blogid=2523

Quon v. Arch Wireless Operating Co., Inc., 529 F.3d 892 (9th Cir. 2008) (2008).

Re, E. D. (1975). Stare decisis. In *Proceedings of the Seminar for Federal Appellate Judges sponsored by the Federal Judicial Center*, (pp. 1-21). Retrieved from http://www.fjc.gov/public/pdf.nsf/lookup/staredec.pdf/$file/staredec.pdf

Reese, G. (2009). *Principles for standardized REST authentication.* Retrieved from http://broadcast.oreilly.com/2009/12/principles-for-standardized-rest-authentication.html

Reith, M., Carr, C., & Gunsch, G. (2002). An examination of digital forensic models. *International Journal of Digital Evidence*, *1*(3).

Rekhis, S., & Boudriga, N. (2010). Formal digital investigation of anti-forensic attacks. In *Proceedings of the Fifth International Workshop on Systematic Approaches to Digital Forensic Engineering*. IEEE Press.

Rice, P. (2005). *Electronic evidence: Law and practice.* New York, NY: ABA Publishing.

Richman, W. M., & Reynolds, W. L. (2002). *Understanding conflict of laws*. New York, NY: Matthew Bender.

Right to Financial Privacy Act, 12 U.S.C. §§ 3401-22 (2000).

Ristenpart, T., Tromer, E., Shacham, H., & Savage, S. (2009). Hey, you, get off of my cloud: Exploring information leakage in third-party compute clouds. In *Proceedings of CCS 2009*. Retrieved from http://people.csail.mit.edu/tromer/papers/cloudsec.pdf

Roberts, J. J. (1974). A practitioner's primer on computer-generated evidence. *The University of Chicago Law Review. University of Chicago. Law School*, *41*(2), 254–280. doi:10.2307/1599148

Robison, W. J. (2010). Free at what cost? Cloud computing privacy under the stored communications act. *The Georgetown Law Journal*, *98*, 1195–1213.

Rodriques v. Furtado, 410 Mass. 878, 575 N.E.2d 1124 (1991).

Rogers, M. (2006). Computer forensics field triage process model. *Journal of Digital Forensics. Security and Law*, *1*(2), 27–40.

Rogers, M. K. (2006). DCSA: Applied digital crime scene analysis. In Tipton & Krause (Eds.), *Information Security Management Handbook* (5th ed.). New York, NY: Auerbach.

Rogers, M. K. (Ed.). (2004). *DCSA: A practical approach to digital crime scene analysis* (5th ed., *Vol. 3*). New York, NY: Taylor and Francis.

Rosenthal Collins Group, LLC v. Trading Technologies International, 2011 U.S. Dist. LEXIS 17623 (N.D. Ill. 2011) (2011).

Roth, T. (2011). Breaking encryption in the cloud: GPU accelerated supercomputing for everyone. In *Proceedings of Black Hat DC 2011*. Black Hat.

Roussev, V., & Richard, G., III. (2004). Breaking the performance wall: The case for distributed digital forensics. In *Proceedings of the Digital Forensics Research Workshop (DFRWS)*. DFRWS.

Roussev, V., Wang, L., Richard, G., & Marziale, L. (2009). A cloud computing platform for large-scale forensic computing. In *Proceedings of the 5th IFIP International Conference on Digital Forensics, Advances in Digital Forensics*, (pp. 201-215). IFIP.

Roussev, V., Wang, L., Richard, G., III, & Marziale, L. (2009). MMR: A platform for large-scale forensic computing. In *Proceedings of the Fifth Annual IFIP WG 11.9 International Conference on Digital Forensics*. IFIP.

RSA. (2009). *Public-key cryptography standards (PKCS)*. Retrieved 21 May, 2012, from http://www.rsa.com/rsalabs/node.asp?id=2176

Ruan, K., & Carthy, J. (2012b). Cloud forensic maturity model. In *Proceedings of the 4th International Conference on Digital Forensics & Cyber Crime*. Lafayette, IN: IEEE.

Ruan, K., Carthy, J., & Kechadi, T. (2011a). *Survey on cloud forensics and critical criteria for cloud forensic capability: A preliminary analysis*. Paper presented at the 6th Annual Conference of the ADFSL Conference on Digital Forensics, Security and Law. Richmond, VA.

Ruan, K., Carthy, J., Kechadi, T., & Crosbie, M. (2011). Cloud forensics: An overview. In *Proceedings of the 7th IFIP International Conference on Digital Forensics, Advances in Digital Forensics*. Berlin, Germany: Springer.

Ruan, K., et al. (2012). *Cloud forensics: Key terms for service level agreements*. Paper presented at the Eigth Annual IFIP WG 11.9 International Conference on Digital Forensics. Pretoria, South Africa.

Russell, K., & Hammons, S. (2012). *Citizen engagement platform*. Boulder, CO: Office of Information Technology.

Saliba, J. (2012). *Finding evidence in an online world - Trends and challenges in digital forensics*. Retrieved from http://www.cybercrimetech.com/2012/07/webinar-finding-evidence-in-online.html#!/2012/07/webinar-finding-evidence-in-online.html

Sammes, T., & Jenkinson, B. (2007). *Forensic computing: A practitioner's guide* (2nd ed.). Berlin, Germany: Springer.

Saripalli, P., & Walters, B. (2010). *QUIRC: A quantitative impact and risk assessment framework for cloud security*. IEEE. doi:10.1109/CLOUD.2010.22

Schalk v. State, 767 S.W.2d 441, 454 (Tex.App. 1988), cert. denied, 503 U.S. 1006, 112 S.Ct. 1763, 118 L.Ed.2d 425 (1992).

Scheier, R. L. (2009). What to do if your cloud provider disappears. *Cloud Computing*. Retrieved from http://www.infoworld.com/d/cloud-computing/what-do-if-your-cloud-provider-disappears-508

Schneckloth v. Bustamonte, 412 U.S. 218, 219, 93 S.Ct. 2041, 36 L.Ed.2d 854 (1973).

Schneier, B. (2010). The threat of cyberwar has been grossly exaggerated. *Schneier on Security*. Retrieved from http://www.schneier.com/blog/archives/2010/07/the_threat_of_c.html

Schroeder, S. (2011). *The lure*. New York, NY: Cengage Learning.

Schumacher, M. (2006). *Security patterns: Integrating security and systems engineering*. Hoboken, NJ: Wiley.

Scott, Z., & Dominick, G. (2011). Cyber forensics in the cloud. *Technology (Elmsford, N.Y.)*, *14*(1), 1–36.

Security as a Service. (2011). *Security as a service defined categories of service 2011*. Washington, DC: Security as a Service Working Group. ACPO. (2008). *Good practice guide for computer based electronic evidence*. Washington, DC: ACPO.

Sedona Conference. (2005). *The Sedona guidelines: Best practice guidelines & commentary for managing information & records in the electronic age*. Retrieved from https://thesedonaconference.org/download-pub/90

Sedona Conference. (2007). *The Sedona principles* (2nd ed). Retrieved from https://thesedonaconference.org/download-pub/81

Sedona Conference. (2008). *Framework for analysis of cross-border discovery conflicts: A practical guide to navigating the competing currents of international data privacy and e-discovery*. Retrieved from https://thesedonaconference.org/publication/Framework%20for%20Analysis%20of%20Cross-Border%20Discovery%20Conflicts

Sedona Conference. (2010). *Commentary on legal holds*. Retrieved from https://thesedonaconference.org/download-pub/470

Selamer, S., Yusof, R., & Sahib, S. (2008). Mapping process of digital forensic investigation framework. *International Journal of Computer Science and Network Security*, *8*(10), 163–169.

Services, U. H. (2012). *Health insurance portability and accountability act*. Retrieved from www.hhs.gov/ocr/hipaa/

Shanmugasundaram, K., Memon, N., Savant, A., & Bronnimann, H. (2012). ForNet: A distributed forensics network. In *Proceedings of the Second International Workshop on Mathematical Methods, Models and Architectures for Computer Networks Security*. IEEE.

Shavers, B. (2008). *Virtual machine forensics, a discussion of virtual machines related to forensics analysis*. Retrieved July 30, 2012 from http:// www.forensicfocus.com

Shende, J. R. (2010). *Digital forensic challenges within cloud computing*. Retrieved from http://jonshende.sys-con.com/node/1576458

Shende, J. R. (2011). *The impact of the cloud on digital forensics*. Retrieved from http://www.dfinews.com/article/impact-cloud-digital-forensics-part-1?page=0,2

Shepherd, E. (1994). Records management in Britain – A review of some developments in professional principles and practice. *Business Archives*, *67*, 13–25.

Shepherd, E., & Yeo, G. (2003). *Managing records: A handbook of principles and practice*. London, UK: Facet Publishing. doi:10.1108/00220410310506349

Shinder, D., & Cross, M. (2008). *Scene of the cybercrime*. New York, NY: Syngress Media.

Shipley, T. G., & Door, B. (2012). *Forensic imaging of hard disk drives- What we thought we knew*. Retrieved 15 July, 2012, from http://articles.forensicfocus.com/2012/01/27/forensic-imaging-of-hard-disk-drives-what-we-thought-we-knew-2/

Silvestri v. General Motors, 271 F.3d 583 (4th Cir. 2001) (2001).

Skok, M. J. (2012). *Future of cloud computing 2012*. Waltham, MA: Northbridge Venture Partners.

Smith v. Maryland, 442 U.S. 735, 743-44, 99 S.Ct. 2577, 61 L.Ed.2d 220 (1979).

Smith, S. E. (2011). *What is cyberwar?* Retrieved 28 January, 2011, from http://www.wisegeek.com/what-is-cyberwar.htm

Smith, G. J. H. (2007). *Internet law and regulation*. London, UK: Sweet and Maxwell.

Smith, R. G., Grabosky, P. N., & Urbas, G. (2004). *Cyber criminals on trial*. Cambridge, UK: Cambridge University Press. doi:10.1017/CBO9780511481604

Solomon, A. (2010). *Privacy and the cloud*. Paper presented at the Cloud Computing Conference and Expo. New York, NY.

Sommer, P. (1998). *Digital footprints: Assessing computer evidence* (*Special Edition*, pp. 61–78). Criminal Law Review.

Sommer, P. (2002). Digital evidence: Emerging problems in forensic computing. *University of Cambridge*. Retrieved 15 August, 2012 from http://www.cl.cam.ac.uk/research/security/seminars/2002/2002-05-21.pdf

Sommer, P. (2009). *Directors and corporate advisors' guide to digital investigations and evidence*. London, UK: Information Assurance Advisory Council.

Sommer, P. (2012). *Digital evidence, digital investigations and e disclosure: A guide to forensic readiness for organizations, security advisors and lawyers*. London, UK: Information Assurance Advisory Council.

Spafford, E. H., & Weeber, S. A. (1993). Software forensics: Can we track code to its authors? *Computers & Security*, *12*(6), 585–595. doi:10.1016/0167-4048(93)90055-A

Spyridopoulos, T., & Katos, V. (2011). Requirements for a forensically ready cloud storage service. *International Journal of Digital Crime and Forensics*, *3*(3), 19–36. doi:10.4018/jdcf.2011070102

Sremack, J. (2004). *Formalizing of analysis: A proof-based methodology*. (Master of Science Thesis). North Carolina State University. Raleigh, NC.

St. Clair v. Johnny's Oyster & Shrimp, Inc., 76 F. Supp. 2d 773, 774 (S.D. Tex. 1999) (1999).

Stanfield, A. (2009). *Computer forensics, electronic discovery & electronic evidence*. London, UK: Reed International Books.

State v. Afana, 233 P.3d 879 (Wash., 2010) (2010).

State v. Bellar, 231 Or. App. 80, 217 P.3d 1094 (2009).

State v. Kern, 81 Wash.App. 308, 914 P.2d 114, 117–18 (1996).

State v. Mathe, 688 P.2d 859 (Wash. 1984) (1984).

State v. Miles, 160 Wash. 2d 236, 156 P.3d 864 (2007).

State v. Moore, 871 P.2d 1086 (Wash. App. 1994) (1994).

State v. Morse, 123 P.3d 832 (Wash. 2005) (2005).

State v. Nordlund, 53 P.3d 520, 525 (Wash. App. 2002), *petition for review denied*, 70 P.3d 964 (Wash. 2003) (2003).

States v. Kassimu, 188 Fed. Appx. 264, 2006 WL 1880335 (5th Cir. 2006) (2006).

Steel, C. (2006). *Windows forensics: The field guide for conducting corporate computer investigations*. New York, NY: Wiley Publishing.

Stephenson, P. (2003). A comprehensive approach to digital incident investigation. *Information Security Technical Report*, *8*(2), 42–54. doi:10.1016/S1363-4127(03)00206-1

Stephenson, P. (2003). Using a formalized approach to digital investigation. *Computer Fraud & Security*, *7*, 17–20. doi:10.1016/S1361-3723(03)08010-2

Stippich, M. J., & Stippich, C. J. (2005). A holistic perspective on the science of computer forensics. *Journal of Information Privacy and Security*, *1*(1), 27–39.

Stored Communications Act of 1986, 18 U.S.C. §§ 2701-2712 (2000).

Stylianou, K. K. (2010). An evolutionary study of cloud computing services privacy terms. *The John Marshall Journal of Computer & Information Law*, *27*, 593–612.

Sustainable. (2000). *Dictionary.com.* Retrieved 15 August, 2012 from http://dictionary.reference.com/browse/sustainable

Sutherland, I., Evans, J., Tryfonas, T., & Blyth, A. (2008). Acquiring volatile operating system data tools and techniques. *SIGOPS Operating Systems Review*, *42*(3), 65–73. doi:10.1145/1368506.1368516

SWGDE. (2009). *SWGDE/SWGIT digital & multimedia evidence glossary version: 2.3*. Washington, DC: Scientific Working Group on Digital Evidence.

Swiderski, F., & Snyder, W. (2004). *Threat modeling*. Redmond, WA: Microsoft Press.

Tang, Y., & Daniels, T. (2005). A simple framework for distributed forensics. In *Proceedings of the Second International Workshop on Security in Distributed Computing Systems (SDCS - ICDCSW)*, (pp. 163-169). ICDCSW.

Tapper, C. (1974). Evidence from computers. *Rutgers Journal of Computers and the Law*, *4*, 324–406.

Taylor, M. (2011). Forensic investigation of cloud computing systems. *Network Security*, *3*, 4–10. doi:10.1016/S1353-4858(11)70024-1

Taylor, M., Haggerty, J., Gresty, D., & Hegarty, R. (2010). Digital evidence in cloud computing systems. *Computer Law & Security Report*, *26*(3), 304–308. doi:10.1016/j.clsr.2010.03.002

Taylor, M., Haggerty, J., Gresty, D., & Lamb, D. (2011). Forensic investigations of cloud computing systems. *Network Security*, *3*, 4–10. doi:10.1016/S1353-4858(11)70024-1

Teubner, A. L. (1978). The computer as expert witness: Toward a unified theory of computer evidence. *Jurimetrics Journal*, *19*, 274–297.

Thomason, I. (2010). *Cloud services a decade away from maturity*. Retrieved from http://www.v3.co.uk/v3-uk/news/1999968/cloud-services-decade-away- maturity

Tomlinson v. El Paso Corp., 245 F.R.D. 474 (D. Colo. 2007) (2007).

Truloch v. Freeh, 275 F.3d 391, 403 (4th Cir. 2001) (2001).

Tucker v. Waddell, 83 F.3d 688 (4th Cir. 1996) (1996).

U.S. Const. amend. IV. (1791).

U.S. v. Brown, 52 F.3d 415, 421 (2d Cir. 1995), *cert. denied*, 516 U.S. 1068 (1996).

U.S. v. Buckner, 473 F.3d 551, 555 (4th Cir. 2007) (2007).

U.S. v. Dawkins, 17 F.3d 399, 405 (D.C. Cir. 1994) (1994).

U.S. v. Friere, 710 F.2d 1515, 1519 (11th Cir. 1983) (1983).

U.S. v. Khorozian 333 F.3d 498, 61 Fed. R. Evid. Serv. 980, (2003).

U.S. v. Ladell, 127 F.3d 622, 624 (7th Cir. 1997) (1997).

U.S. v. Matlock, 415 U.S. 164, 171 (1974).

U.S. v. Morning, 64 F.3d 531, 536 (9th Cir. 1995), cert. denied, 516 U.S. 1152 (1996).

U.S. v. Rico, 51 F.3d 495, 501 (5th Cir.), cert. denied, 516 U.S. 883 (1995).

U.S. v. Rith, 164 F.3d 1323 (10th Cir.), cert. denied, 528 U.S. 827 (1999).

U.S. v. Smith, 27 F. Supp. 2d 1111 (C.D. Ill. 1998) (1998).

United States v. Andrus, 483 F.3d 711, 718 (10th Cir.2007), cert. denied, 522 U.S. 12997, 128 S.Ct 1738. 170 L.Ed.2d 542 (2008).

United States v. Bach, 310 F.3d 1063 (8th Cir. 2002) (2002).

United States v. Beddow, 957 F.2d 1330, 1335 (6th Cir.1992) (1992).

United States v. Calandra, 414 U.S. 338, 346, 94 S.Ct. 613, 38 L.Ed.2d 561 (1974).

United States v. Cameron 762 F.Supp.2d 152, 158-159 (D. Maine 2011) (2011).

United States v. Cameron, 573 F.3d 179, 183 (4th Cir. 2009) (2009).

United States v. Drew, 259 F.R.D. 449 (C.D. Cal. 2009) (2009).

United States v. Falcon 766 F.2d 1469, 1476 (10th Cir. 1985) (1985).

United States v. Gorshkov, CR00-550C, 2001 WL 1024026, 3-4 (W.D. Wash. May 23, 2001) (2001).

United States v. Graham CRIM. RDB-11-0094, 2012 WL 691531 (D. Md. Mar. 1, 2012) (2012).

United States v. James 353 F.3d 606 (8th Cir. 2003) (2003).

United States v. Jones, 132 S. Ct. 945 (2012).

United States v. Kassimu, 2006 WL 1880335 (5th Cir. 2006) (2006).

United States v. Leon, 468 U.S. 897, 916, 104 S.Ct. 3405, 82 L.Ed.2d. 677 (1984).

United States v. Mann, 592. F.3d 779, 782 (7th Cir. 2010) (2010).

United States v. Miller, 994 F.2d 441 (8th Cir. 1993) (1993).

United States v. Nafzger, 965 F.2d 213 (7th Cir.1992) (1992).

United States v. Presler, 610 F.2d 1206, 1213-14 (4th Cir. 1979) (1979).

United States v. Richardson, 607 F.3d 357, 363 (4th Cir. 2010) cert. denied, 131 S. Ct. 427, 178 L. Ed. 2d 324 (U.S. 2010) (2010).

United States v. Stephens, 206 F.3rd 914, 917 (9th Cir. 2000) (2000).

United States v. Turner, 770 F.2d 1508 (9th Cir.1985) (1985).

United States v. Ward, 576 F.2d 243, 244-45 (9th Cir.1978) (1978).

United States v. Williams, 2010 U.S. App. LEXIS 1327 (4th Cir. Jan. 21, 2010) (2010).

United States v. Ziegler, 474 F.3d 1184, 1189 (9th Cir. 2007) (2007).

Upward, F. (2000). Modeling the continuum as paradigm shift in recordkeeping and archiving processes and beyond – A personal reflection. *Records Management Journal*, *10*(3), 121. doi:10.1108/EUM0000000007259

Upward, F. (2005). The records continuum. In McKemmish, S. (Eds.), *Archives: Recordkeeping in Society*. New South Wales, Australia: Charles Stuart University.

Upward, F., & Stillman, L. (2007). Community informatics and the information processing continuum. In Stillman, L., & Johanson, G. (Eds.), *Constructing and Sharing Memory: Community Informatics, Identity and Empowerment* (pp. 318–332). Cambridge, UK: Cambridge Scholars Publishing.

Urquhart, J. (2009). *Cloud is an operations model, not technology*. Retrieved July 30, 2012 from http://news.cnet.com/8301-19413_3-10249486-240.html

US Department of Justice. (2009). *Searching and seizing computers and obtaining electronic evidence in criminal investigations*. Retrieved from http://www.justice.gov/criminal/cybercrime/docs/ssmanual2009.pdf

US Government. (2010a). *Federal rules of civil procedure*. Retrieved from http://www.uscourts.gov/uscourts/RulesAndPolicies/rules/2010%20Rules/Civil%20Procedure.pdf

US Government. (2010b). *Federal rules of criminal procedure*. Retrieved from http://www.uscourts.gov/uscourts/RulesAndPolicies/rules/2010%20Rules/Criminal%20Procedure.pdf

US House of Representatives Committee on the Judiciary. (2011). *Going dark: Lawful electronic surveillance in the face of new technologies*. H.R. REP. NO. 112-159. Washington, DC: US House of Representatives Committee on the Judiciary.

USA PATRIOT Act Pub. L. No. 107-56, 115 Stat. 272 (2001).

US-CERT. (2008). *Computer forensics*. Retrieved December 2008 from http://www.us-cert.gov/reading_room/forensics.pdf

USDoJ. (2002). *Prosecuting computer crimes*. Washington, DC: United States Department of Justice, Computer Crime & Intellectual Property Section.

Vaciago, G. (2012). *Cloud computing and data jurisdiction: A new challenge for digital forensics*. Retrieved from http://www.thinkmind.org/index.php?view=article&articleid=cyberlaws_2012_1_20_70033

Van Horenbeeck, M. (2005). *Forensic investigation and its relationship with information assurance and corporate governance*. (Certificate of Multidisciplinary Forensic Investigation Thesis). Katholieke Universiteit Leuven. Flanders, Belgium.

Van Horn, C. (2009). *Chris Coleman documents and search warrants*. Retrieved from http://www.examiner.com/article/chris-coleman-documents-and-search-warrants

Vaquero, L. M. (2008). A break in the clouds: Towards a cloud definition. *ACM SIGCOMM Computer Communication Review*, *39*(1), 50–55. doi:10.1145/1496091.1496100

Veeam Software. (2011). *V-index.com virtualization penetration rate in the enterprise*. Retrieved July 30, 2012 from http://www.v-index.com/pdf/v-index_full_report_q3_2011.pdf?button_btm

Viacom Int'l Inc. v. YouTube Inc., 2008 WL 2627388 (S.D.N.Y. 2008) (2008).

Video Privacy Protection Act, 18 U.S.C. §§ 2710-12 (2000).

Virtual Computing Environment Company. (2012). *VCE company LLC*. Retrieved from http://www.vce.com/

VirtualBox. (2012). *Remote virtual machines*. Retrieved July 30, 2012 from http://www.virtualbox.org/manual/ch07.html

VMware, Inc. (2007). *Understanding full virtualization paravirtualization and hardware assist*. Retrieved July 30, 2012 from http://www.vmware.com/files/pdf/VMware_paravirtualization.pdf

VMware. (2011). *What files make up a virtual machine?* Retrieved July 30, 2012 from http://www.vmware.com/support/ws55/doc/ws_learning_files_in_a_vm.html

Volonino, L. (2003). Electronic evidence and computer forensics. *Communications of the Association for Information Systems*, *12*(27), 457–468.

Vouk, M. A. (2008). *Cloud computing-Issues, research and implementations*. IEEE.

Vyatta. (2011). *On demand networking for virtual environments*. Retrieved July 30, 2012 from http://www.vyatta.com/solutions/virtual

Wang, F., Qiu, J., Yang, J., Dong, B., Li, X., & Li, Y. (2009). *Hadoop high availability through metadata replication*. Shanghai, China: IBM.

Wang, W. Y. C. (2011). Toward the trend of cloud computing. *Journal of Electronic Commerce Research*, *12*(4).

Ward, B. T., Sipior, J. C., Volonino, L., & Peterson, G. (2007). Computer forensics, e-discovery, and spoliation: Impact of the new federal rules. In *Proceedings of the Americas Conference on Information Systems*. Keystone, CO: IEEE.

Ward, B. T., Sipior, J. C., Volonino, L., & Purwin, C. (2010). *Electronic discovery rules and electronic evidence: A United States perspective*. Paper presented at the European and Mediterranean Conference on Information Systems. Abu Dhabi, UAE.

Ward, B. T., & Sipior, J. C. (2010). The internet jurisdiction risk of cloud computing. *Information Systems Management*, *27*(4), 334–339. doi:10.1080/10580530.2010.514248

Warshak v. United States, 490 F.3d 455, 470 (6th Cir. 2007), vacated 532 F.3d 521 (6th Cir. 2008) (2008).

Warshak v. United States, 631 F.3d 266, 286 (6th Cir. 2010) (2010).

Weinstein, J. B., & Berger, M. A. (1995). *Weinstein's evidence: Commentary on rules of evidence for the United States courts and magistrates*. New York, NY: M. Bender.

Welsh v. Wisconsin, 466 U.S. 740, 748, 104 S.Ct. 2091, 80 L.Ed.2d 732 (1984).

Wikipedia. (2011). *Cloud computing*. Retrieved January 10, 2011, from http://en.wikipedia.org/wiki/Cloud_computing

Wiles, J. (Ed.). (2007). *The best damn cybercrime and digital investigations book period*. New York, NY: Syngress Publishing.

Willamette Week. (2011, April 8). You look like Obama: FBI seeks Facebook records for person of interest in mosque arson. *Willamette Week*. Retrieved from http://www.wweek.com/portland/blog-26890-you_look_like_obama_fbi_seeks_facebook_records_for.html

Willassen, S. (2008). Using simplified event calculus in digital investigation. In *Proceedings of the 2008 ACM Symposium on Applied Computing*. ACM Press.

Williams, C. (2011). *Cybercrime gang responsible for a third of all data thefts*. The Telegraph.

Wilsdon, T., & Slay, J. (2005). Digital forensics: Exploring validation, verification & certification. In *Proceedings of the First International Workshop on Systematic Approaches to Digital Forensic Engineering (SADFE 2005)*. IEEE.

WindowsAzure. (2012). *Website*. Retrieved from http://www.windowsazure.com/en-us/home/features/overview/

Wolf v. Colorado 338 U.S. 25, 69 S.Ct. 1359, 93 L.Ed. 1782 (1949).

Wolski, R. (2010). Top 5 questions posted on "cloud computing" (part 1/3). *Eucalyptus*. Retrieved from http://www.eucalyptus.com/blog/2010/05/21/top-5-questions-posed-cloud-computing-part-13

Wolthusen, S. (2009). Overcast: Forensic discovery in cloud environments. In *Proceedings of the Fifth International Conference on IT Security, Incident Management, and IT Forensics*, (pp. 3-9). IEEE.

Wolthusen, S. D. (2009). Overcast: Forensic discovery in cloud environments. In *Proceedings of the Fifth International Conference on IT Security Incident Management and IT Forensics, 2009, IMF 2009*, (pp. 3-9). IMF.

Wood, L. (2009). *Cloud computing and compliance: Be careful up there*. Retrieved from http://www.computerworld.com/s/article/9126934/Cloud_computing_and_compliance_Be_careful_up_there

Xen. (2011). *Xen hypevisor - Leading open source hypervisor for servers*. Retrieved 10 February, 2011, from http://www.xen.org/products/xenhyp.html

Xen. (2012). *Xen hypervisor project*. Retrieved July 30, 2012 from http://www.xen.org/support/documentation.html

Yan, C. (2011). Cybercrime forensic system in cloud computing. In *Proceedings of the 2011 International Conference on Image Analysis and Signal Processing (IASP)*, (pp. 612-615). IASP.

Zissis, D., & Lekkas, D. (2012). Addressing cloud computing security issues. *Future Generation Computer Systems*, *28*(3), 583–592. doi:10.1016/j.future.2010.12.006

Zittrain, J. (2009). Lost in the cloud. *The New York Times*.

Zubulake v. UBS Warburg LLC, 216 F.R.D. 280, 291 (S.D.N.Y. 2003) (2003).

About the Contributors

Keyun Ruan (26) worked as a PhD researcher at Center of Cybersecurity and Cybercrime Investigation (University College Dublin) and Cyber Security Research Lab (EADS) on cloud forensics. She was among the first in the world to work on this emerging area. Keyun has given talks around the world in both academic and industry conferences including CloudEXPO Europe and Silicon Valley, Cloud Futures held at Microsoft Research Headquarters, Cloud Security Alliance Congress, RSAConference Europe, Campus Party Europe, the ADFSL Conference on Digital Forensics Security and Law, the International Conference on Digital Forensics and Cyber Crime, the IFIP International Conference on Digital Forensics, etc. Keyun is now Chairperson and CRO of New York-based XENSIX Inc., Research Scientist at University College Dublin, and Research Partner at EADS. She is an active member of the Cloud Security Alliance, member of the board of Cloud Security Alliance Ireland, and is leading the Cloud Security Alliance Incident Management and Forensics Working Group. She is an active contributor to the NIST Cloud Computing Program, and a Technical Lead of the NIST Cloud Forensics Working Group. She is also a semi-professional artist and holds a diploma in Art and Design from the National College of Art and Design, Ireland.

* * *

Richard Adams is Principal in the Forensic Division of a Big4 professional services organization and is based in Western Australia. He is in the process of finalizing his PhD thesis through Murdoch University on the topic of a new process model for the acquisition of electronic data. His research interests are in the application of technology to digital forensic investigations. Recent projects include applying data analytic concepts, such as Self-Organizing Maps, to the output of keyword searches from several digital forensic tools as a cost-effective aid to prioritizing the analysis process. Richard currently lectures for the postgraduate unit on Forensics and Information Technology at the University of Western Australia and is a mentor for undergraduate computer science students for their professional computing projects. Richard is an active member of the Australian Standards Working Group developing the Guidelines for Identification, Collection, Acquisition, and Preservation of Digital Evidence.

Aaron Alva is a Juris Doctor and Masters of Science in Information Management student at the University of Washington, Seattle, USA. He earned his Bachelor degree at the University of Central Florida studying Political Science with a minor in Digital Forensics (2011). His career interests are in cybersecurity law and policy creation for the federal government. Aaron has cybersecurity research experience at a U.S. national laboratory, and currently conducts research on the legal requirements for cloud forensics and on digital evidence admissibility in U.S. courts. He is a current recipient of the National Science Foundation Federal Cyber Service: Scholarship for Service, and contributor to projects with the Cloud Security Alliance.

Diane Barrett is Adjunct Professor at American Military University (AMU), USA. Prior to working at AMU, Diane was the program champion for the Technology Forensics program and the Faculty Council Chair for the Systems Development Group at the University of Advancing Technology (UAT). While at UAT, she developed a full forensic curriculum for the Bachelor degree program. Diane is a PhD candidate at Northcentral University in the School of Business and Technology Management. She holds many industry certifications including CISSP, ISSMP, MCSE, CompTIA, and Digital Forensic Certified Practitioner. She has co-authored and been the lead author on several computer forensics and security books, including *Computer Forensics JumpStart* (John Wiley & Sons, 2004), *Computer Networking Illuminated* (Jones & Bartlett Learning, 2005), and *Virtualization and Forensics* (Syngress, 1 Ed., 2010). She is also an editor for the *Journal of Digital Forensics, Security, and Law.*

Fred Cohen is well known for his seminal work on computer viruses and defenses, critical infrastructure protection, security governance, and the use of deception and counter-deception in information security. As an educator, he has taught graduate courses in digital forensics for almost ten years, taught California POST certified courses, lectured at the Federal Law Enforcement Training Center, and given talks and guest lectures in digital forensics and related topics all over the world. As an expert witness, he has testified in cases at all levels, ranging from federal criminal to civil disciplinary boards. He has also produced digital forensics tools including the White Glove Linux operating environment, the Unix-based ForensiX toolkit, and ForWord, built special purpose network forensics devices used by law enforcement and in private investigations, published refereed journal articles and conference papers in the digital forensics area, and is on editorial boards for publications in digital forensics and related areas.

Mark Crosbie is a Security Architect responsible for security policy in the IBM Chief Information Office, based in Dublin, Ireland. His responsibility is for the Secure Engineering and Development policies in force in IBM. Previously, Mark was responsible for Ethical Hacking against the IBM Lotus product portfolio. Mark holds a CISSP certification, and has filed numerous patents on key security technologies. He has a Master degree in Computer Science from Purdue University (USA).

Dener Didoné has a Bachelor degree in Computer Science from State University of Mato Grosso (UNEMAT) and a Master degree in Computer Science from Federal University of Pernambuco (UFPE), Brazil. He is specialized in security and forensic computing. Currently, he is working for Bank of Brazil and teaching at the same time.

Josiah Dykstra received a B.S. in Computer Science and a B.A. in Music from Hope College, USA, in 2002. As part of the National Science Foundation Scholarship for Service fellowship, he earned an M.S. in Information Assurance from Iowa State University in 2004. Mr. Dykstra is pursuing a Ph.D. in Computer Science at the University of Maryland, Baltimore County, conducting research on the topic of digital forensics for cloud computing. His research interests include network security, intrusion detection, malware analysis, digital forensics, and cloud computing. Dykstra is a member of the ACM, IEEE Computer Society, American Academy of Forensic Sciences, Cloud Security Alliance, NIST Cloud Working Group, IFIP Working Group 11.9 on Digital Forensics, and American Bar Association E-Discovery and Digital Evidence Committee. His certifications include the Certificate of Cloud Security Knowledge, CISSP, and NSTISSI 4011.

Barbara Endicott-Popovsky is Director for the University of Washington's Center for Information Assurance and Cybersecurity, Academic Director for the Masters in Infrastructure Planning and Management in the Urban Planning Department of the School of Built Environments, and holds an appointment as Research Associate Professor with the Information School. Her academic career follows a 20-year career in industry marked by executive and consulting positions in IT architecture and project management. Her research interests include forensic-ready networks, secure coding practices, and digital forensics. She is a member of the American Academy of Forensic Scientists. Endicott-Popovsky has a PhD in Computer Science from the University of Idaho, USA.

Kirsten Ferguson-Boucher is Programme Advisor for the MScEcon in Information Governance and Assurance at Aberystwyth University, Wales, and heads the UK arm of the Centre of Information Assurance and Cybersecurity, University of Washington (designated by the National Science Foundation as a Centre for Academic Excellence in Information Assurance Education and Research). Prior to her appointment at Aberystwyth University, where she lectures in Records and Information Governance; Digital Risk and Asset Management; Compliance, Law, and Ethics; and Information Assurance, she worked in public, private, and voluntary sectors in research, management, and information roles. Her recent and current research interests include digital/cloud forensics and information assurance; cloud computing and information governance; human rights and the privacy agenda; and the role and purpose of conceptual modeling in describing organizational and individual behavior. Of particular relevance is the publication of preliminary research conducted in the UK into the needs of organizations from a record and information perspective when moving into the Cloud and the publication of a Cloud Toolkit to assist with the governance processes through the lifecycle of the information. Kirsten has an MA (Hons) in Classics (Greek, Latin, and Classical Archaeology) from Edinburgh University, Scotland, and holds Master's degrees from Heriot Watt University, Scotland (MA Leisure Policy and Practice) and Aberystwyth University, Wales (MScEcon Records Management).

Pavel Gladyshev is a Lecturer at the University College Dublin, Ireland, where he is directing the MSc programme in Forensic Computing and Cybercrime Investigation. Dr. Gladyshev is also a co-founder of UCD Centre for Cybercrime Investigation where he is heading the digital forensics research group. He is conducting several research projects on automated malware forensics, high-speed algorithms for automated detection of illegal material, Apple Mac memory forensics, forensics in cloud computing environment, and signature-based algorithms for user activity detection.

Dean Gonsowski, as a former litigator, General Counsel, and AGC, Dean Gonsowski brings over 15 years of eDiscovery consulting and legal experience to his position as Sr. eDiscovery Counsel for Symantec, Inc. Dean Gonsowski is a member of the Sedona Conference Working Group on Electronic Document Retention and Production (WG1), the Electronic Discovery Reference Model (EDRM), and the Association of Corporate Counsel (ACC). He has contributed articles to a number of leading industry publications, including *Business Week, Corporate Counsel, ILTA Peer to Peer, Inside Counsel,* and the *Legal Tech Newsletter.* Mr. Gonsowski received his JD from the University of San Diego School of Law and his BS from the University of California, Santa Barbara. He is a licensed attorney in both California and Colorado, USA.

Giuseppe F. Italiano is Professor of Computer Science at the University of Rome "Tor Vergata," Italy. After obtaining his Ph.D. in Computer Science from Columbia University in 1991, he joined the IBM T.J. Watson Research Center in Yorktown Heights as a Research Staff Member and was later appointed to Professor of Computer Science at University of Salerno, Italy, in 1994. He was Visiting Professor at Max-Planck-Institut für Informatik, Columbia University, and Hong Kong University of Science and Technology. His research interests include computer and network security and the design, analysis, and experimental evaluation of algorithms, areas in which he has published over 200 papers in high quality journals and in proceedings of conferences. He has served on editorial boards and as guest editor of several journals and as chair and member of numerous program committees of leading scientific conferences. He is currently Editor-in-Chief of the *ACM Journal of Experimental Algorithmics.*

Joshua I. James is a Ph.D. researcher with the University College Dublin Centre for Cybersecurity and Cybercrime Investigation, and a seconded researcher with the An Garda Síochána eCrimes Unit in Ireland. Coming from a background in network security and administration, his focus is now on the formalization and automation of digital forensic investigation methods, and the application of these methods in low cost, open source solutions for digital investigators.

Vasilis Katos is Assistant Professor of Information and Communications Systems Security at Democritus University of Thrace, Greece. Prior to this post, he was Principal Lecturer and Course Tutor for the MSc in Forensic IT at the University of Portsmouth in the UK. Dr. Katos obtained a Diploma in Electrical Engineering from Democritus University of Thrace in Greece, an MBA from Keele University in the UK, and a PhD in Computer Science (Network Security and Cryptography) from Aston University (UK). He has worked in the industry as information security consultant and served as an expert witness in a criminal court in the UK. Dr. Katos's research is in the area of information systems security and more specifically in network security, privacy, computer forensics, and incident response.

Fabio Marturana received M.S. degree in Electronic Engineering from the Polytechnics of Turin, Italy, in 1998. He is a PhD candidate at the Civil Engineering and Computer Science Department of University of Rome "Tor Vergata," Italy. He also serves as a senior officer in the Italian Carabinieri Corps, and is currently based in General Headquarters in Rome, Italy. He is a published researcher, and his main research interests include digital forensics, computer security, cloud computing, and cloud forensics.

Ivan Orton recently retired after 30 years as a Senior Deputy Prosecutor with the Fraud Division of the King County Prosecutor's Office in Seattle, USA. In the job, he investigated and prosecuted cases involving complex economic crime, computer crime, and financial abuse of the elderly. He is a co-author of *Cybercrime: The Investigation, Prosecution, and Defense of a Computer-Related Crime* (Carolina Academic Press, 3d Ed., 2009). He was a contributing author and a member of the Planning Panel for "Digital Evidence in the Courtroom: A Guide for Law Enforcement and Prosecutors" (National Institute of Justice, 2007). He regularly teaches computer crime and digital evidence classes to judges, prosecutors, technicians, and the public. He is currently working with co-author Barbara Endicott-Popovsky on the planning and creation of a multidisciplinary Digital Evidence program at the University of Washington School of Law and Information School. He is a 1977 graduate of Harvard Law School.

Ruy José Guerra Barretto de Queiroz is Associate Professor at Federal University of Pernambuco (UFPE), Brazil. He has a Bachelor degree in Electronic Engineering (1980) and a Master degree in Computer Science (1984) from UFPE. He has a PhD from Imperial College London in 1990. He is Editor-in-Chief for *Logic Journal of the IGPL* (Oxford University Press), member of Editorial Board for the *International Directory of Logicians* (College Publicatoins, 2009). He was elected as member of the Council of the Association for Symbolic Logic from 2006 to 2008. In 1994, he created the International Workshop on Logic, Language, Information, and Computation (WoLLIC), which is listed as a B-level conference by the Australian Research Council. In 2006, he was awarded "Edward Larocque Tinker Visiting Professor" from Stanford University, nominated by Solomon Feferman (Rolf Schock Prize Winner 2003) and Grigori Mints. He was a member of the Advisory Group to the Rolf Schock Prize in Logic and Philosophy (2008 and 2011), elected by the Royal Swedish Academy of Science. He is Associate Editor for the *Journal of Computer and System Sciences* (Elsevier). He is also member of the Editorial Board for the LNCS-FoLLI series (Spinger). His research interests include theory of computing, particularly proof theory, computation theory, mathematical logic, model theory, and fundamentals of computer security. He maintains two blogs: http://ciberdominiopublico.blogspot.com and http://osventosdaliberdade.blogspot.com.

Jon Rav Gagan Shende is an executive with over 15 years of business experience, and the youngest VP of a global enterprise based in USA. He commenced his career in medical services before moving into the oil and gas environment, where he was introduced to SCADA and network technologies. He is experienced with the operations of technology startups as well as Fortune 50/100/500 corporations, where he contributed strategy and advisory services at the C and Senior Director levels. As an IT Business Executive, Jon RG Shende has experience with product development and management, virtualization, business and IT strategy, security and risk management, continuity, and compliance. He is a Fellow of the BCS Chartered Institute for IT, holds the Chartered IT Professional designation, as well as SCADA security and CRISC certifications and the HITRUST Certified CSF Practitioner certification. He is also a regular speaker at various conferences. Jon Rav Gagan commenced his formal education with undergraduate studies in Biochemistry and Engineering, is a graduate of the University of Oxford, holds a Masters certificate in Business Administration, as well as an MSc in IT Security, specializing in Computer Crime and Forensics.

Ahmed F. Shosha is a Ph.D. researcher and Teaching Assistant with University College Dublin Centre for Cybersecurity and Cybercrime Investigation, Ireland. His research focuses on formalizing digital forensic investigation methods for malicious software investigation. Ahmed has been working with different antivirus vendors as a part of his research to provide a state-of-the-art solution for malware detection, analysis, and investigation.

Theodoros Spyridopoulos studied Electrical and Computer Engineering at Democritus University of Thrace, Greece, where he continued his studies for a Master in Information Security and Digital Forensics. His Master's thesis was on Cloud Forensics, and his work led to a presentation at a forensics workshop held in London (WDFIA 2011) and also to a publication at the *International Journal of Digital Crime and Forensics* (IGI Global). He is currently pursuing a PhD in System Modeling Techniques of Cyber Security under the supervision of Dr. Theo Tryfonas. The key objective of his research is to examine novel pathways for improving situational awareness in the context of critical information infrastructure, on the premise of systems thinking.

Simone Tacconi holds a Ph.D. in Artificial Intelligent Systems from the Polytechnic University of Marche, Italy, and M.S. in Electronic Engineering from University of Ancona, Italy. He is currently Technical Director of the Computer Forensics Unit at the Italian Postal and Communications Police, Ministry of the Interior. His main research interests include computer security, cryptography, and digital forensics. He is co-author of several refereed scientific papers in international journals and conference proceedings.

Index

D

E

F

www.ingramcontent.com/pod-product-compliance
Lightning Source LLC
LaVergne TN
LVHW060409300926
849162LV00006B/1380